STYLE AND TEXT

STYLE AND TEXT

STUDIES PRESENTED TO NILS ERIK ENKVIST

© Språkförlaget Skriptor AB Stockholm 1975

Published by Språkförlaget Skriptor AB and Åbo Akademi in collaboration.

Editorial Committee:

Håkan Ringbom (chairman)
Alfhild Ingberg
Ralf Norrman
Kurt Nyholm
Rolf Westman
Kay Wikberg

ISBN 91 7282 095 0

Printed in Sweden by Tryckeri AB Allehanda, Trelleborg, 1975

Contents

IV. TEXT LINGUISTICS

THE PUBLISHED WRITINGS OF NILS ERIK ENKVIST

Preface

To mark the occasion of Professor Nils Erik Enkvist's fiftieth birthday on 27 September, 1975, some of his friends, colleagues and former pupils decided to publish this Festschrift. It was felt desirable to restrict the themes of the contributions to stylistics and text linguistics, which in recent years have been the focus of Nils Enkvist's scholarly interest. Contributions were solicited from a number of scholars working in these fields. Among the contributions received, four main groups seemed to crystallize: Stylistic Theory, Style and Literary Criticism, Linguistic Approaches to Style, and Text Linguistics (the term preferred by Enkvist for what others have also labelled Discourse Analysis). These headings were chosen and the material arranged accordingly, although some of the articles could be characterized as border-line cases.

In publishing these essays the editorial committee gratefully wish to acknowledge help from two of the contributors, Dr. Roger D. Sell and Dr. Hans Karlgren. Thanks to generous grants from Stiftelsen för Åbo Akademi and Stiftelsens för Åbo Akademi Forskningsinstitut publication of the work was made possible.

Åbo, January, 1975

HÅKAN RINGBOM
Editor

Editorial Committee:

HÅKAN RINGBOM (chairman) KURT NYHOLM
ALFHILD INGBERG ROLF WESTMAN
RALF NORRMAN KAY WIKBERG

Tabula gratulatoria

Birgitta & Sten-Erik Abrahamsson
Olga Akhmanova
Anna Maria & Bertil Albrektson
Pirkko & Alho Alhoniemi
Sture Allén
Jens Allwood
Inga-Britt Amnell
Maja & Dag Anckar
Olle Anckar
Erik & Ulla Andersson
Håkan Andersson
Sven Andersson
The Duke & Duchess of Anglia de
    Redonda
Raimo Anttila
Mr. & Mrs. William A. Armstrong
Solveig & Rolf Askevold
Helge Aspelund †
Merton & Janet Atkins
Robert & Sylvi Austerlitz
W. D. Bald
Karin & Åke Bamberg
P. O. Barck
Hreinn Benediktsson
Eduard Beneš
Gunilla Berglund
Karl Ove Berglund
Allan Berthelsen
Haralds Biezais
Thora Balslev Blatt
Mr. & Mrs. Morton W. Bloomfield
Margareta Blumenthal
Pat & Ian Borland
Jean & Jeffrey Boughey
Birgit Bramsbäck
Mårten & Barbara Brenner
Roger Broo
Ulli & Patrick Bruun
Malcom & Jane Calder
B. Carstensen
Mr. & Mrs. Francis A. Cartier
Peter Cassirer
Paul Christophersen

Gunnel & Fredric Cleve
Eugenio Coseriu
Dick & Marijke Coutinho
Liisa Dahl
Karl-Hampus Dahlstedt
Fabian Dahlström
František Daneš & Irena Danešová
Peter & Ferelith Davies
Norman & Traude Denison
René & Gabrielle Derolez
Teun A. van Dijk
Ulrika & Carl-August Doepel
Lubomir Dolezel
Scott & Janet Donaldson
H. W. Donner
Ethel & Nils Edelman
Stig Eliasson
Alvar Ellegård
Eva & Gordon Elliott
Ernst & Sigrid Enkvist
Edmund L. & Tegwen Epstein
Erik Erämetsä
Mr. & Mrs. Robert O. Evans
Itamar Even-Zohar
Gunnar Fant
Jan-Erik & Margareta Feldt
Jan & Helen Firbas
Jacek Fisiak
Lisa & Karl-Gustav Fogel
Ivan Fónagy
Roger Fowler
Thorstein Fretheim
Udo Fries
Brita Gardberg
Nanna & C. J. Gardberg
Christine-Louise & Birger Gestrin
Rosemarie Gläser
Åke Granlund
Sam & Eleanor Granowitz
Marja & Raoul Granqvist
Christopher & Ulla Grapes
La Vonne & Gottfrid Gräsbeck
Bo Grönholm

Marita Gustafsson
Rafael & Augusta Birgithe
  Gyllenberg
William Haas
Tom Hagan
Auli Hakulinen
Michael A. K. Halliday
Björn Hammarberg
Eric & Margot Hamp
Ingeborg & Vidar Hannus
Peter Hartmann
Hans H. Hartvigson
Ruqaiya Hasan
Eva & Einar Haugen
Allen & Ruth Pratt Hayman
Adrien Heigho
Orvokki Heinämäki
John Helgander
Astrid Hellström
Mr. & Mrs. George Hendrick
William & Beverly Hendricks
Marita & Runar Hernberg
Malcolm Hicks
Mr. & Mrs. Archibald A. Hill
Risto & Leena Hilpinen
Pekka Hirvonen
Inger & Olof Holmberg
Christina Holmström
Roger Holmström
Lauri & Märta Honko
'Peter' & 'Darby' Horne
Leon & Henrietta Howard
Raimo & Pirkko Huikuri
Lars Huldén
Carita & Leif Hummelstedt
Christer Hummelstedt
Eskil Hummelstedt
Eva & Göran Högnäs
Karl-Johan & Siw Illman
Alfhild Ingberg
Rune Ingo
Ida & Eric Jacobsen
Sibyl C. Jacobson
Sven & Evy Jacobson
Birgitta & Hans Jalling
Kurt R. Jankowsky
Robert & Karin Jansson

Waldemar & Karin Jensen
Sirkka & Carl-Johan Johansson
Stig Johansson
Sune Jungar
Solveig Jungner
Enne-Maija & Osmo Järvi
Eino & Genevieve Kainlauri
Hans Karlgren
Fred Karlsson
Gwen & Göran Karlsson
Kaj Karlsson
Kostas & Maria Kazazis
Ferenc Kiefer
Margareta Kihlman
Mårten Kihlman
Arvi & Kirsti Kiivimaa
Ann & Carl-Erik Kniivilä
Lilja & Viljo Kohonen
Inna Koskenniemi
Mauno Koski
Gillis Kristensson
Auvo Kurvinen
Christiane Käär
Ulla Ladau-Harjulin
Kirsti & Kari Lagerspetz
Mona & John Lagström
Britta & Tor-Erik Lassenius
Ilse Lehiste
Matti Leiwo
Samuel R. Levin
Hans Lindbäck
Karin & Gösta Lindeskog
Marita & Åke L. Lindfors
Kaj B. Lindgren
Rolf Lindholm
Vasthi & Sven Lindman
Pirkko H. Lindqvist
Ritva & Caj-Gunnar Lindström
Birgitta & Sven Linnér
Klaus Krister Lohikoski
Virgil L. & Agnes M. Lokke
Bengt Loman
Herbert & Mary Lomas
Ingmar & Birgitta Lundberg
Agneta & Tony Lurcock
Erika Lyly
Christina & Kurt-Erik Långbacka

John Makin
Bertil & Margit Malmberg
Lars Malmberg
Margareta Mansner
Albert H. Marckwardt
Raija Markkanen
William & Lois E. Matthews
George Maude
Martin Mayer
Silvester Mazzarella
Ian McIntosh
Britta & Donald McNeill
W. R. Mead
Ulla Mickelsson
Louis T. Milic
Thelma S. & Ward L. Miner
Ellen Moers
Karin & Bengt Mossberg
Howard & Marion Munford
Sirkka & Tauno F. Mustanoja
Kerstin & Olof Mustelin
Aino Naert
Carl L. & Charlotte B. Nelson
Saara Nevanlinna
Gerhard Nickel
Sigrid & Oscar Nikula
Valter Nordling
Hans & Kristina Nordström
Ralf & Eva-Liisa Norrman
Liisa Nummenmaa
Tauno Nurmela
Anders & Agneta Nygård
Kurt & Gretel Nyholm
Karl Johan Nylund
Kerstin & Bjarne Nylund
Martti Nyman
Richard Ohmann
Els Oksaar
Ursula Oomen
Erik Palmén
Sari & Niilo Peltola
Anna-Liisa & Esko Pennanen
Rauha Petro
Björn Pettersson
János S. Petöfi
Geoffrey Phillips
Michael Pickering

Leila Pietilä
Elisabeth & Ilpo Tapani Piirainen
Herbert Pilch
Gunn & Hans Pipping
Ida & Knut Pipping
Una Mary Ponsonby
Sigurd Portin
Roland Posner
Göran & Ulla Printz-Påhlson
Christer Påhlsson
Randolph Quirk
Bengt-Olof Qvarnström
Benita Qvarnström
Marita Rajalin
Marianne & Olof Ramberg
Irma Rantavaara
Carin & Ole Reuter
Siv & Mikael Reuter
Martti & Nina Rewell
Thyra Ribbing
Astrid Ringbom
Håkan & Åsa Ringbom
Marianne & Sixten Ringbom
Inga & Helmer Ringgren
Päivi Rintala
Erik B. & Ritva Riska
Matti Rissanen
Peter Roe
John & Gunvor Rosas
Inger & Karl-Erik Rosengren
Hans Rossipal
Pat M. & Jamice Ryan
Mats Rydén
Alarik Rynell
Mirja Saari
Guy Saias
Matti A. Sainio
Kari Sajavaara
Vivian & Paul Salmon
Olli Sampola
Nils Johan Sandberg
Karl Inge Sandred
Constantin-George Sandulescu
Pauli Saukkonen
Hans Saxén
R. A. Sayce
Claes & Ingrid Schaar

Randolf & Karin von Schalien
Siegfried J. Schmidt
Thomas A. Sebeok
Anita & Krister Segerberg
Susanne Segerstråle
Christina W. & Roger D. Sell
Brita & Per Seyersted
Petr Sgall
Birgit Simons
John Sinclair
Paavo Siro
Eva Sivertsen
Folke & Birgitta Sjögren
Kaj Sjöholm
Gunvor & Rainer Sjöström
Sigmund Skard
Kristian Smidt
Helena Solstrand
Karin & Carl Eric Sonck
F. R. Southerington
E. G. Stanley
Wm. T. & Frances M. Stafford
Daniel & Angela Carlucci Stempel
Wolf-Dieter Stempel
Christina & Kurt-Erik Stenbäck
Erik & Eva Stenius
Ardis & Haakon Storm-Mathisen
G. Storms
Siv & Nils Storå
Bertil Sundby
Erna & Carl-Eric Sundman
Gunilla & Jan Svartvik
Sirkka-Liisa Särkilahti
Märta & Torbjörn Söderholm
Knud Sørensen
Sauli Takala
Ashley & Jean Talbot
Gurli & Carl Olof Tallgren
Hillevi & Lars Erik Taxell
Tor Erik Teir
Ulf Teleman
Erik Tengstrand

Jan Thavenius
Robin Thelwall
Dolly Therman
Andrea & Holger Thesleff
Kerstin & Carl-Eric Thors
Nils Thun
Seija Tiisala
Ilpo Tolvas
Päiviö Tommila
Mr. & Mrs. L. T. Topsfield
Knut & Henriette von Troil
Bengt Törjas
Mr. & Mrs. Walter Ullrich
Josef Vachek
Chad & Eva T. Walsh
Winston Weathers
Diana & Michael Webster
Ingeborg & Carl B. Westerberg
Rolf & Nina Westman
Björn Westerlund
Göran & Erica Westerlund
Kristina & Jan C. Westerlund
Robert White
Solveig & Bill Widén
Kalevi & Kirsti Wiik
Kay & Chantal Wikberg
Bo-Jungar Wikgren
Edward & Mary Wilkinson
Ann-Sofie & Stig Olof Winter
Werner Winter
Ullabella & Thomas Wrede
Georg Henrik & Elisabeth von
    Wright
Johnny von Wright
Marianne von Wright
Dieter Wunderlich
Arne Zettersten
Clas & Mona Zilliacus
Sven Öhman
Emil Öhmann
Jan-Ola Östman
Orm Överland

I. *THEORY OF STYLE*

Erik Andersson
Åbo Akademi

Style, optional rules and contextual conditioning

1. STYLE AS VARIATION DUE TO OPTIONAL RULES

The basis of this paper will be the view that *style is a kind of linguistic variation* (Enkvist 1973, p. 17). Style can be viewed as the difference or rather some of the differences between two or more texts, and it is therefore an implicitly relational concept. To state that a text has a certain style is then equivalent to stating that it differs in some respects from other texts. Usually the term *text* is restricted to that member of the comparison that is being studied for the moment, while those discourses that this text is compared to are called *norm*. However, there is no principal difference between the two members of the style relation. In actual research, it is customary and often necessary to choose the norm much bigger than the text to obtain more significant differences, but theoretically, text and norm could perfectly well switch roles. I shall therefore later in this paper prefer the term *texts* or *variants* for both text and norm, partly in order to avoid the evaluative connotations of the term *norm*.

Moreover, the stylistic differences are located *in the text*. Potential *style markers* are therefore the occurrence and frequency of morphemes, morpheme classes, syntactic structural patterns, sequences of such structures, etc. A style marker should not be confused with a contextual factor that correlates with the style marker. On the other hand, such correlations are of the utmost importance to stylistic research.

If we accept the view of style as one kind of textual variation, it is appropriate to ask how this variation is generated. In a formal linguistic theory such as transformational grammar, there are two kinds of rules: obligatory and optional ones. The task of these rules is to generate all the sentences of a certain language. Two sentences can differ from each other only if at least one optional rule has applied in the derivation of one of the sentences, but not in the derivation of the other. According to this theory, stylistics will be concerned with the investigation of optional rules. One example of such an approach is Jacobs and Rosenbaum (1971).

However, all variation within a language has to be generated by optional rules. At the same time, most people are very reluctant to call all variation within their language stylistic. Two sentences might for instance agree in style but differ in meaning. Therefore, we have to specify what other kinds of variation there can be in a language and what variation counts as stylistic. This will be one of the purposes of the present paper. In the following sections, I shall discuss some possible further restrictions on the definition of style. It is not the purpose of stylistics to invent a technical, a priori style definition for its own sake. The definition should rather reflect and perhaps explicate the common usage of the term *style*. The testing of the definition is therefore an empirical question.

2. STYLE AS VARIATION WITHIN ONE LINGUISTIC SYSTEM

One kind of variation that we might not want to label stylistic is variation due to regional, temporal and social dialects (Enkvist 1973, p. 16). One possible way to exclude the study of such differences from stylistics is to state that stylistic variation has to be variation within one single language system. If we regard different dialects as different varieties of the same language defined by different rule systems, dialectal variation will be variation in language rather than in style.

However, such a solution seems quite arbitrary as long as we do not have any independent reasons for describing dialects, and dialects only, as different rule systems. We might equally have said that each style is constituted by a rule system of its own. But we could perhaps suppose that each speaker possesses one single rule system generating all the styles he masters. His grammar would then be some kind of a supergrammar comprising in it several subgrammars for the different styles. The above claim that style is variation within a single linguistic system is then roughly equivalent to the claim that all the styles of a speaker are so similar to each other that they all should be fitted into the same general framework.

If we assume that the grammars we construct should mirror the psychological reality in the speaker's minds, it might not be far-fetched to assume that all those variants of a language that a speaker encounters in his linguistic experience are if possible integrated into one system in his brain. This speaker would then be inclined to regard as a style a variant of his language that he is accustomed to, and to regard as dialects all variants that he is not accustomed to and has not integrated into his linguistic system. Style could then roughly be taken as certain kinds of linguistic variation within a single coherent speech community, since the styles used in such a community are likely to have been heard by the speakers and integrated in their linguistic systems. However, we should be aware that we really have a sliding scale here. Those variants that a speaker uses actively are probably best integrated in his linguistic system, while variants that he only passively receives from his environment are less integrated. Least integrated are probably variants that he very seldom encounters, such as the language of the past, etc. It is almost a matter of taste where we should draw the line between stylistic and dialectal variation.

3. EXCLUDING VARIATION IN MEANING

Another variation that we might not want to consider stylistic is variation in meaning. How to distinguish such a variation from other types of variation is very much an open question. Logicians have proposed that it is identical to variation in intension, the intension of a morpheme being defined as a function that is used in calculating the truth value of declarative sentences where the morpheme occurs. A change of meaning can therefore change the truth value, while a change in style never does. It can only change the appropriateness of the sentence. There is certainly something in the distinction between truth and appropriateness. On the other hand, it is quite hard to explain the difference between these concepts. A getaway not to be contempted is to accept the distinction as intuitive. We do seem to have quite strong intuitions on it. Perhaps it is also possible to say that the meaning of an expression is the information that it gives about its own referent. The expressions *a boy* and *a lad* give roughly the same information on the referent, the boy, but differ in the information they give about the speaker's relations to the listener and the general speech situation. We might also say that the meaning is the *conventional message* of an expression. The conventional message would be that information speakers normally want to convey when they use the expression. It might differ from the actually intended message, since a speaker might intentionally use style differences or even totally different propositions to communicate his points.

The exclusion of variation of meaning from stylistic variation suggests a simple definition of style: linguistic variation within a single rule system minus variation of meaning. Stylistics would under this definition be a waste-paper basket exactly as semantics in earlier transformational theory. Katz & Fodor has defined semantics as "synchronic linguistic description minus grammar" (Katz & Fodor 1963, p. 172). Anything you cannot explain in your syntax and semantics you shove into stylistics for others to worry about. I shall later on argue that this view is mistaken and that stylistic variation can be defined more precisely. However, let us dwell a little on this position in order to investigate its consequences.

4. THE PLACE OF STYLISTIC RULES IN GRAMMAR

Let us for a moment accept the view that stylistic variation equals linguistic variation minus variation in meaning. We can now investigate where in the grammar the stylistic rules have to be placed. In traditional transformational grammar, there are three basic types of optional rules: base rules (i.e. phrase-structure rules), the rule for lexical insertion and transformations.

In the generative semantics framework, some kind of still unspecified formation rules generate a semantic representation. Obligatory and optional transformations, among other things carrying out lexical insertion, then convert this representation into a surface structure. The meaning of a sentence is fully represented in its semantic representation, and all transformations are therefore meaning-preserving. This means that all optional transformations are stylistic.

It would be very nice if semantic representations were unique, i.e. if there did not exist two synonymous semantic representations. If so, nothing but meaning would be represented in semantic representations, and optional base rules would never be stylistic, since they only generate a difference in meaning. This variant of generative semantics thus envisages a very elegant division between base rules and transformations. If semantic representations are given in a notation resembling standard logical notation, however, they will not be unique. There are numerous examples of logically equivalent (i.e. synonymous) well-formed logical formulas. Consequently, even semantic representations might contain stylistic variation, and stylistic rules might be interspersed with meaning-generating base rules.

In Chomsky's extended standard theory the situation is still more complicated (Chomsky 1971). The output of the base rules, deep structure, is not identical to semantic representation. Instead, projection rules operate on deep structures to generate semantic representations, and these rules can of course conflate two deep structures into the same semantic structure in the process. Even if semantic representations were unique, deep structures could contain stylistic variation, and the base rules will be either stylistic or meaning-generating, or perhaps both at once. Similarly, the rule for lexical insertion also gives rise to variation in both meaning and style. In generative semantics on the other hand, lexical insertion was a transformation that did not affect meaning, since it just matched an abstract semantic symbolization with a phonological form. It could generate a style difference, though, by choosing between several synonymous but stylistically non-equivalent alternatives.

In the extended standard theory, not even normal transformations have a single function, but in a way introduce differences in both meaning and style. The reason is that transformations are no longer meaning-preserving, since the projection rules not only operate on deep structure, but also on surface structure. When for instance the passive transformation is applied to sentence (1) yielding (2), it simultaneously changes the meaning:

(1) Many arrows did not hit the target.
(2) The target was not hit by many arrows.

Many transformations thus have a double function giving rise to differences in both style and meaning. However, transformations only affect meaning very indirectly, since no transformation is linked directly to a projection rule, while there is a much clearer correspondence between base rules and projection rules. The generalization rather seems to be that there has to be a certain similarity between surface structure and semantic representation. This is in fact the solution of generative semantics

(Lakoff, 1971). If a transformation destroys this resemblance, the output is regarded as ungrammatical. This derivational constraint in a way restricts the optionality of optional transformations.

It is at least possible that stylistic research might help to decide the stubborn controversy between the extended standard transformational theory and generative semantics. It is of course an empirical question whether it is preferrable to intersperse meaning-generating and stylistic rules in the base and keep syntax and semantics distinct, as in Chomsky's theory, or whether it is better to transfer most stylistic rules in the base to the transformational component and merge syntax and semantics, as in the theory of generative semantics.

5. STYLE AS VARIATION IN THE PRESENTATION OF A MESSAGE

But we cannot state that there is no connection between variation of meaning and variation of style. A certain style can demand that the communicated facts are chosen in some special way (cf. Björck 1953, ch. 1:5). One of the characteristics of *subjective* as opposed to *objective* style, *abstract* as opposed to *detailed* style, etc. is that the choice of facts to communicate is biassed. We could of course state that such a variation is not to be labelled stylistic, but then we would not be concerned with the traditional term *style,* but with an entirely new concept.

It might here be fruitful to consider a more concrete model of linguistic communication. The generation of a message starts out from an extralinguistic context. Given is a speaker and a task for this speaker. He might for example want the window to be shut. The speaker now performs a series of consecutive choices. Should he use communication at all to fulfil his task or should he just shut the window himself? If he chooses the first alternative, he has to choose a receiver, a language, a medium and a general message, a thought to be conveyed. These choices are considerably more linguistic than the first one. Then he chooses a semantic representation for his general message, i. e. determines his strategy for the communication, chooses the type of illocution, fills out details of facts etc. Finally, he should convert the semantic representation into a surface structure. This is only a rough approximation of the process, and the choices might actually be carried out in slightly different order.

We can now observe that the further down in the hierarchy of choices we come, the more stylistic are the decisions. Roughly, the choices leading up to a semantic representation generate variation in meaning, while the choices following the choice of general message are stylistic. The choices between the general message and the semantic representation then have a double function, giving rise to both variation in meaning and variation in style. This view of style is akin to Askeberg's definition of style as the way in which the speaker solves the problem of giving his words the intended effect in a given speech situation (Askeberg 1954, p. 48). Style is viewed as variation that does not change the general message of a text.

But since earlier choices will influence later choices, stylistic decisions might be dependent on the choice of message, medium, listener, etc. This does not mean that these early choices themselves are stylistic choices. But there might be a correlation between the early and the late choices, for instance so that a certain message (or a subject matter) goes together with a late rule, say application of the passive. The early choices will in fact correspond to what has been called contextual features. In other words, stylistic rules can be contextually conditioned.

6. STYLE AS CONTEXTUALLY CONDITIONED VARIATION

We have now adopted the view that stylistic rules are rules that generate a variation that is not in itself a variation in situation or general message, but *might* be dependent on such a variation. One might want to go a step further and state that stylistic variation *must* be dependent on the context. Again, this is an empirical question. Do there exist variations in natural languages that are not dependent on variations in context? If so, do we in practice call them stylistic?

If stylistic rules generally are contextually conditioned, then it is no longer appropriate to call them optional. On the contrary, they might be obligatory, if we consider them in the context of the sentence where they apply. The question whether stylistic rules are always context-dependent can perhaps be regarded as equivalent to the question of whether there are any really optional rules in the grammar, or whether free variation really exists. It is rather unlikely that a rule would give rise to totally free variation. This would mean that different texts have different frequencies for the various options, but that the variation is governed by chance and does not correlate with any contextual feature. But the contextual situations seem to be so manifold that at least some of them must influence the choice of the options. If nothing else will influence the choice, individual idiosyncrasies will make the options correlate with the language habits of the speaker.

Let us leave aside for a moment the question of whether free variation really exists in natural languages. Stylisticians are anyway justified in concentrating on context-dependent variation. The reason is that the correlations between stylistic textual features and contextual features enable him to make predictions. Given a certain contextual situation, the stylistician can predict which textual features will occur in a text uttered in that situation. And given a text with certain textual features, he can predict in what kind of contextual situation the text was uttered. The listeners in the actual communication situation, too, can carry out these predictions. Precisely because of these correlations, style markers can carry information about the context that is not included in the meaning of the sentence. The correlations also justify the terms *stylistic deviance, stylisticity,* and *norm.* A text is deviant if the predictions are not borne out, i. e. if the contextual features of the text are not matched by the normal style markers. If the predictions are borne out, the text has a high stylisticity. This suggests a more narrow use of the term *norm* than is common in style theory. Not just any text can be chosen as norm when we study a certain text, but only a text that agrees in either textual or contextual features with the text under study. All differences between text and norm that are revealed by the comparison can then be labelled *deviance.* However, one might require more of a *good style* than high stylisticity. In addition, one might want the text to be easy to perceive, aesthetically pleasing, etc.

If stylistic variation is to be defined as linguistic variation conditioned by contextual features, it becomes an extremely important task for stylistic research to determine what these contextual features are and to describe the conditioning (Enkvist 173, p. 51). One suggestion of this paper is that the contextual features include the choices a speaker has to make early in a communication situation, e. g. the choice of general message. Observe, however, that all contextual differences are not stylistically relevant. Another interesting observation is the distinction between natural and conventional style markers. Some correlations between style markers and context might have arisen by chance or by social convention, while others are independently motivated. Correlations of the latter kind might be the complicated syntax of abstract style, and the archaic nature of written language. Research on the motivation of correlations might be called *explanatory stylistics.* Observe also, that the correlations enable us to use two different series of style labels. We can identify a style either by mentioning its style markers, e. g. adjectival style, archaic style, emotive style, or by mentioning in which context it occurs, e. g. spoken style, informal style, the style of the author N. N. However, as our communication model implies, there is no clear borderline between style markers and contextual features.

7. PROBABILISTIC RULES

In most cases, one single occurrence of a textual feature is not enough to determine the style of a text. 'Having a certain style' is a property generally attributed to a text long enough to allow for a statistical treatment of the frequency of the options. One might even propose that style should be defined as linguistic variation on a more general delicacy level. If we replace one morpheme in a text with another, this change might affect meaning, but will not alter the total frequencies of the morphemes significantly, and will therefore not affect style. The question is then how far down on the delicacy scale a linguistic category can be placed and still count as a style marker. The frequency of a certain syntactic construction is normally a linguistic feature general enough to be a style marker; the frequency of a specific sentence is too delicate a feature.

However, there are style markers placed on a very delicate level. Often one single occurrence will determine the style rather narrowly. We have to encounter just one *thou* in a text to know that the style is definitely archaic. I think that the solution to the style problem might not be to regard style as a variation on a general delicacy level in long portions of a text. Rather, there are two kinds of stylistic rules, absolute and probabilistic ones. Absolute rules introduce a linguistic option uniformly in a certain context. For instance, the second person pronoun might be *thou* everywhere in an archaic style, *you* everywhere in another style. A probabilistic rule, on the other hand, introduces one option in some of the cases only, and other options otherwise. An example might be topicalization, which fronts a constituent in a sentence, but does not always operate. Different styles will then only differ in the frequency of the different options. In this case, one instance of a linguistic structure is not enough to determine the style. It is rather the ratio between the options that is the style marker. This ratio is of course calculable only from a rather long portion of a text.

A probabilistic rule is then what is left of an optional rule when we have taken into account the contextual conditioning. A probabilistic rule will assign a ratio to each option, telling us how often this option is chosen. In addition, the ratios might be different for different contextual situations. One might argue that probabilistic rules are not to be accounted for in a competence grammar, but should be left to a description of linguistic performance. If this argument is accepted, competence is given a meaning very different from its meaning in everyday language. Certainly we *know* what frequencies of the options are expected, what is stylistically acceptable, just as we know which sentences in the language are grammatical. A competence grammar should reflect our knowledge about what is normal language in different situations. A performance grammar should also describe how this knowledge is actually put to use and how various disturbing factors influence performance. These factors can also affect style and give rise to stylistic deviation. The distinction between expected style and actual style is really a subcase of the distinction between competence and performance. If we want to capture this distinction, expected style has to be accounted for in a competence grammar. Those who place style in performance only impose a fundamental distinction between ungrammaticality and stylistic deviation that is not really arguable.

It is an empirical question whether there are probabilistic rules that are not contextually conditioned, i. e. that do not give rise to stylistic variation. This would happen when the same ratios are valid for all contexts. Such a lack of variation must be distinguished from free variation, which means that the frequencies of the options do vary, but not according to any rule. No fixed ratios could then be assigned to the options. However, even when there are fixed ratios, these ratios do not always have to be followed strictly. A deviance of 5 percent from the fixed ratio might in some cases cause a serious stylistic deviation, in other cases be hardly noticeable. Perhaps a note on the standard deviation should be attached to each ratio. On the other hand, the degree of deviance might often be predictable from the numerical ratios themselves, as we shall see in the next section.

8.   A HYPOTHESIS ON STYLISTIC DEVIANCE

Let us now consider some possibilities for the contextual conditioning of a grammatical rule. Four examples are depicted in (3—6):

(3)

	option A	option B
context A	1	0
context B	0	1

(4)

	option A	option B
context A	3/5	2/5
context B	2/5	3/5

(5)

	option A	option B
context A	1	0
context B	2/5	3/5

(6)

	option A	option B
context A	1	0
context B	1	0

For the sake of simplicity, I have limited the number of options and contexts to two, but in principle there might be any number of them. The only thing to remember is that the sum of the ratios in each horizontal row should equal 1. The ratio for an option is obtained by dividing the frequency of the option in a text with the total frequency of all the alternatives in the same text.

Diagram (3) depicts a situation where the context totally determines the choice. The rule is not really optional at all, but obligatory and context-dependent. We have a different construction in each style, and they never mix. A case in point might be number agreement between subject and verb in Swedish around 1900. In written Swedish, the verb always agreed with the subject in number, in spoken everyday language never. Our hypothesis is now, that a deviation from the general pattern in such a situation will instantly be recognized and felt as an inappropriateness not unlike an ungrammaticality.

Diagram (4) indicates a situation where the two styles are much more similar to each other. In each style, both constructions occur, and there is just a weak preference for one of them. An example is optional deletion of *har, hade* in dependent clauses in written and spoken Swedish. The deletion has traditionally been considered as a style marker of written language, but also occurs in spoken language (Holm 1960). In this case, our hypothesis tells us, a deviation from the expected pattern will hardly be noticed and will certainly not be considered inappropriate.

Diagram (5) depicts a situation where a deviation will be felt inappropriate in one style but not in another. An example is certain reductions in Swedish casual speech. In my dialect, there is only one spelling of *skulle*, but the word can be pronounced either /skulle/ or /sku/. The full pronunciation of course has a flavour of carefulness, but is not at all abnormal even in colloquial speech. The generalized hypothesis is that the more even the balance is between the options, the less severe is a deviation from the expected pattern.

Diagram (6), finally, does not really depict a contextually conditioned rule at all, but a normal, obligatory rule. Option B is not acceptable in any style, and hence ungrammatical. I have included the diagram just to show that ungrammaticality is nothing but the limiting case of stylistic deviance.

9. A HYPOTHESIS ON LINGUISTIC CHANGE

It is certainly reasonable to assume that linguistic change originates as optional variation, i. e. variation to be described by a probabilistic rule. This variation can simultaneously be stylistic, e. g. the new construction might be introduced as a variant in some style only. Little by little the new construction replaces the older one in that style and other styles (cf. Labov 1965). Finally, the optional rule becomes obligatory. If new rules are added last in a grammar, as some linguists have claimed, we should have mainly obligatory rules early in the grammar and mainly optional ones late in the grammar. New optional rules can be added after these, but at the same time, the earlier optional rules are re-structured into obligatory ones.

If our earlier hypotheses about the acceptability of a stylistic deviation are correct, there should be a considerable resistance against a totally new option with low probability. Since the expected pattern of occurrence in such cases is the one given in diagram (6), the new option will be considered ungrammatical. Diagram (6) then depicts an inherently stable situation. Language contains a mechanism that prevents exuberant change. The initial resistance must in some way be broken, e. g. by popularity depending on social status or by perceptual advantages of the new option. It might be easiest to overcome the resistance in some fairly restricted, contextually well-defined style. If this happens, the situation of diagram (6) has been replaced by the situation given in diagram (5). However, this is not a stable situation. If the new option is also accepted in other styles, the result is the situation of diagram (4). *Ha*-deletion in Swedish might be an example. It originated in written language and is now spreading into spoken language (Holm 1967, p. 159). If the option is not accepted in other styles, but replaces the old option in the style where it originated, the result is the situation of diagram (3).

But diagram (4) does not depict an equilibrium state, either. According to our hypotheses, one hardly recognizes deviations from the pattern. It is therefore possible for an option to get more and more unusual and finally disappear totally. An example might be the verb-final word order of Old Swedish, once freely alternating with the order verb — object — adverbial, but now totally obsolete. The outcome is here a situation of type (6), but could also have been a situation such as in (3), where a deviation from the pattern is rather unacceptable. My example above does not seem to confirm that diagram (3) depicts a stable situation, since subject-verb agreement has now disappeared from written Swedish (Ståhle 1970, pp. 35—45). However, the change occurred astonishingly late. Already in the seventeenth century many varieties of spoken language had no agreement. We can also observe, that the result was not a system like that in diagram (4), but rather that of diagram (6). We now have no optionality at all. The process was not gradual, but very abrupt: plural forms of verbs disappeared almost overnight in for instance the newspaper style. We have a sudden reorganization of the grammar: the style of context A was simply introduced in situations of type B also. We have now come full circle, and the gradual process of change can start over again.

There are of course many counter-examples to the rule 'optionality tends to be avoided'. One reason might be that contextual features sometimes really force a variation. This is true of natural style markers, and the above argument can be carried out for conventional style markers only. I have included the above hypotheses just to show what kind of arguments a probabilistic treatment of optionality might lead to. Nothing can be asserted with certainty in this area, before we have more accurate diachronic data to consider.

10. DETERMINING THE CONDITIONING FACTORS

In Swedish, the rule of topicalization fronts a constituent in a main clause, causing subject-verb inversion. The fronted constituents seem to be of two types: a) the focus of the sentence, emphatically stressed and containing new information, is preposed more often than constituents not in the focus, b) constituents high up in the syntactic tree are preposed more often than constituents further down. Examples would be (7) and (8):

(7) Kl. 5 åt jag middag i går. (emphatic)
(8) I går åt jag middag kl. 5. (high up in the structure)
'I had dinner at 5 o'clock yesterday.'

On the face of it, there seems to be just one rule, since either one of the time adverbials in (7) and (8) can be preposed. But the results have slightly different stylistic value: (7) occurs mostly in spoken language and makes an emotive impression that is totally absent from (8).

Topicalization also seems to be a probabilistic rule, which is carried out in some of the cases where it theoretically could apply. But it is impossible to say that the rule applies to a certain percentage of all cases in a certain context. Rather, we should say (a) that topicalization is conditioned by focus-position and that the frequency of the transformation in that environment is further conditioned by the type of context, and (b) that topicalization is also conditioned by the place of the constituent to be moved in the syntactic hierarchy and that the frequency in this case is also affected by the context. Such a double conditioning might be confusing sometimes, but it is important to map it in great detail if one wants to state reliable stylistic correlations.

11. CONCLUSION

In this paper, I have viewed style as a textual variation not affecting the general message, and possibly conditioned by contextual features and the contents of the message. Most traditionally optional rules have to be treated as probabilistic rules, assigning different ratios to the options in different contexts. Some hypotheses about the diachrony of stylistic rules are also presented.

The general conclusion is that style cannot be isolated from grammar. Stylistic rules have to be stated in a competence grammar. Our intuitions on stylistic value do not differ in substance from our intuitions on grammaticality, only in degree. A purely grammatical rule might have been stylistic before it was generalized and lost its optionality. Stylistic conditioning is but a special type of the types of conditioning that are possible in a grammar. Since we cannot draw a sharp borderline between style and grammar, we should accept their unity.

REFERENCES

Askeberg, Fritz. "Stilbegreppet". *Modersmålslärarnas förenings årsskrift,* 1954, pp. 17—50.
Björck, Staffan. *Romanens formvärld.* 1953. New ed. Stockholm: Natur och Kultur, 1968.
Chomsky, Noam. "Deep structure, Surface structure, and Semantic Interpretation". In Steinberg and Jakobovits, pp. 183—216.
Enkvist, Nils Erik. *Linguistic Stylistics.* The Hague: Mouton, 1973.
Holm, Gösta. "Hjälpverbet ha i bildat talspråk". *Nysvenska studier* 39 (1960), pp. 83—93.
— *Epoker och prosastilar.* Lund: Studentlitteratur, 1967.
Jacobs, Roderick A. and Peter S. Rosenbaum. *Transformations, Style and Meaning.* Waltham, Mass.: Xerox College Publishing, 1971.
Katz, Jerrold J. and Jerry A. Fodor. "The Structure of a Semantic Theory". *Language,* 39:2 (1963), pp. 170—210.
Labov, William. "The Social Motivation of a Sound Change". *Word,* 19 (1963), pp. 273—309.
— "On the Mechanism of Linguistic Change". *Georgetown University: Monograph Series in Language and Linguistics,* 18 (1965), pp. 91—114.
Lakoff, George. "On Generative Semantics". In Steinberg and Jakobovits, pp. 232—296.
Steinberg, Danny D. and Leon A. Jakobovits (eds.). *Semantics: An Interdisciplinary Reader in Philosophy, Linguistics and Psychology.* London: Cambridge University Press, 1971.
Ståhle, Carl Ivar. "Några drag i svenska språkets förändring under 1900-talet". *1900-talssvenska.* Eds. Bertil Molde and Carl Ivar Ståhle. Stockholm: Läromedelsförlaget, 1970.

Peter Cassirer
University of Göteborg

On the place of stylistics

What then is style and what does stylistics do? Questions like these very often form the opening of stylistic investigations. This very fact points to two phenomena: firstly, that there is no accepted definition of style and no general agreement on aims, methods, or material for what is known as stylistics;[1] secondly, that there seems to be fairly clear agreement among stylisticians that these questions are problematic.[2] The development of linguistic theory during the last two decades has made stylistics a central topic in linguistics. In early TG theory, style was regarded as a rather unimportant part of performance, but it is now recognised more and more that there is such a thing as stylistic competence and that stylistic competence might be a very important factor. At the same time there are scholars who claim that there is no such phenomenon as style and consequently, no science called stylistics (Gray 1969, 1973). Others endeavour to establish a general style-theory in which the concept is independent of other variables (Trabant 1974) or seen in relation to other sciences (Enkvist 1971). Stylistics is traditionally considered to be a science "which lies astride the border-line between linguistics and literary studies" (Ullmann 1957 Preface; cf Todorov 1966; Sanders 1973).

In this article I shall try to show that the case for this traditional placement can be called in question and that it is to be explained by a fundamental difference between two theoretical aspects of science. This distinction also determines the relationship between text-grammar and stylistics and, furthermore, seems to be the source of the bad reputation from which stylistics suffers.[3]

As the point of departure for an analysis of the ultimate goals of stylistics, the convariance of style-concept with such variables as aims, material, method and science-ideal is discussed as well as what consequences that variation has for the definition of the "elusive concept of style"[4] and for the status of stylistics as an independent science.

Bennison Gray's dismissal of the existence of stylistics coincides ironically enough with an almost incredible increase of interest in this branch of science, as evidenced by the appearance of several new periodicals such as *Style; Poetics; Poetica, Zeitschrift für Sprach- und Literaturwissenschaft; Poetique; LiLi, Zeitschrift für Literaturwissenshaft und Linguistik; Journal of Literary Semantics*, etc. Some of the titles of the most recent years' monographs illustrate the combining of interest in linguistics and literature: *Some aspects of text grammars; a study in theoretical linguistics and poetry* (van Dijk 1972); *Linguistik in der Literaturwissenschaft* (Ihwe 1972); *Sprachliche Konstituten moderner Dichtung* (Kloepfer and Oomen 1970); *Linguistic Structures in Poetry* (Levin

1962), and mention can be made of anthologies such as *Essays on the language of Literature* (Chatman and Levin, eds. 1970) and the four volume work *Literaturwissenschaft und Linguistik* (Ihwe, ed. 1971—1972).

These titles give some illustration of the tendency of linguists and students of literature to devote themselves to the study of common problems; these problems can be considered in the traditional way as stylistic. It does not necessarily follow, however, that stylistics must be characterised as a border-line science between linguistics and literary studies.[5] Certain scholars, perhaps chiefly in the USA, have limited the application of the terms "style" and "stylistics" to the field of "pure" literature, but other scholars, in Sweden at any rate, have applied these terms also to the study of non-literary texts.[6]

An important reason why stylistics has been considered a combined science of linguistics and literature is to be found in the fact that stylisticians traditionally work on *texts*. The modern science of language — i. e. structuralism — was originally founded on detailed research down to the smallest components of language and has only recently begun to tackle problems beyond the limits of the sentence, i. e. on the textual level. Literary scholars like philologists, however, have of course always worked with texts, and whenever a linguist has approached a text with textual methods of analysis, he has been labelled a stylistician. The fact that stylisticians have developed a special interest in texts of a purely literary nature has naturally contributed even more to the interpretation of stylistics as a border-line science between linguistics and literary research: "When pushing upwards towards larger textual units we are also approaching problems traditionally regarded, as literary, not linguistic", Enkvist very significantly notes (1973 p. 88). In cultures where the term stylistics is reserved for literature, the term "rhetoric" has been employed to the study of non-literary texts which have been approached from more or less the same point of view as that used by stylisticians in their study of literature. Historically, however, stylistics is a direct descendant of rhetoric. But since the concept of style — in the case of stylistic value, stylistic level and style type at least — is applied to non-literary texts in cultures where one would first apply stylistics to pure literature (and — to my knowledge — there has never been any recognition of the existence of a comprehensive concept in rhetoric which would correspond to *style*), there is no reason to complicate the debate further by introducing a distinction between stylistics and rhetoric — all the more, since it is impossible to differentiate clearly between pure literature and ordinary prose.

Let us accept then that all texts have style, and likewise that there can be stylistically relevant features at all levels of the text. At the same time, however, it does not necessarily follow that the concept of *style* is usually applied to all levels of the text; a descriptive examination of the traditional use of the term shows that it is applied to the text in the first place; that one does not speak of style until one reaches the level of text (cf Sanders 1973 p. 79). Phonetic (or phonological) and morphematic factors can be "style-markers" but sounds and words hardly "have style" — they can be accorded certain stylistic value and be placed in a style category, at a stylistic level or in a style pattern (for example genre). It is more doubtful whether isolated sentences can be said to "have style" (cf however Enkvist 1973 p. 111), since the distinction between a text and a sentence can hardly be said to be clearly drawn. However, it seems to me that a sentence which is clearly not a complete unit, i. e. a text, should rightly belong IN a style or style type. More simply, one can describe the use of terms thus:

phonetic and phonological items	have	stylistic value;
morphemic items	are on a	stylistic level;
syntagmatic items	can have	style;
texts	have (a)	style

This can also be presented schematically as in figure, below, where the lines from left to right can be read as: *constituted of* or *can be applied to* and from right to left *constitute*.

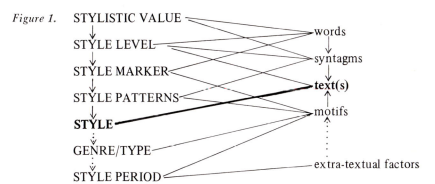

Figure 1.

In as much as linguistics was confined to the framework of the sentence, stylistics could be formally separated from it by means of its concern with texts. The stylistician could thus be a linguist who applied his linguistic terms of reference to a field in which linguists lacked terms of reference. It is not surprising that the results he could achieve by this method often appeared as trivial or irrelevant to the literary scholar as to the linguist.[7] Furthermore, the stylistician had a fundamentally different aim from the linguist, particularly when working with literary texts. This fundamental difference still remains although linguistics has spread over into the area of text-grammar with the result that text-grammar and stylistics are by no means identical branches of science.[8]

The basic distinction between the traditional stylistician and the linguist lies in the difference between nomotetic and idiographic aspects (to use Windelband's terms) or, to use more modern terminology, between *genotype* and *fenotype* respectively.[9] In the case of a nomotetic approach, one deduces general rules, systems and structures from the object of investigation or area of research, whereas the idiographic approach is concerned with the particular: the solution of the idiographic problem is not necessarily to be used as a basis for generalisation. It is possible, however, to trace the advances to different levels of a nomotetic approach in stylistics, for example in the attempt to describe the style of a whole language system or in investigations of stylistic typology and genre studies. But the traditional stylisticians have chiefly worked on a limited number of texts — one (literary) text or a (literary) author. These later stylisticians have often been accused of lacking stringent method and sometimes of lacking an explicit theory. Probably the best example of this is the criticism levelled against Leo Spitzer.[10] This criticism is invalid since it is based on false premises — a point of view that Spitzer tried in vain to clarify to his opponents. From a nomotetic point of view, separate analyses of texts might not be adequate as a basis for a general deductive system (however brilliant and inspired they may be, a quality which Spitzer's adversaries furthermore tend to regard as suspect).

Scholars with a purely nomotetic interest have frequently claimed an exclusive right to the title of "scientific". They have, however, failed to recognize that there are idiographic problems, the solutions of which are as legitimate as those of general problems. Furthermore it is a moot point whether one will ever be able to establish a general descriptive/explanatory system for the humanities which would satisfy this demand, and also whether, from the epistemological point of view, it is even conceivable.[11] As far as stylistics is concerned, the problem has made itself felt in the debate on macro- and microstylistics, in the question of the application of quantitative methods, and in the debate on the meaning of style.

Linguistics is the study of the general in language and as such is a nomotetic science. Stylistics, however, studies parts of what is specific in the language[12] — sometimes very small divisions of language — and thus is, by its very nature, an idiographic science.[13] (That the distinction between nomotetic and idiographic is not a real dichotomy but that the terms suggest the two ends of scale becomes obvious when one considers the fact that the stylisticians' area of interest ranges from the language in its entirety through genre and style-types down to poems of only a few lines.) In the discussion of macro- and microstylistics, it has been maintained that the smaller the unit of text examined, the more specific becomes function, meaning and importance of each element, and thus the less adequate the general-rules description as an explication model. The same goes for text-linguistics or -grammar, which examines what characterises well-structured texts and sets up general rules for text construction. Text linguistics describes general and possibly universal rules. The stylistician has usually worked with a limited number of texts and — by lacking an explicit textual theory — usually establishes certain textual-linguistic patterns, e. g. narratives, in specific texts or genres or in a specific author. The absence of a basic explicit text theory has meant that these observations, from the nomotetic point of view, must be regarded as "ad hoc", however systematised they may be in relation to the examined texts in question. That stylisticians have so much devoted themselves to the analysis of literary texts obviously complicates even further the attempts to generalise or to set up a general style theory. Today it is obvious that an important characteristic — *ipso facto* — of especially modern literary works, is that, in one way or another, they deviate from "the normal", that they are — for example in Prague-structuralist terms — "foregrounding"[14], which means that the results from stylistic research into such material do not lend themselves directly to forming the basis of a text grammar in the generative sense. Of course, *mutatis mutandis*, the same applies to older texts and probably all poetry. It is reasonable to suppose, nevertheless, that text-grammar has a great deal to gain from the type of stylistic research in which, for example, the stylistician is dealing with composition. Here the concept "linguistic stylistics" takes on special interest: in this concept, the two aspects of genotype and fenotype seem to clash. Stylistics, applied to verbal phenomena, has always been linguistically orientated in a closer sense than rhetoric. The stress on linguistics in the term "linguistic stylistics" might thus appear both superfluous[15] and contradictory. The two style theorists who gave this name to their books in 1973 (Sanders: *Linguistiche Stiltheorie* and Enkvist: *Linguistic Stylistics*) also meant two different things by the qualifier "linguistic". Sanders extends linguistics — according to some recent theories of language — to include pragmatics, by which stylistics quite naturally becomes a subsidiary branch of linguistics, irrespective of what material is being examined. For Enkvist, on the other hand, the concept "linguistics" in this context implies the same sense as "objective, scientific" and the meaning in this case of "linguistic" is seen as "with objective methods as in linguistics".[16]

In this connection one can point to a strange tendency in nomotetic-biased criticism to isolate the formal, or immanent, aspects of the language while neglecting the whole.[17] Stylisticians who have not been infected by the positivist disease have always — albeit often implicitly — worked with the theory that language is a means of communication in discussing the authors' intentions or the effect of the text on the recipient. The stylisticians who posed these questions — however "ad hoc" or "unsystematically" they may have worked — have, in principle, a sounder approach than the "isolating" formalists who examined the separate parts of language — however universal they may be — but who did not investigate the functional role of language as language; that is, as a means of communication.[18] The discussion about Nora's line in "A Doll's House". — "I lay the keys here". (Enkvist 1964 p. 53; 1973 p. 33; Cassirer 1970 pp. 41 f) may serve as an example of the problem just mentioned.

The difference of opinion between Enkvist, who in 1964 contended that the interpretation of the import of the utterance in its specific context should not rightly fall within the field of stylistics (not within linguistic stylistics, anyway) but rather within the jurisdiction of literary analysis, and myself, who maintain that stylistics, when describing a text where symbols of a higher order occur, must account for the import of these in the specific context, resolves itself into the question of whether one has a nomotetic or idiographic aim; something which Enkvist explicitly states in 1973: "How far we wish to go in our discussion of an utterance such as this will of course depend on our own purpose" (p. 34). It is simply a question of which level or stratum of the text (and its meaning) we want to reach.[19] No linguistic or semantic theory can reasonably account for all the specific potential imports that words or sentences can yield in specific contexts, but the theory must embrace and account for the possibility that they can acquire those very different and specific imports and contain an explanation of these phenomena, and hopefully, in the final resort, also give certain basic guidelines for interpretation strategies. No linguistic theory can make the claim of completeness (holism), without taking into consideration the fact that language is a social phenomenon — that is a means of communication. "Linguistic competence" consequently must include communicative, social, interpretative and stylistic competence. Nothing has more clearly demonstrated the inadequacies of a linguistic theory that is based only on surface structures than the developments within linguistics in the last decades. The attempt to explain language phenomena through the syntactical approach (with the hope of leaving the semantic factors outside the discussion as far as possible) has shown itself as less than satisfactory. All effort to reduce or eliminate the role of semantics in language theory have shown themselves to be hindrances to the understanding of language as a phenomenon.[20] The linguist cannot possibly evade the responsibility of tackling the capacity of language to create import (as opposed to meaning) claiming that it is the business of some other discipline, e. g. literary science. All communication presupposes an interpretative faculty or competence, and the "literary" seems not to be different in kind from the "linguistic" — if it were, the dividing line between literary and non-literary works could be based on this very difference. But there is no such dividing line (cf Cassirer 1970). Meanings at different levels occur in all types of verbal communication — even if symbols of a higher order occur to a greater extent in lyrics than in directions and instructions. Therefore the demands placed on interpretative competence are higher in the interpretation of literature, which of course makes the problem there more complex, from the interpretative point of view, than if one proceeds from simpler language types.[21] This in turn means that certain linguists have wanted to push the problem into the background for as long as possible. Here too there is a dividing line between mentalist and positivist linguists as well as stylisticians. And these differences of goal and, consequently, approach have meant that different stylisticians have proposed different definitions of style.

Mukařovský has in my opinion convincingly shown (1948 p. 13—28)[22] that a concept is a structural variable the import of which is dependent on the import of the other elements that are included in the structure of concepts in the science, or the branch of science in question. The validity of Mukařovský's theory seems to me to be verified by the fact that it can explain the multiplicity and divergences between the different definitions of style. Of these, there are nearly as many as there are theoretical and/or practical stylistic investigations of some extension, and they are dependent on the stylistician's SCIENTIFIC IDEAL, MATERIAL, GOAL and METHOD just as each of these factors is, in turn, a variable in the structure, so that all are interrelated and interdependent and thus affect each other. All these above-mentioned factors can be — in varying degrees of course — guiding factors in a certain structure. (The PROBLEM is seen here as a function of MATERIAL and GOAL. CONCEPT implies — implicity or explicity — needless to say, THEORY). Schematically, the effects of these complex interdependent relationship for the definition of style can be stated as in figure 2, p. 35.

Let us assume that the prevailing scientific ideal defines science or scientific manner in terms of objectivity and exactness. This means, of course, that theory building and conceptual devices — yes even the definition of the problem[23] — are adapted to such an ideal, and problems and phenomena which do not fit into such an outlook are dismissed from the context as "inoperable" or "non-scientific" factors. An example of this is found in Lyons (1963) where he claims: "We are no longer tempted to invent [!] rather nebulous 'emotive' differences of meaning that can be given no operational significance" (p. 77). Roman Jakobson has characterised another representative of this special approach in an apposite remark in his well-known closing statement "Linguistics and poetics": "Joos is indeed a brilliant expert in reduction experiments and his emphatic requirement for an 'expulsion' of the emotive elements 'from linguistic science' is a radical experiment in reduction — *reductio in absurdum*" (1960 p. 354).

As an example of positivistic stylistics — however much less extreme — one could refer to Louis T. Milic's work on Swift (1967). The first three chapters give a very valuable analysis and criticism of so-called "impressionistic" or metaphoric stylistic criticism, and the quantitative research that Milic undertook is undoubtedly of linguistic and stylistic interest. But "the playfulness, the irony and ultimately the seriousness" which Milic claims made him love Swift's work and engaged him in it (p. 15), are qualities that his (quantitative) method has obviously been unable to describe or explain more closely. The result of the research is — as Milic says himself[24] — of rather a *distinctive* character (see more about this term below). The criticism which he levels against impressionistic metaphoric stylistic criticism fails, thereby, to achieve its desired effect. It seems to me that this "impressionistic" type of criticism — in any case, when it is at its best — is capable of reflecting the critics' fascination with the texts' quality in a more adequate way. At the same time, let it not be thought I do not heartily concur with Milic's view that the judgements that are applied to the style in a work, or of an author, must be firmly attached to an explicit analysis — most impressionistic assessments are nothing more than hypotheses about which features that can be seen as stylistically relevant in a text, and consequently are only points of departure for the scientific description which has the ambition of accounting for, not only the critics' response, but also — and primarily — the stimuli which worked together to form it.

The traditional criticism of quantitative method rests on the assumption that with such a method one is not able to gain access to the very qualities which people like Milic reckon have led them to love Swift. This is by no means necessarily the case. Everything allows itself to be counted in one way or another. The question is only whether the estimations are meaningful. The smaller the text-unit examined, the more specific becomes the function of every element in its specific context (as I have said earlier) and thus the more difficult (but not a priori impossible!) becomes the application of the quantitative method. In any case, every quantification presupposes a qualitative analysis[25] and this qualitative analysis may well be judged to be quite sufficient in many cases.

The idiographically-minded stylistician in general will, in all likelihood, proceed from material in which he finds the most interesting problems — e. g. irony in Swift. His goal will determine his method. If he discovers he can solve the problem by a qualitative method, he will apply it, and assume thereby that the method is justified. The criterion for scientific behaviour in such a case is that the researcher convincingly demonstrates that his thesis is built on real premises (something which, in the light of present psycho-linguistic research should be pretty hazardous for some time) and that the final conclusions are correct. With such a goal, he must meanwhile work with a concept-device which can cope with perceptual aspects since an adequate style concept for an examination of this type must also cover the function and effect of the examined factors as a whole.

By "qualitative" in the preceding passage, I do not of course mean evaluative or so-called tertiary qualities. In itself, an idiographic or mentalist style concept need not consist of evaluative aspects. Stylistics can very well remain descriptive (as opposed to estimative) and ought, of course, to be so if the end in view is descriptive. But it should be equally clear that the investigation must lead to the evaluative qualitative result, if the point of departure, the incitement, of the whole investigation is of such a nature. If Milic (to take his investigation as an example once again) had wanted to examine why he had grown to love Swift, — that is, which factors gave his prose those specific qualities — then obviously it would be unreasonable if he did not include a discussion of the evaluative qualitative factors in the investigation. Here one can consider that a scientific ideal of a positivist nature would forbid stylisticians to discuss style in such terms, since they would be seen as subjective and therefore unscientific. It speaks for itself that the results of such an investigation do not give the solution to the initial problem. Here then a conflict arises between the original objective, the method and the result which can probably be traced in not a few stylistic investigations. There is no stylistic theory about absolute values which reaches beyond the classical rhetorical bounds and perhaps no such theory can be established. From this it does not necessarily follow that a stylistician who takes a value experience as his point of departure should conceal this under the cloak of a pseudo-objective investigation, whereby he would be unable to account for, explicitly, the values which lie behind the choice of the object of investigation and the selection of the features examined. On the contrary, one should actually demand that these evaluative qualitative aspects be stated and explicitly shown throughout the whole investigation. It would be a blatant hypocrisy to maintain that the evaluative qualitative factors in an overwhelming number of cases did not decide the choice of the problem within several, if not all, sciences and within traditional stylistics especially. It would not be too soon if the criteria that make us differentiate between "good" and "bad" texts — literature as well as non-fictive prose — became as acceptable a field of research as the corresponding field in regard of effective versus ineffective advertisements. In this respect, there is some hope to be seen in the fact that in the last ten years there has been a change in the scientific ideal.[26]

As Mukařovský underlined in his previously mentioned work, the result of an investigation can in turn affect the scientific ideal (which is probably affected at least as much by factors outside the scientific field). Perhaps the difficulties that are faced in the construction of a translating machine have been one of the important factors which drove language science theory building back to mentalism. See the arrow to the left of the science ideal in figure 2.

Figure 2.

In brief, the different strategy paths in figure 2 can be exemplified as follows:

Aα) refers to a stylistician who with a given objective — for example, to show the meaning of imagery in a certain material — chooses a suitable method to that end. He can then proceed from and adopt for example Ullmann's thesis; "Imagery takes us to the very heart of an author's style" (1957 p. 15) or he can, with the objective of outlining the fundamentals of a general style theory choose material from differing genres and periods, literary or factual, and apply for example psycholinguistic and/or statistical methods (as in the form of empirical research) and with this point of departure reach a style theory like Enkvist's: for example "Our impressions of styles result from comparisons of densities of linguistic features in the text and in the textually related norm" (1973, p 145).

Aβ) pre-supposes a given objective; one wishes for example to investigate the vocabulary in different genres or in different authors — and has at one's disposal a method and theory which one applies to certain material. Examples of this type of investigation are Guiraud's or Josephine Miles' studies of vocabulary.

For the traditional stylistician, probably the most common approach would seem to be Bα) or Bβ). In the former case, the investigator has found a material that seems to him to be suitable to treat by the method which his scientific-ideal prescribes. As an example of this strategy one can possibly consider the studies of Spitzer (1949) on the Sunkist advertisement, where Spitzer applied "explication-de-texte" to non-literary material in order to explain its effect on its readers. The style concept in such a strategy includes also non-literary texts; the point of emphasis lies in the question of the function and effect of the style in question. The most common of all, however, should be Bβ): the stylistician finds a material which he thinks is interesting from a certain angle and applies the methods his scientific ideal prescribes to solve the problem. He will also adapt the style concept's intension and extension to this end just as he can feel himself forced to formulate a general theory of style on the basis of his objective and his material — which is of course also the case in all the other strategies. Examples of this type of procedure are legion; as a single example Ohmann may be quoted: "The very many decisions that add up to a style are decisions about what to say as well as how to say it" (1962 p xii). A definition of style can hardly be more inclusive and Ohmann concedes: "to give it substance requires critical results as well as critical theory. The inherent interest of such results. . . is a more general *raison d'être* for this book" (ib. p xiii).

The two remaining strategies, Cα) and Cβ) note the cases where the scientific ideal allows only one given method or approach. (This includes scholars who use a science-theory point of view such as the misguided extremists who taboo all quantitative analysis from some incomprehensible aversion to the method itself, as well as those who define scientificness in terms of estimated probability or mechanical quantification).

Such strategies are acceptable of course if the investigator uses them to test the method so as to examine its authenticity and range. (But then, testing the method becomes the goal!) One would like to suppose that a stylistician would select some of the existing textattribution methods and would apply these in an unprejudiced way to different material in order to see what the result would be. Such a course of action seems not only acceptable but also really necessary and has to some extent also been applied to distinctive stylistics.[27] What is less satisfactory, on the other hand, is if a certain method prescribed by the scientific ideal directs the objective as well as the choice of material — in other words, the choice of problem. It is in such a case that one rejects certain problems or issues as unscientific *per se*, which is logically inconsistent (a problem might be wrongly formulated but cannot be in itself unscientific). Moreover, of course, this attitude is totally sterile for a science since then it can only set similar problems and respond to them in a similar way.[28]

Naturally I am fully aware that the preceding account is an outline, and nothing more. In fact — as I pointed out at the beginning of this survey — these allowable factors are interrelated and interdependent in an exceedingly complex manner. For the individual stylistician, concepts and theory building will come to be tested and re-tested continuously; this has been my own experience in any case. And similary, the strategies are never as neatly organized as may be thought from fig. 2.

* * *

The formulation of the PROBLEM — i. e. the function of GOAL and MATERIAL, in the terms I have been using hitherto — is, as Susanne Langer has so very adequately put it in the first chapter of her *Philosophy in a New Key*, a fundamental within the sciences. "The technique or treatment of a problem begins with its first expression as a question. The way in which a question is asked limits and disposes the ways in which any answer to it — right or wrong — may be given" (1953 p. 1). The objective or formulation of one problem should, according to Susanne Langer's science theory from the early 40's, be the guiding factor.[29]

The feasibility of finding a solution to a problem by means of certain methods must not, as in the view of the ultrapositivist scientist, dominate the choice of problem. It is therefore natural that, in order to clarify the different imports of a concept *style*, one examines and classifies the different objectives of stylistics. It is by no means correct that "studies of style can have but a few aims" (Milic 1967 p. 56).

One of the traditional objectives of stylistics is didactic and is a legacy from rhetoric; we can call this type of stylistics *prescriptive*. The art of giving our message the desired effect through a suitable form is achieved from the stylistics we learn — and pass on — at all levels of language learning and teaching, respectively. It includes both oral as well as written language, from sounds to entire texts, from the art of beginning to that of finishing; it precribes *what* to say and *when* to say it as well as *how* to say it. Stylistics of the prescriptive sort, however, is primary only to the extent that it is the first type that we come into contact with — it is built more often on convention and intuition than on the results of research.[30] Prescriptive stylistics applies pragmatic, aesthetic, religious and sometimes national criteria. It poses questions like: Does it sound right? Which word can be used in which context? Is it comprehensible? Will it have the intended effect? Does it fit into the accepted pattern? Does it suit the national system? Does the form fit the content? etc. The style concept in prescriptive stylistics must include the purpose of the speaker and the receiver's reaction (effect). To a high degree it is also a question of the selection of what may be said and what form it can be given when it is said. It would be a serious breach of "style" (or social convention) to start a conversation with a stranger in a lift or at a cocktail party by giving an account of an operation one has recently undergone or by complaining about the promiscuity of one's wife. The style concept here develops into or is subordinate to a general semiotic aspect.

The investigation and formulation of stylistic conventions, codes and systems falls within the realm of *descriptive stylistics*. While a norm is derived from certain evaluations, the description should be illustrative and account for the conventions that the norm is based on. Descriptive stylistics of course covers all levels of language, as has been mentioned before. Its method is qualitative in that it categorises, and generally also quantitative, in that it states frequencies of occurences and connections. It is designed as a description of a certain territory and sets the question: What does the text look like? It is applicable diachronically as well as synchronically. All types of stylistic research include, of course, a descriptive phase.

The purpose of *distinctive stylistics* is to differentiate texts. It is used most commonly in the field of text-attribution but its method is quite often applied to texts of known authors to establish the style differences between them and can in this way, at least partially, serve as a description of elements of style in these texts. For the pure distinctive stylistician the chief purpose however is to separate the texts rather than to examine how they differ. Distinctive stylistics can therefore not be equated with the current comparative method within descriptive stylistics which means that one sets one text, or type of text, in relief against another by means of comparison.

There is a fundamental and vital difference between descriptive and distinctive stylistics: while the former concentrates on the stylistically relevant features — and what is stylistically relevant must be decided in a style theory — everything that can separate texts from each other is relevant to the distinctive stylistician; it may concern the use of meta-

phor, the choice of motif, the composition or even the use of space before and after the comma.[31] For the distinctive approach, all qualities in
the text which point to evidence for classifying it in a certain way become relevant. The style concept in distinctive stylistics becomes thus
strongly operational and must be formulated in quantitative terms.

Argumentative stylistics corresponds to the analytical aspect of classical rhetoric (applied also to written texts). Its objective is to make se-
mantical and logical analyses of argumentative and persuasive (influence-
exerting) texts to investigate which techniques the writer uses in order
to achieve which effect, to reveal and expose illusory objectivity in allegedly factual statements, etc.

Argumentative stylistics is consequently directed towards the question
of the means used to achieve a particular effect and — vice versa — what
these means as used in a text can indicate about a non-explicitly expressed intention or attitude of the writer. Through its analysis of the texts'
import and effect, and the author's intentions, argumentative stylistics
can be said to be a special branch of *interpretative stylistics*, the purpose
of which is to establish the meaning of the text by means of stylistic
analysis, and to establish the writer's purpose and sometimes even his
psyche. Interpretative stylistics is consequently applied to texts whose
import is not immediately clear, and which can be thought to have a so-
called "deeper meaning". By virtue of the fact that a considerable
amount of literature works with and contains this deeper import, interpretative stylistics has of course come to be applied more frequently to
literary than to non-literary texts, but it is by no means restricted to this
particular field. Interpretative stylistics can be one tool in interpretation,
a method of hermeneutics in that certain style-types can be shown to lead
to a certain interpretation of the text, or can be demonstrated to be indicative of an author's intention or psyche. The ultimate goal of interpretative stylistics, however, is not to lead to the conceivable interpretations
of a text but to show by what means the text organizes its content on
different levels.[32] The preceding is summarized in figure 3, p. 40.

Content analysis is, in fact not merely part of the interpretative stylistician's goals but actually, at the same time, a pre-requisite of all style
analysis which is based on a concept of style formulated in terms like
"the way of doing it" (Ohmann 1970 p. 263). Descriptions of only the
first part (*way*) — that is, accounting for the fact that style is verbal,
rather than nominal; that it is characterised by metaphor to a large extent rather than by a lack of metaphor; that it has very largely value-
loaded words as opposed to neutral ones; that the style is simple or complex; that it is marked by having, to a great extent, instances of irony,
paradox, hyperbole, etc. etc. — these descriptions are of course quite sufficient for certain types of stylistic research. On the other hand, twist
and turn the thing as much as you will, the fact is that if one cannot de-

Figure 3.

GOAL	MATERIAL	LEVEL	QUESTIONS	METHODS	CONCEPT
PRESCRIPTIVE	sounds, words, clauses, sentences, text	style-value style-level	does it sound well? is it understandable? does it fit to context?	(evaluative criteria)	"Style is the way in which one solves the problem of giving one's words the intended effect"
DESCRIPTIVE	from sounds to things, from punctuation signs to the intention of the speaker/writer; text (s)	style-elements style	how is the content of the text communicated?	qualitative and quantitative analysis	Style is the aggregate and structure of all stylemarkers in a text. (What gives a text-element the status of stylemarker has to be made clear in a style theory)
DISTINCTIVE	texts	style-elements	who has written ..? has X written ...? what differences are there between text p and q?	comparative analysis with aid of statistics or other quantitative methods	Style is the difference between texts or between a text and a norm
ARGUMENTATIVE	conative and arguing texts, pseudo-objective texts	style-elements relevant for the special issue	is the argumentation correct? which is the purpose of the text and the intentions of the speaker/ writer? what effect does the text have?	semantical and logical analysis, analysis of purpose and effect	Style is the way in which a writer/ speaker affects and/or influences the reader/listener
INTERPRETATIVE	text(s) the meaning of which is not directly apparent	style-elements contributing to the meaning of the text or which give clues to the intention of the	what does the text say and what does it mean? how is the import of the text communicated?	hermeneutics, semantic context-analysis	Style is the way in which a content is presented

termine what content-factors those style-features organise, the information that such accounts put forward becomes rather trivial. As previously mentioned, the smaller the corpus the more obvious this principle becomes. For the classification of style periods like baroque or enlightenment, or genres like the ballad and legal style (the latter terms already including information about the sort of content) such style characteristics are certainly by no means uninteresting. But to describe the style of an author — and even more obviously, of a single text, the statements are insufficient unless the content-factor is included. Since content-analysis is by no means a simple or uncontroversial undertaking (even if one is satisfied with the so-called "manifest content"),[33] the stylistician who has the ambition of clarifying how a text is organised and what effect it has, really faces great difficulties. In a well-known essay, "Generative Grammar and Literary Style," Richard Ohmann discusses the inconsistency between a theory of style that claims that style is a way of putting forward certain contents which also could have been presented in another way (form), and the intuitive feeling that changes in form unavoidably lead to changes in content. Ohmann thought he was able to solve the problem by applying the concept-device of transformational grammar. Having given several examples of paraphrases of the sentence "After dinner the senator made a speech", he asks:

"Which ones represent stylistic variations on the original, and which ones say different things? We may have intuitions, but to support them is no trivial undertaking. Clearly it would help to have a grammar that provided certain relationships, formally statable, of alternativeness among constructions. One such relationship, for example, might be that which holds between two different constructions that are derived from the same starting point. And, of course, a generative grammar allows the formulation of precisely this sort of relationship." (1970 p. 264).

But this is only re-formulating the same crux: are the differences which are brought about through different transformations "from the same starting point" really only stylistic? What Ohmann calls "starting point" must in all likelihood be precisely the same as what many style theoreticians (e. g. Kayser 1962, Ullman 1964) have called the invariant, "the same or similar meaning". That one cannot solve the underlying problem by such reasoning is obvious, something which the recent development of linguistic theory has clearly shown. In his discussion of this very problem, Coseriu emphasises that paraphrases obtained through transformation from a base can certainly be equivalent in reference, but by no means in *meaning* (1970 p. 56).

If the problem had been as straightforward as Ohmann maintains, certainly transformational grammar would have been of immense help to stylistics since it offers an exact and describable alteration model, but that deep structure — in Chomsky's sense — should or could be equated with semantic deep structure in the sense of "underlying sense" would not be claimed by anyone — certainly not by Chomsky himself (1971

p. 89). The type of style description that Ohmann advocates in the work quoted, is definitely not fruitless — it is based on a more stringent and worked-out theoretical method of grammatical investigation — but it corresponds nevertheless to traditional stylistics which has examined, among other things, the very same categories that Ohmann mentions but has found them unsatisfactory. I concur whole-heartedly with Ohmann's general argumentation on the necessity for an explicit text theory (and to a greater extent, style theory) but I must question if one can regard "the move from formal description of style to critical and semantic interpretation" which "should be the ultimate goal of stylistics" as a "first step" (ib. 271). In actual fact the semantic analysis precedes the transformational operations. How otherwise can one know that "the content of the passage remains roughly the same"??? (ib. p. 270).[34] Syntax may well be "a central determinant of style" (ib. p. 276) but it is merely one of several: that syntactical transformations alone or especially could account for "a certain conceptual orientation, a preferred way of organizing experience" (ib. p. 271) I find highly improbable.

One should, however, be able to circumvent or evade the obviously insoluble problem of form and content if one regards style, not as equivalent to form ("What is content and what is form, or style" Ohmann ib. p. 263), and, further, if one does not, in a definition of style as "the way of doing it" assume that "it" is an invariable and "way" is a variable but if one rather considers both the elements "way" and "it" as interdependent variables, and regards style as a relation between them. With a definition such as Steinthal formulated (1866): ".... der Styl ist ein Verhältniss zwischen der Sprache und dem Ausgedrückten" (p. 472), or that style in a text is a relation between form[35] and content, STYLE becomes, consequently, "the WAY of *saying it*" where *saying* corresponds to "form" and *it* corresponds to "content" or "meaning".[36] With a definition like this, there is no desperate need to solve the problem of whether it is possible or impossible to express "the same thing" "in a different way".

The definition of style as the relation between form and content indicates the place of the concept in the system or structure of other concepts: style does not lie on the same level as "form" and "content" since it is regarded as a function of them.[37] Since style in turn, however, can also be a sense- or import-constitutory factor, it is legitimate to consider it as "part of total meaning" (Enkvist 1973 p. 87).

The proposed definition fulfills the demand of being general enough to allow within itself variations or changes of emphasis which are dependent on or required by specific problem-settings. The term "style" takes on, therefore, a different meaning in different contexts and different meaning if it is combined with or applied to different units. Thus it appears — if it comes to nothing else — that the intension and extension of the concept "style" fluctuate together with those elements that are said to have style or be designated by the derivative "stylistic". The meaning of "style" is thus — as already proposed — patently not the same in *style* as in *style-period* or *style-level* and there is also an obvious difference between the meanings of *style-* in the two latter terms. It would seem also that the import of the style-concept is dependent on the size of the corpus that the term is applied to; "the style" of Elizabethan drama can hardly cover the same meaning as "the style" of *Hamlet;* and it in turn probably designates something else than "the style" of Ophelia's song in Act 4 scene 5. The greater the amount of text the more general the problems and the closer the text-system to a language-system. Correspondingly it is natural then that the meaning of the concept "style" comes closer to the meaning of the concept of "language". Not only *style* but also *stylistics* thus gets different meanings in different contexts. Where one draws the line between what should be designated "language" and what "style" depends on whether one can give the two terms, in a particular context, a clearly differentiated import. Style is a cultural concept and it seems just as pointless to quarrel about the "right" style definition as to argue about the height of the world's lowest mountain: "our terms are what we make of them ... and the only criteria are consistency and adequacy, not some discoverable jewel called truth" (Chatman 1967 p. 77).

Now the knotty question remains of what relations between factors of form and content are "stylistically relevant". Generally, one should be able to say that all factors that give, or contribute to giving, the text as a whole a certain effect or import, are stylistically relevant. Many definitions of style have also included this aspect. The very concept "content" or "meaning" or "import" ("Bedeutung" and "Sinn" respectively in Frege's terms) presupposes an interpretant (in one of the senses of the term given by Pierce). "Meaning", "content", "import" designate *a priori* relating concepts; a relation between the signifying (signifikant) and the one to whom it signifies (interpretant). Since style in a text has been defined as a function (in a weak sense) of two variables, one of which at least is obviously perceptual ("content"), it follows that the style concept is also perceptual — this factor need not necessarily be included in the formulation of the definition, but is presupposed by it.

That the proposed definition is broad enough in itself to allow for adjustments and alterations of points of emphasis depending on the formulation of one's problem, (that is Goal and Material),[38] implies also that it does not presuppose any specific method — for example comparison with or without quantitative methods. Neither is stylistics necessarily subordinate to linguistics but rather placed on an equal level to linguistics,[39] and subordinated to general semiotics.[40] Stylistics is autonomous but its field of inquiry has as many links with linguistics, psychology (especially psycho-linguistics), sociology and statistics, as with the aesthetic and literary sciences.[41] From such a view of stylistics, the concepts of *linguistic stylistics* and *literary stylistics* become meaningful in that they indicate different approaches of investigation.[42]

In this connection I would like to add that it might very well be possible to build rather beautiful and theoretically consistent theories about style — what they are really worth will be shown only in action, i. e. when they are applied to actual problems. There has been criticism of stylistic analysis without theory. I would like to claim that style theories without style analysis are as dubious!

REFERENCES

Baumgärtner, Klaus, 1965, Formale Erklärung poetischer Texte". In H. Kreuzer & R. Gunzenhäuser, eds., *Mathematik und Dichtung*. München.
Bense, Max, 1969, *Einführung in die informationstechnische Ästhetik*, Hamburg.
Casirer, Peter, 1970 a, *Deskriptiv stilistik*. Göteborg.
— 1970 b, *Stilen i Hjalmar Söderbergs "Historietter"*. Göteborg.
— 1972, *Modell för struktur- och innehållsanalys av en text* . . . Prolegomena till en stratifiell innehålls- och stilteori. Mimeo. Göteborg [Model for analysis of structure and content of a text . . . Prolegomena to a stratificational theory of style].
— 1974, "Stilistisk analys av Pär Lagerkvists *En hjältes död*". In Ulf Teleman & Tor Hultman, eds., *Språket i bruk*. ·
— forthcoming, "Die Sprache als Fingerabdruck". In *Leuvense Bijdragen*.
Chatman, Seymour 1967, "The semantics of style". In *Social Science Information* VI, 4.
Chatman, Seymour & Levin, Samuel R., eds. 1970, *Essays on the language of literature*. Boston.
Chomsky, Noam 1971, "Deep structure, surface structure and semantic interpretation". In Roman Jakobson & S. Kawamoto, eds., *Studies in general and Oriental linguistic presented to Shiro Hattori*. Tokyo.
Coseriu, Eugenio 1970, "Semantik, Innere Sprachform und Tiefenstruktur". *Folia Linguistica* IV.
van Dijk, Teun 1972, *Some aspects of text grammars: a study in theoretical linguistics and poetics*. Amsterdam.
Enkvist, Nils Erik 1964, "On defining style". In N. E. Enkvist, I. Spencer & M. Gregory, *Linguistics and style*, London.
Enkvist, Nils Erik 1971, "On the place of style in some linguistic theories". In Seymour Chatman, ed., *Literary style: a symposium*. London & New York.
— 1973, *Linguistic stylistics*. The Hague.
Gray, Bennison 1969, *Style. The problem and its solution*. The Hague-Paris.
— 1973, "Stylistics: The end of a tradition". In *Journal of Æsthetics and art criticism* XXXI:4.
Fowler, Roger 1972, "Style and the concept of deep structure". In *Journal of literary Semantics 1*.
Guiraud, Pierre 1954, *Les caractères statistiques du vocabulaire*. Paris.
Hall, Robert A. Jr. 1963, *Idealism in romance linguistics*. Ithaka, N. Y.
Harweg, Roland 1972, "Stilistik und Textgrammatik". In *LiLi 5*.
Hatzfeld, Helmut 1955, Methods of stylistic investigation. In *Literature and science. Proceedings of the sixth tirennal congress, Oxford 1954*.
Havránek, Bohuslav 1964, "The fuctional differentiation of the standard language". In Paul L. Garvin, ed., *A Prague School reader on Esthetics, literary structure, and style*. Wash. DC.

Hoppe, Ottfried 1973, "Triviale Lektüre". In *Linguistik und Didaktik* 13.
Ihwe, Jens, ed., 1971—72, *Literaturwissenschaft und Linguistik.* I—III Frankfurt a. M.
— 1972, *Linguistik in der Literaturwissenschaft.* München.
Jakobson, Roman 1960, "Linguistics and poetics". (Closing statement). In Thomas A. Sebeok, ed., *Style in language.* Cambridge, Mass.
Johannisson, Ture 1973, *Ett språkligt signalement.* Göteborg.
Kaemmerling, Hans-Ekkehard 1973, "Aspekte einer semiotischen Rhetorik und Stilistik". In *Sprachkunst* IV, 1973:3/4.
Kayser, Wolfgang 1962, *Das sprachliche Kunstwerk.* 8. Aufl. Bern & München.
Klœpfer, Rolf & U. Oomen 1970, *Sprachliche Konstituenten moderner Dichtung.* Bad Hamburg.
Kristeva, Julia 1969, Σημειωτιχή (Sēmeiōtike) Paris.
Kroeber, Karl 1969, "Perils of quantification: The exemplary case of Jane Austen's *Emma*". In L. Dolezel & Bailey, eds., *Statistics and style.* N. Y.
Langer, Susanne 1953, *Philosophy in a new key.* N. Y.
Levin, Samuel R. 1962, *Linguistic structures in poetry* 's-Gravenhage
— 1963, "Deviation — statistical and determinate — in poetic language". In *Lingua* 12.
Lili, Zeitschrift für Literaturwissenschaft und Linguistik (1—12 Athenäum, Frankfurt a M., 13— Vanderhoeck & Ruprecht, Göttingen).
Lotman, Jurij 1972 a, *Die Struktur literarischer Texte.* München.
— 1972 b, *Vorlesungen zu einer strukturalen poetik.* München.
Lyons, John 1963, *Structural semantics.* Oxford.
Mey, Jacob 1972 a, "Some practical aspects of a theory of linguistic performance". Mimeo. [To appear in the proceedings of the 11th international congress of linguists (Bologna 1972)].
— 1972 b, "Performansens dialektik". Mimeo. Odense.
— 1972 c, "Wille zum Verstehen oder Verständnis als Wahl". *Linguistische Berichte* 21.
Meyer, W. J. 1974, Randbemerkung zu: J. Trabant, Poetische Abweichung. In *Linguistische Berichte* 32.
Miles, Josephine 1960, *Renaissance, Eighteenth-Century, and modern language in English poetry; a tabular view.* Berkeley, Cal.
Milic, Louis Tonko 1967, *A quantitative approach to the style of Jonathan Swift.* The Hague-Paris.
Mukařovský, Jan 1948: *Kapitoly z české poetiky.* 2. vyd., 1. Praha.
Ohmann, Richard 1962, Shaw, *The Style and the man.* Middletown. Conn.
— 1970, "Generative grammars and the concept of literary style". In Donald C. Freeman, ed., *Linguistics and literary style.* London etc. (First published 1964 in *Word* XX).
Oller, J. W. 1972, "On the relation between syntax, semantics, and pragmatics". In *Linguistics* 83.
Pór, Peter 1973, "Kunstwerk, Stil, Semiotik". In *Sprachkunst* IV 1973:3/4.
Riffaterre, Michael 1966, "Describing poetic structures. Two approaches to Baudelaire's *Les chats.*" In *Yale French studies* 36/37.
Ringbom, Håkan 1973, *George Orwell as essayist.* Acta Academiae Aboensis 44:2. Åbo.
Rosengren, Inger 1972, "Style as choice and deviation". *Style* VI:1.
Sanders, Willy 1973, *Linguistische Stiltheorie.* Göttingen.
Saussure, Ferdinand de 1955, *Cours de linguistique générale* 5ième éd. Paris.
Schlotthaus, Werner 1965, "Stilmerkmale 'zweitrangiger' Literatur". In *Sprache im technischen Zeitalter* 16 (Ed. by W. Höllerer).
Schmidt, Siegfried J. 1971, "Text und Bedeutung". In *Poetics* 1.
— 1974, "Literaturwissenschaft zwischen Linguistik und Sozialpsychologie." In *Zeitschrift für Germanistische Linguistik* II:1.

Spencer, John & Michael Gregory 1964, "An approach to the study of style". In N. E. Enkvist, J. Spencer & M. Gregory, *Linguistics and style*. London.
Spitzer, Leo 1918, "Die groteske Gestaltungs- und Sprachkunst Christian Morgensterns". In *Motiv und Wort. Studien zur Literatur- und Sprachpsychologie*. Leipzig.
— 1948, *Linguistics and literary history*. New Jersey.
— 1949, *A method of interpreting literature*. Northampton, Mass.
Stalnacker, Robert C. 1970, "Pragmatics". In *Synthese* 22, 1970:1/2.
Steinthal, Heymann 1866, "Zur Stylistik". *Zeitschrift für Völkerpsychologie und Sprachwissenschaft* 4.
Stutterheim, C. F. P. 1948, "Modern stylistics". In *Lingua* 1.
Todorov, Z. 1966, "Les anomalies sémantiques". In *Languages* I.
Trabant, Jürgen 1970, *Zur Semiologie des literarischen Kunstwerks*. München.
— 1974, "Poetische Abweichung". In *Linguistische Berichte* 32.
Törnebohm, Håkan 1974, "Paradigm i vetenskapernas värld och i vetenskapsteorin". Mimeo. Göteborg.
Ullman, Stephen 1957, *Style in the French novel*. London.
— 1964, *Language and style. Collected papers*. Oxford.
Windelband, Wilhelm 1911, *Präludien*. Aufsätze und Reden zur Einführung in die Philosophie 4. Aufl. Tübingen.

NOTES

[1] "There is no agreement on the aim of stylistic investigation, consequently there can be none in the methods." Hatzfeld 1955 p 44.

[2] Cf Chatman 1967 p 77.

[3] "A l'heure actuelle, cette discipline [la stylistique] n'a pas une position enviable. Située a mi-chemin entre la linguistique et la littérature, tel un valet à deux maîtres, elle n'est bien accueillie ni par l'une ni par l'autre." Todorov 1966 p 119.

[4] "Style in literature is a recognizable but elusive phenomenon." Spencer & Gregory 1964 p 59.

[5] "Wenn wir auch nur ein einziges Gedicht als Ausgangspunkt nehmen, so ist dies, nach dem von uns gewählten Standpunkt, zugleich und vielleicht auch gleichwertig ein literaturgeschichtliches, soziologisches, psychologisches, ideengeschichtliches, gesellschaftsgeschichtliches, sprachliches oder gar sprachgeschichtliches Phänomen, und diese verschiedenen in sich berechtigten Standpunkte reihen sich heute eher bloss nebeneinander, als dass sie sich in einer harmonischen, endgültig erscheinenden Hierarchie ordnen liessen." Pór 1972 p 177.

[6] In his *Linguistische Stiltheorie* (1973) Willy Sanders devotes a chapter to the point of view that all texts, not only literature, can be considered to have style. This view is almost self-evident for someone trained in the Swedish stylistics tradition but is apparently not so obvious elsewhere.

[7] Todorov 1966 p 119.

[8] Cf Sanders 1973 p 85; Harweg 1972 p 71. With text-grammar linguistics has taken the important step from a Marsian (= context-free) to at least a lunar level. The step to terrestrial linguistics, that is a pragmatic/holistic approach, necessarily includes the stylistic domains.

[9] Other terms for equivalent dichotomies are *analytic-synthetic* (Lotman 1972 a) and *typologisch-topologisch* (Harweg 1972).

[10] Hall 1963 *passim*; Enkvist 1964 p 9; Milic 1967 p 66 — to mention only a few!

[11] Cf Schmidt 1971 p 85.

[12] "Der rhetorische Kode operiert auf dem sprachlichen Kode." Kaem-

merling 1973 p 190 — cf Kristeva 1969, especially 'Le texte clos' pp 113—142.

[13] "A work of literature, indeed any discourse, is unique by virtue of what it says; it is common, and thus comprehensible, by virtue of its being an instance of a particular language. Stylistics, however, tries to apply the concept of uniqueness to the language and commonality to what is said." Gray 1973 p 511.

[14] Havránek 1964 p 9ff. Cf Bense 1969 pp 43ff.

[15] "Stilistik ist, wie jedermann weiss, die Wissenschaft oder Kunde vom Stil — genauer: vom sprachlichen Stil." Harweg 1971 p 71.

[16] "The virtue of linguistic stylistics, as opposed to other kinds of stylistics, rests squarely on its ability to make precise, objectively verifiable statements." Enkvist 1973 p 147; cf also ib p 91!

[17] "If one described something, then this was (as best) an element of "style", not of "a style". Unconnected sentences or parts of sentences were taken from various texts to serve as material for illustration for some stilisticum or other. It was not thought necessary to consider and examine a passage, a poem or a story as a stylistic whole. In other words: the stylisticum remained a style-element, did not become a style-feature or style-moment. Consequently it lacked all the characteristics it might have as part of a whole. This had its consequences again for its subdivisions into classes: this was founded on logical and grammatical, seldom on stylistic criteria." Stutterheim 1948 p 412.

[18] Cf Mey 1972 a, b; Stalnaker 1970.

[19] Cf Schmidt 1971 p 97; Cassirer 1972 *passim*.

[20] Cf Oller 1972.

[21] Sanders (1973 p 35) points out forcefully — but quite rightly — the absurdity of attempting to define "style", a knotty language phenomenon, from the starting point of literature, the most complex manifestation of language. Not only is literature "foregrounding" and "deviant" but it often works with indirect presentational methods, is intended for interpretation.

[22] I have read the part referred to (pp 13—28) in Swedish translation in Kurt Aspelin & Bengt A Lundberg, eds, *Form och struktur*. Stockholm 1971.

[23] Langer 1953 p 10.

[24] Pp 17, 137, 237, 272.

[25] The problem of what is to be considered *stylistically relevant* is in fact the central question for many a stylistician operating with a nonmentalistic concept notion of *style* — see e g Ringbom 1973 p 10. In fact the question seems often enough to be a stumbling-block: references to something undefined called "stylistic effect" tend to pop up even in contexts that are explicitly non-mentalistic and in which style is defined in purely quantitative — not perceptual — terms, e g Rosengren 1972 p 15. It would be so much easier for all of us if it were true that stylistic effect always and only depends upon quantity or density of linguistic features. Since that, however, is obviously not so, there will always remain doubts whether a quantitative definition of *style* is adequate — see e g Levin 1963, Chatman 1967, Kroeber 1969!

[26] Cf Harweg 1972 pp 73f. In fact, what in German is called "Trivialliteratur" is of utmost interest for evaluative stylistics — cf Hoppe 1973, Schlotthaus 1965 and discussions in LiLi 6, 1972.

[27] See Cassirer, forthcoming, "Die Sprache als Fingerabdruck" In *Leuvense Bijdragen*.

[28] Cf Törnebohm 1974. The categorical formulation I am entirely and solely responsible for!

[29] See also Meyer 1974 p 75.

[30] Modern psycholinguistic research is bound to furnish us with relevant information in this respect.

[31] Cf Johannisson 1973 p 467f.

[32] Cf Cassirer 1972, 1974.

[33] As proposed e g in Enkvist 1973 p 90.

[34] "Wir verstehen unter der Erklärung von Texten weitgehend ihren Erzeugungsprozess. Da dieser Prozess in jedem Fall eine strukturelle Interpretation voraussetzt ... ist er genaugenommen der Rückerzeugungsprozess der betrachteten Texte" Baumgärtner 1965 p 79.

[35] "Form" in the meaning of von Humboldt's: "Das, was etwas anderes gestaltet". The meaning of a text or part of a text can become "form" in that sense for another meaning, "deeper", or on another level, so that we get different strata of form and content, the relation between which could be called *style*. See Cassirer 1972. Fowler says it in terms of TG: "Style is presumably a function of the relation of deep and surface structure" (1972 p. 15).

[36] Cassirer 1970 a pp 74—76. NB that this definition explicitly states "style in *a text*".

[37] There has been some criticism of this theory as proposed in my thesis (1970 a) as to the fuzziness of the basic concepts "form" and "content" upon which the theory of style depends. Though I am myself not happy with this state of things there are nevertheless outstanding scholars who claim this procedure to be perfectly all right — e g Robert Stalnaker (1970 pp 287 f).

[38] Cf Sanders 1973 pp 21f.

[39] The difficulty of distinguishing *style* from *language* is illustrated by the frequency with which those terms are used in combination.

[40] Saussure 1955 pp 32ff.

[41] Cf Schmidt 1974.

[42] "Stylistics is not a branch of linguistics; it is a parallel science which examines the same problems from a different point of view. It will therefore have the same subdivisions as linguistics." Ullman 1954 p 10.

As should be quite clear I agree with the first two propositions but not with the following ones (from the relative clause on).

Ruqaiya Hasan
University of Essex

The place of stylistics in the study of verbal art

Of all the applications of linguistics, that to the study of literature is potentially the most challenging and the most fruitful. In literary studies, it might have contributed, at the least, to some explicit formulation of how and why the language of literature differs significantly from language produced in other contexts. In linguistics, it might have had the far-reaching effect of making one reconsider the established views concerning the nature of the human verbal system. The contrast between what might have been and what is, is indeed striking: to date, stylistics remains a subject that has made no significant impact upon what goes on in literary studies or in theoretical linguistics.

When stylistics appeared upon the scene, armed with the objective methods of linguistic analysis and perhaps reasonably proud of its hard-won scientific orientation to language study, its scientific analysis of the language of literature left the literary student cold, if not actively hostile. He remained unimpressed by the carefully prepared tables displaying frequencies of tokens of well-defined types occurring within a text. Highly objective definitions of style (Bloch 1953) failed to evoke a positive response in him, and from the supreme heights of his aesthetic concerns he indifferently surveyed the theoretically valid analytical categories of subject, predicate, transitive, intransitive and suchlike, remarking merely that after all there was more to literature than language. As to the benefits flowing from a scientific analysis of language, would any one seriously propose that the scientific analysis of pigment bears a direct relevance to Renoir as art? Of course one is forced to accept that, unlike pigment, language is itself a symbolic system, but what this might imply for the study of literature is an issue which seldom detains one. Although grossly oversimplified, this account of the literary student's response sums up both his disillusionment with linguistics and his conviction that what goes under the name of stylistics is, at best, only peripheral to the study of literature as an aesthetic object. One may take this kind of analysis of language as the starting point, but to consider it crucial to the study of literature as art would be surely wrong (Wellek and Warren, 1942; Wellek, 1960).

On the other side of the boundary, the linguist tackles the problem of the analysis of language from seemingly opposing angles. One point of vantage sees it as the hunting ground for deviation, distortion and ungrammaticality, though views differ on whether the phenomenon is to be regarded as a crucial characteristic of literature or not. Curiously enough, there are only perfunctory (Chomsky, 1965) or piecemeal (Thorne, 1965; 1970) explanations for the fact that despite ungrammaticality, meaninglessness is not an attribute that could be assigned to a text in literature. Had the implications of this fact been considered seriously, the theoretical linguist might have found good reasons for redefining linguistics as a study of sensicality — the ways in which men, using natural language, manage to mean — rather than that of grammaticality. The second point of vantage in linguistics emphasizes the element of similarity between the language of literature and language elsewhere. In this view, the language data from the domain of literature represent yet another ground for testing the descriptive adequacy of one's categories. A linguist is naturally reassured when the categories, devices and notations designed for the description of language as a whole can be used for the analysis of the language in *Pride and Prejudice* as well as in *Beeton's Book of Household Management*. The sense of reassurance is greater here because for centuries popular and expert opinion alike has claimed the language of literature to be universally and uniformly different from language elsewhere. But the danger of this approach is inherent in its very emphasis on similarity, which cannot after all be equated with identity. So, while it is true that for the description of language at the formal-phonological levels the linguist would use (a selection from) the same set of descriptive categories for both texts, there can be little doubt that the textual function of language in the two is distinct.

Opposed as these points of view appear, it is important to realize that they have essentially the same orientation. Despite appearances, the linguist has not much concerned himself with the qualifier *of literature* in the expression *language of literature* and the wry remark is justified that in both cases the qualifier has a predominantly 'locative' meaning for the linguist, its actual function being to indicate the locale where some more data for testing hypotheses may be found. So far as the term *language* in the expression is concerned, the linguist in both cases starts out with a set of premises about its essential nature. Whatever follows from these premises in the shape of theory or techniques for description is seen as a constant, which admits of no fundamental revision; rather, revision sullies the purity of linguistics as science. That the language of literature defies our accepted views, especially as regards the structure of semantics, has had little or no influence on what we have had to say about semantics in linguistics.

Again, like the summary offered above (p. 49), this account does not do justice to particular scholars. Yet it remains a largely accurate account of the concerns of stylistics from the linguist's point of view, which is implicit in his statements regarding the scope of stylistics — what it can or cannot do. Let me take two such statements and let me refer to them as S1 and S2, standing for two somewhat distinct interpretations of the term. Both have existed concurrently since the revival of interest in the language of literature and are amply represented in *Style in Language* (Sebeok, 1960).

According to S1, the linguistic study of the language of literature involves no more than the use of descriptive categories derived from some theory of language in scientific linguistics. The nature and scope of this application are probably quite faithfully reflected in Sol Saporta (1960): "The linguist cannot study poetry as art without abandoning his position as linguist; he can only study poetry as language ... On the other hand, it may turn out that the analysis of poetry as language will in some way correlate with, or be a complement to, the analysis of the phenomena as art, at the same time utilizing more precise techniques. ... Terms like *value, aesthetic purpose* etc. are apparently an essential part of the method of most literary criticism, but such terms are not available to linguists. The statements that linguists make will include references to phonemes, stresses, morphemes, syntactical patterns etc. and their patterned repetition and co-occurrence." A whole volume could be written concerning the validity of the assumptions underlying these statements. Here, let me just state three reasons why the program suggested in S1 does not deserve serious attention.

As the techniques for the descriptions of language grow in sophistication, it becomes clear that the exhaustive analysis at the levels of semantics, syntax, lexicon and phonology, of even such a simple sentence as *I wonder about the trees.* (Frost) will require a tremendous amount of time and patience (Hudson, 1972). That an exhaustive analysis of every segment at every level is called for in S1 is quite obvious: S1 does not — indeed, *cannot* — provide any guidance regarding the aspects of analysis which are likely to "correlate with, or be a complement to, the analysis of the phenomena as art". Further, in order to claim validity for the final statements, this exhaustive analysis must be carried out over a valid sample. The problems involved in the construction of a valid sample — and there are those who would question whether there could be a valid sample — are not just practical problems: they inevitably involve a theoretical framework within which terms such as Elizabethan, Victorian, romantic, classical, sonnet, epic etc have significance.

Let us, however, ignore the mundane practical problems arising from the requirement of exhaustive analysis and the more theoretical ones arising from the need to construct a valid sample. Let us enquire, rather, into the end-product of such an analysis. Presumably, this would take the form of innumerable tables listing frequencies of tokens of different types from the various levels of language. Now, even at their best, such tables can only possess consistency and accuracy; they provide no motivation for their own interpretation, which has to be based upon some hypotheses. I am at a loss to imagine what kind of theoretical framework could exist here for any hypotheses put forward. So, I would leave this vexing problem with just two comments. To suggest that these frequencies could be contrasted with the norm frequencies of the language, so as to establish those linguistic patterns diagnostic of verbal art, is to delude oneself that one is saying something substantial while actually saying nothing, for the concept 'norm of language' happens to be at least as elusive as that of 'style' in literary studies. Secondly, assuming the impossible to have happened, even if we do emerge with an array of patterns which can be validly said to be unique to literature, how do we hope to explain why these patterns alone have such privilege?

Last of all, there is the curious fact that for S1, the term stylistics is superfluous. Strictly speaking the linguist's job here finishes with the presentation of the tables; as linguist he can say nothing about verbal art. Certainly, as linguist, he does analyse language produced in distinct institutionally recognized domains, but he does not confer a discrete label to the study of the language of each specific domain. Ironically, then, the only rationale for the recognition of the term stylistics lies in the acceptance of the element of art in literature, and yet this is precisely the element about which S1 has nothing significant to say. If the programme of S1 can be followed, we shall certainly have a lot of evidence, but we would be in the position of not knowing what it is evidence of! Note, too, the assumption that the relevant categories for the analysis of the language will have already been enumerated and that these (perhaps with 'deviation') will suffice for the analysis of language in literature. To put it mildly, this assumption is open to question.

In S2, the term stylistics is interpreted as the study of style. The point of contact between S2 and the study of literature would rest upon the assumption that literature is the domain where style matters most. The literary student's deep interest in the concept of style would appear to justify this assumption. However, before the relevance of S2 to the study of literature can be accepted, it has to be shown that both the literary student and the linguist mean the same thing by style. If upon examination we find that under the label of style, the two groups of scholars study distinct phenomena, then quite obviously the contact between S2 and the study of verbal art is thrown into doubt. It is therefore essential to enquire what a linguist normally means by style in S2. So long as the identity of the studied phenomena is not proved, it would be useful to use *style* where style in S2 is concerned, and artistic-style to refer to style in literature.

The study of style in S2 can be seen as a part of 'institutional linguistics' (Hill, 1958). Stylistics in S2 enquires into the nature of the systematic correlation between variation in language and variation in the context in which the language is produced. Roughly the same field of enquiry has been referred to as the study of register, of speech varieties and of diatypic varieties. Thus stylistics in S2 is a new name for some old preoccupations. Whatever the name by which a linguist might refer to this field of study, the basic hypothesis is always that the language of a discourse varies in significant ways in accordance with the variation in the context of situation in which the discourse is embedded. Various schemata for the systematic study of such variation have been suggested (Firth, 1950; Jakobson, 1960; Hymes, 1962; Halliday *et al*, 1964; Fishman, 1965; Gregory, 1967; Crystal and Davy, 1969; Hasan, 1972), but, despite differences, these essentially agree on the relevance of the following factors of the extralinguistic situation to variation in language:

1. what is said (the subject-matter of the discourse)
2. in what setting (the part played by the verbal symbolic system within the total social process)
3. to whom by whom (the social roles of those who function as speaker/ addressee)
4. for what purpose (for exposition, persuasion, seeking information...)
5. through what channel (spoken/written; prepared/extempore...)

The constellation of these five factors can be referred to as 'contextual construct', to be seen as an abstract entity, each element of which is manifested by some particular category in any given verbal interaction. Moreover, these categories can be specified with varying degrees of generality or specificity, depending upon the needs and interests of the analyst. So, the first factor may be specified as *history* or more specifically as *the reign of Mary Tudor*. The second factor may be specified as, say, *pedagogical*, or more specifically as *lecture*. The constellation of particular categories, specified at whatever level of generality, may be referred to as 'contextual configuration'. A contextual configuration is a particular instance of the abstract entity contextual construct and is specific to a class of discourse.

With these basic notions, it is possible to arrive at a definition of style. The style of a discourse — the shape in which the language unfolds itself — is a function of the contextual configuration relevant to the discourse. This manner of approaching style eliminates those variations which arise from the idiolectal, dialectal or sociolectal provenance of the participants of the discourse. It is certainly true that all types of variation are simultaneously manifested within one single discourse, but there is good reason for keeping the '-lectal' and diatypic variation distinct since the underlying social significances of the two appear to be distinct.

It is a common assumption in S2 that the study of style is essentially quantitative, stylistic differences being established empirically by an analysis of the type recommended in S1 for the study of the language of literature. Those patterns which after such analysis are found to correlate with some particular category in the contextual configuration are said to belong to the style of that category. So we might have a style correlating with *setting: lecture,* and this could be referred to as the *style of lecture.* The patterns of language that are specific to one particular style can be regarded as the *crucial distinctive features* of that style. The implication is clear: such patterns are diagnostic and can be seen as the signature of some factor of the contextual configuration upon the language of the discourse. I would draw attention to the similarity between S1 and S2: it would seem to be part of the assumption in S1 that literature is crucially distinguished from non-literature by virtue of possessing a distinct style, and therefore the study of variation in style can be seen as the means to the end of defining the domain of literature linguistically.

Clearly the above conception of the study of style suffers from the same shortcomings stated above for S1. Recently, interest has arisen in another mode of approaching the problem (Hasan, 1972; Halliday, 1975). In the notion of the contextual construct the linguist has a powerful tool. A contextual configuration can be seen as a determinant of the total meaning potential relevant to the discourse, so that each specified category in the contextual configuration can be seen as predictive of that set of components of meaning which will be primarily relevant to the discourse. Because of the realizational relation between meaning and form, it becomes possible to predict, not the actual items and patterns, but rather the range of items and patterns from which some selection will appear in the discourse. Naturally, the more specific the categories in the contextual configuration, the more powerful the prediction will be. Because of this relationship, even if the linguist started with frequency analysis and managed to abstract the crucial distinctive features of a style, he would still be in a better position to explain why these and no other patterns are crucial.

Now, it remains to be seen whether the contextual construct can play the same crucial role in the discussion of artistic-style. An examination will show that, of all the varieties of a language, literature is the one which makes the most tenuous contact with the contextual construct; it is far from easy to specify the contextual configuration relevant to any one particular text. It is not that the questions 1—5 cannot be answered at all, but rather that the answers, unless banal, beg very large questions indeed. What, for example, is the range of categories which may be said to be capable of manifesting the factor *setting* here? There are at least two valid sets of categories which may be considered. One set would emphasize the interaction between language and non-language; examples could be some kind of symposium where verbal artefacts are presented for the first time. This immediately raises the question of the distinction between the production of the text and its presentation and whether the two can be seen as causally related, and if so, to what extent. The second set would emphasize the form of the discourse; examples would be drama, sonnet, epic, novel etc. In saying that the genre itself constitutes the setting of the verbal artefact, we would be saying that just as lecture is a discourse form so also is novel. The difference in the nature of the two kinds of categories — the lecture and the novel — is so obvious that it needs no further comment.

Leaving these problems unresolved, let us consider another difference.

Normally, in those contextual configurations where the setting can be specified as, for instance, lecture, the specification of the first element provides unambiguous information regarding another aspect of the discourse. From the facts that the discourse is in the form of lecture and it is about, say, the human respiratory system, a prediction can be made about at least that section of vocabulary which would be primarily relevant to this discourse. As more elements of the construct are specified, the range of predictions can be narrowed and at the same time syntactic predictions become possible. So that if the purpose is exposition, then in English the declarative clause structure is primarily relevant, whereas interrogatives, if they occur at all, will seldom have the true semantic function of seeking information. They are likely, rather, to indicate the speaker's shift from one sub-topic to another within the discourse. Without going into details, it can be seen that every time the categories lecture and human respiratory system appear within the contextual configuration, certain sections of the verbalizing mechanisms — the syntax, the lexicon, the phonological patterns — can be said to be irrelevant or at least peripheral, while others will be primarily relevant as those from which some selection will have to occur. The situation for a verbal artefact is different. As soon as we begin to ask, say, *what is this novel about?*, we run into difficulties, because the simple-seeming words *about what?* are capable of being interpreted in different ways. So, without any necessary contradiction of facts, one may be justified in maintaining that Golding's *Free Fall* is about (i) a little urchin who goes through a series of experiences in his progress toward adulthood; (ii) the enigmatic nature of what determines the course of events in human life; (iii) the lack of true choice and the notion of free will. Even if making an exception — and why one has to make an exception here, is itself a significant question — we consider all three together as a composite specification of the first element in the contextual configuration of this novel, we are far from having arrived at a paradigm of the type 'lecture on human respiratory system'. In the first place, the constellation (i)—(iii) is not likely to be repeated; secondly, from this type of specification, there is in any case very little likelihood of our being able to make any significant predictions regarding the verbalizing mechanisms which would be primarily relevant to this class of discourse. It would be a waste of time to examine each element in detail — the problems get still more involved, so that one would be wise, long before one reaches that thorny question *for what purpose*, to abandon this line of enquiry with specific reference to texts in literature. It cannot be denied that complex problems arise also in the examination of other varieties such as of religious or conversational discourse. Without going into any details, I would suggest that the relationship of these varieties to social system — which is what the contextual construct is abstracted from — is a direct one. So, the solutions to the problems here would be arrived at by appeal to the social context; I doubt if the same could be said about the problems arising in the examination of the variety literature.

Although I have not defined artistic-style and have no intention of doing so here, it seems undeniable that style in S2 and artistic-style are not identical concepts: the properties of artistic-style do not seem to be determined by the factors of the contextual construct. Therefore, to suggest that S2 can throw light both on classical heroic poetry and on legal discourse (Crystal and Davy, 1969) appears untenable, if there is any implication that the modes of studying the two are identical. Of course, not all linguists interested in speech variation make this assumption (Gregory, 1967; Halliday, 1971; Hasan, 1967; 1971). I must also add that the systematic study of speech variation is a valid and highly important area of theoretical linguistics; this importance is not diminished by the conclusions drawn above regarding its application to style in verbal art. But the point at which it assumes importance in the study of verbal art is a different one: for example, when examining the 'credibility' of an interactional sequence in a novel, the use of the contextual construct could be almost as powerful a tool as it is elsewhere in language. All I am claiming is that just because the study of speech variety is related to style differences between classes of discourse, it does not inevitably follow that this study can function as a diagnostic tool for identifying verbal art for us, or for defining artistic style and, least of all, for pointing out the element of art in literature. If indeed any such assumption is made in S2, then it needs to be pointed out that, in this respect, S2 is as inadequate as S1.

What is wrong with the linguistic analysis of the language of literature is not that it is scientific or objective or 'atomistic' (Wellek, 1960) but rather that it has often approached the study without any clear conception of the role of language in verbal art. In both S1 and S2, the focus of attention is *verbalization*, which I have elsewhere called linguistic execution (Hasan, 1964; 1967; 1971). This focus, I think, is fully justifiable in non-literature, for here there is an immediate relationship between the level of meaning and the level of verbalization — ie the selection of grammatical, lexical, and phonological categories — so, it can be validly maintained that the one is reflected in the other directly. In these discourses, considered as texts alone, there is only one process of symbolization at work, namely that of language itself. Verbal artefacts display a crucial difference in this respect. If we use 'theme' in the sense it is used in literary studies as referring to the deepest level of meaning in a verbal artefact, then the elements of the theme themselves may be said to be realized or articulated by certain events and/or statements verbalized within the work. For any one interested in the theme of *As You Like It*, the interest in the events and statements within the play is primarily an interest in their realizational relationship to the theme. Supposing that one element of the theme of this play is the notion of *order*, then the episodes of the brothers, the character development of Celia and Rosalind, and the four marriages can all be seen as symbolically 'talking about' this theme. So, the level of verbalization in a verbal artefact does not enter into a direct and immediate relationship with the level of theme; between the two lies the mediating level of symbolic articulation.

There is, of course, no new discovery in the above statement; the three traditional categories of *theme, plot* and *diction* would up to a point parallel what I have called *theme, symbolic articulation* and *verbalization*. However, the two ways in which the view expressed here differs from traditional views should be pointed out. I see the relationship between the first and the second member of this triad as having essentially the same nature as that of the relationship between the second and the third member: both are essentially symbolic and it is only in this sense that a verbal artefact may be described as an extended metaphor. This similarity of the relationship is not always insisted upon in the traditional view; in point of fact, I doubt if it has been explicitly stated anywhere. Secondly, there is often an assumption that all three components of the triad are present only in certain genres; this may be because of the more specific nature of the element *plot*, which is certainly not as abstract as *symbolic articulation*. Whatever the reason for the traditional view, I would maintain that all components of the triad are always present within every verbal artefact, irrespective of the genre or the verbal length of the text, though differences clearly exist in the complexity and nature of the *theme* as well as in the modes of *symbolic articulation*. It is not possible to discuss here the full range of implications arising from these two postulates, viz (i) that the presence of the triad is essential to the description of a text as an instance of verbal art and (b) that there is a functional continuity in the relationship existing amongst the three components. I will restrict myself to a few remarks regarding the implications in particular for the place of the study of language in literature.

It is a curious fact that although the above view appears to assign a subsidiary status to the level of verbalization, a closer examination shows that there is nothing to verbal art — qua art — except what is present in its verbalization. To arrive at this conclusion, one has to examine the relationship between *theme* and *symbolic articulation*. Can it really be maintained that there is a symbolic process involved here? I would maintain that this is the case for the simple reason that the relationship between the events, states of affairs and statements which symbolically articulate the theme is essentially an arbitrary one, just as the symbols of language are arbitrarily related to the underlying meanings encoded by these symbols. For example it could be maintained that one element of the theme of Frost's *The Road Not Taken* and *Free Fall* is the same: at the deepest level of meaning both texts are concerned with the lack of true choice and the notion of free will. But a cursory glance is sufficient to show that the events and states of affairs which articulate this theme are far removed from each other. Again the theme of mutability is present in Herrick's *Daffodils*, in Shakespeare's *Sea Dirge* and in Yeats' *Old Men Admiring Themselves in the Water*; but despite this similarity at the level of theme, the articulation of the theme itself is provided by distinct states of affairs. The verbal artist may see as unique meaning in a configuration of events, which could be seen as having a different meaning by some other artist. To Herrick a flower in full bloom is symbolic of flux; to Ghalib — an Urdu poet — a flower in full bloom is symbolic of satisfaction in having attained a predestined stage of fulfillment. Now, it may be argued that a given configuration of events, states of affairs etc has to have some inherent quality which permits the perception of some general underlying meanings. But even if the premise is accepted, the fact remains that the qualities inherent within an entity, a configuration of events, states of affairs may be mutually contradictory; that is to say, the same Thing can be seen from different points of view as having different significance. So, the perception of a particular meaning remains a personal statement; to use Bernstein's formulation, the meaning here is highly individuated and may not be available to others in the same way (Bernstein, 1971). Secondly, the premise is more tenable where the events seem to run parallel to our perception of possible reality, as, say, in *Pride and Prejudice*. How such a premise could be used to discuss Gulliver's last voyage or Kafka's *Metamorphosis* is not at all clear. And yet there is no functional difference between the 'quasi- real' events — running parallel to our conception of every day reality — and the 'fantastic' events, created out of the artist's imagination. In saying this I am not referring to the view that in the ultimate analysis, the shape of imagination itself may be substantially conditioned by social reality, but rather to the fact that the fantastic events possess the same potential for symbolic articulation of the theme as do the real ones. From this point of view, T. S. Eliot's never-arriving traveller (*Four Quartets*) is no less fantastic or real than Kafka's hero-turned-insect. Of course the element of fantasy in verbal art deserves study in its own right, and as it relates to the notion of creativity. My claim here is only that the symbolic function of the fantastic events in verbal art throws doubt upon the premise that events, states of affairs, *per se*, have some inherent qualities which logically determine the range of meanings that can be possibly assigned to them.

Despite this similarity between the symbols of language and of the level of symbolic articulation in verbal art, there is an important difference between the two. The effect of the arbitrariness of the linguistic symbol is counteracted in verbal interaction because as a system for communication language is the property of the community, and there is a substantial degree of agreement as to what linguistic symbol may encode what meaning. In verbal art, if the symbols at the level of articulation can be said to form a system at all, it is a system that is specific to a particular text; besides there is no substantial agreement regarding what events may symbolically encode what thematic meaning. To the extent that the relationship is arbitrary and arises from the unique perception of the artist, it follows that the symbolic entities, events, states of affairs have to be organized in such a way that the theme may be coherently realized by them. It is here that the level of verbalization plays a major role: an artist's success in conveying the deepest meanings of his discourse depends to a large extent upon how he can exploit the verbal mechanisms of the language to impose a definite structure upon the level of symbolic articulation. It is to this artistic need that the code-like regularity in the selection of language categories can be related: the function of the code of the text (Giraud, 1970) is to impose structure and thus create a symbolic system which has no physical or communal existence in the external universe. We can offer this as an explanation for the generally observed characteristic of the language of verbal art, namely that it is highly structured, displaying a formation of patterns from the formal-phonological patterns of language (Halliday, 1964; 1970; Mukarovsky, 1964; Nowottny, 1962).

Perhaps it would be useful to explain what I mean by codelike regularity. It does not mean that the verbal artist is constrained to select the same linguistic category as such, but rather that some element of the semantic import is kept constant in language categories which symbolize those events that articulate some specifiable part of the theme. If we take this triadic relationship of the thematic, the articulatory and the verbalizing components in verbal art as relating to style in verbal art, then any stylistic shift within a discourse is a signal that a move is being made to some other element of the theme (Hasan, 1964; 1967). Such a pattern of shift becomes crucial to the understanding of the work in that it relates to some symbolic events which are themselves crucial to the perception of the theme. To give but one example, the last stanza in Herbert's *Jordan* displays a stylistic shift; every single clause here is a declarative while every single clause in the preceding two stanzas is an interrogative: this observation concerning the selection of language patterns — a fact at the level of verbalization — becomes significant only when its textual function within the poem is examined, how the states of affairs encoded by these categories differ and how this difference relates to the theme of the poem. It is this kind of simultaneous structuring at the levels of articulation and of verbalization which is missing in a precis of *Hamlet*; although the major configuration of symbolic events may be presented in the precis, it will seldom contain the characteristic of imposing structure upon the symbolic events through the exploitation of the verbalizing categories. If Lamb's *Tales from Shakespeare* could be regarded as instances of verbal art, it would be not because of the events selected therein but rather because of the relationship between the events and the theme and the language.

Seen from this point of view the focus on verbalization in S1 and S2 is utterly incapable of making any significant statements about verbal art; however, the shortcoming of the two models does not imply that therefore the study and analysis of language in verbal art is either a waste of time or even peripheral to the interests of the literary student. To move to a more general level of discussion, it seems that art itself cannot be separated here from verbalization, but in order to see the true role of verbalization in literature one has to ask how it relates to the element of art. If the art consists, in literature, of the manipulation of all three levels simultaneously, then it follows inevitably that the only viable model of stylistics would be that which enquires into the fit of the language to the symbolic articulatory events and of the fit of the latter to the theme. There is no true dichotomy between linguistic stylistics and aesthetic stylistics (Wellek, 1960) except of the linguist's making. In as much as this implies *evaluation,* such stylistics will be evaluative; but here the statements could be perhaps more explicit than they have characteristically been in literary studies, though I would add immediately that a close reading of a large part of literary criticism is such as to engender in one a sense of humility, in that it certainly contains some keen insights, which the linguist's mode of approaching the verbal artefact characteristically lacks.

As to the relationship of the model of stylistics being discussed here to literary studies, one must take account of the fact that in literary studies one approaches the study of verbal artefacts from various angles. To a literary student, the verbal artefact is a multifaceted object, which can be seen from various angles. These can be presented as a dazzling set of antinomies. Literature is universal, though it is also culture-bound; literature is shaped by a specific culture, yet in its turn it can shape culture; being specific to a culture, literature is a product of a culture at a specific moment, yet it is also timeless; it is the work of one individual, yet in it reverberates the tradition of centuries preceding it; literature mirrors a culture, yet it is not its copy; literature is above the moral cannons of a culture, yet it has a moral quality; literature is not philosophy, yet it is philosophical. I do not wish to deny that all these angles are valid, but I do think that one has the right to ask which of these observations is an observation specific only to literature and not to anything else. It seems to me that that which is specific to literature alone can be validly thought of as the nucleus of literary studies, its focal point. And I venture to express the hope that the triadic relationship explored here is one such phenomenon, so that it may be said that stylistics is concerned solely with verbal art as art, not as history, cultural evidence, philosophy or catalyst of change; even though a study of any of the angles mentioned above will always lead to a greater understanding of the work *in toto,* its understanding as art requires the techniques of stylistics.

REFERENCES

1. Bloch, B: "Linguistic structure and linguistic analysis" in A. A. Hill, ed., *Report of the Fourth Annual Round Table Meeting on Linguistics and Language Teaching*, Washington, 1953.
2. Bernstein, B: *Class, Codes and Control, Vol. 2*, London, Routledge & Kegan Paul, 1971.
3. Chomsky, N: *Aspects of the Theory of Syntax*, Cambridge, Mass, M I T, 1965.
4. Crystal, D. and Davy, D: *Investigating English Style*, London, Longmans, (English Language Series), 1969.
5. Firth, J. R: "Personality and language in society," *The Sociological Review* 42, 2, 1950.
6. Fishman, J. A: "Who speaks what language to whom and when," *Linguistique* 2, 1965.
7. Guiraud, P: "Immanence and transitivity of stylistic criteria' in S. Chatman, ed., *Literary Style: A Symposium*, New York, Oxford University Press 1971.
8. Gregory, M: "Aspects of variety differentiation," *Journal of Linguistics*, Vol. 3, no. 2, 1967.
9. Halliday, M. A. K., McIntosh, A., Strevens, P: *Linguistic Sciences and Language Teaching*, London, Longmans, (Linguistics Library Series), 1964.
10. Halliday, M. A. K: "Descriptive linguistics in literary studies" in G. I. Duthie, ed., *English Studies Today*, Edinburgh, University Press, 1964.
11. —: "Linguistic function and literary style: an enquiry into the language of William Golding's *The Inheritors*" in S. Chatman, ed., *Literary Style: A Symposium*, New York, Oxford University Press, 1971.
12. —: "The text as semantic choice in social context" in T. A. van Dijk & J. Petöfi, eds., *Grammars and Descriptions*, Berlin, De Gruyter, 1975 (in press).
13. Hasan, R: *A Linguistic Study of Contrasting Features in The Style of Two Contemporary English Prose Writers*, Edinburgh University Ph. D. Thesis (unpublished), 1964.
14. —· "Linguistics and the study of literary texts." *Etudes de Linguistique Appliqueé* 5, 1968.
15. —: 'Rime and reason in Literature' in S. Chatman, ed., *Literary Style A Symposium*, New York, Oxford University Press, 1971.
16. Hill, T: "Institutional linguistics," *Orbis* 7, 1958.
17. Hudson, R. A: "An exercise in linguistic description" in G. Thornton, D. Birk & R. A. Hudson, eds., *Language at Work*, London, Longman, (Schools Council Programme in Linguistics and English Teaching: Paper Series II, vol. 1), 1972.
18. Hymes, D: "The ethnography of speaking" in T. Gladwin & W. C. Sturtevant, eds., *Anthropology and Human Behaviour*, Washington, D. C, Anthropological Society of Washington, 1962.
19. Jakobson, R: "Linguistics and poetics" in T. A. Sebeok, ed., *Style in Language*, Cambridge, Mass., M I T, 1960.
20. Mukarovsky, J: "Standard language and poetic language" in P. A. Garvin, ed., *A Prague School Reader in Esthetics, Literary Structure and Style*, Washington, D. C., Georgetown University Press, 1964.
21. Nowottny, W: *The Language Poets Use*, London, The Athlone Press, 1962.
22. Sebeok, T. A: *Style in Language*, Cambridge, Mass., M I T, 1960.
23. Thorne, J. P: "Stylistics and generative grammars," *Journal of Linguistics*, Vol 1, no 1, 1965.

24. —: "Generative grammar and stylistic analysis" in J. Lyons, ed., *New Horizons in Linguistics*, Harmondsworth, Penguin, 1970.
25. Wellek, R: "From the viewpoint of literary criticism" in T. A. Sebeok, ed., *Style in Language*, Cambridge, Mass., M I T, 1960.
26. Wellek, R. & Warren, A: *Theory of Literature*, New York, Harcourt Brace and World, Inc., (Revised ed.), 1956.

William O. Hendricks

Style and the structure of literary discourse

A basic assumption underlying many approaches to the analysis of style is that "manner" ("expression," "form") can be separated from "matter" ("content") and subjected to independent analysis. The purpose of this paper is to suggest certain necessary qualifications and clarifications of this assumption. One need for clarification is made evident by the occasional explicit acceptance of the manner-matter dichotomy coupled at the same time with the assertion that the notion of style refers to alternative ways of expressing the same content. Such is the case, for example, in Richard Ohmann's article "Generative Grammars and the Concept of Literary Style."[1] It should be obvious that analysis of style in this sense, which requires that one hold the content constant and explore various means of expressing it, cannot be said to be the analysis of expression *independent of* content, at least not in the sense these terms have in linguistic theory.

In linguistic theory "expression" refers to the phonetic aspect of language, that aspect of language with a physical manifestation, as opposed to the content side of language, which is not open to empirical investigation in the same way that sound is. Although it is recognized that content and expression are in one sense inseparable, being comparable to the front and back of a sheet of paper, the fact that there is no bilateral dependency, no exact one-one correlation, between the two planes means that the expression plane, say, can be isolated for study independently of the content plane. Lack of bilateral dependency is illustrated by the fact that no constant meaning difference is associated with the substitution of the English phoneme /b/ for /p/; cf. *bit/pit, bin/pin*, etc. Furthermore, semantic considerations are irrelevant in determining the phonemic distinctness of pairs such as *bit/pit*.[2]

Analysis of linguistic expression is not limited to phonemics. It is assumed that the combination of phonemes into morphemes, morphemes into sentences can be studied without taking into account the meaning of these combinations. Zellig Harris, for instance, has stressed that "The observed co-occurrences [of morphemes] ... have to be taken as raw data for classification and comparison; they cannot be adequately derived from some nonlinguistic source such as 'the desired combination of meanings'."[3]

What, then, are we to make of the assertion that analysis of stylistic variants — different ways of saying the same thing — is independent of content? The solution to this seeming antinomy lies in the recognition of an equivocalness in the terms *form* and *content*. Consider these remarks by Hirsch on Ohmann's suggestion that transformational grammar provides a basis for the distinction between form and content: "the 'meanings' that emerge from his deep-structural analysis are no 'deeper' than 'meanings' that can be gleaned from a casual reading of the sentence."[4]

Hirsch's mistake in equating linguistic deep structure with the literary critic's notion of the "deep" meaning of a literary work — its thematic significance, as distinct from its literal ("surface") meaning — points up the necessity for making a clear-cut distinction between the linguistic and the literary versions of the form-content dichotomy.[5] It is in terms of such a distinction that we can resolve the problem of Ohmann's emphasizing the separability of form and content while at the same time defining style as alternative ways of expressing the same content.[6]

However, Ohmann himself consistently confuses the two dichotomies, as evidenced by his remark that transformational grammar is "powerful enough to set forth, formally and accurately, stylistic *alternatives* to a given passage or a given set of linguistic habits" (p. 438). The difference between alternatives to a passage and alternatives to "linguistic habits" may seem slight, but in the present context it is crucial — the former type of alternatives is congruent with the literary form-content dichotomy, whereas the latter presupposes adherence to the assumption that linguistic form can be studied independently of linguistic content. This assumption, in fact, guided Chomsky's early work in transformational grammar upon which Ohmann drew. In *Syntactic Structures* Chomsky explicitly states that "We considered the problem of syntactic research to be that of constructing a device for producing a given set of grammatical sentences and of studying the properties of grammars that do this effectively. Such semantic notions as reference, signification, and synonymity played no role in the discussion" (pp. 102—03).

Ohmann, perhaps vaguely aware of the expression-centered orientation of early transformational grammar, does shift his conception of style from "alternative ways of saying the same thing" to one that Chomsky's early model can more nearly adequately explicate: "A style is a characteristic use of language, and it is difficult to see how the *uses* of a system can be understood unless the system itself has been mapped out" (p. 425). By the "use of a system" Ohmann specifically means the writer's characteristic choices (= "set of linguistic habits") from among the transformational rules of a language. This conception of style is illustrated in his analysis of a passage from Faulkner's "The Bear," in which he shows that only a very few transformational rules account for the "Faulknerian" quality of the passage.[7] To answer the objection that these particular transformations are so basic that passages from any writer would reflect their extensive use, Ohmann effects the same reduction on a passage from Hemingway, which does not overlap at all in content with the Faulkner passage.

By using transformational analysis to compare different writers saying different things, Ohmann separates linguistic expression from linguistic content and subjects it to independent analysis. In those instances in which Ohmann may be said to examine different ways of saying the same thing — e. g., in his analysis of a passage from Henry James — he is forced to make ad hoc modifications of transformational grammar.

Expression-centered views have dominated much of modern linguistics, and it was inevitable that they influenced work in linguistic stylistics. Other examples of conceptions of style that separate linguistic expression from linguistic content include those that define style in terms of statistical deviations from a "norm" and those that attempt to correlate linguistic features of utterances with the socio-physical context in which they occur.[8] Today the predominant trend in linguistic theory is to assign equal status or even priority to the content plane of language. This shift has mixed implications for the linguistic analysis of style. On the one hand, it has given impetus to the study of the paraphrase relation; on the other, it has led some linguists to pay more attention to the semantic implications of surface structures and to argue that paraphrase is less widespread in language than is commonly assumed.[9]

We consider it an open question whether the concept of style is dependent on or independent of the linguistic plane of content, i. e., whether or not the concept of style is tied to the paraphrase relation (though for convenience we will assume that it is, for the balance of the paper). In either case, one can invoke the literary form-content dichotomy and assert that stylistic variation is independent of literary content. It is the clarification and modification of this particular assertion that will be our primary concern here.

First, by way of clarification, literary content should not be thought of exclusively in terms of "theme" or symbolic significance. Any aspect of a literary work that, in the opinion of a number of literary critics, entails drawing "inferences" from the language itself is an aspect of literary content. What we have in mind are the numerous arguments that have been adduced against a linguistic analysis of literature. Thus, plot and character, which are often said to "transcend" language, constitute part of literary content.[10] In this context language is only the material medium of the literary work. In other words, "literary expression" includes both linguistic expression and linguistic content. One can thus isolate the language of a literary text from its literary content and still base stylistic variation on the paraphrase relation.

As support for this interpretation of the assumption underlying much stylistic analysis, consider Spencer and Gregory's characterization of the concept of style as an abstraction: "It is abstract ... in the sense that style is one quality out of several possessed by any work of literature."[11] They propose that "when the language of a text is examined, not as a source of information about plot or character or thought, but as the major focus of attention in the dialectical process — that is when the response is primarily to the use of language itself — the critic may be said to be examining the style of the text" (pp. 62—63).

In elaboration of this representative view, we can note that in a very general sense the relation between literary content and literary expression is comparable to that existing among a set of stylistic variants. Consider for example the plot unit Propp termed the *function*.[12] A given function has variant manifestations within the plot of a tale or across tales; e. g., among the "species" of the function *Villainy* are such actions as a dragon kidnapping a princess, a stepmother driving her stepdaughter out of the house, etc. These actions represent different ways of "saying the same thing," but not in the same sense in which one speaks of stylistic variation. The locus of stylistic variation, per se, is the linguistic means for signalling each of these actions (species of function). Each action can be encoded by diverse linguistic means — the only requirement being that the "cognitive" content, say the notion of a dragon kidnapping a princess, remain constant. The notion of a kidnapping, therefore, is a variable vis-a-vis the function *Villainy*, but is a constant vis-a-vis variant sentences conveying this event.

The following diagram should provide a clear picture of the relation of language (considered as literary expression) to literary content:

2   E   R   C

1   $\overline{\text{ERC}}$

[handwritten annotation: This looks very much like a Desaussurian approximation to esthetic rotation.]

This diagram is one that Barthes has used to portray graphically Hjelmslev's notion of a *connoted system* of signification.[13] Any system of signification consists of a plane of expression (E) and a plane of content (C); the signification coincides with the relation (R) of the two planes. A connoted system is a complex second-order system, with a first-order system as one component — its plane of expression. In other words, a connoted system of signification is a system whose plane of expression is itself constituted by a signifying system.

In terms of the above diagram, literary content corresponds to the second-order system, and literary form corresponds to the first-order system — "language," the object of conventional linguistic research. The diagram makes clear that literary expression encompasses both the plane of expression and the plane of content of "language."

However, the above diagram is an overly simplified representation of the relation between literary content and its linguistic expression. Although the locus of stylistic variation is the first-order significative system, it is not the case that style per se can be wholly equated with the linguistic features of the "textual surface," the constituent sentences of a text. In other words, it is not the case that the primary data of stylistic analysis are immediately "given" to the analyst, who merely has to discern a recurrent pattern of syntactic choice, etc. Insofar as Spencer and Gregory imply that this is possible, they have a "concrete" conception of style.

The relation between the second-order and the first-order systems is no more simple and direct than is the relation between sound and meaning in the first-order system. To explicate this relationship, we must first note that what we have been referring to as "literary content" is more exactly specified as "literary structure," which is a hyper-structure vis-a-vis language structure. Furthermore, this literary hyper-structure is just one instance of the "macro-structure" that is assumed to underlie any coherent text, providing the controlling plan for the text. As such, the macro-structure is roughly comparable to a resume or summary of an article that may consist of sentences and vocabulary items not occurring in the article itself.[14] The study of macro-structure (second-order significative system) and its mapping onto the constituent sentences of a text (first-order significative system) falls within the scope of what I have termed *semiolinguistics*.[15]

The mapping relation between literary macro-structure and language structure is typically one-many. This disparity reflects the utilization of a number of literary techniques and devices that intervene between the two significative systems, leaving "traces" in the language of the literary text. Insofar as these devices and their linguistic correlates are part of the supra-individual literary tradition, they cannot be considered part of the writer's individual style.

The implication for stylistic analysis is that it cannot proceed as if the underlying (macro) structure did not exist, with the text regarded simply as a simple linear concatenation of sentences. Analysis must take into account the fact that the constituent sentences of a text manifest an abstract underlying structure. In other words, the assertion that stylistics is the study of language independent of literary content is subject to certain crucial qualifications. Complete independence, in a sense comparable to what American descriptive linguists referred to as strict separation of levels, must be rejected in favor of a proposal loosely comparable to Pike's well known argument in the 1940's for grammatical prerequisites to phonemic analysis.

The inadequacy of an overly "concrete" conception of style, one that overlooks the fact that some linguistic features of sentences reflect technique rather than stylistic options per se, has not totally escaped the attention of some stylisticians and literary theorists. Northrop Frye, for example, has observed that "Style exists in all literature . . . but may be seen at its purest in thematic [i. e., discursive] prose: in fact it is the chief literary term applied to works of prose generally classified as non-literary . . . In a novel we are aware of a more complicated problem: dialogue has to speak with the voice of the internal characters, not the author, and sometimes dialogue and narrative are so far apart as to divide the book into two different languages."[16]

Stylisticians at least intuitively aware of the problem posed by dialogue have adopted the strategy of merely eliminating such passages from their corpus.[17] But this expedient will be highly unsatisfactory in the case of literary works with extensive dialogue. And it would fail entirely in more subtle instances in which "decorum" — Frye's term for the writer's "modification of his own voice to the voice of a character," (p. 269) — affects the narrative itself. What we have in mind are narratives in which one or more characters serve as narrator — their share of the narrative is in effect an extended monologue, which implicitly (and sometimes explicitly) is enclosed in direct quotation marks. The consequence of the strategy of simple elimination in this situation would be that a novel such as Faulkner's *The Town* (New York: Random House, 1957), in which the entire narrative is presented through the eyes and language of three characters, would be totally unamenable to an analysis of Faulkner's style.

That the language of a Faulkner narrator who is a character may differ from the language of an anonymous or impersonal narrator (and in ways that transcend or are irrelevant to differences usually discussed in terms of "point of view" or the reliability of the narrator) can be demonstrated by a comparison of the language of Faulkner's story "Mule in the Yard" (in his *Collected Stories* [New York: Random House, 1950]) and the language of Charles Mallison's retelling of the same story in chapter 16 of *The Town* (pp. 231ff). Although no comparative analysis of the two versions has been attempted, one would presumably reveal that the differences are superficial and that underlying them is the invariance that is Faulkner's style.

The basis for this supposition is the fact that dialogue proper in a narrative does not constitute a reproduction of spoken conversational language. Writers utilize certain conventions designed to give the appearance of spoken language. The possibility exists, therefore, that decorum in dialogue (as well as in the narration of a character/narrator) may merely be a matter of sporadic "markers" that could easily be factored out. With such "normalization" dialogue would be amenable to stylistic analysis and would not have to be omitted from the analyst's corpus.

A process of normalization, as a requisite preliminary to stylistic analysis, would give recognition to the fact that the sentences of a text occur as part of a larger whole — a text — which has a determinate global structure underlying it; and would give recognition to the fact that the language of a text is a realization of this global structure, with individual style accounting for only a part of the linguistic characteristics of the sentences constituting the text.

The matter of dialogue is just one instance of the general situation in which we hypothesize that individual style has superimposed upon it language features that reflect the use of various literary techniques or devices. In many cases these non-stylistic aspects of language use have not been intuitively recognized as such, with the result that analysts of style have confused style proper with linguistic correlates of technique.

One striking instance is Ohmann's brief analysis of Hemingway's style — despite the fact that in theory at least Ohmann is well aware of the necessity of a principled limitation of the scope of stylistic variation. And he argues in particular for a distinction between technique and style (see p. 425). But in practice what Ohmann analyzes in the passage from the Hemingway story "Soldier's Home" is a particular technique, in our sense of the term.

According to Ohmann, the transformations primarily responsible for the distinctiveness of the passage are "quotation or reported thought," "indirect discourse," and a deletion transformation (p. 435). Despite his suggestion that stylistic intuition allows one to identify an author by his style, Ohmann has to concede that these transformations "do not in themselves distinguish Hemingway's style from the styles of many other writers (Virginia Woolf, Ford Madox Ford, James Joyce, etc.). But it is interesting, and promising, that a stylistic difference so huge as that between the Faulkner and Hemingway passages can be largely explained on the basis of so little grammatical apparatus" (p. 436).

The reason these transformations do not distinguish Hemingway's style from that of a number of other writers is that, as Ohmann himself states, they are "responsible for what critics call the *'style indirect libre'* " (p. 435). This, in our terminology, is a technique or device. Ohmann apparently is mislead by nomenclature (it is referred to as a "style") and by the fact that it recurs in a passage. Technique need not be sporadic in occurrence as Ohmann implies (p. 425).

Since the Faulkner passage does not utilize the device of style indirect libre, the comparison with Hemingway is spurious. And presumably the similarity between Hemingway, Woolf, and others lies in their use of this device. What Ohmann has presented, therefore, is not an analysis of Hemingway's style per se, but an analysis of the linguistic correlates of this particular device. Our hypothesis is that these linguistic correlates are superimposable upon a wide range of syntactic structures which can be exponents of individual style. Hemingway's style, then, would be an "abstraction," underlying the concrete sequence of sentences constituting a Hemingway text. Ohmann failed to go beyond some of the more obvious "surface" features.

Let us turn now to a consideration of M. A. K. Halliday's analysis of the "style" of Golding's *The Inheritors*, the story of a small group of Neanderthals ("the people") who are invaded and supplanted by a more advanced tribe ("the new people").[18] The long first section of the book is the narrative of the people, while the short final section deals with the new people. Halliday points out that the two sections differ in their language, in the prominent or recurrent clause types. He gives a brief grammatical description of each, referring to them as "Language A" (that of the people) and "Language C" (that of the new people), respectively.

It is obvious that Halliday has not attempted an analysis of Golding's individual style — his study is "stylistic" only in the loose sense of any type of linguistic examination of a literary work. But his study demands examination in the present context, for it implicitly challenges our hypothesis that the literary text is "stratified" — that a clear-cut distinction can be made between literary content and linguistic content; and hence it challenges the very existence of style in the sense of "different ways of saying the same thing." The implicit challenge is summed up in Halliday's assertion that "In *The Inheritors*, the syntax is part of the story" (p. 360). By "the story" Halliday means not only the literal (linguistic) content, the subject-matter, but also the underlying theme (literary content) of the novel:

> We have to do here with an interaction, not of meaning and form, but of two levels of meaning, both of which find expression in form, and through the same syntactic features. The immediate thesis and the underlying theme come together in the syntax; the choice of subject-matter is motivated by the deeper meaning, and the transitivity patterns realize both ... The foregrounding of certain patterns in syntax as the expression of an underlying theme is what we understand by 'syntactic imagery,' ... But in *The Inheritors* these same syntactic patterns also figure prominently in their 'literal' sense, as the expression of subject-matter ... (p. 347).

Let us examine exactly in what respect Halliday considers the syntax of *The Inheritors* to be part of the story. As a first step, we need to consider just what clause types Halliday finds to be prominent in each section. In the first (Language A), there is a predominance of intransitive clauses; and in half of these the grammatical subjects are not people but inanimate objects or parts of the body. In the short final section (Language C), on the other hand, the majority of clauses have a human subject, and of these most are transitive.

These clause types more or less correspond to the options that exist in the base (or phrase-structure) component of the early model of transformational grammar. (We are obviously overlooking the major differences between the grammatical systems of Chomsky and Halliday, focusing instead on the observed output.) The stylistic relevance of such options is briefly considered by Ohmann, who notes that "The various possibilities for rewriting at this stage of the grammar account for some of the major sentence types in English, and since the structural meaning of, say, Vt + NP differs considerably from that of Be + Adj, a writer's preference for one or another of these forms may be a stylistic choice of some interest" (p. 428). For example, one could derive, from the same point of origin (the symbol "VP"), either *Columbus discovered America* or *Columbus sailed* — two clause types that basically correspond to Language C and Language A, respectively, of *The Inheritors*.

Ohmann rejects this source of stylistic option because it does not yield clear-cut synonymous expressions. Ultimately, the basic problem with such options as a source of stylistic variation is that they presumably depend on what one chooses to say, i. e., the subject-matter. Halliday, as we have seen, rejects the dichotomy between literal and thematic meaning and considers choice of subject-matter a "stylistic" choice in his sense.

However, Halliday does point out some instances in which the fore-grounded clause types are not the typical form of expression for the subject-matter, "there being other, more likely ways of 'saying the same thing' " (p. 347). One example is: *A stick rose upright ... The stick began to grow shorter at both ends.* (Although not the typical form of expression for the subject-matter, this clause type does conform to the syntactic norm of the first section of the novel.) A more "expected" phrasing would be: *Someone held up a bow and drew it.*

But even here Halliday says that we cannot talk about a dichotomy between "what" and "how," for in such instances the clause type directly embodies the underlying theme of the novel — in effect, theme is laid bare, not masked by any literal meaning. Thematic significance thus motivates Golding's "syntactic originality" (cf. p. 359).

To explain how syntax could be said to embody theme, we need to consider the notion of "structural meaning" in its modern, revitalized sense. In descriptive linguistics of some decades ago, the subject-predicate construction, say, might be said to have the structural meaning of actor-action. Such interpretations came to be rejected by many linguists (e. g., Chomsky in *Syntactic Structures*, p. 100) because they failed for a wide number of constructions (e. g., *John received a letter*). Halliday's grammatical system (and Fillmore's case grammar, among others) in effect renovates this notion by recognizing that the grammatical subject itself has no fixed semantic significance (except that of "topic"). Instead, a number of different functional roles (= case relations), such as actor, goal, etc. are posited which can occupy the subject position. Also, the notion of action is specified into more refined semantic categories, such as "undirected action," "goal-directed action," "mental process," etc.

The sequence quoted earlier from *The Inheritors* has the structural meaning, in part, of an undirected (self-caused) process, as opposed to that of a goal-directed (externally caused) process in the case of the more expected formulation. The underlying theme of the novel, in Halli-day's interpretation, is in effect a generalization of the sense of the descriptive terms of his grammatical system. Halliday asserts that "The theme of the entire novel, in a sense, is transitivity..." (p. 359). More specifically, "It is ... the lack of transitive clauses of action with human subjects [in the first section] ... that creates an atmosphere of in-effectual activity: the scene is one of constant movement, but movement which is as much inanimate as human and in which only the mover is affected ..." (pp. 349—50). "In Language A there is a level-two theme, that of powerlessness" (p. 357); etc.

What we take issue with is Halliday's assertion that theme is directly embodied in syntax, that "it is the syntax as such ... to which we are responding" (p. 350). Halliday himself hedges somewhat on this at one crucial point when he notes that "the language as a whole is not deviant, and the difficulties of understanding are at the level of ... re-interpretation, as when we insist on translating *the stick began to grow shorter at both ends* as 'the man drew the bow' " (p. 358).

Halliday comes close but fails to recognize that Golding is utilizing a narrative device widely studied by the Russian Formalists, the device of *disautomatization,* which is usually characterized simply as the practice of not referring to objects by their usual name and which is justified by the objects' being distorted through the mental processes of a character who is not familiar with them. Halliday's "process of re-interpretation" requires the reader's intuitive awareness of the utilization of this particular device, which mediates the underlying structure of the novel and the constituent sentences of its textual surface. The reader is thus not directly responding to the syntax. For example, the disautomatized description of bow and arrows allows the reader to infer (in conjunction with textually derived information) that "the people" do not have any knowledge of this implement and hence that the "new people" are at a more advanced stage of technological development.

More generally, Golding uses the device of disautomatization as his means of "reaching out through the imagination into the unknown" (Halliday's quote from a critical study of the novel, p. 348); i. e., it is a conventionalized suggestion, not inherent in the syntax, of the world-view and mental processes of Neanderthal man. As such, the device need not be given any "thematic" interpretation. Furthermore, it is the device itself that provides the motivation for the prominent syntactic options noted by Halliday. His grammar of Language A is a specification of the linguistic features which actualize, in this particular case, the device of disautomatization. The choice he refers to between the "expected" and "unexpected" ways of saying something is primarily a choice between the use or non-use of the device.

Like Ohmann in his analysis of Hemingway, Halliday has failed to get beyond the most obvious linguistic features, features which manifest a device rather than the style of the author. Halliday's analysis therefore cannot be cited as a demonstration of the non-existence of style in the sense of alternative ways of saying the same thing independent of literary content. Golding's own style, we assume, is manifested throughout the novel and can be perceived only after non-stylistic features have been factored out. Support for this assumption comes from the observation (in the edited discussion appended to Halliday's paper) that certain grammatical constructions, such as co-ordinate clauses and verbal groups, seem to recur throughout the novel, as well as in Golding's *Free Fall,* irrespective of shifts in scene or other internal changes (p. 366).

In conclusion, the main thrust, by implication, of our argument in this programmatic paper is that linguists have tried to make analysis of literary style too simple. It might be objected that our proposal would make stylistic analysis hopelessly complicated. However, no one would seriously deny that results obtained from present assumptions and analytic techniques leave much to be desired. It might also be objected that the present proposal, if pushed to its logical conclusion, would see in all aspects of language use the manifestation of one or another device, thus rendering the concept of style superfluous. But this looms as a possibility because of an admitted vagueness in the concept of device, which needs to be carefully defined. Furthermore, we would suggest, in the spirit of Halliday, that language features can simultaneously serve several functions, so that some features that are stylistic can also reflect the use of certain compositional devices. For example, some aspects of "point of view" may overlap with genuinely stylistic features; if so, it would not be a matter of factoring out these features, but rather of analyzing the same set of linguistic features from more than one perspective.

Another possibility that needs to be explored is that stylistic variation, at least in part, may be a matter of linguistically variant manifestations of a given device. For example, there may be room for individual variation in the representation of conversational dialogue. But before there can be a serious exploration of this and other possibilities, much more must be discovered about how the global structure of discourse is mapped onto (first-order) language structure.

NOTES

[1] *Word*, 20 (1964), 423—39; see especially p. 427 & p. 431. All subsequent references to Ohmann's work are to this article.

[2] See Noam Chomsky, *Syntactic Structures* (The Hague: Mouton, 1957), p. 94.

[3] "Co-occurrence and Transformation in Linguistic Structure," *Language*, 33 (1957), p. 285.

[4] David H. Hirsch, "Linguistic Structure and Literary Meaning," *Journal of Literary Semantics*, No. 1 (1972), p. 86.

[5] Of course, it is a mistake to equate Chomsky's deep structure even with linguistic (literal) meaning, but Ohmann seems to have had such an equation in mind.

[6] It should be noted that Hirsch rejects the literary dichotomy and hence the possibility of style in this sense. We will examine this issue below.

[7] Note that the "kernelized" version of the Faulkner passage that Ohmann presents cannot be regarded as a genuine stylistic alternative — Ohmann himself characterizes it as artificial.

[8] An example of the former is Bernard Bloch, "Linguistic Structure and Linguistic Analysis," in *Report on the Fourth Round Table Meeting on Linguistics and Language Teaching*, ed. A. A. Hill (Washington: Georgetown Univ. Press, 1953), 40—44. An example of the latter is Nils Erik Enkvist, "On Defining Style: An Essay in Applied Linguistics," in *Linguistics and Style*, ed. John Spencer (London: Oxford Univ. Press, 1964), 3—56; see especially p. 20.

⁹ See, for instance, Wallace L. Chafe's discussion of what he terms the *"X is really Y* syndrome" in his *Meaning and the Structure of Language* (Chicago: Univ. of Chicago Press, 1970), pp. 86—88. See also his "Directionality and Paraphrase," *Language* 47 (1971), 1—26.

¹⁰ See the discussion of such arguments in my *Essays on Semiolinguistics and Verbal Art* (The Hague: Mouton, 1973), pp. 40f, and also my paper "The Relation between Linguistics and Literary Studies," *Poetics,* No. 11 (1974), 5—22.

¹¹ John Spencer and Michael J. Gregory, "An Approach to the Study of Style," in Spencer, ed., op. cit., p. 59.

¹² Vladimir Propp, *Morphology of the Folktale,* 2nd ed. (Austin: Univ. of Texas Press, 1968).

¹³ See Roland Barthes, *Elements of Semiology* (London: Jonathan Cape, 1967), p. 89. Note that our interpretation of "connotation" differs from that of Hjelmslev and Barthes; the latter refers to it as "at once general, global and diffuse ... the sum of messages in French refers, for instance, to the signified 'French'..." (p. 91).

¹⁴ For more discussion of these points, see my review-article on *Some Aspects of Text Grammars,* by T. A. van Dijk, *Poetica* (Tokyo: Sanseido), No. 1 (1974), 132—41. See also my *Essays,* pp. 57f; and "The Relation...".

¹⁵ In "The Relation..." I proposed calling the study of the mapping relation *stylolinguistics;* however, this term is inappropriate, for reasons that will become obvious in the course of our discussion. Note that *semiolinguistics* is partly synonymous with some scholars' use of such terms as *text linguistics* and *discourse analysis.* However, many practitioners of discourse analysis, particularly in the United States, have largely restricted their investigations to devices of intersentence linkage, such as anaphora, lexical equivalence classes, and so on.

¹⁶ *Anatomy of Criticism* (1957; rpt. New York: Atheneum, 1965), p. 268. Cf. the notion of "contextual cohesion" in Nils Erik Enkvist, *Linguistic Stylistics* (The Hague: Mouton, 1973), p. 122. Note that the "language" of description also differs from that of narration; but the linguistic correlates of these two techniques are so broad that within each there is ample room for stylistic diversity (see ch. VII of my *Essays*). Note too that the "purity" of style in discursive prose may well be an illusion, a reflection of our relative ignorance of the nature of the global structure underlying such discourse and its linguistic manifestation.

¹⁷ Other discussions that touch on aspects of the non-concreteness of style and the problems it poses for analysis include those of John B. Carroll, "Comments to Part Two," in *Style in Language,* ed. Thomas A. Sebeok (Cambridge, Mass.: M I T Press, 1960), p. 52; and Louis T. Milic, "Rhetorical Choice and Stylistic Option," in *Literary Style: A Symposium,* ed. Seymour Chatman (London & New York: Oxford Univ. Press, 1971), 77—88. Carroll's solution is to study the literary artist's "unstudied, nondeliberate materials," e. g., spontaneous conversation, personal letters, etc. The obvious problem with this solution is that such "unstudied" material will reflect supra-individual functional constraints that make language appropriate to situational context (see the work of Enkvist). Milic's solution is to study linguistic features amenable to statistical treatment. The difficulty here is that most statistical approaches are more author-attribution studies than studies of style per se — such studies interpret literally the metaphor of style as verbal fingerprints. However, one can study individual style without assuming that it is unique. And the problem we are dealing with here arises even in the study of group (or period) styles.

¹⁸ "Linguistic Function and Literary Style," in Chatman, ed., op. cit.

J. McH. Sinclair
University of Birmingham

The linguistic basis of style

It is proposed here that literary style, its techniques and its very possibility, arises from the existence of certain properties common to all natural languages. Six properties are outlined and exemplified; the properties are believed to be definable and distinct from each other but they do not form an exhaustive list. The properties are:

1A *arbitrariness* between sign and referent
1B *arbitrariness* between proposition and exponence
2A *structural superfluity*
2B *derivational hierarchy*
3   *idiom*
4   *reference*

All these properties have been noted many times before, indeed several are all commonplace, in literary criticism. The main aim of this paper is to present them in a way which may clarify them as linking concepts between the two disciplines. In conclusion, some more general comments are made on these properties in relation to literary structures and genres.

1A ARBITRARINESS BETWEEN SIGN AND REFERENT

This has been a cornerstone of linguistic theory since Saussure. Linguistic signs have referents outside language, and the relationship between sign and referent is the essential link that allows the language to mean. This relationship is abstract, arbitrary, unpredictable. The learner of a language cannot guess accurately on the basis of the physical features of the signs, what they refer to. The fringe area of moos and miaows, and even some involuntary noises, is language-specific and subject to the normal laws of historical change. There are no direct links from noises within a language system, to noises outside it, or to anything else outside it.

But despite this firm position, speakers of a language persist in sensing an appropriateness of sound to sense, prefer one phrasing to another, and argue from a point of view that seems to be opposed to Saussure's. Far from assuming the theoretical norm of arbitrariness, they seem to work on the principle that the physical features of items in a text can stand in a richly symbolic relationship to their referents. Virtually any quality which can be related to the physical substance of an utterance can be related to the meaning. The relationship may be appropriate, or specifically inappropriate. At a basic level, a contrast may be pointed by the selection of alliterating words, and though we know as readers that the initial sound of a word is not semantically significant at all, we assign meaning to the pattern.

It is not enough to talk of brilliant selection and ordering by writers, or to construct a concept of formal meaning, separate from the usual decoding, where these arbitrary features may become significant. Assuming that there is virtually no total synonymy in natural language, and that literary texts are careful, self-conscious constructs, a linguistic sign cannot be presented simultaneously with full regard to its reference (i. e. arbitrarily in respect to its substance) and meaningfully in terms of its substance. If it appears that something of this nature actually happens, then the descriptive categories are in need of revision.

If it can be argued against the above that the enormous choice available in a language provides enough leeway for signs to be chosen with an eye to their creating additional patterns, it is not clear how the readers or listeners perceive both types of ordering simultaneously. It is unlikely that the total sound wave is retained for examination along a very large number of possible parameters, and so some activating devices must be supposed. Also, we could take a hint from an important feature of visual ambiguity that may well be characteristic of other senses.[1] That is the impossibility of reaching more than one interpretation of an ambiguous figure simultaneously. In the famous duck/rabbit type of drawing, the figure has to be reassessed to move from one interpretation to the other.

It would be a digression to pursue the analogy with visual perception much further at this stage, but possibly helpful to add one or two brief observations. An ambiguous drawing, like a pun, has to be marked out for study or it will be assigned one of its meanings without further ado. For it to be artistically effective, the viewer would have to assign a synthesising interpretation to the phenomenon of the same lines suiting two different simple interpretations. The duck/rabbit would be an unlikely starter, but the famous "wife and mother" might lead to a reflection about beauty ageing, or the athenian boys wrestling may suggest the physical contact which is prominent in the sport. Several artists, notably Escher in representational and Vassarely in geometric forms have exploited some of the possibilities of the visual ambiguity. But note that in studies of visual perception each interpretation seems to be made by the same set of rules in the same medium. In literature the rules whereby we decode the conventional meaning of linguistic signs are at least superficially different from the processes whereby we find meaning in the patterns of language substance. The pun is not typical of the battery of possibilities inherent in a language whose development has followed the Saussurean principle of arbitrariness.

One of Jakobson's pronouncements seems to go contrary to this position on arbitrariness, since he talks of the *identity* of sign and referent and stresses that the language patterns in literature must break this identity.

> The function of poetry is to point out that the sign is not identical with its referent. Why do we need this reminder? Because along with the awareness of the identity of the sign and the reference (A is A₁) we need the consciousness of the inadequacy of this identity (A is not A₁); this antinomy is essential since without it the connection between the sign and the object becomes automatized and the perception of reality withers away.

(Roman Jakobson, "Ce je poesie?" *Volne smery* XXX (1939—4), pp 229—239, quoted in V Erlich *Russian Formalism*, The Hague 1969, p. 181.)

It is clear from the latter part of the paragraph that Jakobson means by identity the conventional association of sign and referent which the literary language must disturb, and that the movement from sign to referent or vice versa is still across an arbitrary relationship (fig. 1).

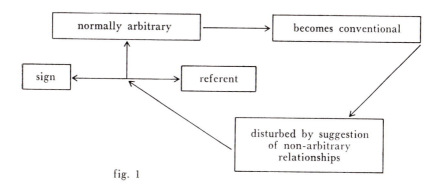

fig. 1

1B ARBITRARINESS BETWEEN PROPOSITION AND EXPONENCE

This property differs from sign/referent arbitrariness in several particulars, although in some respects it is similar. It is the relationship between the propositional content of an utterance and its exponence, or realisation. The main differences are:

(a) propositional content is paraphrasable so that there are many options in realisation. For example, *X is hotter than Y = Y is cooler than X; X is Y = X is not W, and not Z (in a set WXYZ). X kicked Y = Y was kicked by X.*

(b) the scale of exponence relevant here stops short of the physical substance, but remains within the areas of lexis and syntax.

(c) Whereas in sign-referent arbitrariness the normal expectation in nonliterary language is that the relation remains largely arbitrary, in this type, which I shall call *congruence*, the normal expectation is that the "overlaying" propositions will support the underlying (deep) propositional content. So in terms of the native speaker's reactions, congruence and appropriateness are complementary features deriving from properties located in different areas of the descriptive model of language.

The stylistic feature of congruence, or incongruence, can be seen very roughly as a relation between deep and surface structure. Deep structure generates the conventional meanings, but during the unfolding of surface structure it is possible to suggest various surface structures which, although ultimately abandoned, may leave a trace of their embryonic meanings. So that, in a sense, *X is hotter than Y* suggests that X is hot and Y is hot; *X is not W* suggests by collocation that X and W are more closely related than by denial of their identity, *Y was kicked by X* suggests that Y did something. If the last example is hard to accept, one can recall an old teaching grammar that said of the sentence

The missionary was eaten by savages

that the missionary performed the action of being eaten by savages.

Shakespeare's sonnet 116 is one of many poems which proceed largely by negative statements. In a poem about the constancy of love there are the following negative statements (italicised in the text):

> *Let me not to the marriage of true minds*
> *Admit impediments. Love is not love*
> Which alters when it alteration finds,
> Or bends with the remover to remove.
>
> O, no! It is an ever-fixed mark,   5
> That looks on tempests *and is never shaken;*
> It is the star to every wand'ring bark,
> Whose worth's unknown, although his height be taken.
> *Love's not Time's fool,* though rosy lips and cheeks
> Within the bending sickle's compass come;   10
> *Love alters not* with his brief hours and weeks,
> But bears it out even to the edge of doom.
>
>   If this be error, and upon me prov'd,
>   *I never writ, nor no man ever lov'd.*

Except for the second quatrain, all the main clauses are negative, and *love* is collocated with *impediments, alter, alteration, Time's fool,* and *alter* again. Perhaps the quasi-legal language of the first two and the last two lines conceal the basic absurdity of argument by negative assertion. The expected "resolution" of the negatives by subsequent positives does happen — lines 5—8, and line 12. But the strong reciprocating pattern of cognates *alter—alteration* and *remover—remove* is hardly compensated for; the subject becomes *it* rather than *love* so that sabotage by negatives continues in *never shaken* and *worth's unknown*, relegated to the subordinate clauses. One must also point to the brevity of the main negative assertions, leaving much of the text to positive comment on the instability of things in the passage of time. The second positive main clause, in line 12, is not nearly prominent enough to counterbalance 9—11; the subject is understood so that *love* again does not collocate with *bears it out*; the line is even-numbered which, in the way sentences fit lines in this sonnet, suggests a subordinate role.

In the second quatrain the words *ever* and *never* appear, words that one might expect in assertions of constancy. By an effect of the arbitrariness feature, the word *every* in the line 7, bolstered by the superficial similarity of

syllables:	6	7	8	9	10
line 5		ever	fix-ed		mark
line 7		every	wandring	bark	

reinforces the presence of *ever* in the quatrain.

The last line is so packed with negatives that it is difficult to understand fully. The final clause

> *nor   no   man   ever   loved*

is the first place where *love* and *ever* collocate, but the negatives dominate, and, by a neat reversal, the negative moves to the subject position and the word *love* moves to the verb. This parallels the reversal of the sentence syntax. From lines 2—12 the characteristic sentence is main clause first, followed by all sorts of subordinate material eroding the main statements — in contrast line 13 is the only case where a subordinate clause precedes the main clause.

The effect of the negatives in this poem is to exemplify the difficulties of constancy. *Love* and *not* and *alter* are never far apart, the negatives are not adequately balanced by positives and they dominate the last line.

The possibilities under the heading of congruence are very wide — as wide as the range of options from proposition to realisation. The example of negatives sketched out above shows a gross discrepancy, or incongruence, between what we understand of the propositional meaning of the sentences and the effect created by their realisation. But many less obvious tactical choices, from word order to matters such as voice and transitivity, are capable of similar modification of the total impression made by a text.

Of course, in a deep structure that fully specifies the eventual surface forms, such matters would be decided at the outset, but it would be an exceedingly difficult task to recognise them from the deep structure formulae. The problem of how these different strands of meaning are perceived, related and interpreted remains as obscure as the similar problem for sign-referent arbitrariness. And since congruence and arbitrariness may both play a part in the same stretch of text, the situation is further complicated.

2A STRUCTURAL SUPERFLUITY

We turn to the well-known feature of poetic licence, and the important question of how a rule-bound system can interpret rule-breaking. The property of language that gives rise to this possibility is the asymmetry of linguistic networks. Not all combinations of symbols are possible. Categories are properly set up in descriptions to account for necessary differences, but only a few of the possible sequential strings are actually assigned status in the descriptions. The stylistic feature of *deviation* fills the gaps.

There has been much exploration by generative grammarians of the boundaries of grammaticalness,[2] and some suggestion that deviant structures might be assigned analogical meaning on a sliding scale. The fuzzy edges of syntax remain fuzzy, despite the clear requirement of Chomsky's model that grammatical sentences must be sharply distinguished from non-grammatical ones.

It is unprofitable in practice also to retain a concept of "more or less grammatical", because that obscures the issue that arises in stylistics of how deviations are interpreted. The assumption remains that a "fairly grammatical" string will be interpreted principally with reference to wholly grammatical strings, and the evidence for this is not conclusive. Experimental subjects can probably be shown to normalise slightly deviant strings, but that process in relation to literature would be a kind of misinterpretation.

Let us turn from the disputed area on the borders of grammaticalness and consider the general case. Suppose a language has (or its description requires) elements of structure A, B and C at a certain point, and the following structures are grammatical:

ABC,   AC,   BC,   BCA,   C

Then suppose one generates BAC, AB, B, AAC or any of the other possibilities. What sort of meaning can be imagined for these?

The answer seems to be — a great deal, often of a particularly evocative and intriguing type. Once again the native speaker finds interpretations for items which have no recognised meaning. There is certainly an urge to assign a tentative syntax to any string, however random, and no doubt that is a natural extension of the everyday process of decoding, where the raw sound waves or line shapes are assigned structure and meaning, often despite interference. The following casual example was concocted by opening a book on language teaching five times and each time picking a word, all without looking.

Of grading be language grammar

Immediately it has some sort of structure; an intonation pattern is assigned to it. *Of grading* will be some sort of initial adjunct; *be* is the main verb, and its lack of inflexion gives, with the curious word-order, a slightly archaic flavour. The subject might be *language, grammar* or *language-grammar*. Certainly none of this structure was put into the selection of the word-string, and it remains nonsense. But the mind keeps turning it over and over to see what meaning it might yield.

In cases where the interpretation finds meaning, the process is far from merely rewriting the string into an acceptable form. The obvious point is that we assume that a literary author could have written grammatically if he had wished. Norman McCaig is a ready source of small-scale deviations e. g.

A ruined chain lies reptile

Leaving aside the exact meaning of *ruined*, the word *reptile*, normally a noun, is glossed as an adjective or past participle — *lies hidden* or *lies quiet*. Some adjectives end in *-ile*, like *facile, nubile*, and some readers might think *supine* is being hinted at, though the process of interpretation need not be conscious. These suggestions and half-echoes arise from the arbitrariness feature and point the way towards a tentative syntactic structure. But the clause retains its unique form, and does not fit the pattern. We are not so much asking "What is the grammar of this clause?" as "What would a grammar be like if it could cope with this clause?" We are asked to extend our grammars, imaginatively and provisionally, to handle the otherwise meaningless entity.

A skilled speaker of a language, then, retains some sort of agile acquisition mechanism to cope with the deviations. However, it is doubtful that the simple technique of relating a deviant utterance to the "nearest" grammatical one is likely to provide a satisfactory account of the literary effect of deviance. Almost certainly more than one route will be suggested, and the decision about which is either "nearer" or more satisfying is not always going to be easy.

Another point concerns the special status of the syntactic decoding process, in contrast with the other dimensions of meaning discussed here. When faced with a deviant passage where the normal syntactic decoding does not fully apply, the claim for attention by stylistic patterns increases and the total effect of the passage may have little to do with similar non-deviant passages. The motivation in a person to understand and to impose order and meaning causes him to explore possible extensions of his grammar, and other dimensions of meaning. He becomes, momentarily, a speculative linguist. The speed and naturalness of this process should not disguise its character or importance. Once again the skilled speaker finds meaning in an aspect of language patterning that has no meaning, officially. Presumably some of the rich meaning that can arise from deviation is a product of the adjustments in his linguistic co-ordinates giving rise to all sorts of concomitant possibilities.

2B DERIVATIONAL HIERARCHY

The literary feature that arises from this property includes most types of parallelism, antithesis and the like — those that do not rely on aspects of arbitrariness. Again it concerns the meaning-potential of formal similarity, but whereas arbitrariness consider only the final outcome, the linguistic sign, the feature we shall call *matching* considers all similarity on a realisation scale within a grammar.

In one sense all sentences are the same — just in the fact that they are sentences. And each sentence is a unique combination of choices, at least slightly different from all others, sharing perhaps a lot of similarities of structure with certain other sentences, not so much with others, and so on. The derivational tree of any pair of sentences will show points of divergence and possibly later convergence. Since all the choices that are made lead to meaning in the eventual sentence, the fact that similar patterns appear in adjacent structures is quite incidental. However, given circumstances which draw attention to the matching, it becomes a powerful source of further meaning.

In Pope's famous dismissive couplet about women[3]

> *A Fop their Passion, but their Prize a Sot*
> *Alive, ridiculous, and dead, forgot!*

the matchings provide much of the structure. The metre, rhyme and alliteration provide a framework; the repetition of *their* and *a* indicate a chiasmus in the first line, and although the structure is reversible the line tends to be paraphrased *Their passion is a fop . . . .* Between the two lines, the linkers *but* and *and* suggest another similar structure but so compressed that each word in the second line except *and* is a full clause.

The antonymic matching *alive-dead* shows that the selection of semantic features is also relevant, and there is a separate comment later about lexical and semantic patterns. Note that *alive* is a member of the class of adjectives that must be headwords and not noun modifiers, though *dead* is ambiguous. *Forgot* is slightly difficult for the modern reader, but easy to match with *ridiculous*. So three adjectives and a past participle in a row can be paraphrased as

> *When they are alive, they are ridiculous,*
> *and when they are dead, they are forgotten*

The effect of the matching is to take two words, *ridiculous* and *forgot*, which have nothing semantically to do with each other and not much syntactically, and to invest them with a fairly comprehensive pejorative meaning, as if they were complementary concepts that between them summed up the folly and fate of women.

Pope's verse paragraphs often start with a clear matching and develop it gradually, keeping it an important structural feature of the paragraph. Early in the *Epistle to Arbuthnot*, Pope writes

> Is there a Parson, much be-mus'd in Beer,　　　　　15
> A maudlin Poetess, a ryming Peer,
> A Clerk, foredoom'd his Father's soul to cross,
> Who pens a Stanza when he should *engross?*
> Is there, who lock'd from Ink and Paper, scrawls
>
> With desp'rate Charcoal round his darken'd walls?　　20
> All fly to *Twit'nam,* and in humble strain
> Apply to me, to keep them mad or vain.
> *Arthur,* whose giddy Son neglects the Laws,
> Imputes to me and my damn'd works the cause:
>
> Poor *Cornus* sees his frantic Wife elope,　　　　　25
> And curses Wit, and Poetry, and *Pope.*

Line 16 gives the match most succinctly: indefinite article, modifier annd noun. The *a,* annd the *p*-alliteration include line 15 although the noun modifier is more elaborate, comes after the noun and has its own subtle alliteration. This makes a fairly common 3-part couplet, similar to lines 9—10. The model of line 15 is developed in 17—18, where the noun modifier takes up most of the couplet, and various local matchings appear. Lines 19—20 start by repeating the first two words of 15, then proceed like lines 17—18, with parallels such as *foredoom'd/lock'd,* and the slight matching of 18 develops into the fourpart pattern of 20. Line 20 in turn recalls the original model of 16.

Line 21 changes the framing syntax from interrogative to declarative, though the sequence *all, Arthur, poor Cornus* retains at least the selection of nouns referring to human beings. The remainder of each couplet creates a distinct pattern with only slight echoes, e. g. 23—4 and 19—20. Line 25 shows the first main clause that fits the line, and this simple correlation is rounded off, in typical fashion, with a line displaying a 3-noun list.

The way in which matchings are perceived and processed is no clearer than the harnessing of arbitrary similarities or differences, and they may best be considered also as types of illusion. It is clear from the examples that the meaning which can be created through matchings is varied and not necessarily of a different order from that of syntax and semantics — except of course that it is quite local, and is created on the instant of reading by the total environment.

One important feature of visual illusions such as line distortions is that the perceiver can convince himself intellectually that a line is straight, by measurement for example, but still cannot *see* it as straight when it is placed in a distorting environment. The presence in literary texts of similar but separate ordering devices may lead to "distortions of meaning".

The examples of deviation and matching have been predominantly syntactical, but the vocabulary of a language allows similar effects, though less accessible to description at present.

Deviation in vocabulary is unusual collocation, where words occur together that we do not normally associate.

This phenomenon is the basis of many literary figures, which may combine with syntactical ones to make complex effects. In the McCaig quotation above

a ruined chain lies reptile

there is a lexical interest as well as the unusual syntax. *Ruin* and *chain* might have general medieval collocations, but *reptile* is unexpected in that environment.

The lexical equivalent of matching is the familiar thesaurus organisation, particularly the development of that known as structural semantics.[4] Word meanings can be analysed in terms of relations like synonymy, hyponymy, and antonymy, and the occurrence of related words in literary text can create a similar effect to the syntactic matching relations. Another line from Pope's *Arbuthnot* is sufficient to demonstrate.

If Foes they write, if Friends they read me dead

(line 32)

The lexical matching patterns, with supporting alliteration, balance exactly and they isolate the last word most strikingly. The syntax is deviant also, so the last two words are unexpected.

3. IDIOM

The syntactic way of understanding language is through assumptions about the choices that lead up to the final text. Text is evidence of routes through choice networks, and, in that sense each linguistic item is independently selected, according to a known and completely general set of rules. The definite article selects a route as shown in figure 2.

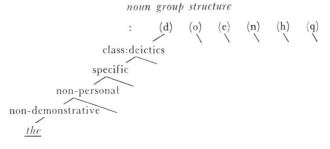

fig. 2

The progressive narrowing down of classes is also a progressive accretion of elements of meaning, and the grammatical value of an item is the total record of its choice pattern. (This statement is generally correct whether or not it is supposed that all choices originate in deep structure and predetermine the route to an item.) In the complexity of syntactic networks lies the main organising power of language.

We are also, however, aware of another type of organisation that involves the same linguistic items, and that can roughly be called idiom. In this type, a single unit of meaning is realised by several items in sequence, not always contiguous and constrained in their variation by rules of a highly specific nature (figure 3).

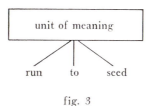

fig. 3

(Notes: *run* can be inflected fully; *to* and *seed* are fixed; sequence is fixed; members of the adverb class including *completely utterly quite* can occur between *run* and *to*, but nothing else can.)

This is a very different process from the typical syntactic one, and may even be considered opposite to it. One characteristic of syntax is that it allows for each utterance to be novel and original, because of the enormous range of combinations of a large number of small elements. In our ordinary language experience, it is a superior stratagem to assume that a sentence is new, than to search for whether one has encountered it before. Idioms, clichés and the like are prepacked language, within which the apparent syntactic signals serve purely to identify the item. They are like letters in words rather than words in sentences, and by pre-empting syntactic choice they reduce the information content of comparable passages.[5]

The task of understanding a text is complicated by having two opposite principles of interpretation available, and in literary texts this tension can be exploited in several ways. One major technique is to create idioms within a text, by repetition in various environments. Refrains, as well as their regular position, can gather text-dependent meaning in this way. The phrase *honourable man* in *Julius Caesar III.* 2 is a famous example. Recurring several times in the early part of Mark Antony's series of speeches, it becomes a jeer taken up by the crowd.

Fourth Plebeian: They were Traitors: Honourable men?

Another productive technique is akin to punning but whereas the pun contrasts alternative meanings, this contrasts idiom and syntax. The idiom *make free (with)*, meaning "take liberties with" has come a long way from the early English meaning of *free* "not in bondage". Vachel Lindsay, in *General William Booth Enters Into Heaven* writes (stanza 2)[6]

> *Hallelujah! It was queer to see*
> *Bull-necked convicts with that land make free.*

Freedom from sin, from the world, etc. is a central theme in the poem and in the evangelism it mimics. The convicts being made free requires that *free* is understood in the sense "no longer in prison". The convicts playing havoc at the Pearly Gates requires the idiomatic meaning.

This effect often involves a slight deviation, to draw attention and make the idiom analysable. In the example above the word-order is odd because *with* doesn't normally precede *make free*.

The popular game of literary echo comes under the general heading of idiom, though it has a wide range of applicability. *The Waste Land* is a monument to echo, and in a modest way the Lindsay poem uses a line from evangelist cliché to telling effect.

Lines 2 and 4 of the first stanza are

> *(Are you washed in the blood of the Lamb?)*

Isolated by brackets, they become part of the jingle, recurring sporadically (last line stanzas 1, 2, lines 6 and 8, st. 5). Lines 6 and 7 of st. 2 are

> *Tranced, fanatical they shrieked and sang:*
> *"Are you washed in the blood of the Lamb?"*

This further reduces the meaning of the line since it is hardly an appropriate question to ask of the angels and saints. But the last 3 lines of the poem run

> *He saw King Jesus. They were face to face,*
> *And he knelt a-weeping in that holy place.*
> *Are you washed in the blood of the Lamb?*

The *you* suddenly refers out to the reader, who has no doubt been enjoying the fun, and the full syntactic meaning of the line returns to it. There are no brackets or speech marks, so the reader cannot escape.

4. REFERENCE SYSTEMS AND THEIR REFERENTS

A reference is a signal at one place in a text that points to another place in the text or to the non-linguistic situation. It is up to the writer or speaker to ensure clarity of reference, to predict the ambiguity of *John saw Clarence and then he hit him* or *Shut the door* when there are three open doors.

If we now turn to the famous opening of Orwell's *Nineteen Eighty-Four* we see the normal process reversed.

It was a bright cold day in April, and the clocks were striking 13.

The first clause, to the comma, describes a normal condition of the British climate and the reader, even if the title has alerted him, assumes that the opening concerns familiar times and places and reads on. *The clocks.* Which clocks? Certainly a bright cold day in April does not entail clocks. The reader imagines perhaps a small town — perhaps nothing so precise, but some area in a known world that boasts more than one large clock. The shock of *13* is all the greater for the reader now has to extend his conventional imaginary world to include a place where clocks strike 13. Present day readers, more accustomed to 24-hour time-table may be less surprised than the original readers.

The normal meaning of *the* is that the noun it modifies is identified. *The* does not actually identify it, but the reader should be able to discover the identification fairly easily. It may be there is only one, *the moon*, or only one relevant, *the queen*, or it may refer backwards in the text, as in *the comma* above, or forward, as in *the noun it modifies*. If there is no obvious referent, the reader has to imagine one, from an assumption of shared experience.

A piece of writing could begin:

There are many design defects in modern houses.
For one thing, the bathrooms are too small . . .

Writer and reader share an assumption that modern houses have bathrooms. If the second sentence above read:

For one thing, the cellars are often damp. . .

there would be a problem of interpretation because modern houses in Britain do not normally have cellars.

Hemingway starts his story "The Short Happy Life of Francis Macomber" as follows:

It was now lunch-time and they were all sitting under the double green fly of the dining tent pretending that nothing had happened.

The reader is a long way behind, and has to construct a provisional universe in which to locate all the hints put forward by the words of reference: *it, now, they, all, the.* There is also something that has happened. The reader must reverse his normal interpretations of the references, and construct the referents in his imagination. The process can be seen as an extension of the "shared assumption" convention, but it is a very considerable extension, and an author is free to manipulate the shared assumptions in order to create effects, of which the opening of *Nineteen Eighty-Four* is a small example.

87

Each of the features that have been outlined arise from six properties of natural language, and so are latent in the structure of every language. Non-literary texts make limited use of them, at least to the extent of contriving their neutrality — by suppressing accidental effects where the writer chooses. Literary texts can develop them into major organisations of meaning.

If we assume that a language contains limitless potential for reasonably precise expression, then the development of these stylistic features must indicate that limitless precise expression is not the aim, and that the quality of mental process necessary to create meaning through these features is an important part of the experience of literature. They are characterised by notions of ambiguity, illusion, imagination; by the intellectual and emotional involvement of the participants.

Literary criticism has kept careful study of the nature of these meanings at bay for centuries, mainly by having names for most of them. Linguistics avoids the area by claiming it isn't there, despite the evidence of informants. There must be something fundamentally wrong with theories of linguistics which offer no explanation for language texts that are held to be the highest achievements of verbal expression.

A subsidiary proposal in this paper is that each of the six properties can be developed until it replaces or almost replaces the recognised meanings as the basic decoding process. The associated features become part of literary structure, not incidental aspects of texts. Sign-referent arbitrariness (1A), when elevated to this position, elicits the genre known as concrete poetry. Proposition - exponence arbitrariness (1B) can give rise to an important type of irony. Deviation taken to extremes could result in utter nonsense, but on the edges of meaninglessness some artifice is possible — for example Beckett's short story *Ping*,[7] or the offerings of Herbert Read in *Encounter* of March 1959. The possibilities of matchings arising from derivational hierarchy are well known to formal poets. Wordsworth in *Tintern Abbey* puts considerable weight of organisation on matchings, and of course heroic couplet poetry is structurally dependent on matchings. Idiom is the basis of ritualistic language (or ritual is the basis of idiomatic language). The exploitation of pseudo-reference is to be found in much folk-tale, science-fiction, and other places where the author is describing a state of affairs to which the reader has access only via the text, in which normal assumptions from experience are invalid.

This paper deals only with stylistic features of a formal kind, arising from the formal properties of language. There is a great deal of work to do to specify them in such a way that particular devices can be analysed. Then there is a need to draft a theory of verbal perception which can explain the origin of their relevance in a text, their inter-relationships and the quality of meaning that they create.

But there are two other tasks that arise from this view of literary style. One is in the area of discourse — to provide a framework for the description of situationally sensitive language in fiction. In some ways this feature is similar to that of pseudo-reference, for the features that conjure up specific types of language are simply those that are characteristic of the type, and do not evoke stylistic meaning in their normal context. But the study of discourse is growing fast, and will be able to make a profound contribution to the elucidation of style.

The other task is to press further with the basic argument of this paper. If the rather abstract properties discussed here can be shown to give rise to style features, what about all the other fundamental properties of natural languages? A sentence is a linear linguistic structure, and so is a novel or an epic or a tragedy. It would be reasonable to suppose that many structural features of literary works are capable of fruitful description by means of extended versions of the categories of grammar, lexis and phonology.

NOTES

[1] There is a succinct and up-to-date account of visual illusion in R. L. Gregory's "The Confounded Eye" in *Illusion in Nature and Art*, ed. Gregory and Gombrich, London 1973. See also G. Leech, *Linguistic Structures in Poetry* London, 1969, pp. 217—220, and A. Cluysenaar, *Aspects of literary stylistics* Batsford, forthcoming.

[2] A convenient statement of the starting position of this work is found in three papers, by Chomsky, Ziff and Katz, in Fodor and Katz (eds) *The Structure of Language*, New Jersey 1964, pp. 384—416.

[3] Moral Essays, Epistle II *To a Lady*, lines 247—8.

[4] See particularly Lyons, *Structural Semantics*, Oxford 1963.

[5] See Makkai, *Idiom Structure in English*. The Hague 1972, for a thorough account.

[6] Text from Williams (ed), *A little Treasury of Modern Poetry*, London 1947.

[7] In *No's Knife* London 1967, p. 166.

Ulf Teleman
Roskilde University

Style and grammar

In this paper we shall be concerned with the relationship between style and grammar. Our main objective will be to specify what use can be made of grammar in stylistic analysis.

The presentation will be in three parts. We shall start by discussing the concept of style. The next section deals with the possible relations between grammatical competence and stylistic competence within the framework of a verbal communication model. The paper concludes with a few pages which attempt to show how one particular type of grammatical theory could determine stylistic analysis of verbal communication.

1. STYLE

Nils Erik Enkvist has eminently reviewed and classified a great many definitions of style suggested by various scholars during the history of linguistic stylistics.

One major type of style definition is the one that regards style as a result of choice between different ways to express "the same thing". Within this definition of style synonymy and ambiguity are key concepts. This must also be the case where style is defined as the relation between meaning and expression.

It is obvious that these two concepts of style go quite well with the general idea of what a scientific grammar is. (Cf. Ohmann 1964, 1966; Hayes 1966.) Grammar should describe how in a given language meanings are connected with expression. It should register which sentences are synonymous and which are ambiguous. This is accomplished by a coherent system of rules which specify semantic, syntactic, lexical and phonological structures and their interdependence.

Grammar is then a description of the abstract, static system of relations between meaning and expression (Saussure's langue), or of an idealized speaker's knowledge of these relationships (Chomsky's competence). Style is the realization of language in texts, or the use of competence in actual verbal performance by speakers, writers, listeners and readers.

We cannot however leave it at that. If style is understood as choice, we are sooner or later forced to answer questions like: "What kind of choice?", Why that particular kind of choice?" etc. Our definition yields a remarkably empty, formal concept, which does not help us very much if we want to describe positively what style is. How could it tell us anything about, for instance, congruence of style ranging over the lexical, syntactic and orthographic choices of one long text?

If we conceive of style as the relation between meaning and expression, our principal problem will be to distinguish between style value and other kinds of meaning. Our definition is of no help if we want to describe the semantic contrasts in the following two pairs of sentences:

(1a) Would you pass me the H_2O, please?
(1b) Would you pass me the water, please?

(2a) Would you pass me the H_2O, please?
(2b) Would you pass me the $KMnO_4$, please?

Let us therefore proceed to another kind of definition, rightly given credit by Enkvist. Style is here defined positively as the set of associations attached to an expression, associations which are determined by the linguistic and nonlinguistic contexts in which an expression is normally used. In the spirit of this definition, style value could also be called associative meaning. The style of a text is then the system of the associations, evoked by its expressions, relating to other contexts of the same kind or of another kind than the one where the text is produced. The stylistic effect of various expressions can be specified qualitatively (which contexts is there an association with?) and quantitatively (how restricted is the set of contexts there is an association with?).

The notion of context has to be qualified a bit further, since in a sense the true semantic meaning of an expression can also be regarded as the system of contexts where the expression can be used. To describe the meaning of, e. g., *pail* we would have to refer to all contexts where a pail can be referred to.

It is certainly beyond the scope of this paper to discuss the problems of linguistic semantics in any detail. Some remarks are necessary, though. Obviously stylistic meaning is non-denotative meaning: its function is not to tell us anything about the persons, things, qualities or actions referred to. Instead the stylistic meaning of an expression tells us something about the person who uses the expression, and this it does in reminding us of other speech situations where the same expression is used and particularly of the language users in these other speech situations. Style is then an associative bond between the actual speaker and other language users (including the speaker himself in earlier, different or similar, speech situations). What he says links him with his own biography and personality as well as with other men or women whose use of language he copies, deliberately or unconsciously. Any sound or word or phrase or construction can theoretically be the carrier of such associations in addition to the denotative meaning it might have. Even where ungrammatical sentences or bold metaphors are created, their structures could be broken down into elements carrying associations to language users in other contexts. This does not exclude, of course, the creation of new stylistic meanings, since each new verbal communication act is itself a new context and may provide the basis for the formation of new associative meanings. Style is then the result of a dialectic interplay between the actual context and history, i. e., the contexts which have preceded it.

Normally the range of stylistic variation possible within a language is regulated by language-specific conventions. For instance, it is mostly a matter of historical convention that religious, psychological or everyday prose can express the same facts in stylistically different texts. The different ways of greeting are likewise language specific. The jargon of one special group of people is characterized by a set of arbitrary expressions or pronunciations by which the group deviates from other people in the community.

There are some important exceptions, though, to the principle of the arbitrariness of stylistic meaning. Notice that a given expression may be stylistically loaded even where no alternative expressions can be imagined. A noun like $KMnO_4$ has no everyday language counterpart in the way that H_2O corresponds with *water*, but it carries all the same an associative meaning similar to the one of H_2O. In this case there is a close connection between denotative meaning and stylistic value: the former determines the latter, since $KMnO_4$ could not have the stylistic meaning it has if it did not refer to $KMnO_4$. Similarly the different stylistic values of H_2O and *water* are accompanied by differences in denotative meaning. While H_2O denotes idealized — or at least distilled — water, the fluid we call *water* can be all sorts of mixtures from a scientist's point of view.

Another type of style variation is rooted in universal conditions determining the use of the human language apparatus. These conditions underlie the kinds of style which we label as complexity, hesitation, dreaminess, talkativeness and the like where our impression is triggered by the same type of syntactic and prosodic phenomena in structurally different languages. (Cf. for some examples Hayes 1966; Osgood 1960; Carroll 1960; consider also for example psycholinguistic work on readability or theories of the physiological and psychological bases of rhythm and meter.)

Our discussion brought us to the conclusion that style is the system of associations evoked by a text to language users in other similar or different contexts. I regard this definition only as a development of those definitions where style is conceived as the relation between meaning and expression. Neither does it contradict the definition of style as choice. It is obvious that our definition presupposes linguistic variation: if different speakers in different contexts could not express themselves differently from each other, the results of their choices could not be systematically loaded with associations to those speakers in their contexts.

2. GRAMMATICAL AND STYLISTIC COMPETENCE

To analyze style we must know the answers to the following questions:

(a) What are the elements and structures of language, i. e., what are the potential carriers of stylistic value?

(b) What stylistic values are carried by what elements or structures?

Obviously question (a) is the one where grammatical theory is involved.

Let us look at a simple model of verbal production before we try to understand the possibilities and limitations of grammar as a guide in stylistic research:

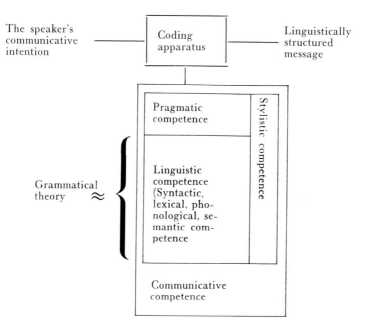

(On communicative competence see for instance Hymes 1971.)

The starting-point of the model is the linguistically unstructured communicative intent of the speaker to inform somebody of something, to ask, to order, to warn, to wish etc. His message is then linguistically structured by a coding mechanism, with strategies drawing upon various kinds of competence. The function of the pragmatic competence is to offer the basic alternatives — be they linguistic or non-linguistic — of action. If the speaker's intention is to warn somebody of something, he can accomplish this in a number of ways: by a gesture, by a scream, by different kinds of sentence (imperative, declarative, interrogative). The choice among these alternatives depends upon various factors of the extralinguistic context. One aspect of pragmatic competence is text structure competence, which includes the rules of how the flow of thoughts can be segmented into sentence units and of how the structure of individual sentences interacts with its linguistic context. The sentences are linguistically structured according to the possibilities specified by the rules of the linguistic competence. The result of this coding process is a linguistically structured message which can be transformed into temporally ordered impulses to the articulatory muscles.

We return now to our questions at the outset of this section. The rules of linguistic competence define psychologically real elements and structures, which can be carriers of stylistic value. But such elements or structures are found not only within sentences but also in the domains organized according to the rules of pragmatic and text structure competence. Two examples: the grammar cannot describe the following warnings as alternatives:

(5) Mind the step!
(6) There is a step in front of you.
(7) Can you see the step in front of you?

These sentences are registered as alternatives by the pragmatic component. Now consider the following utterances:

(8) I don't feel well. I will stay at home to-day.
(9) I will stay at home to-day, since I don't feel well.

Only text structure competence could relate these utterances as alternatives in relation to a particular communicative intention. However, in both these cases it is obvious that we want to be able to assign different stylistic values to the alternative expressions.

We are now ready to discuss the stylistic competence of the speaker and also indirectly the basis for answering our second question.

Notice first that associative meaning must be assumed to be present already in the communicative intention of the speaker. (My use of "intention" is a bit misleading since I do not presuppose that the speaker is consciously aware of all details in the message he sets out to communicate.) During the coding process those expressions are chosen which cover as much as possible of what the speaker intends to communicate. In other words the speaker tries to find those elements and structures which, in addition to their denotative meaning, convey the right associations. Such associations may be attached to pragmatic alternatives, text structures, syntactic phenomena, words or phrases, orthography, phonology, articulation.

Associations are sometimes rather straightforward as in archaisms, dialect words, the vocabulary of chemistry, music etc. But they can also be more vague, for example associations linked to certain syntactic and prosodic characteristics, or for that matter to particular words such as *type-writer* or *snake*.

Style is determined not only by the occurrence of particular structures but also by the relative frequency of these. One passive sentence is uninteresting from a stylistic point of view, but if a significant number of sentences in a text are passives, this has stylistic consequences. (Cf. especially Doležel 1969 and Rosengren 1972.)

Another important fact about style is that it can be attached to structures or elements which are not generated by the kinds of competence that we have postulated.

What consequences have such facts for the status of stylistic competence? Should stylistic values be generated along with the elements or structures in the various types of competence organizing these elements and structures? Or should stylistic intuition be considered as a special component consisting of rules differing from those of the other components? I will summarize the arguments for choosing the latter alternative:

(a) The same style value can be expressed through elements and structures defined by different types of competence.

(b) The associative network around lexical elements cannot be formalized within the framework of present semantic theory.

(c) The vague and individualistic character of stylistic value makes it different from other kinds of meaning.

(d) Transformations do not carry denotative meaning in present grammatical theory. (That they can indirectly affect the meaning of surface structure in the so-called extended standard grammar of Chomsky and Jackendoff does not alter this fact.) But it is generally assumed that stylistic value is directly attached to some optional transformations.

(e) Frequency of an expression does not affect its denotative meaning but can be the sole basis of assignment of stylistic value.

(f) Deviations from the rules of pragmatic, text structure or grammatical competence can carry stylistic value although they are excluded from these competences by definition.

(Rosengren 1972 also postulates a separate stylistic competence, though not quite of the same type as the one I have in mind. Some of the above arguments are identical with hers.)

I have little to say about the formal structure of stylistic competence. If it is imagined as attached to a grammatical competence of the form hypothesized in extended standard grammar, it ought to be construed as operating interpretively upon the structures generated by the other competences, just as the semantic component interprets the deep and surface structures within the syntactic component.

I may have given the impression — by choosing a model of verbal production as my point of departure — that stylistic *competence* is used primarily in this kind of performance. If so I would like to stress that stylistic competence like other types of competence postulated is to be regarded as neutral in this respect. I have not been able to comment upon the *style-forming process* (cf. Doležel 1969) of the speaker-writer any more than the *style-perception-interpretation process* of the listener-reader. These are different performance processes determined by different (coding and decoding) strategies. But the stylistic competence of the speaker-hearer is assumed to be independent of the kind of performance he is involved in.

Before concluding the discussion of this section we shall return once more to the status of grammar. We must bear in mind that grammar is not equal to grammatical competence; it is only a hypothesis of it. Grammars are primarily axiomatic systems generating the possible grammatical sentences of the language. Only if a grammar generates these sentences with the same structure, via the same categories and rules as real human competence, can it provide the right answer to our first question.

There are other important problems concerning grammar which are relevant to the theme of this paper, but I will only mention one of them. Generative grammar is and must be built upon grammatical intuition operationally defined as the competence of the speaker to judge some sentences as grammatical and others as ungrammatical, some sentences as synonyms and others as not etc. But is this capacity to judge really the kind of psycholinguistic competence that we employ when we produce and interpret verbal messages? Is not judging sentences as grammatical etc. rather a specific ability related to but not identical with the kind of knowledge that we use in real communication? All I can do here is to mention the discussion of these vital problems in e. g. Lyons & Wales 1966 passim and Maas & Wunderlich 1972 pp. 90 ff. (The only defence that could perhaps be put forward here is that the "judging competence" underlying generative grammar in any case must be quite relevant as a basis for stylistic studies of such texts where the author has processed his language in a conscious, deliberate way and where the reader is expected to work on deciphering it with the same conscious, deliberate effort.)

3. STYLISTIC ANALYSIS: A FIRST STEP BASED UPON A GRAMMATICAL THEORY

In this section we shall sketch briefly how a part of one grammatical theory can be used to specify which elements or structures are the potential carriers of stylistic value. We shall limit our interest to "true grammar", i. e. grammar minus lexicon. True grammar defines the regularities of language, leaving the non-generalizable facts to the domain of the lexicon. One reason for drawing a line between lexicon and the rest of linguistic competence is provided by language acquisition: true grammar is acquired in a few years during childhood while our lexicon is enriched through the whole of our lives.

Grammatical categories and structures are quite general features of language in the sense that they are not to any notable degree determined by the denotative contents of the text. This is interesting from a stylistic point of view: any difference in the writer's use of true grammar is then a suitable candidate as a carrier of stylistic value. The generality of its categories and structures makes it furthermore possible to quantify the characteristics even of a relatively short text.

For the demonstration I have chosen the grammatical theory called extended standard transformational grammar (EST), described by Chomsky and Jackendoff in several publications. The structure of the EST can be rendered in the following way:

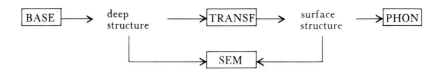

We shall concentrate here upon syntax (base + transformations), since it is the autonomous part of the rule system. It is characteristic of generative transformational grammar that structures of different depths are ascribed to one and the same sentence: the deep structure of a sentence is mapped by transformations into more shallow structures until the surface structure of the sentence is reached. If we use EST in quantitative stylistic analysis we assume then that deep structure and surface structure are both psychic realities as are also transformations or transformed structures linking them together. This is a necessary consequence if we claim EST to be a model of human grammatical competence.

In a stylistic study of two texts we should therefore, in accordance with such assumptions, compare not only the surface structures but also the deep structures of sentences. Since deep structure and surface structure are formal entities of the same kind, they can be described along the same variables:

complexity (e. g. total number of nodes per sentence or per total number of terminal nodes)
orientation (i. e. complexity in relation to time = linearity)
categories and features (i. e. constituent classes, word classes, morpheme classes, selectional features)

It is equally important to compare the relations between deep structure and surface structure in the two texts with each other. This could be done in two ways. One way is to relate the structures directly to decide how and how much surface structure differs from deep structure in one text as against the other: in terms of complexity and orientation. It also seems reasonable to study grammatical ambiguity, i. e. to what extent surface structures of the text could have had other deep structures, as well as the use of structural cues, i. e. transformationally inserted markers which make it easier for receivers to get at deep structure from surface structure.

The relation between surface and deep structures can also be studied via the apparatus provided by the EST itself, i. e. the transformations. We could then register which transformations or families of transformations are needed how many times to describe the relations between deep and surface structures. Another possibility is to group together transformations according to the kind of difference between the structures matched by them:

> deletion
> substitution
> insertion
> permutation

Up till now we have assumed the sentences of the texts to be grammatical. If they are not, our next step is to relate the quasi-grammar underlying the deviant sentences to standard grammar. Here the formal machinery of EST provides us with a long range of possibilities to characterize the kinds and degrees of deviation in a general way. We can ask first, which rules are offended:

> categorial rules
> subcategorization rules
> cyclic T-rules
> post-cyclic T-rules

(Cf. Chomsky 1965, 148ff.; Weinreich 1966.) The deviation can often be described in the same way as linguistic development by diachronic linguistics. Our question is now how the system of standard grammar rules must be altered to generate the deviant sentences:

> order between rules changed
> rule deleted
> context of old rule generalized
> context of old rule restricted
> new rule added

(Cf. Kiparsky 1968; King 1968.)

This sketch was intended as a demonstration of how a grammatical theory could provide a *first step* towards stylistic analysis. (The reader may have noticed that many of my hints above should have been preceded by the proviso "in principle". Equally the theory underlying EST is not yet sufficiently worked out in detail, nor do we have a complete grammatical description according to EST of any particular language.) *The next* — and perhaps more interesting — *step* will be to find out which stylistic values are attached to the elements and structures identified, in short: what the differences between the texts mean.

The considerations in this paper have drawn our attention to an important point. To do stylistic research we need grammatical theory as a hypothesis of the psychologically real linguistic categories and structures in the texts which we analyze. But stylistic analysis can also be used to evaluate grammars: any fruitful use of a grammatical theory in stylistics can be regarded as a validation of that grammatical theory in the same way as psycholinguistic studies can be used to evaluate grammatical theory. If the categories postulated by the grammatical theory employed had not been psychologically real, they would not have been able to carry associative meaning and the quantitative analysis based upon them would not have given systematically organized, interpretable data.

REFERENCES

Carroll, J. B., "Vectors of Prose Style". In: Sebeok, Th. A., ed., *Style in Language*, Cambridge, Mass. 1960.

Chomsky, N., *Aspects of the Theory of Syntax*, Cambridge, Mass.: The MIT Press 1965.

Chomsky, N., "Remarks on Nominalizations". In: Jacobs, R., & Rosenbaum, P., eds., *Readings in Transformational Grammar*, Waltham, Mass.: Blaisdell 1970, 184—221.

Chomsky, N., "Deep Structure, Surface Structure, and Semantic Interpretation." In: Steinberg, D., & Jakobovits, L., eds., *Semantics*, New York: Cambridge University Press 1971, 183—216.

Doležel, L., "A Framework for the Statistical Analysis of Style". In: Doležel, L., & Bailey, R. W., eds., *Statistics and Style*, New York 1969, 1off.

Enkvist, N. E., Spencer, J., & Gregory, M., *Linguistics and Style*, London: Oxford University Press 1964.

Enkvist, N. E., *Stilforskning och stilteori*, Lund: Gleerups 1973.

Enkvist, N. E., *Linguistic Stylistics*, Haag: Mouton 1973.

Hayes, C. W., "A Study in Prose Styles: Edward Gibbon and Ernest Hemingway". In: *Texas Studies in Literature and Language* VII 1966, 371—386.

Hymes, D. H., *On Communicative Competence*, Philadelphia: University of Pennsylvania Press 1971.

Jackendoff, R. S., *Semantic Interpretation in Generative Grammar*, Cambridge, Mass.: The MIT Press 1972.

King, R. D., *Historical Linguistics and Generative Grammar*, Englewood Cliffs, N. J.: Prentice-Hall 1969.

Kiparsky, P., *Linguistic Universals and Language Change*. In: Bach, E., & Harms, R. T., eds., *Universals in Linguistic Theory*. New York: Holt, Rinehart and Winston 1968.

Lyons, J., & Wales, R. J., eds., *Psycholinguistic Papers*, Edinburgh: Edinburgh University Press 1966.

Maas, U., & Wunderlich, D., *Pragmatik und sprachliches Handeln,* Frankfurt am Main: Athenäum 1972.

Ohmann, R., "Generative Grammars and the Concept of Literary Style". In: *Word* XX 1964, 424—439.

Ohmann, R., "Literature as Sentences". In: *College English* 27 1966, 261ff.

Osgood, Ch. E., "Some Effects of Motivation on Style of Encoding". In: Sebeok, Th. A., ed., *Style in Language*, Cambridge, Mass. 1960.

Rosengren, I., "Style as Choice and Deviation". In: *Style* 6 1972, 3—17.

Weinreich, U., "Explorations in Semantic Theory". In: Sebeok, Th. A., ed., *Current Trends in Linguistics* III, Haag: Mouton 1966.

Josef Vachek
J. A. Comenius' University, Bratislava

Some remarks on functional dialects of standard languages

In the pre-war Prague linguistic group interest in problems of style was never lacking. In accordance with that group's functionalist approach, the Prague people laid special emphasis on the existence in languages of "functional styles", which they distinguished from "special languages" (cf. Enkvist 1973, 79).

One interesting point concerns the question raised by Enkvist in connection with Boh. Havránek's (1932) distinction of functional styles and special languages. According to Enkvist this distinction "tends to separate descriptions of individualistic styles from those of impersonal styles" (Enkvist 1973, 39). This may indeed be so; still, it should be noted that in his later writings Havránek duly distinguishes between the conventions of the individual style and those of the interindividual "special languages" which, still later, he prefers to denote as "functional dialects" (a term used also by P. L. Garvin in his abridged English version of Havránek's paper, see Havránek 1964). It should also be noticed that in Havránek's opinion the language means which function as instruments for stylistic purposes constitute, for all their conventionality, only a specific manner of organization of concrete utterances (cf. Havránek 1942).

The distinction between stylistic approaches which are individual and much less conventional, and those which are interindividual and more highly conventionalized was also underlined by another Prague scholar who devoted much thought to problems of style, Vilém Mathesius. In his extensive paper on language and style (V. Mathesius 1942) he draws a distinct line between the individual, inimitable style of a creative artist, and the interindividual kind of style which should be mastered by every member of the given language community during his or her school years. This "style of simple exposition", as Mathesius calls it, is indeed imitable, can be learned and must be learned. Among its features, special stress is laid, above all, on the clarity of syntactic structures, on proper differentiation by language means of thematic and rhematic elements of utterances (according to other terminology, proper differentiation of topic and comment), and on other prerequisites of efficient communication.

By characterizing the individual style as a purely personal, inimitable affair Mathesius, so to speak, drew a fairly distinct line between what is collective and thus conventional, implementing a certain stylistic norm of this or that "functional dialect" (to use the term later introduced by

Havránek) and, on the other hand, what is found to overstep this norm and even intentionally deviates from it for specific aesthetic purposes. One important conclusion follows from this distinction. Since it is universally admitted that language constitutes the most essential instrument of communication within a certain community, the primary concern of the linguist is necessarily the functional dialect as an inter-individual system of means of communication, as a kind of a more or less normalized system of values. This, of course, does not at all mean that the personal style of this or that individual using the given language (particularly the personal style of a creative artist) should lie outside the scope of interest of the linguist. As a matter of fact, even in the pre-war Prague group a large number of papers were devoted to concrete analyses of such concrete personal stylistic means (among the scholars who dealt with such issues may be mentioned again B. Havránek and especially J. Mukařovský). However, such concrete analyses concentrate mainly on the ascertainment of the artists' deviations from the established norm (Mukařovský even spoke, less aptly, about the "deformations" of that norm) of the corresponding functional dialect and on the aesthetic effect of such deviations. From this it naturally follows that even such analyses of personal stylistic means can be successful only if the norm of the corresponding functional dialect has been established to such a degree that the deviations of the individual language user can stand out against the background of this norm with sufficient clarity.

So much for the general standpoint of Prague linguists in matters of style. The functionalist basis of this standpoint is obvious: the differences ascertainable between the functional dialects of one and the same standard language (to which we limit our discussion) are due precisely to the differences of aims pursued by these functional dialects. As these aims are seen to differ most appreciably, it is obvious that one cannot support the traditional belief (even now maintained in some practical handbooks of stylistics) that only one functional dialect may be classified as "good", and thus should rank as a kind of model to be adhered to by all other functional dialects which rank as "less good" of even "bad". Some earlier handbooks of English style, for example, classify as model of such good style the means of expression contained in the Authorized Version of the English Bible (cf. G. T. Warner 1915). It is obvious that the simple monumental flavour of these means, though undoubtedly of high stylistic quality, would be unable to cope with the aims followed by contexts of what is commonly called "the journalese", "the oratorical style", "the moralizing style", etc. It is precisely the specialized functions of such specialized functional dialects which may fully justify most of their lexical, phraseological and sometimes even grammatical deviations from the recommended "model style".

Another problem that interests the linguist is that of the classification of functional dialects. It appears that a reliable overall classification can only be obtained if more than one classificatory criterion is applied. Havránek (1932) distinguishes four functional dialects: conversational, workaday, scientific and poetic (we use here the terms by which Garvin interpreted Havránek's Czech terms in the English translation of the Czech scholar's paper). Clearly, the classificatory criterion has been here the milieu in which the dialects are employed. This milieu appears to be closely similar to what D. Crystal and D. Davy 1969 call "the province" dimension of the message (other functionally orientated discussions of stylistic issues also appear to be based mainly on this criterion — see, e. g., I. R. Gal'perin 1971). Other important issues, based on other criteria, are only mentioned in Havránek's classification of functional styles, e. g., exhortation (appeal), suasion, as well as the differentiation of oral and written messages. In other words, these other features are regarded by him as specific functions of "speech" (parole), not of "language" (langue). Still it can hardly be doubted that the language expression of these other features is also conventionalized in the language community and thus must be included in the make-up of functional dialects, i. e. in facts lying within the sphere of "langue".

It appears to us, then, that a different scheme might perhaps more aptly cover the facts to be classified, and possibly do so in a more general and more exhaustive way. In our opinion, there are three main criteria that should be applied in classifying any message from the stylistic point-of-view. The first is the language user's approach to the content handled by the message, the second is the language user's approach to the recipient of the message, and finally, the third is the choice of the medium employed in transmitting the message.

To start with the last-mentioned criterion, each message can of course be either spoken or written. This difference is not merely material but also has its important stylistic consequences, mainly in the selection of different syntactic patterns (length and complexity of sentences, etc.). — The second classificatory criterion, the approach by the language user to the recipient of the message, distinguishes those messages which appeal to the recipient from those which lack any such appeal: for want of a better turn, one might speak here, perhaps, of the opposition "appellant" vs. "non-appellant". The category appellant may be further subdivided into propagandist and non-propagandist — specimens of the former can be represented by what is traditionally called oratorical style, while the latter covers roughly the same field as what is currently denoted as directive style (various instructions, recipes, also legal texts, etc.). It is hardly necessary to prove that the differences of the functional dialects here mentioned are characterized by the differences of language means employed in them.

Somewhat more complicated is the classification of functional dialects according to the first of the above-mentioned criteria, i. e. according to the approach by the language user to the subject matter transmitted by the message. Here one must distinguish the content of the message from the form in which this content is organized for presentation. Though, generally speaking, some content must be present in every message, the form of its organization for presentation purposes may differ widely. In simple narratives or descriptions it is presented in a relatively clear and simple manner which, however, does not aim at exactness and exhaustiveness in tracing all the essential items of the treated subject and the mutual relations of these items. The functional dialect characterized by these features may be denoted as "simple communicative". — If, on the other hand, the author of the message *is* aiming at such exactness and/or exhaustiveness, one has to do with a different category, with a functional dialect that may be called "argumentative". (It may, of course, be implemented either by a spoken or by a written variant; an interesting spoken variant of it is constituted by what is traditionally called "oratorical style", where an additional feature, referred to here above as propagandist, enters the picture.)

It will have been noted that the mutual relation of the simple communicative and the argumentative functional dialects can hardly be expressed in binary terms; rather one has to do here with a case of relation denoted by the Trubetzkoyan term "gradualness" (N. S. Trubetzkoy 1969, 75): the amount of exactness and/or exhaustiveness, relatively small in the simple communicative dialect, is seen to increase considerably in the functional dialect here called argumentative. — The assumption that the mutual relation of these two dialects is indeed not binary is also confirmed by another interesting fact. There exists a fairly well established functional dialect which, although again presenting information, aims at exactness and exhaustiveness even less than the one here called simple informative. It is the dialect traditionally called "journalese style", whose abundant use of clichés and highly abstract, mostly foreign lexical items admittedly serves the purpose of only roughly approximating the communicated content. Such rough approximate reference is indeed necessary because an average journalist can hardly ever work at sufficient leisure to ascertain the more exact nature of the facts to be communicated, of which he himself usually has only a rough-and-ready, second-hand knowledge. Obviously, this kind of functional dialect represents another extreme case of communication, placed on the opposite side of the simple communicative dialect than the argumentative dialect is located. We suggest that this opposite extreme should be called by the term "a purely informative dialect".

Theoretically, there is another possibility of a functional dialect which, however, can be only rarely met with. This would be a dialect in which the content would be shifted into the background to such a high degree that the attention of the recipient of the message would concentrate exclusively on the form by which this irrelevant content would be transmitted. Concrete instances of such a stylistic approach can of course be found in some specimens of decadent, purely formalist literature. However, they hardly ever develop a norm which would be socially binding for other writers — rather they constitute idiolects of individual authors whose only common feature is negative, i. e., opposition to the otherwise universal supremacy of content of message over its form. (Admittedly, artistic mastery in literary activity lies exactly in the harmonious coordination of content and form, a coordination in which, naturally, the content of the message restricts the range of choice for the form of that message.)

One more remark should be adduced to the classificatory scheme outlined here. The enumerated categories of functional dialects, especially those established according to the criterion of "approach to the subject matter" and "approach to the recipient", should not be regarded as watertight compartments into which all messages to be classified should be shelved at all costs. Undoubtedly, a number of messages will be found to constitute transitional phenomena in which features characterizing two or even more categories will appear to be closely linked. For instance, there will be some specimens of simple communicative functional dialect which will be seen, at times, to present some argumentative features; similarly, the opposition of appellant vs. non-appellant messages will not always be easy to assert, because the tendency inherent in the message to be classified may not be outspoken at all but rather very much subdued, and its very presence may be at times a matter of dispute. In other words, one must become reconciled to the fact that not only "all grammars leak" (as was seen already by E. Sapir 1921, 39) but all stylistic classifications leak as well. To admit this fact does not amount to helpless resignation by the linguist but to his doing justice to the dialectic, i. e., dynamic, nonstatic, character of the phenomena to be subjected to classification.

The last remark to be added here concerns the problem of whether, among all the functional dialects enumerated here, the linguist can pinpoint one of them as "unmarked", i. e., as one which is least committed to function in specialized situations or circumstances and which, in case of need, can be substituted for those dialects which function exclusively in such specialized situations or circumstances. This problem is not only of theoretical interest but has also some practical significance: if this particular functional dialect is least committed to specified situations, it will be possible to employ it in virtually all circumstances, and so it will obviously be useful to take it up as the first target in teaching the practical stylistics of the given language.

If all the enumerated functional dialects are scrutinized one by one, it soon becomes obvious that the only one that can claim the unmarked status is the one we termed simple communicative style (whether in its narrative or descriptive variety). Undoubtedly, this dialect can, in case of need, replace other, specialized functional dialects, while the reverse substitution cannot be made. Naturally, such substitution can only be evaluated as an emergency measure: in normal cases it is the specialized, marked functional dialects that are indicated for functioning in them. In view of this fact, every foreign learner of the given language, after having mastered its unmarked functional dialect, is also expected to acquire some of its marked dialects, mainly those which lie within the scope of his linguistic and/or practical interests. Needless to say, both the unmarked functional dialect and its marked alternatives should be mastered both in their spoken and in their written implementations (if, of course, both these media are used within the given functional dialect).

From the purely theoretical viewpoint, of course, the status of the unmarked functional dialect can only belong exclusively to the *spoken* variety of the simple communicative dialect. This is so because the written variety of that functional dialect, catering for more specialized communicative situations, must necessarily possess the marked status. Still, being functionally closely linked to the corresponding spoken variety by way of functional complementation (on this point some comment may be found in Vachek 1959), it preserves its importance for the learner and is something he or she must acquire. — Besides, the written variety of the simple communicative dialect has the status marked only as long as it is opposed to the latter's spoken variety. When opposed to the written varieties of other, specialized functional dialects, then this same written variety certainly ranks as much less marked than they. As a matter of fact, the written variety of the simple communicative functional dialect might, in emergency cases, replace the written varieties of more specialized functional dialects, and with regard to them is therefore seen to behave as if it possessed the unmarked status. All these facts seem to corroborate what was said here about the theoretical and practical importance of the simple communicative functional dialect, which may thus be safely evaluated as the unmarked member of the whole system of functional dialects of the standard language.

The above brief remarks could naturally not exhaust all aspects of the problems involved. Their modest aim was simply to demonstrate once more the fruitfulness of the functionalist approach to problems of style, the approach that has been pursued for decades by members of the Prague linguistic group.

REFERENCES

Crystal, D. — Davy, D. 1969: *Investigating English Style*. London (Longman).
Enkvist, N. E. 1973: *Linguistic Stylistics*. Janua linguarum, ser. critica 5, The Hague (Mouton).
Gal'perin, I. R. 1971: *Stylistics*. Moscow (Higher School Publishing House).
Havránek, B. 1932: "Úkoly spisnového jazyka a jeho kultura". In: Pražský linguistický kroužek: Spisovná čestina a jazyková kultura. Praha (Melantrich), pp. 32—84.
Havránek, B. 1942: "K funkčnímu rozvrstvení spisovného jazyka". Časopis pro moderní filologii (Praha) 28, 409—416.

Havránek, B. 1964: "The Functional Differentiation of the Standard Language". In P. L. Garvin (Ed.): *A Prague School Reader on Esthetics, Literary Structure, and Style.* Washington, D. C. (Georgetown University), pp. 3—16.

Mathesius, V. 1942: "Řeč a sloh". In: Čtení o jazyce a poesii I (Praha, Družstevní práce), pp. 11—102.

Sapir, E. 1921: *Language.* New York (Harcourt, Brace & Co.)

Trubetzkoy, N. S. 1969: *Principles of Phonology* (transl. by Chr. A. M. Baltaxe). Berkeley and Los Angeles (Univ. of California Press).

Vachek, J. 1959: "Two Chapters on Written English". Brno Studies in English 1 (Praha, Stát. pedag. nakladatelství), pp. 7—38.

Warner, G. T. 1915: *On the Writing of English.* London (Blackie).

II. STYLE AND LITERARY CRITICISM

Assumes 'proposition' and 'semantic structure of sentences' are distinct concepts.

František Daneš *(Prague)*
Czechoslovak Academy of Sciences

An attempt at characterizing dramatis personae in terms of their semantic roles

*   One way to describe the propositional aspect of the semantic structure of the sentence is to assign various "semantic roles" (syntactico-semantic functions) to different participants (actants) in the "state of affairs" rendered by the given utterance. One may assume that any character (dramatis persona, DP) in a work of literature appears in different semantic roles (SR) in various contexts; i. e., in any sentence (utterance) in which a DP is referred to by means of an denominating expression, a certain SR will be ascribed to this DP, according to the position the corresponding expression occupies in the semantic structure of the given sentence. Consequently, it is possible to discover a set of different SR's for every DP in a given literary work (text). And it may reasonably be assumed that, at least in typical cases, the particular composition of such a set of SR's may serve as a differential characteristic of the given DP. Furthermore, one might also expect that systematic statements of this kind could furnish objective means for characterizing not only a particular personage, or a type of it, but the whole structure of characters,[1] and the literary type of the given text (its genre, etc.).

Ascribing SR's to the participants is only one possible way of describing semantic (propositional) sentence structure. The other ways are: the ascertainment of the semantic relations between the participants, or the ascertainment of the syntactico-semantic class of the predicate, or the global syntactico-semantic characteristic of the given sentence type (cf. Daneš, Hlavsa, Kořenský et al., 1973). These different descriptive approaches may be viewed as complementary, and the following sketch of a classification tries to combine them in a specific way.

The classification of predicates may be accomplished in terms of 5 distinctive semantic features: (1) dynamicity, (2) mutation, (3) articulatedness, (4) intended activity, (5) involvement of more than one participant. Between this set of features certain correlations obtain, mainly: (-1) excludes $(+2)$, $(+4)$; and the other way round $(+2)$ as well as $(+4)$ imply $(+1)$; (-3) excludes (± 5). — The basic predicate classes are:

A.   static "situations", characterized by (-1)

B.   dynamic "processes", characterized by $(+1)$:
    I.   simple processes: $(+1)$, (-2)
    II.   mutations (processes involving a change or transition): $(+1)$, $(+2)$

** *Neglects Universe of Discourse and Genre.*

111

By applying further distinctive features, we arrive at the following sub-classification:

A. Situations:
   I.   articulated (+ 3): 1, with a single participant (— 5) *(He is ill; She is sitting)*, 2. with more than one participant (+ 5) *(Milk contains water)*
   II. inarticulated (—3) *(It is warm)*

B. Processes:
   I.   Simple processes
       1. articulated (+ 3):
       a) non-active (—4), (aa) restricted to a single participant (— 5) *((The fire is burning)*, (ab) not restricted (+ 5) *He suffers from malaria)*
       b) active (+ 4), (ba) restricted to a single participant (— 5) *(He jumped up), (They marched)*, (bb) not restricted (+ 5) *(They pursued the thief)*
       2. inarticulated (—3) *(It freezes)*
   II. Mutations:
       1. articulated (+ 3)
       a) non-causatives (—4) *(The milk turned sour. The brontosaurus died out)*
       b) causatives (+ 4): (ba) "autocausatives", i. e., restricted to a single participant (processor) (—5) *(He went out. She stopped dancing)*, (bb) not restricted (+ 5) *(They built a new house. She washes the children. He marched the soldiers. She pacified him. She made breakfast ready. They will buy a new car)*
       2. inarticulated (—3) *(It grew dark)*.

"Situations" (either as self-contained simple predicates, or as components of complex mutational predicates) are mostly relations (the most typical relators are: qualification (Q), location (L), possession (P), with different modifications); besides, two types of non-relational situations should be assumed (namely, existential and positional situations). — Predicates of "mental" character (verba cogitandi, putandi, sentiendi, dicendi) may be regarded as a parallel system to A, BI, BII.

The syntactico-semantic functions (semantic roles, such as agent, patient, instrument ...) of the particular participants follow from the semantic class of the predicate and from the semantic type of implied relations. Thus, the semantic roles may be viewed rather as labels with a practical "mnemonic" function; they may be established on different levels of generality and their number depends on the depth of detail of our analysis. Different aims of investigation may lead to the establishment of (partially) different sets of semantic roles. — In our present attempt, we shall confine our analysis to one piece of literature, namely a classical Czech ballad (of mythological character) "The Willow", by K. J. Erben,[2] with the aim of examining and evaluating the personages from the point of view of the different degrees of activity they display in the plot. For this purpose we propose the following simplified classification of the predicates and of the corresponding set of semantic roles (of a rather general character):

(A)   Situations: the only participant is the bearer of a quality (of a position, of a possessional relation, etc): BA ("Like a corpse you are at night")

(B)   PROCESSES:

(1) the only participant performs the role of the (non-active) bearer of a process: BP ("E'en as if to dust it came")

(2) the only participant performs an action with himself: PR (the processor: "I rise at morn")

(3) the participant performs an action (directed beyond him): the agent AG; the other participant(s) (if any) is (are) either affected or effected elements, or elements participating in the action in another non-active (passive) way: PP.

Now we may try to establish a tentative hierarchy of semantic roles as to the degree of their activity: AG, PR; BP, BQ, PP.

The following matrix presents the frequencies of occurrence of the particular personages, i. e., of "mistress", "husband", and various "magical elements" (such as "herbs", "a potent spell", "fate", "God's might"), in different semantic roles. Naturally, it takes into account all cases in the text where a personage is referred to irrespective of the types of referential means employed, i. e., semantic (intensional) synonyms, "denotative synonyms" (e. g. "mistress": její tělo (her frame), vrba (the willow), žluté proutí (yellow bough), etc.), pronouns, inflectional suffixes.

personages \ semantic roles	AG	PR	BP	BQ	PP	Sum
"paní (mistress)"	4	5	9	9	15	42
"pán (husband)"	10	2	—	—	4	16
magical elements	11	—	—	—	—	11

It appears that the personage of "mistress" conducts itself as a predominantly non-active element: it occurs 9 times (4 + 5) in an active role, while 33 times in a non-active one; it shows the highest frequency of occurrence in the least active role of PP. — The personage of "husband", on the other hand, appears as a mostly active element (12 occurrences), while its non-activity is restricted to the fourth part of all occurrences. — The magical elements perform altogether the highest active role of AG.

Such a highly differentiated distribution of semantic roles between different personages is hardly a fortuitous phenomenon and certainly has some bearing on the literary character of the given text. Not being a specialist in literary studies, I do not dare to present a reasoned interpretation of these connections. The only point that seems to me certain is that the above statements obviously support the mythological interpretation of Erben's ballad.[3]

The aim of my contribution was rather modest: to hint — by way of illustration — at a possibility of applying linguistic facts (from the area of linguistic semantics) to the literary interpretation of texts. Only further investigations done on the basis of detailed analyses of a large and representative body of texts can show the possible value of such an approach.

K. J. Erben *Vrba*	*K. J. Erben* *The Willow*
Ráno sedá ke snídaní, táže se své mladé paní:	In the morn he sat at meat; Thus his youthful spouse did greet:
"Paní moje, paní milá! vždycky upřímná jsi byla,	"Mistress mine, thou mistress dear. Thou in all things wert sincere.
vždycky upřímná jsi byla — jednohos mi nesvěřila.	"Thou in all things wert sincere, — One thing ne'er thou let'st me hear,
Dvě léta jsme spolu nyní — jednoho nepokoj mi činí.	"We have now years been wed, Only one thing brings me dread.
Paní moje, milá paní! jaké je to tvoje spaní?	"Mistress mine, O mistress blest, With what slumber dost thou rest?
Večer lehneš zdráva, svěží, v noci tělo mrtvo leží.	"In the evening fresh and bright, Like a corpse thou art at night.
Ani ruchu, ani sluchu, ani zdání o tvém duchu.	"Naught has sounded, naught has stirred Nor is trace of breathing heard.
Studené jest to tvé tělo, jak by zpráchnivěti chtělo.	"Filled with coldness is thy frame, E'en as if to dust it came.
Aniž to maličké dítě, hořce plačíc, probudí tě. —	"Nor doth rouse thee from thy sleeping Our young child, with bitter weeping.
Paní moje, paní zlatá! zdali nemocí jsi jata?	"Mistress mine, thou wife of gold, Doth some sickness thee enfold?
Jestli nemoc ta závada, nech at přijde moudrá rada.	"If by sickness thou'rt dismayed, Let wise counsel be thine aid.
V poli mnoho bylin stojí, snad některá tebe zhojí.	"Many herbs are in the field, Thou perchance by one art healed.

Pakli v býlí není síly,
mocné slovo neomýlí.

Mocné slovo mračna vodí,
v bouři líté chrání lodí.

Mocné slovo ohni káže,
skálu zdrtí, draka sváže.

Jasnou hvězdu strhne s nebe:
slovo mocné zhojí tebe." —

" "O pane můj, milý pane!
nechtěj dbáti řeči plané.

Co souzeno při zrození,
tomu nikdež léku není.

Co Sudice komu káže,
slovo lidské nerozváže!

Ač bezduchá na svém loži,
vždy jsem přece v moci boží.

Vždy jsem přece v boží moci,
jenž mne chrání každé noci.

Ač co mrtvé mi je spáti,
ráno duch se zase vrátí.

Ráno zdráva vstáti mohu:
protož poruč pánu bohu!" "

Darmo, paní! jsou tvá slova,
pán úmysl jiný chová.

Sedí babka při ohnisku,
měří vodu z misky v misku,

dvanáct misek v jedné řadě.
Pán u baby na poradě.

"Slyšíš, matko! ty víš mnoho:
víš, co potkati má koho,

víš, kde se čj nemoc rodí,
kudy smrtná žena chodí.

Pověz ty mi zjevně nyní,
co se s mojí-paní činí?

Večer lehne zdráva, svěží,
v noci tělo mrtvo leží,

ani ruchu, ani sluchu,
ni zdání o jejím duchu;

"But if herbs can naught avail,
A potent spell can never fail.

"Clouds to a potent spell will yield,
That ships in the raging storm can shield.

"A potent spell, o'er fire holds sway,
Rocks can shelter, dragons slay.

"A gleaming star from heaven can rend
A potent spell thy weal can send."

"O husband mine, so dear to me,
Let no vain word trouble thee.

"What was fated at my birth,
To no balm will yield on earth.

"What has been decreed by fate,
At man's word will not abate.

"Tho' lifeless on my bed I lie,
Ever 'neath God's might am I.

"I am ever 'neath God's might,
Who protects me night by night.

"Tho' I sleep as dead, at morn
My spirit back to me is borne.

"I rise at morn from weakness freed
For 'twas thus by God decreed."

Wife, these works of thine are naught,
For thy husband guards his thought.

At a fire an aged soul
Water pours from bowl to bowl.

Cauldrons twelve stand in a row,—
The husband for her aid doth go.

"Mother, hear! thy skill is great,
Know'st what each has to await.

"Know'st how plague comes into being,
Where the Maid of Death is fleeing.

"Tell me, now, with clearness, this:
What is with my bride amiss?

"In the evening fresh and bright,
Like a corpse she lies at night

"Naught has sounded, naught has stirred,
Ne'er a trace of breathing heard.

studené jest její tělo, jak by zpráchnivěti chtělo." —	"Filled with coldness is her frame, E'en as if to dust it came."
" "Kterak nemá mrtva býti, když má jen půl živobytí?	"How can she be aught but dead, Since her life but half is led?
Ve dne s tebou živa v domě, v noci duše její v stromě.	"She dwells by day at home with thee, At night her soul dwells in a tree.
Jdi k potoku pod oborou, najdeš vrbu s bílou korou;	"Go to the stream beyond the park, Thou find'st a willow with shining bark.
žluté proutí roste na ní: s tou je duše tvojí paní!" " —	"A yellow bough the tree doth bear, The spirit of thy bride is there."
"Nechtěl jsem já paní míti, aby s vrbou měla žíti;	"I have not espoused my bride, That with a willow she might abide.
paní má at se mnou žije, a vrba at v zemi hnije." —	"Near to me my bride shall stay, The willow in the earth decay."
Vzal sekeru na ramena, utal vrbu od kořena;	In his arm the axe he held, From the root the willow felled.
padla těžce do potoka, zašuměla od hluboka,	In the stream amain 'twas cast, From the depths a murmur passed.
zašuměla, zavzdychala, jak by matka skonávala,	There came murmur, there came a sigh, As of a mother whose end is nigh.
jak by matka umírajíc, po dítku se ohlédajíc. —	As of a mother in death's embrace, Who to her infant turns her face.
"Jaký shon to k mému domu? komu zní hodinka, komu?" —	"Round my dwelling what a throng, Wherefore sings the knell its song?"
" "Umřela tvá paní milá, jak by kosou st'ata byla;	"The wife thou lovest is no more, As by a sickle smitten sore.
zdráva chodíc při své práci, padla, jako strom se kácí;	"At her toil she bore her well, Till like a tree hewn down she fell.
zavzdychala umírajíc, po dítku se ohlédajíc." " —	"And she sighed in death's embrace, And to her infant turned her face."
"O běda mi, běda, běda! paní zabil jsem nevěda,	"Ah, woe is me! Ah, grievous woe; My bride, unwitting, I laid low.
a z dět'átka v túž hodinu učinil jsem sirotinu!	"In that same hour, thro' me was left My child of mother's care bereft.
O ty vrbo, vrbo bílá! což jsi ty mne zarmoutila!	"O thou willow, willow white, Why did'st bring me to this plight?
Vzalas mi půl živobytí: co mám s tebou učiniti?"	"Half my life thou took'st from me; What shall I do unto thee?"

" "Dej mne z vody vytáhnouti,	"Let me from the stream be drawn,
osekej mé žluté proutí;	And my yellow bough be sawn.
dej prkének nařezati,	"The wooden strips thou then shalt take,
kolébku z nich udělati;	And thereof a cradle make.
na kolébku vlož děťátko,	"Lay the child therein to sleep.
at nepláče ubožátko.	That the poor mite may not weep.
Když se bude kolébati,	"When he lies in slumber there,
matka bude je chovati.	He shall find his mother's care.
Proutí zasad podlé vody,	"Plant the boughs by the water-side,
by nevzalo žádné škody.	That no evil them betide.
Až doroste hoch maličký,	"Till he to a stripling grown,
bude řezat píštaličky;	Frame a reed-pipe for his own.
na píštalku bude pěti —	"On the reed pipe he will sing,
se svou matkou rozprávěti!"	To his mother answering."

REFERENCES

Daneš, F., Hlavsa, Z., Kořenský J., et al.: *Práce o sémantické struktuře věty. Kritický přehled a rozbor.* A critical survey and analysis of studies concerning the semantic structure of the sentence. Praha 1973. (Preprint.)

. van Holk, A. G. F.: "A semantic discourse analysis of The Coffin-Maker", *Dutch contributions to the 7th International Congress of Slavists*, 1973, 86—109.

NOTES

[1] A slight indication of such a possibility may be found in van Holk's contribution (1973, 103 ff.).

[2] The full Czech text of the ballad "Vrba" with a parallel (though not fully adequate) English version (taken from P. Selver's book *An anthology of Czechoslovak literature*, London 1929, pp. 46—51) is appended.

[3] This topic was discussed in detail by M. Otruba in *Česká literatura*, Praha, 1972, pp. 50 f.

Louis T. Milic
The Cleveland State University

A propositional analysis of Steele's *Guardian* No. 12

1. PURPOSE

This paper is an application of the method of Propositional Reduction[1] to a prose work by Richard Steele for a double purpose: to attempt an examination of the style of this neglected writer and to demonstrate the functioning of the method.

2. RICHARD STEELE.

Although Steele is responsible for the discovery of a new genre, the periodical essay, he seldom receives adequate credit for it. He began the *Tatler* in 1709 and was soon joined by Joseph Addison, who was also his partner in the *Spectator* and in the *Guardian*. The three periodicals comprise about 1000 papers, of which Steele produced more than half, a hundred more than Addison. For various non-literary reasons, including his own generous compliment to Addison's ability after his death,[2] Steele's reputation has become completely overshadowed, to such an extent that he is the victim of a curious paradox. It is claimed that his style is both inferior to that of Addison and indistinguishable from it.[3] Though Addison's style has often been commented on and at times excessively praised, Steele's has been almost ignored. Lannering, who has written a monograph on the prose of Addison,[4] makes only slight mention of Steele and devotes little space to a comparison of their styles. He quotes Steele's praise of Addison as a sufficient depreciation of Steele's own style. It appears that there is a place for a discussion of Steele's prose to determine what its own peculiar qualities might be.

For this purpose, I have selected Steele's essay on criticism, *Guardian* No. 12, as a typical performance, dating from a time (March 25, 1713) when the writer's ability to turn out essays should have become second nature. It is not his best piece, but it is certainly far from his worst. It is what a man writes when he is a professional.

3. PROPOSITIONAL REDUCTION.

As is well-known, there are many procedures available for the study of style. These fall essentially into two classes: methods which consider the entire text as a set of units, such as words and sentences, to be treated quantitatively, and some which examine sentences in their context. These latter are generally consistent with the nature of text-grammars in that they take account of the structure of units greater than the sentence. Although it is true that sentence-grammars are inadequate to characterize the style of a *composition,* they are adequate to characterize the style of a *writer,* provided certain aspects of the context are not neglected. As rhetoric, for example, is a text-grammar, it compels attention to forms of parallelism (e. g., *anaphora*) which may involve successive sentences. Unfortunately no attempt at text-grammar beyond classical rhetoric has had much general acceptance. The method I propose to use, despite its apparent lack of rigor, has certain advantages for the examination of brief works. It is thorough and generates conclusions which can be verified in larger samples by more scientific methods. It is, in addition, of value in pedagogical situations, for elementary instruction in stylistics.

Propositional Reduction is a close stringent paraphrase of any given "text" sentence from which anything not absolutely essential to the cognitive meaning is omitted and everything at all elaborate is replaced by its simplest equivalent. Imagery is made literal, ellipses are restored, and qualifications usually left out. The end result of this process (a "base") is something like the intended thought of the writer, what he "had in mind" when he framed each sentence. If it were possible to write in a neutral language, without style, the reduced sentence (the "base") would be this styleless form. But of course every natural sentence, even the simplest, instances a number of stylistic choices. Apart from the sort of conversion I have described, there is no way to represent the thought that underlies a text except with a metalanguage of zero redundancy in which a given message can have only one possible form, and such a thing does not now exist. But Propositional Reduction should not be confused with the process used in Transformational-Generative grammar of searching for a kernel sentence in the deep structure. The deep and surface structures of a sentence are identical in meaning; only the forms differ, but they are connected by obligatory rules. In other words, a given deep structure plus certain transformations must always result in a specific surface structure. A base, however, can manifest itself as a variety of different texts. The *base* is the idea or concept; the *text* is the linguistic realization. This should become clear if we consider a variety of texts all with the same base, a Latin aphorism of great antiquity:[5]

> TEXT X1: "Every man is the architect of his own fortune." [Proverb]
>
> TEXT X2: "A man's own manners do shape his his fortune." [Taverner]
>
> TEXT X3: "The mold of a man's fortune is in his own hands." [Bacon]
>
> TEXT X4: "Each person is the founder / Of his own fortune, good or bad." [Beaumont and Fletcher]
>
> TEXT X5: "Every man is the maker of his own fortune." [Steele][6]

There should not be much disagreement about the assertion that the base of all these texts is the following neutral and literal formulation:

BASE X: — each person controls his own success —

Each of the texts represents an attempt to translate the Latin original of which Base X is equally the foundation. Three of the five texts have adopted the Latin copulative construction and have variously rendered *faber* as *architect*, *founder* and *maker*, while keeping *fortune* constant. Taverner and especially Bacon reveal a better appreciation of the difference between Latin and English by adhering more closely to the semantic level and adapting the saying to their native idiom. The apparent congruity of Texts X1, X4 and X5 to the Latin form is deceptive, for these actually diverge further from the base. What is unquestionable is that the five texts are all attempts to realize the same base. It is the standard assumption of this kind of analysis that what a writer does he does regularly, and that the findings, taken all together, are reliably typical.

Although there is no known grammatical transformation which will produce any one of the Texts from Base X, any reader can recognize the relationship between them. Thus, the Propositional Reduction procedure, despite its dependence on intuition, exploits an actual fact of the language, the validity of paraphrase and the unity of synonymous renderings. The application of this method to the text under study may reveal whether anything of interest can be learned by this means.

4. THE ANALYSIS

Guardian No. 12 consists of five paragraphs totalling 30 sentences, averaging 40 words each. The first paragraph (A) deals with the difficulty of criticizing poetry and the quantity of bad criticism that poetry elicits. This paragraph contains three sentences of which the following is the first:

TEXT A1: "When a poem makes its first appearance in the world, I have always observed, that it gives employment to a greater number of criticks, than any other kind of writing."

The first step in Propositional Reduction is to delete all unnecessary flourishes, such as the parenthetical "I have always observed," the superfluous "that" and the redundant "in the world," leaving:

A1a: "When a poem makes its first appearance, it gives employment to a greater number of criticks, than any other kind of writing."

In the second stage, the imagery of the poem as a debutant and the critics as society gossips is replaced with literal equivalents:

A1b: "When a new poem is published, it receives more criticism than any other kind of writing."

The last step in this case involves the condensation of the syntax from a complex sentence to a simple declarative and the omission of the now-redundant "is published," as well as the non-essential comparative:

BASE A1: — a poem always receives much criticism —

COMMENT: The 30 words of the text have been reduced to six without omitting any significant part of the meaning. What has disappeared is the part of the writing that fills out the bare skeleton of the basic syntax with the structures that make it typically Steele's. It is also the imagery: the lighthearted likening of the poem to a young man being presented to society and of the critics as idle old crones awaiting the opportunity to pounce.

The second sentence:

TEXT A2: "Whether it be that most men, at some time of their lives, have try'd their talent that way, and thereby think they have a right to judge; or whether they imagine, that their making shrewd observations upon the polite arts, gives them a pretty figure; or whether there may not be some jealousie and caution in bestowing applause upon those who write chiefly for fame."

Leaving out the intervening stages we arrive at

BASE A2: — men criticize poetry because they have: experience as poets, desire for reputation, envy of fame —

COMMENT: The "sentence" is really a sequence of three parallel subordinate complex clauses each introduced by *whether*, but the parallelism is weak and each of the subordinate structures differs from the others. The diction is diffuse: *that way* means *in writing poetry; pretty figure* is an idiom for *reputation*; and *jealousie* is used in the older sense of *envy*.

TEXT A3: "Whatever the reasons be, we find few discouraged by the Delicacy and Danger of such an Undertaking."

BASE A3: — the risks of criticizing poetry discourage few —

COMMENT: The first clause is a summary reference to the previous text (A2). There is an alliterative doublet *(Delicacy and Danger). Such an Undertaking* refers vaguely to the criticism of poetry.

In this first paragraph, Steele has erected his target (bad critics of poetry) and has gently prepared the ground for an attack (or counterattack) against them. The approach is good-natured, as the diffuseness of Text A2 reveals. Having indicated the target, Steele proposes in the second paragraph to examine more closely the ways of bad critics.

TEXT B1: "I think it certain, that most men are naturally not only capable of being pleased with that which raises agreeable Pictures in the Fancy, but willing to own it."

BASE B1: — most readers enjoy poetry —

COMMENT: The initial framing clause of the text reveals uncertainty about how to proceed, the assertion of certainty being a usual indication of doubt. Steele creates an antithesis between the enjoyment of

121

poetry and the acknowledgment of that enjoyment, which is unnecessary except to provide a transition to B2. He circuitously refers to poetry as "that which raises agreeable Pictures in the Fancy," in accord with an aesthetic theory of the period.

> TEXT B2: "But then there are many, who, by false applications of some Rules ill understood, or out of Deference to Men whose Opinions they value, have formed to themselves certain Schemes and Systems of Satisfaction, and will not be pleased out of their own way."

> BASE B2: — some readers of poetry use dogmatic rules or the guidance of critics to justify their dislikes —

COMMENT: Steele places in parallel here two thoughts of quite different types: false use of misunderstood rules; care for the opinions of others. By means of one of these or the other, the uninformed readers Steele criticizes avoid giving an objective judgment of poetry. Regrettably for the parallel, only the former motive (rules) is reprehensible; there is nothing in itself wrong with following the opinion of a critic. There might be, if the "men whose opinions they value" were not critics but, for example, politicians. The expression *pleased out of their own way* is an idiomatic substitute for *hard to please*. *Schemes and Systems of Satisfaction* is both an alliterative doublet and an alliterative sequence.

> TEXT B3: "These are not Criticks themselves, but Readers of Criticks, who, without the Labour of perusing Authors, are able to give their Characters in general; and know just as much of the several Species of Poetry, as those who read Books of Geography do of the Genius of this or that People or Nation."

> BASE B3: — these readers are ignorant of critical principles and of the writers they criticize —

COMMENT: This complicated sentence has as its purpose the indictment of these hard-to-please readers by calling them ignorant and by crediting them with only a second-hand knowledge of literature derived from reading critics. Since, in fact, this is not a very telling charge, Steele shifts ground by introducing an analogy he is confident will be effective, that of the armchair traveller, which has always called forth ridicule. It is not clear what the reference of the pronoun *these* might be: whether the hard-to-please readers or the critics depended on by these readers. I have concluded that it is the former.

> TEXT B4: "These Gentlemen deliver their Opinions sententiously, and in general Terms; to which it being impossible readily to frame compleat Answers, they have often the Satisfaction of leaving the Board in Triumph.

> BASE B4: — those who criticize in generalities are hard to answer —

COMMENT: Steele here sounds like a man who has been overcome by a better talker. Opposing the arguments of those who deliver their

122

opinions in axioms and generalities — note the pleonastic parallelism — requires only ordinary skill in debate. Either Steele did not have it or assumes his audience lacked it and would welcome some means of frustrating the man who always leaves the "board" in triumph (after-dinner conversation?).

> TEXT B5: "As young Persons, and particularly the Ladies, are liable to be led aside by these Tyrants in Wit, I shall examine two or three of the many stratagems they use, and subjoin such Precautions as may hinder candid Readers from being deceived thereby."
>
> BASE B5: — I shall analyze and refute their arguments —

COMMENT: The introductory clause displays the attitude toward this audience that Steele and Addison made famous in the *Spectator*. It diminishes the triumph of the critic ("tyrant in wit") by showing him overcoming the young and the ladies that he misleads. Steele's role (that of a "guardian") is to protect the young and innocent, here archaically termed *candid*. The reference to "two or three of the many stratagems they use" is the studied carelessness of the essayist. In fact he is going to take up the three critical questions he wishes to discuss. The pretense of protecting the weak against tyranny provides a framework within which Steele can give a lecture on a rather dry subject. This is what distinguishes a periodical essayist from a professor of criticism.

The question of rules is the topic of the third paragraph.

> TEXT C1: "The first I shall take Notice of is an Objection commonly offered, *viz. That such a Poem hath indeed some good lines in it, but is not a regular-Piece.*"
>
> BASE C1: — a common criticism of a poem is that it breaks the rules though part of it is good —

COMMENT: What is presented as a quotation is doubtless Steele's own language, though it probably resembles the conversation of the period and is a critical issue of interest. The sentence reveals some of the carelessness typical of this writer in this genre, for example, in reference: *the first* fails to add something like "of these critics' stratagems." The quotation has an unnecessary synonym: if *poem*, why *piece*? *Regular* is a literalism for "according to rule" (Latin *regula*).

> TEXT C2: "This for the most part is urged by those whose Knowledge is drawn from some famous *French* Critics, who have written upon the Epic Poem, the Drama, and the great kinds of Poetry, which cannot subsist without great Regularity; but ought by no means to be required in Odes, Epistles, Panegyricks, and the like, which naturally admit of greater Liberties."
>
> BASE C2: — rules are favored by those familiar with French critical statements about epic and drama —

123

COMMENT: This sentence exemplifies the double technique typical of the *Spectator:* informing while amusing or distracting. As Steele has no reason to believe his readers are acquainted with French classical criticism and as his argument rests on a distinction he wishes to make within its limits, he must tell them enough about it so that they will accept his argument and believe that they understand it. Within the essay, this problem exists only in this particular paragraph which deals with the rules. The other two critical questions in this paper (the ancients and "ease" as a poetic ideal) can be treated with the mixture of common sense and homely analogy that his readers have come to expect. Steele approaches the difficulty first, in good military manner, but also because he counts on tainting his opponents with foreign French ways, appealing to British insularity and xenophobia. The structure of the sentence is antithetic, balancing the greater forms against the minor ones. Having listed the drama and epic, he identifies them in an appositive "continuator"[7] which defines them, and describes their relation to the rules in a relative clause. After a semi-colon followed by an adversative *but*, he reverses the process and defines the inapplicability of the rules to the minor forms, which he lists, and which with another relative clause he exempts from the tyranny of the rules. It is interesting to observe how much detail has ingeniously been inserted in this sentence partly by means of the device of antithesis. It should be noted, however, that the antithesis is not central but peripheral. It operates within the relative *who*-clause not against the main predication ("those whose Knowledge . . .").

> TEXT C3: "The Enthusisasm in Odes, and the Freedom of Epistles, is rarely disputed; But I have often heard the Poems upon Publick Occasions written in Heroic Verse, which I chuse to call Panegyricks, severely censured upon this Account; the Reason whereof I cannot guess, unless it be, that because thay are written in the same kind of Numbers and Spirit as an Epic Poem, they ought therefore to have the same Regularity."
>
> BASE C3: — occasional poems need not be regular —

COMMENT: In this very long sentence, the main effort is in the direction of definition. The reader is told that odes may be enthusiastic and epistles informal, that rhymed couplets on topical subjects are called "panegyricks" by Steele, and that this same poetic instrument is also used in epic poems. The references to disputes and censure are not basic; they are again the pretext for the entire sentence. The structure of this sentence begins antithetic and proceeds to sequential relative modification ("which I chuse . . . the reason whereof . . .") and concludes with a set of subordinates ("unless . . . that because") and the illative *therefore*. The eight clauses of this sentence because of their essentially linear disposition do not challenge the reader's ability to follow the meaning, even despite the vague reference of *upon this Account* and *the Reason whereof*.

> TEXT C4: "Now an Epic Poem, consisting chiefly in Narration, it is

necessary that the Incidents should be related in the same Order that they are supposed to have been transacted."

BASE C4: — an epic follows a chronological sequence —

COMMENT: *Now* signals the beginning of a line of argument, the preliminary exposition having been made. Steele's interest in his argument may have enticed him into creating the awkward verb cluster *are supposed to have been transacted.*

TEXT C5: "But in Works of the above-mentioned kind, there is no more Reason that such Order should be observed, than that an Oration should he as methodical as an History."

BASE C5: — occasional poems need not be chronological —

COMMENT: Matching the previous *now*, Steele poses an initial *but* showing adversative deviation from the implication of C4. His habit of vague reference is again in evidence: *works of the above-mentioned kind* may be *odes and epistles* or *panegyricks* or both. The evidence for the proposition in this sentence is an analogy: epic is to occasional poem as history is to oration. Many today would think of an oration as requiring closer construction than any history.

TEXT C6: "I think it sufficient that the great Hints, suggested from the Subject, be so disposed, that the first may naturally prepare the Reader for what follows, and so on; and that their Places cannot be changed without Disadvantage to the whole."

BASE C6: — occasional verse need only have some logic of its own —

COMMENT: A rather vague and pleonastic sentence recommending that the topics on which the occasional poem is based be in some order, not merely put helter-skelter. Such a requirement seems to be a minimum condition of any composition. The second half (after the semicolon) is clearly a restatement of the first half.

TEXT C7: "I will add further, that sometimes gentle Deviations, sometimes bold and even abrupt Digressions, where the Dignity of the Subject seems to give the Impulse, are Proofs of a noble Genius; as winding about, and returning artfully to the main Design, are Marks of Address and Dexterity."

BASE C7: — apparent disorder can be justified in occasional poems —

COMMENT: The opening words reveal Steele's awareness that the paragraph is getting too long. The uncertainty is suggested both by the pleonastic *further* after *I will add*, when neither is, in fact, needed. It is not clear what the purpose of the second segment (after the semicolon) may be. If digression is laudable, how is meandering different, as Steele suggests by seeming to contrast "noble Genius" with "address and dexterity?" Of course, the *as* segment may simply be a restatement of the opening phrase of the sentence. There is, incidentally, an alliterative tendency manifested in the nouns *deviations, digressions, dignity, design, dexterity,* all of them placed in emphatic positions.

This rather wordy paragraph has presented two things: an argument in favor of the freedom from rules of occasional poetry, and a review of the traditional kinds of poetry and their standing with reference to rules. The rules themselves seem to involve mainly the arrangement of the parts of a narrative, whether chronological or otherwise. In concluding the' paragraph as he has, Steele has not taken care to prepare a transition to his next subject, the influence of the ancients.

> TEXT D1: "Another Artifice made use of by Pretenders to Criticism, is an Insinuation, *That all that is good is borrowed from the Ancients.*"

> BASE D1: — some wrongly claim that all good writing is influenced by classical writers —

COMMENT: Steele casually begins his fourth paragraph with a statement of his second critical topic introduced by the phrase *another artifice*. He used a similarly direct approach in the introduction to the previous paragraph (C1), also by means of a (doubtless made-up) citation, here referred to as an *insinuation*. Though the sentence is casual to the point of awkwardness, its very simplicity allows it to contrast emphatically with its more elaborate neighbors.

> TEXT D2: "This is very common in the Mouths of Pedants, and perhaps in their Hearts too; but is often urged by Men of no great Learning, for Reasons very obvious."

> BASE D2: — the inferiority of modern poetry is maintained by both learned and ignorant readers —

COMMENT: The initial vague reference *(this)* appears once again, followed by a double antithesis about the source of the opinion cited in D1. Such a view as Steele mentions would be naturally held by the learned *(pedants)*, therefore in their *mouths*. The reference to their *hearts* is a sneer implying the hypocrisy of the learned who often speak what they do not believe. The slur in the second member, at the non-learned, asserts obvious reasons for their view (e. g., desire to seem learned). By a bit of trickery, which includes the antithetic content, Steele damns both sides: the learned, who are hypocrites, and the ignorant who wish to seem learned. Steele himself is learned enough to be able to criticize the pedants and to gather to his side the honestly ignorant readers, who can now feel superior to both camps.

> TEXT D3: "Now Nature being still the same, it is impossible for any Modern Writer to paint her otherwise than the Ancients have done."

> BASE D3: — modern poetry must resemble ancient poetry, since mankind has not changed —

COMMENT: Having set up the argument with the two propositions in D1 and D2, Steele signals the turn to a conclusion with an initial *now*. "Nature is ever the same" is the major premise and the conclusion seems inevitable that ancients and moderns must therefore be writing alike. The unexamined minor premise (that writers paint nature) hardly needed stating for either Steele or his readers. Even the force of *paint* to mean *describe* and *Nature* to mean *mankind* was felt by Steele and his contemporaries to be more literal than metaphoric.

> TEXT D4: "If, for Example, I were to describe the General's Horse at the Battel of *Blenheim*, as my Fancy represented such a noble Beast, and that Description should resemble what *Virgil* hath drawn for the Horse of his Hero, it would be almost as ill-natured to urge that I had stolen my Description from *Virgil*, as to reproach the Duke of *Marlborough* for fighting only like *Aeneas*."
>
> BASE D4: — a description of a modern warrior might be expected to resemble one done by an ancient writer —

COMMENT: That Steele should use the Duke of Marlborough as an example is not surprising given Steele's political views and the part that great man played in the politics of the day. That he should likewise select Virgil as a literary example is not surprising either considering the Latinity of the English Augustans. The hypothesis behind this sentence has as an important secondary motive the political rehabilitation of Marlborough. The equation is defective since the bravery of Aeneas might be measured on a linear scale (from zero to very brave) whereas the description of the horse cannot, though Steele may assume that it varies from not accurate to very accurate. The analogical method shown here was previously used in C5.

> TEXT D5: "All that the most exquisite Judgment can perform is, out of that great Variety of Circumstances, wherein natural Objects may be considered, to select the most beautiful; and to place Images in such Views and Lights, as will affect the Fancy after the most delightful manner."
>
> BASE D5: — even the best poet is limited to selecting and arranging beautiful images —

COMMENT: Since Steele here concedes that the poet selects those aspects of the object which have the greatest impact on the reader, it is evident that he is not claiming, as might have been thought from his earlier remarks, that a description can only be either accurate or the opposite. The sentence has unusual word order in that it contains between the main verb *(is)* and its complement *(to select...)* a long adverbial clause which normally would belong after the end of the complement (i. e., just after *beautiful*). It is possible that the purpose of this manoeuver is to achieve a kind of parallelism between the two infinitives around the semi-colon, perhaps matching the pleonastic doublet *views and lights*.

> TEXT D6: "But over and above a just Painting of Nature, a learned Reader will find a new Beauty superadded in a happy imitation of some famous Ancient, as it revives in his Mind the Pleasure he took in his first Reading such an Author."
>
> BASE D6: — a learned reader of poetry enjoys both the beauty of the poem and its allusion to the ancients —

COMMENT: Again the learned reader is introduced, this time to stand as a superior consumer of poetry since he enjoys both the description and the literary allusion. The subordinate clause (*as ...*) gives as an explanation for this effect one which is less offensive to the unlearned reader. It stresses not the literary but the human side of learning.

> TEXT D7: "Such Copyings as these give that kind of double Delight which we perceive when we look upon the Children of a beautiful Couple; where the Eye is not more charm'd with the Symmetry of the Parts, than the Mind by observing the Resemblance transmitted from Parents to their Offspring, and the mingled Features of the Father and the Mother."

> BASE D7: — imitation of the ancients has an effect similar to perceiving beauty in the resemblance of a child to its parents —

COMMENT: This restatement of D6 is probably calculated to win the attention of women readers. It consists of a set of parallels and antitheses (perhaps symbolized by the reference to *double delight*): *eye/mind, parents/offspring, father/mother*. This is accomplished fairly compactly with a series of connected subordinate clauses: *which we perceive, when we look, where the eye is*. The process is consistent with Steele's earlier uses of analogy.

> TEXT D8: "The Phrases of Holy Writ, and Allusions to several Passages in the Inspired Writings (though not produced as Proofs of Doctrine). add Majesty and Authority to the noblest Discourses of the Pulpit: In like manner an Imitation of the Air of *Homer* and *Virgil* raises the Dignity of modern Poetry, and makes it appear stately and venerable."

> BASE D8: — imitation of the ancients makes modern poetry more dignified —

COMMENT: The first two phrases are synonymous (even *holy writ* doubles *inspired writings*), and the two parts of the sentence reflect each other, one sacred, the other secular. The doubling is emphasized by such doublets as *majesty and authority, Homer and Virgil, stately and venerable*. In fact, the entire paragraph contains a pairing that symbolizes the ancient-modern symmetry, especially notable in the parent-child image in D7, which is the most explicit. Structurally, of course, the paragraph is deceptive in that it begins by offering to treat the ancients as the previous one treated the rules, i. e., as inapplicable. Steele scorns the ancients argument by presenting it as another trick of the false critics. He does not sustain this position, however, contending that both ancient and modern imitate nature and then acknowledging that the modern is the child of the ancient. It is inconsistent but to Steele's audience may not have been objectionably so. For his readers, it is the padding that counts.

The final paragraph announces itself by an initial reference to its conclusive nature.

> TEXT E1: "The last Observation I shall make at present is upon the

Disgust taken by those Criticks, who put on their Cloaths prettily, and dislike every thing that is not written *with Ease.*"

BASE E1: — some critics like only poems written with 'ease' —

COMMENT: Steele's third topic is a critical term *(ease)*[8] rather than a critical issue. Again he ridicules his antagonists, this time by likening them to fops. As in C1 and a few times elsewhere, Steele places himself in the foreground with a first-person pronoun. He may well have felt irritated about this matter, which he has brought in as if it were a weighty critical question rather than a faddish piece of critical jargon.

TEXT E2: "I hereby therefore give the genteel part of the learned World to understand, that every Thought which is agreeable to Nature, and exprest in Language suitable to it, is written with Ease."

BASE E2: — every natural idea expressed in appropriate language has 'ease' —

COMMENT: Steele makes his rather tame statement about the general applicability of *ease* in the form of a challenge to the faddish proponents of erroneous criticism, here referred to as the *genteel part of the learned World*. The vague language *(thought agreeable to nature, language suitable to it)* leaves everything undefined and inexact. To the careless reader it seems plausible; in fact, it is either an untenable claim (if the key terms are defined) or a tautology.

TEXT E3: "There are some things which must be written with strength, which nevertheless are easie."

BASE E3: — strong writing may have 'ease' —

COMMENT: Steele's irritation with the idea of "easy writing" leads him into a paradox whose absurdity he hopes will reflect on the critics.

TEXT E4: "The Statue of the *Gladiator,* though represented in such a Posture as strains every Muscle, is as easie as that of *Venus*; because the one expresses Strength and Fury as naturally as the other doth Beauty and Softness."

BASE E4: — representations of both strength and beauty can reveal 'ease' —

COMMENT: This sentence amplifies and illustrates E3. The Gladiator statue is contrasted with that of Venus; the doublets *strength and fury* contrast with *beauty and softness:* these pairings maintain the antithesis found throughout this essay.

TEXT E5: "The Passions are sometimes to be rouzed, as well as the Fancy to be entertained; and the Soul to be exalted and enlarged, as well as soothed."

BASE E5: — poetry may rouse as well as soothe —

COMMENT: Though the reference is unspecific, it is probable that Steele is here explaining the implications of E4 and his objections to the theory of 'ease'. The structure of the first half of the sentence is a complex antithesis of two elements: *passions/fancy, rouzed/entertained.*

The second half adds the complication of a third substantive *(soul)*, followed by an alliterative doublet *(exalted/enlarged)* with a trailing element *(soothed)*, which repeats in the second half the structure of the whole (three nouns).

> TEXT E6: "This often requires a raised and figurative Stile; which Readers of low Apprehension, or soft and languid Disposition (having heard of the Words *Fustian* and *Bombast*) are apt to reject as stiff and affected Language."
>
> BASE E6: — rousing poetry requires figurative writing which is sometimes mistaken for affectation —

COMMENT: Once again the grammatical subject is a detached *this*. The sentence is rich with doubling: *raised/figurative, soft/languid, Fustian/Bombast, stiff/affected.* Everyone of these doublets is pleonastic. It almost appears here as if Steele had been preparing a defense of non-easy writing.

> TEXT E7: "But Nature and Reason appoint different Garbs for different Things; and since I write this to the Men of Dress, I will ask them if a Soldier, who is to mount a Breach, should be adorned like a Beau, who is spruced up for a Ball?"
>
> BASE E7: — different themes require different styles —

COMMENT: The conclusion of the paragraph is cast in the form of a clothes metaphor which explains the use of a variety of clustering vocabulary items *(garb, dress, adorned, beau, spruced, ball)* unrelated to the actual subject of the sentence. In fact, Steele is here concluding his attack on the critics "who put on their cloaths prettily", now referring to them as "Men of Dress" and putting his objections to the language they favor in the form of a reductive analogy having to do with dress. The sentence is a question (rhetorical, to be sure) but presented in the doubling manner characteristic of the entire essay: *nature/reason, different garbs for different things, soldier/beau, breach/ball* and the parallel adjectival *who*-clauses. The carelessness about exact diction characteristic of Steele's manner is shown in his selection of the weak general-purpose word *things* instead of the more precise *situations* or *uses*.

5. CONCLUSION

To determine whether this analysis has accomplished one of its purposes, let us summarize the indications about the style of Steele that have been derived from it. These range from matters of diction to the over-all rhetorical strategy of the essay. Although Steele announces that he is writing to protect the helpless reader from the tyranny of critical bullies by exposing their methods, this is not really what he does or means to do. Rather it is the framework for a popular treatise on several critical questions likely to interest his audience provided these are offered in an acceptable way. As a result of making a propositional analysis of the essay, we know as certainly as if we had eavesdropped on his editorial conferences that his stated intention was not his real one. This is evident in many aspects of the writing, some of which have been pointed out above. In addition, and perhaps most convincing in this regard, is the instability of Steele's names for his targets and his audience. The former are originally called *Criticks* (A1) and *Readers of Criticks* (B3). Later they are *Tyrants in Wit* (B5), later still *Pretenders to Criticism* (D1) and *Pedants* (D2). At this point, the *learned Reader* (D6) is called on to help with a point that Steele needs to make, but in the next paragraph he seems to be included in the challenge that Steele ironically addresses to the *genteel part of the learned World* (E6). By now, Steele seems to have extended his condemnation to everyone: *Criticks* with pretty clothes (E1), *Men of Dress* (E7) and the *Readers of low Apprehension* (E6) who might well be part of his actual readership. In reality, Steele was not aiming at any of these but merely using them as a pretext for his exposition of modern critical theory.

Given the audience he is addressing in this covert and indirect manner, it is not surprising to find that the ratio between the quantity of text and base (in number of words) is 1170 to 311 or 3.8, which suggests a "dilute" substance — as opposed to a "dense" — one suitable to this kind of popularization. Also consistent with this purpose is the procedure of image, analogy and example (A1, B3, C5, D4, D7 and paragraph E). Typical of the posture of the periodical essayist as instructor is a certain indifference to accuracy in pronoun reference (A2, A3, B3, C1, D2, E6), as well as occasional recourse to first-person address, both of the "framing" type (e. g., A1) and the predicative type (e. g., B5).

Harder to reconcile with the genre and its purpose are certain other features which may be unconscious stylistic habits of Steele's prose. The clothes imagery in paragraph E may well be deliberate, but the antithesis which proliferates in paragraph D is probably not merely an effort to support the opposition between ancient and modern which is its subject. For one thing, this figure occurs elsewhere (B1, C2 . . .) and it is for the most part strained and decorative. It may well be an unconscious habit of our author, as the tendency to use doublets in quantity (A3, B2, D5, D8 . . .)[9] and to be fond of alliteration probably are. Similarly, the imperfect parallelism of sequential clauses (A2, B2, B4, E7) appears to be a habit or even a vice. One is reminded of Wimsatt's account of Johnson's addiction to antithesis, which caused him in successive clauses to state an important argument and to conceal it for the sake of this formal symmetry.[10]

This simple outline sketch of Steele's prose style in this essay may be deprecated by some on the ground that the features mentioned are more characteristic of the genre or the period than of the writer. This is possible, though contrary to all that we know about stylistic con sistency in prose writers. Perhaps some estimate could be made of the force of this charge if it were possible to compare a sentence by Steele with one of Addison's. Fortunately, Addison earlier wrote a *Spectator* on the subject of bad critics.[11] In it appear these two sentences, whose relationship to Steele's D3 and D5 is obvious:

> TEXT Y1: "It is impossible, for us who live in the later Ages of the World, to make Observations in Criticism, Morality, or in any Art or Science, which have not been touched upon by others."
>
> TEXT Y2: "We have little else left us, but to represent the common Sense of Mankind in more strong, more beautiful, or more uncommon Lights."

Even a cursory inspection of the two sets of sentences reveals that they are surprisingly different in style. With essentially the same bases, Addison has made Y1 more generally applicable, more philosophical than D3, and has shaped Y2 to follow more strictly the implication of the previous sentence. In other words, the reasoning is closer. Steele's D3 is more narrowly focused on the argument, followed by an extensive illustration in D4 and capped by a diffuse conclusion of a more general kind than Addison's. In pictures, Addison's way is that of a funnel right side up and Steele's of one upside down.[12] There is not space for a more extensive demonstration here but it is hoped that the above will be suggestive of the difference between these two authors and will allow the inference that the stylistic features derived from the analysis in this paper are those of Richard Steele.[13]

Finally, I must answer the question that some readers may have formulated: "Is Propositional Reduction essential to discover features of style?" Of course it is not, though it provides a method for doing so. Any method which conveniently permits the separation of the surface structure from the propositional level can produce similar results. This method has the advantage that it places at the disposal of the student the experience of his predecessors in the study of style. This experience states that no appreciable understanding of the style of a writer can occur in the absence of a method which permits — nay, compels — the serious consideration of alternative phrasings of the text.

NOTES

[1] The method of Propositional Reduction is explained in Milic, *Stylists on Style* (New York, 1969), pp. 18—21 and in Chisholm and Milic, *The English Language: Form and Use* (New York, 1974), pp. 417—420. I have been much enlightened by the use of this method by one of my students, Mary P. Hiatt, "Locke on Language Via Propositional Reduction," *Style*, V (1971), 284—299.

[2] "...the elegance, purity and correctness which appear'd in [Addison's] writings, were not so much to my purpose, as in any intelligible manner as I could, to rally all those singularities of human life..." *Correspondence of Richard Steele*, ed. Rae Blanchard (Oxford, 1941), pp. 510—511.

[3] The relation of these writers under the aspects of reputation and style has been treated more fully in my "Steele vs. Addison: A Lesson in Reputation" (forthcoming).

[4] Jan Lannering, *Studies in the Prose Style of Addison* (Upsala, 1941).

[5] Attributed to the Roman censor Appius Claudius Caecus (4th Cent. B. C.) under the form "Faber quisque fortunae suae," although several variants exist ("Faber quisque fortunae propriae," "Fortunam sibi quisque fingit").

[6] *Tatler*, No. 52.

[7] A continuator is a structure of the type *etc.* The phrase "and the great kinds of Poetry" serves to inform even the simplest reader how he (or she) should classify epic. The parallel phrase "and the like" gives no such help. See R. Ohmann, *Shaw: The Style and the Man* (Middletown, Conn., 1962), p. 9, and Milic, *A Quantitative Approach to the Style of Jonathan Swift* (The Hague, 1967), pp. 95—98.

[8] Samuel Johnson, half a century later (*Idler* No. 77, October 6, 1759), defines easy poetry as having 'natural' diction, without "harsh or daring figures ... transposition ... unusual acceptations of words [or] any license, which would be avoided by a writer of prose." It is probable that 'ease' had achieved respectability as an ideal of poetry by then. In Steele's time it seems rather to have been a cant term. Steele also makes references to 'easy writers' in *Tatler* No. 9 (April 28, 1709) and *Spectator* No. 109 (July 5, 1711).

[9] The eighteen doublets in this essay (counting only pairs of words of the same grammatical class separated by a conjunction) are nearly all of the "pleonastic" type. Eight of them occur in the last half-paragraph. The ratio of 1.70 per hundred words is consistent with the figures for Addison found by Lannering (pp. 25ff.) and Milic, *Swift* (p. 90). It may be worth remembering that criticism was not Steele's preferred topic but Addison's.

[10] W. K. Wimsatt, *The Prose Style of Samuel Johnson* (New Haven, Conn., 1941), pp. 48—49.

[11] No. 253 (December 20, 1711). This resemblance was brought to my notice by Daniel McDonald's edition of Addison and Steele's *Selected Essays* (Indianopolis, 1973), p. 592

[12] In the terms that I use for my Logical Diagram (*Stylists*, pp. 21—22, *The English Language*, pp. 469—479). Addison moves from his 'initial' to an 'illative' whereas Steele proceeds to an 'illustrative' and an 'exploatory'.

[13] It should be kept in mind that the style of Steele is whatever must be added to the base in order to create the text, not merely what appears in the Comments.

Irma Rantavaara
University of Helsinki

Virginia Woolf, diarist, novelist, critic

A study of some stylistic aspects.

While still a writer of more or less conventional novels — *The Voyage Out* and *Night and Day* — Virginia Woolf is already in her Diary pondering over ways in which to find her own way to handle "this loose, drifting material of life" (April 20, 1919). She finds writing a diary good practice: "finger exercises" she much later (May 31, 1940) calls her daily half-hour at it.

> What sort of diary should I like mine to be? Something loose knit and yet not slovenly, so elastic that it will embrace any thing, solemn, slight or beautiful that comes into my mind. I should like it to resemble some deep old desk, or capacious hold-all, in which one flings a mass of odds and ends without looking them through. /— — —/ It loosens the ligaments. Never mind the misses and the stumbles. Going at such a pace as I do I must make the most direct and instant shots at my object, and thus have to lay hands on words, choose them and shoot them with no more pause than is needed to put my pen in the ink." (April 20, 1919)

When writing *Jacob's Room*, the first novel in which she uses the technique that was to become her hallmark, Virginia Woolf writes in her Diary, on February 18, 1922:

> My only interest as a writer lies, I begin to see, in some queer individuality; not in strength, or passion, or anything startling, but then I say to myself, is not 'some queer individuality' precisely the quality I respect?

And a little later, on July 26, more sure of herself by now:

> There's no doubt in my mind that I have found out how to begin (at 40) to say something in my own voice; and that interests me so that I feel I can go ahead without praise.

Her ambition is to create a style "so fluent and fluid that it runs through the mind like water". And not only *a* style but a variety of styles that would reflect her "squirrel cage mind", which compels her "to follow, blindly, instinctively with a sense of leaping over a precipice the call of — the call of —" (Nov. 7, 1928). The words she is trying to find come a little later: "these mystical feelings."

Style is, for Virginia Woolf, as for Proust, not a question of technique but of vision.

> Why admit anything to literature that is not poetry — by which I mean saturated? Is that not my grudge against novelists? that they select nothing? The poets succeed by simplifying: practically everything is left out. I want to put practically everything in: yet to saturate. That is what I want to do in the Moths [later to be called *The Waves*]. It must include nonsense, fact, sordidity: but made transparent. (Nov. 28, 1938)

Art is not preaching, she emphasises. Art is something in itself, *das Ding an sich*. "Multitudinous seas" is beauty in itself. Imagery, the choice of words, are the work of imagination, of vision, and their task is to suggest, to work under ground. As Dr. Johnson, Coleridge, and the ancient Greek and Roman stylists said of images in poetry, so, in the novel, images are made of the fusion of many different ideas; that is how and why they say more than they state. To say more than the words themselves convey, to "make words transparent" was Virginia Woolf's ambition as a writer.

— — —

Between the Acts (BA) is Virginia Woolf's last, posthumously published novel. It is a finished piece of art, composed between April 1938 and November 1940, as the Diary tells us on November 23:

> Having this moment finished the Pageant — or Poyntz Hall? — (begun perhaps April 1938) my thoughts turn well up to write the first chapter of the next book (nameless) Anon, it will be called /— — —/ I am a little triumphant about the book. I think it is an interesting attempt in a new method. I think it's more quintessential than the others. More milk skimmed off. A richer pat, certainly a fresher than that misery *The Years*. I've enjoyed writing almost every page. This book was only (I must note) written at intervals when the pressure was at its highest, during the drudgery of *Roger*.

But although finished, the book needed some final brushing up. On February 26th, 1941, almost exactly a month before her suicide on March 28th, she writes: "Finished Pointz Hall, the Pageant; the play — finally *Between the Acts* this morning". We can legitimately consider her last novel to be a thoroughly worked-out achievement. It deserves full attention as a work of art created with mature and perfected skill, with great intensity and a definite sense of goal.

The working process of *Between the Acts* can be followed in the Diary; it entitles one to believe in the goal-consciousness with which the artist developed both her theme and its form. On August 6th, 1937, she writes:

> Will another novel ever swim up? If so how? The only hint I have towards it is that it's to be dialogue: and poetry: and prose; all quite distinct. No more long closely written books. But I have no impulse; and I shall wait; and shan't mind if the impulse never formulates; though I suspect one of these days I shall get that old rapture. I don't want to write more fiction. I want to explore a new criticism. One thing I think proved, I shall never write to 'please', to convert; now I am entirely and for ever my own mistress.

It took some months before the initial steps were taken, but then, right away, the main ideas were shaping and the nucleus started formulating. On April 26th, 1938, the Diary gives us a short summary of the outlines:

> Why not Poyntzet Hall: a centre: all literature discussed in connection with real little incongruous living humour: and anything that comes in-

to my head; but 'I' rejected: 'we' substituted: to whom at the end there shall be an invocation? 'We'... the composed of many different things... we all life, all art, all waifs and strays — a rambling capricious but somehow unified whole — the present state of my mind? And English country; a scenic old house — and a terrace where nursemaids walk — and people passing — and a perpetual variety and change, from intensity to prose, and facts — and notes; but eno'.

The epithets that characterise the incipient new novel are "fantastic" (April 26, 1938), "airy" (May 20, 1938), "PH poetry" (August 28, 1940). Writing it is "a frisk" (October 6, 1938), "a relief after a long pressure of Fry facts [the biography of Roger Fry she was writing, finishing off in June 1940] (Dec. 19, 1938), "a holiday from Roger" (Feb. 28, 1939), "playing with words" (May 31, 1940). It gave her a feeling of happiness even in the middle of air raids, both in London where their home in Mecklenburg Square was demolished, and in their country home at Rodmell, near Lewes, where Virginia and Leonard Woolf had to fight fire bombs in their garden many nights in succession.

> My first solitary morning, after London and the protracted air raid — from 9.30 to 4 a. m. — I was so light, so free, so happy I wrote what I call P. H. POETRY. Is it good? I suppose not, very. (August 28, 1940)

At the start it was "the mildest childbirth I have ever had" (June 5, 1938), and she enjoyed the writing all along, though she was sure "it won't please anyone, if anyone should ever read it" (Aug. 7, 1938). As usual, she had no illusions about her popularity and, as usual, her self-criticism was awake despite her enjoyment:

> — it remains to be seen if there's anything in PH. In any case I have my critical brain to fall back on. (Nov. 22, 1938)

When she had written 120 pages, she has the whole of it formulated in her mind. She wants to make it

> a 220 page book. A medley. I rush to it for relief after a long pressure of Fry facts. But I think I see the whole somewhere — it was simply seized, one day, about April, as a dangling thread: no notion what page came next. And then they came. To be written for pleasure. (Dec. 19, 1938)

She, like Miss La Trobe in the novel, had her vision.

After a pause in 1939 when the first version was finished, rewriting was taken up with great concentration.

> Began PH again today and threshed and threshed till perhaps a little grain can be collected. (May 25, 1940)

And two days later:

> Scraps, orts and fragments, as I said in PH, which is now bubbling. I'm playing with words: and I think I owe some dexterity to finger exercises here. (May 31, 1940)

At times she feels "loosely anchored", especially when she has reached the point of finishing off the novel.

> The end gives its vividness, even its gaiety and recklessness to the random daily life. This, I thought yesterday, may be my last walk . . . (June 22, 1940)

The end of the novel, however, is not an end but a link in the chain, emphasising the dominating theme: the unity of everything. Towards the end of the book there is this typical passage:

> Like quicksilver sliding, filings magnetized, the distracted united. The tune began; the first note meant a second; the second a third. Then down beneath a force was born in opposition; then another. On different levels they diverged. On different levels ourselves went forward; flower gathering some on the surface; others descending to wrestle with the meaning; but all comprehending; all enlisted. The whole population of the mind's immeasurable profundity came flocking; from the unprotected, the unskinned; and dawn rose; and azure; from chaos and cacophony measure; but not the melody of surface sound alone controlled it; but also the warring battle-plumed warriors straining asunder; To part? No. Compelled from the ends of the horizon; recalled from the edge of appalling crevasses; they crashed; solved; united. And some relaxed their fingers; and others uncrossed their legs.
>   Was that voice ourselves? Scraps, orts and fragments, are we, also, that? The voice died away. (BA, 220—21)

The passage quoted serves also as an illustration of Virginia Woolf's manner of writing in this last novel of hers. Practically all the "style markers" are there: the ample use of semi-colons and commas; the short sentences for the impressionistically, even pointillistically created atmosphere; the use of comparisons and metaphors to make the text convey more than it states; the repetitions; the sudden jumps from the transcendental-metaphysical to trivial and realistic, from "the whole population of the mind's immeasurable profundity" to "scraps, orts and fragments". In what follows an attempt is made to study her style in a greater detail.

— — —

"Poyntzet Hall: a centre: all literature discussed in connection with real little incongruous living humour" became in the novel Pointz Hall where the yearly village festival takes place, a pageant, composed and directed by Miss La Trobe with great ambition and little chance of giving form to her great vision. The play takes, off and on, some 140 pages out of the 256 pages of the novel. It contains the little poems that Virginia Woolf was composing in her leisure hours, and covers, like *Orlando*, though in a different manner, the history of England from the times immemorial ("Sprung from the sea / Whose billows blown by mighty storm / Cut off from France and Germany / This isle.") through different ages till the present day.

> Suddenly the tune stopped. The tune changed. A waltz, was it? Something half known, half not. The swallows danced it. Round and round,

in and out they skimmed. Real swallows. Retreating and advancing. And the trees, O the trees, how gravely and sedately like senators in council, or the spaced pillars of some cathedral church ... Yes, they barred the music, and massed and hoarded; and prevented what was fluid from over-flowing. The swallows — or martins were they? — The temple-haunting martins who come, have always come ... Yes, perched on the wall, they seemed to foretell what after all the *Times* was saying yesterday. Homes will be built. Each flat with its refrigerator, in the crannied wall. Each of us a free man; plates washed by machinery; not an aeroplane to vex us; all liberated; made whole ... (BA 212—13)

What the message was did not become very clear to the audience, but one thing reached practically everyone: "Each is part of the whole," or as the Rev. G. W. Streatfield in his vote of thanks tried to formulate it: "Yes, that occurred to me, sitting among you in the audience. Did I not perceive Mr. Hardcastle here" (he pointed) "at one time a Viking? And in Lady Harridan — excuse me, if I get the names wrong — a Canterbury pilgrim? We act different parts; but are the same. That I leave to you ... (BA, 224)

It was an ingenious device to use a village pageant as a means of bringing together the different layers of English society, at "half-past three on a June day in 1939", on the premises of a large country house. The audience could be made a motley crowd, and the actors could also represent a cross-section of the villagers, including even the most humble, the village idiot. The whole thing could be made what the author had in her initial plan aimed at: "dialogue: and poetry: and prose; all quite distinct", "a rambling capricious but somehow unified whole." It gave her a natural opportunity to include "variety and change, from intensity to prose, and facts," to create "something loose knit and yet not slovenly, so elastic that it will embrace any thing, solemn, slight or beautiful that come into my mind" — just like her Diary. The style had to be "fluid and following the flight." Its task was to suggest, not to state.

— — —

Practically any page of the novel could be chosen to serve as an example of her style: the characteristics are ubiquitous. Let us first take the description of nature. It, too, varies from impressionistic matter-of-factness to poetical, imaginative "flights of the mind":

Beyond the lily pond the ground sank again, and in that dip of the ground, bushes and brambles had mobbed themselves together. It was always shady; sun-flecked in summer, dark and damp in winter. In the summer there were always butterflies; fritillaries darting through; Red Admirals feasting and floating; cabbage whites, unambitiously fluttering round a bush, like muslin milkmaids, content to spend a life there. Butterfly catching, for generation after generation, began there; for Bartholomew and Lucy; for Giles; for George it had begun only the day before yesterday, when, in his little green net, he had caught a cabbage white. (BA, 70—71)

"The forecast," said Mr. Oliver, turning the pages till he found it, "says: Variable winds; fair average temperature. Rain at times." He put down the paper, and they all looked at the sky to see whether the sky obeyed the meteorologist. Certainly the weather was variable. It was green in the garden; grey the next. Here came the sun — an illimitable rapture of joy, embracing every flower, every leaf. Then in compassion it withdrew, covering its face, as if it forebore to look on human suffering. There was a fecklessness, a lack of symmetry and order in the clouds, as they thinned and thickened. Was it their own law, or no law, they obeyed? Some were wisps of white hair merely. One, high up, very distant, had hardened to golden alabaster; was made of immortal marble. Beyond that was blue, pure blue, black blue; blue that never filtered down; that had escaped registration. It never fell as sun, shadow, or rain upon the world, but disregarded the little coloured ball of earth entirely. No flower felt it; no field; no garden. (BA, 30)

The use of semicolons and commas, and of colours, are favoured devices in impressionistic description, to be met on practically every page of the novel. Repetition, another popular device, covers all the parts of speech:

— a tarnished, a spotted soul (22)
— an unusual, an agreeable sensation (56)
— the ravaged, the silent, the romantic gentleman farmer (19)
— And she loathed the domestic, the possessive, the maternal (25—6)
— But what did he do with his hands, the white, the fine, the shapely (64)
— in that deep centre, in that black heart (55)
— this ripe, this melting, this adorable world (70)
— Nothing changed their affection; no argument; no fact; no truth. (33)
— The room smelt warm and sweet; of clothes drying; of milk; of biscuits and warm water. (88)
— Across Africa, across France they had come (129)
— Change is not; nor the mutable and lovable; nor greetings; nor partings; nor furtive findings and feelings (181)
— She had come into the stable yard where the dogs were chained; where the buckets stood; where the great pear tree spread its ladder of branches against the wall. (182)
— what a cackle, what a raggle, what a yaffle — as they call the woodpecker, the laughing bird that flits from tree to tree. (214)
— Faster, faster, faster, it whizzed, whirred, buzzed ... (21)
— beat, beat, beat; repeating that if no human being ever came, never, never, never (23)
— The cook's hands cut, cut, cut. (43)
— Only at Giles he looked; and looked and looked. (127)

Thanks to the small details, reality is anchored to the flights of the mind. The unimportant and sordid are linked to the elevated and valuable. Jumps and jerks are used to shock the reader into awareness:

— And the audience turning saw the flaming windows, each daubed with golden sun; and murmured: "Home, gentlemen; sweet..." yet delayed a moment, seeing through the golden glory perhaps a crack in the boiler; perhaps a hole in the carpet; and hearing, perhaps the daily drop of the daily bill. (229—30)
— The Home would have remained; and Papa's beard, she thought, would have grown and grown; and Mama's knitting — what did she do with all her knitting? — Change had to come, she said to herself,

or there'd have been yards and yards of Papa's beard, of Mama's knitting. Nowadays her son-in-law was clean shaven. Her daughter had a refrigerator... Dear, how my mind wanders, she checked herself. What she meant was, change had to come, unless things were perfect; in which case she suppose they resisted Time. Heaven was changeless. (202—3)

— "It's very unsettled. It'll rain, I'm afraid. We can only pray," she added, and fingered her crucifix. "And provide umbrellas," said her brother. Lucy flushed. He had struck her faith. (31)

The bare, matter-of-fact description is given in short, abrupt, rythmical sentences.

— While the chorus was sung, the picnickers assembled. Corks popped. Grouse, ham, chickens were sliced. Lips munched. Glasses were drained. (198)
— Water boiled. Steam issued. Cake was sliced. Swallows swooped from rafter to rafter. And the company entered. (121)

The short descriptive sentenes, however, are rare in comparison with the richly metaphoric idiom of the novel. In fact, the whole book is a long metaphor, anchored to reality with scattered pieces of matter-of-fact information.

Characterizations of people and the net of human relationships are almost always given obliquely, by means of comparisons and metaphors. Isa and Giles Oliver, the protagonists, are a youngish couple, young enough to have a love-hate passion for each other, yet at the same time having some vague desire to escape from conventional life.

— Giles glared. With his hands bound tight round his knees he stared at the flat fields. Staring, glaring, he sat silent. Isabella felt prisoned. Through the bars of the prison, through the sleep haze that deflected them, blunt arrows bruised her; of love, then of hate. Through other people's bodies she felt neither love nor hate distinctly. Most consciously she felt — she had drunk sweet wine at luncheon — a desire for water. (81—2)
— Isa raised her head. The words made two rings, perfect rings, that floated them, herself and Haines, like two swans down stream. But his snow-white breast was circled with a tangle of dirty duckweed and she, too, in her webbed feet was entangled, by her husband, the stockbroker. Sitting on her three-cornered chair she swayed, with her dark pigtails hanging, and her body like a bolster in its faded dressing-gown. (9—10)
— "In love," she must be; since the presence of his body in the room last night could so affect her; since the words he said, handing her a teacup, handing her a tennis racket, could so attach themselves to a certain spot in her; and thus lie between them like a wire, tingling, tangling, vibrating — she groped, in the depths of the looking-glass, for a word to fit the infinitely quick vibrations of the aeroplane propeller that she had seen once at dawn at Croydon. Faster, faster, faster, it whizzed, whirred, buzzed, till all the flails became one flail and up soared the plane away and away... (20—21)

The tension between man and wife and the jealousy of the husband are in the following passage revealed through a combination of imagery, inner monologue and behavioristic means.

140

— Words this afternoon ceased to lie flat in the sentence. They rose, became menacing and shook their fists at you. This afternoon he wasn't Giles Oliver come to see the villagers act their annual pageant; manacled to the rock he was, and forced passively to behold indescribable horror. His face showed it; and Isa, not knowing what to say, abruptly, half purposely, knocked over a coffee cup.

William Dodge caught it as it fell. He held it for a moment. He turned it. From the faint blue mark, as of crossed daggers, in the glaze at the bottom he knew that it was English, made perhaps at Nottingham; date about 1760. His expression, considering the daggers, coming to this conclusion, gave Giles another peg on which to hang his rage as one hangs a coat on a peg, conveniently. A toady; a lickspittle; not a downright plain man of his senses; but a teaser and twitcher; a fingerer of sensations; picking and choosing; dilly-ing and dallying; not a man to have straightforward love for a wo-man — his face was close to Isa's head — but simply a —. At this word, which he could not speak in public, he pursed his lips; and the signet-ring on his little finger looked redder, for the flesh next it whitened as he gripped the arm of his chair. (74—5)

Irony, never very far off in Virginia Woolf, is not a characteristic trait in this novel. There are shades of it only in the delineation of Mrs. Manresa, who represents a vulgar, nouveau-riche type of a snob.

— Her hat, her rings, her finger nails red as roses, smooth as shells were there for all to see. But not her life history. That was only scraps and fragments to all of them, excluding perhaps William Dodge, whom she called "Bill" publicly — a sign perhaps that he knew more than they did. Some of the things that he knew — that she strolled the garden at midnight in silk pyjamas, had the loud speaker playing jazz, and a cocktail bar, of course they knew also. But nothing private; no strict biographical facts. (50)

— So with blow after blow, with champagne and ogling, she staked out her claim to be a wild child of nature, blowing into this — she did give one secret smile — sheltered harbour; which did make her smile, after London; yet it did, too, challenge London. For on she went to offer them a sample of her own life; a few gobbets of gossip; mere trash; but she gave it for what it was worth; how last Tuesday she had been sitting next so and so; and she added, very casually, a Christian name; then a nickname; and she'd said — for, as a mere nobody they didn't mind what they said to her — and "in strict confidence, I needn't tell you," she told them. And they all pricked their ears. (52—53)

Self-irony can be read into the picture of Miss La Trobe and her great vision which nobody understood and valued.

— No, I thought it much too scrappy. Take the idiot. Did she mean, so to speak, something hidden, the unconscious as they call it? But why always drag in sex... It's true, there's a sense in which we all, I admit, are savages still. Those women with red nails. And dressing up — what's that? The old savage, I suppose... That's the bell. Ding, dong. Ding... Rather a cracked old bell... And the mirrors, Reflecting us... I called that cruel. One feels such a fool, caught unprotected... (233)

— Miss La Trobe stood there with her eye on her script. "After Vic." she had written, "try ten mins. of present time. Swallows, cows, etc." She wanted to expose them, as it were, to douche them with pre-

> sent-time reality. But something was going wrong with the experiment. "Reality too strong," she muttered. "Curse 'em'." She felt everything they felt. Audiences were the devil. O to write a play without an audience — *the* play. But there she was fronting her audience. Every second they were slipping the noose. Her little game had gone wrong. If only she'd a back-cloth to hang between the trees — to shut out cows, swallows, present time. But she had nothing. She had forbidden music. Grating her fingers in the bark, she damned the audience. Panic seized her. Blood seemed to pour from her shoes. This is death, death, she noted in the margin of her mind; when illusion fails. Unable to lift her hand, she stood facing the audience. (209—10)

Even when the reader might expect irony, for instance in the picture of Mrs. Swithin with her naïve religious-anthropological ruminations, he encounters gentle humour, without malice. Mrs. Swithin is one type of human being complete, with her own idiosyncrasies, which have to be tolerated, even if not shared. This is what her down-to-earth, agnostic brother is thinking of her:

> why, in Lucy's skull, shaped so much like his own, there existed a prayable being? She didn't, he supposed, invest it with hair, teeth or toenails. It was, he supposed more of a force or a radiance, controlling the thrush and the worm; the tulip and the hound and himself, too, an old man with swollen veins. It got her out of bed on a cold morning and sent her down the muddy path to worship it, whose mouthpiece was Streatfield. A good fellow, who smoked cigars in the vestry. He needed some solace, doling out preachment to asthmatic elders, perpetually repairing the perpetually falling steeple, by means of placards nailed to Barns. The love, he was thinking, that they should give to flesh and blood they give to the church... (32—33)

In fact, Mrs. Swithin represents, treated in a humorous light, something essential in the novel, something that Isa, too, is brought to understand:

> But none speaks with a single voice. None with a voice free from the old vibrations. Always I hear corrupt murmurs; the chink of gold and metal. Mad Music... (183)

Including the humorous picture of Mrs. Swithin, an almost Jungian concept of racial memory can be read into the novel, both into the message of the pageant and the ubiquitous imagery in the description of that particular day in June in 1939.

— — —

While finishing off *Between the Acts* Virginia Woolf was pondering over the possible re-creation of her critical idiom. The same problems and the same passion "to be herself" were occupying her till the end of her days.

> I wish I could invent a new critical method — something swifter and lighter and more colloquial and yet intense: more to the point and less composed; more fluid and following the flight, than my C. R. essays. The old problem: how to keep the flight of the mind, yet be exact. All the difference between the sketch and the finished work. (22.6.1940)

Within this limited space, I have chosen only one collection, *The Death of the Moth*, as an example of her critical idiom. Published posthumously in 1942, it yet contains essays from a long period, from 1919 to 1940. Out of the 26 essays only four come under observation here: 'Henry James' (1919), 'The Novels of E. M. Forster' (s. a.), 'The Art of Biography' (s. a.), and 'Craftsmanship' (a broadcast on April 20th, 1937).

It is interesting to notice that it looks — only looks — as if the theme influenced the reviewer's style. When discussing Henry James the essays contain an abundance of adjectives, repetitions, and of long rambling sentences, reminding one of the famous Jamesian style:

> A spectator, alert, aloof, endlessly interested, endlessly observant Henry James undoubtedly was. (95)

Virginia Woolf speaks admiringly of Henry James's "genius to analyse shades and subtleties majestically rolling the tide of his prose over the most rocky of obstacles" (85), something that she herself was striving towards. Her use of repetitions and her verbosity are very much like James's.

> — The mellow light which swims over the past, the beauty which suffuses even the commonest little figures of that time, the shadow in which the detail of so many things can be discerned which the glare of day flattens out, the depth, the richness, the calm, the humour of the whole pageant — all this seems to have been his natural atmosphere and his most abiding mood. (87)
> — The tendency perhaps was rather to a good fellowship in which the talk was wide-sweeping, extremely well informed, and impersonal than to the less formal, perhaps more intense and indiscriminate, intimacies of to-day. (88)

Virginia Woolf's comparisons and metaphors are quite as numerous and telling as those of the master stylist himself:

> — A "cosmopolitanized American," as he calls himself, was far more likely, it appears, to find things flat than to find them surprising; to sink into the depths of English civilization as if it were a soft feather bed inducing sleep and warmth and security rather than shocks and sensations. (93)
> — But Henry James had neither roots nor soil; he was of the tribe of wanderers and aliens; a winged visitant, ceaselessly circling and seeking, unattached, uncommitted, ranging hither and thither at his own free will, and only at length precariously settling and delicately inserting his proboscis in the thickset lusty blossoms of the old garden beds. (95)

As stylists, Henry James and Virginia Woolf are born soul-mates. As early as 1919 Virginia Woolf already reveals the characteristic stylistic traits that we are to find in all her later writings. In connection with Henry James it seems as if she had been infected with some of the Jamesian idiosyncrasies, but in fact they were all genuinely her own.

When writing on E. M. Forster, however, Virginia Woolf's style is much less verbose and she uses metaphors more sparingly; repetitions and the wayward construction of sentences are there to hammer in important facts.

> — Sawston implies Italy; timidity, wildness; convention, freedom; unreality, reality. (105)
> — It is the soul; it is reality; it is truth, it is poetry; it is love; it decks itself in many shapes; dresses itself in many disguises. (105)
> — Here, then, is a difficult family of gifts to persuade to live in harmony together: satire and sympathy; fantasy and fact; poetry and prim moral sense. (106)

"The Art of Biography' is an essay on Lytton Strachey's *Eminent Victorians, Queen Victoria* and *Elizabeth and Essex*. They are deemed to be "of a stature to show both what biography can do and what biography cannot do" (121). *Eminent Victorians* was at the time of its publication, 1918, a landmark, a revelation, an example to be followed. Today it has been reduced and put to its proper place as an example of "debunking", well-written and amusing, but not by any means the whole truth and nothing but the truth. The Victorians, eminent and otherwise, have been brought to proper perspective through a distance in time. Already in the 1930's Virginia Woolf saw that "fact and fiction refused to mix" (123) in Lytton Strachey's brilliant essays. Her definition of the genre of biography in general is as good as any definition earlier or since, but it also serves as an example of her style in this estimation of her friend's work:

> The artist's imagination at its most intense fires out what is perishable in fact; he builds with what is durable; but the biographer must accept the perishable, build with it, imbed it in the very fabric of his work. Much will perish; little will live. And thus we come to the conclusion, that he is a craftsman, not an artist; and his work is not a work of art, but something betwixt and between. /— — —/ But almost any biographer, if he respects facts, can give us much more than another fact to add to our collection. He can give us the creative fact; the fertile fact; the fact that suggests and engenders. (125—6)

This is still true of Lytton Strachey, despite the changing fashions.

'Craftsmanship', a broadcast on April 20th, 1937, is an interesting essay, particulary interesting from the point of view of this article, for it deals with aspects that are relevant for Virginia Woolf's own ambitions in the use of words: the nature of words "is not to express one simple statement but a thousand possibilities" (127). It is in the nature of words to mean many things:

> Thus one sentence of the simplest kind rouses the imagination, the memory, the eye and the ear — all combine in reading it. /— — —/ In reading we have to allow the sunken meanings to remain sunken, suggested, not stated; lapsing and flowing into each other like reeds on the bed of a river. /— — —/ Words are full of echoes, of memories, of associations, so stored with meanings, with memories, that they have contracted so many famous marriages. (129—30)

144

What Virginia Woolf was trying to convey in her *Between the Acts* on a wider sphere — the unity of everything — she is also stressing when smaller items, words, are in question: a word is not just a single and separate entity, but part of other words, to be seen in a larger context. The central problem of a writer, of Virginia Woolf herself, is: "How can we combine the old words in new orders so that they survive, so that they create beauty, so that they tell the truth? That is the question." (130) The question, in fact, which Virginia Woolf was trying to solve in all her writings whatever the genre, in all her attempts to find an adequate manner in which "to handle this loose, drifting material of life."

Claes Schaar
University of Lund

Vertical context systems

My starting-point is the concept 'allusion' regarded as a literary device and defined by the OED as 'a covert, implied, or indirect reference';[1] by Littré as a 'figure de rhétorique consistant à dire une chose qui fait penser à une autre'.[2] Major dictionaries and encyclopedias in other languages provide similar definitions; like Littré, Alonso regards allusion as a rhetorical figure.[3] These definitions must be modified and amplified. For one thing, so far as I know, 'allusion' is not an accepted term in rhetoric, and Littré and Alonso are possibly thinking of the word in its older sense of 'pun', 'play on words'. Secondly, in view of general usage, a full description should make it clear that allusions in the proper sense of the word are i n t e n t i o n a l: when we say that poet A is alluding to passage B we are implying that he does so deliberately. This is an important point.

In a great many cases the word allusion, so understood, can be used without much difficulty. Faced with a collection of statements like, 'In *The Waste Land* 366 ff. T. S. Eliot alludes to the chaos of eastern Europe'; 'This poem contains allusions to the Great Fire of 1666'; or 'In the *Paradiso* 3.118f. Dante alludes to Emperors Barbarossa, Henry VI and Frederick II', few readers are likely to deny that there is a very high degree of probability that the respective authors knew perfectly well what or whom they had in mind, referring as they do to certain specific phenomena or people. Like Eliot, they could have said so in explanatory notes. But there are other instances of what is called 'allusion' which are not easily covered by the definition formulated and commented on above. In his book on the classical background of *Paradise Lost*, D. P. Harding supplies a good many examples of two groups called 'direct' and 'surreptitious' allusions to the *Aeneid*. As an instance of surreptitious allusion he cites a reference to the legend of Tityos 'hidden away' between the lines on Satan prostrate on the burning lake (1.193ff.): 'Tityos' . . . prostrate body in Tartarus, according to Virgil, occupies "over nine full acres".[4] Harding points out that since Milton uses the same unit of land measurement as Virgil does, the reader is likely to think of Satan's size but also, by way of natural association, of his punishment. In his study of Vida's *Christiad* and the *Aeneid*,[5] Di Cesare divides the Neo-Latin poet's imitation of Virgil into three categories: the commonplace phrase, the echo, and the evocative allusion. The third of these is described as 'a correspondence in language which, by recalling a passage, draws on the emotions or meanings attached to that passage. It may operate by similarity of context, in which case

the evocation adds to the desired effect; it may operate also by mutation, surprise, or contrast'.[6] An example is *Christ.* 4, where John
enumerates Christ's twelve followers, briefly characterizing each one,
and ending his list with the words, ... *et ipse mali fabricator Iudas*
(274), closely resembling Virgil's words about the last of the warriors
to emerge from the wooden horse *(et ipse doli fabricator Epeos,* from
Aen. 2.264). 'Nothing else in John's list', says Di Cesare, 'even vaguely
suggested the Greek warriors; the surprise caused by this final line
gives the reader, as nothing else can, the feeling of the deceitful cunning of Judas and his relationship to the other Apostles, unsuspecting
until this very night but nonetheless not wholly easy about him' (p.
152).

It can be argued that the parallels discussed by Harding and Di Cesare are in a different category from the examples of allusion I have
mentioned by way of introduction. There may be borderline cases, but
these do not concern us here. In Harding's and Di Cesare's instances
there are no references to specific historical names or occurrences
which the poets can be assumed to have had in mind; instead, it is a
question of resemblances between word-combinations in purely literary
contexts. Such instances call for some comments intended to supplement
Wimsatt and Beardsley's classic discussion of the 'intentional fallacy'.[7]

Whether the so-called allusions in Milton and Vida — word-groups
suggesting other word-groups — are intentional or not, and thus deserve that name, is a question easier to ask than to answer. How are
we to say in each particular case whether we have to do with deliberate imitation? There is no way of knowing if Milton was aware of the
Virgilian parallel to *PL* 1.193ff., or if there was deliberate intention behind Vida's bringing out the cunning of Judas by making his line similar to some words in the *Aeneid.* Yet this unfruitful problem arises automatically as soon as we use the word 'allusion', provided the word has
the meaning we have assigned to it in accordance with usage. As everybody knows, learned poets in the 16th and 17th centuries were so im-
bued with impressions from classical, biblical, patristic, and other comparable literature that there are few lines in their work which are not
somehow coloured by such impressions. They all had, indeed, a dyer's
hand, and images, formulas, and motifs were common property to an
extent difficult to imagine for a modern reader. Possibly, intention is
more easily ascertainable in modern poets since the background texts
on which they draw do not similarly form part of a common cultural
heritage. Their working out of 'allusive' techniques may thus be more
deliberate than corresponding processes in Renaissance authors. In any
case, whether we are discussing old poetry or new, if we use the word
'allusion' for certain literary similarities, we must also in each case be
prepared to answer questions as to whether and to what extent they
are fully intentional, semi-intentional, subconscious, unconscious, and

so on. Some readers are likely to regard such questions as futile and immaterial, a view I am inclined to share. The problem of intention, recently — not without bias — discussed by E. D. Hirsch,[8] tends to overshadow the problem of function. The point is how literary similarities work, not if they are deliberate. And, as Wimsatt and Beardsley observe in the case of Eliot's poems, 'they work when we know them'.[9] On the other hand I would not go so far as to subscribe to these critics' addition, 'and to a great extent even when we do not know them, through their suggestive power' — in such cases the effect is hardly due to their evocative, but to their poetic power. These things are only in part identical. If not recognized, the similarity cannot contribute to the meaning of a piece of language, and therefore in a sense does not exist: if it exists, it may with some exaggeration be said to do so in the same way as a defunct and unknown language exists in its mute inscriptions, in a set of symbols not yet interpreted. As soon as we can identify and interpret the language its written remains spring to life, existing as an active instrument in communication. So even if we cannot tell if a literary similarity is intentional or not, and thus if it is an allusion, we can always, if we have the necessary knowledge, establish its existence, describe it and analyse its function in the text.[10]

Thus the question, 'Is this passage an allusion?' does not always make sense, but the question, 'Does this passage suggest some other passage?' always does and, if it can be answered in the affirmative, leads on to other meaningful questions. It does not matter that situations can arise where readers judge differently, one reader claiming a similarity which another denies. Both can defend their respective views in ways which lend themselves to analysis, referring as they can to a concrete material available to everybody. Discussions about intention cannot have a similarly objective basis. Since 'allusion' as a term for the phenomena referred to by Harding and Di Cesare is thus found to be scientifically unsatisfactory, we can easily do without it and instead concentrate exclusively on the *function* of literary similarities of the type indicated here. By 'the function of literary similarities' we mean the imparting to word or word-group A of additional meaning derived from word or word-group B, so that A is invested with additional meaning by being like B. B 'rubs off' on A[11]. The meaning involved in such transmission is practically always of the connotative rather than of the denotative kind. Only very exceptionally does the denotation of words or word-groups seem to be affected by this kind of similarity.

In cases where additional meaning is derived from earlier texts — no matter *how* much earlier[12] — there is thus a 'vertical' relationship between the elements resembling one another. A vertical context system emerges, a semantically connected whole made up of surface context and deep context, here to be called infracontext, investing the surface context with connotative meaning. We should speak of context, not text, since we are concerned with environmental entities. The process is not fundamentally different from pieces or blocks of language charging one another with connotative meaning on the horizontal level. 'Infracontext' should not be confused with 'source', being a much larger concept, though of course 'source' often coincides with at least part of this concept. While the search for sources is concerned with the tracing of origins, the quest for infracontexts is an attempt to enlarge and stratify meaning. Infracontexts often cover matter which was not and could not have been known to the author of the surface text. Looking for infracontexts we work like archaeologists delving far down through the strata of the past, laying bare traces of cultures which throw light on later civilizations, endowing them with a meaning they would not otherwise possess. The study of infracontexts is in fact *text archaeology*, and the past becomes the key to the present. Connotations emerge, operating within larger literary systems made up of groups of texts available to homogeneous groups of readers with the same cultural background, readers likely to recognize relevant pieces of language and to respond in a similar way to them. An unresponsive reader, in whose mind no associations arise, derives a narrower and more limited meaning from his study of the surface context. The enrichment of its meaning is due to a Gestalt appreciation of the infracontext evoked by it, but it is hardly possible in each particular case to trace and describe the entire associative pattern. In the present paper, at least, I must confine myself to providing a bare minimum of quotation and comment, and to mapping out the main features. Some cases, however, are highly complex, with different strata of infracontexts branching out, pyramid-like, underneath one another. Such complex systems resemble a Calder mobile, 'Five branches and a thousand leaves'.

Analysis of the vertical systems does not profit much from use of the term 'code' for the system of surface contexts. These contexts in relation to the infracontexts can only constitute a connotative code of a trivial character (trivial if regarded as a code, but not trivial in other respects). A non-trivial member of a code points beyond itself, a = b, whereas the surface context, like the ordinary linguistic sign, already has a meaning of its own. What happens is that this meaning is in various ways amplified, reinforced, or modified by the infracontext. Thus on the infracontextual level there is no meaning which does not already somehow, on the denotative level, form part of the semantic area of the surface context. Using an analogy from music we might say that a theme given out by a certain instrument group is picked up by another or by several others joining in, so that an augmented version of the theme emerges. The relationship between surface context and infracontext is thus not a = b, but a < A: within its framework, a vertical system is *isosematic*. We shall later return to the problem as to whether use of the term 'code' is meaningful in some other sense than that discussed here.[13]

A study of the nature of infracontexts should, then, deal with the ways in which they affect the connotative meaning of the surface con-texts. It follows from what has been said previously that an allegedly 'allusive' text like *The Waste Land* paradoxically does not lend itself so well to such an investigation since the system of infracontexts does not naturally form part of the reader's frame of reference, but has been deliberately constructed by the poet.[14] It does not meet the demands that should be made on a cultural heritage proper. An ideal period is the Renaissance and the time up to about 1700, a period when we can assume that the literary 'living past' I have discussed above was a power-ful factor in the experience of learned readers. As any reader of *Stil-forskning och Stilteori* knows, its distinguished author, recipient of this miscellany, recommends those who propound theoretical models to present material sufficient to enable others to reinterpret it, to modify the model proposed, or to suggest other and better models (p. 168). It is in conformity with this sound piece of advice (all the more noteworthy as the present 'model' is by no means complete) that we shall study examples of different vertical context systems in *Paradise Lost* and above all in the *Strage degli Innocenti*, the 17th-century religious epic by Giambattista Marino. Examples will be taken from the first book, the *Sospetto d'Herode*, translated by Crashaw. Original as well as translation will be considered.[15]

Text archaeology reveals that the following variables can be isolated in vertical context systems: S setting, F focus, U unifunctionality or Mu multifunctionality, P polyphony, A authority, I impact, and M mood. There may be yet other variables, but a study of those enumerated here is sufficient for our present purposes. Setting is scenery or loca-lity described in more or less detail; Focus, emphasis on thematic con-tent, often of a moral character; Unifunctionality, a marked homoge-neousness in character, tenor, and modus operandi of the infracontexts involved; Multifunctionality, various differences in these respects, though not great enough to disrupt the isosematic framework; Poly-phony, related to degree of complexity in setting and functionality; Authority, related to degree of general validity; Impact, the combined 'weight' of the infracontexts involved (thus a narrower concept than the ordinary 'poetic impact'), and Mood, the atmosphere and emotive character of a system. No two variables cover each other, though there may occasionally be some measure of overlapping, and U and Mu are mutually exclusive, but it is impossible to illustrate the interrelation-ship and intensity of the variables graphically — combinations are too numerous and too complex.

Vertical context systems characterized by these variables can be roughly divided into four grops of increasing complexity. An instance of the first and simplest type, where I is always strong, is the system involving *PL* 1.263, *Better to reign in Hell, than serve in Heaven*, a sur-face passage which forms part of Satan's well-known speech to Beelze-bub. The line is one of several maxims which make up the speech and give it an air of finality intended by the speaker to strengthen character and courage and tighten discipline. Infracontexts[16] reach down into deep strata involving Aeschylus' *Prom.* 965, where Mercury, taunting Prometheus, sarcastically remarks to the proud hero that he seems willing to serve his rock rather than be Zeus' messenger. Younger strata include Plutarch's *Life of Caesar* 11.2: Caesar, travelling through a poor and barbarian village, would rather live first there than second in Rome. The formula recurs in a larger number of Renaissance texts dealing with the fallen Lucifer: *Purple Isl.* 7.10 *In heav'n they scorn'd to serve, so now in hell they reigne; Apollyonists* 1.20 *To be in heauen the second he disdaines: / So now the first in hell, and flames he raignes.* Similar formulas occur for instance in Valvasone's *Angeleida* and in the *Sospetto d'Herode* 34, and, together, make up a comprehensive pattern of infracontexts. A is fairly strong: the formulaic statement, like a faithfully copied inscription, appears in approximately the same form everywhere and derives its force from suggesting a universally valid, proverbial truth. S is not conspicuous owing to some degree of abstraction, though the scenes where the conversations including it occur are in part graphic enough. F is strongly on pride; there is M of a highly emotive type, but P stands in inverse relation to U and in direct relation to weak S.

Another more concrete example of the simple group is the system of which *PL* 1.299ff. forms the surface context. This is where Satan addresses the fallen angels who, in a Homeric multimembered simile, are compared to ¹) autumnal leaves strewing the brooks in Vallombrosa, and ²) scattered sedge afloat when violent *Orion armd / Hath vext the Red-Sea Coast, whose waves orethrew / Busiris and his Memphian Chivalrie*, when full of hatred they went after the 'Sojourners of Goshen' who beheld from the shore carcasses and broken chariots littering the sea. The infracontexts here provide not only strong I but also P by the scenes being superimposed on one another, thus affording a kind of stereoscopic effect: the *Gerusalemme Liberata* 9.66 on the *Inferno* 3.110ff., the *Inferno* on the *Aeneid* 6.309f., the *Aeneid* on the *Iliad* 6.146ff. In the lowest stratum Homer uses the image of autumnal leaves when making Glaucus ponder the transitoriness of man in his between-the-armies dialogue with Diomedes; Virgil and Dante, when describing the innumerable souls of the dead waiting for Charon's boat; Tasso, when depicting the evil spirits driven back to the Underworld by the Archangel Michael. S in this system is thus marked. There is very strong A due to the echo from Exodus suggesting evil designs on God; Busiris is a figure for the devil (and his unmentioned slayer, Hercules, for Christ). Associations converge, affording U and M: defeat and ruin are connected with withering and transitoriness, the situation in the nether world links up with Hades in Virgil and the Inferno in Dante; the fall of the angels with the scene in Tasso. At the same time, the enormous number of fallen angels, and consequently the threat to Heaven, is emphasized. On every point the meaning of the surface context is reinforced by the analogues: infracontexts provide a bass accompaniment, and the cluster of interrelated themes emerges as a fully integrated motif. F is on defeat and the transitoriness of power, both on an enormous scale.

The second of our four main groups is slightly more complex in that the infracontexts are partly submerged; this is the synecdochic type.[17] Here, I and other variables are made prominent not only by infracontexts coinciding with the surface but also by stretching as it were beyond it and supporting it. Thus in the *Sospetto d'Herode* the poet lists a number of miracles taking place on the occasion of the Nativity (16—17): a threefold sun, a collapsing heathen temple, toppling idols, annihilation of unnatural love, the appearance of the star of Bethlehem. The *Legenda Aurea* — the ultimate original for these stanzas — enumerates these miracles and subsequently a great many others: darkness turns to light, the water of a well in Rome to oil, the vines of Engaddo come into bloom and bear fruit overnight, Joseph's ox and ass bend their knees and worship the Saviour, etc. etc. If familiar to the reader, these details add to the effect of those directly paralleled in the surface context, which consequently operate as *pars pro toto*. Nearly all variables are represented here, though S is not very pronounced since the enumeration is a fairly bare one. U, as a reflection of I, is fairly strong. F is on the Miracle of the Nativity. There is some degree of P owing to the variety and richness of the miracles attending the great Miracle. A is not particularly marked, the episodes being post-biblical; nor is M: the system is too abstract. Another example is the *Sospetto* 44, an Underworld description of the forest surrounding Cruelty's palace which immediately suggests a number of infracontexts of varying depth: the wood of the Suicides in the *Inferno* and the forest of Mars in Marino's *L'Adone*, in Boccacio's *Teseida*, and in Statius' *Thebaid* (the source for Boccacio and Marino). In Crashaws version we read about *a black wood,/Which nods with many a heavy headed tree*, a passage paradoxically suggesting *locus amoenus* scenery in Claudian's *De Raptu Properpinae* (2.110) *Fluctuat hic denso crispata cacumine buxus*. This is one out of many details in the rich description of the vernal scenery in the *De Raptu* where Proserpine and her companions are gathering flowers. But it is only superficially that the echo here contrasts with the tenor of the infra- and surface contexts. Claudian's description leads up to a similarly detailed paragraph on Pluto appearing in smoke and thunder while the universe trembles, and this submerged part of the context thus reinforces the infernal theme, providing I and P and adding M in so doing. S is naturally pronounced; F is on the weirdness of the Underworld. The complexity of the details involved, particularly the element deriving from Claudian, provides Mu. Owing to the echo from Dante, A must be regarded as strong. Some of the infracontexts in this system are reminiscent of half-obliterated but not undecipherable inscriptions.

The synecdochic type is interesting, and I shall give one more example.

The *Sospetto d'Herode* describes Satan in fetters. Sitting on his throne, he is bound for ever by *A curl'd knot of embracing Snakes, that kisse / His corresponding cheekes* and keep him in 'eternal ties'. Infracontexts are provided by Revelations, various Apocrypha, and the *Inferno*, thus affording strong A. In Rev. 20.1f. the visionary sees *angelum ... habentem ... catenam magnam in manu sua. Et apprehendit draconem serpentem antiquum ... et ligauit eum per annos mille, et misit eum in abyssum.* No infracontext depicts Lucifer himself fettered by snakes, but in the *Inferno* 24.94ff. serpents shackle the hands of the damned. The chasm of serpents mentioned in this passage is compared by Dante to the snake-infested Libyan desert described in detail by Lucan in the *Pharsalia* 9. This description in its turn underlies st. 48 in the *Sospetto*, where Cruelty on her devil-inspired mission to Herod, with snakes for hair like Medusa, comes close to petrifying the universe. The effect of the system thus has a 'subterranean' dimension; it points forwards as well as backwards, and it is from a reading of the entire poem that the pattern emerges. The infracontext in Lucan establishes a connection between Lucifer, Cruelty, and Herod, thus making not only I but also F, on the punishment of evil, strongly prominent. As to other variables, U is crowded out by Mu and P, allowing great complexity. S and M are marked. As in many similar cases, the vertical-horizontal connections here may seem remote and far-fetched to some readers, less so to those whose frame of reference allows them to respond to the suggested contexts in the Bible, in Dante, and in Lucan.

In the third group there are contrasts between surface context and infracontext. The *Sospetto d'Herode* 60 describes Herod's nightly torments and insomnia after his fear of the alleged Infant-usurper has been roused by Cruelty. His bed, *benche ricco e morbido, gli sembra / Siepe di spine, e campo di battaglia*; he is badly shaken by Cruelty's message, he rages and shouts for arms. The quoted words in the Italian context suggest a double infracontext of an uncommon type, one incorporated into the other. In a well-known courtesy-book by Stefano Guazzo, the *Civil Conversatione*, an unhappy lover's torments are described, insomnia among them: *Le piume del letto mi sono pungenti spine.* It is added that unhappy lovers are poor eaters, something which aggravates sleeplessness: *Et duro è di battaglia il letto.* These words are derived from the last line of a Petrarch sonnet on the unhappy lover's plight: weeping, pain, food = poison, a life in grief. What in Guazzo-Petrarch is a symptom of hopeless love becomes a sign of hatred and fear in Marino, and the word-for-word similarity between surface and infracontext serves to set one very sharply off against the other. S is suggested by the descriptive, non-abstract character of the contexts, P is weak, and there is little A (which of course has nothing to do with the contrast effect). There is U due to the contrast, and I, F and M are strong.

Another example of a similar type, though without word-for-word similarity, is met with two stanzas further down in the same poem. The scene is still Herod's bedchamber, the tyrant is wide awake, impatiently awaiting the morning when he will deal effectively with the threat to his power. 'Jealous envy and unrest' ... *Makes him impatient of the lingring light, / Hate the sweet peace of all-composing Night*. The infracontexts evoked by contrast here are those provided by the *alba* genre, the dawn song, in which the lover traditionally laments the coming of dawn which puts an end to the amorous bliss of night. This is the kind of poetry to which Petrarch alludes in *Canz.* 255: *La sera desïare, odiar l'aurora / Soglion questi tranquilli e lieti amanti*. On every point Herod does and is the opposite: excited and wrathful instead of calm and happy; hating night, he is eagerly waiting for dawn. Again, the amorous activities to which dawn puts an end benefit procreation and life, whereas Herod is preparing for a mass murder of Infants and, of course, is trying to kill Life itself. The contrast here is likely to have struck a 17th-century reader accustomed to 'baroque' conceits, and brings out the tenor of the surface context in full relief. There is S for the same reason as in our first example; P is not very marked, but I, F and M are again strong. So is U, and there is some degree of A in view of the weight of the *alba* genre. It is important to remember that the contrast character of the third type in no way reduces its isosematic quality since the contrast does not invalidate, but on the contrary brings out F more clearly.

We come to the last and most complex group of vertical context systems. All possible variables here are of some intensity. Within the usual homogeneous semantic frame, there is a certain amount of mobility of meaning or semantic elasticity emerging as a result of the contact between surface context and infracontext. My two instances are to some extent thematically interrelated. In the beginning of the *Sospetto d'Herode* the fallen Lucifer is looking back at his and his followers' experiences before and after opposing God. In st. 11 of the Italian version he is watching from the Underworld the preparations for Salvation that are being made on earth, *onde nel petto / Rinouando dolor, crebbe sospetto*. The words in Marino's stanza take on different meanings as we read them in the light of different infracontexts. Owing to the almost proverbial *rinovare-dolorem* formula (cf. below), I and A are both strong. There is identity of scene and sense, S and F, in the nearest analogue, the *Gerusalemme Liberata* 4.12, where Satan in his speech to the demons rejects the unnecessary and painful thinking of past sufferings: *Ma che rinouo i miei dolor parlando?* But the perspective changes as we think of the deepest layer of infracontexts, the basis for the phrase: *Aen.* 2.3, *Infandum regina iubes renouare dolorem* — the beginning of Aeneas' description of the fall of Troy — indescribable is the pain renewed at the thought of defeat and treason. Lucifer being the speaker in Marino's poem, the irony is heavy; at the same time, from Lucifer's point of view, his and the apostate angels' fall was ultimately due to a

treacherous act on the part of God — did not God, announcing the In-
carnation, intend to disgrace the entire angelic race by investing pure
angelic essence with vile human substance? Text archaeology, however,
reveals yet another infracontext embodying the *Aeneid* line: *Inf.* 33.4f.
This is where the traitor, Ugolino, laments when compelled by Dante to
renew his grief: *Tu vuoi ch'io rinovelli / Disperato dolor che il cor mi
preme*. The reader knows Ugolino's sins; the traitor himself in his
speech throws the blame on others and dwells in detail on the horrors
of his death. This infracontext, then, strongly and directly reinforces
the surface context. Obviously in view of the different interpretations
of the infracontexts, U is not characteristic of this system, which on the
contrary is clearly Mu, and the meaning is dependent on the shifting
F into which the surface context is brought. The different passages suggest visual, concrete scenes, and thus S; M is also present, and the
varying character of the scenes in the context afford P.

A somewhat different instance involves *PL* 1.84ff. as surface context.
'Weltering by his side', Beelzebub is thus addressed by Satan: *If thou
beest hee; But Oh how fall'n! how chang'd / From him, who in the
happy Realms of Light, / Clothed with transcendent brightness didst
outshine / Myriads though bright*. The nearest infracontext here is st.
10 in the *Sospetto d'Herode*, where the poet apostrophizes Lucifer: *Misero,
e come il tuo splendor primiero / Perdesti, ò già di luce Angel più bello*,
which Crashaw renders by *Disdainefull wretch! how hath one bold
sinne cost / Thee all the beauty of thy once bright Eyes!* The lines in
Milton and Marino — and the entire situation in *PL* — strongly suggest
one of the deepest infracontexts, *Aen.* 2.274ff., where the phantom of
Hector, gory and disfigured, appears in Aeneas' dream: *Hei mihi, qualis
erat, quantum mutatus ab illo / Hectore, qui redit, exuvias indutus
Achilli / Vel Danaum Phrygios iaculatus puppibus ignes!* These lines,
again, are representative of an entire group of formulas, the *ubi sunt*
group: the first lines of the *Sospetto* poet's apostrophe to Lucifer, and
even more Satan's words to Beelzebub suggest, like Aeneas' exclamation, melancholy feelings caused by the transitoriness and emptiness
of glory. So far, F is unequivocally centred on this motif. The infracontexts evoked by Crashaw's version, on the other hand, are based on
Is. 14.12, where the prophet apostrophizes the king of Babylon: *Quomodo cecidisti de caelo Lucifer, qui mane oriebaris? corruisti in terram,
qui uulnerabas gentes*, a passage which was later, in patristic texts,
taken to refer to the apostate angel.

Renaissance infracontexts suggested by this last-mentioned passage
include Valmarana's *Daemonomachiae* (1, p. 15), a close imitation of
Isaiah: *Quomodo de caeli cecidisti, Lucifer, astris, / Qui super impositus
dextram tentare Parentis, / Ausus*, etc.; further the *Gerusalemme Liberata* 4.2 *Come sia pur leggiera impresa, hai stolto!, / Il repugnare a la
divina voglia*; and Fletcher's *Apollyonists* 1.19 *Ah wretch, who with
ambitious cares opprest, / Long'st still for future, feel'st no present*

good. These infracontexts, embedded in layers superimposed one upon the other, are thus in the nature of philippics and invective, taking up the spirit and tenor of the verses in Isaiah, a triumphant diatribe suggesting hatred of the tyrant and joy at the victory of God. These meanings colour the surface context. Here we are far from the *ubi sunt* idea of the classically inspired context. The respective situations make S fairly strong, and I and A are both secured owing to the biblical version of the formula. There is Mu if original and translation are considered together; there is clearly M, due to S, and P emerges as a result of infracontextual variations.

We return, finally, to the question of whether these different vertical context systems can in any sense constitute a code. Though surface contexts cannot make up a non-trivial code owing to their isosematic relation to the infracontexts, it would seem that surface context and infracontext *together* can. It is precisely due to their isosematic nature that they form complex and comprehensive yet homogeneous signs. The answer to the question how this is possible obviously lies in F, the variable which is most closely bound up with sense. F in fact indicates the meaning of the sign. Thus in the first example of group I the meaning indicated is *superbia* bringing its own revenge; in the second example, the meaning is the defeat and transitoriness of evil and worldly powers. In the first example of group II, F indicates the power of the Divine Miracle; in the second, damnation; in the third, the punishment of evil. In group III the meaning indicated in the first example is 'sinner tormented by sin' (a well-known Platonic-patristic conception), in the second, vindictiveness and hatred of God. In group IV the first example suggests treason and subsequent defeat, but mobility of meaning makes one possible sense ironical, depending on a Virgilian infracontext. In the last example, *ubi sunt* melancholy or else hatred of evil are possible meanings according as we 'tilt' the surface context in the direction of the classical or the biblical infracontext.

Thus surface context and infracontext merge into entities with at least some measure of denotative, non-trivial meaning. As in Paleo-Christian iconography, the initiated recognize collocations of figures, objects, and scenes, and understand the hidden meaning.[18] The signs making up the code depend for their effectiveness on complexity, just as in music full and rich orchestration elicits deep and strong esthetic response. The vertical context systems provide one of the more sophisticated codes contained in the texts we have examined.

NOTES

[1] OED *allusion* 4.
[2] *Dictionnaire de la langue Française* 1, ed. Paris, 1956, p. 339.
[3] *Enciclopedia del Idioma* 1, Madrid, 1958, p. 295.
[4] *The Club of Hercules. Studies in the Classical Background of Paradise Lost.* Urbana, 1962, p. 60.

[5] *Vida's 'Christiad' and Vergilian Epic.* New York and London, 1964, p. 141.

[6] *Ibid.* pp. 149f.

[7] *The Verbal Icon. Studies in the Meaning of Poetry.* Univ. of Kentucky Press, 1954, repr. 1960, pp. 3 ff.

[8] *Validity in Interpretation.* New Haven and London, 1967, repr. 1971. I cannot here, of course, discuss the numerous articles on Wimsatt & Beardsley's and Hirsch's ideas.

[9] *The Verbal Icon,* p. 15.

[10] A useful summary of various recent discussions of the nature of allusions is to be found in L. Vinge, 'Om Allusioner' (*Tidskrift för litteraturvetenskap* 3, 1972—73, pp. 138 ff.).

[11] For a similar view of the function of 'allusions' cf. Kittang & Aarseth, *Lyriske strukturer, Innföring i diktanalyse,* Oslo, 1968, pp. 97 ff. (referred to by Dr. Vinge). Like the metaphor, 'allusion' involves expansion of meaning ('meningsutvidelse', pp. 97 f., 103).

[12] This of course is not necessarily so: a text may quite well derive additional meaning from a contemporary or even a later work.

[13] 'Code' here is of course used in the sense 'system of signs', not 'system of norms'. Connotative codes of a trivial kind are discussed at some length by Eco in *La Struttura Assente* (Milan, 1968), Barthes in *Littérature et Société. Problèmes de méthodologie en sociologie de la littérature* (Brussels, 1967, pp. 31ff.), and in many later semiotic studies. I cannot here discuss the code problem in any detail.

[14] One critic dealing with allusions in *The Waste Land,* S. Bergsten in "Illusive Allusions. Some Reflections on the Critical Approach to the Poetry of T. S. Eliot' (*Orbis Litterarum* 14, 1959, pp. 9 ff.), distinguishes between on the one hand an allusion proper, 'intended by the author and depending on its source for its full meaning', which is present when a 'source may throw considerable light on the whole context of the borrowed words', and on the other 'incidental, perhaps unconscious' reminiscences which cannot be called allusions, 'the source being of no significance to the meaning' (p. 10).

[15] As energetic readers know, I have earlier discussed the *Sospetto d'Herode* and the two versions' relation to the literary background (*Marino and Crashaw: Sospetto d'Herode. A Commentary.* Lund, 1971).

[16] Needless to say, I have little to add to the results of text archaeology as far as *Paradise Lost* is concerned: from Hume in the sixteen-nineties onwards, industrious digging has revealed all infracontexts of any relevance.

[17] Dr. Vinge (*ibid.* p. 142) regards synecdoche as a characteristic feature of 'allusions' generally. In my system, the synecdochic type is only present when we can move outwards horizontally *after* completing the vertical movement.

[18] Cf. particularly A. Grabar, *Christian Iconography. A Study of Its Origins* (Bollingen Series XXXV, 10), Princeton, 1968.

Roger D. Sell
Åbo Akademi

Two types of Style Contrast in *King Lear:*
A Literary-Critical Appraisal

I

In drama, stylistic variation may be potentially more frequent than in other genres. Useful distinctions are sometimes drawn between an essayist's style of reasoned exposition and the same essayist's style of impassioned peroration, or between a narrative writer's different styles for different subject-matter — setting, action, conversation. Nevertheless, in the essay, in narrative, in poetry, all action and all argument, everything seen, heard and thought, is usually mediated through the one author or authorial persona, so that there inevitably occurs a certain amount of smoothing or filtering. Works departing from this convention gain no small part of their literary effect by doing so. In drama, on the other hand, the audience is placed in direct contact with a number of different stage personalities who can, if the dramatist so chooses, express their fluctuating moods and experiences more "in the raw", the fluctuation profiled by style contrasts.

Many dramatists reject or only half accept this option. Neo-classical drama, for instance, has a strict notion of decorum which, carried to the extremes of some English Restoration tragedy, makes any expression of emotion sound like any other expression of any other emotion by any other character, and can even make a straightforward piece of information sound like emotion too. Such indiscriminate heightening or filtering is what makes possible Fielding's parody in *The Tragedy of Tragedies, or Tom Thumb the Great.* A different but no less restrictive filtering takes place in some of the plays of Pinter, in those sequences which seem deaf to almost every feature of conversation apart from its occasional inconsequentiality and communicative failure, features which Pinter renders systematic. And again, stylistic uniformity sometimes probably results from sheer lack of technical resource. Admittedly Kyd's and Marlowe's strutting ranters were what the audience wanted. On the other hand, Shakespeare had not yet shown the way to anything different. Just how different things could be is amply illustrated by *King Lear,* and in what follows I shall try to show how certain style contrasts are integrated into their contexts in that play.[1]

Because of the space limit, and also as a suggestion that the range of stylistic variation integrated into the play may be very considerable, I have chosen two, widely different style contrasts. The first is the contrast between what I call the "imperative-exclamatory style", i. e. the use of imperatives and exclamations as a stylistic device, and the "cumulative-balanced style", of which I do not attempt a summary definition. The second contrast is that between verse and prose.

II

Shakespeare sometimes plays off a style which, in its syntax and rhetoric, is to some extent balanced and cumulative against a style which is coloured by the use of imperatives and exclamations. (The terms "balanced" and "cumulative" are vague here, but will become clearer as the discussion proceeds.) The balanced, cumulative style correlates with characters being reasonable, calm, un-self-centred and alive to the realities of past and present. The imperative-exclamatory style is used by characters in moments when, ignoring or spurning the present, they hope to shape the future.

The first scene presents an interesting case in point. There, Lear has a compelling vision of the future. In the long term, having shaken off the cares of office, he will "Unburthen'd crawl towards death". More immediately, his three daughters shall contest in words as to which of them loves him most; Cordelia shall win the contest; she shall receive the richest third of the divided kingdom, in which he himself will reside with her; and her pre-eminence shall be marked by the award, either to herself or to the consort whom she shall now choose, of a coronet. And almost as soon as this plan misfires, Lear recoups, improvises a new future, and dictates accordingly.

The language he speaks suitably expresses his precipitate haste. A more delicate analysis of it would highlight several features active in this, but at least some part is played by imperatives and exclamations. The prompt realization of his plans necessitates a series of commands, which begins from his first entrance: "Attend the Lords of France and Burgandy, Gloucester"; "Give me the map there. Know that . . ."; "Tell me, my daughers, . . ."; "Our eldest-born, speak first"; "what can you say to draw/A third more opulent than your sisters? Speak". When present reality proves an obstacle, he expresses his surprised distaste by an exclamation: "How, how, Cordelia!" And his redoubled eagerness for the second, re-planned future is expressed in commands and exclamations still more peremptory: "Peace, Kent!"; "Hence, and avoid my sight!"; "Call France. Who stirs? Call Burgandy."[2] This last order, which the courtiers are apparently too astonished to obey, contrasts with the very first command, "Attend the Lords of France and Burgandy, Gloucester". It represents the same wish, but Lear would now feel that escorts and titles are a ceremonious waste of time. And at the end of the same speech, his contempt for reality is so great that he even issues a command whose fulfilment is impossible. Confirming the two-fold division of the entire kingdom between Goneril and Regan, he says to their husbands, "This coronet part between you". The Fool later has some bitter comments about what happens when you try to split crowns in the middle. In conjunction with this command, the coronet ironically becomes a stage symbol of far greater suggestiveness than if Lear had been able to put it to the more conventional use he had first intended. In sum, then, Shakespeare's use here of imperatives and exclamations is one small indication of the homogeneity of style, action and character. They help to pinpoint Lear's headstrong rush into the future.

Now that rush is something in which Goneril, Regan and Burgandy willingly acquiesce. They say what he wants them to. But Cordelia, Kent and France try to impede it. They try to force his mind upon the realities of the situation. Cordelia says that a wife cannot love her father to the exclusion of her husband; Kent that empty vessels make most sound; and France that modesty has its value.

The language of Goneril, Regan and Burgandy could of course be partly differentiated from that of Lear. In particular, Goneril's extraordinary piece of flattery itself gives an instance of an expressive change in style. Its rhythm is different, and it is profiled by its use of comparatives and comparative constructions, and by being a very elaborate epanalepsis: it has only one main verb, "I love", which is first placed at the very beginning and is then recapitulated, after the hyperbolical comparisons, at the very end. But in a broad sense, Goneril, Regan and Burgandy are stylistically neutral. Lear calls their tune.

At all events, opposition to his wishes is pointed by much sharper breaks with his style. The first break, wich is also Lear's first twinge of pain in the play, is sharpest of all. However, discussion of it does not really belong here, since it is an excellent example of what Shakespeare can achieve by variation from verse to non-verse:

Lear ... what can you say to draw
    A third more opulent than you sisters? Speak.
Cor. Nothing, my lord.
Lear Nothing?
Cor. Nothing.
Lear Nothing will come of nothing: speak again.
Cor. Unhappy that I am, I cannot heave
    My heart into my mouth ....

The first real interruption of Lear's charge towards ruin is also the first interruption of the blank verse rhythm since his entrance. But then, when the verse rhythm is restored, the first lines of Cordelia's, Kent's and France's subsequent interventions or replies present style contrasts which are hardly less marked:

Lear ... Mend your speech a little,
    Lest you may mar your fortunes.

Cor.   Good my Lord,
   You have begot me, bred me, lov'd me: I
   Return those duties back as are right fit,
   Obey you, love you, and most honour you.

Lear This coronet part between you.
Kent   Royal Lear,
   Whom I have ever honour'd as my King,
   Lov'd as my father, as my master follow'd,
   As my great patron thought on in my prayers, —
Lear The bow is bent and drawn; make from the shaft.

Lear [to Burgandy] Then leave her, sir . . .
   . . . *[to France]* beseech you
   T'avert your liking a more worthier way
   Than on a wretch whom Nature is asham'd
   Almost t'acknowledge hers.
France   This is most strange,
   That she, whom even but now was your best object,
   The argument of your praise, balm of your age,
   The best, the dearest, should in this trice of time
   Commit a thing so monstrous, to dismantle
   So many folds of favour . .

Again the point can be made with crude descriptive tools. Each time, the opposition begins by wresting the last one-and-a-half or two feet of a line from Lear, and using it for some expression which can be followed by a strong terminal pause. This is almost as effective an impediment to Lear's haste as the first a-metrical "Nothing" passage. An actor can dramatize it with facial expressions and gestures suggesting a perplexed attempt to get things straight and an appeal for understanding in others. Then follows the deliberate rehearsal of fact upon fact, to be carefully weighed together. Just as the first speech of acquiescence in Lear's folly, Goneril's, was the most sharply profiled, so it is Cordelia's opening thrust for sanity which most clearly exhibits the stylistic principle of accumulation with balance: the "I" is poised antithetically at the end of the line against the initial "You"; the three perfect-tense verbs plus "me" syntactically mirror and semantically add to each other; and they are weighed against the three present-tense verbs plus "you" in the line following that which explicitly states the reciprocity. Yet in Kent's and France's speeches too, some parallelism, some marking of points equally worth consideration by means of iconic linkage, is still clearly noticeable: there is Kent's "*perfect-tense verb as my noun, perfect-tense verb as my noun, as my noun perfect-tense verb, as my [adjective] noun perfect-tense verb [adverbial phrase]*"; and there is France's "The *noun* of your *noun, noun* of your *noun*, The *superlative used as noun*, the *superlative used as noun*". The stylistic similarity between the three characters is further enforced by Kent and France's subsequent use of striking antitheses and parallelism, e. g. "maid,/That justly think'st and hast most rightly said"; "Fairest Cordelia, that art most rich being poor;/Most choice foresaken; and most lov'd despis'd". Standing out against Lear's predominant style, it intimates that the three characters are "on the same side", and strengthens the triadic narrative pattern of the three unsuccessful attempts to make reason prevail. The style contrast inheres in the structure of the scene and in the personalities and issues involved.

However, the exclamatory-imperative style is not Lear's prerogative. Indeed, one small feature of his clash with Kent is Kent's impatient adoption of that very style — "Reserve thy state; ... check this hideous rashness"; "See better, Lear"; "Kill thy physician, and thy fee bestow/ Upon the foul disease. Revoke thy gift". Conversely, the cumulative-balanced style is sometimes used by Lear:

> *Lear* To thee [*i. e. Regan*] and thine, hereditary ever,
> Remain this ample third of our fair kingdom,
> No less in space, validity, and pleasure,
> Than that conferr'd on Goneril. Now, our joy, [*to Cordelia*]
> Although our last, and least; to whose young love
> The vines of France and milk of Burgandy
> Strive to be interess'd; what can you say . . .

This is a strongly marked climax to the triadic love-contest. Lear is now arriving at one of the points in the future he was most looking forward to: listening to Cordelia tell her love for him. "Now, our joy" is in the same metrical position as Cordelia's later "Good my Lord", Kent's "Royal Lear" and France's "This is most strange", and there is a similar pause after it. Lear slows himself down to dwell for once in the present. The savour of the present is deliberately relished in the phonetically and semantically almost identical "last" and "least", which he juxtaposes for consideration, and in the next line's witty parison, the figure *par excellence* of cumulative balance. Such context-inherent style changes by one and the same character sound like a counterpoint to his main tune, and account for much of Shakespeare's stylistic richness.

Later in the play, Lear learns more of present reality; he begins to understand the error of his ways, the true nature of each daughter, and how powerless he has made himself; and he tries to accept all this with patience. But at the same time, he can also be convulsed with wrath and visions of a future revenge.

In these circumstances, what was earlier only an occasional variation between styles can sometimes become more like a fundamental dichotomy. When told that Cornwall cannot see him because of illness and that he should bear in mind Cornwall's fiery temper, he responds:

> Fiery! the fiery Duke! Tell the hot Duke that —
> No, but not yet; may be he is not well:

Infirmity doth still neglect all office
Whereto our health is bound; we are not ourselves
When Nature, being oppress'd, commands the mind
To suffer with the body. I'll forbear;
And am fall'n out with my more headier will,
To take the indispos'd and sickly fit
For the sound man. *[Seeing Kent in the stocks]* Death on my state!
                                                                    Wherefore
Should he sit here? This act persuades me
That this remotion of the Duke and her
Is practice only. Give me my servant forth.
Go tell the Duke and's wife I'd speak with them,
Now, presently: bid them come forth and hear me,
Or at their chamber-door I'll beat the drum
Till it cry sleep to death.

The fluctuation between anger, an attempt at patience and back again could not be more marked. As always, there is a change in rhythm. But also, the fluent exclamations and imperatives are in strong contrast to the three antitheses. That Lear finds complete calm unattainable may be subtly suggested by his failure to push the antitheses towards fuller isomorphism.[3] Thus stylistic variation helps express a character's inner struggle.

Shortly afterwards, the same dichotomy helps to make our two glimpses of Lear in the storm, III ii and III iv, punctuated as they are by the short prose scene, III iii, interestingly contrast with and complement each other. In the first scene, Lear wants to bring about the apocalyptic end of the world; there shall be a universal judgement, which will of course take care of his daughters. As he encourages the roaring elements to this end, the exclamations and imperatives reach a kind of peak, both by their density of occurrence and by their semantic strength — all the verbs have a fairly restricted collocative range: "Blow, winds, and crack your cheeks! rage! blow! You cataracts and hurricanoes, spout"; "You sul'phrous and thought-executing fires/ . . ./Singe my white head! And thou, all-shaking thunder,/Strike flat the thick rotundity o' th' world!/ Crack Nature's moulds, all germens spill at once/That makes ingrateful man!": "Rumble thy bellyful! Spit, fire! Spout, rain"; "Tremble, thou wretch"; "caitiff, to pieces shake"; "close pent-up guilts,/Rive your con-cealing continents, and cry/These dreadful summoners grace". Yet even here it is explicitly suggested that Lear can change his mood, that he might achieve moments of acceptance and pity for others: "No, I will be the pattern of all patience; I" — and this is an a-metrical line in which he perhaps half-conciously imitates Cordelia — "will say nothing"; "My wits begin to turn./Come on my boy. How dost, my boy? Art cold?/ . . . Poor Fool and knave, I have one part in my heart/That's sorry yet for thee". And these suggestions provide a kind of bridge across III iii

to the second storm scene, where they are realized. Now we glimpse
Lear concentrating on the physical sufferings inflicted by the storm,
in an attempt to control his mental anguish and desire for revenge;
moreover, his further concentration on the plight of the Fool is the
catalyst for a pity hardly less universal than his earlier call for doomsday.
This is a context in which the cumulative-balanced style, in its turn,
reaches something of a climax:

> Thou think'st 'tis much that this contentious storm
> Invades us to the skin: so 'tis to thee;
> But where the greater malady is fix'd,
> The lesser is scarce felt. Thou'ldst shun a bear;
> But if thy flight lay toward the roaring sea,
> Thou'ldst meet the bear i' th' mouth. When the mind's free
> The body's delicate . . .

There is a most dramatic contrast between the poise of these lines
and the continuing fury of the storm, a reminder of Lear's earlier mood.
The dualism of mental and bodily suffering, which was only half-articu-
lated in Lear's attempted patience on the news of Cornwall's indisposition,
is now given greater stylistic expression by means of extended iconic
interplay: between "greater" and "lesser", semantically opposite but
morphologically equivalent; between "is fix'd" and "is felt", parallel
morphologically, but not quite phonetically; between "Thou'ldst shun a
bear" and "Thou'ldst meet the bear"; locally, between the isomorphic
yet semantically contrasting "the mind's free" and "The body's delicate"; and on a larger scale, between the clausally isomorphic "where the
greater malady is fix'd,/The lesser is scarce felt" and "When the mind's
free/The body's delicate", an isomorphism pointed metrically by the
repeated use of the line-end to separate one clause from the other. And
then, as Lear's mind reaches out into the present which surrounds him —

> Poor naked wretches, whereso'er you are,
> That bide the pelting of this pitiless storm,
> How shall your houseless heads and unfed sides,
> Your loop'd and window'd raggedness, defend you
> From seasons such as these? —

the basic facts represented by the nouns are dwelt on and explored,
particularly in the accumulating adjectives; fact is weighed together
with fact in a movement of mind linguistically and rhetorically conveyed
by pairings: the wretches' poverty or piteousness is added to their naked-
ness by simple juxtaposition of adjectives; the storm's pelting to its
pitilessness partly by alliteration; the houseless heads to the unfed
sides by parison; and the clothes' visual appearence to their lack of
weather-proofing by the two stages of a sylleptic semantic progression.[4]
As with the first storm scene, this scene would be less than Shake-
spearian if Lear's mood and style were rigidly unfluctuating. He still

164

shows traces of anger and of the exclamatory-imperative style — "filial ingratitude!"; "O Regan, Goneril!". But it is perhaps noteworthy that in

    ... Take physic, Pomp;
    Expose thyself to feel what wretches feel ...

he is commanding, albeit indirectly, himself, and the command is the more temperate for a hint of balance in the polyptoton. Thus, then, the succeeding phases of the play are articulated partly in different stylistic colouration.

III

However, dramatic opposition between the cumulative-balanced and the exclamatory-imperative in *King Lear* is only occasional. It is only one type of Shakespeare's integrated style shifts, one of the more subtle, though others may be still more subtle. Altogether more obvious and widespread is, of course, the alternation between blank verse (of which the two styles already discussed can be viewed as sub-styles) and prose.[5]

It is a cliché of criticism that Shakespeare's prose is used where a lower tone seems to be needed, or that it can also mark some other kind of strong contrast.[6] Certainly, the prose-verse-prose alternation of *King Lear's* first scene can be read as tuning the audience's receptive power by successively relaxing and bracing it. Both plots are partly touched on in the relaxed prose conversation between Gloucester and Kent. Then the sennet signals the change of level, and the main part of the scene, which sets the Lear plot in headlong motion, takes place in verse. And the subsequent prose conversation between Goneril and Regan adds nothing; it allows the audience to sit back and feel they were right about these two sisters' duplicity and Lear's folly. Again, in the middle of the play, the prose of II iv 61—87 and of III iii and v seems to slacken the rope momentarily only so that it can be notched all the tighter; the first passage, which punctuates a scene built on a whole succession of dramatic moments and culminating with Lear's departure into the storm, is a wry choric interlude between the Fool, Kent and a Gentleman; III iii and v punctuate the great storm scenes and the mock-trial scene with the shady double-dealing of Edmund. And again, it is particularly noticeable that in Acts IV and V, where the audience is likely to be so absorbed in the movement towards the climax that any prolonged change of tension would be inappropriate, there are only four instances of prose, three of which create brief special contrasts, so that the fourth, Lear's reason in madness during the scene with the blind Gloucester (IV iv), is all the more prominent; and this again makes for special effect — for even greater pathos.

But explanations which focus exclusively on the likely audience reaction, an extrinsic factor, become too reductive. Shakespeare, of all dramatists, never forgets the audience. But he would not be the mature

Shakespeare if his style shifts had no inner logic, dictated by factors intrinsic to characterization and action. Extrinsic and intrinsic factors must be weighed together. After all, if it were not for what the style shifts connoted intrinsically, they would have no effect on the audience in the first place.[7]

Thus the prose section of I iv, where Lear hires the disguised Kent, is insulted by Oswald, and listens to the Fool and the Knights commenting on his situation, certainly does contrast in tone with the preceding verse episodes, in which Goneril tells Oswald to slacken his services to Lear, and Kent soliloquizes on how he will redouble his; but the point is also that, whereas Goneril means to play her game seriously and Kent realizes that Lear's situation may be dangerous, Lear himself *wants* to keep the tone low. He wants to enjoy his crawl towards death — his hunting, his dinner, his jester. He wants to ignore the insubordination of menials or, when he has to see it, he is reluctant to attribute it to any abatement of kindness in his daugher. On Goneril's entry, he chides her fairly gently in prose. But she, not only out of immediate distaste for the Fool's prose-and-sing-song interruption, launches into indictments and threats in verse. She has meant business all along, and now she forces Lear to take her full measure, and to speak verse. This is as dramatic as Cordelia's break with Lear's verse rhythm in I i.

These are actually the first two of several instances in which Shakespeare so exploits the prose-verse contrast in dialogue. There are several more in Lear's subsequent passages with the Fool, and here again criticism has fastened on the likely audience reaction. For example, because we laugh at the Fool's prose jests we do not laugh at the bathos of Lear striving "in his little world of man to out-storm/The to-and-fro-conflicting wind and rain" in verse. Yet the Fool is not only the audience's safety-valve. He is a real character of flesh and blood. He pines away at Cordelia's departure. He cannot hide his bitterness at Lear's folly. On the contrary, he goads Lear himself into seeing it. He has enough worldly wisdom to foretell the result of remaining loyal to Lear. But loyal he remains. He alone stays with Lear at the very height of the storm, and he tries to "out-jest/His heart-strook injuries". True, by a paradoxically human touch, he finally succeeds, not by his jests, but by his silent presence as an object for Lear's pity. But for all that, the jests were his attempt to help, to lower the tone where Goneril and Regan had insisted on raising it. They may be a ploy in Shakespeare's relations with the audience. They are a ploy in the Fool's with Lear too.

Morover, as with the cumulative-balanced/exclamatory-imperative style shifts, the prose/verse alternation expresses, not only such contrasts between characters, but also ambiguities in a single character; and as these ambiguities are developed or resolved by the unfolding action, the prose/verse alternation helps to structure what is happening. Very broadly speaking, a character is likely to be more himself when he speaks verse. When he speaks prose, his nature can be in one way or another obscured. And if we now study the main characters it will become clear that a vital aspect of the unfolding action is the development and removal of such obscurities. The terminal movement towards verse, significantly interrupted only by Lear's reason in madness, and noted earlier as a possible concession to the mood of the audience, is of the play's very essence. Style change springs from within.

Edmund's self-revelatory opening soliloquy is in verse. He changes to prose when he dupes his father and brother, and returns to verse soliloquy at the end of the scene. It is, in a sense, during the apparently framing soliloquies that the action of the sub-plot is actually instigated. It is almost as if the central prose section were the creation of Edmund's own mind. He hides his true nature, and Gloucester, with his convoluted meanderings, and Edgar, with his blank astonishment, are his puppets —

> *Edmund* . . . Edgar —
> > *Enter Edgar*
> — and pat he comes . . .

The incongruity between the determination and scope of evil expressed in his verse and the mundaneness of the prose section testifies to the ease of his deception — it is reminiscent of the alternation between Iago's prose conversation with Roderigo and his verse soliloquy.[8] There is a similar case at the beginning of II i, where Edmund, apparently in all innocence, asks Curan for the latest news in prose and then soliloquizes on how it suits his schemes in verse. Verse is also spoken during his subsequent staging of the mock-fight with Edgar and his lying about it to Gloucester and Cornwall. But this, precisely, is the enactment of his hidden designs, and there is an analogous pattern in Act III. In III iii and v he works his deception in prose conversations with Gloucester and Cornwall; but his soliloquizing comment on his progress (iii 24—27) is in verse, and, although he himself is not actually present, the realization of his plan for Gloucester's disinstatement takes place in verse (III vi). Henceforth, in soliloquy (V 55—68) and dialogue alike, Edmund speaks only verse. Most of his goals attained, he is fully fledged. Goneril and Regan may fight over him as they will. In giving the order for Lear's and Cordelia's death, he takes the law into his own hands. He will be dependent on none.

Gloucester's nature, unfortunately for him, is flawed, and this is intimated in some small degree by the distribution of prose and verse. In I i 1—33, I ii 23—123 and III iii he is, respectively, unduly pleased with the sexual infidelities of his youth, feebly superstitious and credulously blind to Edgar's love, and unduly intimidated and somewhat ignoble in his attempt to help Lear.[9] At these low points he speaks prose. Lear does bring out something better in him. He always addresses Lear in verse. He speaks publicly on Lear's behalf in verse. And he speaks verse when he directly witnesses, pities and helps Lear in his sufferings. But he can still relapse, and speak prose. It is only when, somewhat later than Lear, he himself really begins to suffer, not in deluded anger, and not so much from his physical torments as from remorse of conscience, that he achieves true stature. Despite everything that is grotesque in his fate, and despite his wavering towards suicide, he is henceforth never less than dignified, though piteous. His sheer weight of knowledge, both of himself and others, makes him an awe-inspiring figure. And henceforth he speaks only verse.

Kent's soliloquy (I iv 1—7) revealing that he has returned to help Lear in secret is, as we should now expect, in verse. But in order to make his disguise complete he must "other accents borrow", and during the section where he is hired by Lear and rebuffs Oswald he accordingly speaks a racy prose. The style change here is a dramatic prop no less explicit than the change of clothes. The two are actually coefficient. On his second skirmish with Oswald (II ii), Kent sustains his prose. This fight-that-is-not-a-fight is a stage parody of the apparently much more serious non-fight between Edmund and Edgar in the previous scene, and Kent's boisterously abusive prose, although in substance not at all departing from some of the play's great themes, and although he means every word he says, enforces the farce. But gradually the true seriousness of the situation, and Kent's native dignity assert themselves. When he describes Oswald to Cornwall he reverts to his true verse idiolect (ll.73—81). He deviates from it twice, once ironically, for a verse panegyric to the astonished Cornwall when Cornwall objects to his bluntness, and then for a final fling of prose — the style changes are as obvious as a change of hat. But after this he speaks verse, not only in soliloquy, but also in commenting on or addressing Lear, and even in trying to help Lear behind his back — the equivalent of some of the passages in which Gloucester speaks prose. Kent's is a nobility that will out, and it is all the more poignant that, as he feels his grief for Lear's suffering bringing on the hour of his own death, he cannot make Lear, also on the point of death, see that Kent and his servant Caius were one and the same man. The disguise, initiated partly by prose, had worked all too well.

The persecuted Edgar also speaks a verse soliloquy (II iii) announcing a planned disguise. It is specific both as to dress — or rather lack of it — and speech: "roaring voice", "lunatic bans", "prayers". He sustains his linguistic disguise, prose interspersed with jingles, during the second storm scene, where he makes it as opaque as possible, and has no asides, in the presence of the father still thirsting for his blood, and also during the mock-trial scene. Yet during the latter he has a blank verse aside to the effect that his pity for Lear will mar his counterfeiting, and, left on his own at the end, he soliloquizes on Lear's sufferings in heroic couplets — a typical example of the cumulative-balanced style. He has other important choric asides in verse later on. When we next see him (IV i) he resumes his soliloquy in a stoical spirit, this time in unrhymed verse, only to be further cast down by the spectacle of his blinded father. While Gloucester and his old servant stand on one side of the stage, Edgar comments in blank verse asides on the other. Gloucester is then presented to what he takes to be the Tom o' Bedlam, and Edgar's reluctance to resume his counterfeiting is poignantly expressed in these lines:

> *Glou.* As flies to wanton boys are we to th' Gods;
>   They kill us for their sport.
> *Edg.* [*Aside*]   How should this be?
>   Bad is the trade that must play the fool to sorrow,
>   Ang'ring itself and others. [*Aloud*] Bless thee master!
>   . . .
> *Edg.* Poor Tom's a-cold. [*Aside*] I cannot daub it further.
>   . . .
> *Edg.* [*Aside*] And yet I must. Bless thy sweet eyes, they bleed.

Here he speaks some words aloud in the role of Tom, but emotionally he cannot break back into that style, as witness the inclusion of Tom's words in Edgar's private blank verse metre. "Bless thy sweet eyes, they bleed" actually seems to be spoken in both roles. Thus when he manages it, the return to prose is very marked. However, the next time we see him and Gloucester, he has received new clothes and is speaking blank verse. Gloucester still does not know who he is, but the time for disguises will soon be over. Gloucester's mind is becoming ripe for it, and Edgar is emerging in his true nature. Again, Shakespeare makes deliberate play on the style change. Gloucester thinks that Edgar's voice has changed and his phrase and matter much improved. Edgar says that he is only changed in his garments, but his speech on the imaginary cliff is enough to disprove that; clothes and style again work together. And when Gloucester thinks he has fallen over the cliff, Edgar, now assuming the role of a man walking along the imaginary beach, distances the phase of prose still further by his epitaph on Tom as a devil Gloucester is well rid of. After this, his only brief prose passage is that in regional dialect by which he disguises himself from Oswald. In all but name he is now, more than ever, Gloucester's true son.

Finally, there is Lear himself. After Goneril has forced him into blank verse in I iv, he has a short scene (I v) in which he speaks some prose and manages to join in the Fool's jesting. Yet at the end of it he suddenly breaks into two ominous lines of verse:

> O! let me not be mad, not mad, sweet heaven;
> Keep me in temper; I would not be mad

And throughout his mounting anger in II iv, his imprecations in the storm in III ii and his milder sentiments in III iv, he still speaks verse. He is still in control of himself, conscious that his fury may lead to madness, partly indulging it, but also at several points trying to rein it in. Then his pity for the Fool calms him and universalizes itself as pity for suffering humanity, of which he is now suddenly confronted with an even more startling instance, in Edgar disguised as Tom. Tom is the thing itself, naked, and speaking a prose which expatiates on the unspeakable in man. And it is this that finally unsettles Lear's mind, in a process of three-fold identification with Tom. First he declares, still in verse, that Tom must also be the father of "unkind daughters". Secondly, Edgar shows us things as they really are, so that we must tear off the trappings which conceal us. Thirdly, there are trappings woollen and trappings stylistic, for the speech which preludes his furious disrobing is partly reminiscent of Tom's in rhythm and imagery,[10] and is in prose. In a way, Lear has actually de-natured himself. This is his fullest rejection of royalty. By the end of the scene, however, and during the mock-trial scene, he achieves a crazed dignity and his verse re-establishes itself, his hallucinations gaining a piteous intensity. But then his grasp slackens as his paranoia and physical tiredness increase. He speaks prose. He sleeps. When we see him again, in the scene with the blinded Gloucester, he fluctuates between verse and prose. His verse is frequently reminiscent of prose, his prose of verse, and editors have devoted great ingenuity to relineating passages one way or the other. The uncertainty is precisely the point — just as he speaks "reason in madness", just as he is "every inch a king", dignified and profound, and a madman "fantastically dressed with wild flowers". Again, style, dress and psychological stance are univocal. And when deep sleep, music, and the restoration on Cordelia's lips bring him to himself, he awakes, dressed in his new garments, to speak verse.

IV

I have concerned myself with style shifts as an expressive device from a frankly literary point of view. It seemed possible to establish the first type of shift with a minimum of linguistic and rhetorical description, and the second needed none at all. But if, as I have tried to show, the stylistically obvious does not correlate with the dramatically facile, if, on the contrary, it is subtly integrated with characterization and action, that is perhaps the strongest proof of Shakespeare's opportunistic genius. He sees the possibilities in dramatic speech as unfiltered language, and he maximizes them. What would now be interesting is a full account of style shift and style-shift context in all his work,[11] together with comparative studies of other dramatists — interesting, though its main finding is perhaps predictable: a development in Shakespeare towards a mastery which no other dramatist has equalled.

NOTES

[1] The text used is Kenneth Muir's Arden edition, special school edition, London, 1961.

[2] In the punctuation conventions of Jacobean printers, ? and ! are sometimes interchangeable. I have quoted only some of the obvious exclamations.

Some expressions, such as "Who stirs?" here, could be either exclamatory or interrogatory, or, indeed, both.

[3] Contrast, at any rate, the "Thou think'st 'tis much" passage, which is discussed in the next paragraph.

[4] Loop = 1) *mod. E.* loop, 2) an opening in a wall to allow for the passage of a missile for defence purposes — cf. "How shall ... /they/ defend you ...?" (See *NED* loop *sb.*[2] 1.) Window = 1) window, 2) wind-eye. The holes are useless for defence but excellent for admitting the attacking winds.

[5] Perhaps the best treatments of Shakespeare's prose are Elizabeth Tshopp, *Zur Verteilung von Vers und Prosa in Shakespeares Dramen* (Bern, 1956), and Brian Vickers, *The Artistry of Shakespeare's Prose* (London, 1968). Vickers is especially relevant to my argument, since he describes the development of imagery, linguistic play and rhetorical structuring through the prose of all Shakespeare's plays. This means that he, on a very large scale, does for the prose what I, very limitedly in section II above, have attempted for the verse: he points out subtle and dramatic contrasts and similarities of style within it. His description of the prose of *King Lear* (pp. 352—371) is characteristically excellent. However, on the broader contrast between verse and prose, Vickers (pp. 16—18 and 351—352 on this contrast in Shakespeare as a whole and in *King Lear* respectively) is perhaps rather summary. At all events, I hope that a few points about its integration into *King Lear* can still be developed, and they will perhaps gain prominence by being treated in isolation from the descriptively more detailed question of style variation within the prose only.

[6] See Vickers pp. 5—6.

[7] For this reason, it would be preferable to speak of style shifts, not as "marking", "indicating", "signalling", "having an effect", but as expressing", "embodying", "representing". If the second set of terms is applicable at any point, then the functions indicated by the first set have in any case been fulfilled. An all-embracing term would of course be "communicates". — However, habitual ways of speech are sometimes likely to militate against theoretical considerations. Vickers, though commendably stressing homogeneity of style, character and action, sometimes falls victim to habit, and I have probably done so myself.

[8] *Othello* I iii at the end.

[9] Gloucester does help Lear. But compared with Kent's constant resoluteness and bold defiance his efforts have an air of scheming. Moreover, earlier (II i) he was servile towards Cornwall, protesting only feebly. It incensed Lear that Gloucester was so cringeing (II iv 95—104).

[10] Cf. Tom's "hog in sloth, fox in stealth, wolf in greediness, dog in madness, lion in prey" and Lear's "Thou ow'st the worm no silk, the beast no hide, the sheep no wool, the cat no perfume".

[11] As noted, Vickers admirably does much of the basic work as far as the prose is concerned.

III. STYLE AND LINGUISTIC ANALYSIS

Eduard Beneš
Prague

Elliptical sentences in German technical and scientific style

1. The term 'ellipsis' is employed in different meanings. In the widest sense of the word it denotes omission of any part of the sentence. The parts that can be omitted are, for instance, components occurring in two (or more) clauses or sentence parts (shared sentence parts in compound and complex sentences, an attribute common to several nouns or a noun common to several attributes), or expressions normally required by the valence of the governing member, or even some morphological devices (the article, auxiliaries, pronominal subject).[1]

1.1 The term 'elliptical sentence' is also conceived differently; this is connected with the different conceptions of the sentence in general. The problem of the definition of the sentence is not solved by the fact that generative grammar defines the sentence recursively. For by his generative rules the linguist defines a set of such 'well-formed' sentences as he has a priori (intuitively) included in the concept of the sentence. It is thus, as has been pointed out by Heringer (1970, 105), a circular definition, as are also the attempts at defining the sentence in different languages according to their grammatical structure. For example, such grammatical definitions state that the German sentence (or the Indo-European sentence in general) has two parts and hence exclude a priori one-member sentences from the concept of the sentence.

1.1.1 Heringer (1970, 107), after a critical survey of different definitions of the sentence, returns to Jespersen's (1924, 307): "A sentence is a (relatively) complete and independent human utterance — the completeness and independence being shown by its standing alone or its capability of standing alone, i. e. of being uttered by itself". A similar definition of the sentence has been given by Bloomfield ("an independent form", 1933, 170).

1.1.2 This communicative conception of the sentence allows conceiving the sentence not only as the highest unit of the syntactic organization of words, but also as the basic unit of the text (and communication). This conception thus implies that expressions like *au!, ja!, schön!, Treffer!, noch ein Bier!* can be evaluated as sentences, although they represent a special type. An explicit distinction between two types of sentences had already been made by Brugmann (cf. his "Vollsatz und

Kurzsatz", 1925, 200) and later by Bloomfield, who distinguished between "full and minor sentences" (1933, 171).[2]

1.1.3 A major contribution to the study of minor sentences in German has been made by Sandig (1971). In her work "Syntaktische Typologie der Schlagzeile" she distinguishes (a) verbless minor sentences ('verblose Kurzsätze, verkürzte Verbalsätze'): *De Gaulle nach Moskau;* (b) nominal sentences ('Nominalsätze') with a noun as the syntactic nucleus: *Unruhen in Schanghai;* (c) fragments, "bei denen der Mangel auf der Ausdrucksseite nicht durch Implikation ausgeglichen ist" (p. 51): *Der CSU beigetreten.* She distinguishes newspaper headlines with sentence value ('Satzwert') (displaying, besides other characteristics, the feature [+ neu]) from titles ('Themaüberschriften') without sentence value (with the feature [— neu]), e. g. *Aus dem Studentenparlament* (p. 109).

1.2 In the present article I follow up the ideas expressed in Sandig's study, but unlike Sandig I conceive of the sentence as including signs, notices and titles. In my opinion signs like *Eingang* or titles like *Aus dem Studentenparlament* have sentence value, since they imply: /Hier ist/ Eingang. /Hier wird/ aus dem Studentenparlament /berichtet/. They represent, of course, a borderline case. However, a non-sentence conception of signs, notices and titles is also held by some Czech linguists who regard them as denominations.[3]

In the present study the elliptical sentence will include:

A) one-member sentences which may be realized by: (a) interjections *(Ach!);* (b) vocatives or nominatives of address *(Meine Damen und Herren!),* (c) adverbs *(Nein),* (d) adjectives *(Phantastisch!);* (e) a noun in a case other than the vocative *(Endstation!);* (f) infinitive *(Aussteigen!);* (g) participle *(Aufgepasst!);*

B) two-member verbless sentences *(Eingang links).*

1.3 The term 'elliptical sentences' is somewhat unsuitable but persists for lack of a better one. It presupposes ellipsis, i. e. omission ('Auslassung'), although in many cases the point in question is economy ('Ersparung'), since, as a result of an implication on the level of content, economy occurs only on the level of expression (Sandig 1971, 23). It cannot be proved that 'elliptical sentences' are really due to omission of certain parts; in many types, this assumption is even improbable. Though it is theoretically possible to regard 'elliptical sentences' as "capable of expansion to a longer underlying form" (Gunter 1963, 137) this transformation involves various difficulties.

1.3.1 Essentially we have to do with the long-discussed problem of whether it is possible and useful to treat apparently incomplete sentences against the background of 'ideally' complete sentences.[4] For generative grammar this question has again become topical, whereas the

Neogrammarians were reluctant even to recognize ellipsis, owing to their positivistic approach to facts. 'Ellipsis' in their conception was a manifestation of language activity fully justified and hence accounted for psychologically.[5]

1.4 This is connected with the question of whether ellipses can be divided into contextual and situational. It may be objected that the influence of the context and of the situation cannot often be distinguished, that they overlap. Nevertheless in many cases a decisive influence is obviously exercised by the context (e. g. in answers in a dialogue[6]), while in others by the situation (e. g. in telegrams[7]).

1.5 Attention should also be paid to the question of whether the sentence is a unit of langue or parole. The opinion of Gardiner (1932, 88) that "The sentence is the unit of speech and the word is the unit of language" has been opposed by a number of linguists,[8] who made a distinction between the sentence as a type and the sentence as a token. More recently, Daneš (1964, 229) has postulated the triad: the utterance-event, utterance and the sentence pattern. Another triple division has been proposed by Heringer (1970, 110): 'Satzäusserung' or 'Satzverwendung (der parole)' — 'Satz (der langue)' — 'Satzform (Abstraktion aus Sätzen)'. Here we shall be concerned with elliptical 'Satzverwendung', but we shall inquire whether it is incidental or whether it realizes an elliptical 'Satzform'.

1.5.1 Early observations that elliptical sentences are characteristic of the first stage of child language have been confirmed by Stampe (1969), who points out that children apply the rules of ellipsis to the largest extent, restricting their uses in later stages only under the influence of adult speech. Then the rules of ellipsis would be an innate principle of the omission of what is semantically obvious. Learning would have to take place only in regard to the restrictions operating in the application of this principle in different languages (Dressler 1972, 34).

2. However, the degree and manner of the employment of elliptical sentences apparently also depends on the style. Professor Enkvist (1964, 28) has given the following definition of style: "The style of a text is the aggregate of the contextual probabilities of its linguistic items". In stylistic research it is important to study "style markers as those linguistic items that only appear, or are most or least frequent in, one group of contexts" (p. 34).

2.1 I propose that the occurrence of elliptical sentences is a style marker that distinguishes different styles. Here I draw on the theory of functional styles developed by the Prague School.[9] In its approach to the questions of style the Prague School has anticipated many questions of style that are now being elaborated by different theories: the British linguistic theory of registers, the attempts of sociolinguistics and pragmatic linguistics at analysing the factors affecting linguistic utterances, and the endeavours of text linguistics to distinguish the 'Textsorten' (sorts of text), i. e. text typology.[10] Particularly noteworthy is the critical reception and further fruitful development of the ideas of the Prague School by Sandig (1970) and Barth (1971). Barth (1971, 212) defines functional style "als einen funktionalen Typ des Sprachgebrauchs, der durch soziale Regeln sprachlichen Verhaltens konstituiert wird".

2.2 The Prague School distinguishes essentially three functional styles: colloquial, technical and literary. Now ellipses obviously occur on a large scale in the spoken colloquial style, above all in dialogue, but also in monologic utterances. In spite of their frequent occurrence they have so far received little attention.[11] In literary style elliptical sentences also appear frequently as a stylized reflection of colloquial speech in dialogue (in novels and plays). However, they can also be a specific device which in different literary genres (e. g. in lyrics) different literary trends and authors put to diverse uses. For instance, the use of nominal sentences was typical of impressionism.[12]

3. Technical style as conceived by the Prague School is further subdivided into practical working style and theoretical or scientific style. However, even in these spheres it undergoes further manifold differentiation. The question of further subclassification of technical style (i. e. its text typology) is still quite open. We can classify the different 'Textsorten' of technical style according to various text-external criteria and examine their text-internal structure. Here we shall inquire how elliptical sentences operate in technical style as a potential 'style marker'.

3.1 I shall leave aside the newspaper style, which owing to its specific properties is often regarded as an independent functional style.[13] In some of its forms elliptical sentences play a major role (even quantitatively), e. g. in headlines (Beugel 1969, Sandig 1971), advertising or tabloid press. Römer (1968, 168) has counted 36.1 % of elliptical sentences in advertisements with longer text, the percentage in advertisements with little text being as high as 55.3. In BILD-Zeitung Mittelberg (1967, 184) has found 13.6 % of elliptical sentences ('Setzungen').

3.2 In technical and scientific style proper, elliptical sentences are used relatively seldom. According to Eggers (1961, 54) the so-called 'Setzungen' account for only 2.5 % of all sentences in his corpus of popular scientific writing in German. However, this overall finding calls for supplementation and correction. In certain strictly definable cases (or 'Textsorten') elliptical sentences occur quite regularly and with a high density. These instances include:

1) Explanations written in an abbreviated dictionary style:

> /1/ *Böhmen (tschechisch Čechy), nördl. und westl. Teil der ČSSR,*
> *... 52 062 km², rd. 6 Mill. E., ... Vorwiegend paläozoische*

> *Rumpfscholle,... Stark entwickelte Landwirtschaft (Getreide, ...Hopfen, Zuckerrübe), Wald; Erzbergbau...*

> /2/ *Novalis, eigtl. Friedrich Leopold Freiherr von Hardenberg, * Oberwiederstedt bei Mansfeld 2. Mai 1772, † Weissenfels 25. März 1801, dt. Dichter; aus altem Adelsgeschlecht, im Elternhaus Herrnhuter Glaube; Studium in Jena,...; befreundet mit Schiller,...; nach tiefer Erschütterung durch den Tod der Braut (Sophie von Kühn), Wendung zur Mystik, Entdeckung J. Böhmes.*

2) Descriptions in certain text forms written according to an established pattern, e. g.:

a) in medicine, anamnesis, diagnosis, results of medical examinations:

> /3/ *Komplikationen: Rhinitis, Pharyngitis, selten Laryngitis, Lungenkongestionen und Bronchopneumonie. Ab und zu gesteigerter intrakranieller Druck mit bombierter grosser Fontanelle. Lumbalpunktion nicht sehr günstig. Exitus in 6 Fällen.*

b) in the natural sciences, descriptions of organisms, chemical substances, crystalline systems, and the like:

> /4/ *Rhombisches System (3 Kristallklassen)*
> *3 aufeinander senkrecht stehende, ungleich lange Achsen.*

c) in meteorological reports and weather forecasts:[14]

> /5/ *Vorhersage für Mittwoch und Donnerstag*
> *Rhein-Main-Gebiet*
> *Aufgelockerte Bewölkung, zum Teil sonnig. Höchsttemperaturen 20 bis 24 Grad, nachts Rückgang auf 17 Grad.*

Descriptions in tabular form will be described in Section 5.

3) Records and minutes, brief statements in reports. Here also belong entries in diaries, log-books and memoirs which represent a borderline case between practical working, colloquial and literary style:

> /6/ *Haupteindrücke des Luxembourg. ... Manet, von Velasquez und Goya kommend, allmählich in die Gegenwart übergehend. Monet, ungleich, weil Dränger, dafür vielseitig, Sisley verfeinert!*
>
> (Klee 191)

4) Brief drafts, theses, syllabuses and surveys:

> /7/ *Zahlentafel*
> *1536 Erasmus von Rotterdam gestorben*

> /8/ *Die Anschauung von der Gestalt der Erde hat folgende Stadien durchlaufen:*

1) Die Erde eine Scheibe; primitive Vorstellung, erwachsen aus dem Augenschein, da ...

2) Die Erde eine Kugel.

3) Die Erde ein Sphäroid (an den Polen abgeplattete Kugel), seit dem Ende des 17. Jahrhunderts.

5) Instructions, directions for use, medical prescriptions, cooking recipes,[15] etc., e. g.:

/9/ *Erste Hilfe bei Unfällen*
Wunden. Eventuelle Blutung stillen (siehe oben); Verschmutzung vermeiden, ...; steriler Verband (Mull).

6) Brief communications and announcements; a special type of this group is the telegram[16]; e. g.:

/10/ *Über Verkehrsstörungen liegt uns folgende Meldung vor: Bayern. Auf der Autobahn München-Salzburg in Richtung Salzburg zwischen ... und ... 2 Kilometer Stau. Keine Ausweichempfehlung.*

7) Slogans,[17] e. g.:
/11/ *Kampf dem Verderb!*

8) Titles, section headings, marginalia, captions to illustrations and diagrams, e. g.:

/12/ *Abb. 1: Schema des Technologie-Transfers.*

This enumeration is far from complete; it might be extended and supplemented by the different 'Textsorten' of commercial style, military style, etc. However, it is sufficient to give an idea of the wide possibilities of the employment of elliptical sentences in technical style.

4. Let us further examine which types of elliptical sentences technical style displays.

4.1 In instances given in 3.2 there is an overwhelming preponderance of one-member nominal sentences. The most common case is provided by nominative sentences, mostly in declarative function. The nucleus is a noun:

a) with no attribute: *Komplikationen* /3/;

b) with adjectival attribute: *aufgelockerte Bewölkung* /5/;

c) with substantival attribute: *Wendung zur Mystik* /2/;

d) with substantival and adjectival attributes: *erste Hilfe bei Unfällen* /9/;

180

e) with adjectival or participial postmodification: *primitive Vorstellung, erwachsen aus dem Augenschein* /8/;

f) with apposition: *Ein kleines Erlebnis als Beispiel* (Becker 152);

g) coordinate conjunction of nouns: *Rhinitis, Pharyngitis,...* /3/.

Some of these nominative sentences have introductory function, whether operating as headings or introducing, after a colon, one-member sentences (frequently in the form of enumeration /3/) or even two-member sentences.

4.2 Nominative one-member sentences pass gradually into two-member incomplete, verbless sentences. Nominative sentences, even denominative, may be considered to involve a latent predicative relation. If two nominatives are found in close vicinity, separated only by a punctuation mark (full stop, comma, colon, dash or brackets), they can be interpreted in two ways: the second nominative may be regarded as an independent apposition to the preceding nominative (conceivable as the predicate) or as the predicate noun of the preceding subjective nominative: *Lewandowsky, der tänzelnde Cellist* (Klee 227).

The predicative relation is obvious in the case of a verbless minor sentence.[18] Technical style displays types similar to those found by Sandig (1971) in headlines. I also avail myself here of Heringer's (1970) notation:

A) Ellipsis of the predicate:

1) Ellipsis of the auxiliary, E_1 /Vf/ //A// Partizip 2/ Adj2, e. g.:
   Erasmus von Rotterdam gestorben /7/.

2) Ellipsis of a bivalent verb governing an accusative, E_1 /P_{22}/ E_2, e. g.:
   Inspektion: Sehr wenig ausgeprägte Befunde (sc. *ergibt*).

3) Ellipsis of the verb in the so-called Gleichsetzungssätze, E_1 /P_{26}/ E_6, e. g.:
   Die Erde eine Scheibe /8/.

4) Ellipsis of a bivalent verb governing a prepositional case, E_1 /P_{25}/ E_5, e. g.:
   ..., wir im Wagen unter rotblühenden Kastanien hindurch zum Bahnhof (Klee 193).

B) Ellipsis of the predicate and the subject (E_1):

1) /E_1/ /Vf/ A Partizip 2 /Adj2, e. g.:
   ..., zum Teil sonnig /5/.

2) /E_1/ /Vf/ E_2/E_3/E_5 Partizip 2, e. g.:
   Sofort ans Werk gegangen und im Araberviertel Aquarell gemalt (Klee 297).

3) /E₁/ /P₂₅/ A E₅ //A//, e. g.:
Dann zurück ins Städtchen (Klee 301).

4.3 Besides these types of elliptical sentences we also often find — mostly in instructions and directions — imperative one-member sentences in the form of the nominative (*Vorsicht!, Achtung!*) or infinitive (cf. /9/) or verbless minor sentences:

/13/ ...; *beim Nachlassen der Erstarrung vorsichtige Massage.*

5. The character of elliptical sentences in tables is not so clear. We can trace a gradual transition from complete linguistic expression to abbreviated formulation in tabular form:

/14/ *Der Kältetod bei Pflanzen*

Es erfrieren:	bei
Gurke	+ 2—3°
Bohne	+ 1.5°

/15/ *Pilzzüchtende Insekten*

Insektengruppe:	Art der Pilzzucht:
Zweiflügler: viele Gallenmücken	Pilzsporen durch Larven in die Gallen eingeschleppt; ...

/16/ *Vargänge bei der Abenddämmerung*

Sonnenhöhe:	Am Westhimmel:	Am Osthimmel:
+ 5°	Gelber Abendschein	Letzte direkte Bestrahlung
— 7 bis — 8°	Auftauchen des 2. Purpurlichtes	Schwächeres Nachglühen

/17/ *Lurche*

Art:	Körperlänge:	Lebensraum:	Fortpflanzung:
Feuer-salamander	bis 20 cm	feuchte Bergwälder	lebendgebärend

5.1 A comparison of examples /14/—/17/ shows how the finite verb gradually recedes into the background, being replaced by nonfinite verbal forms or actional nouns or adjectives. It is precisely the use of tabular form that permits the verb — as a merely formal and linguistic connective — to be largely omitted, since the reader supplies it himself; moreover, in most cases, the verb is unnecessary for the comprehension of the table. Tables can be "read" in different ways, e. g.:

Der Lebensraum des Feuersalamanders sind feuchte Bergwälder.
Der Feuersalamander hat als Lebensraum feuchte Bergwälder.

The data in tables refer to two headings, one of which applies to columns and the other to rows. In the horizontal reading of the row in example /17/ the expression *Feuersalamander* is always the theme; something new is said about it with respect to *Körperlänge, Lebensraum, Fortpflanzung.* In the vertical reading of the column headed *Lebensraum*, this expression is the theme, which is further specified by the denotation of the particular zoological species in each row. Tabular (cross) arrangement of data allows combining them quickly and readily in different ways, whereas in the case of full linguistic expression we would invariably be limited to one particular combination. The 'sentences' made up from data given in tables have a character typical of scientific style: x in relation to y = z.[19]

5.2 Actually, however, verbalization of these 'sentences' does not take place at all. In the tables the reader finds data largely in the form of elliptical sentences; the connection of the data, however, is implemented as an act of thought, not of language. This clearly shows that the graphic form of language essentially differs from the acoustic form: the difference consists not only in the fact that the graphic form lacks certain devices appropriate to the acoustic form but also in the existence of certain specific graphic means that are lacking in speech.[20]

In technical style, these possibilities are made full use of, cf. the different types of print (italics, interspaced or boldface print, brevier, capital letters), certain types of punctuation marks used with a specific function, in particular brackets, dashes, the colon or even an exclamation mark or question mark in brackets (as mentioned in several places here), or abbreviations and special graphic signs *, †, §, % and the like. As for tabular arrangement, it is also typical of technical style; as we have seen, it compensates for the monodimensional character of speech and endows the communication with two dimensions, viz. the possibility of simultaneous cross-connection of facts. It breaks the principle of text construction derived from timeboundedness, which necessarily governs any spoken utterance, and gives rise to a new principle of text construction, which takes advantage of the visual projection of the text on a surface and of the possibility of its optical perception. The possibilities of print are also widely and specifically utilized in newspapers, which is in turn important for the use of elliptical sentences (cf. headlines, advertisements).

On the other hand, it should be pointed out that in some cases graphic form is not a necessary condition for the occurrence of elliptical sentences in technical style. Some of the above instances (3.2) of elliptical sentences are just as feasible in speech as in writing. A weather fore-cast /5/ has the same form whether printed or broadcast on the radio, and the traffic report /10/ is usually also given out in the acoustic form.

6. Apart from newspaper writing, elliptical sentences further occur in certain other transitional and peripheral spheres of technical style which have so far received little attention. I have in mind texts aimed at attracting the reader, gaining his personal interest, as is the case of popular scientific style with a specific colouring, or of texts with a pronounced subjective standpoint, which is found in critiques and pole-mics. A sphere bordering on colloquial or even literary style is found in diaries and memoirs; scientific treatises in literary form occur in essays. al colouring can be made use of in a measure otherwise unusual in In all these spheres the element of subjectivity and expressive-emotional colouring can be made use of in a measure otherwise unusual in standard technical writing. Such texts have a special mixed transitional character, but their specific features are recognized only against the background of the impersonal character of technical style. Not infrequently elliptical sentences are employed in such texts for expressive or rhetorical effect.

6.1 We have here to do with different types of elliptical sentences, even with such as do not occur in other sorts of technical style.

Of nominal sentences, there is a predilection for qualifying sentences, which endow the judgement they express with a particular pregnancy and force:

> /18/ ... *Woyzeck* ... (New paragraph:)
> *Die erste soziale Tragödie der deutschen Bühne. Kein soziales Tendenzstück und überhaupt kein Thesenstück. Noch in der aphoristischen Andeutung, ... eine Dichtung von weitestem Wurf.* (Rilla 152)

6.2 Various stylistic effects are achieved by nominal interrogative sen-tences. The question serves as a means of internal dramatization of the text:

> /19/ *Der Ton des Briefes? Es ist der Ton des jugendlichen Revolu-tionärs, ...* (Rilla 143)

How are these questions to be understood? Does the author ask the question of himself or of the reader? This point cannot usually be settled. However, this is hardly necessary, because such questions are fic-titious. They could of course be expressed even by complete statements. Yet in the form of elliptical sentences they have more appeal.

A fictitious question is sometimes intended to evoke in the reader a certain emotive attitude underlying the question, whether uncertainty or perplexity, or astonishment and confusion at a lack of understand-ing, etc.:

> /20/ "... *selig unter dem tödlichen Kuss der Schönheit vergeht,*" ...
> *Der tödliche Kuss der Schönheit? O, keineswegs, dass Herr Spi-nell sich persönlich bemüht hätte.* (Rilla 275)

184

In this manner, it is possible to introduce objections, guesses, etc.:

/21/ *Nur eine Kleinigkeit? Aber nur daran, ...* (Rilla 283)

6.3 In fact, a fictitious question is always one that the author asks' himself, but sometimes it creates the impression that he is doing so on behalf of the reader. ("The reader may ask ...") Since the question gives rise to tension and expectation, this stylistic trick stresses the novelty and unexpectedness of the following reply, especially if it has elliptical form.[21]

In this case technical style displays context-dependent elliptical sentences, which are otherwise typical of colloquial dialogic speech. The answers to the questions are sometimes expressed by sentences containing adverbs of affirmation, negation or others:

/22/ *Genügen diese Bemerkungen? Natürlich nicht.* (Becker 288)

/23/ *Ist nun deswegen die Widerspiegelungstheorie falsch oder unzureichend? Keineswegs.*

24/ *Ob in einer Sprachlehre auch über das Fremdwort zu sprechen ist? Bestimmt, denn ...*

/25/ *Oder sträubt sich da bei Ihnen das Sprachgefühl?*
Schade! (Becker 291)

In other cases the answers contain only the sentence part that is the focus of the preceding question:

/26/ *Wen zeichnet Wedekind? Keinen Repräsentanten, sondern einen Aussenseiter der Gesellschaft, ...* (Rilla 196)

/27/ *Was hält diese bürgerliche Welt zusammen? Der Geschlechtstrieb und der Besitztrieb.* (Rilla 207)

/28/ *Was gehörte alles zur Sprachentstehung schon an physischen Voraussetzungen! Vor allem das Wichtigste: der aufrechte Gang.* (Becker 7—8)

In this manner the writer achieves a more plastic and effective presentation of the utterance (together with a more lively curve of the immanently inherent intonation), as can be demonstrated by the transformation of the question and answer into statement. In example /26/ the contrast is thus emphasized, in /27/ and /28/ the subject is rhematized.

6.4 The texts discussed in Section 6 sometimes also exhibit nominal exclamatory sentences, e. g. *Thalatta!!* (Klee 301), *Aber Byron! Byron!* (Klee 221), *Dann Daumier!!* (Klee 227).

Even a qualifying nominative sentence may be expressed in the form of an exclamation:

/29/ *Ist es recht, ... zu benennen? Dumme Frage! In dieser Sprachschicht ist alles recht, was Spass macht.* (Becker 110)

/30/ *Mochte solche Rechteckigkeit doch zerfallen! Triumph des Verfalls!* (Rilla 346)

6.5 A specific type of one-member exclamatory sentence is provided by inserted warnings with an exclamation mark; these represent accompanying comments by which the author wishes to advise the reader "telegraphically" to pay attention to a particular point ("Mark ..., Note ..., Recall ..."):

/32/ *Männchen sind nur vorübergehend vorhanden (Hochzeitsflug!)*
/33/ *Oft benutzt man ... auch ... offene Profile ... (keine Rohre, dann Unfallgefahr!)*

6.6 In texts written in scientific style with a rhetorical perspective we can even find interjections and vocatives, weakened into sentence parts; these instances, however, are rare; cf. e. g. /20/ or:

/34/ *Ach, wenn wir keine weiteren Sorgen hätten!* (Becker 91)

6.7 Expressive colouring can accompany not only one-member sentences but also verbless minor sentences, e. g.:

/35/ *Otto Eisfeldt 70 Jahre!*
/36/ *Ein ganzer Pariser, dieser Sonderegger.*   (Klee 227)

7. Elliptical sentences often occur in parentheses (cf. examples /1/, /9/, /32/, /33/); in technical style they are especially common. Closely connected with elliptical sentences are 'Herausstellung' (prolepsis, often the so-called nominativus pendens) and 'Nachtrag'. Isolated, independent sentence parts can easily become separate elliptical sentences, cf. e. g /19/ or:

/37/ *Lessing; Herder; Goethe: das ist die klarste Kampfansage; die tiefste geschichtlich-philosophische Begründung; die vollkommenste sinnliche Realisierung des Vorgangs.*   (Rilla 43)

/38/ *..., weil er (sc. Lessing) es war, der die Parolen ausgegeben hat. Die Parolen des Kampfes, die Parolen des Gedankens, die Parolen der poetischen Praxis.*   (Rilla 43)

Ellipsis is sometimes confused with aposiopesis, which is a forced, inorganic interruption of a sentence at any point of its linear progress; in technical style, this stylistic device is uncommon.

8. Observation of the employment of elliptical sentences in technical style leads to the following conclusions.

8.1 Technical style is richly differentiated. It is necessary to distinguish its centre and the peripheral areas. In the centre of technical style, which is characterized by a relatively stable neutral standard, typical of technical style as a whole, the occurrence of elliptical sentences is restricted to certain strictly definable cases in which, however, they are the norm. In the peripheral spheres of technical style, we find even other types of elliptical sentences, which are normally characteristic of colloquial or literary style, because these spheres represent transition belts or shifts to other styles.

8.2. Within one relatively homogeneous style the same device, in our case the elliptical sentence, can be put to very diverse uses. It is thus not sufficient to study the degree of occurrence of a certain stylistic means; it is necessary to investigate the manner of its integration in the whole, its function, invariably with respect to the stylistic norm valid in the particular 'Textsorte'. Professor Enkvist (1964, 39) has justly emphasized that "The same linguistic element may appear as a style marker when matched against one norm, and as stylistically neutral when compared with another."

NOTES

[1] Cf. Duden 1973, 585—590; Erben 1972, 248—9, 309—313.

[2] See the discussion of this question with references to literature in Heringer 1970, 111.

[3] This is the opinion held e. g. by Hausenblas 1958; an opposite view, however, was expressed by Šmilauer 1947, Kopečný 1958, Mrázek 1962.

[4] Cf. Delbrück 1900, 112—117, who criticizes the opinions of ellipsis held by 16th and 17th century grammarians.

[5] Cf. Paul 1886, 263.

[6] Cf. Isačenko 1965.

[7] Cf. Gunter 1963, who distinguishes contextual and telegraphic, i. e. situational, ellipses.

[8] See the discussion of this question with references to literature in Heringer 1970, 110. Gardiner's view has also been opposed by Mathesius 1936.

[9] For a recent detailed presentation of its principles, see Dubský 1972.

[10] See Gülich-Raible 1972 for references to further literature.

[11] A monographic study of ellipsis in colloquial English has been made by Bowman 1966. For ellipses in spoken German, see Zimmermann 1965.

[12] Cf. Thon 1928. For elliptical sentences in modern fiction, see Adamová 1971.

[13] This view is held especially by Riesel 1963.

[14] Cf. Rath 1968, Sandig 1970.

[15] Cf. Sandig 1970.

[16] Cf. Brandstetter 1968.

[17] Cf. Klotz 1963.

[18] Cf. Grosse 1968, Daniels 1972.

[19] Cf. also Beneš 1973, Fries 1973.

[20] Cf. especially Vachek 1948, 1959.

[21] Cf Regula 1953.

REFERENCES

Adamová, Eva: Neslovesné věty v současném německém literárním jazyce /Verbless Sentences in Present-Day Literary German/, Philosophical dissertation, Praha 1971.

Barth, Erhard: "Die funktionale Differenzierung der Sprache." In: *Die Neueren Sprachen 69*, NF. 19, 1970, 186—191.

Barth, Erhard: "Fachsprache, eine Bibliographie." In: *Germanistische Linguistik* 1971, Heft 3, 205—363.

Beneš, Eduard: "Thema-Rhema-Gliederung und Textlinguistik." In: *Studien zur Texttheorie und zur deutschen Grammatik. Festgabe für Hans Glinz,* Düsseldorf 1973, 42—62.

Beugel, Gabriele: "Zur Syntax der Schlagzeile. Perfekt, Präteritum und Partizip II." In: *Neue Beiträge zur deutschen Grammatik. Hugo Moser zum 60. Geburtstag gewidmet.* Mannheim 1969, 9—21.

Bloomfield, Leonard: *Language*, New York 1933.

Bowman, Elizabeth: *The Minor and Fragmentary Sentences of a Corpus of Spoken English,* The Hague 1966.

Brandstetter, Alois: "Das Telegramm und seine syntaktische Situation." In: *Duden-Beiträge* 33, Mannheim 1968, 23—43.

Brugmann, Karl: *Die Syntax des einfachen Satzes im Indogermanischen*, Leipzig 1925.

Daneš, František: "A Three-Level Approach to Syntax." In: *Travaux linguistiques de Prague* 1, 1964, 225—240.

Daniels, Karlheinz: "Das Substantiv in der deutschen Gegenwartssprache, Ergebnisse und Aufgaben der Forschung." In: *Zeiten und Formen in Sprache und Dichtung. Festschrift für Fritz Tschirch zum 70. Geburtstag*, Köln/Wien 1972, 432—450.

Delbrück, Berthold: *Vergleichende Syntax der indogermanischen Sprachen* III. Teil, Strassburg 1900.

Dressler, Wolfgang: *Einführung in die Textlinguistik*, Tübingen 1972.

Dubský, Josef: "The Prague Conception of Functional Style." In: *The Prague School of Linguistics and Language Teaching*, London 1972, 112—127.

Duden, Grammatik der deutschen Gegenwartssprache. Der Grosse Duden, Bd. 4, Mannheim/Wien/Zürich ³1973.

Eggers, Hans: "Zur Syntax der deutschen Sprache der Gegenwart." In: *Studium generale* 15, 1962, 49—59.

Enkvist, Nils Erik: "On Defining Style." In: *Linguistics and Style*, London 1964, 1—56.

Erben, Johannes: *Deutsche Grammatik, Ein Abriss*, München 1972.

Fries, Udo: "Zum Thema Stilistik und Textlinguistik." In: *Festschrift Prof. Dr. Herbert Koziol zum 70. Geburtstag /Wiener Beiträge zur englischen Philologie* Bd. 75/, Wien 1973, 74—86.

Gardiner, A. H.: *The Theory of Speech and Language*, Oxford 1932.

Grosse, Siegfried: "Mitteilungen ohne Verb." In: *Festgabe für Friedrich Maurer*, Düsseldorf 1968, 50—68.

Gülich, Elisabeth — Raible, Wolfgang /Hrsg./: *Textsorten, Differenzierungskriterien aus linguistischer Sicht*, Frankfurt/M. 1972.

Gunter, Richard: "Elliptical Sentences in American English." In: *Lingua* 12, 1963, 137—150.

Hausenblas, Karel: "Syntaktická závislost, způsoby i prostředky jejího vyjadřování" /Syntactic Dependence, Ways and Means of its Expression/. In: Bulletin VŠRJL 2, 1958, 23—48.

Heringer, Hans Jürgen: *Theorie der deutschen Syntax /Linguistische Reihe* Bd. 1/, München 1970.

Isačenko, A. V.: "Kontextbedingte Ellipse und Pronominalisierung im Deutschen." In: *Beiträge zur Sprachwissenschaft, Volkskunde und Literaturforschung* /Festschrift Steinitz/, Berlin 1965, 163—174.

Jespersen, Otto: *The Philosophy of Grammar*, London 1924.

Klotz, Volker: "Slogans." In: *Sprache im technischen Zeitalter*, Heft 7, 1963, 538—546.

Kopečný, František: *Základy české skladby* /Foundations of Czech Syntax/, Praha 1958.

Mathesius, Vilém: "On some Problems of the Systematic Analysis of Grammar." In: TCLP 6, 1936, 95—107.

Mittelberg, Ekkehart: *Wortschatz und Syntax der BILD-Zeitung /Marburger Beiträge zur Germanistik* Bd. 19/, Marburg 1967.

Mrázek, Roman: "K otázce českých větných schémat a typů, zvláště neslovesných" /On the question of Czech sentence patterns and types, with special reference to verbless structures/, In: *Slovo a slovesnost* 23, 1962, 21—36.

Paul, Hermann: *Prinzipien der Sprachgeschichte*, Halle /Saale/ ²1886.

Rath, Rainer: "'Unvollständige Sätze' im heutigen Deutsch, Eine Studie zur Sprache des Wetterberichts." — In: *Duden-Beträge* 33, Mannheim 1968, 9—22.

Regula, Moritz: "Die Rolle der Frage im Sprachleben." In: *Sprachforum* 2, 1956, 11—19.

188

Riesel, Elise: *Stilistik der deutschen Sprache*, Moskau ²1963.

Römer, Ruth: *Die Sprache der Anzeigenwerbung /Sprache der Gegenwart Bd. 4/*, Düsseldorf 1968.

Sandig, Barbara: "Probleme einer linguistischen Stilistik." In: *Linguistik und Didaktik 1*, 1970, 177—194.

Sandig, Barbara: *Syntaktische Typologie der Schlagzeile /Linguistische Reihe Bd. 6/*, München 1971.

Šmilauer, Vladimír: *Novočeská skladba* /Syntax of Contemporary Czech/, Praha ²1966.

Thon, Luise: *Die Sprache des deutschen Impressionismus*, München 1928.

Vachek, Josef: "Written Language and Printed Language." In: *Recueil linguistique de Bratislava* 1, 1948, 65—75.

Vachek, Josef: "Two Chapters on Written English." In: *Brno Studies in English* 1, 1959, 7—38.

Zimmermann, Heinz: *Zu einer Typologie des spontanen Gesprächs*, Bern 1965.

SOURCES

Becker = Becker, Henrik: *Sieben Sprachbriefe zur Gegenwart*, Halle /Saale/ 1956.

Klee = *Tagebücher von Paul Klee* 1898—1918, Köln 1957.

Rilla = Rilla, Paul: *Essays, Kritische Beiträge zur Literatur*, Berlin 1955.

Rosemarie Gläser
Karl-Marx-University, Leipzig

Emotive features in technical and scientific English

0. In recent research in the field of text theory and stylistics, attention has been focused on the linguistic structure of scientific and technical texts. As such texts are expected to provide the specialist with up-to-date and relevant information, they must meet certain communicative requirements which are reflected in specific features of style. Every scientific and technical text, whether it be a monograph, an article in a learned journal, a lecture or public address, a book review or operating instruction for a machine or laboratory equipment, is subject to stylistic and rhetorical rules. The most important features of texts of this kind are objective information, the statement of facts, brevity and authority. Therefore a wordy, imprecise and flowery style would be inadequate and would violate stylistic norms.

1. Since scientific publications are mostly objective factual reports, linguists commonly hold the opinion that this sort of writing is entirely rational and without emotional features. Jackson E. Morris calls for the "cultivation of a simple, correct, and vigorous scientific and technical writing style",[1] and Rufus P. Turner states categorically: "Good technical writing is unemotional and unadorned".[2] On the whole, this view is also shared by a number of Soviet linguists, among them I. A. Volnina and V. M. Avrasin.[3] Emphasis is put on such stylistic features as "jasnost', točnost' " and "ob-ektivnost' izloženija" (i.e. clarity, preciseness and objectivity of presentation) of scientific and technical texts. The Soviet authors maintain that emotive features and colloquial elements would be incompatible with the objective character of technical writing and distract from its basic content. A somewhat different opinion is held by the Soviet linguist M. N. Kožina.[4] She tries to prove that although scientific discourse tends to make abstractions and generalizations it is not necessarily free from emotive features which express the author's personal ideas and assessment of the subject. Thus emotive features may occur as occasional figures of speech such as metaphors, similes and epithets, i. e., tropes increasing the communicative effect of the text. Because scientific and technical texts tend to emphasize objectivity and avoid stylistic variation, A. E. Darbyshire concluded that discourse of this kind has "anti-style", by which he means the absence both of imagery and of the individual way of expression. The author seems to misinter-

190

pret the general conventions in scientific and technical writing when he states:

"Much, indeed most, of the scientific and technical prose that can be found nowadays in the language of information and instruction, in contributions of learned journals, in the textbooks intended for advanced students, and those encyclopaedic volumes which record the vastness of modern scientific discovery, presents the reader with an anti-style. And the presentation of an anti-style shows an attitude which is timid, lawabiding and uncreative. The language which embodies the myths of modern science and technology becomes petrified, for the writers are apparently aghast with horror at the thought of straying too far from the narrow and virtuous path of orthodoxy."[5]

On closer inspection, those linguistic features which Darbyshire wrongly describes as "anti-style" prove to be rhetorical and stylistic regularities of the register of such prose.

2. In view of such a diversity of opinions among linguists, the crucial problem arises of investigating to what extent scientific and technical texts are in fact strictly rational and free from emotive features. The object of the present article is to analyse various kinds of English texts taken from chemistry, physics and biology and to describe the relationship between emotional and non-emotional passages. The texts under analysis are textbooks intended for students and scientists, articles from learned journals, monographs, lectures, reports and scientific book-reviews. The problem under discussion has at least two aspects: (1) emotive features of texts, and (2) emotive features in the word-stock, especially in the process of designating new concepts.

3. As operational terms the linguistic key-words "emotive features", "emotionality" and "rationality" with regard to style call for a definition. Under the heading of "expressiveness" Stephen Ullmann groups a large number of linguistic features which are a special dimension of a t e x t. As Ullmann puts it: ". . . they do not directly affect the meaning of the utterance, the actual information which it conveys. Everything that transcends the purely referential and communicative side of language belongs to the province of expressiveness."[6] Expressiveness may be linked with a special register or with the author's social setting. As various linguists have shown, it is not limited to texts of prose fiction. According to the German style specialists Siegfried Krahl and Josef Kurz, emotionality and rationality ("Emotionalität" and "Rationalität") are varieties of expressiveness ("Expressivität").[7] They are not abstract stylistic categories, but denote characteristic features of t e x t s, i. e., they are context-bound. Thus emotionality is brought about by recurrence of emotionally coloured elements of a text. Rationality is expressed by the combination of intellectually motivated elements and segments of texts, especially of scientific statements, definitions, tenets and theorems. The illustrative example adds to clarity and exactitude.

4. A qualitative analysis of scientific and technical English texts reveals that in various genres of prose writing there is an interrelation between rational and emotional elements. The author of a text may be a representative of a work team or a research group and may therefore share the register characteristic of his field of work, but — and to a no lesser degree — he also communicates as an individual who expresses his personality by developing an argument or in his approach to a scientific or technical problem. Another point corroborates the assumption that rationality and emotionality as textual features cannot be strictly separated. In understanding and describing complex problems, the human mind is prone to use analogous concepts. It is a well-known fact that abstractions are derived from incidental individual phenomena. Thus many technical terms were coined as picturesque metaphors or comparisons which made the meaning of the object denoted self-explanatory. If we signify new concepts by way of analogy resulting in bold metaphors, this cognitive process obviously has both a rational (intellectual) and an emotional side. In the light of semantics and stylistics, the categories of emotionality and rationality should rather be understood as two complementary sides of the same cognitive process as reflected in the communicative and cognitive functions of language. This assumption can easily be proved by the observation that various linguistic structures may serve as both rational and emotional elements of a text. The syntactic strucucture of a question placed at the beginning of a new passage may be used for the sake of logical argument or for posing a relevant problem; likewise it may be an emotional appeal to the reader in that it arouses his curiosity and interest, which is typical of rhetorical questions in textbooks. Parallelisms on the other hand may contribute to the intelligibility of a text by emphasizing items of information. Parallel ideas may be presented in parallel structures, paragraphs and larger segments of texts. Thus Jackson E. Morris recommends parallelisms as a legitimate stylistic device in scientific and technical prose:

"The principle of parallelism can be applied at all levels of structure; that is, to ideas, to paragraphs, to sentences, to clauses, to phrases, to individual words, to the headings and subheadings of an outline, to briefing posters, to table entries, to simple lists, and to items of a series. Anywhere coordinate, or equal, ideas are associated in writing, their statement is best made in parallel grammatical form. This principle is very powerful in obtaining clarity. The idea of parallelism also involves the idea of subordination. That is, express parallel ideas in parallel grammatical form, and subordinate ideas in a subordinate or modifying form."[8]

The emotional stimulus initiated by parallelisms may result in a memory effect, in particular, for didactic objectives. Therefore, semantic and syntactic parallelisms are used to good purpose in academic and school textbooks.

A typical example of parallel construction may be found in *A Hand-*

book of Systematic Botany by Subhash Chandra Datta. The author draws a comparison between the administrative subdivision of geographical and residential areas on the one hand and the plant kingdom on the other:

> "Just as a continent is divided into countries, countries into nations or states, states into provinces, provinces into divisions, divisions into sub-divisions, sub-divisions into districts, etc., so the plant kingdom is divided into a number of categories which differ in size, rank and nature".[9]

The subsequent passages in which the terms *species, genus, family, cohort* and *order* are defined, strictly follow the principle of parallelism in that they place the *explicandum* at the beginning of the sentence.

As a rule, emotional elements are absent in definitions, tenets and theorems. A definition is characterized by an objective statement of facts. It is a normative semantic fixation of a concept. Typical examples may be found in such textbooks as *Organic Chemistry* ed. by F. Degering:

> "An atom is a positively charged nucleus surrounded by negative electrons, the number of electrons being just sufficient to balance the positive charge on the nucleus. The positive charge of the nucleus of the uranium atom, the heaviest of atoms, is 92 times that of the hydrogen atom, the lightest of atoms."[10]

5. Within the register of scientific and technical writing, a variety of literary (formal) English, the distribution of rational and emotional features will vary in different genres of texts. In explanatory and descriptive scientific texts, emotional elements are implicit rather than explicit features. As the author wishes to direct the reader's interest towards the subject and to develop his understanding step by step, he chooses examples for illustrating a complex chemical, physical or mathematical problem. For pedagogical reasons he often prefers the personal pronoun *we* in order to address the reader personally. This principle is even followed by textbooks of theoretical character such as *English — German Chemical Terminology* by Fromherz and King[11] which is an introduction to the terms of elementary, inorganic, organic and physical chemistry in the two languages. Quite often the authors use phrases like *we assume, if we begin with, we presently reach, we would conclude that...* Other emphatic elements may occur in conclusive and affirmative statements: *we have seen that..., now, ice and steam are substances with entirely different physical properties from water.* The communicative effect of a statement may be increased by corroborative adverbs (*of course, naturally*). These textual features also hold true for the textbook *Vitalized Physics* by Robert H. Carleton. This is intended for future students of physics. For this reason the author aims at an appropriate presentation of his material. Very often he uses the pedagogical and conjectural *we*, e. g. *force is known to us as a push and as a pull, ... temperature tells us what is happening to the individual molecule, ... the marvels of our present electrical age are possible as a*

result ... Included in the text are everyday examples which may strike the adult reader as trivial but which may have some cognitive value for the undergraduate. They help to vary a technical text by alternating between deductive and inductive passages. The example given may illustrate a general principle:

> "Examples of capillary action are the penetration of oil between the leaves of automobile springs when sprayed on the surface; the rise of water in soil and in the roots and stems of plants; the rise of oil in the wick of an oil lamp; the absorption of water by filter paper or a towel".[12]

It is also possible to make up examples which appeal to the reader's imagination. They are introduced by a stimulus, e. g.,

> "Imagine a 1-foot cube of aluminium submerged in water ...".

Texts of this kind are not necessarily popular-scientific writing, but quite typical of teaching material for adult education both in Great Britain and especially in the United States.

5.1. In the logical presentation of a scientific and technical text, question sentences play an important part. They may be rhetorical questions introducing a new complex of thoughts, *wh*-questions followed by a definition, or *yes/no*-questions which subdivide a semantic complex into known and unknown information, e. g.,

> "Does water lift the stone, or does gravity pull the stone down with less force when it is in the water? It is easy to prove that the force of gravity doesn't change ..."[13]

5.2. In scientific and technical journals, rationality prevails on principle. The contents must be presented in a concentrated, precise and objective way. As Rufus P. Turner aptly puts it:

> "The purpose of all technical writing is to explain something. This type of writing is devoted mainly to engineering and allied subjects, but its techniques have been used to advantage in such diverse fields as accounting, home economics, and nursing ... A good technical style is one that guarantees quick, accurate, honest communication."[14].

Therefore, emotive features and verbose and colloquial elements would contradict the objectivity of technical writing in the strict sense of the word. Clarity, brevity and authority are norms which are binding on the author of a technical text. The freedom of an individual author's style is delimited by the register of scientific English. Economical use of linguistic means of expression is desirable in the light of the huge amount of information which must be conveyed.

5.3. In scientific and technical texts, however, authors tend to use the first person plural *we* for the sake of the argument. This personal pronoun may stand for the author as a representative of a research group, or it may be an expression of himself in the *plural majestatis* or *modestiae,* or even be the pedagogical address in nondidactic texts. One very frequently encounters such sentences as *we have neglected several reactions that may be responsible for this situation . . . We must realize that for certain problems no simple solution, no simple "wonderdrugs" are available . . . We should not turn away from procedures which appear complex at present.* Sometimes the author of a scientific article inserts such emphatic elements as *hopefully* and *personally* which express his personal views or experience:

> "Personally, I like to use a foot switch because I like to use both hands to hold a delicate syringe, get it inserted in the septum properly without bending the needle".

The adverbial *hopefully* is believed to be slightly colloquial, and some critical linguists even reject it as an Americanism. Undoubtedly, the adverbial adds to the emotional emphasis of the statement:

> "Hopefully, an open mind toward any scheme can be preserved . . . The specific system employed — ethanol and γ-alumina — is familiar but hopefully not shopworn."

This example may have occurred originally in an oral report.

6. Narrative scientific prose may be regarded as a genre of discourse in its own right. It may comprise descriptions of explorations, expeditions, discoveries and experiments. At great detail, including technical comment, the author depicts the situation and the sometimes unfavourable conditions under which scientific advances were made. Narrative prose as represented by J. D. Bernal's series *Science in History*[15] includes elements of literary journalism, although basically it remains scientific and technical discourse because the narrative descriptive passages will alternate with explanatory and argumentative passages. Bernal enlivens his style by using metaphors, personifications, well-chosen comparisons and syntactic inversions.

7. Book reviews on scientific and technical publications are another essential genre in the register of scientific discourse. In contrast to documentary texts (*abstracts, précis, summaries*), a book review in a technical journal implies the author's personal assessment of the publication under review and thus an individual, emotive way of writing. The book review is expected to convey objective information to a fairly wide readership of specialists, to judge a new book against the background of previous research work, and to evaluate its methods and findings. Emotive features are linked with the reviewer's attempt to express his own opinion in the most convincing manner. Revealing in this respect are the reviews on scientific and technical books published in such journals as *Scientific American, New Scientist, Archive for History of Exact Sciences,* and the UNESCO Bulletin *Nature and Resources.* The reviewer may express his opinion impersonally by describing himself as "the reader" or "the reviewer", or he may speak polemically in the

first person singular. This habit is illustrated by the following example:

> "The migration of animals is a subject of great interest about which
> many books have been written, some good, some not so good; this
> book, I regret to say, falls into the second category".[16]

Characteristic of review articles are indirect statements, sometimes
even euphemisms and mitigating expressions. Obviously they add to the
emotive colouring of the text. The categorial tone of a statement can be
weakened by the use of modal verbs or restrictive adverbs expressing
modality (*nearly, perhaps, maybe*). On the other hand, the reviewer is
free to vary his evaluation by means of synonyms. Shortcomings of a
book may be called "a blunder", "a wrong statement of facts", or "defects", or they may be politely circumscribed as "inaccuracies", e. g.

> "... the book is marred by innumerable inaccuracies of detail. On
> nearly every page there is some blunder or wrong statement of fact
> — so many that it would be unprofitable, and perhaps unkind,
> to quote even a sample. It may be that some of these defects are
> due to the translator[17] ..."

Emotional concern on the part of the reviewer may lead to his using
elements which otherwise chiefly occur in oral speech. These may be
insertions of emphatic words and phrases such as "well", "of course",
"it's a pity that", or interjections like "yes, indeed!" or "please!". As
for punctuation, the exclamation mark increases the emotional effect.
The following example is by no means an exception:

> "Obviously the meteorologist has to find out all the details of reality
> later, but not at the same time as the basic principles, please!"[18]

In some cases the reviewer may choose to emphasize his ideas by
means of a bold comparison. He must bear in mind, however, that too
much emotionality could impair the objectivity, clarity and authority
of a review article. Moreover, stylistic comparisons may increase undesirable redundancy in a technical text, even if it is a book review. The
following example may be regarded as not so typical, although the comparison will strike the reader as expressive and original:

> "The art of separating out essentials lies in handling them in a
> simple way, and the reader cannot be blamed if he feels like Pavlov's
> dogs — illogically rebellious — for he just begins to feel secure in
> a basic idea when all sorts of extraneous information is piled upon
> him and he will be confused".[19]

This comparison taken from a scientific field (psychology, cybernetic
reactions) seems to be well-suited in the given context. Its effect is surprising, but persuasive.

Occasionally a reviewer's positive evaluation of a book may result in
an advertising appeal to the reader. Such examples will even occur in
quality technical journals. They are, however, on the verge of advertising
English, which is a variety of journalism, thus deviating from the regis-

ter of scientific and technical English. Examples are to be found in *New Scientist:*

> "This is an important subject affecting every citizen and *The Politics of American Science* will be a welcome addition to any bookshelf".[20]

In a different issue, a book review on demographic problems in the People's Republic of China ends as follows: "Well, this was supposed to be a review of a book. It has, instead, turned out to be more of a contemplation of the man who wrote the book. But this may be no bad thing if it helps an appreciation of what the man has written. I hope you will spend 35 s on Dr Horn's saga".[21]

Book reviews of this sort show that there is a zone of transition between the register of scientific and technical writing and that of journalism. Moreover, there is a large scale of variation between rationality and emotionality within the genre of a book review. Emotive elements in a text may contribute towards clarifying the reviewer's theoretical standpoint and conveying his persuasion to the reader. But emotionality should not be the predominant impression of a scientific book review.

8. In documentation texts meant for special bibliographical purposes or for reference cards, emotive features of style are not permitted. An author's *abstract* (*précis* or *summary*), preceding the main body of a paper, must be in accordance with the rules laid down by the UNESCO Conference in 1966. Based on this set of regulations, various international journals have issued guidelines which are binding on an author. For example, the *Guidelines for Preparing Abstracts for the MLA Abstract System* (= *Modern Language Association*) and the journal *Language and Language Behavior Abstracts* at the University of Michigan have limited the length of an abstract to 200 words. The abstract must be written as a coherent text of complete sentences, in one paragraph. Variation in tenses and between the active and passive voice is not allowed. Redundancy is undesirable, e. g. the naming of the author in phrases like *the author concludes ..., in this article, I ...* Figures of speech will be completely out of place.

9. A different set of problems touching the relationship of emotionality and rationality arises from scientific and technical vocabulary, in particular from the process of designating new objects and phenomena. It is a matter of experience that every technical word-stock has a considerable number of words which are in fact bold metaphors or comparisons. To the specialist they are everyday expressions whose stylistic expressiveness has faded away in the course of time and usage, whereas to the layman they may still appear as emotionally coloured words. In most cases these technical metaphors show a motivation based on the principle of analogy, i. e., some similarity in shape, position, function or material, between the designated object and a familiar one. Transfer of meaning conditioned by similarity is widely known in non-technical

usage too. Stephen Ullmann has described these types of semantic transfer.[22]

9.1. In technical English, metaphors go back a long way, dating from the days of early manual work. In modern technology we speak of *a saddle* (of a suspension bridge), *bubble-caps* (of a distillery), *a ladle* (in a blast furnace) *the memory of a computer, the stripping of an atom.* In general, the norm-fixing bodies who are responsible for technical terms and nomenclatures are not inclined to admit metaphorical expressions for coining new technical terms. According to binding international standards, a term should meet the following requirements: it should be defined, precise (having only one meaning), systematic, stylistically not coloured, in other words, emotionally neutral. These requirements only hold for word-formation in vocabulary belonging to the *literary or formal level* of the register of scientific and technical English, but they do not to the same extent concern *workshop language* where jargon and even slang words will occur. These different levels of usage, which ultimately reflect a socio-linguistic stratification, should be taken into account when we speak of the colourful motivation of technical vocabulary. The internal stratification of scientific and technical usage was suggested by a number of applied linguists, among them Heinz Ischreyt, E. Beier and Manfred Gerbert.[23] It is customary to distinguish between "scientific discourse" or "laboratory language" (in German "Prüffeldeutsch") as the upper stratum, "workshop language" (in German "Werkstättensprache") as the next stratum closely linked with the sphere of production, and finally "sales language" (in German "Verbraucher- und Verkäufersprache"), which is the field of commercial advertising. It goes without saying that the term "language" in these expressions does not imply an independent linguistic system in the sense of the national standard language, but only refers to varieties of English (or German) characterized by specific words and phrases and perhaps a different frequency of occurence of morphemes (in word-formation) and syntactic structures.

In a number of cases, the metaphorical expression may be regarded as an adequate way of designating a new concept in that the figurative word may signal the proper associations among those who use it in a particular field of activity. Even among linguists and technicians there are divided views about metaphors in technical vocabularies. Based on actual observation of the living language, the following opinion is held by Jackson E. Morris: "Some usage of metaphor — figures of speech — is proper, however. Metaphor is defined as the transference of meaning between words and phrases by analogy, or by a comparison which shows some unsuspected likeness. The language of the scientist and engineer would be poorer, indeed, without the use of phrases such as *boster skirt, engine apron, rocket tail, wind sock,* and *belly tank.* The comparisons are conventional now, but at one time they had to be invented by some mind busy at analogical extension of the language from the old to the new".[24]

9.2. It is true that in most textbooks on semantics, technical vocabularies are not included, which is a shortcoming, since semantic processes affect the whole field of lexis of all registers. So far, chiefly poetic diction, advertising English and everyday usage have been under analysis. In a few cases, workers' jargon was even included in the description of slang (under such heading as "special slang", cf., the dictionaries by Partridge and Berrey-Van den Bark[25]).

9.3. The vocabulary of mining, geology and minerology provides plenty of examples of figurative expressions, most of them occurring in *workshop language*, e. g. *barnyard* (interglacial soil horizon), *dog-house* (drilling workers' hut), *mud smeller* (petroleum geologist), *toadstone* (melaphyre), *niggerheads* (a certain shape of coal).

In different technical vocabularies patterns of semantic transfer are frequently used, the most typical being anthropomorphisms, among them metaphors derived from parts of the human body, animal metaphors (including a subgroup of metaphors derived from parts of the animal body), plant metaphors (and those derived from parts of a plant), and metaphors derived from an article of clothing or from another artifact. The last two categories of metaphors are often motivated by some similarity of shape or position to adjacent objects, e. g., the idea of enclosing or shielding is suggested.

Anthropomorphic metaphors may occur as single words or compounds. They are also found among terms in chemistry and geology. It may be understood as a reflection of original expressiveness that in chemistry many figurative expressions are trivial names, whereas the stylistically neutral expression is the systematic name used in a nomenclature (e. g. *hybrid ions, zwitter ions*, as opposed to *amphoteric ions*). Other typical anthropomorphisms are: *twin crystal, compound twins* (geology), *volcanic embryo, rock tribe, river beheading* (*river piracy, river capture*). In various fields we speak of a *cattle population*, a *tractor population* or of a *bacterial colony*. In typography the specialist will talk of the *head-and-tail portions* of an article and of a *widow* (according to Webster "a short line ending a paragraph and appearing at the top or bottom of a printed page or column").

Animal metaphors are often based on similarity of appearance: *hogback* (crested hill-ridge), *horseback* (fossil water-course in coal), *lambskin* (inferior variety of anthracite in Wales), *whisker* (a form of crystal), *coontail ore, peacock coal, cat's eye quartz, toad's eye tin.*

Plant metaphors occur in various natural sciences: *flowers of sulphur, antimony bloom, ice fern, mushroom rock, haematite rose.* Metaphorical expressions derived from articles of clothing are often associated with the idea of similar shape or protection and shielding, e. g. *water jacket, alluvial apron, ice cap, iron hat, vein skirts* (in mining). Also other physical objects may be linked with metaphorical designations of scientific or technical concepts. The *tertium comparationis* in this case may be similarity in form or function: e. g. *crystal lattice, gravel fan, glacier mill, drainage blanket*, or simplex words such as *gun, bed, saddle* in a transferred meaning.

199

10. Conclusion

10.1 With regard to the relationship between emotional and rational elements in scientific and technical writing it is necessary to distinguish between the linguistic level of the text and that of lexis. As to the stylistic side of the text, it would be a simplifying statement to declare *a priori* that scientific and technical English is devoid of emotive features. This register is varied enough in itself, since it includes monographs of a highly theoretical character, treatises, textbooks for academic studies or self-instruction, articles of scientific and technical journals, reports on experiments, explorations and discoveries, papers presented at conferences, book reviews, reference articles in encyclopaedias, formulae for laboratories, and such borderline genres of technical texts as applications for a patent, or commercial advertising for technical equipment. If the information conveyed in a technical text is condensed as in an operating manual for a machine or in a recipe, it is subject to language economy which excludes redundancy and thus emotive features. On the other hand, scientific articles, reports, monographs and papers which are less subject to specific conventions binding on the linguistic structure of a text will allow some kind of stylistic variation.

10.2. As scientific and technical discourse has a different communicative function than journalism or prose fiction for example, it follows that the range of the author's linguistic and stylistic creativity in writing such a text is limited by the strict logical sequence of items deriving from a complex theoretical problem. A certain degree of self-restraint and self-control in thought is reflected in the development of an argument, e. g. the principle of parallelism, of thesis-antithesis, emphatic stress (often brought about by stylistic inversion) or in analogous examples. Scientific and technical English as a functional variety ("functional style") or register has a rhetoric of its own — whether it occurs in an oral or written form. The requirements of a text (clarity, brevity, authority) in this field have resulted in a set of linguistic regularities and conventions ("impersonality" by preference of the passive voice, complex sentences etc.), but it would be entirely wrong to describe these features as "anti-style". Every linguistic utterance, every text, has style. Stylistic devices necessarily vary, depending on the subject of the text, the personality of the author, the province of discourse, in short — the socio-linguistic setting of the text.

10.3. Even in scientific and technical English, emotive elements do occur. In the given context they have a communicative function. Emotive features are justified whenever they help in conveying information and in facilitating the communicative effect on the part of the recipient of the message, in other words, the listener or reader of such a text.

10.4. With regard to the relationship between emotional and rational elements in the vocabulary of technical and scientific English, metaphorical designations of new concepts reflect a still productive semantic process. Also in recent publications in the field of chemistry, according to the principle of analogy, phenomena of abnormal conformations of molecules are described in terms of metaphors (e. g. *chair conformation, boat conformation* in the case of cyclohexane). Since the scientific and technical word-stock is an open system similar to that of the national standard language, it is likely to be affected by the same semantic and word-building processes which are operative outside this variety of English. It will be up to the "norm-fixing" bodies of engineers and scientists to decide on the specific technical neologisms and whether their figurative origin will be misleading or appropriate. To the specialist, the stylistic colouring of a technical word will fade away in the course of time and usage.

NOTES

[1] Jackson E. Morris, *Principles of Scientific and Technical Writing.* New York, . . . London, 1966, preface, p.V.

[2] Rufus P. Turner, *Technical Writer's and Editor's Stylebook.* Indianapolis — New York, 1964, p. 16.

[3] V. M. Avrasin, "Charakteristika teksta i sistema stilevych čert", p. 101—107, I. A. Volnina, "K voprosu ob opredelenii ponjatija 'stil' 'v lingvističeskoj terminologii," p. 20—26, cf. Proceedings of the Moscow Style Conference, held in 1969, cf. *Sbornik naučnych trudov, Uypusk 73,* Moskva, 1973.

[4] M. N. Kožina, *O specifike chudožestvennoj i naučnoj reči v aspecte funkcional'noj stilistiki,* Perm' 1966, p. 182 ff.

[5] A. E. Darbyshire, *A Grammar of Style.* London 1971, p. 129.

[6] Stephen Ullmann, *Language and Style.* Part II. Problems of Style. Oxford 1964, p. 101.

[7] Siegfried Krahl — Josef Kurz, *Kleines Wörterbuch der Stilkunde.* Leipzig 1973[2], cf. pp. 39 and 84.

[8] Morris, cf. Note 1, p. 74.

[9] Subhash Chandra Datta, *A Handbook of Systematic Botany,* London 1965, pp. 3 and 4.

[10] *Organic Chemistry.* An Outline of the Beginning Course Including Material for Advanced Study. Keyed to Standard Textbooks. Ed. by F. Degering. New York 1955 [14], p. 6.

[11] H. Fromherz and A. King, *Englische und deutsche chemische Fachausdrücke. English-German Chemical Terminology.* Weinheim/Bergstrasse 1968 [5].

[12] Robert H. Carleton, *Uitalized Physics.* Preparation for College Entrance Tests in Physics. New York 1960 [4], p. 12.

[13] ibid., p. 27.

[14] Turner, op. cit., p. 14.

[15] cf. J. D. Bernal, *Science in History.* Volume 2: *The Scientific and Industrial Revolutions.* Penguin Books. Harmondsworth, Middlesex, 1969.

[16] *New Scientist,* 4 December 1969, p. 520.

[17] ibid.

[18] *New Scientist,* 12 March 1970, p. 520.

[19] ibid.

[20] *New Scientist,* 4 December 1969, p. 520.

[21] *New Scientist,* 18 December 1969, p. 612.

[22] Stephen Ullmann, *The Principles of Semantics.* Glasgow—Oxford 1959 [2].

[23] H. Ischreyt, *Studien zum Verhältnis von Sprache und Technik. Institutionelle Sprachlenkung in der Terminologie der Technik.* Düsseldorf 1965. — Manfred Gerbert, *Besonderheiten der Syntax in der technischen Fachsprache des Englischen.* Halle/Saale 1970.

[24] cf. Morris, op. cit., p. 80.

[25] Lester V. Berrey and Melvin Van den Bark, *The American Thesaurus of Slang.* New York 1953. Repr. 1962. — Eric Partridge, *Slang To-day and Yesterday.* London 1950 [3].

Kirsti Kivimaa
Helsinki School of Economics

Notes on sentence patterns and style in
Purity and *Patience*

Of the works generally attributed to the *Gawain*-poet, *Sir Gawain and the Green Knight, Pearl, Purity* and *Patience*,[1] the two former have been treated in a great number of studies, some of them dealing with aspects of style.[2] The editor of *St. Erkenwald* is inclined to think that this work was also composed by the same poet,[3] but his view has not been commonly accepted. All the works are written in a north-west Midland dialect, but a precise location is difficult to ascertain.[4]

There is no doubt that the *Gawain*-poet is one of the greatest in Western literature, in creative imagination as well as in craftsmanship. *Gawain*, with the marvellous and the fanciful, the splendid courts and the wild woods, the exciting and the puzzling, is the work that most readily arouses the reader's admiration. *Pearl*, skilful and much praised as it is, seems to the present writer to possess less of the striking freshness of expression of *Gawain*, perhaps because of the conventional dream-vision and the elegiac-homiletic subject-matter, which may demand a more subdued treatment. *Purity* and *Patience*, with paraphrases of biblical stories, differ markedly from the others, but both of them contain passages that are comparable in expressive power to the best in *Gawain*.[5] These are the passages in which the author elaborates the Vulgate text and creates a "realistic" picture of happenings and events, the realism being a product of his imagination. It is particularly in the descriptions of dramatic events that the author seems to delight, and uses the full measure of his poetic skills. The aim of the present paper is to examine some syntactic patterns from a stylistic viewpoint in these works. In the editions used, *Patience* has a stanzaic form of four lines, whereas *Purity* is not divided into stanzas.[6]

Parallelism, the repetition of a syntactic pattern, has been a favourite rhetorical pattern since ancient times, and has been used in English since the earlist period, for instance by Ælfric and Wulfstan, to our day, notably by T. S. Eliot. In *Purity* and *Patience* the parallel schemes vary, and those consisting of sentences are especially frequent. A prime illustration of this is the passage in the Prologue of *Patience* (13—28) paraphrasing *Matt.* v. The repetitive pattern in the Gospel has been welded to the verse pattern of *Patience*, simply and effectually, as in

Pat 13   Thay arn happen þat han in hert pouerte,
For hores in þe heuen-ryche to holde for euer.
Pay ar happen also þat haunte mekenesse,
For þay schal welde þis worlde and alle her wylle haue.

Matt. v. 3—4: Beati pauperes spiritu quoniam ipsorum est regnum cae-
lorum. Beati mites quoniam ipsi possidebunt terram.

A related pattern, with parallelism in every second line, also occurs in
[byþenk þe]

Pur 583   Wheþer he þat stykked uche a stare in uche steppe yȝe,
ȝif hymself be bore blynde, hit is a brod wonder;
And he þat fetly in face fettled alle eres,
If he hatz losed þe lysten hit lyftez mervayle.

More common than the above kind is a repetitive pattern of two
successive lines or half-lines, as e. g. in

Pur 588   Per is no dede so derne þat dittez his yȝen;
Per is no wyȝe in his werk so war ne so stylle

Pat 274   And stod vp in his stomak þat stank as þe deuel;
Per in saym and in sorȝe þat sauoured as helle

On the whole, in *Patience* groups of two lines frequently form a
unity — not unexpectedly, considering its stanzaic form of four lines;
in *Purity* groups of three and even more are common. A very frequent
pattern consists of a relative clause after the caesura in successive lines.
In this instance *Patience* also has a tendency towards twos:

Pat 485   I keuered me a cumfort þat now is caȝt fro me,
My wod-bynde so wlonk þat wered my heued.

Though three relative clauses in successive b-verses are uncommon
in *Patience*, the continuation of 274-5 reads (276) *þer watz bylded his
bour þat wyl no bale suffer.* In *Purity*, however, relative clauses abound.
Clausal parallelism is often accompanied by other repetitive patterns,
as in the following with three relative clauses in successive b-verses.

Pur 530   Uche fowle to þe flyȝt þat fyþerez myȝt serve,
Uche fysch to þe flod þat fynne couþe nayte,
Uche beste to þe bent þat bytes on erbez.

In the superb passage relating the painless delivery of the Virgin,[7]
the poet uses parallel sentences of two and three:

Pur 1075   Watz never so blysful a bour as watz a bos þenne,
Ne no schroude-hous so schene as a schepon þare,
Ne non so glad under God as ho þat grone schulde.
For þer watz seknesse al sounde þat sarrest is halden,
And þer watz rose reflayr where rote hatz ben ever,
1080   And þer watz solace and songe wher sorȝ hatz ay cryed.

The first three a-verses form a repetitive pattern (though 1075 differs
somewhat from the following two); they are all emphatic negative pe-
riphrases, followed by antithetical *as*-comparisons. The following three

a-verses (1078—80) are parallel, affirmative, followed by antithetical relative clauses. The b-verses also form groups of two and three introduced by *as* (1075—7), *þat* (1077—8) and *wher* (1079—80. The repetitive syntactic patterns contribute greatly to the beauty of the passage.

In addition to many instances of three (see e. g. *Pur 375—7, 920—2, 994—6*, etc.), there are also sequences of four and five relative clauses in the b-verse:

> *Pur 973* Þe segge herde þat soun to Segor þat ȝede,
> And þe wenches hym wyth þat by þe way folȝed;
> Ferly ferde watz her flesch þat flowen ay ilyche,
> Trynande ay hyȝe trot þat torne never dorsten.

> *Pur 257* For hit was þe forme-foster þat þe folde bred,
> Þe aþel aunceterez sunez þat Adam watz called,
> To wham God hade geven alle þat gayn were,
> Alle þe blysse boute blame þat bodi myȝt have,
> And þose lykkest to þe lede þat lyved next after.

The verse flows smoothly, but the impression given is one of monotony. Sequences of relative clauses in *Purity* seem occasionally to be routine mannerism. But the device is indeed effective when used with discipline, as most examples on the preceding pages show.

Just as parallel sentence structure is one of the markers of style in *Purity* and *Patience,* so it is also in *Gawain* and *Pearl.* The long description of the Green Knight and his horse (138—220) contains shifting patterns, of which the passage below serves as an example:

> *Gaw 203* Wheþer hade he no helme ne hawbergh nauþer,
> Ne no pysan ne no plate þat pented to armes,
> Ne no schafte ne no schelde to schwue ne to smyte,

Two additional passages may be quoted to illustrate repetitive syntactic units in *Gawain* and *Pearl*:

> *Gaw 2077* Þay boȝen bi bonkkez þer boȝez ar bare,
> Þay clomben bi clyffez þer clengez þe colde.

Sir Gawain is riding to meet the Green Knight.

> *Pearl 607* He laueȝ hys gyfteȝ as water of dyche,
> Oþer groteȝ of golf þat neuer charde.
> Hys fraunchyse is large þat euer dard
> To Hym þat matȝ synne rescoghe.

The Pearl is describing God's mercifulness.

Parallelism may be combined with lists of words (as in *Pur 530* ff., *Gaw 203* ff. above). Lists or catalogues of things and phenomena in realistic descriptions are traditional.[8] Catalogues in Old English were particularly favoured by Wulfstan in his homilies (e. g. in *Sermo Lupi ad Anglos*). In *Purity* and *Patience* there are lists of the conventional literary type, such as the one in *Purity* describing the holy relics of Jerusalem (1271—80); the magnificence of Babylon and Belshazzar's palace (1377—92); the spendid table vessels and the musical instruments at the banquet (1404—16); the description of the holy relics again with their wonderful engravings and precious stones (1451—88).[9] In *Patience* the conventional lists are fewer and shorter, but see e. g. the allegorical "dames" of virtues in the Prologue (31—33); the appeal to gods (165—167); God's attributes (417—20). Some also occur in the Vulgate, as e. g. the last-mentioned, but in *Purity* and *Patience* the lists of the Vulgate are frequently elaborated or added entirely by the poet, conforming to contemporary fashions.

There are instances of catalogues that are not so stereotyped as the ones mentioned above in *Purity* and *Patience*, though not all seem particularly inventive. Lists of sins are conventional, but the passage below includes kinds that are elaborated by the poet. The grouping of sins in twos and threes, the repetition of *and* and *for*, the adjectival or genitival attribute in b-verse contribute to smooth rhythm. But in thought the effect is hardly convincing, as the wages of sins are out of proportion to their severity: because of sloth, boasting and pride, man plunges violently into the devil's throat, but because of a worse sin, such as man-slaughter, he may only come to harm (183).

Pur 177   For fele fautez may a freke forfete his blysse,
         Þat he þe Soverayn ne se — þen for slauþe one,
         As for bobaunce and bost, and bolnande pryde,
    180   Þroly into þe develez þrote man þryngez bylyve;
         For covetyse, and colwarde and croked dedez,
         For mon-sworne, and men-scla3t, and to much drynk,
         For þefte, and for þrepyng, unþonk may mon have;
         For roborrye, and riboudrye, and resounez untrwe,
    185   And dysheriete and depryve dowrie of wydoez,
         For marryng of maryagez, and mayntnaunce of schrewez,
         For trayson and trichcherye, and tyrauntyre boþe,
         And for fals famacions and fayned lawez —
         Man may mysse þe myrþe þat much is to prayse
    190   For such unþewez as þise, and þole much payne,
         And in þe Creatores cort com never more,
         Ne never see hym with sy3t for such sour tornez.

In all, the sins are enumerated haphazardly: perjury, man-slaughter and too much drink (182) form one group, in which the last seems catachrestic, especially as *drynk* is not required by alliteration; theft and quarrel (183) on one hand, and robbery, lechery and lying (184) on the other, are combined. The last group of sins, false report or defamation and false laws (188) are an anticlimax; so is the punishment for the long list of sins: after the suffering of pain comes the litotes, the missing of the praiseworthy joy of arriving in the Creator's court (191; cf 178—80). As a summary the sins are called *unþewes*, literally 'unvirtues' (190) and *sour tornez* 'dirty tricks' (192),[10] which expressions weaken, instead of reinforcing, the effect of the many severe breaches against the Lord and man. Even taking into account the exigencies of alliteration, it seems that the poet was not inspired by cataloguing man's sins and their consequences.

However, the poet was clearly inspired by elaborating one of the Virgin's five joys, the Nativity (see the excerpt above, *Pur* 1075 ff.), and the listing of the Ark's animals (*Pur* 530—9). The drama of the flood is described in vivid terms of the terror and destruction of all that lived, the land that was, the river banks, dales, mountains (*Pur* 375—402), till the silence of death had enveloped all (403—8). The way Sodom and Gomorrah were destroyed is described in detail (*Pur* 947—68), the people of Jerusalem, the girls, babies, priests, women killed cruelly (1247—52), the prisoners (1297—303), the sick coming to be healed by Christ (1093—7) are enumerated carefully.

In *Patience* the storm scene, as can be expected, has aroused the poet's imagination, and he lists the things tossed overboard by the sailors in peril of their lives:

> *Pat* 157 Þer watȝ busy ouer-borde bale to kest,
> Her bagges and her feþer-beddes and her bryȝt wedes,
> Her kysttes and her coferes, her caraldes alle,
> And al to lyȝten þat lome, ȝif leþe wolde schape.

Parallel enumeration may be combined with emphatic negation (see also *Gaw* 203 ff. above):

> *Pat* 391 Seseð childer of her sok, soghe hem so neuer,
> Ne best bite on no brom ne no bent nauþer,
> Passe to no pasture, ne pike non erbes,
> Ne non oxe to no hay, ne no horse to water.

> *Pur* 522 Multyplyez on þis molde, and menske yow bytyde,
> Sesounez schal yow never sese of sede ne of hervest,
> Ne hete, ne no harde forst, umbre ne droȝþe,
> Ne þe swetnesse of somer, ne þe sadde wynter,
> Ne þe nyȝt, ne þe day, ne þe ȝerez,
> Bot ever renne restlez — regnez ȝe þerinne!

The corresponding passages in the Vulgate are much more concise. The passages mentioned and the quotations given as examples show that catalogues — frequently combined with parallelism — may do much to lend the narratives realistic plausibility, bring them close to the audience's own experiences or make it see them with "sight of his eyes" (*Pur* 576 *wyth syȝt of his yȝen*). But catalogues of the conventional type, as for example the descriptions of the holy relics (*Pur* 1451—88), or clumsily combined (e. g. *Pur* 177—192 above), however fresh they may have seemed to the mediaeval audience, tend to give the reverse impression to the modern reader.

Purity and *Patience* differ in sentence structure in that the former uses polysyndeton not infrequently, whereas the latter shuns it. In passages describing calmly flowing movement, the syntactic units are linked with a conjunction; in passages of exciting content, the structures tend to be without. The polysyndetic conjunction is generally *and*. The variation of polysyndeton with asyndeton is illustrated below with descriptions of three different ways of feasting; the first is from the noble Wedding Feast, the second and third from Belshazzar's Feast, the early part and the mad revelling later, the drinking from the sacred vessels.

The Wedding Feast:

Pur 119   Clene men in compaynye forknowen wern lyte,
        And ʒet þe symplest in þat sale watz served to þe fulle,
        Boþe with menske and wyth mete and mynstrasy noble,
        And alle þe laykez þat a lorde aʒt in londe shewe.
        And þay bigonne to be glad þat god drink haden,
        And uch mon wyth his mach made hym at ese.

The calm delight of those participating in the Wedding Feast, made at ease and happy by the drink and other treats in the royal surroundings, is not only expressed by the vocabulary but also by the complete unabridged sentences, each linked to the following with a connective. *And* contributes particularly to the unhurried impression given by the passage.

Belshazzar's Feast, early:

Pur 1417   So watz served fele syþe þe sale alle aboute,
         Wyth solace at þe sere course bifore þe self lorde,
         Per þe lede and alle his love lenged at þe table.
    1420   So faste þay weʒed to him wyne, hit warmed his hert,
         And breyþed uppe into his brayn and blemyst his mynde,
         And al waykned his wyt, and wel neʒe he foles.

In this part of Belshazzar's Feast the drinking is just beginning, and the author uses both asyndeton and polysyndeton, asyndeton in 1420 to emphasize the swiftness of the pouring of the drinks for Belshazzar and the first effect, "it warmed his heart"; the following clauses are connected with *and* at the beginning and at the caesura (1421—2); these clauses are short and accumulative, ending in a climax. Therefore, their effect is one of swiftness, contrary to the longer leisurely ones, also connected with *and*, in the Wedding Feast. The climax "very nearly he goes mad" is followed by Belshazzar's ordering the sacred relics to be fetched, their description (51 lines, 1437—88), and later the strong contrast of sacrilege in

Pur 1499   Now a boster on benche bibbes þerof,
         Tyl he be dronkken as þe devel, and dotes þer he syttes.

These lines, the second extra long with four complete units, give a comic effect, perhaps so intended by the author: a mighty king, but a foul blasphemer, is ridiculous when drunk, and that destroys his image more devastatingly than horror at his despicable behaviour. Spearing finds comic, even farcical passages in *Patience* written intentionally,[11] as is no doubt the case.

Belshazzar's Feast, late:

Pur 1507   Baltazar in a brayd bede bus þerof —
         'Weʒe wyn in þis won — Wassayl!' he cryes.
         Swyfte swaynes ful swyþe swepen þertylle,
    1510   Kyppe kowpes in honde kyngez to serve;
         In bryʒt bollez ful bayn birlen þise oþer,
         And uche mon for his mayster machches alone.
         Per watz rynging, on ryʒt, of ryche metalles,
         Quen renkkes in þat ryche rok rennen hit to cashe,

1515   Clatering of covaclez þat kesten þo burdes,
        As sonet out of sauteray songe als myry.

In the sacrilegious revelling, the author uses asyndeton to underline its wild atmosphere of bustle and noise. Lexically asyndeton is frequently associated with an abundance of verbs, as this passage also shows. But the author is careful not to overdo either device, asyndeton or poly-syndeton, and variation in linking is found throughout Belshazzar's story, as well as elsewhere in *Purity*. Another example is where the attack and attackers on the Chaldeans are carefully described, the silent stealing into the city using ladders to climb the walls, the sudden blasts of the trumpets and the shouts (1769—84), and then

Pur 1785   Segges slepande were slayne er þay slyppe myȝt,
          Uche hous heyred watz wythinne a hondewhyle;
          Baltazar in his bed watz beten to deþe,
          Pat boþe his blod and his brayn blende on þe cloþes;
          Pe kyng in his cortyn watz kaȝt bi þe heles,
    1790   Feryed out bi þe fete, and fowle dispysed,
          Pat watz so doȝty þat day and drank of þe vessayl;
          Now is a dogge also dere þat in a dych lygges.

One sentence in the Vulgate,

Dan. v *Eadem nocte interfectus est Baltassar rex Chaldaeus* has inspired the author to visualize the entire happening, culminating in Belshazzar's gory end, and transmit it in vocabulary and syntax admirably suited to the context, alternating normally linked and asyndetic sentences. The laconic statement at the end, the association of the once powerful king with the dead dog in a ditch, finishes the story in a striking antithesis. Many passages in Belshazzar's Feast illustrate clearly how a few statements, mere recordings in the Vulgate, have been expanded by the poet into pictures and sounds in which vocabulary and syntax share equally in creating vivid scenes of terror and excitement.

Other instances of asyndeton together with an abundance of verbs in *Purity* occur in dramatic passages, such as Lucifer's Fall (217—23), the Flood (e. g. 363—70), the destruction of the cities (947—60), the siege and battle of Jerusalem (1185—214), the slaughter of its people (1247—51), the seizure of the holy relics (1263—8). But the passages are interwoven with expressions linked by connectives, as pointed out above.

In contrast to the swift movement generally associated with asyndeton, a "still-life" using this device occurs at the beginning of the section telling of Abraham's entertaining the three angels. The Vulgate here only states the facts.

Pur 601   Olde Abraham in erde onez he syttez,
         Even byfore his hous-dore, under an oke grene;
         Bryȝt blykked þe bem of þe brode heven,
         In þe hyȝe hete þerof Abraham bidez,
   605   He watz schunt to þe schadow under schyre levez.
         Penne watz he war on þe waye of wlonk wyȝez þrynne.

The sweltering scene is painted with a few masterful strokes for the reader to see: the hot sun shining from the bright sky, old Abraham sitting in front of his house-door amidst the familiar English landscape with the green oak, the shade of its shining leaves. When the scene is set, then (*þenne*) the action begins. Thus the same kind of stylistic device can create opposite effects depending on the vocabulary, as in the above instance the verbs of rest, the adverbial expressions, contribute to the impression of static motionlessness.

In *Patience* polysyndeton, in the way it is used in *Purity*, does not occur. It is true that many stanzas begin with *and*, but very rarely are more than two successive clauses linked by it. Asyndeton is common, however; the story of Jonah opens:

> Pat 61 Hit bi-tydde sum-tyme in þe termes of Jude,
> Jonas joyned watʒ þer-inne jentyle prophete;
> Goddes glam to hym glod þat hym vnglad made,
> With a roglych rurd rowned his ere:

The suspicions of Jonah if he obeys God and goes to Niniveh:

> Pat 77 When þat steuen watʒ stynt þat stowned his mynde,
> Al he wrathed in his wyt, and wyþerly he þoʒt:
> 'If I bowe to his bode and bryng hem þis tale,
> And I be nummen in Nuniue, my nyes begynes.

The story progresses in this manner, in relatively short linked or unlinked sentences, of a line or half-line, regardless of whether the contents describe swift motion or not: the storm-scene, the throwing overboard of the packages and bags (157 ff. above), and of Jonah (249 ff.), his passage into the whale's belly and his sojourn there (265 ff.), the whale spitting him ashore (339 ff., see note 11), and so forth, even the grief of Jonah when his beloved woodbine is gone:

> Pat 477 And þen hef vp þe hete and heterly brenned;
> Pe warm wynde of þe weste, wertes he swyþeʒ.
> Pe man marred on þe molde þat moʒt hym not hyde,
> His wod-bynde watʒ away, he weped for sorʒe.

Syntax with main and sub-clauses, complete with connectives, is most common in the Prologue and in the oral exchanges between God and Jonah; thus e. g. in Jonah's prayer in the whale's belly (305—64), his angry words after the disappearance of the woodbine and God's answers.

We may wonder why clausal length and linkage in *Patience* differ on the whole from those in *Purity*. The former illustrates the virtue of patience with one story, the latter the virtue of spiritual cleanness with the parable of the Man without a Wedding Garment, and three narratives from the Old Testament, and in addition, introductions and deviations. The design of *Patience* is compact, whereas that of *Purity* is loose, the narrative at times rambling. The syntactic structures of the works second their thematic design. In *Patience*, discounting the Prologue (1—

60) and considering only the story of Jonah, we encounter a man brought to submission by God through bizarre adventures. Jonah is a simple man in *Patience*, who thinks himself shrewd, wary even of God, and certainly not to be trapped into ill fate, so he reasons with his horse sense. The story is told as if of an obstinate child[12] and as if to children, using simple sentence structures. The work is thoroughly thought out, finished and polished, to express the poet's intention, to exemplify patience, to the point of the first and last lines being almost identical (531 *patience is a nobel poynt, paȝ hit displese ofte;* the first line omits *nobel*).

Purity, with its less disciplined thematic design also has more variation in syntax, long drawn-out sentences with polysyndeton, and short sentences with asyndeton. The shifts of the stylistic devices agree, though not entirely consistently, with the shifts of contents. The work has passages of superb beauty in both content and form, manifesting truly fresh inspiration disciplined by craftsmanship, and others that seem careless, not worked over, as if the poet had written them out of duty to his intention and then abandoned them (see e. g. 177 ff. above).

In *Gawain* asyndeton is the general rule, as e. g. in the following lines from the hunting scene:

Gaw 1697   Hunteres vnhardeled bi a holt syde,
             Rocheres roungen bi rys for rurde of her hornes;
             Summe fel in þe fute þer þe fox bade,
    1700   Traylez ofte a traueres bi traunt of her wyles;
             A kenet kryes þerof, þe hunt hym calles;
             His felaȝes fallen hym to, þat fnasted ful þike,
             Runnen forth in a fabel in his ryȝt fare.

Though polysyndeton is rare, it occurs occasionally:[13]

Gaw 936   Þe lorde laches hym by þe lappe and ledez hym to sytte,
           And couþly hym knowez and callez hym his nome,
           And sayde he watz þe welcomest wyȝe of þe worlde;
           And he hym þonkked þroly, and ayþer halched oþer,
           And seten soberly samen þe seruise quile.

In *Pearl* neither polysyndeton or asyndeton are striking features, but the clauses tend to observe what we could call normal patterns of linkage or non-linkage. This may be due to the debate form, both the Pearl and the father trying to persuade one another in carefully wrought sentences.

The present paper has tried to demonstrate the stylistic effects of some syntactic devices in *Purity* and *Patience*. In so doing, evaluations of what is successful and what is not have also been made. But the evaluations are those of a present-day person who is bound to her time and the tastes of her time, in addition to an individual taste. Impressions created by the style of a poet who wrote about 600 years ago may, and probably do, differ from those experienced by his contemporary audiences. But *Purity* and *Patience* have qualities, however they are defined, in content and expression that have made them survive and speak to present-day audiences, too, with the indisputable voice of a poet.

NOTES

¹ The editions used in the present article: *Sir Gawain and the Green Knight*, ed. J. R. R. Tolkien and E. V. Gordon, 2nd ed. revised by Norman Davis, Oxford 1967; *Pearl*, ed. E. V. Gordon, Oxford 1953; *Purity*, ed. Robert J. Menner, *Yale Studies in English* LXI, New Haven and London 1920; *Patience*, ed. J. J. Anderson, *Old and Middle English Texts*, general ed. G. L. Brook, Manchester 1972 (1969). They are all contained in the unique MS Cotton Nero A X, in the same hand, from about 1400. The MS is not the author's original (Davis, *Gawain*, xi, xxv). In the present paper, textual emendations by the editors have not been pointed out in the quotations.

² See e. g. Benson, Larry D., *Art and Tradition in Sir Gawain and the Green Knight*, New York 1965; Bishop, Ian, *Pearl in its Setting*, Oxford 1968; Borroff, Marie, *Sir Gawain and the Green Knight: a Stylistic and Metrical Study*, *Yale Studies in English* 152, New Haven and London 1962; Burrow, J. A., *A Reading of Sir Gawain and the Green Knight*, London 1965; Id., *Ricardian Poetry: Chaucer, Gower, Langland and the Gawain Poet*, London 1971; Everett, Dorothy, *Essays on Middle English Literature* (ed. Patricia Kean), Oxfors 1955; Pearsall, Derek A., "Rhetorical 'Descriptio' in 'Sir Gawain and the Green Knight' ", *The Modern Language Review* 50, 1955, 129—34. Most of the Studies also have references to *Purity* and *Patience*.

³ *St. Erkenwald*, ed. Henry L. Savage, *Yale Studies in English* LXXII, New Haven and London 1926, lviii, lxv. The MS is Harley 2250 (British Museum), from about 1470—80.

⁴ Angus McIntosh, "A New Approach to Middle English Dialectology", *English Studies* XLIV, 1963, 1—11, narrows the area to SE Cheshire or NE Staffordshire, but this has not, so far, been proved. On the whole, even taking into account that alliteration has evidently dictated the use of some rare words and the stretching of meaning of some more common ones, the vocabulary is to be considered difficult.

⁵ A. C. Spearing, "*Patience* and the *Gawain*-Poet", *Anglia* 84, 1966, 305—29, has made a fine analysis of *Patience*, with references to some stylistic aspects, but not to the ones dealt with in the present paper.

⁶ Everett, (74) thinks that *Purity* also has a tendency towards lines grouped in fours, but such a tendency does not seem very marked to the present writer.

⁷ Menner (102) comments that "the poet frequently renders homage to the Virgin (cf. *Pearl* 423 ff., 453 ff.; *Gaw.* 647 ff.); but nowhere has he written fairer lines in her praise than this series of contrasts describing her joy in the birth of Christ."

⁸ Lists also occur in *Gawain* and *Pearl*; see e. g. Borroff, p. 123 ff. A prime example is the description of the Green Knight and his horse referred to in this article; Pearsall (130) comments on it as "this description through enumeration of detail". In Western literature, the device goes back to the earliest Greeks (Homer).

⁹ Menner (109—10) points out that the poet's description of Belshazzar's Feast was influenced by Mandeville's account of the Great Chan's palace.

¹⁰ Menner (72) thinks that *sour tornez* probably means 'evil devices'.

¹¹ As one example of the comic, even farcical, Spearing (311) quotes the passage describing Jonah's being spat ashore:

> *Pat* 339 Þe whal wendeȝ at his wylle and a warþe fyndeȝ,
> And þer he brakeȝ vp þe buyrne as bede hym oure lorde.
> Þenne he swepe to þe sonde in sluchched cloþes;
> Hit may wel be þat mester were his mantyle to wasche.

Indeed, the housewifely thought does astonish in that situation!

¹² Spearing (315) comments on Jonah's childlike behaviour in the last section of the poem (IV, 409 ff.), but it seems that his childishness is visible throughout in *Patience*.

¹³ Benson (154) finds ellipsis and asyndeton common in *Gawain*, and points out that when clausal linkage occurs, it is generally *and*; he quotes 1187—93 as an example (155—6).

Inna Koskenniemi
University of Turku

On the use of repetitive word pairs and related Patterns in *The Book of Margery Kempe*

In a passage describing a sea voyage made by Margery Kempe and her fellow pilgrims we read:

> Hyr felaschep was *glad & mery,* and sche was
> *heuy & sory* for dred of þe wawys.   (233.1)[1]

The balanced, antithetical sentence construction is a well-known feature of the book. The use of semantically related words in pairs is another typical stylistic device, which *The Book of Margery Kempe* shares with a number of Late Middle English prose writings. The device in fact goes back to Old English[2] and is a linguistic pattern favoured by many different literary periods and styles. Repetitive word pairs — particularly those in common use, e. g. *odds and ends, part and parcel* — have also been termed *binomials,* especially since the appearance in 1959 of Yakov Malkiel's article "Studies in Irreversible Binomials".[3] In the present paper the term *word pair* will be used, because in *The Book of Margery Kempe* the majority of these combinations probably do not have the degree of formulaicness that the term *binomial* would suggest.

Several critics have commented on the device of word pairing in Late Middle English prose. The most detailed analysis so far is perhaps Ernst Leisi's study of tautological word pairs in Caxton's *Eneydos.*[4] Chaucer's 'untransposable binomials' have been recently discussed by Simeon Potter.[5] In his article "Three Middle English Mystics"[6] R. M. Wilson singles out the use of word pairs, or 'doublets', as a typical feature in mystical prose. A recent study by R. K. Stone[7] dealing with the styles of Margery Kempe and Julian of Norwich contains extensive lists of alliterative as well as non-alliterative word pairs from the writings of both female mystics. In examining different levels of usage discernible in *The Book of Margery Kempe,* Shōzo Shibata mentions the synonymic pairs as "features which can hardly be termed colloquial".[8]

In view of the curious manner in which the work was composed, the autobiography of Margery Kempe should in fact provide interesting material for a study of different varieties of fifteenth century usage. As is generally assumed, Margery Kempe, illiterate herself, dictated her memoirs to two different persons, one of whom, the priest, also revised the sections written down by the other amanuensis. Hence the book may reflect the speech habits of at least three different persons. However, many critics consider that, in its general character, the book represents, as R. M. Wilson says, "the kind of prose that Margery herself would have written had she not been illiterate".[9]

The present paper is an attempt to examine certain semantic and lexical aspects of the use of word pairs in *The Book of Margery Kempe*. It is hoped that the study may perhaps throw light on whether or not this well-known stylistic trait is essentially a literary and non-colloquial feature.

The following observations are based on a material of 262 word pairs collected from *The Book of Margery Kempe*. As several word pairs are used more than once, the total number of occurrences comes to 391.

In addition to combinations of two words, repetitive patterns consisting of a word and a roughly synonymous phrase (or in the reverse order) have also been considered. In *The Book of Margery Kempe*, as in medieval prose in general, they represent a fairly common variant of the word + word pattern:

> The company was *wroth* & *in great angyr*. (64.11)
> þer was a monk whech bar gret offyce in
> þat place *despysed* hir & *set* hir *at nowt*. (25.31)
> sche cryid ful lowde & sobbyd ful boystowsly
> *many tymes* & *ofte*. (152.2)

The remarks made below on the currency of certain word pairs in the ME period are based on occasional examples of such combinations as listed in the *MED* and the *OED* and also on a corpus collected by the present writer from a selection of ME prose of the period 1340—1500.

The question of which word pairs should be regarded as a tautological device formed the main issue in Leisi's study of Caxton's style. When one examines the combinations found in *The Book of Margery Kempe*, it seems extremely difficult to say anything definite about the degree of closeness of two synonyms. For this reason, it may perhaps suffice to classify the word pairs into three main types, as regards the semantic relationship of their components:

	Number of word pairs
1. Synonymous or nearly-synonymous	159
2. Metonymic (associated by contig- uity of meaning)	77
3. Complementary or antonymous	26
Total	262

The following examples will illustrate the three varieties:

> 1. in many a place wher sche was neuyr *kyd ne knowyn*.
> (244.9)

þu xalt haue þe same *mede* & *rew+* in Heuyn

(186.19)

2. "Modyr, I drede me to be *deed* & *slayn* wyth enmyis."

(100.35)

Sche wyl boþe *smytyn* & *bityn*, & þerfor is sche
manykyld on hir wristys. (178.2)

3. wythowtyn hyndryng of *body* er of *catel* ... may gon
hom a-geyn in-to owr lond. (100.10)

& þer had sche gret cher, bothyn *bodily* & *gostly*

(110.29)

In a large majority of the pairs, the components are thus synonymous,
or roughly synonymous. In a number of cases, e. g. *hindren* & *lette, kyd
ne knowyn, secret* & *prevy*, the two words can perhaps be said to have
one and the same referent. The fact that one member is often a Romance
loan and the other a native word may indicate, however, that they had
different connotations and were not completely synonymous.

This type of varied repetition is seen in the passages below:

Also þe Saraȝines mad mych of hir & *conueyd* hir & *leddyn*
hir abowtyn in þe cuntre wher she wold gon.

(75.15)

— owr Lord, þat sent hir *help* and *socowr* in euery nede,

(243.5)

þu art weyke j-now of wepyng & of crying, for þo makyn
þe *febyl* & *weyke* anow. (162.24)

whan þe creatur sey þe *worshep* & þe *reuerens* þat
þei dedyn to þe ymage, (77.35)

As may be seen from these examples, the loan-word can take either
the first or second place in the word pair. The position of the components, on the whole, is more dependent on rhythm and euphony than on
etymological factors. There is a general tendency in word pairs and binomials — unless semantic or other important factors intervene — to
give the second place to the longer word.[10] In the present material,
about 54 % of the examples follow this pattern. This figure must be
regarded with some reservation, however, because it is often very difficult to compare the lengths of two ME words, particularly those containing an equal number of syllables.

But an etymological analysis of the word pairs may throw some light
on the use of this device in *The Book of Margery Kempe*. In the following table each word pair has been counted once, and words of Greek
origin which have come to English through Latin, have been classified
under "Romance". The table also shows the order in which the etymo-
logically different components appear.

Etymological Distribution of Word Pair Components

Number of Word Pairs

Anglo-Saxon + Romance	65 ⎫ 112
Romance + Anglo-Saxon	47 ⎭
Anglo-Saxon + Anglo-Saxon	86
Romance + Romance	52
Norse + Anglo-Saxon	4
Anglo-Saxon + Norse	3
Norse + Romance	3
Romance + Norse	2
Total	262

The large proportion of word pairs consisting of purely native or purely Romance elements indicates, first of all, that the device is not primarily used to interpret loan-words by means of native synonyms. This agrees with the comments made by Jespersen[11] and others on the purpose of word pairing in Late ME texts. The fact that the sequence Anglo-Saxon + Romance is somewhat more common than the reverse type may be taken as a further proof of this assumption.

It is also interesting to note that nearly 33 % of the word pairs found in *The Book of Margery Kempe* are purely native in origin. Among these one finds certain phrases that seem to have been quite common in the period:

þe creatur al *hol* & *sownd* thankyd hym of hys *cher* & hys *charyte*, (22.4)

And hastily aftyrwarde sche was *heyl* & *hoyl*. (104.37)

þer was neuyr childe so buxom to þe modyr as I xal be to þe boþe in *wel* & in *wo*, (87.21)

owr Lord þat had ȝouyn hir not lettryd *witte* & *wisdom* to answeryn so many lernyd men (128.28)

& so to folwyn hym as I *kan* & *may*. (246.12)

And þe sayd creatur thowt þat sche ran euyr *to* & *fro* as it had be a woman wyth-owtyn reson, (194.5)

Of these combinations, *heyl* & *hoyl*, *hol* & *sound*, *wel* & *wo*, *to* & *fro*, *can* & *may*, *witte* & *wisdom*, appear already in Old English or Early ME texts.[12] Furthermore, they seem to be irreversible, at least when used in prose texts. In poetry, considerations of rhyme or alliteration may occasionally cause the traditional order to be reversed.

One may thus assume that a certain number of word pairs occurring in *The Book of Margery Kempe* were set phrases of the period not limited to any particular literary genre. Further examples of this type include: *helth & welth, ese & comfort, cher & contenawns,*[13] *joy & blisse, joy & gladness, mihti & strong, sygnys & tokenys.* Some combinations of this kind originated in religious contexts, and a few are translation loans from Latin (e. g. *hol & sound* representing *sanus et salvus*). Nevertheless, by the end of the Middle English period, they may already have become part of the spoken idiom.

Another, perhaps more 'literary' type of word pair is seen in combinations referring more exclusively to concepts of the Christian faith or morality. Some of these also go back to OE, or Early ME, and are based on Biblical usages. The following, for example, occur frequently in late ME texts: *payn & passyon, mede & meryte, feyth & beleue, grace & mercy, pite & compassyon, humbely & mekely.* In particular, the writers of the period make use of antonymous word pairs when referring to the dichotomy of body and soul, thought and deed, the religious and the secular, the active and the contemplative life:

> & so þei abedyn þer xiiij days in þat lond,
> & þer had sche gret cher, bothyn *bodily & gostly,*
>
> (110.28)
>
> he suffyrd it ful mekely & paciently & so dede many
> a worthy clerk, bothyn *reguler & seculer,*   (167.26)
>
> Sche sey hem [apparitions of spirits] many dyuers tymes
> & in many dyuers placys, boþe in *chirche* & in hir
> *chawmbre,*   (88.12)

Certain features of the use of vocabulary and grammatical forms are typical of the mystical writers both in Germany[14] and in England. One is a predilection for nominal verb forms, in English particularly verbal nouns and participles. In his study of the style of Richard Rolle of Hampole, Antonie Olmes notes the frequency of such word pairs as *ledand* and *lerand, waxand* and *noght wanande, herken* and *here,* in *greting* and in *langyng.*[15] Similar paired expressions are common also in *The Cloud of Unknowing* and in the *Revelations* of Julian of Norwich. The abstract and elusive nature of the mystical revelations has given rise to special types of verb pair, some of which are modelled on Latin originals. When describing her religious experiences, Margery Kempe speaks, for example, of hyr *meuynggys* & hyr *steringgys* (3.19). The expression is found in a similar context in *The Cloud of Unknowing.*[16] Some word combinations relating to mystical experiences are almost uniquely employed in *The Book of Margery Kempe.* An example is the noun *dalyawns,* which appears in the meaning 'spiritual dialogue with God' and often forms a word pair with such near-synonyms as *speech* and *communicacyon:*

> So be holy *dalyawns* & *communycacyon* sche felt wel he
> was a good man.   (96.35)
>
> þes swet *speech* & *dalyawns* had þis creatur at owyr
> Ladijs graue,   (73.20)

S. B. Meech remarks that the word "was not used for mystical experience by Rolle but appears, in Margery's sense, in the elevated last chapter of the *Scale of Perfection* of Walter Hilton".[17] In another passage of *The Book of Margery Kempe*, the corresponding word combination occurs in a more ordinary sense, without reference to a mystical communion with God:

> þe good preste of Inglonde *dalying* & *comownyng* in
> her owyn langage, Englysch. (97.23)

It is also interesting to note that in the *Promptorium Parvulorum* (c. 1440), which was compiled in Lynn, Margery Kempe's home town, the verb is glossed as follows: "*Daplyyn or Talkyn: fabulor, confabulor, ... colloquor*".[18]

A conspicuous type of word pair in *The Book of Margery Kempe* consists of expressions describing the emotional manifestations of the mystic's religious experiences. Passages such as "þer *cryed* sche & *wept* wyth-owtyn mesur" (71.27) occur throughout the book and contribute to the monotonous tone of large portions of the narrative. These repetitive patterns stem from the mystical tradition of 'religious tears' and are not limited to *The Book of Margery Kempe*.

A more personal stylistic trait can perhaps be seen in the equally numerous synonym pairs through which Margery Kempe expresses her sense of being slandered and held in contempt by others, particularly by her fellow travellers during the pilgrimages. This attitude is of course a well-known psychological theme in the mystic's autobiography. The following examples will illustrate typical word combinations used in such contexts:

> þan was sche *slawnderyd* & *repreuyd* of mech pepul
> for sche kept so streyt a levyng. (12.29)

> & þerfor many man & many woman wondyrd up-on hir,
> *skornyd* hir & *despised* hir, *bannyd* hir & *cursyd* hir
> (107.13)

> For sche xuld ben holdyn a fool & þe pepyl xuld
> not *makyn of hir* ne *han hir in reputacyon*.
> (62.17)

The above comments thus suggest that repetitive word pairs and other parallel constructions as employed in *The Book of Margery Kempe* represent different stylistic levels of Late Middle English vocabulary, ranging from the colloquial to specific areas of mystical 'jargon'. A number of phrases have the character of set phrases and could perhaps be termed binomials. Several of these have been inherited from Old or Early Middle English, and some persist even today. In spite of this colloquial element, the more literary type of word pair, however, predominates in the book. As Margery Kempe, in spite of her illiteracy, is known to have been familiar with some other mystical writings, it is probably futile to speculate about which word pairs she may have used in dictating her experiences and which came into the narrative when it was written down by her amanuenses. In any case, a study of word pairs in *The Book of Margery Kempe* shows that a device originating as a means of emphasis has developed, in this late medieval prose work, primarily into a decorative element, reflecting the general tendency towards mannerism common in the literature as well as the pictorial arts of the period.

NOTES

[1] All line references are to *The Book of Margery Kempe*, ed. S. B. Meech and H. E. Allen, EETS 212, 1940, reprinted 1961.

[2] On the early history of this pattern in English see, for example, I. Koskenniemi, *Repetitive Word Pairs in Old and Early Middle English Prose: Expressions of the Type "Whole and Sound" and "Answered and Said", and Other Parallel Constructions*, Annales Universitatis Turkuensis, B 107, Turku 1968.

[3] First published in *Lingua* 8, 1959, 113—160; reprinted in *Essays on Linguistic Themes*, 311—355, Oxford 1968.

[4] *Die tautologischen Wortpaare in Caxton's "Eneydos"*, Zürich diss., Zürich and New York 1947.

[5] "Chaucer's Untransposable Binomials", in *Studies Presented to Tauno F. Mustanoja on the Occasion of His Sixtieth Birthday*, NM 73, 1972, 309—314.

[6] *Essays and Studies*, N. S. 9, 1956, 87—112, *passim*.

[7] *Middle English Prose Style: Margery Kempe and Julian of Norwich*, The Hague and Paris 1970, pp. 93, 113—114, 122 ff.

[8] "Notes on the Vocabulary of *The Book of Margery Kempe*", in *Studies in English Grammar and Linguistics: A Miscellany in Honour of Takanobu Otsuka*, Tokyo 1958, 209—220; see pp. 209—211.

[9] Wilson, p. 105.

[10] On the position of the components in OE and EME, see Koskenniemi, pp. 81—88, and in binomials in general, Malkiel, pp. 338—350.

[11] *Growth and Structure of the English Language*, 9th ed., Oxford 1948, pp. 89—90.

[12] See Koskenniemi, p. 125 (*can* & *may*); p. 135 (*hal* & *gesund*); p. 159 (*witte* & *wisdom*); and *MED, from* adv. (*to* & *fro*); *MED, heil* adj. (*heil* & *hol*); *OED, weal* sb. (*weal* & *woe*).

[13] In his article "Zur Bedeutungsgeschichte des englischen Wortes *countenance*", *Archiv* 203, 1966, 32—51, Werner Habicht considers that the frequent ME collocation *chere and countenance* may have influenced the semantic development of the word *countenance*: "Es ist, als ob dabei *countenance* durch die Bedeutung von *chere* ('Gesicht') infiziert würde, als ob eine semantische Assimilation vorläge" (p. 38).

[14] On the vocabulary of the medieval German mystics see, for example, Hermann Kunisch, "Spätes Mittelalter", in Maurer—Stroh, *Deutsche Wortgeschichte*, Vol. I, 2nd ed., Berlin 1959, pp. 246—267.

[15] *Sprache und Stil der englischen Mystik des Mittelalters, unter besonderer Berücksichtigung des Richard Rolle von Hampole*, Halle 1933, p. 68f., 73—78.

[16] *The Cloud of Unknowing and The Book of Privy Counselling*, ed. Phyllis Hodgson, EETS 218, 1944, reprinted 1958; see p. 162, line 11. The word pair *meven* & *steren* is used, however, also in non-religious contexts. (See, for example, *Paston Letters and Papers of the Fifteenth Century*, ed. Norman Davis, Part I, Oxford 1971, Letter No 40, line 81).

[17] *The Book of Margery Kempe*, Notes, p. 256.

[18] Ed. A. L. Mayhew, EETS, ES 102, London 1908; col. 135.

Bengt Loman
Åbo Akademi

Prosodic patterns
in a Negro American dialect

"Such matters as the fate in the New World of the tonal elements in West African speech, where, as has been indicated, tone has semantic as well as phonemic significance, remain to be studied. — — — That the peculiar 'musical' quality of Negro-English as spoken in the United States and the same trait found in the speech of white Southerners represent a nonfunctioning survival of this characteristic of African languages is entirely possible, especially since the same 'musical' quality is prominent in Negro-English and Negro-French everywhere."

M. J. Herskovits, The Myth of the Negro Past (1941)

1. PROSODIC AND SYNTACTIC FEATURES

The present paper is part of a preliminary report from a study of the stress and intonation patterns in a Negro American dialect, especially as it is spoken by ten-year-old children. The dialect is spoken in the central, low-income area within Northwest Washington, D. C., and the description is based on a series of recorded conversations, which have been transcribed and published in a separate volume, *Conversations in a Negro American Dialect* (Washington, Center for Applied Linguistics, 1967).

The introduction to this volume contains a short presentation of the recordings and the informants, and also of the principles used in the transcription of the texts, including a few remarks on the system for prosodic notation. As is pointed out there, the texts have been transcribed in a modified standard orthography, while the prosodic transcription is an adaption of the Trager-Smith system (with some important modifications). A short summary of the working procedure is given here.

First of all, in connection with the transcription of the segmental material, all pauses (p) have been marked, tentatively dividing the material in word groups, "phrases". A phrase consists of: (a) an intonation contour, (b) a terminal juncture, (c) a stress pattern, (d) segmental material. The intonation contour is analyzed as a sequence of pitch levels; the pitch levels are four: /4/ extra high, /3/ high, /2/ central, /1/ low. The pitch levels are always marked on the following syllables in a phrase:

(a) the first syllable
(b) the last syllable
(c) every syllable with primary stress.

If there is a clear fall and/or rise in the intonation between any of the mentioned pitch points, this change will also be marked in the transcription, for instance:

5.150. if shé lèt me stày dis lóng

A clear rise or fall within one syllable from one pitch level to another has been marked by two numbers as the example shows. Such intonation patterns are particularly frequent in syllables with primary stress in phrase final position, for instance:

10.14. I dìd wéll

As a rule, terminal junctures have only been marked in the position immediately before a pause: the juncture system is used to describe characteristic features in the articulation in this position. These features may be described in terms of a double set of contrasts:

The double bar juncture / ‖ / is characterized by short final rise in the fundamental frequency; this rise opposes the double bar juncture to the two other types of terminal juncture.

The single bar juncture / | / is characterized by sustained or increased intensity combined with sustained fundamental frequency.

The double cross juncture / # / is characterized by absence of final intensity, while the fundamental frequency may be either sustained or, more often, lowered (changes in frequency, in this case, are always marked by numbers indicating pitch levels).

In the analyzed texts, the terminal junctures / # / and / ‖ / normally occur at the end of complete sentences, while / | / normally occurs within sentences, dividing them into two or several phrases. For this reason, / # / and / ‖ / may be regarded as final junctures, and / | / as a non-final juncture.

An intonation contour may be divided into two parts:

(a) the onset — the part which precedes the (last) syllable with primary stress

(b) the primary contour — the part which starts with the (last) syllable with primary stress and ends with the terminal juncture.

There are several reasons for this division. First of all it simplifies the description. If we take whole phrases as the basic unit, we must deal with a great variety of contours. By dividing the contours, we may describe them as combinations of a more limited set of onset patterns and primary contours. Also, experience shows that it is easier to hear or to react to the various pitch levels in the primary contours than in the onset, and especially to hear a rise or fall between the (last) syllable with primary stress and the end of the phrase. This part of the phrase intonation also seems to contain more information, which is reflected especially in the large variety of pitch combinations in the primary contours. The onsets, on the other hand, are far more monotonous.

The main purpose of this report is to describe how speakers of the dialect combine various types of primary contours with various types of sentence units.

The sentence units are primarily various types of complete sentences: declarative sentences, special questions, general questions and commands. Among the general questions, the so-called reiterative formulas (*didn't she*) have been classified as a separate group. Direct adresses, interjections and "fragments" have also been segmented as separate sentence units. These categories have been found necessary and sufficient for a segmentation of the text into contingent but not mutually overlapping elements. A passage from the conversations demonstrates the segmentation procedure.

Extract from Conversation 5, sentence units 29—44

29. Ǐ ca' béat hér #   (decl. sent.)

30. yèh   (interj. *yeah*)

31. shé bèat you úp   (decl. sent.)

32. dí'n' shè #   (reit. form.)

33. nó #   (interj. *no*)

34. lás' tíme she dì' | (decl. sent.)

35. bu' nòt dàt tìme when Ǐ was in Miss Mérl's hòuse   (decl. sent.)

36. hóney chì' #   (dir. address)

37. Ǐ tóre hèr úp #   (decl. sent.)

38. shè ain' nèver tàlk to mé agàin #   (decl. sent.)

39. [mmm]   (interj. [mmm])

40. Ǐ 'on' knów #   (decl. sent.)

41. shè was scáred o' mè dàt tìme | when wè was in
    Miss Mérl's hòuse #   (decl. sent.)

42. gír' #   (dir. address)

43. she stàrte' crýin' an' àll at jàm #   (dir. address)

44. she wen' ou'síde   (decl. sent.)

221

45. an' Llóy' was óut dère #   (decl. sent.)

46. wáit'n' for mé an' Jánie #   (fragment)

47. bu' Í knòw who pùt us' ùp to fíght'n' #   (decl. sent.)

48. whó #   (fragment: spec. q.)

49. Dóris #   (fragment)

This extract consists of 21 sentence units: 12 declarative sentences, 1 reiterative formula, 2 direct adresses, 3 interjections, and 3 fragments. Fifteen sentence units are terminated by juncture / # / and one ends in / | /. Five sentence units are connected with the following unit without any intermediate juncture.

The introduction of terminal junctures serves one important purpose at this stage of the analysis. All sentence units are not terminated by a final juncture, but a final juncture always marks the end of a sentence unit. This means, for instance, that sentence unit 45 ends with the word *dere*, and that the following sequence is considered an independent sentence unit (in this case a fragment). If, however, the two sequences had been separated by the non-final juncture / | /, then the sequence *wait'n' for me an' Janie* would have been regarded as a part of the same sentence unit as *an' Lloy' was out dere*. It was necessary to introduce this phonological criterion to avoid subjectivity and confusion in separating fragments from complete sentences.

Special questions are questions which begin with an interrogative word, such as *what, who, why*, while general questions do not begin with an interrogative word. General questions may be answered by *yes* or *no*, while special questions require more specific information as an answer. Both types of question may be constructed without the auxiliary *do*. For this reason, a general question may lack all morphological and syntactical indications of its interrogative character. The *yes*- or *no*-reaction from the interlocutor can not be taken as evidence of a preceding question, because these utterances may also occur as confirmations or rejections of statements in the form of declarative sentences; for instance, *he was there — yes/no*. In such cases, the intonation becomes a necessary criterion for classification: the general questions are characterized by a rising primary contour, or by a primary contour consisting of pitch level /3/, for instance:

10.22. when you gèt 'em àll rígh' she pùt in |

yés òn i' #

10.43 éverybody go óut at de sàme tíme #

Two types of fragments have been separated within the larger category: fragments implying a special question and fragments implying a general question. The special question fragments can be identified by the presence of interrogative words, for instance

1.27.   whó $\#$

5.181.   whére $\#$

5.244.   how múch $\#$

10.78.   hòw abou' Mársha' $\#$

The general question fragments can be identified by the intonation (and by the speech situation).

Finally, it should be pointed out that non-question fragments have been registered only when they are terminated by a final juncture. The reason for this is the difficulty of separating unspecified fragments in non-final position from regular elements of a sentence. Question fragments, on the other hand, have been registered when terminated by a non-final juncture or by a zero juncture, as well as by final juncture.

2. THE TEXTS

It is evident that the conversations are not uniformly valuable for a study of the Washington Negro Dialect spoken in its genuine setting. In the conversations with the adults, the children are, as a rule, the more passive partners; they listen and answer, but they take few initiatives. This restricts their syntactic repertoire considerably with respect to questions, commands, and direct addresses. This is the case with conversations 6—8, where a mother is one of the participants, conversation 10 (a father-and-son dialogue), and conversations 11—14, where the white research assistant interviews the children actively. At the same time, some of the recordings with children as main participants are also limited in this respect, as a large part of the conversations consists of story telling, where questions and commands occur primarily as quoted utterances in the stories. Conversations 1 and 5 are certainly the most representative examples of uninhibited language behavior in daily conversations among Negro children in the area investigated. These two texts have therefore been chosen as the material for the more detailed study of intonation patterns. As it is of interest to include a Negro adult in this basic study, conversation 10 has been selected av a complement. The conversation between AJ and GJ seems to be far more natural than the conversation between HJ and MJ, where the boy is obviously influenced by earlier experiences in interview situations.

The more detailed study is therefore based on the material in this limited corpus, including utterances of one male adult (AJ), two boys and one girl about ten years old (MJ, GJ, JD), and one girl six years old (BS).

3. THE JUNCTURES

The material for the present study is the sentence units. The study focuses on the primary contours ending these sentence units. Because the character of a primary contour may have some correlation with the following juncture, the juncture system has been included in the analysis, but only to the extent that it is related to the primary contours. So only those junctures have been counted which are correlated with a primary contour ending one of the specified sentence units. Given these restrictions, the terminal juncture / # / is by far the most frequent in the texts.

In the 18 cases of juncture / ‖ / two specific functions may be noted. Sometimes this juncture ends a phrase which belongs to a listing sequence; as a rule the speech tempo may be very slow and sustained here (for instance 5.6—10). Other times it occurs in phrases which are pronounced in an excited mood, and here the juncture may be regarded as an intensifying element, for instance:

1.75. you ^{3}'on' ^{2}knòw what you are ^{3}tálkin' ^{2}abou' ^{2}‖

1.178 I ^{2}bét ^{3}you I ^{2}wòn a ^{4}fóotba' ^{3}‖

The material permits one comparison between the use of non-final / ‖ / and the use of zero juncture: there are more cases of non-final juncture / ‖ / than of zero juncture on the borderline between two sentence units (91 cases against 51). The zero juncture occurs especially under the following conditions:

(a) after an interjection, (17 cases), for instance:

10.117. well ^{2}Térry ^{4}nòt ^{2}in de ^{4}kínny^{2}garden^2 |

(b) after or before direct addresses, (10 cases), as:

5.140. ^{2}hère I ^{3}cóme ^{2}téacher^2 #

5.180. ^{2}tèacher can I ^{3}páss ^{3}óu'^{2} #

(c) after a sentence of the type *I say, I think,* followed by a sentence unit which is formally identical with an independent main clause, (10 cases), for example:

10.158. I ^{2}thínk ^{3}she ^{2}dòin' ^{3}fí'^{1} #

224

(d) before *an'* coordinating two sentence units, (5 cases), for instance:

5.16. yeah Í tòok my fís' an Í kep' on púnchin' hèr #

Other phenomena connected with the use of various junctures probably deserve special attention. It could be interesting, for example, to measure the average length of the phrases uttered by various speakers and in various speech situations. For the preliminary report only a few isolated pages have been studied in this respect, indicating that the average phrase is 3 or 4 words long. It could also be of interest to study the average length of the sequences which are terminated by a final juncture. Of greater relevance, however, is a study of the average length of the syntactic macroconstructions, the sentence units.

Table 1. Primary contours in declarative sentences and non-question fragments.

	Decl. sent. junct. #	Decl. sent. junct. / | / or zero junct.	Non-q. fragm. junct. #	TOTAL
A. Falling PC				
—43	8	6	1	15
—42	14	7	2	23
—32	128	42	40	210
—41	1	—	—	1
—31	32	—	12	44
—21	1	—	1	2
Total	184	55	56	295
B. Rising PC				
—34	—	—	—	—
—24	—	—	—	—
—23	11	1	27	39
Total	11	1	27	39
C. Level PC				
—4	1	2	—	3
—3	27	23	27	77
—2	20	3	19	42
—1	—	—	—	—
Total	48	28	46	122

4. THE PRIMARY CONTOURS

4.1. The frequencies of various primary contours (PCs) in declarative sentences and in non-question fragments are registered on Table 1. As the following analysis will show, there are reasons for grouping these two categories together in a description of the functions and character of the PCs. A few general observations may be made on the basis of this table.

The most frequent PCs are /—32/, /—3/, /—31/, /—2/ and /—23/. In declarative sentences, there is a higher frequency of PCs combined with final juncture than of PCs combined with non-final juncture (243:84). The main difference between PCs occurring with non-final juncture and those occurring with final juncture is that no PCs ending on pitch level /1/ occur in non-final position, while there are altogether 81 such contours in final position. The material is in general too limited to permit any significant comparisons between various speakers. It may however be noticed that PC /—32/ has the highest frequency in the material of each speaker.

Before the character of /—32/, the most frequent PC, is described, a few of the less frequent PCs will be described.

PC /—3/ is used particularly with listing. BS and GJ use it frequently in this way in conversations 5 and 10. The primary contour is usually preceded here by an onset containing several syllables on pitch level /3/, for instance:

10.171—2.   we háve # (p) geógraphy tés' one dáy #

10.173—74.   den we hà' # (p) spéllin' tès' one dáy #

Pitch level /3/ starts on the first syllable with primary stress, which as a rule is identical with the first primary stress syllable of the word or word group that indicates the listed item.

PC /—23/ is used particularly in the following three contexts which are of course not mutually exclusive:

(a) in answers; this category is perhaps the most characteristic for the use of /—23/ in declarative sentences and non-question fragments, for instance:

5.48.   whó #

5.49.   Dóris #

(b) at the end of an utterance containing several preceding phrases, for instance: 5:46, 82, 121, 186.

(c) in listing, and here usually in variation with other contours, like /—32/:

5.273—4. trée # óne #

5.300—1. trée # óne #

JD does not use this contour very often in her conversation with BS, but more frequently in her conversation with PJ. This may be taken as an indication that the contour is used especially when a younger person is talking to an older. It is also noticeable that GJ normally uses the /—23/ contours in the *yes-* and *no-*responses he gives to his father in conversation 10.

That PCs ending in pitch level /1/ function as a finality marker, is partly shown by their appearance in combination with the final juncture / # /, but not with non-final juncture / | / or with zero juncture. PC /—32/, on the other hand, is combined with / | / as well as with / # /. Another indication of the final character of pitch level /1/ is the fact that it only occurs once in the onset of an intonation contour (1.218). Furtemore, the PCs with final level /1/ occur as a rule at the end of an utterance (consisting of one or several phrases), or in the middle of an utterance in which the speaker changes the subject (after a marked pause). The following sequences are typical instances: 1.52—59, 5.51—53, 10.89—91. Relatively often the adverbs *now* and *too* in final position are pronounced with PC /—31/. There may be an element of emphasis implied in at least some of these cases. The more frequent marker of emphasis is, however, falling PCs starting on pitch level /4/, for instance:

1.174. yóu didn' wìn nóne #

The instances of PC /—2/ are a rather diffuse group, where it is difficult to find the common denominators. The PC is used to some extent in listing, especially of shorter units like numbers (see for instance 1.52—59). In other cases a special effect seems to be implied in the use of this PC, for instance:

1.5. MJ: bèt you a níckel # da Í'm lòokin' shàrper dan yóu #

GJ: nó you wàsn' #

The instances are, however, rather scattered in the texts, and the recorded texts must be checked again before any specific claims can be made concerning the character of the contour. This is also the case with the other PCs that have been found only in isolated instances.

PC /—32/ is the normal contour in declarative sentences and in non-question fragments; its functions need not be analyzed in subcategories. It occurs in the material with almost all the functions to which the other less frequent PCs are more or less restricted. Thus, it is used in both utterance final and non-final position, in listing, and in answers. Because of its general, unspecified character, however, it seems to have no emphatic or special effect connotation.

To the standard speaker, PC /—32/ sounds particularly strange and unfinished when the syllable with primary stress and pitch level /3/ is followed by several syllables with pitch level /2/ in utterance final position. For example:

1.12.   I áin' ha' my plày clothes òn #

10.111—2.   wè ha' twó | fóurf gráde tèachers an' | twó thír' gràde

tèachers # an' | twó | kínnygarden tèachers #

4.2. In spite of the limited material, there seem to be some significant tendencies in the distribution of PCs in various types of questions, and in the character of the onsets.

PC /—32/ is the most frequent in special questions (incl. fragments), both in final and non-final position. The next most frequent PC is /—2/. The interrogative word in the onset is usually pronounced on pitch level /3/ or /4/, even if the stress of the word is secondary or weak. For instance:

1.198.   whò slug yóurs in yóur little bòxer héa' #

5.56.   how òld are yóu Jáckie #

5.225.   whàt you dó |

In some cases pitch level /3/ starts on the interrogative word in the onset and then continues until the final fall to /2/ in the primary contour:

1.120.   hów did yòu like Màrsha' Háll | Grégory #

This gives the whole question a falling contour. There are also variations of this general pattern, such as the choice of pitch level /4/ in the onset (which seems to intensify the question):

1.197.   who slúg your héad ín #

228

In general questions /—3/ is the most frequent PC. As a rule pitch level /3/ starts already on the first syllable with primary stress in the question, for instance:

10.161.   you ²àll have a ³hómework ³èvery ³évening #

Sometimes pitch level /3/ is reached already on unstressed syllables preceding the first syllable with primary stress, so that the whole question may be pronounced on pitch level /3/:

10.80.   ³is [zæt] de ³sáme ³clàss ³Térry in #

In other cases there may be a momentous fall in the unstressed syllable immdialety preceding the PC:

10.133.   i' ²Mó³jo in ne sàme [ə:#] ²fírs' ³gràde as ²Lár³ry in #

In another variation, pitch level /3/ is preceded by pitch level /4/ in the onset:

5.97.   you ⁴knòw wha' de ³mán | ³sit'n' ³dówn | ³báck

dère | ³dó³in' #

The exceptions from the general pattern with level PC are mostly sentences in which the syntactic construction in itself is a clear indication of the interrogative character of the utterance:

5.180.   ²tèacher can I ³páss ³²óu' #

The interrogative marker may also be a lexical item, such as *any* in the following question:

5.163.   ³wè gonna ²dò any ³prín'n ² #

4.3. Various PCs occur before final juncture in commands. Here /—32/ and /—2/ are the most frequent PCs. For instance:

1.231.   ³come ²ón |

5.187.   go ²héa' ³² #

A characteristic feature in the commands is the frequent use of pitch level /3/ in the onset. This gives the command a falling total contour of the same type that has been found in special questions, for instance:

1.41.   ³shùt ²úp #

1.227.   ³gì' me twén'y ³² #

4.4. The direct addresses in the conversations are pronounced with a wide variety of contours. As a rule the addresses are attached to another sentence unit, containing the message to wich the speaker wants to draw the addressed person's attention, as in *Gregory come on*. In the texts the address generally follows the message. It very often has a level intonation contour which is a continuation of the last pitch level of the preceding unit. The pitch level is either /3/ or /2/, in the examples, and the address may be more or less closely connected to the message by arrangements in juncture and stress pattern. For instance:

5.104. hé còlor so déep # gír' #

5.155. okáy # téacher #

There are some instances where the address is pronounced as a separate phrase and has a more independent contour. This is the case especially when the address is an isolated utterance. The intonation can be either falling or level here (rising contours have not been found in the material):

1.139. Grégory # Grégory #

1.119. Grégory #

There are also cases where the direct address precedes the message, with or without a terminating juncture, with or without primary stress, and with or without pitch level /3/, for example:

1.210. Grégory | we don' knów whàt to sáy like dá' #

1.215. bòy we hàd some fún | dídn' we #

There are fewer than 100 instances of direct addresses in the entire corpus (*Conversations in a Negro American Dialect*). The material is therefore too limited and at the same time too heterogeneous to allow anything more than a few descriptive remarks. The same is of course true of the interjections.

5. ON THE RELATIONSHIP BETWEEN PITCH AND STRESS.

A full treatment of the prosodic system of the dialect must include a study of how the stress patterns are correlated with the segmental material in various syntactic constructions, for instance, the occurrence of double primary stress in modifier-noun-constructions, like *cásh móney*, *Míss Brówn*. A second requirement would be to correlate these stress patterns with the intonation contours, and particularly to study the interrelationship between various degrees of stress and various levels of pitch in various positions within phrases. In this preliminary study, however, the task has been considerably simplified: the starting point is not an analysis of the rules for the distribution of various degrees of stress, but acceptance of the stress notation in the transcriptions. The main problem is therefore to describe how various degrees of stress in the texts are correlated with various levels of pitch.

First it may be pointed out that primary stresses have a high frequency in the continuous speech of the dialect. A phrase may contain several syllables with primary stress, as in the following utterances of various speakers:

1.95.   (MJ)   I don' líke Grégory to tálk to mé like dá' #

5.89.   (JD)   wáit till I fínish dís dumb pí'ture #

5.107. (BS)   dís how Í còlor ápple #

10.130. (AJ)   an' nén ney got anóther fírs' gráde #

10.196. (GJ)   Í saw dém on ne pláygròun todáy #

This high frequency of primary stresses seems to be one of the most characteristic features of the prosodic system of the dialect, especially when it is compared with American standard pronunciation.

The examples given also demonstrate another characteristic feature: the primary stresses are generally combined with pitch level /3/, while the other syllables are generally pronounced on pitch level /2/. The examples also show how a falling or rising primary contour is materialized as a glide on a final syllable with primary stress, while the primary contour may dominate several syllables if unstressed syllables follow the syllable with primary stress.

The general observations may be supported here by some statistical data. Table 2 shows the occurrences of various pitch levels in combination with a syllable with primary stress. If there is a rise or fall on the syllable, the highest pitch level has been regarded as relevant in the counting; so that

dáy

for example, has been classified as a syllable with primary stress in combination with pitch level /3/. Table 2 (a—b) shows that of the 1220 syllables with primary stress in three conversations, 908 are pronounced with pitch level /3/ (74.4 % of the total material). This tendency is particularly strong in the conversation between GJ and his father AJ, where both speakers combine primary stress with pitch level /3/ in almost 90 % of the cases. In his vivid conversation with MJ, however, the boy GJ makes a more varied use of pitch-stress combinations. MJ combines primary stress with pitch level /3/, in 63 % of his primary stressed syllables, while in 13.9 % of these syllables, primary stress is combined with /2/, and in 23 % of the cases with /4/.

Table 2 (a) Number of syllables with primary stress combined with various pitch levels.

1. Syllables with primary stress combined with	Conv. 1		Conv. 5		Conv. 10		Total
	MJ	GJ	JD	BS	AJ	GJ	
1.1. pitch level /4/	53	36	3	45	6	2	145
1.2. pitch level /3/	145	123	106	237	125	172	908
1.3. pitch level /2/	32	18	36	50	8	23	167
Total	230	177	145	332	139	197	1220

Table 2 (b) Percentage of syllables with primary stress combined with various pitch levels.

1. Syllables with primary stress combined with	Conv. 1		Conv. 5		Conv. 10		Total
	MJ	GJ	JD	BS	AJ	GJ	
1.1. pitch level /4/	23.0	20.3	2.1	13.6	4.3	1.0	11.9
1.2. pitch level /3/	63.0	69.5	73.1	71.4	89.9	87.3	74.4
1.3. pitch level /2/	13.9	10.2	24.8	15.1	5.8	11.7	13.7
Total	99.9	100.0	100.0	100.1	100.0	100.0	100.0

Pitch level /4/ is used only in a few utterances in the conversation between AJ and GJ, which is an indication of the somewhat stiff and formal atmosphere. AJ uses pitch level /4/ once on the stressed syllables of an utterance, as a substitution for pitch level /3/:

$$
\overset{2}{\text{well}} \ \overset{4}{\text{Té}}\text{rry} \ \overset{2}{\text{nòt}} \ \text{in de} \ \overset{4}{\text{kí}}\text{nny}\overset{2}{\text{garden}} \ \overset{2}{|}
$$

10.117.

$$
\overset{4}{\text{hé}}\text{'s} \ \overset{2}{\text{in}} \ \text{fìrs'} \ \overset{4}{\text{grá}}\text{de} \ \overset{2}{\text{àin}}\text{' }\overset{3}{\text{'e}} \ \|
$$

The utterance constitutes a (slightly indignant) correction of GJ's preceding utterance, and it expresses a sudden commitment in the conversation. This may be compared with an earlier situation in the conversation. AJ asks one of his stereotyped questions about the child-

ren in school; then he suddenly becomes interested in one item, interrupts himself, and switches to a higher pitch:

10.71.
       2 3   3   2 3 2 2
do yóu sèe Míchael an' áll o' [bm] #

    2   4   4 2
is Míchael in your clàss #

Here pitch level /4/ continues on the subsequent unstressed syllables.
The final example from AJ's contributions to the conversation also
shows how the speaker changes to a higher pitch in an outburst of
personal interest (this sudden interest is also marked by the interruption of the preceding sentence unit):

10.183.
           2   3   2
when you gìt to de síx gràde yòu [ɑ:#] (p)

   3   2   2   4   4   2
léave Fòster an' # (p) hòw hígh do you go in [ɑ:#]

     2   3 2
(p) òver at Fóster #

In his daily life in discussions with his peer group, AJ uses pitch level
/4/ far more extensively than this short extract from an uncommited
conversation shows. It is an interesting feature in the speech behavior
of the Negro men, that pitch level /4/ is typically pronounced in the
falsctto register. This is how pitch level /4/ is expressed in AJ's utterances, and more examples can be found in the utterances of his brother,
HJ, in conversation 9. This phenomenon can also be heard whenever
there is a group of Negro men talking spiritedly at the street corner.

GJ makes use of pitch level /4/ only in isolated utterances while
talking with his father. In these cases, the pitch level is used for contrast or emphasis:

10.206.
       3 2   2   2   4 3 2
Máurice knòw how to | prin' hís wéll #

      2   4 2
èvery time sòmebody try to tèach Léwis |

     3 2 2   3   2   2
Léwis make | létters báckwar's #

In one case pitch level /4/ falls on an unstressed syllable:

10.151.
      2   3   4 3 2
dey páss | dìs tí' #

In the conversation between the two boys, pitch level /4/ sometimes
seems to have an emphatic-contrastive function, as in

1.153.
      4   2 2
tén dòllars

1.157.
      4   3 3   2
Mórt'n sált bòx

In other cases it may be regarded simply as an expression of the excited mood of the speaker, especially when a phrase or an utterance contains several subsequent syllables on pitch level /4/, like:

1.110. I tréw yóur ténnis báll úp on ne róof |

  yóu gòt Hàrry Lée ténnis bá' #

1.166. bu' Í stìll béat dat ráce an' gót mè a níckel #

In the conversation between the two girls, BS makes frequent use of pitch level /4/ on stressed syllables, while JD's utterances contain only a few cases. This is obviously an expression of her grudging attitude towards the childish (but talkative) interlocutor. JD uses pitch level /4/ with an obviously emphatic function:

5.134. I áin' gon béat you #

5.182. yòu jus' wànt to be góin' |

5.272. jùs sáy # thrée # an pùt [ə] óne #

In BS's utterances, finally, pitch level /4/ very often has the character of a non-functional but emotionally loaded variation to pitch level /3/, for example:

5.41. shè was scáred o' mè dát tìme |

5.133. hére de rúler you bèat us wìt #

The combination primary stress plus pitch level /2/ is related to the segmental or syntactic material in a complex fashion. (It is at least not possible to explain its use in terms of emphasis or excitement.) Some common phrases are however normally pronounced with pitch /3/ on the first syllable and pitch /2/ on the stressed second (final) syllable:

okáy (5.132, 176, 220, 251), *come ón* (1.231, 5.130), *shùt úp* (1.41), *thát's áll* (5.183). Cf. also the listing of numbers (1.52—58), and the use of direct addresses pronounced on pitch level /2/:

1.212. Grégory # did you líke Màrsha' Háll góo' #

For further examples, see 1.121, 213, 221, 5.36, 42, 137, 155.

As mentioned earlier, both constituents are very often pronounced with primary stress in a modifier-noun construction. In these cases the first constituent may have pitch level /3/ while the second constituent has pitch level /2/; this intonation contour seems to be especially frequent immediately preceding a final juncture; for example:

$\overset{3}{fi}\overset{2}{fty}\ \overset{}{cén}$ # (1.47), $\overset{3}{six}\ \overset{2}{cén}$ # (1.62), $\overset{3}{tén}\overset{2}{nis\ bá}$ # (1.107)

$\overset{3}{sált}\ \overset{2}{bóx}$ # (1.156), $\overset{2}{lást}\ \overset{2}{tíme}$ # (5.64), $\overset{3}{hér}\ \overset{2}{smóke}$ # (5.70)

$\overset{3}{Miss}\ \overset{2}{Brówn}$ # (5.76), $\overset{2}{blúe}\ \overset{2}{cráyon}$ # (5.203), $\overset{3}{dís}\ \overset{2}{númber}$ # (5.269).

Another characteristic group consists of the cases where a phrase ends with the primary contour /23/. In some cases this implies a rising glide on the last syllable, if it has primary stress. If the final syllable has secondary or weak stress it is pronounced on pitch level /3/, while pitch level /2/ lies on a preceding syllable with primary stress. For example:

5.46 $\overset{3}{wáit'n}$ for $\overset{3\ 2}{mé\ an'}$ $\overset{2\ 3}{Jánie}$ #

The cases of the final pattern $/\overset{2\ 3}{xx}$ #/ are also registered on Table 3, as category 2.2.c. From the table it is obvious that this prosodic combination is used especially by BS and GJ in their conversations with older persons. (Cf. p. 227.)

There are still many cases of the combination primary stress plus pitch level /2/ that remain to be classified. The use of this feature seems to be associated with special speech situations. In Conv. 5, JD makes frequent use of the pattern, and it reflects to some extent the low, uncommitted voice quality she uses in her conversation with the little girl. BS, on the other hand, shifts frequently and unpredictably between various pitch levels, for instance:

5.1. $\overset{3}{I'm}\ \overset{3}{á'}\overset{2}{way}\ \overset{2}{gèt'n'}\ \overset{2}{béat'n'}$ #

5.3. $\overset{4}{whó}\ \overset{2}{mòre}\ \overset{2}{béat}\ \overset{3}{me}\ \overset{2}{úp}$ #

5.5 $\overset{4}{I}\ \overset{3}{knów}$ who $\overset{3}{béat}$ me $\overset{2}{úp}$ #

It is possible that this constant variation in the use of prosodic patterns gives her speech a special artificial or childish touch.

Syllables with secondary or weak stress have, as a rule, pitch level /2/. As all the syllables have not been counted, no percentage figures can be presented indicating how often various pitch levels are combined with syllables with secondary or weak stress. Table 3 shows to what extent those syllables are combined with pitch levels /3/ and /4/. Here it has been found necessary to distinguish between various positions in relation to the stressed syllable. Categories 2.1.b. and 2.2.b. contain the cases where a syllable (or a sequence of syllables) with secondary or weak stress is combined with pitch level /4/ or /3/ in the position immediately after a stressed syllable with the same (or higher) pitch. For instance:

1.182. I wón a fóotbà' an' Mársha' tréw it ùp òn ne róof #

1.67. I bét yòu it ís #

Table 3. Number of syllables with secondary or weak stress with various pitch levels and in various positions.

2. Syllable (or sequence of syllables) with secondary or weak stress combined with	Conv. 1		Conv. 5		Conv. 10		Total
	MJ	GJ	JD	BS	AJ	GJ	
2.1. pitch level /4/							
2.1.a. preceding stressed syllable	7	2	—	16	1	1	28
2.1.b. immediately following stressed syllable w/ pitch level /4/	7	2	1	6	1	—	17
2.1.c. immediately following stressed syllable w/ pitch /3/ or /2/	—	—	—	1	—	—	1
Total	14	4	1	23	2	1	46
2.2. pitch level /3/							
2.2.a. preceding stressed syllable	16	24	26	65	10	23	164
2.2.b. immediately following stressed syllable w/ pitch /4/ or /3/	53	24	14	59	37	21	208
2.2.c. immediately following stressed syllable w/ pitch level /2/	—	2	1	8	1	12	24
Total	69	50	41	132	48	56	396

In some cases this pattern may have a functional relevance, for instance in general questions, where the interrogative character may be marked by a sequence of stressed and unstressed syllables on pitch level /3/ or /4/. For example:

10.161.   you àll have a hómework èvery évening #

In other cases the choice of pitch level /3/ may simply be a nonfunctional variant of the more frequent shift to pitch level /2/.

It may perhaps be regarded as a sort of pitch level assimilation (where a high pitch on a syllable with primary stress influences the choice of pitch for the following syllables). A long sequence of unstressed syllables on pitch level /3/, may however be an expression for a strong emotion, for example:

1.23.   Greg Bárber look bètter dan yóu #

yòu cóme in dère wit your clòthes |

hàngin' dówn àll le way dówn to here #

Table 3 shows that following a stressed syllable with pitch /3/ or /4/, unstressed syllables on pitch level /3/ are frequent for all the speakers, while pitch level /4/ occurs here only in isolated cases (this is of course a result of the lower frequency of /4/ altogether).

Categories 2.1.a. and 2.2.a. on Table 3 contain cases where a syllable (or a sequence of syllables) with secondary or weak stress is combined with pitch level /3/ or /4/ in a position where it precedes (not necessarily immediately) a stressed syllable, for example:

5.191.   Ì 'on' knów hòw to dó dà' júnk #

5.186.   Ì 'on' wànna be góín' #

(If a syllable with the combination secondary or weak stress plus pitch level /3/ or /4/ takes the position between two stressed syllables, it has been counted as a case of categories 2.1.b—c. or 2.2.b—c.)

In conversations 1,5, and 10 there are altogether 192 cases of categories 2.1.a. and 2.2.a. In about 130 of these cases the syllable with pitch level /4/ or /3/ consists of a pronoun, usually a personal pronoun functioning as the subject of a sentence. In other cases, the syllable may be an adverb, especially an interrogative adverb (14 cases), or an imperative verb form in a command construction (14 cases), for example:

5.225.   whàt you dó |

5.252. whàt is dís #

1.231. come ón |

5.302. lòok at dís one #

A fourth characteristic category is the first constituent in a modifier + noun construction, for example:

1.51. bìg móuf #

10.39 twò tímes #

In several cases this constituent is of course a pronoun:

5.24. dàt chíld

5.85. hèr hóuse

5.113 sòme ápple |

As mentioned earlier (p. 234), the first constituent in such constructions may also have primary stress.

Of the remaining material, two categories may be specially noted. One is the interjection *okay*, wich as a rule is pronouced with the prosodic pattern

okáy #

The other is the phrase *I don't know*, wich as a rule has the following typical pronunciation in the Negro dialect:

5.40. I 'on' knów #

6. ON THE PROSODIC PATTERNS IN A CONTINUOUS TEXT

After performing the prosodic analysis and description of isolated utterances, it is of interest to see how the various patterns are combined in an extract from a continuous conversation. Such a study may verify whether the categories that have been specially pointed out in the preceding analysis can really be regarded as frequently recurring and hence typical elements in the prosodic system of the dialect. For this final test, sentence units 29—49 of Conversation 5 have been chosen — the same passage that was included earlier for the demonstration of segmentation into sentence units (pp. 221 f.) The sentence units will be analyzed here with references to relevant pages in the preceding chapters.

29. BS: Ì ca' béat hér #

Pitch level /3/ on syllables with primary stress (p. 231)), and also on the pronoun subject in the onset (p. 237). Pitch level /2/ on unstressed syllable (p. 231). The primary countour /-32/ has high frequency in declarative sentences (p. 228).

30. JD yèh
     ²

Interjection *yeh* with secondary stress and pitch level /2/, connected with following sentence unit without intermediate juncture (p. 224).

31. JD: shé bèat you úp
         ³ ²   ³

Declarative sentence with /3/ on syllables with primary stress, otherwise /2/, connected with following sentence unit without intermediate juncture. Primary contour /-3/ is also frequent in declarative sentences (especially before non-final or zero juncture (p. 225, 226).

32. JD: dí'n' shè #
         ³   ²

Reiterative formula with /3/ on syllable with primary stress and /2/ on following syllable with secondary stress (p. 231).

33. BS nó #
        ²³

Interjection *no* used with rising intonation, PC /-23/, in answer to an older person (pp. 226 f.).

34. BS: lás' tíme she dì' |
         ³⁴   ³   ³

Declarative sentence with non-final juncture. Primary stress on both constituents in a modifier-noun construction (p. 234); rising intonation on the first constituent, which gives it a higher pitch level hhan the following noun (p. 234 f.). Level PC as a result of pitch assimilation (p. 237).

35f. BS: bu' nòt dàt tìme when Ì was in Miss Mérl's hòuse hóney chì' #
         ²   ³   ²   ²   ²

Declarative sentence combined with following direct address, without intermediate juncture (p. 224). Pitch level /2/ on syllables with secondary or weak stress (p. 231); pitch level /2/ on the syllable with primary stress in the direct address (whose primary contour is a continuation of the last pitch level of the preceding sentence unit). (p. 224).

37. BS: Ì tóre hèr úp #
            ³ ²   ²

Pitch level /3/ on the pronoun subject in the onset; pitch level /2/ on the following syllables with primary or secondary stress — an artificial or emotional intonation? (p. 235).

38. BS: shè ain' nèver tàlk to mé agàin #
  ^{3 2}   ...   ^{3 2 2}

Declarative sentence with /3/ on syllable with primary stress, and /2/ on other syllables, except for /3/ on the pronoun subject in the onset.

39f. JD: [mmm] I 'on' knów #
  ²   ³   ^{3 2}

Interjection combined — without a primary contour of its own — with following declarative sentence, which has the intonation pattern normally attached to the expression *I 'on' know* (with /3/ on the auxiliary, constituting the unstressed syllable immediately preceding the primary contour. (p. 238).

41f. BS: shè was scáred o' me dát tìme | when wè was in Miss Mérl's
  ⁴ ² ⁴ ² ^{4 2}   ³

  hòuse # gír' #
  ²   ²

Declarative sentence followed (without intermediate juncture) by a direct address. Pitch level /4/ or /3/ on syllables with primary stress, except for the stressed syllable in the direct address (where the primary contour continues the final pitch level of preceding sentence unit). Pitch level /4/ also on the pronoun subject in the onset.

43f. BS: she stàrte' crýin an' àll lat jàm #
  ³ ² ³   ³

  she wen' ou'síde
  ³   ³

  an' Llóy' was óut dère #
  ² ³ ³ ³

Declarative sentences pronounced on pitch level /3/, except for a few unstressed syllables; the extensiv use of pitch level /3/ has been regarded as a characteristic feature in listing sequences (p. 226). Sentence units 43 and 44 begin with unstressed syllables on pitch level /3/ containing the pronoun subject.

46. BS: wáit'n' for mé an' Jánie #
  ³   ^{3 2} ^{2 3}

Fragment with continuous use of pitch level /3/, but fall to /2/ on the unstressed syllable immediately preceding the primary contour. PC /-23/ is a characteristic contour at the end of a long utterance, or before a shift of topic (p. 226).

47.   BS: bu' Í knòw who pùt us ùp to fíght'n' #

Declarative sentence in which the speaker shifts the topic. The
new topic is emphatically presented with pitch level /4/ on the
stressed syllable. PC /3/ on stressed syllable in the onset.

48.   JD: whó #

Special question fragment consisting of one syllable, pronounced
on pitch level /2/ (p. 228).

49.   BS: Dóris #

A bisyllabic fragment with PC /-23/, typical of answers from
a younger person to an older (pp. 226, 227).

Thus, it seems possible to describe and explain the intonation patterns
in this extract from a spontaneous conversation in terms of the descriptive rules which have been formulated in the preceding anlysis.

Note. A COMMENT ON THE MOTTO

The introductory motto is a quotation from M. J. Herskovits' standard work on the African heritage of the American Negro. The purpose
of the motto was originally just to keep a door open to the fascinating
problems concerning the origin of the Negro American dialects. The
experiences and results of a year's work with the intonation patterns
in a modern Negro American dialect permit some final comments which
relate to Herskovits' statement.

First of all, Herskovits' terminology is of course rather unspecific. The
concept "musical" occurs sometimes as a general semi-professional description of the intonation of various languages and dialects, and it is
not always easy to understand in individual cases which features in the
prosodic system are causing this impression or this judgment. Furthermore, it may be a difficult or even impossible task to find traces of the
tone system of West African languages in the modern Negro American
dialects, which are not tone languages.

Of course there is a possibility that some features in the prosodic
system of Negro American dialects have an African origin, a direct
historical connection with corresponding features in West African
prosody. The task in proving such a relation will be to isolate and define
the features of the dialects which seem to deviate most obviously from
white standard pronunciation, and then to study the frequency and distribution of similar features in West African languages. It seems to
me that in this respect three phenomena deserve special attention in

the Negro dialect of the United States — as I have heard it spoken especially by Negro children and teenagers in schools in Washington, D. C., in Clinton, Tennessee, and in Jackson, Mississippi.

1. The high frequency of primary stresses (Cf. p. 231).

2. The constant and marked shift between pitch levels /3/ and /2/ which basically is correlated with the shift between syllables with primary stress and with weaker stress, and which therefore may give the impression of a "musical rhytm" in the speech. (Cf. p. 231).

3. The frequent use of pitch level /4/ pronounced in the falsetto register, as a substitute for pitch level /3/, and typically occurring in the excited speech of Negro men. (Cf. p. 223).

One may make a comparison with the case of the Swedish dialect spoken in Finland, which is usually described by Standard speaking Swedes as "singing" or "musical". The basic intonation pattern of this dialect consists of a marked shift between high pitch on stressed syllables and low pitch on unstressed syllables, while the intonation of Standard Swedish is more gliding, with constant rises and falls, not necessarily related to the stress system. The gliding character of Standard Swedish intonation is also particularly accented by the functional contrast between the two word tones, tone I and tone II, which does not occur in the Swedish dialect of Finland (with some exceptions).

The constant shift between pitch levels /2/ and /3/ may constitute the "musical" character of the Negro dialect — especially as pitch levels /2/ and /3/ have a somewhat different distribution in the dialect as compared with standard American pronunciation. These differences in distribution make it easier for the Standard speaker to pay attention to or to react to particular shifts between the two levels.

REFERENCES

Bengt Loman. 1967. *Conversations in a Negro American Dialect.* Washington D. C., Center for Applied Linguistics.
—   . 1967. "Intonation Patterns in a Negro American Dialect: A preliminary Report." Washington, D. C., Center for Applied Linguistics, Unpublished manuscript.

Håkan Ringbom
Åbo Akademi

The style of Orwell's preface to *Animal Farm*

When we meet a text whose authorship is uncertain we may neverthe-less often have a fairly clear idea of who wrote it. There may be certain Shavian or Hemingwayan features, for instance, that make Shaw or He-mingway seem the probable author of such an unknown text. But very often it is difficult to say exactly why this seems to be so.

Some of the vital questions in stylistic analysis are thus the following: How do we arrive at the conclusion that it was one particular author who wrote the text and not another? On what concrete criteria, lexical, syntactic, and/or textual, do we base our hypothesis? How can we verify whether our intuition proved correct?

These questions prompt themselves at a reading of the essay recently published in *The Times Literary Supplement* entitled "The Freedom of the Press" (15 Sept., 1972). An elucidating commentary by Bernard Crick in the same issue provides strong evidence that the essay is a hitherto unknown preface to *Animal Farm* by George Orwell, even though it might seem strange that hardly anybody appears to have known about such a preface. Apparently Orwell — wisely enough — decided not to include the preface after all. A miniature masterpiece such as *Animal Farm* can perfectly well stand on its own, without any prefatory com-ments. Anyway, although Crick's evidence is not based on the style of the essay, it is difficult to imagine that anyone at all familiar with Orwell's style would doubt that it was Orwell who wrote it.

But what, then, does this unmistakably Orwellian flavour consist of? One possible answer might refer to the polemical nature of the essay. A collection of the abusive words and phrases used in "The Free-dom of the Press" (hereafter abbreviated FP) results in quite an im-pressive list: *cowardice* (2), *sinister, conspiracy, servility, complete disregard to historical truth or intellectual decency, libelled, scandal, boycotted, falsify, dishonest, sordid motives, blasphemy, denigration, a dull, silly book and a disgraceful waste of paper, acres of rubbish, scurrility, slipshod writing, foolish, intolerant, despise, crush its ene-mies, conscious lying, yelping, outrage, agitation, unscrupulousness, de-liberate falsification of history, forgery, dishonesty* (2), *evil* (3), *deadly sin, cowardly, timidity, nonsense, to do dirt on.* But Orwell is, of course, not the only writer to make such violent attacks in his argumentation.

243

Similar lists could easily be compiled from Shaw's prefaces, for instance.

Since most of the words above occur only once in FP, which comprises little more than 3600 words, we can hardly say with certainty that any one of them belongs to Orwell's favourite words, or pluswords, as I shall call them. Such a statement might, perhaps be made about certain nouns with a relatively high frequency, such as *intelligentsia* (10 occurrences), *liberty* (9), *censorship* (9), and *intellectual*(s) (11), but regular use of these words reveals more what the author wrote about than how he wrote it. This is, indeed, a main problem whenever word-frequencies are analysed for a stylistic purpose.

In order to find out about the style of FP rather than its content it might be possible to start with the high-frequency words, that is, the words occurring more than twenty or twenty-five times in the essay. We can begin comparing the commonest words in FP with a rank list containing the words with the highest frequency in a large collection of essays, such as Section G in Kučera-Francis, *Computational Analysis of Present-Day American English*.[1] (K—F) Considering the different sizes of FP and K—F, one can calculate the expected frequency for individual words in FP, taking K—F as the norm and assuming that

Word	Frequency in FP	Expected freq in FP based on K—F	Plusword[3] or minusword in FP	Word freq. in K—F	
1. The	254	262	—0	1. The	10758
2. Of	139	155	—0	2. Of	6378
3. To	114	102	+0	3. And	4460
4. And	87	109	—?	4. To	4164
5. It	85	33	+	5. A	3458
6. Is	78	44	+	6. In	3409
7. In	70	83	—?	7. That	1960
8. A	70	84	—?	8. Is	1815
9. That	63	48	+?	9. He	1536
10. Not	50	20	+	10. Was	1470
11. Was	41	36	+0	11. His	1447
12. This	36	19	+	12. It	1372
12. But	36	19	+	13. For	1291
14. Be	30	21	+?	14. As	1261
15. They	29	15	+	15. With	1095
16. One	27	13	+	16. I	845
16. Or	27	15	+	17. Be	844
				19. Not	832
				22. This	791
				23. But	772
				29. They	609
				31. Or	597
				32. One	550

the data conform to a "normal" distribution. The expected frequencies in such a comparison can be regarded only as rough guidelines, however, since a simple regula de tri calculation of the expected frequency is not an adequate procedure,[2] when the norm is a sample more than forty times as large as the text compared with it.

A glance at this table already reveals something about the favourite words in FP. But the frequencies in themselves do not give sufficient information. They need to be supplemented by other investigations, for instance, as to whether the words are found in regularly recurring syntactic constructions. In particular, it might be worth looking at such constructions in FP where one can find several high-frequency words marked + in the table. An obvious collocation is *it is*, and other words with which this collocation is combined are *to*, *not* and *that*. From the examples in the text some recurring syntactic formulae can be made up:

Examples in FP	Syntactic formula
It is quite safe to attack Churchill	
It is important to distinguish	
It is important to realize	It is (adj.) to (vb.)
It is very rare for anything of an anti Catholic tendency to appear	
It is "not done" to say it	
It is not because	
It is obviously not the whole of the story	It is not
It is not the same in all countries	
It is not so in the United States	
It is not desirable that	It is (adj.) that
It is true that	

(Eleven other examples of *it is*)

Then, the next question to be asked is whether these constructions are also characteristic of a representative body of Orwell's essays, such as his *Collected Essays* (CE), as compared with K—F. We get the following table:

	Actual frequency in CE	Expected frequency in CE	Actual frequency in K—F	χ^2
Is	3355	1743	1815	1491
It is	693	286	298	638
It is not	62	25	26	55
It is (adj) to	120	46	48	219
It is (adj) that	90	29	30	128

245

Now, if we calculate the expected frequencies of these constructions in FP according to the norms of both CE and K—F, there can be no doubt about which norm comes closer.

	Actual frequency in FP	Expected frequency acc. to CE	Expected freq. acc. to K—F
Is	78	84	44
It is	22	17	7
It is (not, to or that)	11	7	2

The expected figures according to CE lie well within the standard deviation, whereas the expected figures according to K—F are far outside the probability of a statistical significance test.[4] In other words, the collocation *it is*, including the syntactic formulae where *it is* is combined with *not, to* or *that*, is a typically Orwellian construction.

Granted that the construction *it is* (adj.) *to/that* ... is characteristic of Orwell's style, one might proceed to find out whether any adjectives occur particularly frequently in these constructions. Figures for such an investigation would have to be taken from a large sample such as CE, since the seven examples in FP are obviously much too few. The following table shows that there are some commonly recurring adjectives in these contexts:

It is (adj.) *that*			*It is* (adj.) *to* (vb.)		
	CE (90 occ.)	K—F (30)		CE (120)	K—F (48)
Possible	8	6	Significant	5	—
Probable	9	2	Possible	10	6
Certain	8	—	Impossible	8	1
			Difficult	20	10
			Easy	17	5
Obvious	8	2	Hard	2	4
Clear	13	2	Necessary	9	3
True	16	5	Important	8	2

Many of these constructions may well be typical of argumentative essays in general, but we may especially note Orwell's regular use of categorical expressions, such as *it is clear/obvious/certain that* (29) and *it is impossible to* (8). *Obviously* and *impossible* have previously been noted as pluswords in Orwell[5] and the use of categorical words of this type very much contributes to the impression of Orwell's style as assertive.

This assertiveness is certainly a most conspicuous feature of FP and it can also be seen in nearly all examples of the syntactic formulae given above. FP also has several phrases expressing obligation or necessity which contribute to the same effect: there are as many as five instances of *ought to*, three of *have to*. Again these verbs are characteristic of Orwell's essays, as compared with K—F.[6] Phrases expressing obligation or necessity are frequently part of Orwell's persuasive devices.

Another example, also connected with an assertiveness of style. When the collocation *it is not* is used in FP, *not* tends to be heavily stressed. This stressed *not* also occurs elsewhere in FP, e. g.: "the chief danger to freedom ... is not the direct interference of the MOI," "one does not say that a book 'ought not to have been published' merely because it is a bad book," "this kind of thing is not a good symptom". The stressed *not* forms an essential part of an argument by elimination, a method commonly met with in Orwell's essays. Also, *not* is often (10 times in FP) combined with *but*, another plusword in both FP and CE, to form an antithetical construction ("it is not because they are frightened of prosecution but because they are frightened of public opinion").

Making use of my previous study of Orwell's essays I shall proceed to give a brief list of some words and stylistic traits in FP which have already been established as characteristic of Orwell's essay style. Going back to the high-frequency words in the table on page 000, we may further note some recurring contexts for *one* and *or*. Nearly half of the occurrences of *one* in FP (13 out of 27) are the indefinite pronoun. Very much the same proportion (52 %) is found for the indefinite pronoun in the significantly many occurrences of this word in CE, whereas the percentage in K—F is only 15. Thus, in both FP and CE it is the use of *one* as indefinite pronoun that explains the high frequency of this word.

With *or*, too, we can point to a regular employment of this word for the same recurring purpose. What comes after the conjunction modifies or restricts the preceding part. Out of the 27 occurrences in FP, 9 are of this restrictive type. Five of these *ors* are immediately followed by *at any rate* or *at least*, which further stresses the restrictive sense. Some examples are: "the intelligentsia, or most of them," "only, or at any rate chiefly," "it is harmless or at least it is understandable".

A typical argumentative device of Orwell's is to build up an imaginary situation and tell the reader what would have been said. In FP there are several of these situations, one of which contains three fictitious quotations:

> "Put it in that form and nearly any English intellectual will feel that he ought to say 'Yes'. But give it a concrete shape, and ask, 'How about an attack on Stalin? Is *that* entitled to a hearing?', and the answer more often than not will be 'No'."

Imperatives (5 instances in FP) are essential means in Orwell's build-up of such imaginary situations where the imaginary reader frequently is asked to take an active part. The pronouns *you* (10) and *one* (13), but rarely *we* (4), may also occur, and direct questions are frequent (8). All these are important elements in creating the peculiar atmosphere of intimacy between Orwell and his reader. The reader has an impression of a speaking voice, and such a conversational effect is also achieved by other means in both FP and CE. One can mention adverbs such as *actually* and *simply* (both used twice in FP), dashes (13) and italics (3), and the introduction of sentences with *and* (7) and *but* (10).

Almost any stylistic investigation suffers from the drawback that an insufficient number of features are commented upon. In this paper only relatively few Orwellian features are dealt with. Of some other characteristic traits our notions may be so vague and impressionistic that it is difficult to verbalize them. For others, only isolated instances can be found in an essay as brief as FP. But when investigating what is genuinely characteristic of an author's style, the procedure outlined here might be worth developing further. A frequency list of the commonest words in the language is compared with a similar list drawn up from a suitable norm. Marked variations in rank order and frequency then form the starting point for an investigation of the contexts in which these words regularly recur. In this way truly typical words and constructions may be found. Particularly when computer-made concordances of the works of individual authors and of whole collections of texts making up a norm are more readily available than at present, the approach outlined above could lead to truly efficient use of concordances for stylistic purposes. For such an approach the statistical apparatus would have to be more elaborate than the very simple calculations I have made here, although statistics in literary studies must never be regarded as an end in itself.

NOTES

[1] In Kučera-Francis, Section G, "Belles Lettres", contains 75 samples of about 2.000 words each. All the texts were published in the United States in 1961. In my recent study, *George Orwell as Essayist: A Stylistic Study* (*Acta Academiae Aboensis* ser. A, 44:2, Åbo 1973) Section G was taken as the "essay norm" against which individual word-frequencies in Orwell's *Collected Essays* (ab. 146.000 words) were compared.

[2] See Sture Allén, "Om textattribution. Kring en avhandling av Marina Mundt," *Arkiv för Nordisk Filologi* 86 (1971), 82—113.

[3] In order to decide whether a word is a plusword or a minusword a statistical significance test has to be applied. The most usual test assessing the significance of the difference between actual and expected frequencies is the χ^2-test. If the value for χ^2 exceeds 6.6 the difference is significant at the 1 % level, if it exceeds 10.8, at the 0.1 % level. However, if the expected frequency is 5 or lower the value is not reliable. One needs to be careful even if the expected frequency is between 6 and 10. For a fuller account of this simple statistical procedure, see *George Orwell as Essayist*, p. 67 (cf. pp. 27 f.).

In view of the different sizes of FP and K—F, the χ^2-values are only approximate. The words with the highest values in the table are *it* (81.9), *not* (45.0), *is* (6.3), *but* and *this* 15.2, *one* 13.5, *they* 11.7, *or* 9.6, all of which can be regarded as pluswords. The remaining words in the table cannot on the basis of this calculation be regarded as clear pluswords or minuswords in FP.

[4] If FP is taken as the stylistic norm and each of the 75 samples in K—F is matched against this norm, one sample ought to contain 12 occurrences of *it is*. In actual fact, only one sample (nr 13) contains 12 or more occurrences (one has 11, two 10 and two 9, the rest fewer than 9 occurrences). No sample in K—F has as many as 6 occurrences of the formula *it is* + *not, that* or *to*.

[5] See *George Orwell as Essayist*, p. 69.

[6] The following table shows the distribution of important verbs expressing obligation and necessity in CE and K—F:

	Actual frequency in CE	Expected frequency acc. to K—F	Actual frequency in K—F	χ^2
Have to	112	58	60	50
Ought to	68	6	6	
Obliged to	15	7	7	
Bound to	16	1	1	195
Forced to	7	12	12	
Compelled to	2	6	6	
Made to	3	1	1	
Total	223	89	93	202

Matti Rissanen
University of Helsinki

"Strange and Inkhorne Tearmes"

Loan-Words As Style Markers in the Prose of Edward Hall,
Thomas Elyot, Thomas More and Roger Ascham

INTRODUCTORY

The primary purpose of the use of loan-words is probably to refer accurately and effectively to concepts which lack a satisfactory native equivalent. In addition, loan-words are often used to give variety to expression and to make the style of the text more elevated and refined. In Renaissance English, for obvious reasons, both these functions of loan-words were of particular importance. The use and acceptability of neologisms formed part of a wider topic: the question of the adequacy of the English language to express abstract ideas in a noble and elevated style.[1]

As Professor Nils Erik Enkvist has emphasized in several contexts,[2] the systematic study of style is essentially comparative. The texts of the four sixteenth-century authors discussed in this paper[3] seem to offer a satisfactory basis for stylistic comparison, both as concerns the date of composition and subject-matter. The fifty years separating More and Ascham do not affect the vocabulary to a disturbing degree. Hall and More are historians; Elyot and Ascham write about education. This makes it easier to estimate the influence of the subject-matter on the results achieved.

The most important characteristic in these four authors is that they were conscious of their style and represented two different attitudes towards the use of loan-words. Ascham's often-quoted criticism of Edward Hall's "Indenture Englishe" and "strange and Inkhorne tearmes" (*Schoolmaster*, p. 260) shows his dislike of the decorative use of loan-words and also confirms the impression that Hall used loan-words as a stylistic device. Elyot's and More's views on loan-words are illustrated by their own comments: Elyot accepts their use without hesitation, though he criticizes the misuse of neologisms; More is more reserved and expresses his confidence in the adequacy of native vocabulary.[4]

The basic material for the present survey consists of three samples of 1000 words of continuous text from each of the four authors.[5] These samples should represent the "normal" prose, the basic type of presentation,[6] of the works studied. For this reason, the passages were chosen so that they did not contain anecdotes, the author's addresses to the reader, long quotations of direct speech, or lists of names. As there was no reliable criterion to define which loan-words were significant as style markers, it seemed advisable to concentrate on all non-Germanic loans first recorded in Middle English or Renaissance writings. From the point of view of style, loan-words from Germanic languages or borrowings dating from Old English do not seem to be comparable with the Romance or later Latin or Greek loans. In many cases, they were probably quite indistinguishable from the native vocabulary.

In the present study, no systematic distinction was made between words borrowed from the Romance languages and those derived straight from Latin. It is possible that these two categories of loan-words had a slightly different stylistic effect, but it is unlikely that this would have been of decisive importance to the author's selection of words. Furthermore, it is very difficult, in many cases, to define the source of the loan-word with any certainty. That no essential difference existed between these two groups of loan-words, is implied by the list of words in Robert Cawdrey's *Table Alphabeticall... of Hard Usuall English Wordes* (London, 1604). Its first hundred entries contain 59 words of French origin, 38 borrowed straight from Latin, and three from other sources. In many cases the information given by Cawdrey on the origin of the word does not coincide with that of the *Oxford English Dictionary*.

NUMBER OF LOAN-WORDS

Table 1 gives the number of loan-word occurrences in the three samples of 1000 words from each of the four texts.

		Hall	Elyot	More	Ascham
Sample	I	221	241	139	162
„	II	246	203	178	155
„	III	253	205	161	176
Total		720	649	478	493
Average		240	216	159	164

Table 1. Number of loan-word occurrences in samples of 1000 words

The figures show, even without mathematical estimates of reliability, that Hall's and Elyot's use of loan-words differs sharply from More's and Ascham's. The frequency of loan-words does not primarily depend on the subject-matter: the two historians or the two educationalists do not belong to the same group. The arithmetic mean of the loan-word usages is 19.5 per cent out of the total number of words in the samples. Hall and Elyot keep above, More and Ascham well below this average in all their samples (as can be seen, the arithemetic means of the loan-word occurrences of the four authors are 24.0, 21.6, 15.9, and 16.4 per cent).

The figures of the occurrences of loan-words do not, of course, tell the whole truth about their use as style markers. Many of these words obviously have very little or no stylistic significance. Words used a long time, and particularly those in frequent use, naturally lose their loan-word character. To obtain some information on the connection between the "age" and the stylistic characteristics of the loan-words, the words were arranged according to date of first occurrence, following the datings of the *Oxford English Dictionary*.[7] In Table 2, the numbers of the loan-words and their occurrences are given. The percentages show each author's share of the total number of the loan-word occurrences in each period.

	HALL		ELYOT		MORE		ASCHAM		ALL	
	words	occ.	words	occ.	words	occ.	words	occ.	words	occ.
—1299	111	220	86	189	103	209	85	143	252	761
		28.9		24.8		27.5		18.8		100.0
1300—49	125	223	108	186	89	142	84	176	275	727
		30.7		25.6		19.5		24.2		100.0
1350—99	91	142	100	141	54	87	60	97	232	467
		30.4		30.2		18.6		20.8		100.0
1400—49	39	49	47	65	19	22	25	27	115	163
		30.1		39.9		13.4		16.6		100.0
1450—99	35	56	22	31	8	9	15	23	73	119
		47.1		26.0		7.6		19.3		100.0
1500—	29	30	29	37	7	9	18	27	75	103
		29.1		35.9		8.8		26.2		100.0
Total	430	720	392	649	280	478	287	493	1022	2340
		30.8		27.8		20.4		21.0		100.0

Table 2. Numbers of loan-words and their occurrences grouped according to the date of first occurrence.

Table 2 shows that Hall's text contains the highest number of even pre-1300 loans. His share of the loan-words of all periods is high and fairly uniform, which suggests that not only the latest — essentially Latin — borrowings are significant as style markers. It is of interest that More's figures for pre-1300 words and occurrences are higher than Elyot's or Ascham's. A plausible explanation, supported by a comparison of the figures of these three authors' fourteenth-century loans, would be that the fairly abstract vocabulary which forms the bulk of Elyot's and Ascham's loans was not introduced into English until the fourteenth century.

On the whole, Table 2 shows that while the earliest stratum of loan-words — those borrowed before 1300 — is of minor significance from the point of view of style, fourteenth-century loans should not be overlooked as possible style markers. Out of the total number of 1194 occurrences of fourteenth-century loans, 58 per cent was found in Hall and Elyot. The real watershed seems to be found at the loans first recorded in later fourteenth-century texts (mostly, of course, in Chaucer): Hall's and Elyot's figures are close to each other and clearly higher than those of More and Ascham. Fifteenth-century loans are, however, even more significant in this respect. Hall's and Elyot's texts contain some 71 per cent of the total number of occurrences dating from this period.

Additional information on the stylistic significance of loan-words dating from different periods can be obtained from Cawdrey's list of "hard" words. Its method of compilation was necessarily unsystematic and not based on stylistic considerations, but we can safely assume that the majority of the words included in a dictionary of this kind were stylistically significant. A study of the first hundred words in Cawdrey's list gave nine pre-1300 words, 37 dating from the fourteenth century and 54 with a later first occurrence.

Omission from Cawdrey's list does not indicate that the word could not be stylistically significant. Yet the figures of Table 3, based on the fairly high number of loans in the samples, are not without interest.

	HALL		ELYOT		MORE		ASCHAM		ALL	
	wds	p.c.	wds	p.c.	wds	p.c.	wds	p.c.	wds	p.c.
—1299	13	(11.7)	5	(5.8)	5	(4.9)	4	(4.7)	21	(8.3)
1300—99	52	(24.1)	61	(29.3)	26	(18.3)	30	(20.9)	140	(27.6)
1400—99	30	(40.5)	38	(57.6)	12	(44.4)	9	(22.5)	89	(47.3)
Total	95	(23.7)	104	(28.7)	43	(15.8)	43	(16.0)	250	(19.2)

Table 3. Loan-words included in Cawdrey. The percentages in brackets show the proportion of these words of all loan-words dating from the same period in each author's text.

Less than ten per cent of the pre-1300 loans of the samples, more than a quarter of the fourteenth-century loans and almost a half of the fifteenth-century borrowings can be found in Cawdrey. These figures support the suggestions made above: pre-1300 words are of secondary importance from the point of view of style; many fourteenth-century words are no doubt significant, but the main attention must be paid to post-1400 words. It is of interest, too, that about one-fourth of Hall's and Elyot's pre-1500 loans are so "hard" as to be included in Cawdrey. The bulk of More's and Ascham's borrowed vocabulary is obviously of a simpler stock — only about one-sixth can be found in Cawdrey. In particular, the low percentage of Ascham's fifteenth-century words should be noted.

In the following list, exampes are given of the four authors' loan-words dating from different centuries.[8]

Twelfth- and thirteenth-century words:
HALL: advance v., affection, arrive, ascent, besiege, dignity, discord, intent, malicious, march n., planet, recoil, relief
ELYOT: advance v., communalty, dignity, discord, sovereign
MORE: accord v., alliance, discord, distance, stably
ASCHAM: arithmetic, distance, empire, intent

Fourteenth-century words:
HALL: accept, alarum, ambassador, broach, communication, deface, demonstration, deprive, despair v., distant, encounter v., exile, furious, germain, glorify, hazard, important, inform, jeopardy, martial, etc.

ELYOT: account v., actual, administration, ambition, annex, approve, artificer, ascend, comprehend, define, discern, discuss, disposed, distribution, divine, divinity, exclude, execution, expedient, incline, etc.
MORE: adultery, assay v., compel, conspire, construe, contrive, credence, depose, desolate, determine, dissimulation, induce, obstacle, protector, resort n., reverently, sanctuary, succession, etc.
ASCHAM: apply, civil, chronicle, comedy, diet, durable, eschew, express, felicity, geometry, humanity, inquisitive, moderately, moment, pamphlet, poet, prose, purgation, solitary, temperate, etc.

Fifteenth-century words:
HALL: advertise, advertisement, ambassade, amity, amplify, apparently, bark n., conflict, delude, detriment, disloyal, dismiss, dominion, elect, enterprise, expedition, fidelity, fraternal, incontinent, instantly, etc.
ELYOT: affability, amity, assertion, commodious, competent, congruence, consequently, consultation, culture, deformity, demeanour, difficile, distribute, dominion, elegant, elevate, enterprise, exploit, immediately, industry, etc.
MORE: amity, attendant, brigander, contriver, custody, delude, immediately, incontinent, instinct, jeopardous, object, solemnisation
ASCHAM: admiration, direction, inventive, moderate, propriety, prosecute, sensibly, servile, superfluous

This list of words supports the evidence given by the figures above. Hall's and Elyot's loans represent a variety of fields, whereas a fairly high proportion of More's and Ascham's loans are closely tied to the subject-matter. The list shows the high degree of abstractness in Elyot's borrowed vocabulary — a feature which perhaps explains the high percentage of his words in Cawdrey. That this characteristic is not necessarily linked with the subject-matter is shown by Ascham, whose effort to use simple and unaffected vocabulary can be clearly seen in his choice of loan-words.

Sixteenth-century words were not included in the preceding discussion because the differing dates of composition reduce the comparability of the texts. These words reflect the readiness of the author to introduce new words into the language and to make use of the latest coinages. A roughly equal number of sixteenth-century loans occur in Hall's and Elyot's texts, but Elyot's words are more often repeated (*beneficence* 3, *efficacy* 2, *gravity* 2, *neglect* 2, *participate* 3, *partly* 2, *undoubtedly* 4). The only late loan occurring twice in Hall is *intimate*. Even short samples prove Elyot's skill in introducing new words; the following are given by the *OED* as being first recorded from Elyot's *Governor: beneficence, decerpt* v., *education, entertainment, frequent, frugality, infrequent, levigate, participate, placability*. In addition, *pestiferous* and *separately* are dated later by the *OED* (1542 and 1552).

Hall is less creative in his vocabulary: only *circumvoisin, lethargious* and *propagate* are first quoted from Hall by the *OED*. *Frivolous* is given a later date (1549).

Judging by the *OED*, More's liking for neologisms is remarkable — despite his own statements praising the adequacy of native resources. More's sample contains three first occurrences: *attonement* (borrowed suffix), *persuade, uncontrolled;* and three words recorded from later texts by the *OED: allective* (*OED* 1531), *adhibit* (*OED* 1542), *partly* (*OED* 1523).

Ascham's tendency to avoid "strange and inkhorn terms" can be seen in his sixteenth-century words. Though he wrote almost forty years later than Elyot and some twenty years later than Hall, the number of his late loans is lower by one-third than that of those two authors. The only first occurrence in his sample is *neatly* — a word which is not comparable to the heavy Latinate loans of the other authors. In addition, there is one word not recorded by the *OED: Nimium,* p. 261 top (cf. *OED nimiety, nimious*).

It is natural that many of the sixteenth-century words of the four authors can be found in Cawdrey: sixteen from both Hall and Elyot, eight from Ascham, but none from More. (The absence of More's words is probably just due to the very low number of his sixteenth-century loans.) In all probability many of the late loans were not included in Cawdrey simply because they were not "usuall" enough from his point of view.

In the following, the sixteenth-century loans not mentioned in the above discussion are enumerated:

HALL: assist, attempt v. and n., closely, consist, contented, confiscate, delate, desist, disburse, dispatch, dissuade, expectation, gain v., intimate v., invasion, partly, persuade, situate, success, summary, valiantly, variety, viceadmiral, vicewarden

ELYOT: allective, appropriate, aptly, attempt v., extol, neglect, partly, persuade, prepence, superiority, tractable

MORE: undoubtedly

ASCHAM: aptly, confute, considerately, Epitome 6, inventor, lament, mathematical, obscurely 2, phrase 2, placing n., place v., privately, scene 2, severely, silent, temperate v.

REPETITIVE WORD PAIRS AND PARALLELISM

An important question in the study of the stylistic characteristics of the loan-words is to what extent their occurrence correlates with the use of other rhetorical devices typical of the prose of the period. Space does not allow any detailed analysis of this problem; only two rhetorical features, fairly easily definable and closely connected with aspects of vocabulary, are briefly discussed here.

Binomials or repetitive word pairs were very popular both in mediaeval and Renaissance prose.[9] In the sixteenth century, word pairs were largely used for decoration, but also to introduce and interpret unfamiliar words. Thus there seems to exist a natural connection between the use of loan-words and word pairs: firstly, borrowed words are likely to be found in explanatory binomials of the type L(oan)/N(ative), or N/L; secondly, the search for synonymous words to create decorative binomials called forth the use of loan-words; and finally, coupling offers a natural means to give extra emphasis to loan-words used for stylistic elevation.

Table 4 illustrates the use of repetitive word pairs in the samples studied.

	HALL	ELYOT	MORE	ASCHAM
N/N	4	1	1	6
L/N (N/L)	22	23	9	15
L/L	56	34	7	13
N/N/N ...	1	—	—	—
L/L/L ...	8	2	—	1
N/L/L ...	8	3	—	4
Total	99	63	17	39

Table 4. Occurrence of repetitive word pairs. The last three lines indicate series of more than two members. The last line includes any combination of three or more with both native and borrowed words.

The high number of L/L pairs in Hall and Elyot is not surprising in view of these authors' frequent use of loan-words. The use of combinations of more than two members is typical of Hall, while Ascham seems to be the only one to use the N/N combination as a stylistic device *(high and hard, heady and brainsick, only and wholly, fat and fleshy, liked and followed, wise and ware)*. In comparison to Hall, Elyot, More and Ascham have a proportionally high number of L/N (N/L) combinations, no doubt largely explanatory.

Hall probably uses coupling as a means to give additional emphasis to his decorative words; twelve of his 29 sixteenth-century loans occur in binomials (*attempts* and *invasions; delate*, amplify or *propagate; frivolous* and trifling; proclaim and *intimate*; aid, *assist* and help; *contented* nor pleased; declare and *persuade*; usage, trust and *expectation; circumvoisin* and adjoining; *intimated* and made; the sixteenth-century words are in italics; the last two pairs are perhaps explanatory in character). In addition, post-1400 loans occur in 27 pairs. The total number of post-1400 words is 47, or over 27 per cent of all loan-words in the binomials, while the proportion of post-1400 words of all loans in Hall is only 18.8 per cent.

Elyot, too, couples late loan-words for stylistic purposes (*instructed* and *furnished*). But only five of his sixteenth-century loans occur in binomials and they are in general linked either with a native word or with a very early loan-word (virtue, discretion and *gravity; infrequent* or strange; *decerpt* or taken; power or *efficacy*; think, consider and *prepense*). In all, 27 post-1400 loans can be found in pairs (26.5 per cent of all loans in binomials; the corresponding percentage of the whole text is 20.5). The examples given above also illustrate Elyot's fondness for the *or*-link in binomials. In his pairs containing post-1400 loans there are thirteen *or*-links and 11 *and*-links, while Hall has only three *or*'s and 37 *and*'s. In a way, this detail can be said to reflect the difference in the two authors' attitude towards the use and function of repetitive pairs.

A large number of the schemes typical of Renaissance rhetoric were

256

based on parallelism and symmetrical, balanced structures.[10] An emphatic position could be given to a loan-word by placing it in the focus of a parallel structure — as one of the elements carrying the syntatic balance. A good example of this is given by the following quotation from Elyot's *Governor:*

But sens one mortall man can nat . . . discusse all controversies,
refourme all transgressions,
and exploite al consultations,

The typographical arrangement shows the balanced arrangement of the loan-words.

A systematic analysis of parallelism is difficult and any figures given are easily misleading because parallelism, even when accentuated by syntactic symmetry, is a very wide concept consisting of a variety of types and degrees of emphasis. In the following discussion, binomials are, of course, omitted, and only such cases are included in which the symmetrical arrangement is perfectly obvious. Table 5 shows the number of loan-words in symmetrical positions.

Cases of parallelism	HALL	ELYOT	MORE	ASCHAM
	26	18	18	75
Loan-words				
—1399	41	39	34	152
1400—	19	17	6	33
Total	60	56	40	185

Table 5. Loan-words in symmetrical positions in parallel structures.

Ascham's prose is much more clearly marked with parallelism than that of the other writers — a feature which no doubt denotes a basic difference in style, the development of a new, antithetical way of expression. Though parallelism is not a conspicuous feature in Hall's and Elyot's basic type of presentation, it is of interest to see that more than thirty per cent (Hall 31.7; Elyot 30.4) of their loan-words in this position represent the post-1400 stratum. (As mentioned above, the corresponding percentages of the whole text are 18.8 and 20.5, respectively.) In Ascham the percentage is only 17.8 and does not differ much from that of the whole text (15.8).

It seems obvious that both Hall and Elyot made use of the emphatic positions offered by parallelism in their use of loan-words as style markers. The following occurrences of sixteenth-century words in symmetrical positions were recorded in Hall and Elyot:

HALL:
there the Englishmen sore assayled, and the Scottes *valiantly* resisted
Sigismund sagely *dissuaded* hym and wisely counsailed him
if they nothing *gained*, yet ever somewhat they lost
ELYOT:
must be the more perfect and of a more *efficacie*

a man sturdie, of oppinioun inflexible, and of soure countenaunce and speche,
with him that is *tractable* and with reason *persuaded* and of a swete
countenaunce and *entretaynement*
that, whiche the one for a vertue embraceth, the other contemneth, or at the
laste *neglecteth*

The sixteenth-century words are in italics. These examples also show
how effectively even earlier loan-words were used in emphatic positions
of symmetry.

TYPES OF PRESENTATION

It is a well-known fact that a single prose text may contain different
types of presentation which also affect the style of the text (cf. n. 6
above). The use of loan-words as style markers can be further illustrated
by the study of their occurrence in passages calling forth elevated rhetorical style and, conversely, in passages suggesting simple expression,
in one and the same text.

Typical passages of heightened rhetoric are the author's addresses
to the reader — often moralizing comments echoing pulpit oratory. A
contrast to the author's address is offered by a type of presentation
which could be called the anecdote; a fairly detailed description of an
incident, often dramatic and with shortish utterances of direct speech.
Samples of roughly one thousand words were taken of both the addresses
and anecdote-type narration of the authors (no author's address of
sufficient length was found in More's *Richard III*).[11] The figures in
Table 6 show the occurrences of loan-words in these passages.

| | HALL | | ELYOT | | MORE | | ASCHAM | |
	addr.	anecd.	addr.	anecd.	addr.	anecd.	addr.	anecd.
—1399	232	168	204	157	—	117	163	120
1400—99	43	16	44	17	—	4	13	5
1500—	10	3	15	6	—	2	7	3
Total	285	187	263	180	—	123	183	128
Percentage of all words	28.5	18.7	27.5	18.0	—	12.3	17.8	12.8

*Table 6. Loan-word occurrences in author's addresses and anecdote-type
passages.*

Hall's and Elyot's figures show very marked differences in the loan-
word usage between the addresses and the anecdotes. In addresses, the
number of occurrences approaches thirty per cent, which means that
the text is very heavily loaded with these words. In anecdote-type passages, the percentage of loan-words sinks below twenty. Ascham's and
More's anecdote figures are low, too, but Ascham's address style does
not affect the number of his loan-words as markedly as Hall's and Elyot's.

In addresses the proportion of post-1400 loan-words is not essentially
higher than in the basic type of presentation, but in the anecdotes it

is very much lower: only a little more than ten per cent in Hall and 12.8 per cent in Elyot. The difference between the addresses and the anecdotes is also clearly shown by the figures of the sixteenth-century occurrences.

The following sixteenth-century loan-words were recorded:

Address:
HALL: diabolical, insurge, pestiferous, renowned, credit, faction, intestine
ELYOT: divulgent, except v., excogitate, frequently, grave, imminent, industrious, lament v., neglect, pernicious, suppression, transgress, terribly
ASCHAM: Anabaptist, barbarous, displace, Epicure, neglect, persuade, questionist

Anecdote:
HALL: counterpain, regicide, suspect
ELYOT: entertainment, expectation, miserable, obtestation, persuade, rosial
MORE: sorcerer
ASCHAM: Ambassage, lament v., severe

Though no definite conclusions can be drawn on the basis of only a few words, it seems that the higher number of loan-words in the addresses is partly due to the occurrence of emotive terms (Hall: *diabolical, pestiferous, renowned;* Elyot: *lament, pernicious, terrible*). In the anecdote, the low number of technical terms is perhaps one reason for the decrease in the percentage of loan-words. This should be particularly significant in Elyot's and Ascham's texts in which the type of presentation changes from non-narrative to narrative.

The occurrence of repetitive word pairs and parallelism correlates positively with the shift of the type of presentation in Hall's and Elyot's texts. The figures in Table 7 show the number of binomials per hundred words in samples representing the different types of presentation:

	HALL	ELYOT
Basic sample	3.3	2.1
Address	4.3	2.6
Anecdote	2.7	1.9

Table 7. Binomials per 100 words in samples of different types of presentation.

It is worth pointing out that the number of L/N (N/L) pairs in the anecdote samples of both authors is remarkably high: thirteen in Hall and eight in Elyot. This seems to support the assumption that the decorative use of the binomials — and the loan-words — is of minor importance in the style of the anecdotes. The use of the loan-words in pairs occurring in the addresses does not essentially differ from that discussed on pp. 00—00 above.

Intensified use of parallelism is a typical stylistic feature in Hall's addresses. His *Introduction to the Life of Henry IV* begins with a series of parallel structures and is worth quoting because it gives a good, though rather extreme, example of the use of loan-words in symmetrical positions:

What mischief hath insurged in realmes by intenstine devision,
what depopulacion hath ensued in countries by civil descension,
what detestable murder hath bene committed in cities by desperate factions,
and what calamitee hath ensued in famous regions by domesticall discord and
unnaturall controversy: Rome hath felt . . .

Hall's address sample consists of at least 24 occurrences of parallelism (many of them formed with several members like the one quoted above) and no less than 118 words in symmetrical positions. The figures in Elyot are less dramatic, though they, too, show a considerable proportionate increase when compared to the basic sample (Table 5, above): fifteen instances of parallelism with 39 loan-words in focus, in a sample of 953 words.

In the anecdote, where the flow of narration is of primary interest, parallelism is not favoured. Parallel arrangements can be found mostly in utterances of direct speech and they are only occasionally accentuated by loan-words in symmetrical positions. Typical examples of this are, for instance, "my herte was heavye, my lyfe stoode in jeopardie, and my combe was clerely cut"; "have I no faitheful frende whiche wil deliver me of hym whose life will be my death, and whose death will be the preservacion of my life" (both examples are from Hall).

FINAL REMARKS

The present survey was based on small samples of text and thus did not aim at statistical exactness or validity. Nevertheless, it seems to prove that a systematic study of the stylistic aspects of loan-words gives concrete and logical results which offer a basis for more general conclusions about a Renaissance author's choice of words and his attitude towards stylistic flourish. Hall's and Elyot's ready acceptance of foreign elements in their vocabulary is proved by their ample use not only of neologisms but also of loan-words dating from the preceding centuries. Ascham's consistent avoidance of decorative borrowings — which does not mean indifference to matters of style — also becomes evident, and so does More's double role as an innovator of vocabulary and as a believer in native resources.

Yet a mere count of words dating from different centuries does not explain why Hall is traditionally labelled as a latinizing decorator whereas Elyot is not (cf. Gordon, p. 76). To approach this problem, a close analysis of the types of presentation within a single text and of the intertwining and cumulative effect of various rhetorical devices is needed — and in this field, much work is still to be done. The answer can probably be found in Hall's habits of decorating his prose with repetitive word pairs and more elaborate forms of parallelism, and of using these rhetorical devices to give additional emphasis to his loan-words. This floridness of style is intensified in passages, more frequent in Hall than in the other authors studied, which call forth rhetorical elevation. Ascham's statement that in addition to changing Hall's "strange and inkhorne tearmes" to commonly used words, he would also "wede out that, that is superfluous and idle, not onelie where wordes be vainlie heaped one upon an other, but also where many sentences, of one meaning, be... clowted up together", is thus to the point. But it is good to remember that when the type of presentation requires it, as for instance in his anecdotes, Edward Hall writes almost as simply and with as few inkhorn terms as Roger Ascham himself.

NOTES

[1] This topic is excellently discussed, with reference to contemporary statements, by R. F. Jones in *The Triumph of the English Language*, Oxford 1953. Good summaries of the dispute are given by A. C. Baugh, *A History of the English Language*, 2nd ed., London, 1959, pp. 240—82, and I. A. Gordon, *The Movement of English Prose*, London, 1966, pp. 73—84.

[2] Most recently in his *Linguistic Stylistics*, The Hague and Paris, 1973, pp. 21—25, and *Stilforskning och stilteori*, Lund, 1974, p. 107.

[3] Edward Hall, *The Union of the Two Noble and Illustre Famelies of Lancestre and Yorke*, London, 1550 (first ed. 1548); Thomas Elyot, *The Booke Named The Governor*, Everyman ed., 1907 (first ed. 1531); Thomas More, *The History of King Richard III*, ed. R. S. Sylvester, New Haven and London, 1963 (first printed by Grafton in 1543, dated 1513 by the *OED*, 1514—18 by Sylvester); Roger Ascham, *The Schoolmaster*, in *The English Works*, ed. W. A. Wright, Cambridge, 1904 (first ed. 1570; dated 1568 by the *OED*).

[4] See Jones, pp. 55—6, 78—82, 89, 107.

[5] Hall: (1) *Henry IV*, 16v—17v; (2) *Henry V*, 21r—22r; (3) *Henry VII*, 11v—12r.; Elyot: (1) pp. 15—17 and 19; (2) pp. 161—4; (3) pp. 275—8; More: (1) pp. 15—18; (2) pp. 44—6 and 52—4; (3) pp. 64—6 and 68—9; Ascham: (1) pp. 188—90; (2) 260—2 and 263; (3) 286—8. As an attempt was made to keep the samples as representative as possible of the basic type of presentation, some of them consist of two extracts instead of one. In a study of loan-words, it would also have been possible to define the length of the samples on the basis of the number of the nouns, adjectives, verbs and adverbs, but the method applied in the present paper gives a better view of the clustering effect which is an important feature in the use of loan-words.

[6] For an introductory discussion of the types of presentation in sixteenth-century English historical prose, see the present writer's *Studies in the Style and Narrative Technique of Edward Hall's Chronicle*, Helsinki, 1973, pp. 14—15 and *passim*.

[7] The *OED* is, of course, unreliable as a source of the dates of first occurrence, but very accurate dating is of no vital importance in a study of this kind. In the datings, the only practicable method seemed to be to ignore earlier first occurrences of related words. In some isolated cases, this may locate the word in what seems to be a wrong category (*partly* is given as a sixteenth-century loan though *part* goes back to the thirteenth), but dating all derivatives by their stems would have resulted in even greater inaccuracies (is, for instance, the sixteenth-century *beneficence* an independent loan or derived from the fourteenth-century *benefit?*). At any rate, the number of these cases is so low that they do not distort the total picture.

The grouping of the dates according to centuries is arbitrary, too — a word first recorded from a text written in 1399 can hardly have a stylistic value different from one recorded in a 1401 text. Yet when a fairly large number of words is studied, this kind of rough classification is illustrative of the author's use of loan-words.

In the present paper, the conclusions based on the *OED* data are drawn with these reservations in mind, even though the reader is not each time reminded of them.

[8] All these words are included in Cawdrey.

[9] See, for instance, Inna Koskenniemi, *Repetitive Word Pairs in Old and Early Middle English Prose* (Annales Universitatis Turkuensis B 107), Turku, 1968. Edward Hall's use of word pairs is briefly discussed by the present writer in the work mentioned in note 6, pp. 26—8.

[10] See, for instance, Brian Vickers's useful discussion of Renaissance parallelism in *Francis Bacon and Renaissance Prose,* Cambridge, 1968, particularly pp. 96—140.

[11] In Hall's Chronicle, six short passages of moralizing comment, totalling 490 words, were studied *(Henry IV* 11r., 14r., 15r., 20v., 25v., and 32 r., see Rissanen, the study mentioned in note 6, p. 72, n. 1), in addition to a 510-word extract of his introductory passage commenting on concord and discord *(Introduction to the Life of Henry IV,* 1r.). Four shortish addresses were stmpled from Elyot and Ascham (Elyot, pp. 110—11, 114, 117—18, 145—47, altogether 953 words; Ascham, pp. 205—6, 220, 265—6, 281, altogether 1029 words).

Anecdote-type narration was studied on the basis of samples totalling 1000 words from each author. Hall, The Duke of Exeter and his wife; the Duke of York and his son *(Henry IV,* 12v.); the assassination of Richard II *(Henry IV,* 14v.). Elyot, an extract from the story of Titus and Gisippus, pp. 167—69. More, part of the account of the Council in the Tower, pp. 46—9. Ascham, part of the account of the dinner party, in the Preface, pp. 175—8.

The present writer is aware of the unevenness and insufficient length of these samples, his only excuse being that the types of presentation of Renaissance English prose have not yet been adequately mapped. Care has been taken, however, to refer only to such stylistic features as are obvious even in these small samples.

Vivian Salmon
University of Edinburgh

The representation of colloquial speech in *The Canterbury Tales*

As long ago as 1920, it was argued that a valuable contribution to the study of the English language would be a historical account of collo-quial speech as recorded in documents of the past. H. C. Wyld, pointing out the inadequacies of his own attempt to describe, "even in the merest outline" the "genius of the English colloquial idiom" during several centuries, acknowledged that all possible sources of information would need to be exploited to the full, and that the "various aspects of collo-quial speech life must be examined, and the different elements arranged and grouped according to some principle of classification."[1] His own categories, very few in number, included e.g. greetings, endearments, oaths and expletives; several studies, especially of idiomatic usage, have been published since these words were written, but most of them are unsystematic, not usefully related to one another, and not based on any theoretical view of the characteristics of spoken, as opposed to written, communication. It is evident, however, that an adequate account of the development of English speech can only be based on a general approach; it will enable the register of informal conversation to be described con-sistently and coherently for all periods for which documents survive, and it will also make it possible to assess the extent to which an author has succeeded in depicting naturalistic speech.

Attempts have recently been made within the field of socio-linguistics to present a systematic description of conversation, treating the "com-ponents of face-to-face interaction as they bear on, or are affected by, the formal structure of speech. These exponents may include the per-sonnel, the situation, the function of the interaction, the topic and mes-sage, and the channel ... [Socio-linguistics] is concerned with *charac-teristics of the code* and their relationship to characteristics of the com-municators or the communication situation, rather than with message, or communication functions and processes alone."[2] Socio-linguistics is also concerned, however, with the contemporary language, and has not yet devoted much attention to earlier periods of English; but the in-sights it has offered into characteristics of living speech enable us to approach with greater confidence the language of the past. In parti-cular, we can be more fully aware of precisely those features where a poet or dramatist is likely to deviate from the norm, for artistic reasons, in his portrayal of conversation; and acquainted with the potential devia-tions, we need not dismiss literary records of past centuries as necessarily inadequate evidence of natural speech, as has sometimes been the case. One attempt has already been made to offer a systematic account of Elizabethan speech;[3] the present study of fourteenth-century London English, although based on a slightly different approach, is intended to supplement it as a foundation for a comprehensive account of the development of the register of conversation.

The realism of the dialogue in *The Canterbury Tales* has already been the subject of comment by several literary critics, whose opinions, though based on subjective impressions, provide valuable corroborative evidence for the linguist who is trying to fit this data into a general pattern of development. Critic after critic praises Chaucer's "developed art of giving his realistic characters colloquial speech";[4] and they argue that "the more we know and understand the actual world and language of Chaucer's age, the more we can see that he habitually used 'a selection of the language really used by men'."[5] One reason for Chaucer's realism, it has been claimed, is that he was in all likelihood reading his poem aloud to an audience who would demand "the familiar phrase," since they were unable to "go back over something which they failed to comprehend. They needed a surface simplicity, a texture which was thin or, if full and ornate, was mostly in language in common use, interspersed with formulae and synonymous doublets."[6] Not only, therefore, does the dialogue of *The Canterbury Tales* give the impression of realism, but the narrative sections also attempt to reproduce the language of the teller of the tale as the Pilgrims journeyed to Canterbury, the only fundamental deviation from the norm of colloquial speech being the fact that the order of elements can be, and often is, subordinated to the requirements of metre and rhyme. The other characteristics of genuine spontaneous conversation which are absent, or inadequately represented, will be considered below.

Literary critics have also remarked on the possibility that Chaucer's representation of speech might have been affected by various artistic considerations. First, there was the common mediaeval convention of the "three styles" of poetry, on which Chaucer himself comments, counselling one of the Pilgrims to "Keepe ... in stoor" his "termes", "colours" and "figures" until he needs to use "Heigh style, as whan that men to kynges write" (*ClT* 16—18). It might be argued that the realistic representation of speech could be affected by the need to coordinate style and subject-matter; but it has been shown that "principles of stylistic classification" tended to change into "principles of characterization"[7] so that "heigh style" would be associated with the speech of upper-class figures such as the Knight and the Squire, rather than with any one kind of subject-matter. This development brings into consideration a second factor which might be thought to distort Chaucer's representation of speech — i. e. that it could be so deliberately aimed at characterization that it could become merely a caricature of the norm. The extent to which Chaucer in fact adapted speech to character has been debated; Eliason, for example, claims that his language does not reflect the individuality, sex, occupation or, except rarely, the local dialect of the speaker, the only significant differences depending on whether the character is "low-minded" or otherwise.[8] On the other hand, Elliott argues that "Chaucer is keenly aware of the way different people speak and there are many indications that he is creating different idioms or, if we so prefer, different registers, for his various characters."[9] But whether Chaucer was representing the speech of an aristocrat or a "cherl", both forms of language, it is argued here, would differ from written communication in the same ways. The differences between them would arise either from the use of different exponents of the various theoretical categories such as "asseveration" or "pause-filler", or the extent to which realisation is given to a category, such as "incomplete sentence." Moreover, whoever the speaker, the representation of his speech is likely to share with that of other characters in *CT* certain divergences from natural speech, e. g. a marked decrease in prolixity, ungrammaticality and repetitiousness, for obvious artistic reasons.

A few scholars have also commented from a linguistic, rather than a literary point of view, on Chaucer's representation of colloquial speech. Apart from Ralph Elliott's recent book on Chaucer's language, there is a brief treatment of the specifically colloquial language by Eliason, in which the following characteristic features are listed in random order: short sentences, frequent use of terms of address, the use of *thou*, homely comparisons, words confined to spoken usage, exclamations, "name-calling", swearing, exuberance, and indication of gesture.[10] There is also an important article by Margaret Schlauch on certain grammatical structures in Chaucer's colloquial English,[11] and some useful notes in various recent editions of the separate *Tales*. Other linguistic commentaries, most of which are listed in Elliott's bibliography, have tended to deal with individual features such as the use of pronouns of address, (i. e. *you* or *thou*), oaths and proverbs, and dialect. The present study attempts to incorporate all these features within an overall framework and to show how they arise, at any period of the language, from inherent characteristics of communication between two speakers. Those sections of the *CT* which will be examined in detail are those which represent direct speech in the form of conversations between two Pilgrims, as in the links between *Tales*, or between characters whose conversation is reported within the individual *Tales*. The narrative portions of the *Tales*, even though they seem to present monologue of a highly colloquial nature, will be cited only where other evidence of any particular feature is lacking.

Whatever the idiosyncrasies of the speaker, and whatever the historical period of speech, there are three fundamental distinctions between the register of conversation and that of any written form of communication (with some exceptions in respect of private correspondence of a familiar kind), which the poet, dramatist or novelist who aims at a

265

realistic representation of speech must reflect in his writings.

The are the following:

1. Differences arising from the nature of the media of communication, i.e. phonic or graphic.
2. Differences arising from the fact that conversation requires two participants, communicating within a situation which itself can affect the nature of the language used.
3. Differences arising from the fact that the participants will normally display attitudes towards one another, the situation, and the message conveyed within the conversation.

The remainder of this study is devoted to exemplifying these differences as they are represented by Chaucer in *The Canterbury Tales.*

1.00 *Differences arising from the nature of the media of communication*

Spoken language, unlike written, is impermanent; it cannot, once uttered, be deleted; and it requires a far more rapid mode of production than written communication. Consequently, a speaker's linguistic performance can be affected by difficulties of recall — for speaker or hearer; by the impossibility of jettisoning without trace unwanted utterances; by the necessity of carrying on a verbal exchange without always having adequate opportunity to formulate grammatical sentences; and by the need to avoid silence by the use of repetition and "pause-fillers."

1.10 As a result of the impermanence of the medium, speakers may find it desirable to "reinforce" their message by devices which will clarify its meaning. Their addressees, unlike readers, cannot of course repeat it for themselves.

1.11 Reinforcement can take the form of an explanatory sentence interpolated within an original statement, e. g.

> And therfore may ye se that oure preyeres —
> I speke of us, we mendynantz, we freres —
> Been to the hye God moore acceptable.   (*SumT* 1911)[12]

1.12 It may also take the form of a paraphrase introduced by *This [that] is to seyn,* e. g.

> And somtyme han we myght of bothe two,
> This is to seyn, of soule and body eke.   (*FranklT* 1492)

> And which of yow that bereth hym best of alle,
> That is to seyn, that telleth in this caas
> Tales of best sentence . . .   (*GenPro* 796)

1.13 Reinforcement may arise from the grammatical device of cross-reference, where the element to which attention is to be drawn is placed outside the sentence boundary and a related pronoun within, e. g. *Virginitee, thanne wherof sholde it growe? (WBT* 72), where the subject-noun precedes the pronoun: *Of alle men yblessed moot he be, The wise astrologien*... (*WBT* 323), where the subject-noun follows: *"The smok," quod he ... "Lat it bi stille ..."* (*ClT* 890), where the object-noun precedes its pronoun.

1.20 The non-deletable nature of the medium may result in the speaker's embarking on a sentence, interpolating another, and finally returning to the original — or even a third — sentence. Such interrupted structures occur fairly frequently in *CT* in certain conditions.

1.21 The speaker begins a sentence and interrupts it in order to comment on some action contemporaneous with the utterance, e. g.

> Ther walken manye of whiche yow toold have I —
> I seye it now wepyng, with pitous voys —
> That they been enemys of Cristes croys ...   (*PardT* 530)

1.22 They also occur when the speaker breaks off to comment on the topic under discussion, sometimes expressing approval, e. g. *My lord youre fader — God his soule blesse! — And eek your mooder*...(*NPT* 3295): sometimes disapproval, e. g. *A teyne of silver — yvele moot he cheeve! — Which that ne was*... (*CYT* 1224): and sometimes regret, e. g. *Ther I was bred — allas, that ilke day! — And fostred*... (*SqT* 499).

1.23 Other interpolations include comments which in the written language would probably be expressed as grammatically subordinate clauses. In the following example, the speaker gives a reason which might be expressed more formally in an adverbial clause:

> Ye mowe, for me, right as yow liketh do;
> Avyseth yow — ye been a man of age —
> How that ye entren into mariage.   (*MerchT* 1554)

1.30 The rapidity with which speech must be produced has varying effects on the utterances of different speakers, and to some extent Chaucer utilises such differences as a mode of characterisation. In the speech of the Wife of Bath, for example, undisciplined fluency of utterance may be regarded as indicative of undisciplined thought and emotion.

1.31 The necessary rapidity of speech production may result in ungrammaticality, e. g. lack of concord between subject and verb, or lack of logical cohesion between clauses in a sentence. In this respect Chaucer's representation of speech deviates from natural conversation most markedly, but there are some occasions in *WBT* where a structure would not now be acceptable, although it might have been so in ME, e. g. *For whoso wolde senge a cattes skin, Thanne wolde the cat wel dwellen in his in* (*WBT* 349), where *whoso* = "if anyone." More often a speaker may produce sentences which, though not strictly ungrammatical, are unacceptable because they consist of a string of simple sentences, linked by coordinating conjunctions. This characteristic of natural conversation is also most fully realized in the Wife of Bath's speech, e. g. ll. 543—549. At one point, her incoherence becomes obvious even to the speaker, and she exclaims: *But now, sire, lat me se, what I shal seyn? A ha! By God, I have my tale ageyn* (*WBT* 585).

1.32 In attempting to avoid ungrammatical or unacceptable sentences the speaker may need to pause, and to avoid silence, often makes use of "pause-fillers." The typical pause-fillers of contemporary English — *er* and *um* — are not exemplified in *CT*, but there are comparable uses of three sentence-initial adverbs, *well, now, why:* "*Well,*" *quod oure Hoost . . .,* "*Now, sire*" *quod he . . ., Why, yis, for Gode . . .,* where referential meaning is minimal. Phrases which often act as pause-fillers at the end of a line include *I gesse,* e. g. *litel hevynesse/Is right ynough to muche folk, I gesse* (*NPT* 2769), and *I dar seyn,* e. g. *Hire beautee was hire deth, I dar wel sayn* (*PardT* 297). Other phrases used as pause-fillers with no semantic content, occurring in any position, include *by your leve,* e. g. *So God me save, Thomas, by youre leve* (*SumT* 2112); *God wot,* and *to seyn the sooth.* Another very common phrase, usually considered a mere pause-filler, but recently alleged to have referential meaning, is *for the nones.*[13]

1.33 Similar to pause-fillers in their function of allowing speech to continue at speed without interruption are idiomatic phrases of various kinds. One group has the general meaning of "in all circumstances", and includes some alliterative antitheses, e. g. *for lief ne looth, for foule ne faire,* as well as pairs only semantically contrasted, e. g. *in heigh and lough, in ernest and in game, alle and some.* Rapidity of utterance is also assisted by the use of dead metaphors such as *go pipen in an yvy leef* (*KnT* 1838), *make his berd* (*WBT* 361), and to *blere the eye* (*RvT* 3865); by conventional emphatic negators, e. g. (not worth a) *bene, leek, straw, boterfleye;* and by conventional similes such as *black as a sloe, busy as bees, doumbe as a stoon, trewe as steele.* Conventional adjectives, strictly limited in number, also allow the rapid flow of speech. *Gentil* is probably the commonest, and seems to retain so little semantic content that it can be applied to such ungentle figures as the Cook and the Shipman. Another repeated adjective, varying in meaning from "innocent" to "foolish," is *sely. Hende* is almost automatically applied to Nicholas in *MillT,* but seems here to be used with a parodistic intention. Idiomatic usages of these kinds, though obviously likely to occur in informal conversation, are to be distinguished in function from slang usage; clichés, dead metaphors and similes are comparable with pause-fillers in preventing hiatus, whereas slang is the choice of an item, from a roughly synonymous set, which is understood as indicating an attitude of familiarity towards the addressee.

1.40 The impermanence, non-deletability and rapidity of the spoken medium have linguistic effects which are related to a speaker's mental

abilities. His *physical* ability to utter sounds is affected by other inherent differences between the spoken and written media. First, the phonetic realisation of individual morphemes may vary in accordance with
the context of utterance, e. g. *does* in *does it* differs from *does* in *does
she*. Secondly, intonation patterns may affect grammatical or affective
meaning, e. g. in changing a statement to a question. Thirdly, weak
stress in the spoken language produces special forms of negated auxiliary verbs, prepositions, etc. Assimilation of contiguous sounds, intonation patterns and unstressed forms are sometimes reflected in the
written medium where the poet or dramatist is aiming at an effect of
naturalism. The following are the most important of Chaucer's attempts
to approximate the written and spoken forms.

1.41 Phonetic change due to context of utterance is represented in *elision*
and *assimilation*. Whereas in current RP there is juncture between word-
final and word-initial vowels, it seems to have been absent in Chaucer's
form of speech. Initial vowels are elided in an unstressed pronoun, e. g.
so thee'ch (*PardT* 947 and *CYT* 929), rhyming with *beech* and *breech;*
and final vowels are elided in unstressed articles, pronouns and negatives, e. g. *th'encheson, th'honour, m'athynketh, m'astert, if I th'excuse,
n'of his olde saw, n'acheveth, n'yn, t'acord, t'espien*. Assimilation
of Θ to /t/ is frequently represented in *artow, maistow, hastow,* etc.

1.42 Intonation functions as marker of question in *"Ye shal?" quod
Proserpyne, "wol ye so?"* (*MerchT* 2264), and also in the numerous
occurrences of echoed phrases, e. g. *Ful blisfully in prison maistow dure,
— In prison? certes nay, but in paradys!* (*KnT* 1236).

1.43 Weakly stressed denasalised prepositions are indicated for *in
(yfayth)* and *on (a Goddes name)*. *Ye* occurs as an unstressed form of
you in *that I parte fro ye* (TC.i.5), where *fro ye* rhymes with *Troye*
and *joie*.

2.00 *Differences arising from the interrelationship of two speakers in
a situation*
Because conversation takes place within a context of utterance and
situation there is likely to be an interrelationship of speech and situation
which may affect speech in ways which are not possible in the written
medium.

2.10 Since certain situations occur with great frequency, conventional
"ritual" utterances may become associated with them. Among the limited
number of situations exemplified in *CT* are meetings, for which a reference to the time of day is common: e. g. *Good morwe, good day*. Less
formal is: *How (now):* e. g. *John also, how now, what do ye heer?*
(*RvT* 4024); *How, Alison! how, John!* (*MillT* 3577). *Hail* (ON *heill*),
as in *hayl, and wel atake*, can receive the rejoinder *welcome* (*FrT* 1384).
Greetings are also initiated by the latter, e. g. *Ey, maister, welcome be*

ye ... (SumT 1800). A different set of greetings consists of blessings of various forms: e. g. *God yow see*, which is answered by *Benedicitee!* (SumT 2169). A group of people is greeted by: *God save ... this joly compaignye!* (CYT 583), as also in *TC*.2.1713. Following the greeting, an enquiry can be made after the health of the addressee or his family, e. g. *how fare ye, hertely?* (SumT 1801), answered by *right weel; Hou fares thy faire doghter?* (RvT 4023, no response).

2.11 A second set of ritual utterances is associated with leave-taking. Quoted as a typical parting formula in *KnT* (2740) is *Fare wel, have good day! Farewell* can be followed by *til we meete* (ShipT 364). The only reference to any other time of day is in *Have now good nyght* (TC.3.341). Blessings are also common: *God thee speede, God be with yow, wher ye go or ryde* (PardT 748), *God thee save and kepe* (RvT 4247). These formulas are sometimes associated with, or replaced by, a dismissal: *Go now thy wey, and speed thee heer-aboute* (MillT 3562).

2.12 A common situation is one where a solemn agreement is made which is accompanied by a ritual utterance — presumably requisite in an age where not all were literate and able to deal with written contracts. The usual form is: *[I] plighte yow my trouthe* (ShipT 198), which was accompanied by a handshake, e. g. *Everych in ootheres hand his trouthe leith* (FrT 1404). Alternative formulas included: *Have heer my trouthe, Have heer my feith to borwe, Lo, heer my feith.*

2.13 Formulas for the expression of gratitude normally incorporate *mercy*, originally meaning "reward", e. g. *graunt mercy of your love*, i. e. "(may God give you) great reward for ...". A form with assimilation of /t/ and /m/ occurs in *gramercy*.

2.14 Situations marked by distress and alarm may be accompanied by the cry *harrow* (OFr *haro*), e. g. *Out! harrow and weylaway!* (NPT 3380), uttered when the fox is seen by the widow and her daughters, *Out! help; allas! harrow!* (MerchT 2366) is uttered by January on seeing his wife with her lover, and more publicly, Nicholas and Alison shouted *"out" and "harrow" in the strete* (RvT 3825).

2.15 Mealtimes and drinking are unfortunately not exemplified, but among the more trivial situations are: enjoining silence *(pees, hold thy pees, hust; clom; Stynt thy clappe)*; summoning *(what! how!)*: telling the time *(it is pryme of day, it is half-wey pryme, it is passed pryme, it was ten of the clokke, at cokkes crowe, about corfew-tyme)*: encouraging horses to effort *(Hayt, Brok! hayt, Scot! FrT* 1543) and attempting to stop them *(Keep! keep! Stand! stand! RvT* 4101).

2.20 Conversation is also distinguished from written language because parts of an utterance may sometimes be inferred from the context of utterance or situation.

2.21 The subject pronoun *thou* in *hast?* (*RvT* 4268) and *arte a person?* (*ParsT* 23) can be deleted in the presence of an addressee, but more frequent is the deletion of part of a sentence because of its dependence on the preceding utterance: e. g. *Can he oght tell a myrie tale? ... Who, sire? my lord? ye, ye ...* (*CYT* 597): *asked ... whiderward she went; And she answerde... "Unto the gardyn..."* (*FranklT* 1510).

2.22 Deletion of a lexical verb often occurs in replies, in which an auxiliary alone represents *aux+V:* e. g. *Tel forth thy tale ... So I shal!* (*SumT* 1763): *This Lollere heer wil prechen us som what. Nay ... That schal he nat!* (*MLT* 1177). The current word-order with *do* substitute is found in *TC* (2.1284): *Lo, yond he rit! Ye ... so he doth!*[14]

2.23 Deletion may also occur when the addressee repeats part only of an utterance by the other speaker: *"how thynke ye herby?" "How that me thynketh?" quod she ...* (*SumT* 2204); *"... strugle with a man" ... "Strugle!" quod he ...* (*MerchT* 2374).

2.30 The presence of two or more participants in a situation entails the directive function of language, including the grammatical expression of their interrelationship as speaker and hearer. Commands, questions and exclamatory sentences require the presence of an addressee; even where they occur in narrative portions of the *Tales*, the Pilgrim is regarded as addressing his monologue to his companions.

2.31 Commands may involve the speaker and addressee (*we*) or the addressee alone; as wishes rather than direct commands they can refer to someone either present in the situation, or referred to in the general context of utterance. In commands involving speaker and addressee *CT* illustrates the choice available in 14th century English: *Sitte we doun, and lat us myrie make* (*CYT* 1195), where the two different choices are clearly due to metrical requirements, although in normal usage they might depend on the degree of familiarity between the speakers. The second person command can be marked for emphasis, where the verb is followed by subject pronoun; it can also be marked for number, where a plural (addressee) is indicated by inflectional *-eth*. (The plural can of course be used for a single addressee in formal speech). The most significant difference from current English in the expression of commands is the greater likelihood of the performative's occurring in surface structure, usually as *I pray, I charge: Wyte it the ale of Southwerk, I yow preye* (*MillT* 3140); *Go lede hym to the deeth, I charge thee* (*SumT* 2026). The performative of wishing may on the other hand be deleted, as in *Mercy! and that ye nat discovere me ...* (*MerchT* 1942). The third-person command/wish is expressed without a performative, and with the subjunctive form of the verb (where it survives): *God yeve hym meschance* (*MLT* 914).

2.32 The performative is normally deleted in questions, although at least once it occurs in surface structure in full: *I pray thee, tel me than, Is he a clerk, or noon?* (*CYT* 615). Where it is deleted, its occurrence in underlying structure can be attested by the frequent use of such phrases as *by youre fey*, e. g. *Wher shal I calle you my lord daun John ... Of what hous be ye, by youre fader kyn?* (*MkT* 1929). The underlying structure here is presumably *I command you by youre fader kyn/You tell me.* Compare the frequent command form: *Tel me ... by youre fey; sey nay, upon thy fey*, where the underlying performative implies adjuration (*I charge you*) *by your faith*. It appears that *do*-support in questions was just entering the language in Chaucer's time; there are two examples (among the earliest recorded in English), and, interestingly enough, spoken by a child: *Fader, why do ye wepe?* (*MkT* 2432).

2.33 Responses to questions are also characteristic of conversation; in the case of alternative questions, they are more closely linked to the question form than in current English. There is a fourfold choice of *ye, nay, yis, no* used as follows (positive question + ye or nay: negative question + yis or no): *Can he oght telle? ... Ye, ye ...* (*CYT* 597); *Make ye yow newe bodies? ... Nay.* (*FrT* 1505); *May I nat axe a libel? ... Yis ...* (*FrT* 1595); *Hastow nat had thy lady? ... No, no ...* (*FranklT* 1589).

2.34 Exclamatory sentences normally depend for utterance on the presence of another speaker; the performative, e. g. *I exclaim, I lament, I regret*, is not usually realised in surface structure. One type, which survives, is regularly marked in ME by inversion of verb and subject: e. g. *Lo, which a greet thyng is affeccioun!* (*MillT* 3611); *How greet a sorwe suffreth now Arcite!* (*KnT* 1219). A type which is extremely common in *CT*, and which does not survive, is: *Allas! ... that evere was I born!* (*FranklT* 1463).

2.40 The interaction of two participants in a situation entails their acknowledgement of each other's presence, and their direction of each other's attention, by means of various forms of address. The reasons for choice are complex; the terms available include: Christian and/or surnames, terms of family relationship, generics, occupational terms, courtesy titles, a group of adjectives or nouns denoting attitudes ranging between love and hatred, and in some dialects of English, a choice of personal pronoun (*you* or *thou*).

2.41 A frequent form of address among the Pilgrims is a Christian name, often accompanied by an occupational term, e. g. *Roger Cook*. The Host is addressed once by both Christian name and surname: *Herry Bailly* (*RvT* 4358); it is not in fact clear whether all the Pilgrims had yet adopted stable surnames, since they occur so rarely. Roger (the) Cook refers to himself without a surname as *Hogge of Ware* (*CkT* 4336), *Hogge* being a familiar form of *Roger*. When speakers change from a

Wherefore, sire Monk, or daun Piers by youre name ... (*NPT* 2792): formal to a personal mode of address, the formula *by your name* is used: "*Doghter,*" *quod he, "Uirginia, by thy name* ..." (*PhysT* 213). The use of Christian names rather than a title by the Host clearly indicates social status (e. g. he uses them to the Cook but never to the Knight); and within the Tales it can indicate either social status or intimacy. In address by a Christian or surname, ME differs from current English (except with a limited set, e. g. *poor, dear*) in allowing an adjective to precede or follow the noun modified, e. g. *gentil Roger* (*CkT* 4353), *hooste deere* (*RvT* 4131), *good Yeman* (*CYT* 652).

2.42 Occupational terms are frequently used in address, either preceded by a personal pronoun (*thou Cook, thou Summoner, thou Preest*) or alone (*Hooste!*). They are often accompanied by a title of courtesy, *sire*, which appears to have little more significance than *Mr* at the present, e. g. *sire Cook, sire Summoner*; though it seems to belong more properly, and was at first restricted to, occupational terms denoting higher social status, e. g. *sire Clerk, sire Man of Law, sire Knight, sire Parish Preest, sire Frere*. It can also be used in the plural to address a group, not as a title of courtesy: *taketh heed, sires* ... (*MancT* 41).

2.43 Titles of courtesy of greater importance are *lord, lady, master, dame, daun. Lord* is frequently used to a superior (lay or cleric), e. g. *my lord so deere* (*MerchT* 2194 — from a wife to a husband), *My lord, the Monk* (*MkT* 1924), *my lord daun John* (*MkT* 1929); it does not necessarily imply any official title, and neither does *lady*, which is regularly used in address to senior members of religious orders, e. g. *my lady Prioresse,* and to a lover's mistress or a young wife, e. g. *my sovereyn lady* (*FranklT* 1325), *my righte lady* (*FranklT* 1311), *my lady free* (*MerchT* 2138). *Master* can be used in its literal sense in addressing the holder of a master's degree, as appears from a conversation involving a monk: "*Now, maister,*" *quod this lord* ... "*No maister, sire*" *quod he, "but servitour, Thogh I have had in scole that honour.*" (*SumT* 2185). It is also used by a young boy to a student (*Maister Nicholay*); and the Friar is often addressed as *leeve maister deere*. It is not apparently in use as the title of all males of some standing, as it was by 1600; and its use to the Shipman — *Sire gentil maister, gentil maryner!* (*ShipT* 437) seems odd, unless ironic. *Madame* was the correct form of address to an alderman's wife — the lowest rank with which it was associated by right, and one on which the Wife of Bath comments: *It is ful fair to ben ycleped 'Madame,' And goon to vigilies al bifore* ... (GenPro 376). *Madame* may imply a slightly higher social status than *dame;* the wife of the Miller, who was the illegitimate daughter of a parson, was so proud of her social status that *Ther dorste no wight clepen hire but "dame"* ... (*RvT* 3956). The joint term of address for a man and woman of some standing was *sire and dame* (*SumT* 1869). *Dame* is sometimes prefixed to a Christian name, e. g. *Dame Alys. Daun*

(Lat. *dominus*) is prefixed to the Christian name of a monk, e. g. *daun John, daun Thomas, daun Piers*; to the name of a man of learning, e. g. *daun Salomon (WBT* 35); and to that of a master craftsman, e. g. *daun Gerveys (MillT* 3761), a smith.

2.44 Terms of relationship were more frequently used than at present. Husbands and wives address one another as such, or as *spouse*; parents address children as *doghter* and *sone*, and children parents as *fader* and *mooder;* anyone with a remote claim to blood relationship may be addressed as *cosyn*, as the Monk explains: *I clepe hym so (ShipT* 151) because he and his 'cousin' *Were bothe two yborn in o village ... (ShipT* 35). The Monk calls his "cousin's" wife *nece*, which, denoting "granddaughter" in early ME as well as "niece," apparently came to be used as a general form of address to any woman (presumably with an affectionate connotation). *Mooder* is used as a term of respect to any elderly woman (*WBT* 1005), *suster* to one's wife or mistress (*WBT* 804), and *brother* to a comrade and friend (*Brother Osewold, MillT* 3151).

2.45 Generic terms often used in address include *man, woman, freend,* and *lordynges*. The Pardoner addresses his congregation as *Goode men and wommen (PardT* 377), and the Host addresses the Pilgrims (*MLT* 1174) as *goode men. Freend* was the form of address to a male of (apparently) equal status whose name is unknown, as when (*CYT* 593) the Host so greets the Yeoman who has just ridden up to the Pilgrims on their way. It is also used between males on friendly terms, e. g. *Freend so deere (MillT* 3775), from Gerveys the smith to Absolon. *Lordynges* (plural only) is a regular form of address to the Pilgrims as a group (i. e. including female members of the party).

2.46 Finally, of all the various modes of address, the most frequent is the personal pronoun, either *thou* or *ye*. Besides denoting singular or plural addressee, they could be used in expressive function, i. e. *ye* could refer to single addressee with deferential or formal connotation, while *thou*, if used in a formal context to a single addressee, could carry an implication of contempt and dislike.[15]

3.00 *Differences arising from the expression of attitudes*

The third major distinction between conversation and written modes of communication is that the former normally expresses the attitude of the speaker, not only, as often with the writer, to the message conveyed, but also to the other participants in the situation, and to the situation itself; conversation, in fact, more consistently than written language is concerned with the "expressive" or "affective" function of language.

3.10 Attitudes towards the other speaker may depend on some permanent relationship between the participants, such as employer to employee, or to some temporary emotional state. Feelings towards the other speaker ranging from loving to hostile may be expressed by the particular choice made from among the various forms listed above, e. g. in ritual utterances, while *How now* seems to indicate familiarity, *God save yow* seems more appropriate to an attitude of deference. The expression of the performative in a command, i. e. *I pray yow* possibly expressed greater politeness than the simple imperative verb, and questions with *do* support were (as far as the evidence goes) of an informal nature. Attitudes to the other speaker are also expressed by the particular selection of forms of address, e. g. of a Christian name rather than *sire* + occupational term. They are demonstrated more frequently by the choice of *thou* or *ye* to a single addressee, and even more obviously by the selection of a term of endearment or abuse. Among the former occurring in the *CT* are *lemman* (OE *leof man*), *my deere love, deerelyng, sweete, herte deere*, all of which are common, and the apparently affected forms used by Absolon (*MillT*), i. e. *honey-comb, faire bryd, sweet cynamome*. The terms of abuse are more varied, and include in particular references to human beings under animal names (*olde stot* "stallion", *stynkyng swyn, thou swynes-heed*); to old age and foolishness (*sire olde kaynard* "dotard", *olde virytrate* and *olde rebekke*, of uncertain meaning, *olde dotard, Jakke fool*); and to disloyalty and social class (*false traitour, olde cherl, false cherl*).

3.11 Lexical choice in general demonstrates the degree of intimacy the participants in a situation feel towards each other, the selection of slang terms (of which there are several in *CT*)[16] indicating familiarity of attitude. Good or ill-will is also denoted by the selection of items representing a blessing or a curse, e. g. *faire yow bifalle!* (*ParsT* 68) and *fy, foule moot thee falle!* (*MancT* 40). Only a close and detailed study, which cannot be attempted here, of the selections made by individual characters in *CT* — in particular of their use of *thou* and *ye* — can reveal the various attitudes to one another, whether permanent or temporary, hostile or friendly, which Chaucer intended to portray.

3.12 Attitudes towards the situation and the message conveyed are expressed by different means, i. e. by a set of spontaneous exclamations uttered in the appropriate situation, or with reference to a particular message.[17] These range from interjections devoid of referential meaning to exclamatory sentences, and represent the speaker's immediate reaction to an action or utterance. The attitudes expressed include, for example, triumph and amazement, both indicated by *A!*, amusement (*ha! ha!, tehee*), regret (*allas! weylawey*), surprise (*O!, Lo!, Ey! What!*), contempt (*fy, avoy*), annoyance and impatience (*What! devil of helle, for cokkes bones, for Cristes passioun, for Goddes dignitee*). One exclamation, *Benedicitee!*, occurs frequently in reaction to a number of different situations. Responses to some element or person in the situation or message are often represented by curses or blessings, e. g. *Unthank come on his hand . . .* (*RvT* 4082), *Yvel thedam on his monkes snoute . . .* (*ShipT* 405).

3.13 Altogether different from these expressions of attitude are those exclamations, usually classified with them as "oaths", which assert the truth of what the speaker is saying rather than his reaction to a situation. These asseverations vary considerably according to the social class and character of the speaker, the strongest, and those most generally condemned by Church reformers, being assertions made by parts of the body of Christ (*blood, armes, herte, bones*). These characterise the speech of the Host, the Summoner and the Reeve. Less objectionable are asseverations made on the name of a saint, either one whose attributes are appropriate to the subject in hand, or one who is a regional patron, e. g. St Cuthbert, in the case of the northern scholar in the *RvT*. Thirdly, asseverations could be made on any object, abstract or concrete, which a man particularly esteemed, e. g. by his *feith, life, croun, head* — even by his *pan* "head," or his *hat*. A man could also swear by his status in life, e. g. *as I am trewe smyth* (*MillT* 3781), *as I am a knyght* (*KnT* 1855). Lastly a speaker could call God to witness to the truth of his words, e. g. *So wisly God my soule brynge in blisse* (*Merch'T* 2175), or could lay claim to prosperity in so far as he was speaking the truth, e. g. *So moot I thryve* (*MillT* 3675), *also moot I thee!* (*MerchT* 1226), *So moot I gon . . .* (*MillT* 3114).

Limitations of space preclude anything but a mere outline of the characteristics of Chaucerian conversation, but it does at least indicate the most important of them, with minimum exemplification. It cannot give any idea of their actual frequency of occurrence, although it can be said that they are all reasonably typical of the speech of the Pilgrims. Some of them are indubitably restricted in occurrence; comparing transcriptions of tape-recordings, one notices the far greater frequency in them of certain characteristics such as interrupted and incomplete sentences, pause-fillers, repetition of sounds, words and subject-matter. Geuine speech also fulfils a "phatic" function which is poorly represented in literature; it enables satisfactory social relationships to be established and continued between two speakers, though there may be very little information to be conveyed. Even this function is not altogether disregarded in the *CT;* although no one talks about the weather while a social relationship is being established, there is an occasional enquiry after the health and welfare of the other speaker or of his family. Genuine speech is also characterised by the random direction in which ideas, argument and communication of information proceed; where the function of literary dialogue is at least partly to carry on the plot, as in the *CT*, lack of logical progression would create intolerable prolixity unless it had some definite function, such as characterisation. Nevertheless, ungrammaticality, "phatic communion" and random progression of ideas are all represented at least marginally in the *CT*, and provided due allowance is made for the under-representation of all such features which retard the development of plot in dialogue, there is no reason why speech in the *CT* should not be accepted as valuable evidence of the way in which Englishmen spoke in the later 14th century.

NOTES

[1] H. C. Wyld, *A History of Modern Colloquial English* (Oxford, 3rd ed., 1936, repr. 1953), p. 361.

[2] Susan M. Ervin-Tripp, "Sociolinguistics," in *Advances in the Sociology of Language*, ed. Joshua A. Fishman, I (The Hague and Paris, 1971), p. 16.

[3] Vivian Salmon, "Elizabethan Colloquial English in the Falstaff Plays," *Leeds Studies in English*, N. S. I (1967), 37—70.

[4] Charles Muscatine, "*The Canterbury Tales:* style of the man and style of the work," in *Chaucer and Chaucerians*, ed. Derek S. Brewer (London, 1966), p. 91.

[5] Nevill Coghill, "Chaucer's narrative art in *The Canterbury Tales*," ibid., p. 117. As Coghill stresses, it was indeed a "selection". The differences between literary and authentic speech are demonstrated, for example, by the transcriptions of tape-recorded conversations in David Crystal and Derek Davy, *Investigating English Style* (London, 1969), pp. 97—102. On the representation of speech in the novel, cf. Norman Page, *Speech in the English Novel* (London, 1973).

[6] "Chaucer's Imagery" by the editor in *Companion to Chaucer Studies*, ed. Beryl Rowland (Toronto, New York and London, 1968), p. 114.

[7] John H. Fisher, "The Three Styles of Fragment I of the *Canterbury Tales*," *The Chaucer Review*, VIII (1973), 119. Cf. n. 2, p. 126.

[8] Norman E. Eliason, *The Language of Chaucer's Poetry:* Anglistica, XVII (Copenhagen, 1972), p. 108.

[9] Ralph W. V. Elliott, *Chaucer's English* (London, 1974), p. 370. This work was not available when the first draft of the present article was completed. Its publication has entailed few alterations, however, since Elliott, while giving a wealth of detail on colloquial speech in two chapters entitled "Cherles Terms" and "Many a Grisly Ooth" does not give a systematic account of the register of conversation.

[10] Eliason, op. cit., pp. 114—5.

[11] "Chaucer's Colloquial English: its structural traits," *PMLA*, LXVII (1952), 1103—1116.

[12] Quotations are from *The Complete Works of Geoffrey Chaucer*, ed. Fred N. Robinson (2nd ed., London, 1957). References to links, prologues and epilogues are quoted under the title of the relevant Tale. Exemplification is restricted for reasons of space.

[13] On the meaning of "for the nones", cf. R. M. Lumiansky, "Chaucer's 'for the nones'," *Neophilologus*, XXXV (1951), 29—36.

[14] Quoted by F. Th. Visser, *An Historical Syntax of the English Language*, I (Leiden, 1963), p. 178, as the first recorded occurrence as a response.

[15] Cf. Thomas Finkenstaedt, *You und Thou. Studien zur Anrede im Englischen:* QF (NF), 10 (134) (Berlin, 1963), pp. 74—87.

[16] e. g. *jape, daf, pan, lousy, tredefowl, viritoot* and the phrasal verbs, *come off, give up, be about.*

[17] T. Mustanoja, in *A Middle English Syntax*, I: Mémoires de la Société Néophilologique de Helsinki, XXIII (1960), pp. 620—640, comments on a large number of these exclamatory terms under the heading "Interjections".

★ ★ ★

I should like to thank Professor Angus McIntosh for some very helpful comments on this paper.

Holger Thesleff
University of Helsinki

Notes on the rise of rhetoric as a stylistic genre

Greco-Roman rhetoric and the history of its influence upon European linguistic habits offer abundant material for a discussion of problems relating to language and style. The following notes concern the earliest stages of Greek rhetoric from a stylolinguistic point of view. I do not expect to reveal facts that are really unknown to specialists in Greek philology. But here as elsewhere it might be useful to try to apply concepts of modern linguistics to the results of philological research.[1]

In a recent book, Nils Erik Enkvist har rightly insisted that "each stylolinguist owes to his readers an explicit report of precisely what he means by style".[2] Here is my report. In dealing with societies like Greco-Roman antiquity, where the use of language is very largely connected with traditional manners of speech or genres of literature, it is convenient to make a distinction between *individual style* and *generic style* (stylistic genre). Theoretically, individual style consists of the sum of linguistic characteristics of a given text as compared with a norm;[3] in practice, observation has to be concentrated on what I, with a certain narrowing of Enkvist's handy concept, would call 'individual style markers', i. e. "those linguistic features whose densities in the text are significantly different from those in the norm".[4] Generic style is a level of abstraction. Theoretically, again, it consists of the sum of linguistic characteristics of a set of texts belonging to a certain genre or type of linguistic behaviour as compared with other genres or types; but in practice it is necessary to limit attention to certain significant 'generic style markers'. It follows that a high frequency of generic style markers, and a low frequency of individual style markers in a text would be a general sign of the text's adherence to conventional patterns. But individual variation in the use of generic style markers is of course normal in conventional texts too, and this variation may in itself constitute individual style markers. Typical 'style mixers' (as distinct from both individualists and conventionalists) in classical Greek literature are Aristophanes (ca. 450—385 B. C.) and Plato (427—347 B. C.),[5] whereas for instance Isocrates (436—338 B. C.) painstakingly follows the rhetorical patterns developed by his predecessors and himself. — It is often difficult to decide how a generic style should be delimited, but a consideration of characteristic generic style markers on the one hand and the

context on the other will usually suffice to objectify the intuitional idea
one has of the central area, the core, of the generic style: thus every
classicist would know what is meant by 'Homeric style' or 'Herodotean
narrative', as every grown-up European has a general idea of 'sermon
style', though the boundaries of the genre may be vague and varying.
— The difference between 'generic style' and what sociolinguists call
'functional varieties of language' or 'sociolects' is more problematical.
From a stylolinguistic point of view it seems often useful to speak of,
say, 'colloquial style' or even 'slang style' where a sociolinguist would
prefer speaking of different 'sociolects' or, perhaps, 'colloquial language';
also 'dialects' may sometimes function as 'generic styles' when the
'individual style' of a text is viewed against its generic background. The
stylolinguistic and sociolinguistic approaches necessarily overlap in
part.[6]

It is customary to refer to 'rhetorical style' as a style (individual or
generic) where several of the manners of expression discussed and recommended in traditional handbooks on rhetoric occur frequently or
pointedly. Rhetorical clichés are then taken as style markers. Since the
handbooks were originally derived from public oratory and were also
intended to be applied in that field, it is natural that rhetorical style
should be found especially in formal speeches and similar genres. This
of course applies to Greek literature too. The Greek word *rhetor* means
a "public speaker", and in ancient Greece the term *rhetorike* (current
since Plato) referred, principally, to the art of speaking in public. But
ever since antiquity, and up to recent times, rhetorical instruction has
affected other genres of literature as well, including high poetry. So it
is often reasonable to describe the style of a piece of poetry or historical
writing as 'rhetorical' or at least as 'coloured by rhetoric'.

Caution, however, is warranted here. The term should be applied only
if it is probable that the style markers concerned really have been supplied by traditional rhetoric. This is usually the case when the author has
had a rhetorical training, as in belletristic literature of the Roman empire, renaissance poetry, or French classical drama. It is less obviously
the case with later seemingly 'rhetorical' texts, though it is true that an
unbroken rhetorical tradition has been at work in some fields until very
recently, for instance in French, British, and American political oratory.
Often rhetorical features have been transmitted to a text by a mediating
genre, such as sermon style or rhetorical poetry; sometimes, indeed,
they are accidental. Again going back to classical Greece, the picture is
complicated by a number of facts.

Though Aristotle (384—322 B. C.) in his *Rhetoric* discusses many
of the rhetorical clichés and patterns (tropes, figures, etc.) adopted in
later handbooks on rhetoric, it is clear, considering the text material
which is contemporary with or earlier than Aristotle, that the majority
of the features later known as 'rhetorical', are rather more frequently
used in Greek poetry than in Greek prose. Homer and, perhaps even

279

more so, tragedy abound in 'rhetorical style markers' that are notably rare or even non-existent in classical Greek oratory. In fact many of Aristotle's examples are taken from poetry.

I pick out from Lausberg's *Elemente*[7] a few examples of 'rhetorical' features that are definitely not typical of classical Greek oratory: *periphrasis* or *allegory*, "she'll not be hit with Cupid's arrow"; *synecdoche*, "mortales" = homines; *antonomasy*, "divum pater" = Juppiter; *metonymy*, "Mars" = bellum; *distinctio*, "o child, my soul, and not my child!"; *epitheton ornans*, "umida vina"; *anastrophe*, "the upright heart and pure"; *simile*, "like a tower"; *aposiopesis*, "quos ego!"; *personification*, "Patria" speaking.

In classical Greece, such features must be labelled generic style markers of high poetry (aposiopesis is of course colloquial, too), not of rhetoric. They were later included in the rhetorical handbooks because the teachers of rhetoric gradually paid more and more attention to poetry as a model of oratory; and at the same time the writing of poetry came to be more and more influenced by rhetorical instruction. On the other hand, working backwards from late classical oratory, notably the speeches of Demosthenes (384—322 B. C.), whose register of style is fairly wide, through Isaeus, Isocrates, and Lysias (ca. 459—380 B. C.) to 5th century oratory, it seems that the assortment of generic style markers of public speaking gets still narrower.

But before I attempt a description of early rhetorical style markers, and indeed, before I can try to persuade the sceptic that there existed such a genre of style, it will be necessary to go still farther back in time and consider the various texts from which we can possibly derive a picture of pre-classical and early classical oratorical practice. Unfortunately the sources are scarce and mostly indirect.

Naturally there had always existed in Greece some kind of public oratory or, at least, public speaking. It might perhaps be expected that the old aristocratic society had developed far more strict rules for correct or impressive speaking than what democratic Athens ever reached. I do not find this particularly likely, considering above all the speeches of Homer's (7th century B. C.?) heroes. As far as I can see, there is nothing to indicate any trace of 'rhetorical instruction' in pre-classical Greece. There were "good" speakers such as the Homeric Nestor (whose manner is described as "honey-sweet"[8] which implies a characteristic of individual style) and "bad" speakers such as Thersites (who was "measureless in speech" and "confusedly babbling"[9]), and ambitious young speakers of course tried to imitate good speakers; but the existence of any kind of systematic teaching cannot be assumed.

An examination of some large and typical speeches in the *Iliad* and the *Odyssey*[10] will convince the reader that Homer did not let his speakers conform to strict patterns, in spite of the formulaic nature of Homeric style. Yet it may be possible to trace a few style markers that these speeches have in common. And one of the lengthy speeches in the

Iliad, Achilles' famous announcement of his decision to sail home (9.308 —429), is worth particular notice because it also contains several of the style markers which we meet in later oratory. I shall return to these below. At any rate, this is an important speech, and the poet has obviously made efforts to be impressive. It is reasonable to think that he has modelled the speech, to some extent, on general stylistic patterns current in oratorical practice in his own days. If this is true, it seems to imply that the roots of Greek rhetorical style reach back in the 7th century B. C.[11]

With this possibility in mind, I have examined a number of post-Homeric texts in order to trace generic style markers of early rhetoric. Here I shall first present the sources, and then give a conspectus of some typical features and trends of style.

In the Homeric *Hymn to Hermes* (probably 6th century B. C.) there occur some speeches by Hermes the cattle-thief that have been taken as early parodical reflections of forensic oratory.[12] Some style markers may be found in them, but they do not add very much to our picture of early rhetoric. — Solon's trochaic and iambic poems (early 6th century) are potentially more relevant. The extant fragments give some glimpses of what could be called a politician's apology to the public. The trochaic and iambic genres of poetry allow some degree of approximation to spoken language and, thus, to a realistic speech situation: in fact there are 'rhetorical' features in the fragments that are probably not conditioned by the poetic genre. — Two or three generations later the poet Xenophanes offers us some 'rhetorical' periods in a fragment (2 Diehl) whose tone is argumentative; cf. Ps.-Tyrtaeus fr. 9 D. — But otherwise Greek literature of the archaic age cannot really be expected to yield material of use to our purpose.[13]

Coming down to the 5th century B. C. we meet a greater variety of literary genres where traces of rhetoric can be sought for. We know that there existed, since the second third of the century (beginning with the Sicilian rhetors Tisias and Corax), an ever growing body of rules for public speaking, but little is known of the details. The first 'rhetorical handbooks' preserved to us are some pages in Plato's *Phaedrus* (ca. 370 B. C.), Aristotle's *Rhetoric* (ca. 330 B. C.), and the *Rhetorica ad Alexandrum* (of disputable origin and date, possibly somewhat earlier than Aristotle's *Rhetoric*).[14] Apparently style was not the main concern of the early teachers: they were more interested in matters of disposition and ways of argument in forensic oratory in particular. But the development of democracy and forensic practice since the 6th century, and the sophists' habit of giving public lectures, manifest since the middle of the 5th century, make it seem a priori likely that more or less established patterns of oratorical style were widely current before the Sicilian Gorgias' first appearance in Athens in 427 B. C.: this date is traditionally regarded as the first fixed signpost in the history of Greek rhetorical style.

From the 'pre-Gorgian' period of the 5th century, approximately 500—425 B. C., we have generally speaking four groups of relevant sources: the fragments of philosophical poetry and prose, Attic tragedy (comedy belongs rather to the next period), historical prose (mainly Herodotus), and political pamphlets (represented to us by Pseudo-Xenophon).

What is here particularly interesting about the two philosophical poets, Parmenides (ca. 470 B. C.) and Empedocles (ca. 450 B. C.), is that both lived in the Greek West where rhetorical instruction is said to have originated,[15] and that both present their teaching in the form of a speech. Extensive argumentation is now for the first time introduced in philosophy. It seems probable that the speech form is somehow connected with this fact: in choosing the speech form the philosopher consciously or subconsciously adopted devices of argumentation current in public debate. Though both poets use Homeric hexameter and, hence, Homeric features of style, they have made efforts to free themselves from the traditional Homeric manner of expression: this is true of Parmenides in particular. It is unclear what Aristotle meant by saying that Empedocles "invented rhetoric",[16] but it is fairly clear that the work of Empedocles to some extent reflects middle 5th century Sicilian oratory. — The style of 5th century philosophical prose seems to represent a different kind of compromise: it may be possible to see here a combination of the old aphoristic prose tradition with contemporary 'rhetoric'.[17]

As for Attic tragedy, Aeschylus (first half of the 5th century) perhaps could not be expected to afford material for a history of rhetorical style to the same extent as Sophocles and Euripides (who both died in 406 B. C.). It is true that most of the speeches in Aeschylus' plays are primarily high poetry. Yet there seem to occur occasional touches of rhetorical style markers, as in the opening speech of Eteocles in *Seven against Thebes* (467 B. C.). The *Eumenids* (produced in 458 B. C.) is interesting because of its trial scene (397 ff.), which quite obviously tends to imitate the practice and style of forensic oratory. In *Prometheus Bound* (date unknown) there occur speeches that are still more 'rhetorical' in style (especially 436—506), in fact rather unexpectedly, considering the context; this has been used as an argument against Aeschylean authorship.[18] — Sophocles is on the whole restrictive with oratorical devices. The most rhetorical passage is probably the speech of Creon on tyranny in *King Oedipus* (584—615; the play was produced soon after 430 B. C.). — Euripides no doubt makes a large use of rhetorical patterns; see for instance Iason to Medea in *Medea* 522—575 (431 B. C.), Hippolytus to Theseus in *Hippolytus* 983—1035 (428 B. C.), the speeches of Theseus and the Herald in *Supplices* 426—510 (ca. 420 B. C.), and Tyndareos to Menelaus and Orestes in *Orestes* 491—541 (408 B. C.).

Most of the speeches in the *History* of Herodotus (written perhaps 450—430 B. C.) are brief and rather artless in style. Some evident examples of rhetoric are to be found especially in the later books: note the speeches of the Persians in Book 7 (8—10, 16), Artemisia to Mardonius in Book 8 (68), and Alexander of Macedonia to the Athenians in the same book (140). The reason for this is not necessarily a 'development' in Greek rhetoric between, say, 450 and 430 B. C., as is sometimes believed, but simply the fact that political and military history is in the foreground in the later books, whereas the earlier parts of the work are concerned mainly with ethnology and legend. The occasional instance of a political debate in Book 3 (80—82) shows clearly that Herodotus considered this the proper context for rhetorical style.

Ps.-Xenophon's political pamphlet on the Athenian government (sometimes called the 'Old Oligarch'; published probably soon after 430 B. C.) is a very valuable source for the present purpose: it extensively employs various generic style markers of rhetoric yet without having the polished form of post-Gorgian oratory.

The development of rhetoric during the last quarter of the 5th century and the beginning of the 4th has been very much discussed and fairly well mapped out.[19] During this period the genre established itself in literature. The earliest direct sources we have for classical oratory are some discourses of Antiphon the Orator (who died in 411 B. C.), Andocides, and Lysias, and a few other speeches and fragments of speeches that can possibly be dated in the late 5th century.[20] The texts preserved under Gorgias' name are difficult to date; and the extant speeches of Isocrates are from the 4th century. Valuable material is also supplied by the speeches in Thucydides' *History* (which received its present form ca. 400 B. C.), though they seem to be heavily coloured by the author's individual stylistic mannerisms. Only fragments exist of the early sophists' publications. It is clear, however, that the sophists produced themselves in different genres: for instance, Antiphon the Sophist rather followed the stylistic tradition of philosophical prose in his treatise *Truth* whereas some other fragments are manifestly rhetorical; and Plato gives a magnificent pastiche of a Protagorean speech (*Protagoras* 320c—328d) which begins in the style of story-telling and ends up in rhetoric. Additional material for the history of late 5th century rhetoric can be found in various other texts, such as some argumentative tracts in the Hippocratean Corpus,[21] and parabasis sections[22] and parodical passages in the comedies of Aristophanes.

Considering now the picture afforded by this material in combination with 4th century oratory, the following general facts may be noted. Insofar as generic style is concerned, it seems unnecessary to differentiate between forensic (dicanic) and deliberative (symbuleutic) style: the distribution of the generic style markers indicates that these two genres are very closely related. The third genre of classical rhetoric, epideictic oratory, is considerably more difficult to grasp, first. because of the scarcity of our sources, and secondly, because this genre is naturally liable to greater stylistic variety according to the theme, the mood

283

of the speaker, and current fashion. There are great differences between, say, Pericles' funeral speech in Thucydides Book 2 (which is stylistically of course Thucydides and not Pericles who died in 429), Gorgias' *Encomium on Helen*, and Pseudo-Demosthenes' *Eroticus*. But except for the very specific style of Gorgias, which forms a branch of its own, it seems to me that many of the generic style markers of forensic and deliberative rhetoric occur in epideictic oratory, too, as a basic pattern.

∗

It is time to attempt a presentation of the generic style markers that can be extracted from the texts reviewed above. The following conspectus is restricted to a few examples and notable features, and little or no account can be taken of individual variation even in the generic patterns (not to speak of properly individual style markers).

A. Phonology and morphology. Both poetic and vulgar features were probably avoided in real speech situations. This is conjectural for the early period (since the poetic form of the texts preserved necessarily draws with it poeticisms), but obvious as regards classical Attic oratory.

B. Vocabulary and phraseology. The same as A, except for Gorgias and his 'school', who had a certain predilection for poeticisms and neologisms.[23] The use of metaphor forms a specific problem which cannot be entered on here. — A close analysis would reveal a great number of words and phrases (some connected with the syntactic patterns discussed below) that are more or less characteristic of this genre. A few examples. Phrases of the type "(Now) I shall speak of ...", "(Now) you will learn that ..." can be traced since the earliest texts. References to "witnesses" or the "truth" occur since the 6th century, references to a "proof" ("indications", *tekmérion, semeîon*) since Aeschylus. Apparently in accordance with the earliest rules laid down for rhetorical argumentation,[24] words for "probably", "it seems" are frequent in the genre since the latter part of the 5th century. The listeners are frequently addressed with vocative phrases (Attic *ô ándres* is a style marker of rhetoric just as modern English "gentlemen!" is indicative of a certain formal level of speech). A number of specific phrases that seem to be characteristic of the rhetorical genre at least since the middle of the 5th century are particularly interesting from a stylolinguistic point of view, since they do not seem to be conditioned by the theme or the speech situation at all. A typical example is the elaborate phrase pattern (Herodotus 7.9.3, 16.3) *es toûto thráseos anékei (hóste)* ..., approximately "(he) has reached that point of insolence (where ...)", which is found almost exclusively in rhetoric as a substitute for the simple idea *thrasýs estin* "(he) is insolent". The seemingly banal combination "not only ... but also ..." appears to have originated in rhetorical style in the 5th century (an early example is Herodotus 7.9), probably as a variation of the type "not A but B" (for which see below); Roman rhetoric has transmitted this pattern to various literary styles of European languages. In fact the generic style markers of ancient rhetoric largely consist of such phrases, though little notice has been taken of them in the traditional handbooks.

C. Syntactic patterns and sentence construction.

1. Sentence periods. The 'invention' of the hierarchic, balanced, many-level period characteristic of classical oratory, is traditionally ascribed to the sophist and orator Thrasymachus (late 5th century B. C.). It is true that conscious art in the arrangement of clauses and subclauses is not found before the time of Thrasymachus and Isocrates. But weighty periods do occur since Homer, particularly in deliberative passages. It seems that periods which include argumentation with hypothetical clauses or antithetic parallel clauses are somehow typical of rhetorical style at least since Solon. Since the 5th century there occur specific patterns such as opening a period with a *hóti* ("that") clause which is clearly a generic style marker.

2. Structuring the exposition by means of words or phrases for "first", "secondly", "most important is" and the like: traceable since Parmenides and Aeschylus, common later.

3. Various forms of antithesis (cf. also 4 and 6) are common in rhetorical style of all periods, but do also occur in different genres of poetry, aphoristic prose, and legal style. It seems that some specific types were favoured in 5th century oratory.[25] In general a large and pointed use of the particles of antithesis (*mén* and *dé* in combination) may be taken as a rhetorical style marker, if there are other rhetorical style markers to support it. 5th and early 4th century rhetoric also makes frequent use of phrases such as *toûto mén ... toûto dé ...*, "on the one hand ..., on the other ...".

4. The type "not A but B" is a variant of antithesis (so-called 'correctio') which is sufficiently common in rhetorical texts, and sufficiently rare elsewhere, to be regarded primarily as a rhetorical style marker. The negative part of the pattern is often expanded ("nor A^1 nor A^2 nor A^3 but B"). The inverse type, "B, not A", is rather more characteristic of poetry.

5. So-called 'synonymy' (or 'hendiadys' in one of the senses of this term), particularly the type "he is a nice and fine man", "we have been working and toiling", is a common feature since Homer. After Homer it seems to be preferred in rhetorical contexts. In classical oratory it is subject to considerable elaboration and variation; also specific phrases such as *pollà kaì megála, pollà kaì kalá* ("many and great", "many and beautiful") may have originated in this pattern.

6. So-called 'polar expressions' — the coupling of antithetic concepts for positive or negative emphasis, as "both gods and mortals", "neither men nor women" — are used frequently in speeches since Homer and may be classed as a generic style marker of rhetoric, though they are not exclusively restricted to it.

7. 'Hyperbaton', the complication of the 'natural' word-order, is normal in poetry but seems to have been to some extent adopted in prose oratory. Perhaps certain types of hyperbaton could be taken as generic style markers.

8. Rhetorical questions, i. e. unanswered questions inserted for positive or negative emphasis, occur since Homer as a rather clear generic style marker.

9. The only kind of repetition that can claim inclusion among the generic style markers of early rhetoric, is anaphora. But it is not a very distinct feature before the 4th century.[26]

D. Sound patterns and rhythm. Various forms of assonance[27] are found in different poetic, ceremonious and aphoristic genres. Except for Gorgias and his followers, orators do not seem to be very fond of such devices; but in particular alliteration is not uncommon in emphatic passages. A sparing use of alliteration seems to be generic in rhetoric. — Greek prose rhythm is a much-discussed problem: since Isocrates, but hardly before him, there occur rhythmical patterns that might be labelled generic.

This list could be easily expanded. and an analysis of details would certainly complicate the picture. Yet, if my expose is, as I hope, approximately correct in its general lines, it may be possible to make from it some general conclusions.

∗

There appears to have existed since the times of Homer, and probably long before this, a genre of public oratory. Though only a few generic style markers can be extracted from the earliest texts (the speech of Achilles, *Iliad* 9.308--429, gives examples of B ["I shall speak"], C 1, 3, 4, 5, 6, and 8, and one or two others not considered here), some of these early style markers recur later again and again and gradually include more and more linguistic features. The rise of explicit public argumentation for "truth" or "probability" (since the 6th century, perhaps systematized in 5th century handbooks), added considerably to this body of style markers (cf. B, C 1, 2). The rise of epideictic oratory and the establishing of rhetoric as a conscious art in the late 5th century led to a still wider register of generic markers.

The specific style of Gorgias implies, partly, an exaggeration of old generic features such as C 1 (balanced antithetic clauses and similar, so-called 'isocolon'), 3, 6, and partly, an introduction of new features such as poeticisms and various patterns of the D class.[28]

However, disregarding Gorgias and his followers, the genre of early rhetoric does not seem to have very much in common with what is now usually associated with 'rhetorical style'. From a stylolinguistic point of view it is interesting to note that most of the generic markers considered here (and in fact some others that I have not discussed) are not empty clichés or mere 'embellishment'. Some reflect a tendency to systematization of thought (cf. B, C 1, 2, 3, 4, 6), some a tendency to emphasis (cf. B, C 2, 4, 5, 6, 7, 8, 9, D [alliteration]). Lucidity and dignity of expression is aimed at (cf. A, B, C 1, 2, 5, 6, 7, D [rhythm]), not shock or surprise.

Pre-classical and early classical oratory exercised an essentially healthy influence upon Greek manners of speech. Rhetoric developed a kind of 'standard language' to be used in public communication. The later, well-known history of ancient rhetoric, with its far-reaching and sometimes disastrous consequences to linguistic behaviour, began with the establishment of systematic instruction in the 4th century B. C. and the tendencies to dogmatism and inflation to which this inevitably led.

NOTES

[1] A good introduction to Greek rhetoric for non-specialists: George Kennedy, *The Art of Persuasion in Greece*, Princeton 1963. Kennedy does not consider details of style. Some of the general facts and details mentioned below have been discussed in the vast and heterogeneous philological literature to which Kennedy makes some references. Important analyses and further references to the older discussion will be found in Wilhelm Schmid, *Geschichte der griechischen Literatur* I:1—5 (Handbuch der Altertumswissenschaft VII.1. 1—5), München 1929—1948. For recent bibliography *L'Année philologique* is indispensable. J. Martin, *Antike Rhetorik* (Handbuch d. Alt. wiss. II.3), München 1974, lacks a diachronic approach. I have not seen F. H. Turner, *The Theory and Practice of Rhetorical Declamation from Homeric Greece through the Renaissance*, Diss. Temple Univ., Philadelphia 1972 (cf. DA 32, 1972, 7119A).

[2] *Linguistic Stylistics* (Janua Linguarum, Series Critica 5), The Hague 1973, p. 147.

[3] Of course the norm is preferably to be chosen among texts of the same period and with approximately similar contextuality.

[4] Enkvist op.cit. p. 146.

[5] In *Studies in the Styles of Plato* (Acta Philosophica Fennica 20), Helsinki 1967, I made an attempt to classify the generic styles employed by Plato in his individual styles.

[6] J. Frösén, *Prolegomena to a Study of the Greek Language in the First Centuries A. D.*, Diss. Helsinki 1974, has tried to apply sociolinguistic categories, rather than stylolinguistic ones, to post-classical Greek.

[7] Heinrich Lausberg, *Elemente der literarischen Rhetorik*, München 1963.

[8] *Iliad* 1.248 f.; cf. 3.212—224, on Menelaus and Odysseus.

[9] *Iliad* 2.212, 246.

[10] Notably *Iliad* 1.149—171, 254—284, 9.115—172, 225—306, 308—429, 434—605, *Odyssey* 2.40—79, 6.149—185.

[11] The theories of later interpolation, applied to this speech in the 19th century, are not particularly well-grounded. But of course, Homeric chronology is very problematical indeed.

[12] See Kennedy, op.cit. p. 40.

[13] The fragments of lyric, elegy, iambography (on the whole), philosophical prose, and prose narrative do not seem to be contextually relevant. Early philosophical prose is clearly aphoristic. But there may occur occasional reflections of rhetoric in all of these genres (cf. e. g. Archilochus P. Oxy. XXII 2310).

[14] See references in Kennedy, op.cit.

[15] Cf. Kennedy, op.cit. p. 26 ff. There were democratic movements in the Greek colonies in Italy and Sicily since the early 5th century, and the development of judicial practice apparently encouraged some kind of systematization of rhetorical technique. To be sure, this is somewhat conjectural.

[16] Cf. Empedocles A 1, 19 DK. Aristotle may have been thinking of the *Katharmoi* of Empedocles, a public speech in poetic form; but the fragments preserved to us are hierophantic rather than 'rhetorical' in style. Probably Aristotle was concerned with attitude, not with style.

[17] I have argued this in *Arctos* N. S. 4, 1966, 92 ff.

[18] The champion of this line of thought is Wilhelm Schmid, op.cit. I:3, 281 ff.

[19] See the references in note 1, above. The much-quoted work of E. Drerup al., *Die Anfänge der rhetorischen Kunstprosa,* Jahrbücher für classische Philologie, Suppl. 27, Leipzig 1902, p. 219 ff., is not to be relied on.

[20] The chronology is problematical, as is also the question of the authentic wording of the speeches. They were probably not written down exactly as they were held, and in some cases they may have been revised by a teacher of rhetoric who applied to the text his own ideas of style.

[21] See my *Arctos* article, note 17, above.

[22] A central section where the poet, through the chorus leader, addresses the audience.

[23] The occasional so-called 'poeticisms' found in 5th century oratory outside the school of Gorgias, are on the whole disputable; some (possible) cases may be due to an attempt to avoid vulgarisms. Poeticisms for the sake of ornament do not seem to occur outside the Gorgian tradition.

[24] Cf. Kennedy, op.cit. p. 30 ff.

[25] References in Kennedy, op.cit. p. 33 ff.

[26] The material has been collected by D. Fehling, *Die Wiederholungsfiguren und ihr Gebrauch bei den Griechen vor Gorgias*, Berlin 1969.

[27] Some material in W. B. Stanford, *The Sound of Greek* (Sather Classical Lectures 38), Berkeley 1967.

[28] Cf. J. D. Denniston, *Greek Prose Style*, Oxford 1952, p. 10—13.

Winston Weathers
University of Tulsa

The construction of William Blake's "The Tyger"

"The Tyger" — without question William Blake's most popular single lyric — is a remarkable stylistic achievement. Praised in Blake's own lifetime as "glorious,"[1] "truly inspired and original,"[2] full of "vigour and force,"[3] "The Tyger" has penetrated the aesthetic sensibilities of readers for over a century and a half, less by what it has to say, far more by the way it is stylistically constructed. The power of the poem is the result not of "its thoughts"[4] but of its being put together in such a way that "thoughts" are stimulated by it. That is, its power is not in its meaning but in a stylistic generation of meaning that remains operative, reader after reader, age to age. Even when readers feel they are responding to the poem's "content," they are, in truth, responding to the stylistic activity of the poem and are, in truth, themselves constructing the content and meaning of the poem. The powerful and exciting meanings that readers find in "The Tyger" are reflections of a style that makes quite different but always vigorous meanings possible — meanings gestated and born, as it were, within and from the poem's stylistic body.

This body — or "total stylistic identity" — of the poem is best understood, a la constructionist theory, as a structure rising from an underlying ground of stylistic possibilities, a structure selected, part by part from all available parts, the final poem being "that which was selected from" a larger body of stylistic material. The poem is a product of stylistic decision-making (part conscious, part unconscious) in which the creative artistry is a process of elimination on the one hand, retention on the other hand — a laboring through options.

Indeed, from a constructionist point of view, all artistry — and certainly that of "The Tyger" — begins with the poet's mastering of stylistic "things to do." This mastery involves a sensitivity to stylistic materials on the poet's part and the capacity to arrange materials into stylistic units or "sets." The capacity to arrange "sets" is accompanied by the capacity to select — on any given creative occasion — particular "sets" as useable stylistic units. And finally, the artistry involves the combining of selected "sets" — by a kind of interweaving, intersplicing, overlaying, and interfacing process — into a stylistic complex that is the final product: the poem itself. Fundamentally, from a constructionist point of view, all artistry begins with the mastery of "things to do" and ends with the selecting and combining of "sets" in some effective way, which is most commonly — but not exclusively — the way that "gives rise to meaning" for readers, i. e. gives rise to semantic experience.

Blake, of course, is often denied the very capacity to be such a constructionist. Because of his own rejection of unbridled reason (in his myth of Urizen, for instance), Blake is too often seen as a stereotypical "inspired" poet who would in no way be involved in any calculated process.[5] Yet Blake was the tremendously disciplined artist, concerned with the maintenance of the clear "line" in all his creative efforts (in his drawings, in his poetry, perhaps even in his music), and is certainly too successful an artist in all media to be explained away as an "accidentalist," someone who accepts, without thinking, the accidents of inspiration and creative randomness. Blake was, I am convinced, a "thinking" artist who — as I believe a constructionist analysis of "The Tyger" will show — mastered stylistic techniques, engaged in creative decision making (at all levels of the psyche), and *worked at* the construction of poems that would be aesthetically functional, aesthetically "well made," and ergo: potentially meaningful.

To reveal Blake's constructionism and to reveal the power of "The Tyger," I wish to identify the major stylistic "sets" in the poem and to analyze each set by considering (a) the stylistic materials involved in constructing the set, (b) the arrangement of the materials or the relationships established among the materials to effect the set, (c) the semantic potential — if any — within the set, and (d) the interfacing or conjunctive aspect of the set, i. e. its relatability to other sets in the poem. This schema of analysis is the key to constructional criticism and provides, I believe, a more truthful insight into the creation of poetry than other modes of criticism generally allow.

2.

Blake's "The Tyger" comprises three major stylistic sets — that of the phonemes (in particular, the frequency of consonants); that of the serials (in particular, the two-part series and the plethora series); and that of the metaphors (in particular the non-explicit and personifying metaphors). Other sets are involved in the total substantiality of the poem, but these three sets create, I believe, the particular effectiveness of the poem and demonstrate, as well as a total and definitive stylistic analysis would do, the general constructional method Blake used.

THE PHONEMIC SET

1. *Stylistic Materials.* No one can read — or listen to — "The Tyger" without being aware of the rich sounds of the poem, and it is the "sounds" of the poem that Blake used as a primary stylistic material, making of them a variety of phonemic sets, the most provocative of which

— in this poem — is that of consonant frequency. All poems, of course, have phonemic sets, but in few poems are the sets as important as they are in "The Tyger."

In spreading out all the English phonemes in front of him, Blake retained nearly every one — yet he reduced the incidence of some of them so much that their presence is practically non-existent. Keeping in mind G. Dewey's *Relative Frequency of English Speech Sounds,*[6] we notice that Blake let the phonemes "e," "v," "l," "k," "p," and a few others drop below the normal incidence level to a state of minimal presence in the poem. On the other hand, he over-used such phonemes as "i," "g," "f," "h," "w," and particularly "r"and "t."

Making such a selection, Blake was on his way to the construction of a phonemic set, that is — a group of privileged phonemes to be used in some stylistic way.

2. *The Set Arrangement.* The poem's prime stylistic set, based upon phonemes, is a hierarchy of dominant consonant phonemes. Again according to Dewey's table of English speech sound frequencies, the usual or average hierarchy of consonant phonemes in English — to the sixth instance (and that is far enough to go so far as our analysis of Blake's poem is concerned) — reads as follows: "n," "t," "r," "s," "d," "l." This frequency hierarchy is a stylistic set and it is one of the sets Blake could have constructed in his poem. But obviously other sets are possible; even within these top six phonemes other arrangements can be made: the dominance of "n" can be negated; the sequence of the order can be altered, e. g. n-t-r-s-d-l can become t-s-l-n-r-d, etc.; or some "outside" phoneme, normally supressed or with lower incidence, can be substituted for one of the dominant phonemes, e. g. "k" could be installed in the place of "s," or "v" could be installed in place of "r," etc.

In many of his poems, Blake retained the normal frequency of consonants as a phonemic set, and in such poems the phonemic set does not emerge as a major constituent of the poem's stylistic body. But in certain poems, Blake radically violated the normal frequency to achieve powerful and important phoneme sets — such as he did in his poem "The Lamb," wherein the phoneme "l" is elevated from its normal sixth place to first place, and wherein the whole "top six" are radically altered to become l-d-m-th-t-n, with the omission of "r" and "s" and with the inclusion of "m" and "th."

In "The Tyger," we find a less radical set, yet one that deviates from the norm in an interesting way. The frequency set in the poem is r-t-n-d-h-w, with the omission of "s" and "l" and with the inclusion of "h" and "w." The main characteristic of the set is the elevation of the "r" into dominant position, with a frequency percentage of 9.8, higher far than the 7.24% of the "r" in Dewey's table. Likewise, Blake's use of "t" is higher, at 8.4% than the expected percentage of 7.1.

A good way to see the particular quality of frequency set in "The Tyger" is to graph it in comparison with the Dewey norm and in comparison, say, with "The Lamb." Converting the top six phonemes of the two poems and the norm to a graph, we see the stylistic set in visual terms:

	0	1	2	3	4	5	6	7	8	9	10	11	12	13	14

"n"
Norm ——————————————— 7.2
Lamb ——————— 3.8
Tyger ————————————— 6.6

"t"
Norm ——————————————— 7.1
Lamb ——————————— 5.4
Tyger ————————————————— 8.4

"r"
Norm ————————————— 6.8
Lamb ———— 2.2
Tyger ——————————————————— 9.8

"s"
Norm ————————— 4.5
Lamb ——————— 3.5
Tyger ———————— 4.1

"d"
Norm ———————— 4.3
Lamb ————————————— 7.0
Tyger ——————————— 6.2

"l"
Norm ——————— 3.7
Lamb ——————————————————————————————— 3.3
Tyger ———— 1.9

"m"
Norm ————— 2.7
Lamb ————————————— 6.6
Tyger ———— 2.5

"th"
Norm ——————— 3.4
Lamb ————————————— 6.6
Tyger ———————— 4.1

"h"
Norm ——— 1.8
Lamb ——————— 3.5
Tyger ——————————— 5.6

"w"
Norm ———— 2.0
Lamb — 0.6
Tyger ———————— 4.3

Looking at the graph, we see the salient features of Blake's phonemic frequency set to be (1) the outstanding dominance of "r," and (b) the outstanding dominance of the "r" and "t" together — they being the only phonemes that rise above all others in the poem and also above their counterparts in either the Dewey scale or in "The Lamb."

(c) *Semantic Potential.* These two salient characteristics — dominant "r" and dominant "r" and "t" together — create a semantic potential for the set. Having made his poem an "r" poem, Blake opened the door, consciously or unconsciously, to the archetypal and/or symbolic meanings for "r" that have been suggested at various times in literary history, especially in that famous passage in Plato's *Cratylus,* when Socrates says, "the letter *rho* seems to me to be an instrument expressing all motion."[7] Plato interpreted the "r" sound as fluidity, movement, action, just as Robert Graves, in *The White Goddess,* has done.[8] Given this interpretation for the "r" sound, the idea of *activity* may enter into a reader's ultimate understanding of the poem, his ultimate identification of content.

Likewise, having set up the "r" and "t" in dominant position *together,* Blake opened the door to the "meaning" of contrast: the contrast between the "go" of the "r" and the "stop" of the "t." The idea of *activity meeting its limit,* the idea of a tension in the universe between energy and entropy becomes a possibility so far as what the poem may ultimately "say."

Pushing "r" and "t" into dominance via the phonemic stylistic set of consonant frequency, Blake established a semantic ground upon which a semantic surface can be built. The contrast between movement and the braking of movement, between energy and the limitations of energy, is at least a possibility for a reader; if the reader does ultimately find the poem "saying" something about such a tension, such a contrast, he will find the phonemic aspect of the poem to be compatible with that "saying."

(d) *Interfacing.* The dominant contrastiveness of the "r" and "t" phonemes in "The Tyger" provides interfacing with a second major stylistic set, which uses phonemes as a portion of its stylistic material and develops aesthetic tension. The first and second stylistic sets overlap.

II. THE SERIAL SET

(a) *Stylistic Material.* Series — sequences of essentially coordinate language/verbal units — served Blake throughout "The Tyger" as stylistic material, from the opening alliterative serial of the "t" phonemes, "*T*yger, *t*yger," the consonant serial of the "r," "*T*yge*r*, tyge*r*, bu*r*ning b*r*ight," and the alliterative serial of the "b," "*b*urning *b*right," through the seriality of the questions asked in the poem and even through the seriality of metrics, rhyme scheme, and stanza structure. Present in the poem are serials of all "kinds" (i. e. of all kinds of unit material) and serials of two basic lengths — the two-part serial and the five-or-more-part serial.

(b) *The Set Arrangement.* Of these two length groups of serials, Blake created a stylistic set that is duplex. First he created a sub-set of gemination, a high two-partness, obvious in the opening "Tyger, tyger," maintained throughout the poem in balances, e. g. "Hand or eye," "deeps or skies," "what shoulder & what art," and in parallel sentences, "On what wings dare he aspire?/What the hand dare sieze the fire?" This twoness" of the poem is supported in every way, in the very rhythm of the lines broken by their caesuras; in the very stanzaic construction of the poem, e.g. opening stanza balanced by closing stanza and in the symmetrical design of the over-all poem, six stanzas divisible into sets of three, etc.

Interlocking with this whole sense of gemination and balance, however, is Blake's use of the long series — most apparent in the series of questions that make up the body of the poem, the plethora of the series accentuated by the use of "what" as anaphora. The fifteen question marks in the poem indicate the great length of this one series, and the number fifteen is obviously in sharp, startling contrast to the number two supported by the gemination in the poem.

Finally, we note that there is, so far as set arrangement is concerned, a near-chiasmus achieved with (a) a plethora of two-part series and (b) a singleness of the plethora series.

(c) *Semantic Potential.* This total stylistic set of high contrast between the gemination sub-set and the plethora sub-set creates the semantic potential of "paradox." In two previous articles, "The Rhetoric of the Series,"[9] and "The Rhetoric of Certitude,"[10] and in a text co-authored with Otis Winchester, *The Attitudes of Rhetoric*,[11] I have demonstrated the semantic potential of all such serials — the two-part series suggesting the ideas of dogma, absoluteness, certainty, and the many-part serial suggesting the ideas of humanity, comedy, the unknown, the questioning not of rational inquiry but of emotional and psychological frustration. Pitting these two serials against each other creates a stylistic set that generates paradox, confusion, and enigma as a potential "meaning" within the poem.

(d) *Interfacing.* The "questioning" aspect of the long series serves as an interface with the next stylistic set, which is one of metaphors.

III. THE METAPHOR SET

(a) *Stylistic Material.* Just as Blake had access to all phonemes in selecting the phonemic material and access to all serials in selecting his major serial groups, so he has access to all "kinds" of metaphors — that is to the full range of metaphorical forms from the explicit metaphors (i. e. regular metaphors wherein the tenor is stated as being the equivalent of the vehicle, either the moon *is* a ship, $A=B$, or similes, wherein the tenor is compared via "like" and "as" to a vehicle, the moon *is like* a ship, A *is like* B) to the condensed forms of metaphors (i. e. metaphors wherein the tenor and vehicle are put in oblique relationships, such as "the sailing moon" or "the bright sails of the moon" or "the moon ship" or "the yellow ship in the sky" with tenors and vehicles being placed in adjective/noun or noun/verb relationships) and on to the symbol metaphors (i. e. metaphors that are presented only in their vehicles and not in their tenors, such as "the yellow ship sails west across the dark blue sea," wherein the identification of the tenor, in this case "moon," is only faintly suggested if suggested at all, so that the metaphorical vehicle can be taken literally or figuratively, and if taken figuratively must be subjected to interpretation.)

(b) *The Set Arrangement.* The great metaphor in "The Tyger" is the tiger itself, which is, of course, the vehicle for an unstated tenor. This large symbol-metaphor contains all other metaphors in the poem, and the stylistic set can best be described as metaphor-within-metaphor.

The reconstituted metaphors are these: (1) X_1 tenor [outside the poem] *is* [unstated] the tyger. (2) The tyger *is* [unstated, condensed] a fire. (3) The tyger *is* [unstated, condensed] a metal that can be hammered on an anvil. (4) Night *is* [unstated, condensed] a forest containing a tiger. (5) Stars *are* [unstated, condensed] warriors or beings, personified, who throw spears. (6) X_2 tenor [outside the poem] is a smithy who operates a furnace.

Diagramatically, the metaphors appear this way:

Outside the Poem		*Inside the Poem*		
x_1 (unnamed tenor) [is—]		tiger	in the forest [—is]	night with stars
		[is]		[are]
	[is]	metal in		
	fire	furnace operated by		unspecified beings who throw spears.
x_2 (unnamed tenor) [is—]		blacksmith		

This complex metaphorical set is characterized by (1) its implicit rather than explicit presentation of the metaphors, with the major continuing metaphor — the blacksmith forging the tiger-metal — indicating two unnamed tenors; (2) the use of dual metaphorical direction, with some images, e. g. "forest," serving as vehicles for more than one tenor, i. e. "forest" is part of the vehicle for X_1 tenor, but is also the vehicle for "night"; (3) a general intricacy of metaphor presentation in that metaphors overlap, e. g. tiger is a vehicle for X_1 but is the tenor for "fire," and is also the tenor for "metal being forged in the furnace"; and (4) a high degree of personification informing the metaphors.

(c) *Semantic Potential.* One can possibly read in this metaphorical complex something about *complexity* not only as it pertains to the universe in general but to the human condition in particular. The very presence of the symbol-metaphor suggests a "meaning" that "all is symbol" in the universe in which we live, that the essential identity of things is yet to be given or is to be created by us. Yet, at the same time, the universe is "personal" and animate."

All this does not indicate that Blake was playing a riddle-game with us, with his knowing what or who the "x" or unknown happens to be. I am more inclined to believe that Blake erected a metaphorical structure that we can simply use as a dramatization of the complex configurations of our existence, the meaning of which is yet to be established; a dramatization of the possibility that "vehicles" precede "tenors" just as often as "tenors" precede "vehicles," and that the metaphorical direction of reality is dual if not even pluralistic; a dramatization of the possibility that we live in the midst of the vehicular aspect of metaphors and that the tenors of metaphors, or the "meanings," are essentially a process of post-vehicular discovery, both in poetry and in life.

(d) *Interfacing.* The "tension" of the dual metaphorical directions interfaces with the tensions found in the serial stylistic set and in the phonemic set. The "mystery" of the absent tenors interfaces back with the "paradox" and "enigma" of the serial set.

3.

As I have already indicated there are other stylistic sets within "The Tyger," but these three sets — phonemic, serial, and metaphor — are the main pillars, I believe, upon which the semantic surface of the poem rests. By the semantic surface I mean the total semantic potentiality of the poem, the stimulative aspect of the poem that prods the reader into making meaning for himself. I believe the stylistic sets in Blake's poem serve, in their separateness and in their compositeness both, as the intellectual ingredients which, when placed in the context of the reader's mind and its knowledge and needs, can "spark" meaning into existence.

Blake's own drafts of "The Tyger" suggest that in his revisions he was working from a stylistic base rather than a semantic base. The changes made in the last line of the fourth stanza, for instance, are revealing: The original word "could" is changed to "dare," so that the line, in the final version, reads "Dare its deadly terrors clasp?"[12] The revised line gives us (1) an alliterative "d" as an example of gemination (in contrast with the earlier "Could its deadly terrors clasp" that would give a consonance of "d" but not a balanced alliteration), and (2) a consonance of "r"'s to maintain the dominant position that the "r" phoneme has in the entire poem (in contrast with the earlier "Could its deadly terrors clasp" that would give an alliterative gemination of "c" [k] but too far spread apart, and would have given three "d"'s to two "r"'s in the line and hence an undesired emphasis on "d" and an undesired suppression of "r"). And we note, in his drafts, that a first version had six stanzas and a second draft had five stanzas, but that Blake went back to the six stanzas with their quality of symmetry and evenness, a part of the total gemination picture in the poem.

There are other significant revisions but these suggest that Blake was working toward the perfecting of stylistic sets, and that the differences in the options — e. g. the differences between "could" and "dare" — were seen as one of stylistics not semantics.

I think Blake himself acknowledges such a constructionist approach to art when he says, in his *Public Address*, "I have heard many people say, 'Give me the ideas; it is no matter what words you put them into.' And others say, 'Give me the design; it is no matter for the execution.' These people know nothing of art. Ideas cannot be given, but in their minutely appropriate words, nor can a design be made without its minutely appropriate execution," and when he says, in his *Annotations to Reynolds*, "Invention depends altogether upon execution or organization; as that is right or wrong so is the invention perfect or imperfect. Whoever is set to undermine the execution of art is set to destroy art." Execution is Blake's word for construction, and he is saying that one cannot be given an idea and then proceed to construction; that the "doing" of the art precedes all else; that the invention — and I think he means by that the overall experienceability of a poem, both in its stylistic and semantic aspects — follows *after* the construction and the organization of the poem.

Blake was a constructionist, I believe, (in contrast with Wordsworth perhaps) and his procedures were and are viable. We too often think, I feel, that the stylistics of a poem are the orchestration of something the poet has to say; that the poet begins with his "idea" and then achieves some appropriate orchestration and manifestation via style. But surely it is just as reasonable to suppose the alternative is possible — especially in the light of many artists' comments that their creations begin, not with "meaning" but with their own "playing around" with sounds, rhythms, images, or what have you. It is reasonable to suppose that artists — at least some artists — are not necessarily ideologists exploiting style but stylists exploring through media toward the unknown and undetermined meaning.

Even those monistic-minded critics who believe there is "one true meaning" for the poem will surely allow that the "one true meaning" can be the result of style as well as the cause of style. And those of us who are pluralistic — and relativistic — minded, who see all meanings as ultimately variable and subjective, dependent upon the particular transaction one reader makes with a poem and dependent upon the context of experience and knowledge into which the reader places the poem and negotiates with it — those of us who *so believe* will see constructionism, as demonstrated in Blake's most famous poem, as an eminently reasonable kind of creativity, not only for the late eighteenth century when Blake wrote "The Tyger," but for other poetic times and climes as well. And we will also see constructionism as a mode of critical analysis that recognizes the poet as the "maker" he has essentially always been.

NOTES

¹ Charles Lamb, Letter, May 15, 1824, in G. E. Bentley, *Blake Records* (Oxford: Oxford University Press, 1960), p. 285.

² Henry Crabb Robinson, *Essay on Blake*, in G. E. Bentley, *Blake Records* (Oxford: Oxford University Press, 1969), p. 454.

³ Allan Cunningham, Lives of the Most Eminent Brittish Painters, Sculptors, and Architects, in G. E. Bentley, *Blake Records* (Oxford: Oxford University Press, 1969), p. 479.

⁴ *Ibid.*

⁵ Yet Blake revealed his own calculated artistry in his "To the Public" preface to the first chapter of *Jerusalem*, when he says, "Every word and every letter is studied and put into its fit place..." *The Complete Writings of William Blake*, ed. Geoffrey Keynes (London: Oxford University Press, 1966) p. 621.

⁶ G. Dewey, *Relative Frequency of English Speech Sounds* (Cambridge, Mass: Harvard University Press, 1923). I am using the Dewey table as presented in George Miller, *Language and Communication*, (New York: McGraw-Hill Book Company, 1951), p. 86.

⁷ Plato, *The Cratylus*, in *Plato with an English Translation* by Herbert North Fowler (Loeb Classical Library) Vol. 6 (Cambridge Mass.: Harvard University Press, 1953), p. 145.

⁸ Robert Graves, *The White Goddess* (New York: Vintage Books, 1948), p. 140.

⁹ Winston Weathers, "The Rhetoric of the Series," *College Composition and Communication*, Vol. XVII, No. 5 (December, 1966), pp. 217—222.

¹⁰ Winston Weathers, "The Rhetoric of Certitude," *Southern Humanities Review*, Vol. 2, No. 2 (Spring, 1968), pp. 213—222.

¹¹ Winston Weathers and Otis Winchester, *The Attitudes of Rhetoric*. (Englewood Cliffs, New Jersey: Prentice-Hall, 1970).

¹² It is interesting that Wordsworth, in his copy of "The Tyger" made from Malkin's copy, changed the word "Dare" to "Did" — thereby eliminating by error the necessary third "r" in the line. Obviously, Wordsworth did not hear the "r"-ness that Blake was making dominant in the poem, but heard instead a "d"-ness contrary to Blake's phonemic set. Much could be said, I think, about Wordsworth's converting the line to a "d" dominance — interferring with the "motion" and "action" aspect of the poem and increasing the dental hardness and haltingness. See G. E. Bentley, *op. cit.*, p. 430.

Werner Winter
Christian-Albrechts Universität Kiel

Intralanguage variation and interlanguage comparison

Languages may be compared for a variety of reasons; depending on the specific purpose, the investigation may be concerned primarily or exclusively with properties of the respective systems, or questions of usage may be of considerable importance. Thus, comparative linguistics in the narrower, historical-genetic sense of the term, will explore whether forms found in several of the languages under study can be shown to correspond to one another in a systematic fashion; as a rule, it will suffice to know that a given form exists, and peculiarities of its occurrence will be, at best, of only marginal interest.

In contrastive linguistics, on the other hand, a comparison of the systems of two or more languages, and of parts of these systems is not enough; quite generally, the purpose of contrastive investigation is also an eminently practical one, and a study of how forms confronted in the languages studied are actually used in each of them plays a very important role.

Typological comparison, the third major type of comparative language study, for a long time was concerned almost exclusively with features of languages as parts of their respective systems and inventories. It was a significant advance in typological work when Joseph H. Greenberg found a way to incorporate a study of usage; his pioneering paper entitled 'A quantitative approach to the morphological typology of language' first appeared (in 1954) in the festschrift for W. D. Wallis (*Method and perspective in anthropology*, University of Minnesota Press) and subsequently reached a larger audience through a second printing in the *International Journal of American Linguistics* (26.1960. 178—194). Greenberg was not satisfied with noting the presence of a given morphological property, but was just as much concerned with measuring the incidence of this property in actual text. His approach enabled him to make a clear distinction between a language in which a given phenomenon occurred only in a few instances, and another where the same phenomenon was extremely common; while a system-oriented investigation would have been forced to assign the two languages to one and the same class, he was now able to place them at quite different points of a usage-determined scale.

Greenberg himself always viewed his paper as a pilot study; it would therefore not be justified to blame him for the somewhat uncritical acceptance it received from a number of other scholars. In my contribu-

299

tion to the Bucharest congress (*Actes du Xe Congrès International des Linguistes* 3.545—549), I discussed some of the problems that seemed to arise if Greenberg's method was adopted without some rather thorough changes. One of the points mentioned only briefly deserves further elaboration.

Toward the end of his paper, Greenberg touched very briefly upon the question of whether the results obtained for a language were seriously affected by the nature of the text actually evaluated. The figures obtained for the index of synthesis (number of morphemes divided by number of words) for three one-hundred word samples each of English and German seemed to indicate a high degree of stability within the two languages: the ratios found were 1.62, 1.65, 1.60 for English, and 1.90, 1.92, 2.11 for German.

An extensive reconsideration of Greenberg's approach, the results of which will be presented elsewhere, showed that more intralanguage variation was found than seemed to be suggested by Greenberg's preliminary observations.

In various seminars conducted at Texas, Hamburg, Yale, and Kiel, I had Greenberg's finding subjected to further scrutiny. For reasons that cannot be given here, we decided to increase the size of the individual text sample from one hundred to five hundred words. In the case of one language, English, we analyzed a much larger number of texts than had been inspected by Greenberg; for other languages, control counts were performed for a somewhat smaller group of texts, and for all languages investigated, a minimum of three texts (the equivalent of Greenberg's maximum number) were evaluated.

Taking into account only the index of synthesis (with the modification that the ratio of morphs to words rather than that of morphemes to words was established in our counts), the following values were obtained:

Text	M/W
International Law [textbook]	1.62
Salinger, *Frannie and Zooey*	1.36
James, *The Madonna of the future*	1.37
Schulz, *Peanuts*	1.46
Faulkner, *As I lay dying*	1.49
Williams, *The night of the iguana*	1.41
Eliot, *Murder in the cathedral*	1.46
Joyce, *Ulysses*	1.21
Milne, *The house on Pooh Corner*	1.27
Whatmough, *Language*	1.81
New York Times	1.70
[A Physics text]	1.60
Hemingway, *A farewell to arms*	1.32
London *Times*	1.57
Chomsky/Halle, *The sound pattern of English*	1.65
Carroll, *Alice in Wonderland*	1.34
Schulz, *Peanuts* [second sample]	1.35

The figures given are raw figures, obtained from a number of different individuals. As we were in the unusually fortunate position that control counts could be performed, which allowed us to determine, within certain limitations, the idiosyncratic behavior of the individual investigator, and to introduce adjustment factors, the list given may be supplemented by a second one which contains figures as might have been supplied by an idealized counter; this list reads:

Law	1.82	Whatmough	1.57
Salinger	1.36	*New York Times*	1.50
James	1.43	Physics	1.60
Peanuts (I)	1.38	Hemingway	1.33
Faulkner	1.41	London *Times*	1.62
Williams	1.47	Chomsky/Halle	1.70
Eliot	1.52	*Alice*	1.38
Joyce	1.36	*Peanuts* (II)	1.39
Pooh	1.27		

Although the individual values vary from the raw to the adjusted list, the overall result remains virtually unchanged: Instead of the great stability suggested by Greenberg's findings, which would indeed permit us to suggested by Greenberg's value for English without risking any serious distortion, we find that the texts assembled here yield figures which differ considerably from one another. The range in the raw table is 1.21 — 1.81, in the adjusted one, 1.27 — 1.82. The overall averages are: raw, 1.47, adjusted, 1.48 (the adjustment, in addition to being highly impractical, thus has a negligible impact). In the case of the raw table, only ten out of 17 values are within a $\pm$ 10 % band around the average (the situation is somewhat improved for the adjusted table), and the degree to which each individual value is representative for any other individual figure from the table is relatively low; it follows that recourse to one single value, be it even an average obtained from the observation of a fair number of individual texts, would obscure the fact that there is a rather great diversity among texts from contemporary English with respect to their morphological complexity.

What therefore seems appropriate, if one sets out to compare English with other languages, is not to try to plot one value per language on a complexity scale, but to take each individual language as represented by a set of values manifested as a band, the width of this band being determined by the amount of stylistic differentiation found within the texts investigated. If the dot on the scale as obtained by Greenberg is replaced by bands placed alongside other bands, it goes without saying that instead of the relatively neat Greenbergian picture of usually discrete entities there will be now very much overlap between languages. This may in some ways be an unsatifactory outcome of the modified approach; however, there are means to introduce further distinctions and thereby disentangle, to some extent, what seems to be unnecessarily confused.

Instead of comparing any English text with any text from another language (as Greenberg did), or of comparing as many different texts as possible jointly (as has been advocated here), it seems possible to select texts of specific types from all languages to be compared and place them side-by-side. The results then will of course not be statements about English, French, etc., as such, but about, say, scientific English, French, etc. Obviously not all languages can be compared in all respects; but as an addition to the band-matching approach, such a specified comparison is likely to yield far from trivial results.

IV. TEXT LINGUISTICS

E. L. Epstein
Queens College, City University of New York

Syntactic laws and detemporalized expression in modern literature

I saw a staring virgin stand
Where holy Dionysus died,
And tear the heart out of his side,
And lay that heart upon her hand
And bear that beating heart away;
And then did all the Muses sing
Of Magnus Annus at the spring
As though God's death were but a play.

Another Troy must rise and set,
Another lineage feed the crow,
Another Argo's painted prow
Drive to a flashier bauble yet.
The Roman Empire stood appalled:
It dropped the reigns of peace and war
When that fierce virgin and her Star
Out of the fabulous darkness called.[1]

This poem, the first of "Two Songs from a Play," was written by William Butler Yeats in 1926 and was first published in 1927. It was later sung as epilogue by the Chorus of Musicians in Yeats' play *The Resurrection*, first performed in 1934. *The Resurrection* deals with Yeats' belief that the advent of Christianity ushered in a new state of history, one in which the classic age which culminated in the Roman Empire gave way to a new historical cycle. As with all new stages of history in Yeats' historical system (as enunciated in his theoretical work *A Vision*), the actual period of transition from one stage of history to another is marked by a supernatural invasion of human activities; at the turning point itself, according to Yeats, no human life can exist — it is the stage of spirits interacting.

"Two Songs from a Play" describe such a turning point, in the life and resurrection of Christ. In the play the resurrected Christ appears to a Greek, a Syrian, and a Hebrew. The Greek, sceptical of the nature of the apparition, predicts that the apparition will be hard as marble, and touches it. He then recoils and screams, "The heart of a phantom is beating!" It is this climax that is described in the first of the "Two Songs."

The period from Good Friday to Easter Sunday is *in* time, but not *of* time — eternity enters time, and supernatural modes of succession take the place of normal quotidian expectation. The resurrected Christ is both of heaven and earth, a phantom with a beating heart. This unprecedented combination predicts a radical historical shift, from the Roman Empire to the Christian era.

As in all of his poems that celebrate such turning points, or intrusion points, in history — "The Cold Heaven," "Leda and the Swan," "The Second Coming," "Byzantium," and others — Yeats employs heterodox linguistic techniques, to convey, and to mirror, the unusual mode of perception during such times. This necessarily involves a type of "sabotage" — subtle but powerful — of the "normal" operations of the English language, since the statistically or regularly normal operation of the language does not seem to convey more than normal states of mind and social interaction. The regular succession of the tenses, the psychologically appropriate reflections of the act of attribution displayed in the creation of nominal and modifying structures, all of these operate in one way in casual conversation and another in these climactic points of history.

A. EXPRESSION OF TEMPORAL SUCCESSION IN ENGLISH

Of all the quotidian marks of speech, the expression of the passing of time is the most affected by the situations in these poems. Time does not appear to "pass" normally in these periods — it is modes of eternity that operate. It seems that there is succession of some sort, but it is not the sort of moment-by-moment seriation that is expressed by normal language.

There are a number of different methods by which the passing of time is represented in language, and each of them is altered or sabotaged in these climactic situations, for necessary dramatic purposes.[2]

(1) First of all, the passing of time is expressed most precisely by adverbials — of time, duration, frequency (except for the adverb of frequency "once"), either specific or general:

Temporal Adverbials

	Specific	General
time	yesterday tomorrow two days from now on Sunday	when Bill saw Mary when the old barn burned down after the cat ran away before you leave
dura-tion	for two minutes for three hours for twenty months	for as long as it takes for as short a time as possible
fre-quency	twice three times a minute	as often as possible as seldom as convenient

In addition to these specific and general temporal adverbials, there is a class of markers by which sequence is marshalled — "first," "then," "in the meantime," "finally," "suddenly" (this last much employed by Yeats). For a technical reason — their occasional inability to act in context as answers to the appropriate temporal interrogatives — these sequence markers should not always be regarded as "adverbials." Often they do not refer to external states of affairs, but rather mark internal points of transition in the presentation of the discourse itself, and therefore mark the temporal succession of the discourse.

(2) These temporal references, especially the specific adverbials, are so precise that, on their own, they can provide the temporal backbone of a great many discourses. Indeed, they make unnecessary *sequence of tenses,* the second method of indicating temporality. In the absence of temporal adverbials, the establishment of temporal frames can be established, when tense is combined with the participial aspects of perfected or progressive action. The tenses themselves indicate two or three separate fields of reference, and the participials assist in the movement, or lack of it, from one stage to the next.

· However, the phenomenon of "historical present" shows how subordinate sequence of tenses is to temporal adverbials. In an historical-present passage, both tense and aspect are neutralized, but the temporality of the situation is quite adequately conveyed by other means. (In several Chinese dialects and in some African languages, *all* temporal sequence is conveyed by adverbials, and *all* tense is neutral.) Yeats employs heterodox sequences and varieties of tense in such poems as "Byzantium" to achieve a dream-like succession of images.

(3) When an impression of orthodox temporal sequence is not desired, these two means of conveying sequence can easily be omitted or neutralized or confused, as in "Byzantium." However, other means of expressing temporality are not so easily evaded. A large number of verbs possess inherent temporality — "walk," for example, suggests at least two or three strides, which take place through time (and space). "Ponder" is a verb of mental action which is held to take place in more than one moment of time. "Sing" (a "point-action verb" like "shout"), "stare" (as against "glance"), "pound" (as against "knock," in one of its meanings), "whisper" (as against "hiss") — all convey action through time (or through space and therefore through time). Of course, deverbal nouns and gerunds derived from these temporal verbs ("singing," "staring," "pounding," and so on) keep their temporality. Stative verbs or verbals like "inherit" have no inherent temporality, not because, like "point-action verbs," they take place in an instantaneous transition, but because in themselves they represent the apprehension of a general state, one whose genesis, if not specified adverbially, is not clear enough to act as the beginning of a temporal sequence. And of course they have no termination, as do the temporal verbs.

We shall see how careful Yeats is with temporal verbs, and how cunningly he sets about robbing them of their temporality.

(4) With a little care, a poet who wishes to avoid the impression of the ordinary passing of time may be able to avoid the use of temporal verbs, as well as the use of temporal adverbials, sequence-markers, and sequence of tenses. However, there are features of English which are much more difficult to avoid while still producing recognizable varieties of English. (What follows below seems to be generally true of the other Indo-European languages as well as English, and a great many more.)

Temporality is one of the irreducible requirements for a well-formed referential utterance in English, since an utterance is not a sentence in (Standard) English without a finite verb, a unit morphologically marked for temporality. (Even the "historical present" is morphologically marked for tense, although semantically neutral.)

The idea of a minimal sentence is as old as Plato, who observes, in the *Sophist* (262 c, d), that single expressions ("dogs") cannot express truth — only binary expressions may be assented to ("dogs bark"). One of the two minimal propositional representatives in the minimal sentence is, therefore, a bearer of the reminder of temporality. A succession of sentential utterances is marked, sentence by sentence, with a sequence of temporally marked units. Of course, the surface form of the utterance may conceal the actual temporal pattern. If surface structure were all, the sentence "John, Mary, and Bill left the room at different times" would seem to refer to only one set, that associated with the single finite verb "left," rather than with three temporally separate acts. Therefore, to determine the precise number of temporal assertions in any surface utterance, it is necessary to consider its underlying structure. This may be accomplished by representing the utterance as a transformational-generative phrase-marker, a structure in which each structure dominated by the symbol S would be required to have its own

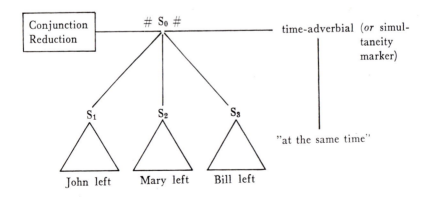

tense-marker, and therefore its own finite verb and its own assertion of temporality. It is likely that by this means it would be possible to recover the pattern of minimal binary utterances organized into the surface sentence, and therefore recover every expression of temporality in the final utterance.

With this qualification in mind, a further assertion can be made. Each minimal utterance will, all things being equal, be found to suggest a different temporal stage from the other minimal utterances in the discourse. The sequence can be recaptured easily from surface utterances that are not heavily "transformed," i. e., conjoined to others or embedded in them. In this case, the left-to-right movement of orthographic symbology would express movement forward in time, and in the base of spoken discourse the last spoken utterance would express the last temporal assertion in a series. Thus, in the following discourse, a temporal succession would be (weakly) suggested from left to right:

1. John *stood up*. 2. Mary *went* to the window. 3. Charles *yawned*. [finite verbs in italics]

There is no reason why these acts could not have taken place simultaneously, but in the absence of specific assertions of simultaneity ("John stood up *as* Mary went to the window, *while* Charles yawned"), the suggestion expressed in the sequence is that the three acts were either sequential in reality (*temporal succession*) or sequentially observed by the speaker (*psychological*, or *spatial*, *succession*).

Events which are in truth simultaneous may not be perceivable as such by any given viewer, who may have caught aspects of each act as he turned his eyes from John to Mary to Charles. The temporality of the situation, therefore, is still a true temporality, but one tied to the action of the viewer and not of the actors.

Before a pattern of temporal succession can be discerned, conjoined utterances must be "unconjoined," and the reduced or deleted elements reconstituted. Coordinate conjoinings are no problem to interpret, but subordinate ones may provide clues to temporal interpretation that contradict what would be the pattern of successivity of the base minimal utterances themselves.

> John, Mary, and Bill *laughed* = [the observer notes successively the laughing of John, of Mary, and of Bill]
>
> Before John *laughed*, Bill *sighed* = [the observer notes that, in temporal succession, first Bill sighed and then John laughed]
>
> Bill *sighed* because John *laughed* = [the observer notes, in reverse, a temporal succession of John laughing and Bill sighing, with a causal connection]

Embedded constructions provide a more complex situation, as in Pope's couplet

> The thriving plants ignoble broomsticks made,
> Now sweep those Alleys they were born to shade.

The first follows temporal order; the second reverses it.

These constructions do generally suggest a temporal succession forward, finite verb by finite verb, if only weakly so, in the sense that, with the proper markers, they could be held to express a simultaneous state of affairs. However, there are some locutions which express a temporal succession strongly (*strong succession*). In this situation the series of locutions cannot possibly be made to express a simultaneous state of affairs.

John sat down.　　John stood up.　　John walked to the window.

It makes no sense to introduce simultaneity-markers, or syntactic orderings of obligatory simultaneity:

* John sat down, while he stood up.
* Standing up, John sat down.

These sequences do not, in the ordinary sense of the word, express logical contradictions. They depend on antonymic relations rather than true contradiction. A true (surface) contradiction expresses no sequence at all:

* John stood up.　　* John did not stand up.

Strong succession can be described as roughly, the subjective effect of temporal succession produced by two or more minimal sentential units of a specific form, whose semantic elements bear a strong resemblance to each other when expanded into intensional sets (or definitional sets) revealing at least one stretch of definition in which there is an exact repetition of units in both, except that one stretch contains a negative that the other does not.

Problem:　are S_x and S_y in strong succession? [For the sake of demonstration, the subjects of the sentences will be held to be the same].

Method:　express the verbals as intensional sets,

$$x \left\{ \ a_x \quad b_x \quad c_x \ldots n_x \ \right\}$$
$$y \left\{ \ a_y \quad b_y \quad c_y \ldots n_y \ \right\}$$

Solution:　is there a pair of intensional units $i_x i_y$ such that $i_x =$ $-(i_y)$, all other pairings being identical in all respects as well as to sign. If so, S_x and S_y are in strong succession. (Note: this is highly oversimplified).

This antonymic relation cannot appear as a surface negative — otherwise a true (sterile) contradiction will emerge. This antonymic requirement for strong succession is capable of being represented with considerable surface diversity. However, it is not the purpose of this paper to define strong succession explicitly (although I am sure it can be done) but rather to establish the notion intuitively, and to apply this knowledge to a description of Yeats' poem.

B. YEATS' MODIFICATION OF THE VERBAL STRUCTURES EXPRESSING TEMPORAL SUCCESSION

All of the above devices express a quotidian trundling forward into the future, a "normal" state of affairs. For the poet who wishes to express an *abnormal* state of affairs, these devices are traps to be avoided, or "sabotaged" where unavoidable (like finite-verb successions). In the first of "Two Songs from a Play," Yeats performs brilliant feats of avoidance and sabotage to avoid commonplace temporal succession in the expression of a highly unusual situation.

(1) Yeats' use, or rather avoidance, of temporal adverbials is characteristically bold and ingenious. There are two temporal adverbials in the poem, both "general": "at the spring" and "when that fierce virgin and her Star/Out of the fabulous darkness called." The first does not specify a time but rather a stage in a recurrent cycle, in Magnus Annus, the Platonic Great Year which, in Yeats' historical system, comes round ceaselessly. The second temporal adverbial is also robbed of specific temporality, by a device to be described below.

However, the most unusual temporal adverbial is one that is not there. If one were to construct a scenario of the events in the poem, it soon would become clear that the place-adverbial "where holy Dionysus died" is a substitute for a more complex temporal adverbial:

> I saw a staring virgin [come up and stand by]
> holy Dionysus [when/as he died]
> And tear the heart out of his side . . .

The place-adverbial somewhat misrepresents the expected sequence of events; the virgin could have stood where Dionysus had died a century before.

The substitution of a spatial expression for a (superficially more adequate) temporal expression is not unique in post-Symbolist poetry. Robert Lowell employed the same effect in an early poem, "Children of Light":

> . . . They [the Puritan settlers of America]
>   planted here the Serpent's seeds of light.
> And here the pivoting searchlights probe to shock
> The riotous glass houses built on rock . . .

The repetition of "here . . . here" instead of "then . . . now," which the sense demands, is similar to Yeats' spatialization of a temporal process.

Yeats here, therefore, neutralized two temporal adverbials and "falsified" a third. (His use of the "sequence-marker" *then* will be described below.)

(2) Sequence of tenses is also sabotaged, with equal originality and boldness as in his use of temporal adverbials. The simple past in the first stanza abruptly alters to the future (or to what could be termed an "advanced present") in the four-line passage beginning "Another Troy must rise and set." The simple past then returns, but the unorthodox, block-like tense sequence effectively removes the poem from the category of the quotidian.[3]

(3) Yeats employs verbs with inherent temporality with great skill. A verbal noun-modifier, with its freedom (in English) to appear either pre- or post-nominally acquires a significance depending on which position it chooses. A prenominal ("attributive") position can sometimes indicate a permanent characteristic of the nominal, while a post-nominal ("predicative") position almost always indicates a temporary state.[4] "Staring," promoted to pre-nominal "attributive" position, suggests a permanent characteristic of "staring" to the virgin, even though, in normal circumstances, staring is an act limited in time. (The effect is reminiscent of archaic Greek sculpture).

The use of "stand" is also heterodox. In the realistic scenario for the poem the observer ("I saw") could not see the virgin come to a halt ("stand") unless she had drawn near. The use of "stand" however, has her appear without temporal preliminary.

(4) The most impressive use or abuse of language occurs with Yeats' avoidance of finite verbal movement. The finite verbals in the poem generally outline what has been called above "strong succession": the virgin stands, tears, lays a heart upon hand, bears it away — *then* the Muses sing, then there is a prophetic outburst, itself strongly successive internally (Troy rises and sets), then a further description of the virgin, performing an act subsequent to her action in the first stanza (as I believe). This highly "stroboscopic" texture could produce an equally highly charged kinetic motion through time. Yeats, however, retains an iron control over temporal sequence by a series of subterfuges.

The virgin's actions are robbed of finite-verbal temporality by the simple device of destroying the finiteness of the verbals expressing her actions. What would be the finite verbals — "stand," "tear," "lay," "bear" — are essentially infinitives, dependent upon "I saw." What would outline a strongly successive series in the first five lines now contains a series of actions which cannot take place simultaneously (by antonymic tests), but which are expressed by non-finite clauses, which do not express such movement forward morphologically, not being marked for tense. The effect is that of a purer type of succession than normal, which is entirely appropriate to the situation. It is a supernatural, ritualistic motion for a ritual action at a nodal point in history.

The polysyndeton of the first stanza — the four "ands" — increases the pressure on the passage to express temporal succession. The effect of "and" is complex, but one characteristic of this conjunction is to reinforce the normal successivity — temporal or spatial, weak or strong — of the items it conjoins. "And" generally has the significance of "and then" or "and in addition." This can easily be demonstrated by the oddness of expressions that contravene this rule:

* I went to Chicago and Chicago
* He died and kicked the bucket
* He hurt his foot and stubbed his toe.

"And" imposes a successivity on series of repeated identical verbs or adjectives.

He ran and ran and ran =	He ran, and then he ran some more, and then he ran yet some more.
Curiouser and curiouser =	More curious, and even more curious than that.

Therefore, the polysyndeton should reinforce the strong succession of the verbals in the lines one through five of the first stanza. The tension between the devices suggesting succession and the detemporalization of the verbals, therefore, creates a powerful impression of a succession of events occurring out of time, a supernatural, ritualistic motion.

Yeats ends this hieratic motion out of time with a sequence-marker deliberately introduced ("then"), to begin time again. As far as the movement from finite verbal to finite verbal is concerned, the "action" has proceeded from "I *saw*" to "then *did* all the Muses sing" without finite verbality and its accompanying commonplace successivity, but with the accompaniment of other devices which would, in other circumstances, suggest intensely strong succession.

Note also that although there are finite verbs (necessarily, or else Yeats would be blatantly engaged in un-English language play), they are de-emphasized or otherwise rendered unimportant and unnoticeable. The action of "seeing" is not at all where the dramatic focus of the first stanza is, and the tense-marker for the Muses' singing is assigned to an auxiliary, because of inverted word order ("did" instead of "sang"). The last finite verb in the first stanza is not even in the indicative voice but the subjunctive — "As though God's death *were* but a play."

Imagine how breathless and commonplace the stanza would be if Yeats had not been so careful with sequence convention. A version of it, disregarding rhyme and metre, would read like this:

> The Virgin Mary came and stared
> As holy Dionysus died
> Then tore the heart out of his side,
> And laid the heart upon her hand,
> And bore it, beating, far away;
> Then all the Muses quickly sang
> Of Magnus Annus at the spring,
> Because God's death was but a play.

The flatness and foolish haste expressed in this version owes, I feel, a good deal to the cancelling of Yeats' brilliant expedients for evading commonplace movement through time.

The same devices are employed, rather more loosely, in the prophetic lines in the second stanza. All of the verbals are dependent upon the colorless finite verbality of the auxiliary "must." With this requirement out of the way, Yeats can express violent action — Troy rising and setting, carrion birds feasting on dead noble warriors, the hysterical thrust of the Argo's prow ("painted" freezes past action) — without finite movement. Again we have non-finite strong succession, a detemporalized, supernatural movement out of time.[5]

Finally, in the last four lines of the last stanza, a normal successivity begins to reassert itself, reminding the reader of the abnormal situation he has just left. The Roman Empire stands appalled and drops the reigns (or "reins") of peace and war, as the Virgin calls from the darkness. However, it seems likely that this calling is not a separate action but is rather a continuation of the action expressed in the first stanza; the heart, having been borne away into the darkness, begins to shine. While the reader was following Yeats into the future, the action in the past was continuing. (For a similar evasion of commonplace methods of narrative succession, see "Leda and the Swan.") The general temporal adverbial in the last two lines, therefore, is also "sabotaged"; the change of voice or point of view in the prophetic lines causes a dislocation in narrative sequence which is interpretable by the reader as a gap in narrative time. A gap in reading time — the gap between the last line of the first stanza and the fifth line of the second — is felt as a gap in the narrative, with the action then taking up after the real/fictive gap. This confusion is typical of later Yeats; a similar effect occurs in "Byzantium," accomplished by rather different means.

The total effect of these linguistic devices is, at the very least, to make the passing of time a much less ordinary phenomenon than the great majority of utterances would suggest, and at the very most, that a highly unusual utterance is created and preserved, in which passage through time is mimed carefully, but with such alterations in regular linguistic devices that quotidian time is avoided and a new type of succession is presented.

C. SOME REMARKS ON THE STATUS OF GRAMMATICAL RULES AND RULES OF DISCOURSE

This description of the language of a Yeats poem seems to reveal a number of linguistic irregularities — the oddity of "staring" in attributive position, the apparent substitution of a place-adverbial for a time-adverbial, noticeably excessive polysyndeton, "strong succession" expressed in non-finite verbals and a general evasion of semantically rich finite verbals, the postponement of a noun-modifier, "beating" (not discussed above), an introduction of four lines in a future tense in a generally past-tense context and a return to past tense, with the gap expressing a true passage of time. It is a difficult question to determine whether these constitute a violation of linguistic "rules" or not.

It might be necessary to make a (perhaps artificial) distinction between true rules and other regulative generalizations. The distinction between a rule, and a device like a law or a custom, is that by its nature a rule cannot be broken. As Wittgenstein has said, "A thought contains the possibility of the situation of which it is the thought. What is thinkable is possible, too. Thought can never be anything illogical, since, if it were, we should have to think illogically." (*Tractatus*, 3.02, 3.03). In his later work, Wittgenstein modifies this stand, which underlies the nature of rules of the language-game, by suggesting a multiplicity of language-games; therefore, there is a possibility that if a rule of one game seems to have been broken the players simply retreat to another type of language-game where the nomoclastic event is not forbidden by a rule. It is as if a chess player would pick up his rook and, instead of moving it along a rank of the chessboard, would fling it into the face of his opponent. This would be an event which would not be covered by any of the rules of chess, and therefore could be held to be breaking the rule of chess, but perhaps obeying one of the rules of the game of Assault and Battery.

The difficulty about applying this notion of a "retreat to another game", as it perhaps can be called, to the violations in poetry is that the retreat from rule-break to rule-whole situations is random, as in the case of the retreat from chess to Assault and Battery, and the rules and their effects bear no necessary relationship to each other. However, the violations of the "rules" of language, if that is what occurs in the Yeats poem, is followed by consequences which seem to be related to the nature of the rules broken — time, which is normally suggested by devices of language, is make to halt or speed ahead, but the effect of "rule-breaking" is still in the area of the conveyance of time, not in some randomly chosen area.

This suggests to me that rules are indeed unbreakable for language, that there is only one language-game, that if a rule is violated it stops the language-game dead (that is, if the rule is broken, no phonological or syntactic hypothesis about the nature of the string presented can be formed and that therefore the assignment of meaning to the string can not even begin). However, if what is violated is not a rule but a *law* of language, then what follows *is* part of the game, the part called the penalty. Lack of meaning is not a penalty but a sign of the cessation of the language-game; violation of a law of language brings a less drastic consequence in its train — one that perhaps a poet willingly incurs, for his own special ends. This suggestion avoids the difficulty with the multiple-game-retreat suggestion above, in that the law and its violation can be held to bear some stateable relationship to each other, one that by repetition becomes as much of the game as the strategy and the laws of the game themselves. (Indeed, until a few years ago, there was a favorite violation of the "rule" forbidding revoking in bridge, when the penalty for revoking was gladly accepted by a player who would lose more points by following suit. I believe the penalty was eventually made much more prohibitive, that is, it was made into a pseudo-rule, a law whose penalty was so extreme that it would never have been strategically appropriate to break it.)

Poets, therefore, break laws of language rather than rules of language. In the case of Yeats in this poem, the penalty for avoiding and sabotaging the discoursal "rules", really "laws", of temporal succession, is a type of succession which is not temporal. This state of affairs is gladly accepted by Yeats, for his own thematic and aesthetic purposes. Perhaps this notion of laws and penalties can be extended to all literature, as examples of controlled use of penalties in the language game for private ends. Indeed, perhaps all discourse, literary or not, provides penalties for the listeners, if the discourse has any informational novelty in it for them. Rousseau suggested that anyone who speaks to someone else and alters the content of his memories is thereby committing an aggression upon him; perhaps he is only forcing him to pay a small penalty for the sake of human expression.

NOTES

[1] Text from *The Collected Poems of William Butler Yeats* (New York: The Macmillan Company, 1951), p. 210.

[2] For some treatment of this topic, see Otto Jespersen, *The Philosophy of Grammar* [1924, 1934] (New York: W. W. Norton & Co., 1965), pp. 276 ff. See also E. L. Epstein, "Blake's 'Infant Sorrow' — An Essay in Discourse Analysis," in *Current Trends in Stylistics*, eds. B. Kachru and H. Stahlke, Papers in Linguistics Monographs, Linguistic Research Incorporated, Edmonton, Alberta, Canada, pp. 231—241; and also E. L. Epstein, "Yeats' Experiments with Syntax in the Treatment of Time," in *Modern Irish Literature: a William York Tindall Festschrift*, eds. R. Porter and J. Brophy (Iona College Press: New Rochelle, New York, Twzyne Publishers, 1972), pp. 171—184.

[3] The four-line prophetic passage is a highly charged paraphrase of a well-known passage from the Fourth Eclogue of Virgil, which has often been interpreted as a prediction of the coming of Christ. Yeats' version is close to that of Shelley in the final chorus of *Hellas*. The "resonance" of such an allusive passage adds a great deal to the total effect of the poem, but it is not really germane to the issue I am treating. See Jon Stallworthy, *Vision and Revision in Yeats' Last Poems* (Oxford, The Clarendon Press, 1969), p. 23, and Harold Bloom, *Yeats* (New York: Oxford University Press, 1970), p. 335. (I owe these references to my student, Robert Zafran).

[4] The major treatments of the position of noun-modifiers are Dwight Bolinger, "Linear Modification," *PMLA* 67 (1952), 1117—44 (esp. 1133—37), and (also by Bolinger), "Adjectives in English: Attribution and Predication," *Lingua* 18 (1967), 1—34.

[5] For a similar effect from similar structures, see T. S. Eliot, *Burnt Norton*, 11. 25—41, where a similar succession out of time is expressed, culminating in the same sequence-marker, "then." In this passage, however, the finite verbals are not morphologically detemporalized.

Jan Firbas
University of Brno

On the thematic and the non-thematic section of the sentence

In an earlier paper of mine,[1] I defined the theme of a sentence/clause in terms of communicative dynamism (= CD), stating that the theme of a sentence/clause is constituted by the element(s) that carries (carry) the lowest degree(s) of CD within the sentence/clause. Elaborating this delimitation, I will attempt to throw some further light on the boundary between the thematic and the non-thematic sections of a sentence/clause. I shall do so mainly by demonstrating how the concepts of the theory of functional sentence perspective (FSP) can be applied in an analysis of a piece of Modern English prose. I have discussed these concepts in other papers of mine.[2] As these papers may not always be easily accessible, I will first summarize at least those discussions which I find most relevant to the problem in hand. The idea of trying to specify the boundary between the thematic and the non-thematic section of a sentence/clause was suggested to me by N. E. Enkvist during his visit to Brno in November 1971.[3]

I

Let me first recall that the concept of CD is based on the fact that communication is not a static, but a dynamic phenomenon. By CD I understand a quality displayed by communication in its development (unfolding) of the information to be conveyed and consisting in advancing this development. By the degree of CD carried by a linguistic element, I understand the relative extent to which this element contributes to the further development of the communication.

Communicative dynamism manifests itself primarily in the operation of three phenomena: context, linear modification (linearity), and semantic structure. It is not difficult to see that context-dependent elements, i. e. such as convey information derivable from the preceding context, contribute less to the further development of communication than context-independent elements, i. e. such as convey information underivable from the preceding context. The former carry a higher degree of CD than the latter.

D. L. Bolinger[4] has developed the concept of linear modification. The "gradation of position (i. e. in direction towards the end of the sentence — J. F.) creates gradation of meaning when there are no interfering

317

factors" (p. 288). *He slowly backed away, He backed away slowly; They left out both pages, They left both pages out.* Gradation of meaning contributes to the further development of the communication. In this respect, gradation of position involves a rise in CD. Bolinger is of course well aware of interfering factors. Let me add that the most powerful factor working counter to linearity is context. Irrespective of position, a context-dependent element becomes "dedynamized" and carries the relatively lowest degree of CD. (Cf. the "dedynamized" *He, him, the boy* in *He saw him, He saw the boy.*) The other important factor capable of working counter to linearity is the semantic structure itself.

As has been shown in a number of places,[2] there are types of semantic content that, as long as they are context-independent, will carry certain relative degrees of CD irrespective of position; if deviating from the positional gradation of CD, they will in fact work counter to linearity. For instance, a context-independent element expressing a phenomenon "appearing/existing on the scene" is communicatively more important and carries a higher degree of CD than the element merely expressing the appearance/existence itself (*A boy came, A boy stood at the corner*). A context-independent element expressing the goal of a motion is communicatively more important and carries a higher degree of CD than the element merely expressing the motion (*He went to Prague, Er fuhr nach Prag, Er ist nach Prag gefahren*).

Context, linearity and semantic structure are the most important means involved in signalling degrees of CD.

At this point, let me insert a note on context, a highly complex phenomenon indeed. The common experience (knowledge) shared by speaker and listener establishes the context of common experience. This involves the context of the immediate situation in which the utterance is produced. In its turn, the context of immediate situation involves the preceding verbal context.

As used in this paper, the designations "context-dependent" and "context-independent" are to be understood in the n a r r o w e s t[5] sense possible. An utterance element is context-dependent if it conveys a piece of information derivable (recoverable) from the preceding verbal context and/or if it refers to a conspicuously obvious item that belongs to the immediate situational context and through its conspicuous immediacy simultaneously captures the speaker's and the hearer's attention. In deciding context dependence or independence, the last court of appeal is the communicative purpose imposed upon the utterance by the immediate communicative concern of the speaker. Hierarchically speaking, the context of immediate situation can come fully into play only in the absence of the preceding verbal context.

Two examples must suffice. In *Bob rushed to the window,* the information conveyed by *window* may be known, but as goal of Bob's motion derivable neither from the context of immediate situation nor from the preceding verbal context, it is unknown and will be context-independent. *He must have broken it* may have been elicited as an immediate reaction to the fall of a boy carrying a fragile object, the immediate situational context fully taking over the role of "dedynamizer" and presenting *He* and *it* as context-dependent.

Let me for a moment return to the operation of the semantic structure within context independent sections of the communication, and in addition to the concepts of "appearance/existence on the scene" (= Ex) and "phenomenon appearing/existing on the scene" (= Ph) briefly discuss the concepts of "quality" (= Q), "specification" (= Sp) and "setting" (= Set).

Taken in a wide sense, Q can be understood as a transient or a permanent aspect (trait) of a phenomenon that has been introduced onto the scene.[6] (A permanent aspect is mostly expressed by an adjective, a transient aspect is mostly expressed by a verb. The possible overlap does not affect the argument.) A Q can be modified. Provided the modification is context-independent, it can be regarded — in view of the dynamics of the discourse — as a Sp.

Further context-independent information conveying important limiting circumstances may serve as F(urther) Sp. An example will illustrate: *He* (B = quality bearer) *offended* (Tr[ansiant]Q: action) *an old gentleman* (Sp: context-independent affected goal of action) *in a most outrageous way* (FSp: context-independent manner). It is important to note that, as used here, "specification" is linked with context-independent information. Context independence, together with suitable semantic content, is considered a prerequisite to specification.

On the other hand, semantic contents that in the act of communication convey mere background information, i. e. purely concomitant circumstances, can be regarded as Set's. In contrast with Sp's, Set's can be either context-dependent or context-independent.

Under the contextual conditioning indicated in brackets, the temporal adverbial *yesterday* serves as a Set in I (d = context-dependent) *met* (i = cont.-indep.) *a friend* (i) *yesterday* (i), but as a Sp in *I* (d) *met* (d) *him* (d) *yesterday* (i), *It* (d) *was* (i) *yesterday* (i) *that I met him* (d). In the following two examples, the adverbial element of purpose serves as a Set in the first and as a Sp in the second, while the local adverbial *to town* (expressing the goal of a motion) and the temporal adverbial *yesterday* respectively serve as a Sp and a Set in both examples: *In order to buy a car* (i), *he* (d) *went* (i) *to town* (i) *yesterday* (i), *He* (d) *went* (i) *to town* (i) *yesterday* (i) *in order to buy a car* (i).

The scope of the present paper does not permit a detailed demonstration of the interplay of context-independent semantic content and linearity. By way of illustration let me mention that a context-independent adverbial of direction will always be a Sp, irrespective of sentence position. On the other hand, the context-independent adverbial of purpose will be a Set if occurring initially (provided the rest of the sentence/clause retains a due degree of context independence), but a Sp if occurring fi nally.[7] A case of even more subtle interplay is presented by context-in-dependent *yesterday*. For instance, if occuring with a context-independent goal of action, it will act as a Set; in co-occurrence with a verb of existence, however, it will serve as a Sp (*It happened yesterday*).

Inquiries into the operation of semantic contents and relations within the context-independent sections of the discourse permit the construction of two scales which can be conveniently fused into one. The scales represent a generalization of the CD relations within the non-thematic sections. They reflect a gradual rise in CD.[8] Needless to say, in actual occurrence they need not necessarily be realized in their entirety.

Scale One: SCENE (settings) — APPEARANCE/EXISTENCE — PHENOMENON APPEARING/EXISTING (possible prospective quality bearer).

Scale Two: SCENE (settings) — QUALITY BEARER — QUALITY (permanent/transient) — SPECIFICATION — FURTHER SPECIFICATION(S).

The resultant (fused) scale:

SCENE (settings) — APPEARANCE/EXISTENCE — PHENOMENON APPEARING/EXISTING/ /QUALITY BEARER — QUALITY (permanent/transient) — SPECIFICATION —FURTHER SPECIFICATION(S).

At this point, a word must be added on the relation between semantic structure and grammatical structure. The latter is rooted in the former.[9] As A. Reichling has pointed out and F. Daneš emphasized, grammatical structure does not merely combine forms as such, but with the aid of formal relations effects a s e m a n t i c connexion, i. e. a connexion of m e a n i n g s. "These meanings might be called *syntactic meanings* and characterized as the generalization of lexical meanings contained in the sentence, accomplished by the relational structure of the . . . grammatical sentence pattern."[10]

It must be borne in mind that apart from its role in syntax, an item of meaning continues to refer to an item of the extralingual reality and in this way continues to convey a piece of information. The semantic structure is then constituted by all the items of meaning (information) and the relations into which these items enter within the formal framework of grammatical structure.

In the act of communication, the formal framework of grammatical structure provides fields and units within which and over which CD is distributed, and which are in consequence made to function in a definite kind of perspective. The distributional fields are provided by explicit or (as has been shown by A. Svoboda[11]) implicit predication. A distributional field of the former type is a sentence/clause, one of the latter type an attributive construction (head element + its attribute).

Regarding predication as creator of distributional (communicative) fields entails the neccessity of regarding sentence elements as communicative units, i. e. as elements that on the formal level are to be primarily looked upon as carriers of degrees of CD. It follows that the communicative units are constituted by the subject, verb element, complements (subject complement, object complement), objects, adverbials. As will be exemplified later, the creation of distributional fields by predication makes it possible, or even necessary, to split up the verb element into two communicative units: one constituted by the notional component of the finite verb, the other by its auxiliary (flexional) component. The latter can be realized by a verbal auxiliary and/or a bound morpheme and/ or a submorphemic feature, and will be referred to as the temporal and modal exponent(s) of the finite verb,[12] or for short TEM(s). As to the communicative units within a distributional field provided by an attributive construction, they are constituted by the head element and the attribute.

As A. Svoboda[11] has shown, the distributional fields with their communicative units are hierarchically ordered. A distributional field provided by a subordinate clause or an attributive construction constitutes a subfield within the distributional field provided by the superordinate structure. Within a superordinate field, a subfield operates as o n e communicative unit. As will be amply illustrated by the analysis, grammatical subordination does not prevent a subfield from carrying the highest degree of CD within the superordinate field.

A distributional subfield can also be provided by a semi-clausal structure, such as an infinitival, participial, or gerundial construction. Strictly speaking, the designation "distributional semi-subfield", or "semifield" for short, should be applied here. Like a subfield, the semi-subfield constitutes o n e communicative unit within the respective superordinate distributional field. An unfinished (truncated) sentence/clause would provide a truncated distributional field.

Let me now turn to the prosodic features borne by the communicative units.[13] A gradual increase in prosodic weight (conspicuousness) is shown by the following series: (i) absence of stress and pitch prominence; (ii) secondary stress unaccompanied by pitch prominence, (iii) pitch-prominent secondary accent, pitch prominence being achieved by means of a change of pitch, (iv) primary (nuclear) stress. For the purposes of the present paper, the relevant syllables can, for short, be referred to as, respectively, (i) "unstressed" and left unmarked, (ii) "partially stressed" and marked , or ,, or •; (iii) "stressed" and marked '; (iv) "bearing a nucleus" and marked ^{r} or ^{f} or ^{v} or $_r$ or $_f$ or $_v$. The marks are placed before the syllables concerned and employed as superscripts or subscripts according as they indicate high or low pitch. The letters $^r/_r$ and $^f/_f$ stand for "rise and "fall"; the mark $^v/_v$ indicates a fall-rise; the mark $\wedge$ indicates a high-pitched syllable followed by a gradual descent of unstressed syllables. The series represents A. C. Gimson's four degrees of accentuation.[14] The tonetic realization of the analysed text is that given by J. D. O'Connor.[15]

It should be added that if there are two or more prosodic features occurring within one and the same distributional field and which, in terms of the above description, appear to be phonically equivalent, the feature occurring nearer the end of the distributional field is considered to be weightier (more conspicuous) than its predecessor. This implies that if there are two or more nuclei within a distributional field, the one occurring last will be the weightiest (the most conspicuous) — the intonation centre (IC) — of that field.[16] Further research may have to modify this statement,[17] but the extent to which it is valid is undoubtedly very great. Perhaps the most important modification is the following. If within one and the same distributional field a low rise occurs after a fall, the former will be less weighty (less conspicuous) than the latter.

A communicative unit may bear several prosodic features. The weightiest of them will indicate the prosodic weight of the unit in relation to the other units of the communicative field. This integrates a unit functioning as a subfield into a superordinate field, at the same time permitting it to display an autonomous distribution of CD. This will be amply illustrated by the analysis offered below.

II

The subject of the analysis is a piece of English prose, an extract from John Wain's *The Contenders*, which — together with the tonetic marks — is quoted from J. D. O'Connor[15] (see pp. 14—15 and 40—41). The analysis is presented in three sections, Section A primarily determining the distribution of CD within fields and subfields, Section B offering their semantic interpretation and Section C tabulating their prosodic weight. Necessary explanations concerning the applied procedure as well as the conclusions that can be drawn from the analysis are adduced in a commentary placed after Section C.

A (Distribution of CD)

(1) It^{10} was^{20} a 'warm 'summery $_f$evening^{30}, (2) and when$^{12.21}$ I$^{12.10}$
    Th   Tr   ''$_f$Rh   (Th   Th
got$^{12.21-22}$ to the $_r$telephonebox$^{12.30}$ there^{11} were^{20} a 'couple of $_r$chaps$^{31.10}$
'Tr $_r$Rh)^{i}Th   Th   Tr (',$_r$Th
,standing$^{31.20}$ 'quite con'tentedly$^{31.31}$ out$_f$side it,$^{31.32}$ while$^{32.21}$ a $^\wedge$woman
((,Tr   '',$_f$Rh))^{iv}Rh)^{ii}Rh (Tr
^{v}inside$^{32.11}$,stared$^{32.21-22}$ 'raptly$^{32.31}$ be$_f$fore her,$^{32.33}$ 'holding$^{32.34.20}$ the
$^{\wedge v}$Th   ,Tr   'Rh $_f$Rh,   (('Tr
'instrument$^{32.34.31}$ to her $_f$ear.$^{32.34.32}$ (3) I^{11} ^{f}join^{30}ed^{20} them^{12} (4) and
   'Rh $_f$Rh))^{v}Rh)^{iii}Rh. Th ^{f}Rh Tr Th

we^{11} ,struck up$^{21-22}$ 'quite a $_f$friendship,^{30} ,,during those ,,long ,,minutes
Th   ,Tr   '$_f$Rh,
on the $_r$pavement.^{12} (5) From the ^{v}weather^{12} we^{11} ,pass^{22}ed^{21} ,on^{22} to
        ,, ,, ,, $_r$Th ^{v}Th   Th   , ,Tr
'inter·national ^{r}politics, eco^{r}nomic a·ffairs, ^{r}sport - and $_f$agriculture.^{30}
                                                        '·'r·r·r-$_r$Rh.
(6) ^{v}One of them^{10} was^{20} a ^{f}Scotsman,^{30} (7) and ^{v}he^{11} was^{21} ,able^{22} to
    ^{v}Th   Tr ^{f}Rh, ^{v}Th Tr ,Tr   (
,,add$^{30.20}$ va^{f}riety and ^{f}breadth$^{30.31}$ to our ,little sym,posium$^{30.12}$ by
,,Tr ^{ff}Rh   , ,Th   ((
,giving$^{30.32.20}$ the 'characte'ristic 'North ^{f}British ,view.$^{30.32.30}$ (8) [^{10}
,Tr   ' ' ' ^{f},Rh))^{ii}Rh)^{i}Rh   Th
be'gan$^{21-22}$ to 'question$^{30.21}$ him$^{30.10}$ ^{f}keenly$^{30.31}$ a,,bout the ^{f}nationalist
'Tr   ('Tr   Th ^{f}Rh
,movement,$^{30.32}$ and the ex,tent$^{30.33.10}$ to which$^{30.33.30.12}$ 'he$^{30.33.30.11}$ ^{v}per-
,, ^{f},Rh,   ((,Th   (((Th   'Th
sonally$^{30.33.30.11}$ con,sider$^{30.33.30.22}$ed$^{30.33.30.21}$ 'Home 'Rule$^{30.33.30.31}$
^{v}Th   ,Tr   ' 'Rh
de^{r}sirable ˉor $_f$feasible.$^{30.33.30.32}$ (9) 'Now and a^{r}gain^{12} we^{11} 'glanc^{22}ed^{21}
    ^{r}-$_f$Rh)))^{iii}Rh))^{ii}Rh)^{i}Rh .   '^{r}Th Th   'Tr
at the 'woman in'side the $_f$box; (10) she^{10} ^didn't$^{21-31}$ ·seem^{22} to be
                            ' '$_f$Rh;   Th   ^· Tr-Rh
^{v}talking ,much^{30} — (11) if$^{12.20}$ she$^{12.10}$ ^{v}was$^{12.30}$ we^{11} could^{21} ^only
    ^{v} ,Rh   (Tr Th ^{v}Rh)^{i}Th, Th Tr
con^{v}clude^{22} that she$^{30.10}$ had$^{30.21}$ ^learnt$^{30.21-23}$ ·some tech^{v}nique of
^^{v}Tr   (Th   Tr   ^Tr
'talking wi·thout 'moving he$_ı$ ^{f}mouth;$^{30.31}$ from a ven^{f}triloquist,$^{30.32}$ no
                · v '·'^{f}Rh; ^{f}Rh,
,doubt.$^{30.22}$ (12) ,,This^{11} led$^{21-23}$ our ,,discourse^{12} ^{r}naturally^{22} into the
,Tr)^{ii}Rh.   ,,Th Tr   ,,Th ^{r}Tr
,,realms of ,,enter^{f}tainment and the ^{f}arts,^{31} our Cale^{v}donian ,friend$^{32.10}$
                                ,, ,,^{ff}Rh, (v , Th
con,,tributing$^{32.20}$ a ^{f}spirited de$_r$fence of the tra'ditional 'songs and
,, Tr
^{r}dances of his 'native ^{f}heath$^{32.30}$ (13) ,What$^{30.11}$,sound$^{30.22}$ed$^{30.21}$ like
    ^{f}$_r$ ' '^{r} '^{f}Rh)^{i}Rh.   (,Th   , Tr
a 'peal of ^{f}laughter$^{30.30}$ 'reach^{22}ed^{21} us^{11} through the $_f$glass;^{12} (14) my
            '^{i}Rh)^{i}Rh.   'Tr Th $_f$Th;
^fellow ^{v}Englishman^{10} sug,gest^{22}ed^{21} that the ^lady's ^unseen
        ^^{v}Th   ,Tr   (
inter^{v}locutor$^{30.10}$ must$^{30.22}$ be$^{30.21}$ a 'witty ·fellow in^{f}deed$^{30.30}$ (15a)
^^^{v}Th   Tr   a 'witty ·fellow in^{f}deed   ' ·'^{f}Rh)^{i}Rh.
'Suddenly^{12} un'able$^{13.20}$ to 'stand$^{13.31}$ it$^{13.10}$ ·any ·longer,$^{13.32}$ I^{11} 'went$^{21-22}$
ι 'Th   ('Tr   'Rh Th :^{r}Rh)^{i}Th Th 'Tr
$_f$up to the ki,osk^{31} (15b) and ^{f}lean^{31}ed^{20} a,gainst it,^{10} my ^{r}face$^{32.10}$ a
    $_f$,Rh ^{f}R   ,Th ('Th

'few 'inches from the $_f$woman's.$^{32.30}$ (*16*) At ^{v}first^{12} she^{11} 'didn't $^{20-31}$
                       $_f$Rh)^{i}Rh. ^{v}Th   Th   'Tr-Rh

^{f} see^{32} me,^{12} (*17*) and I^{10} was^{21} 'able^{22} to 'study$^{31.20}$ her$^{31.10}$ in^{f}tently$^{31.30^r}$as,
^{f}Rh Th   Th Tr   'Tr   ('Tr   Th ^{f}Rh)^{i}Rh (^{r}Tr

'shoulders^{r}hunched,$^{32.13}$ she$^{32.11v}$held$^{32.21-22}$ the ,telephone$^{32.12}$ in a 'tense
(('Th ^{r}Rh))^{iii}Th Th ^{v}Tr   .Tr

$_f$grip$^{33.31}$ 'jammed a·gainst her $_f$ear.$^{33.32}$ (*18*) $^\wedge$Possibly'through
'$_f$Rh   '$_f$Rh)^{ii}Rh.

fa^{v}tigue,^{13} she^{11} ^{f}was$^{20-32}$ not^{31} $_r$standing,^{12} but ^{f}leaning^{33} ^{f}rigidly^{34}
$^{\wedge \cdot v}$Th   Th ^{f}Tr—Rh $_r$Th, ^{f}Rh ^{f}Rh

a·gainst the ^{f}wall of the ,box;^{35} (*19*) she^{10} ,look^{22}ed^{21} like a ,roll of
             '^{f},Rh;   Th   ,Tr

'frozen li^{f}noleum in the 'hold of a ^{f}liner.^{30} (*20*) Her 'un'seeing 'eyes^{10}
                 ,^{f,f}Rh.   '''Th

were^{20} 'slightly^{32} $_f$rais^{33}ed,^{20} as if$^{33.21}$ 'staring$^{33.22}$ at an i'maginary
Tr   'Rh $_f$Rh,   (Tr   'Tr

ho$_r$rizon.$^{33.30}$ (*21*) In a^{r}flash^{12} I^{11} 'knew$^{21-22}$ her $_f$secret.^{30} (*22*) She^{11} was^{20} ·
'$_f$Rh)^{i}Rh ^{r}Th Th 'Tr $_f$Rh.   Th Tr

'one of 'those ^{r}women$^{30.11}$ who$^{30.11}$ are$^{30.20}$ 'all $_f$soul,$^{30.31}$ 'all 'fire and $_f$radian-
(''^{r}Th T$_1$ '$_f$'$_f$Rh)^{i}Rh.

ce.$^{30.32}$ (*23*) 'Nothing$^{11-31}$ could^{21} as'suage^{22} that 'wild 'thirst for 'beauty
         'Th—Rh   Tr   'Tr

and pro'fundity^{12} except the 'master·pieces of the 'great 'Russian$_f$nove-
         ''''Th

lists.^{30} (*24*) ^{r}But^{21} — 'child of a 'harsh civili^{r}sation 'ceaselessly de'nying
'·''$_f$Rh. ^{r}Tr

the 'generous 'impulses of its ^{r}people^{12} — she^{11} had^{21} ,,never $^{23-31}$ been^{21}
                   '' ^{r} :''' ^{r}Th   Th   Tr ..Tr—Rh   Tr

,,taught$^{22-21}$ to ^{f}read.^{32} (*25*) So 'each $_r$night^{12} she^{11} 'went$^{21-22}$ to the
,,Tr ^{f}Rh.   ,^{r}Th   Th   'Tr

$_r$telephone,^{30} (*26*) and her ^{v}cousin-in-,law,^{12} the 'one with the ^{v}stam-
  $_r$Rh, ^{v},Th,

mer,^{13} read$^{21-22}$ her^{11} 'half a 'dozen 'chapters of 'Dostoi$_f$evsky.^{30} (*27*)
$^{\wedge v}$Th,   Tr   '''',$_f$Rh.

A'flame with 'knowledge and 'sympathy,^{12} I^{11} 'flung$^{21-22}$ 'open^{31} the 'door
                         ''''Th Th   'Tr   'Rh

of the $_f$box.^{32} (*28*) But^{21} be$^\wedge$fore$^{12.21}$ I$^{12.31}$ could$^{12.21}$ find$^{12.22}$ words$^{12.31}$
   '$_f$Rh.   Tr ($^\wedge$Tr   Th   Tr   ·Tr $^\wedge$Rh

to 'tell$^{12.32.20}$her$^{12.32.11}$ that I$^{12.32.31.11}$ ^{v}knew$^{12.32.31.20-30}$ her ,secret$^{12.32.31.12}$
(($^\wedge$Tr   Th   (((Th ^{v}Rh   ,Th)))^{iii}Rh

and that it$^{12.32.31.11}$ was$^{12.32.32.20}$ ^{v}safe$^{12.32.32.30}$ with ,me,$^{12.32.32.12}$ the
     (((Th   Tr ^{v}Rh   ,Th)))^{iv}Rh))^{ii}Rh)^{i}Rh

'woman^{11}·put$^{21-22}$ the 'telephone^{31} 'back in its ^{f}rest.^{32} (*29*) I$^{30.10}$
'Th ·Tr   'Rh   '^{f}Rh.   (Th

,,can't$^{30.21-31}$ get$^{30.22}$ ^{f}through'',$^{30.32}$ she^{11} ,said$^{21-22}$,wonderingly.^{23}
,,Tr—Rh   Tr ^{f}Rh)Rh   Th   ,Tr   ,Tr.

B (Semantic Interpretation)

(*1*) Sc [indicated by a semantically empty element] (Th), Ex(Tr), Ph(Rh). (*2*) Set : temporal (Th)[i], Sc(Th), Ex(Tr), Ph(Rh)[ii], Sp : temporal, contrastive [presenting another Ph] (Rh)[iii]. (*2[i]*) B(Th), TrQ : motion, Sp : direction (Rh). (*2[ii]*) B(Th), Q(Rh)[iv]. (*2[iii]*) B(Th), TrQ : action (Tr), Sp : manner (Rh), FSp : place (Rh), FFSp : manner (Rh)[v]. (*2[iv]*) Ex(Tr), Sp : manner (Rh), FSp : local (Rh). (*2[v]*) TrQ : action (Tr), Sp : affected goal (Rh), FSp : direction (Rh), (*3*) B(Th), TrQ : action (Rh), *affected goal* (Th). (*4*) B(Th), TrQ : action (Tr), Sp : effected goal (Rh), *Set : temporal* (Th). (*5*) Set : place (Th), B(Th), TrQ : action : motion (Tr), Sp : direction (Rh). (*6*) B(Th), A of Q(Tr), PQ(Rh). (*7*) B(Th), A of Q(Tr), TrQ(Tr), Sp of Q(Rh)[i]. (*7[i]*) TrQ : action (Tr), Sp : effected goal (Rh), *direction* (Th), Sp : manner (Rh)[ii]. (*7[ii]*) TrQ : action : producing (Tr), Sp : effected goal (Rh). (*8*) B(Th), TrQ : action (Tr), Sp : effected goal (Rh)[i]. (*8[i]*) TrQ : action (Tr), *affected goal* (Th), Sp : manner (Rh), FSp affected goal (Rh, Rh[ii]). (*8[ii]*) B(Th), TrQ(Rh)[iii]. (*8[iii]*) B(Th), TrQ action : ascription of quality (evaluation) (Tr), Sp : affected goal : evaluated phenomenon (Rh), FSp : ascribed quality (evaluation). (*9*) Set : temporal (Th), B(Th), TrQ : action (Tr), Sp : affected goal (Rh). (*10*) B(Th), TrQ + negation focus anticipator (Tr + Rh), Sp of Q, negation focus (Rh). (*11*) Set: condition (Th)[i], B(Th), TrQ : action (Tr), Sp : effected goal (Rh)[ii]. (*11[i]*) B(Th), Assertion of Q (Rh). (*11[ii]*) B(Th), TrQ : action : acquiring (Tr), effected goal (Rh), Sp : local : source (Rh), attitudinal indication (Tr). (*12*) B(Th), TrQ : action (Tr), *affected goal* (Th), attitudinal indication (Tr), Sp : direction (Rh), FSp : essential circumstance (Rh)[i]. (*12[i]*) B(Th), TrQ : action (Tr), Sp : effected goal (Rh). (*13*) Ph(Rh)[i], Ex(Tr), *persons present at the appearance* (Th), Set : local (Th), (*13[i]*) B(Th), TrQ(Tr), Sp by comparison (Rh). (*14*) B(Th), TrQ : action : producing (Tr), Sp : effected goal (Rh)[i]. (*14[i]*) B(Th), PQ(Tr), Q(Rh). (*15a*) Set : cause (Th)[i], B(Th), TrQ : motion (Tr), Sp : goal of motion (Rh); (*15b*) TrQ : action (Rh), *direction* (Th), Sp : local (Rh). (*15a[i]*) Set : temporal (Th), TrQ(Tr), Sp of Q (Rh), *affected goal*, Sp : temporal (Rh). (*15b[i]*) B(Th), Sp : local (Rh). (*16*) Set : temporal (Th), B(Th), negation focus anticipator (Rh), TrQ, negation focus (Rh), *affected goal* (Th). (*17*) B(Th), TrQ(Tr), Sp of Q (Rh[i]), FSp : essential circumstance (Rh)[ii]. (*17[i]*) TrQ : action (Tr), *affected goal* (Th), Sp : manner (Rh). (*17[ii]*) Set : concomitant circumstance (Th)[iii], B(Th), TrQ : action (Tr), *affected goal* (Th), Sp : manner (Rh), FSp : imposed Q (Rh), FFSp : direction (Rh). (*17[iii]*) B(Th), TrQ(Rh). (*18a*) Set : cause (Th), B(Th), A of Q + negation focus anticipator + negation focus : negative assertion (Tr + Rh), *TrQ* (Th); (*18b*) TrQ : action, contrasted (Rh), Sp : manner (Rh), FSp : direction (Rh). (*19*) B(Th), A of Q (Tr), Sp of Q by comparison (Rh). (*20*) B(Th), A of Q (Tr), Sp : manner (Rh), Q(Rh), FSp : comparison. (*20[i]*) TrQ : action (Tr), Sp : affected goal (Rh). (*21*) Set : time and manner

(Th), *B*(Th), TrQ : action (Tr), Sp : affected goal (Rh). *(22)* B(Th), A of Q (Tr), Q(Rh)[i]. *(22[i])* *B*(Th), A of Q (Tr), Q(Rh). *(23)* B + negation focus anticipator (Th + Rh), TrQ : action (Tr), *affected goal* (Th), Sp : manner : exclusion (Rh). *(24)* Set : cause (Th), *B*(Th), A of Q + negation focus anticipator (Tr + Rh), TrQ : experienced action (Tr), Sp : effected goal (Rh). *(25)* Set : temporal (Th), *B*(Th), TrQ : action : motion (Tr), Sp : direction (Rh). *(26)* B(Th), TrQ : action (Tr), Sp : effected goal (Rh). *(27)* Set : concomitant circumstance (Th), *B*(Th), TrQ : action (Tr), Sp : effected quality (Rh), FSp : effected goal (Rh). *(28)* Set : temporal (Th)[i], *B*(Th), TrQ : action (Tr), Sp : affected goal (Rh), FSp : direction (Rh). *(28[i])* *B*(Th), TrQ : action : producing (Tr), Sp : effected goal (Rh), FSp : purpose (Rh)[ii]. *(28[ii])* TrQ : action : producing (Tr), *affected goal* (Th), Sp : effected goals (Rh)[iii,iv]. *(28[iii])* *B*(Th), TrQ : action : perception (Rh), *affected goal* (Th). *(28[iv])* *B*(Th), A of Q (Tr), TrQ (Rh), Set : local (Th). *(29)* Effected goal (Rh)[i], *B*(Th), TrQ : action : producing (Tr), Sp : manner (Tr). *(29[i])* *B*(Th), negation focus anticipator (Rh), TrQ : action + negation focus (Rh).

C (Prosodic Weight)
BASIC DISTRIBUTIONAL FIELDS

	Theme	Transition	Rheme
(1)	0	0	2+3
(2)	$(2+3)^*,0$	0	2+3
(3)	$0,\ 0_d$	x	3
(4)	$0,\ 1_d^3$	1	2+3
(5)	$3^*,0$	1	2+3
(6)	3^*	0	3
(7)	3^*	1	1+2+3
(8)	0	2	1+2+3
(9)	$(2+3)^*,0$	2	2+3
(10)	0	$1+2^{NegFAnt}$	1+3
(11)	$(0+3)^*,0$	$(0+2+3)^*$	1+2+3
(12)	$1^*,\ 1_d$	$0,\ 3^*$	1+2+3
(13)	$0_d(1+3)_d^*$	1	$(1+2+3)_d$
(14)	$(2+3)^*$	1	1+2+3
(15a)	$(2+3)^*,0$	2	3
(15b)	1_d	x	2+3
(16)	$3^*,0\ 0_d$	$2^{NegFAnt}$	3
(17)	0	1	1+2+3
(18a)	$(1+3)^*,0\ 1_d^3$	—	1+3
(18b)	—	—	1+2+3
(19)	0	1	1+2+3
(20)	1^*	0	2+3
(21)	$3^*,0$	2	3
(22)	0	0	2+3
(23)	$1^{NegFAnt},\ 1_d$	1	2+3
(24)	$(1+3)^*,0$	$1^{NegFAnt}$	3
(25)	$3^*,0$	2	3
(26)	$(1+3)^*,\ 0_d$	0	2+3
(27)	$2,\ 0$	2	2+3
(28)	$(1+2+3)^*,2$	1	2+3
(29)	0_d	$0_d,\ 1_d$	$(1+3)_d$

DISTRIBUTIONAL SUBFIELDS

	Theme	Transition	Rheme
(2^i)	0	1	3
(2^{ii})	$2+3$	—	$1+2+3$
(2^{iii})	$(2+3)^*$	1	$2+3$
(2^{iv})	—	1	$2+3$
(2^v)	—	2	$2+3$
(7^i)	1_d	1	$1+2+3$
(7^{ii})	—	1	$2+3$
(8^i)	0_d	2	$1+2+3$
(8^{ii})	1	—	$1+2+3$
(8^{iii})	$(2+3)^*$	1	$2+3$
(11^i)	0	—	3
(11^{ii})	0	$1, 1_d$	$1+2+3$
(12^i)	$(1+3)^*$	1	$1+2+3$
(13^i)	1	1	$2+3$
(14^i)	$(2+3)^*$	0	$1+2+3$
$(15a^i)$	$1, 0_d$	2	$1+2+3$
$(15b^i)$	3^*	—	$2+3$
(17^i)	0_d	1	3
(17^{ii})	$(2+3)^*, 0, 1_d$	3^*	$1+2+3$
$(1\,7^{iii})$	2	—	3
(20^i)	—	2	$2+3$
(22^i)	$(2+3)^*$	0	$2+3$
(28^i)	0	1	$1+2+3$
(28^{ii})	0_d	0_d	$1+3$
(28^{iii})	$0, 1_d$	—	3
(28^{iv})	$0, 1_d$	0	3

COMMENTARY

(i) The text analysed comprises 29 basic distributional fields and 26 subfields, including 12 semifields. Basic field are referred to by bracketed Arabic numerals (1, . . . , 29(. In referring to subfields, Roman superscripts are added to the basic numeral (e. g., $2^i, 2^{ii}, 2^{iii}$). Subfields constituted by attributive constructions consisting of the headword and an adjective or adjectives, or their simple equivalent, or a prepositional noun-phrase, are not further analysed.

The communicative units within the fields are also indicated by super-scripts. In indicating the grammatical hierarchy of the units, small (low-er case) letters could be used, *a* indicating a communicative unit on the basic distributional field level, *a. b* a unit within a distributional subfield that is constituted by an *a*-unit, *a. b. c* a unit within a distributional sub-field constituted by an *a. b* unit, etc. In the analysed text, the small let-ters are replaced by two digit numbers (e. g., 11, 12.21, 22, 33, 31.32, 30.33.11). They indicate relations in CD, i. e. the degrees of CD. The assignment of degrees will be discussed here under (v).

(ii) Semantic characterizations of the distributional fields and subfields are added in a separate table (Section B of the analysis). They are an attempt to interpret the dynamic aspect of the semantic structure of the distributional fields. They are expressed in terms general enough to match the generality of the syntactic descriptions. They naturally admit of par-ticularization.[18] Some of the abbreviations used have been explained ear-lier (see here p. 319). Let me add the following explanations: A of Q = ascription of quality; FFSp = specification modifying a further specifi-cation; PQ = permanent quality; Sc = scene; Sp of Q = specification of quality.[19]

(iii) The semantic interpretation goes hand in hand with the determina-tion of context dependence and independence. Context-dependent units of any rank carry the lowest degree of CD within their r e s p e c t i v e fields. In the semantic interpretations of the fields, the representations of the context-dependent units are italicized.

(iv) Within the context-independent part of a distributional field, rela-tions in CD, i. e. the degrees of CD, are determined by the interplay of semantic structure and linearity. Special mention should be made of those cases in which one of two elements will carry a higher degree of CD as long as it remains context-independent. (For instance, a context-inde-pendent element expressing a goal of motion will carry a higher degree of CD than the element expressing the motion, irrespective of the con-textual status of the latter; cf., *And then he went to Prague, Und dann ist er nach Prag gefahren.*) Under such circumstances, the CD relation can safely be determined even if uncertainty arises as to the contextual status of the latter element.

(v) An inquiry into the interplay of context, semantic structure and linearity within the basic distributional fields makes an important phe-nomenon come to the fore. In terms of the context-independent semantic scale, a verb element expressing Q cannot become carrier of the highest degree of CD if accompanied by a Sp. Similarly, a verb element express-ing Ex cannot exceed in CD a context-independent element expressing Ph. On the other hand, if context-independent, a verb will naturally ex-ceed all context-dependent elements and/or context-independent Set's and/or a context-independent B. All this makes the verb suitable for a central position in the distribution of CD within a distributional field. Even more suited for this role are the TMEs. In communicative impor-tance, they are exceeded in CD by the notional component of the verb.

329

They will retain this central position (in terms of CD, i. e. i r r e s p e c - t i v e of linear arrangement) even if the notional component comes to carry the highest degree of CD within the distributional field. They are a linking, i.e. transitional, element *par excellence*. They serve as Transition Proper (TrPr).[20] They cease to perform this function only in second-instance[21] sentences, which can show only two degrees of CD, the lowest and the highest, and in consequence dispense with a transition.

Within first instance, the TMEs constitute a border-line between two sections within a distributional field, differing in CD. The one carrying the lower degrees of CD can be termed thematic (the theme = Th), the other carrying higher degrees of CD non-thematic (the non-theme = non-Th). ("Section" is to be understood here in terms of CD relations, not in those of linear arrangement or contiguity.) The unique role of the TMEs within first instance can further be illustrated by the following striking phenomenon. In *My fellow Englishman* (Th) *suggest-*(non-Th)-*ed* (non-Th, TrPr) *that the lady's unseen interlocutor must be a witty fellow in-deed* (non-Th), *That ... indeed* (Th) *was* (non-Th, TrPr) *suggest*(non-Th)-*ed* (non-Th, TrPr) *by my ... Englishman* (non-Th), *It* (Th) *was* (non-Th, TrPr) *my ... Englishman* (non-Th) *that suggested that ... in-deed* (Th), *Nicht mein Vater, sondern mein Bruder* (non-Th) *ist* (non-Th, TrPr) *krank* (Th) *gewesen* (non-Th, TrPr), ... *daß mein Bruder* (Th) *krank* (non-Th) *gewesen ist* (non-Th, TrPr), all fields functioning within first instance, the TMEs continue to serve as Tr Pr, whereas the other elements may under different contextual conditions perform diametrically opposed functions. This necessitates regarding the TMEs as a communicative unit *sui generis*.

Within first instance and in the presence of the TMEs, non-Th is never homogeneous in CD, the TMEs carrying the lowest degree of CD within non-Th. Let me recall that if accompanied by a Sp or a context-independent Ph, the notional component of the verb element is transitional. Units exceeding it in CD then form the rheme (Rh), the one carrying the highest degree of CD serving as Rh Pr/oper/. On the other hand, as has already been pointed out, the notional component of the verb element may itself become RhPr if not exceeded by any unit in CD. If consisting of more than one unit, Th may not be homogeneous in CD either, the unit carrying the very lowest degree serving as ThPr. Th, Tr and Rh can respectively be denoted by the superscripts [10], [20], [30], replaceable by [11], [12], ..., [21], [22], ..., [31], [32], ... in case it appears necessary to indicate possible heterogeneity in CD.

Closer inquiry[22] has shown that the TMEs themselves are not homogeneous in CD, being capable of pointing to (participating in) Th and/or even Rh. But this is in no way in contradiction with their transitional, i. e. linking, character. In any case, the very l i n k they establish between Th and non-Th is a piece of context-independent information and constitutes a suitable b o u n d a r y between Th and non-Th. Considerations of space do not permit a discussion of the dividing line between Tr and Rh.

330

This may not appear to be distinct enough in some cases, but this is not in contradiction with the linking character of transition.[23]

(vi) We can now turn our attention to the prosodic features, which in spoken language co-operate in signalling degrees of CD and which to a considerable extent remove multifunctionality.[24]

In the analysed text, the prosodic features of Th, Tr and Rh are indicated interlinearly and summarized in two special tables. The numerals 0, 1, 2, 3 respectively stand for "unstressed", "partially stressed", "stressed", "bearing a nucleus". As to Tr and Rh, their prosodic weight is — with two exceptions — given summarily, the "unstressed" (0) feature being recorded only in the absence of a weightier feature. On the other hand, the prosodic weight of Th is consistently particularized. The superscript[3] indicates a low fall that occurs after a high fall within one distributional field and is in consequence regarded as having little prosodic weight (cf. here p. 322). A cross (x) placed in the "transition" column indicates that Tr is expressed only by TMEs appearing in the form of a bound morpheme or a submorphemic feature.

Unless accompanied with the subscript $_d$, standing for "deviation from the Th-Tr-Rh sequence", the tabulated items reflect the order actually realized in the distributional fields. In the analysed text, the number of deviations is strikingly low. This shows that the examined fields, of no matter what rank, show a high degree of conformity with what has come to be termed the basic distribution of CD. (In its fully developed shape, this distribution can be given as ThPr — rest of Th — TrPr — rest of Tr — Rh to the exclusion of RhPr — RhPr.) In the analysed text, it is mostly the thematic elements, less frequently the transitional elements, and only once a rhematic element, that display deviation.

Tr is expressed by the TMEs and/or the notional verb form (nonfinite in semi-fields), the latter being in three cases (7, 15a[1], 17) replaced by an adjective (*able*, *unable*). The prosodic features of Tr are strikingly less weighty than those of Rh. In this respect, both show perfect congruence between the gamut of CD and that of prosodic weight.

Absence of congruence between the two gamuts is indicated by an asterisk in the prosodic table. It is displayed comparatively often by Th and in three cases by Tr. But as has been explained in greater detail elsewhere,[25] deviations from the mentioned congruence do not necessarily hinder the signalling of degrees of CD. They do not do so in the examined text. Owing to the interplay of non-prosodic and prosodic means (mainly owing to the operation of the semantic contents of the TMEs and the notional verbal component and owing to the occurrence of a nucleus or nuclei later in the field), the deviations are to be regarded as prosodic intensifications, not effecting a change in the thematic or transitional status of the elements concerned.

It is of particular interest to examine the thematic elements that in the examined text show prosodic intensification and do not by themselves constitute the theme. They all deviate from the basic distribution of CD. Within Th, however, their prosodic weight is in perfect harmony with their degrees of CD.

III.

I believe I am right in concluding that the offered analysis has corroborated the interpretation that within a sentence, which provides a basic distributional field, or within a clause, which provides a distributional subfield, the theme is constituted by units carrying the lowest degress of CD.

Within first instance, the TMEs, showing congruence between their grammatical function of expressing predicative categories and that of a link between theme and non-theme, in fact simultaneously prove to be a dividing line between these two sections. The designations "thematic section" and "non-thematic section" do not necessarily apply to uninterrupted stretches of units, but respectively cover all thematic and all non-thematic units within a distributional field, irrespective of their linear arrangement. The following types of unit qualify for functioning as constituents of the theme: context-dependent units irrespective of their semantic content, settings, notional verbal components expressing appearance or existence on the scene in the absence of a setting, units expressing quality bearers in the presence of context-independent qualities and/or specifications.

The absence of a finite verb form within a subfield provided by an attributive construction (head element + attributive element) accounts for the absence of an explicit link between the possible thematic and the possible non-thematic unit within this type of subfield.

As has been explained in greater detail elsewhere, the TMEs cease to function as a link within second instance, which permits only two degrees of CD, distributing them irrespective of semantic content.

In all the above types of distribution, within first or second instance, a thematic and a non-thematic section are discernible, the former carrying the lowest degrees within the field.

Frequently interpreting an entirely context-independent distributional semifield as themeless and in any case as having no transition proper is not in contradiction with the above conclusions. On the contrary. Provided by a semiclausal structure of divided grammatical dependence (simultaneously relating to the finite verb and the subject of its superordinate clause), a semifield is not a subfield in its own right.

NOTES

[1] See my "On Defining the Theme in Functional Sentence Analysis", *Travaux linguistiques de Prague*, 1(1964), 267—80.

[2] See, e. g., my "Non-Thematic Subjects in Contemporary English," *Travaux linguistiques de Prague*, 2(1966), 239—56; "A Note on Transition Proper in Functional Sentence Analysis," *Philologica Pragensia*, 8(1965), 170—76; "On the Interplay of Prosodic and Non-Prosodic Means of Functional Sentence Per-

spective," in *The Prague School of Linguistics and Language Teaching* (London: Oxford Univ. Press, 1972), pp. 78—94.

[3] I must add here that the present paper is based on my researches carried out during my resident fellowship at the Netherlands Institute for Advanced Study at Wassenaar, taken up with the consent of the Ministry of Education of the Czech Socialist Republic. My grateful thanks are due to both institutions.

[4] D. L. Bolinger, "Linear Modification", in his *Forms of English* (Cambridge, Mass.: Harvard University Press, 1965), pp. 279—307.

[5] The concept of "contextual boundness" as employed by P. Sgall, E. Hajičová and E. Benešová in their *Topic, Focus and Generative Semantics* (Kronberg, Taunus: Scriptor Verlag, 1973) is wider than my concept of "context dependence". See also my notes on the narrow scene in "Non-Thematic Subjects..." (quoted here in note 2), esp. pp. 246—47.

[6] Cf. V. Mathesius, *Obsahový rozbor současné angličtiny na základě obecně lingvistickém* [A Functional Analysis of Present-Day English on a General Linguistic Basis], ed. by J. Vachek (Prague: Academia, 1961), esp. pp. 62—63; and its recently published English translation, *A Functional Analysis of Present Day English on a General Linguistic Basis,* prepared by L. Dušková and ed. by J. Vachek (Prague: Academia 1975), esp. pp. 57—58.

[7] See E. Golková, "On the English Infinitive of Purpose in Functional Sentence Perspective," *Brno Studies in English,* 7(1968), 119—128.

[8] For a more detailed discussion of these scales, see my "A Functional View of 'Ordo Naturalis'," to be published in Volume One of a new series of the University of Groningen to be called *Archives de Phonétique et de Linguistique Expérimentales.* Their construction is an outcome of my earlier researches. The credit for first constructing such a scale must, however, go to P. Sgall et al.; see their book, quoted here in note 5, esp. p. 67. Like Sgall, I am well aware of the necessity of further elaboration and verification.

[9] Cf. I. Poldauf, "Podíl mluvnice a nauky o slovníku na problematice slovesného vidu" [The Share of Grammar and Lexicology in Questions of Verbal Aspect], *Studie a práce lingvistické 1* (Prague: Academia, 1954), esp. pp. 200—06.

[10] See A. Reichling, "Principles and Methods of Syntax: Cryptanalytical Formalism," *Lingua,* 10(1961), 1. Quoted after F. Daneš, "Some Thoughts on the Semantic Structure of the Sentence", *Lingua,* 21(1968), 56.

[11] A. Svoboda, "The Hierarchy of Communicative Units and Fields as Illustrated by English Attributive Constructions," *Brno Studies in English,* 7(1968), esp. pp. 50—52.

[12] Cf. B. Trnka, "Some Thoughts on Structural Morphology", *Charisteria Guilelmo Mathesio... oblata* (Prague, 1932), esp. p. 58.

[13] See my "On the Prosodic Features of the Modern English Finite Verb as Means of Functional Sentence Perspective (More Thoughts on Transition Proper)," *Brno Studies in English,* 8(1968), 11—59.

[14] See A. C. Gimson, *An Introduction to the Pronunciation of English,* 2nd ed. (London: Edward Arnold, 1970), esp. p. 267.

[15] J. D. O'Connor, *Advanced Phonetic Reader* (Cambridge, Eng.: Univ. Press, 1971). For typographical reasons, the set of tonetic marks used by J. D. O'Connor has had to be replaced by another one in the present paper.

[16] A term introduced by F. Daneš; see his *Intonace a věta ve spisovné češtině* [Sentence Intonation in Present-Day Standard Czech] (Prague: Academia, 1957), pp. 27, 153.

[17] A case in point seems to be the prosodic pattern of (13) (see here Table B). For want of evidence the solution must remain pending. The non-prosodic means, however, signal the degrees of CD with sufficient adequacy.

[18] Such particularization will primarily have to take into account the types of semantic content of the verb. For instance, F. Daneš's and K. Pala's inquiries are relevant here. See the former's "Pokus o strukturní analýzu slovesných významu" [An Attempt at a Structural Analysis of Verbal Meanings] *Slovo a slovesnost*, 32(1971), 193—207, and the latter's "Semantic Classes of Verbs and FSP", in *Papers on Functional Sentence Perspective* (Prague: Academia, 1974), pp. 196—207.

[19] The abbreviation NegFocAnt stands for "negation focus anticipator". By negation focus I understand the element that within the non-thematic section of a negative sentence/clause carries the highest degree of CD. The negating element is then regarded as the NegFocAnt. Anticipator is to be understood in terms of the gamut of CD, not in terms of linear arrangement. Examples: *I 'didn't 'meet ₍f₎John ,yesterday, I didn't 'meet 'John ₍f₎yesterday, ᶠI ,didn't ,meet him; didn't* contains the NegFocAnt, while *John, yesterday,* and *I* respectively function as NegFoc. Cf. my "A Study in the Functional Perspective of the English and the Slavonic Questions," to be published in *Brno Studies in English* 12.

[20] Cf. my "A Note on Transition Proper . . .", quoted here in note.[2]

[21] A detailed explanation of the concept of "second instance" has been given in my "On the Prosodic Features . . ." (see here note 13), pp. 15—18. A distributional field operates within second instance, if induced to appear in h e a v y, *ad hoc* contrast on account of one of its units, which is context-independent, whereas all the other units are context-dependent (*I met HIM yesterday*).

[22] An inquiry into the CD of the TMEs has been carried out in my "A Study . . ." (see here note 19). My inquiries into the CD of the English finite verb are in harmony with L. Uhlířová's inquiries into the function of the Czech verb in FSP; see, e. g., her "On the Quantitative Analysis of Clause and Utterance in Czech", *Prague Studies in Mathematical Linguistics* 4 (Prague: Academia, 1972), 107—28.

[23] An interpration of the degree of CD carried by conjunctions must remain pending. The subordinating conjunctions are tentatively interpreted as related to transition proper owing to similarity in semantic content with the TMEs. This relation seems to be borne out by the dependence of the use of tense and mood on the semantic character of the conjunction.

[24] "Multifunctional" is used here to mean "permitting of more than one interpretation of CD distribution in a particular context". For a discussion of multifunctionality, see my "Non-Thematic Subjects . . ." (quoted here in note 2), pp. 249—253.

[25] For a discussion of prosodic intensification, see my "On the Prosodic Features . . ." (quoted here in note [13]), pp. 21—23.

Hans Karlgren
KVAL, Stockholm

Text Connexitivity and Word Frequency Distribution

It would seem natural, now that linguistics is again raising its gaze to look beyond the sentence boundary, to expect substantial support from statistical methods. There are at least two good reasons for such expectations.

a. It is generally believed that the restrictions on a coherent text as opposed to an arbitrary sequence of immaculate sentences are in some sense of a weaker nature than the restrictions on sentences as opposed to arbitrary sequences of words. It does not seem very likely that the inter-sentence relationship of a proper text — let us call it a *connex* text — could be well described by suprasegmental text rules formally similar to the rules — formulated in a generative or some other framework — which specify grammatical sentences. At least some connexitivity rules seem to be weak in the sense that they apply most of the time but that it is hard to formulate conditions for exceptions. In text linguistics as in stylistics one is therefore inclined to talk about tendencies rather than about binding rules — even though some binding rules could be established, as appears from some other contributions to this book.

Now, stochastic models have in other domains proved capable of describing regularities of a "weak" kind. They are, in fact, almost the only formal tool elaborated for describing what are commonly called tendencies.

Thus, the tendency in some cultures for young men to marry slightly younger women can be expressed in statistical terms; it seems rather absurd to try to account for such observations of cultural pattern in terms of, say, a substitution class of eligible mates for each young man from which he has to draw unless well-defined circumstances authorize him to deviate.

Similarly, the tendency for consecutive passages of a connex text to be semantically close can be expected to be describable in a similar manner. It may be that binding rules can be formulated for the subset of texts in natural language which constitute logically strictly coherent presentations, but as everybody knows many texts show more or less disturbing traits of incoherence without ceasing to be "texts", to be "connex", on that account. Can connexitivity, then, be defined in a useful way?

b. Statistical linguistics as it is known today has been concerned primarily with what is sometimes called *macroscopic* properties of texts (sic!) as opposed to the microscopic properties which characterize individual passages. It would seem, then, that statistical linguistics in describing global instead of local properties of a text has already left the sentence.

Is it true, then, that statistical models are powerful tools for text linguistics? And if so, do there already exist results which are directly relevant to text linguistics?

We shall very briefly try to examine these two questions. We shall discuss openings for research, not report solutions. We focus on the most studied statistical property of language, viz., word frequency distribution. Naturally, we begin by the second question which refers to actual achievements.

Word frequency studies refer to sets, not to individual words. These sets are not sentences.[1]

The statistical model generally adopted for describing word frequency distributions is that of a stable stochastic generator, randomly producing words of a statistically defined "language". The language, then, is thought of as unchanging or at least as changing so slowly that we can assume it to be constant during the production of one text, irrespective of the length of that text.

The simplest generator can be descibed as one where each word has a poisson distribution around a stable mean, varying round this mean independently of other words. This extremely simple model, already formally clarified by Yule (1944), has been successful in describing word frequency observations in a larger number of texts — longer and shorter, though not shorter than some hundreds of words — in a large number of "languages", where "language" may be understood as "style" or "kind of text". Rarely in the humanities does one "formula" explain so much.

Because we consider the frequency of occurrence in texts or text segments of at least some hundreds of words, we have eliminated that local structure in the texts which consists of the structure within sentences or the connections between pairs of consecutive sentences. The text we describe, then, could be said to be the text we would obtain if we took the original text, chopped it into pieces of, say, 500 words and randomly permuted the words in each segment. The assertion that the words have a poisson distribution amounts to saying that such slightly destructured natural texts are insensitive to any further permutations, local or not local: words can unrestrictedly change places in such a text without turning it into an un-text. When we say that there is good evidence that the poisson distribution gives a good fit, as it does

336

for very many mutually different kinds of text, this amounts to saying that we can disregard every long-range lexical structure in all those texts. Or, in other words, a generator which forgets what it produces at the same rate as it proceeds in the text is not a bad model of a human author's behaviour on the lexical level.

This rather frustrating picture is an extreme model of the absolute lack of coherence in a text. It is the extreme opposite of what text linguists are trying to develop, of a model which would account for the interconnections between different parts of one and the same text. It is interesting as such: as a point of reference in judging text linguistic attempts, a formally well-defined antipode.

Naturally, deviations from this basic model have been recorded. In every word frequency count, many words have been found to be more unevenly distributed over the samples than they should be with the poisson model. While the poisson model normally gives a good approximation for the very frequent form words — conjunctions, prepositions, &c — it is customary for several — but not all! — of the words of the next frequency layer to be more concentrated to one or a few samples. They show what we may call a *lumping tendency* in the material.

For an infrequent word — that is for the majority of the words recorded in any count — it is not possible to verify nor to refute a hypothesis of a lumping tendency. A word occurring only once, as most words do, naturally can occur in one sample only, and words occuring twice can not be spread over more than two. But a lumping tendency can be established also for the lower frequency layers of the vocabulary. Thus, for the frequency-2-words, the frequency of word distributions where the two occurrences appear in the same sample is significantly higher than it should be with a mere poisson distribution, although we cannot in this layer point at particular words which reveal a lumping inclination.

This matter is well-known — though perhaps not as well known as it should be, even to compilers of frequency dictionaries — and we are concerned here not so much with the mathematical formulation and quantitative assessment of such tendencies as with their interpretation.

One approach is to say that this lumping shows that the corpus studied was heterogeneous. It was a mixture of texts properly belonging to different "languages". By "language" we shall of course here understand any homogeneous output of one statistical generator. It may be the kind of language which is otherwise called a sub-language or style or individual way of expression — whether the regularities within the "language" and its originality vs. other "languages" are due to historical, social, or individual factors, subject matter or communicative situation, &c, is immaterial for the present discussion.

Now, if we aptly subdivide the corpus into groups of texts of different kinds, we find for each sub-corpus a characteristically more poisson-like picture. A much greater proportion of the words are evenly distributed over the samples within one such sub-corpus than in the indiscriminate statistics for the whole corpus, if the subdivision of the corpus was adequate.

But even if we proceed to classify and subclassify until we have only one coherent text in each subclass, we still retain the lumping phenomena, unless of course we are left with only one sample in the class. For many words, the distribution of occurrences over samples which constitute consecutive segments of "one text" significantly differs from the poisson distribution: these words show a lumping tendency even within one text. This observation seems to be general for all word counts so designed that the distribution over such samples can be observed, which unfortunately is not the case for all word frequency studies.

This phenomenon, too, can be interpreted as an evidence of mixture: the text is composed of sections which, because of subject matter or because of some other more purely stylistic reasons, represent different sub-languages, although they belong to the same document and were produced by the same author on practically the same occasion. He shifted between styles from chapter to chapter, from paragraph to paragraph, as mood and matter directed him.

In that way the poisson distribution can always be warranted: if we accept that "one" text is a sequence of text fragments of arbitrary shortness, it is next to impossible to refute the poisson distribution for any word in any fragment. It may even be meaningful — using a mathematical model of a dual stochastic process, where the frequency of occurrence is determined by a poisson process round a stochastically but "not too fast" changing mean — to calculate with incessant transitions between (in each step moderately different) "languages". Such a model need not at all be formally vague and possibly not even very complicated.

Let us focus on the linguistic implications of what has just been said. If it is common or even inevitable for one text to be described as a conglomerate of text fragments from different "languages", then "language" (or "text type" or "style", if one prefers a less technical term), can no longer be defined as or even characterized by a set of mutually congruent texts. The language then becomes a still more abstract concept, representing rather a tendency acting on the text generator at a certain point of the production procedure.

If we look at it that way, we are led to another interpretation of the lumping phenomenon than as an evidence of a mixture. Instead of considering this effect as the disturbance caused by impurities, we can establish the fact that texts show that kind of heterogeneity; lack of homogeneity can also be expressed as presence of structure, since structure requires an interaction of parts. If we believe that a text is in some sense an organic whole, we must expect a text to be homogeneous in some respect and heterogeneous in some others. The lumping tendency is worth our attention in this perspective: on the macroscopic level, this is one and perhaps the only known reflexion of what is happening in the text, of theme dynamics, as Nils Erik Enkvist phrases it.

We can summarize then and say that the distribution of a word in a text can be described in two ways: by the manner in which it differs from that in some other texts and by the manner in which it varies from one part of the text to another.

The first comparison of the word frequency distributions of one text against a set of background texts to establish words which are characteristically frequent or possibly infrequent is well-known if not always well-performed. Guiraud (1954) already defined keywords on quantitative criteria, and several attempts at specifying the theme of a document (for document retrieval purposes and other applications) are based on the selection on statistical basis of thematic words. (Cf. *Kay & Sparck-Jones*, 1973 and the literature cited there, and *Moskovich* 1971). These words are expected to reveal — indirectly and imperfectly and not always in a lucid manner — what is being talked about in the text.

It should be noted that the thematic words are those which stand out in comparison with a given background. It is in principle impossible, on statistical evidence, to distinguish between words which are preferred because of the subject matter, the author's taste or communicative circumstances. The term thematic may therefore be misunderstood if used without warning in the technical sense we use it in here.

The second comparison remains to be elaborated. The lumping words may be seen as the evidence of what is said in the text about the theme: let us call them *rhematic* words, extending by analogy the opposition theme/rheme from sentences to texts. These concepts at the same time assume a relative nature: what is rhematic for a whole text or a longer portion of one is the theme of one section thereof. We think it may be fruitful to pursue investigations on these lines.

What means do we have, then, to establish statistically the lumping tendency of the words in a text?

If we examine existing accounts for word frequency counts, we shall find that the majority, due no doubt to lack of understanding of the statistical issues, have omitted relevant material on dispersion. Many give only the mean, possibly specified for different kinds of text material, thus tacitly assuming that the variation within one kind of text and even more so within one single text is negligible or uninteresting. Others give not even that but an overall mean, possibly with some sort of dispersion measure added.

Now, a mean taken over different kinds of texts is not only difficult to estimate but meaningless in principle, unless some additional assumptions are added. A mean for "English", based on, say, some proportion of the Holy Bible and daily newspapers, may be meaningful only under certain circumstances; e. g., if we have reason, to accept that proportion as a forecast for a student's further study or a particular printer's production &c, but it is doubtful what "English in General" would stand for. This is an extreme example, but the same objection should be considered against claims of calculating a mean even for newspaper style over a brief period — what further justifications were made to justify the mean at all?

One would expect, therefore that the measures of dispersion in linguistic work would be very carefully chosen and linguistically well motivated. This is not commonly so.

As measures of dispersion frequency several dictionaries use the *range*, the number of samples where a word has a frequency greater than zero, or some other primitive and at best easily computable indication of unevenness, measures which are apparently easy to understand but from which it is so much more difficult to draw statistical conclusions. Of course, a measure like the range is not based on serious statistical considerations. It originates from an exaggerated respect for the difference between some and none, which is alien to statistical reasoning. It is a relapse into non-statistical yes/no-reasoning, in the midst of a statistical study.

We shall not here review the various attempts, some home-made and original in a manner which shows more ignorance than ingenuity. For many purposes, admittedly, the choice of measure is of secondary importance. If we only want an indication that the mean is an extraordinarily incomplete representation of the original observations, many measure do. And it is a legitimate task for a measure of disperssion to warn against bad means: if the disperssion is high, the mean in a way carries less information. Thus, if the variation between observations was high, there would be less reason to include a word with a particular frequency in a language training course, since it is less certain that the word will recur in later reading than another word with the same mean number of occurrences. In short, the exact statistical presentation is not crucial when we look at the lexical items one at a time. The arguments — such as the pedagogical argument sketched — are half-intuitive anyhow, since the data about one particular word are insufficient to give statistical significance even in multi-million word counts, except for the top few hundred words.

But this casuistic approach to frequency studies is a poor defence in a statistical context. It means that the work ceases where statistics should begin. Not even with the best of statistical methods can much be said about individual words which have occurred only a handful of times. Instead of making a statistical study of the properties of the vocabulary as a whole, one presents a dictionary, that is, thousands of parallel studies, almost all with uncertain results. The few million running words which even the large counts can at most cover (equivalent to less than our daily reading in a newspaper during one year) is so obviously insufficient to make a dictionary, a book which can be consulted for information about individual words; anybody who undertook to write a non-statistical dictionary on so meagre a basis of experience would not be taken seriously, and for a statistical analysis of every word's properties one would need more, not less, material than for a sound intuitive investigation. Most frequency dictionaries — bulky as they are, and the more so as computer counting and compter type-setting proceeds — give thousands of pages of more or less insignificant material, which is even misleading to the innocent student, but leaves to the reader to compile for himself such statistical conclusions as can be computed with the often incomplete information supplied on variation between samples.

As soon as we are interested in the over-all properties of word frequency distribution, the measures of sample fluctuation become crucial, and particularly so if we are interested in variation as such, viz., in the difference in variation between texts and between equivalent amounts of material sampled from the same text. The measure must be such that the many small observations can be combined — "added" in a literal sense or by some other arithmetical operations — into a meaningful and reliably ascertained whole. This combination of many small observations, each insignificant taken *per se*, into a total picture is the very essence of statistical reasoning. If we design our study so that the observations cannot be algorithmically combined, it is no consolation to the statistician that they are many; that is merely cumbersome. This is the fundamental difference between statistical and non-statistical work: in a good dictionary, every dictionary article is good reading in its own right, based on sufficient knowledge to support it, and we are only happy and grateful if the volume is bulky.

It is remarkable, therefore, that neither the statistical summaries nor adequate data to summarize are always given. In fact, it is often left unsaid to what extent the observations are made in different texts or in different passages of the same. Thus a recent computer-based frequency study of Swedish texts gives thousands of pages of data on individual words but omits, in the printed addition, such fundamental information as sample lengths, as well as statistical measures to that effect.[2]

We may say, in short, that quantitative linguistics as far as word frequency counts go does not normally supply quantitative macroscopic information about texts. What it aims at doing is to supply quantitative information about a language — either the more or less meta-physical languages like English *an sich* or some sub-language — and from these data the quantitative structure of texts can be derived if and only if we assume that the texts lack a quantitative structure — which we know that they have. By disregarding statistical text structure the estimates of the parameters for the language are also less good than they could have been with the given number of observations.

Let us examine, however, the variations within texts for which statistical records are more complete. I select for this purpose a series of well-designed studies of word frequency properties, made by Carita

Hassler-Göransson (1968—71). Hassler-Göransson made extensive word counts as early as the 1930's, investigations which through her own publications and those of others have had a great impact on teaching and teaching materials in Sweden; the counts were published in full in 1966. But she is not only one of the earlier[3] investigators in this field, but also one of the latest and most advanced. In three studies of Swedish authors she has compared 100 000 running words from 10 different contemporary writers, the same amount from 10 works of one writer and finally, that amount from one text by that same writer. In three little articles on these studies she gives in a way the most exhaustive and statistical treatment so far of Swedish word frequency problems in Swedish, although — or because — she does not give full-size lists of word frequencies but the top of the lists and a statistical summary of the whole, comparing authors, books and text passages on one hand and various statistical parameters on the other.

Carita Hassler-Göransson gives a "lumping index" for each one of the words she accounts for.

The measure of dispersion she uses — we shall here denote it by C_0 — is defined as the chi-square value divided by the number of degrees of freedom. This measure is zero when the occurrences are distributed over the samples according to the poisson law and is greater the further the actual distribution deviates therefrom.

It is clear that C_0 is not independent of the word's total frequency. Words with high frequency tend to have larger C_0 values. The C_0 value of two words, therefore, cannot be compared without caution.

But this value has some very attractive characteristics. It is easy, via the well-known chi-square-function, to derive from a C_0 value the probability to obtain by mere chance as great or greater deviation from an even distribution over samples. And, above all, this index has the desired additive property: the evidence provided by observations of one word can meaningfully be "added" to the evidence provided by another word, so as to obtain a good and safe description of the text as a whole. This is one of the best known and best appreciated properties of chi-square measures in general, and the linguistic investigation here has come into the main stream of research. When the number of degrees of freedom — the number of samples and the number of words considered — is the same for two materials, it is even possible to perform this combination of the evidence by simple addition: the sum or average of the lumping indices may meaningfully be compared (and related to probabilities); in the general case, the chi-square values and the degrees of freedom must be added separately and a chi-square table be consulted with the two pairs of values.

Hassler-Göransson's results show that the lumping tendency as a whole is much stronger in one coherent book than in a material of 10 samples from one author, this latter material being again slightly more lumping than an equivalent amount drawn from different authors.

A close study of the actual words with a rhematic and thematic function is fascinating, but slightly deceptive, since an over-emphasis can easily be placed on the variation of single items. But a student of style can certainly find material for reflexion and fancy on a simple reading of the frequency distribution lists: the words enter and leave the scene in a pattern which characterizes the text in much the same way as the *intrat*'s and *exit*'s determine a play; it would be a fascinating game — and the odds for success would be fairly good — to try and reconstruct the text from this information. At the same time, the words with a more or less stable frequency represent the requisita and the background. They give the atmosphere but since they do not change conspicuously they do not in themselves contribute to the events.

It would be particularly interesting to study systematically the relation of theme and rheme, statics and dynamics, in this quantitative sense, by comparing the distribution over consecutive samples of varying lengths. By way of illustration, we give in Table I a very brief extract from a table of the distribution over consecutive 10 000 word passages from a novel (Ivar Lo-Johansson, Journalisten-Författaren) included in Hassler-Göransson's material[4] and in Table II an extract from a table of the distribution over 2 500 word passages from the same book.[5] The extracts chosen as illustrations are taken neither at the top nor at the bottom of the degressive frequency lists but from a level where the rhematic character of the words are particularly striking.

When we look at the distribution over consecutive samples, we immediately see that the lumping effect not only means an overrepresention of high frequency values but also, naturally, sequences of higher values. The agglomerative tendency operates not only over short distances, within each sample, but also over text portions which cover several samples. This lumping effect is not accounted for by the C_0 value. When the order of the samples is retained from the original text, therefore, one should calculate some kind of measure of the agreement between neighbouring samples and between samples which are separated from each other by one other sample, and so on. Such autocorrelation values, as they are often called, can be designed in various, more or less equivalent ways, all based on the mean of the products $X_i X_{i+d}$ for some "lag" d, compared with the average of all products $X_i X_j$, X_i being the frequency in the i:th sample. We assume here and in what follows that the samples are of equal length, noting that the generalization to arbitrary sample length is trivial. Let us define the correlation measure C_d for a lag $d = 0, 1, \ldots$ as the measure C_0 if $d = 0$ and otherwise as

$$C_d = \frac{2}{n-1} \left(\frac{\Sigma X_i X_{i+d}}{X} - (n-d)\, \overline{X} \right)$$

where X_i is the frequency in sample i, for $i = 1, \ldots, n$; the sum is taken over $i = 1, \ldots, n-d$ and $\overline{X} = \Sigma X_i / n$

These C values add up to zero; a lumping tendency is revealed if the C values are high for small i. The lumping tendency can thus differ not only in overall strength but also in the extension of the passages where the word examined has an over-average concentration.

These C values show that the lumping tendency is different for different words and kinds of words. Carita Hassler-Göransson has shown that there are differences between word classes, as was to be expected, but that clear lumping tendencies appear in all classes. The proportion of lumpers is however greater in some classes. It is especially great among proper names and, surprisingly enough, among personal pronouns, where incidentally, the feminine pronouns lump much more than the masculine ones. The behaviour of pronouns may, as Hassler-Göransson points out, be a consequence of the appearance of proper names.

Just as with frequency, the lumping tendency is only partly an inherent feature of a word. Some words tend to lump in all texts, others do so only in particular texts. Texts differ as to which words in them are frequent and which of them have high lumping indices, and they partially agree as to the distribution over frequencies and lumping indices. In short, the quantitative proportions, representing a more abstract structure, are more stable than the selection of actual words which play the different statistical roles.

In classifying the words from the point of view of lumping inclination, it would be desirable to have an index which is independent of the frequency so that these two dimensions of word occurrence could be studied separately. Nothing could be more easy to find, since the C values increase with the word's total frequency. If we divide by the frequency, we obtain values in the interval $+1$ to -1. If we do so and also eliminate the factor $n/(n-1)$, which is motivated only by attempts to infer from the observations to some population, we obtain attractive descriptive measures, R_d. We have, then,

$$R_0 = \frac{\Sigma X^2}{(\Sigma X)^2} - \frac{1}{n}$$

$$R_d = 2\frac{\Sigma X_i X_{i+d}}{(\Sigma X)^2} - 2\frac{n-d}{n^2}$$

where the sums are taken over $i = 1, \ldots, n$ and $i = 1, \ldots, n-d$, respectively. Obviously

$$\sum_d R_d = 0.$$

The R values are measures of the actual unevenness over the samples. We could interpret R_d in terms of probabilities: $R_d = p_d - q_d$, where p_d is the probability if we draw twice from our material an occurrence of a particular word that these occurrences are placed at such distance that there are d sample boundaries between them; q_d is the corresponding probability for occurrences equally distributed over samples. The R value then is the excess probability of finding occurences of the given word at a particular range of distances.[6]

I said the R values were good descriptive measures. But they are a

poor basis for estimating a population from where the observed cases are considered as taken. The distributions 8 0 0 0 and 1 0 0 0 give the same R values, and in a sense these distributions are equally uneven. But whereas the first one is an argument to expect other forces to have been active than mere chance, the latter is certainly not: the distribution could not be made more even by chance or intelligent manipulation, as long as the frequency is 1. As an argument for a "structure" and against the poisson amorphness 8 0 0 0 is much stronger than 4 0 0 0, whereas 1 0 0 0 is void.

The difference between C and R values — or equivalent measures — may be trivial, since we can turn one into the other if we know the frequency (but not if we only know the mean!). But it may also be an indication of an attitude. The R values, to which the popular Juilland's index is equivalent[7], are natural to those who study a corpus without trying to relate it to some population and who study individual words without trying to combine these results by mathematical means to establish features of the whole vocabulary in the language or the text.

Now, if we want to proceed from a study of the words by means of the texts to a study of the texts by means of the statistical properties of the words, much thought will have to be given to developing appropriate statistical methods. From the C and R values, global measures of a text's cohesion over shorter and longer distances can be estimated, indicating the average lengths of the fibres which bind the text together. Similarly, the strength of the connection between any two parts of the text can be estimated and a segmentation of the text into internally more strongly connected and mutually more loosely connected portions can be tested or even mechanically suggested. We thereby leave the relatively simple statistical problems of word behaviour and enter the domain of automatic classification, sometimes called numerical taxonomy, with a wide range of unsolved and partly unsolvable mathematical problems.

Table I. Word frequencies in consecutive 10 000 word samples from one text (Ivar Lo-Johansson, Journalisten—Författaren; extract from Carita Hassler Göransson, 1969).

Rank	Word	Appr English equiv.	X_1	X_2	X_3	X_4	X_5	X_6	X_7	X_8	X_9	X_{10}	ΣX_i	Index C_0
206	författare	writer	—	1	—	—	—	—	—	9	22	22	54	15,56
207	plötsligt	suddenly	4	—	4	3	9	8	9	6	6	5	54	1,67
208	stå	stand	5	10	6	8	6	4	11	1	1	2	54	2,22
209	ibland	sometimes	2	2	7	7	1	2	4	7	10	11	53	2,45
210	kunnat	could	2	5	3	1	6	8	8	6	7	7	53	1,13
211	köpingen	town	6	4	1	6	21	8	7	—	—	—	53	7,55
212	nästan	almost	4	3	4	3	3	6	5	8	4	13	53	1,89
213	sett	seen	6	9	2	9	5	4	9	4	3	2	53	1,51
214	tänkt	thought	5	5	6	2	6	5	12	4	1	7	53	1,70
215	vet	know	10	3	6	11	6	5	4	1	3	4	53	1,89
216	istället	instead	5	2	5	8	7	2	3	7	7	6	52	0,96
217	Berger	(proper name)	4	1	2	19	4	11	10	—	—	—	51	7,84
218	böcker	books	—	4	2	—	—	2	—	14	20	9	51	9,61
219	hennes	her	7	11	6	2	4	15	4	1	1	—	51	4,51
220	inget	nothing	5	6	6	9	7	11	3	—	4	—	51	2,55
221	journalist	journalist	18	5	5	6	2	7	7	1	—	—	51	5,49
222	nej	no	7	3	7	5	4	7	7	2	4	5	51	0,59
223	nån	some.	5	10	8	10	4	7	7	—	—	—	51	3,14
224	ord	word	5	3	8	4	5	7	10	5	2	2	51	1,37
225	sagt	said	4	7	2	6	10	13	4	2	1	2	51	2,94

Note, i.a., the rhematic words *författare* (writer) and *journalist* which indicate the major roles of the hero of the story; cf. thematic words like *ord* (word), *sett* (seen), *tänkt* (thought).

Table II. Word frequencies in consecutive 2 500 word samples from one text (the beginning of the same text as in Table I).

Word Rank		Appr. Eng. equiv.	X_1	X_2	X_3	X_4	X_5	X_6	X_7	X_8	ΣX_i	C_0	C_1	C_2	C_3	C_4	C_5	C_6	C_7
300	banan	banana	1	1	5	—	—	—	—	—	7	3.408	0.209	0.133	−1.250	−1.000	−0.750	−0.500	−0.250
301	barnen	children	—	—	1	—	1	—	5	—	7	3.408	−1.750	1.459	−1.250	0.633	−0.750	−0.500	−0.250
302	bilder	pictures	—	—	—	—	—	—	—	7	7	7.000	−1.750	−1.500	−1.250	−1.000	−0.750	−0.500	−0.250
303	bägge	both	2	2	—	—	2	—	—	1	7	1.122	−0.444	−1.500	0.709	0.306	−0.750	0.153	0.403
304	Dalarna	(geographical name)	—	4	3	—	—	—	—	—	7	3.081	2.168	−1.500	−1.250	−1.000	−0.750	−0.500	−0.250
305	därinne	in there	—	—	3	2	1	—	1	—	7	1.449	0.862	−0.194	−0.597	−0.020	−0.750	−0.500	−0.250
306	egnahemmare	house owner	—	—	—	4	2	—	1	—	7	2.429	0.862	−0.847	0.056	−1.000	−0.750	−0.500	−0.250
307	föreställde	represented	1	—	—	—	2	—	2	2	7	1.122	−0.444	−0.194	0.056	−0.347	−0.750	0.253	0.403
308	förväg	advance	2	—	—	—	—	3	2	—	7	1.776	0.209	−1.500	−1.250	−1.000	1.209	0.806	−0.250
309	gammal	old	1	3	—	—	—	—	1	2	7	1.449	−0.117	−1.500	−1.250	−1.000	0.226	1.782	0.403
310	händer	hands	2	1	—	2	1	—	—	—	7	0.795	−0.444	−0.847	0.709	0.306	−0.750	−0.175	0.403
311	hörde	heard	1	1	—	2	—	—	2	1	7	1.122	−0.117	−0.847	0.056	0.306	−0.097	0.153	−0.250
312	istället	instead	1	—	2	2	—	—	1	1	7	0.795	−0.117	−0.847	0.056	0.306	−0.097	−0.175	0.075
313	kaniner	rabbits	—	—	—	—	—	7	—	—	7	7.000	−1.750	−1.500	−1.250	−1.000	−0.750	−0.500	−0.250
314	kunnat	could	—	—	1	1	3	1	1	—	7	1.122	0.862	0.786	−0.597	−0.675	−0.750	−0.500	−0.250
315	landsvägen	highway	1	—	1	—	4	—	1	—	7	2.102	−1.423	−0.194	0.056	0.306	−0.750	−0.175	0.075
316	lille	little	—	—	3	4	—	—	—	—	7	3.081	2.168	−1.500	−1.250	−1.000	−0.750	−0.500	−0.250
317	liten	small	—	3	1	—	1	1	1	—	7	1.122	−0.444	−0.847	0.056	−0.675	0.556	0.476	−0.250
318	länge sen	long ago	3	1	—	2	—	—	—	1	7	1.499	−0.770	−0.847	−1.250	−0.675	0.226	0.153	1.709
319	mormor	grandmother	—	—	—	2	4	—	1	—	7	2.429	0.562	−1.500	0.056	−0.347	−0.750	−0.500	−0.250

NOTES

[1] This statement is true also when the frequency counts refer to sentence length — the number of words per sentence. The quantitative statements refer to sets of sentences, not to individual sentences. The quantitative statements about sentences, on the other hand — say, about the permissible length in words or the number of hierarchially ordered s-nodes in a sentence — are not very exciting. Everyone agrees, that on the surface there exist one-word sentences and that there is little sense in defining sentences in such a way that there exists an upper limit to sentence length.

[2] See *Karlgren* 1972.

[3] See my survey of work on Swedish word frequency studies in *Karlgren* 1972, with thorough methodological comments, and in *Karlgren* 1973, with an introduction to the theory. In these surveys are left unmentioned the statistical studies made by Jan Thavenius on Swedish poetry, not because they are less valuable but because they are less easily comparable with the rest.

[4] See *Carita Hassler-Göransson*, 1971.

[5] By courtesy of Carita Hassler-Göransson, from unpublished material.

[6] R_0 is never negative, which would mean that there could never be an underrepresentation of occurrences close to each other, which though linguistically rare (unless a peculiar kind of rhythm or horror of repetition has governed the text production) is logically possible; the reason is that drawing twice, as I carefully put it, includes finding the same occurrence twice. It is of course trivial to modify the measure so as to compensate for this effect.

[7] Juilland's dispersion index, used in, e. g., S Allén, *Nusvensk frekvensordbok*, Uppsala 1967—69, can be defined as $1 - \sqrt{R_0}$ or, to be exact, $1 - \sqrt{C_0/\Sigma X}$. It thus also varies between 0 and 1 inclusive, but the direction of change is inverted so that greater values indicate that the occurrences are more evenly spread over the samples. This is, of course, completely immaterial, but it is slightly confusing that this measure is still referred to as a measure of dispersion. Now, it is naturally just as reasonable to say that the dispersion is high when the occurrences are well spread over the samples, so that the sample frequencies are concentrated round their mean, as it is to say that the dispersion is high when the sample frequencies are spread over values further apart, because the word occurrences concentrate to a few samples. This is merely a trivial matter of convention, but it is an evidence of the cultural isolation of linguistics that a convention could spread here which is contrary to the terminology of science at large.

Hassler-Göransson, Carita, Ordfrekvenser i nusvenskt skriftsspråk, Lund 1966.

eadem, Försök till kvantitativa studier av nusvenska författares ordförråd, Nusvenska studier, årg 47, ss. 173—200, Lund 1968.

eadem, Kvantitativa studier av Ivar Lo-Johanssons prosa, I i Nusvenska studier, årg 49, ss. 78—218, Lund 1970, II i Nusvenska studier, årg 50, ss. 5—30, Lund 1971.

Karlgren, Hans, Latskrift, Iisalmi 1973.

idem, Ord, massor av ord, i Språkvård 3-1972, ss. 8—17, Stockholm 1972.

Kay, Martin & Sparck-Jones, Karen, Linguistics and Information Science, 1973, report from the international committee on linguistics in documentation (FID/LD) to the Fédération internationale de documentation (FID).

Moskovich, Wolf, Informacionnye jazyki, Moskva 1971.

Yule, Udny, The Statistical Study of Literary Vocabulary, Cambridge 1944.

FERENC KIEFER

Hungarian Academy of Sciences

Coordination within sentences and sentence combinability within 'texts'

1. In spite of the great efforts made by many linguists toward a linguistic model of text as opposed to sentence,[1] the arguments which are generally brought up in order to justify a particular text grammar are at least dubious;[2] they would be convincing if it could be shown that the phenomena on which they are based can only be accounted for by rules going beyond those of sentence grammars. In other words, observations with respect to deictic elements, pronominalization, the use of articles, topic-comment structure, emphasis, etc., which we very often encounter in the pertinent literature, all refer to properties of sentences which may but need not be conditioned by the linguistic context of the sentence in question.

If, for example, we want to argue that an adequate theory of pronominalization requires an apparatus that goes beyond sentence grammar, it must first be shown that there are certain facts about pronominalization that can be accounted for in a text grammar but not in a sentence grammar. As we know, every theory of pronominalization which has been propounded so far fails in one aspect or another.[3] But no 'text linguist' has thus far managed to show that this failure is due to the fact that the theory of pronominalization has been based on sentence grammar rather than on text grammar. Grammarians who confine themselves to sentence grammar may still feel that they have good reasons to believe that there is nothing which 'text grammarians' can do and which they could not do equally well.[4]

the difference between pheme and dolewe.

The unclear status of text grammar is partly due to the fact that the differences between 'sentence' and 'text' are as yet poorly understood. Intuitively it seems to be rather clear that there are essential differences between a sentence and a text. But nobody has been able to say exactly what these differences are.[5] One also has the feeling that an adequate 'text grammar', whatever it is, could not be in the same way a grammar as sentence grammars are.[6] Text grammar could possibly be conceived as a set of semantic rules operating on sentences. The super-sentence constitution of a text is a semantic phenomenon *par excellence*. Texts do not seem to have a syntax, a morphology and a phonology as sentences do.[7] According to this view, sentences but not texts can be grammatical

349

or ungrammatical and texts can only be acceptable or unacceptable. Instead of trying to work out a text grammar, one should rather attempt to establish the conditions under which a set of sentences may form a piece of coherent text. These conditions would be part of a theory of text.

In particular, we shall investigate some aspects on the combination of sentences by coordination.[8] First, we shall try to answer the question of whether the restrictions for coordination are of essentially the same character as other regularities accounted for in sentence grammar. Second, we shall investigate to what extent the restrictions found to be valid for combining sentences by conjunctions into larger sentences do also hold for other ways of combining sentences into 'texts'.

Let us consider some conditions for sentence coordination and then discuss whether these conditions refer to individual sentence structure or to super-sentence text structure.

2. The conditions for coordination we shall be concerned with are the following: semantic distinctness, inclusion and contradiction. Furthermore, we shall restrict ourselves to the conjunction "and" and to coordination of exactly two sentences, S_1 and S_2, called *conjuncts*. We shall give "and" the following operational meaning: take the propositions represented by S_1 and S_2 as being simultaneously true.[9]

2.1. The conjuncts of a coordination must be semantically distinct. Semantic distinctness means that /a/ the conjuncts must have different meanings and /b/ they must have different references.[10] Thus, sentences /1//a/ are unacceptable because condition /a/ fails, sentences /1//b/ because condition /b/ fails.

/1//a/   Eva is pretty and pretty.
John smokes and smokes a cigarette.
Bill owns a car and an automobile.
/b/   I live in Budapest and in the capital of Hungary.
I have met Palme and the Swedish Prime Minister.

Though this seems to be the basic rule there are several exceptions to which we shall turn immediately. Notice, however, that all these exceptions seem to be semantically describable in general terms.

One type of exception seems to involve tense and a certain type of referentially identical nominal constructions which are, however, different as to meaning. Compare the unacceptability of /2/ with the acceptable sentence /3/:

/2/   I see the morning star and the evening star.
/3/   I have seen the morning star and the evening star.

Referential identity seems to be allowed whenever different aspects are involved, depending to some extent on the verb employed. Thus, though the expressions 'Palme is a man' and 'Palme is the Prime Minister of Sweden' are referentially identical one can very well say

/4/   I like Palme as a man and as the Prime Minister of Sweden.
It is also possible to say

/5/   This is my house and my home.

The other type of exception seems to involve 'phrasal conjunction'
rather than coordination ('sentence conjunction'). Consider

/6/ /a/   John walked and walked and walked all day.
   /b/   She talked and talked and talked.
   /c/   I like her and I like her and I like her.

Notice that /6/ /a/ seems to be unacceptable if complete conjuncts
(sentences) are repeated:

/7/   John walked all day and John walked all day and John walk-
         ed all day.

The fact that /6/ /b/ and /c/ are acceptable, though whole conjuncts
are repeated, can be explained if we observe that pronouns are clitics,
they do not carry stress /under normal intonation/. If we replace the
pronouns in /6/ /b/ and /c/ by full noun phrases we get unacceptable
sentences:

/8/ /a/   My grandmother talked and my grandmother talked.
   /b/   My father likes Mary and my father likes Mary.

This fact seems to indicate that this (emphatic) conjunction is a sort
of phrasal conjunction. This seems to allow the repetition of certain constituents where a sentence, too, may be considered as a constituent provided it contains only one single full word, the other words in the sentence being clitics. The repeated constituent is always emphatic. In
fact, emphasis seems to be introduced here by repeating a constituent.
Thus, it is clear that we have here another "and", different from that
we are concerned with in this paper. It is an interesting fact that this
repetition, too, underlies severe semantic constraints. Thus, factive,
implicative and performative verbs as well as verbs expressing propositional attitudes[11] cannot be repeated:

/9/ /a/   I realized and I realized that ...
   /b/   I managed and I managed to solve the problem.
   /c/   I said and I said that she should come.
   /d/   I believe and I believe that ...

The exceptions to the main principle are thus not real exceptions. The
cases where referential identity is allowed can be accounted for by general principles while sentences containing repeated constituents do not
fall under the heading of sentence coordination.

2.2 If one of the conjuncts entails the other one we get unacceptable sentences:

/10/ /a/   John bought a Volvo and a car.
    /b/   John bought a car and a Volvo.

/11/ /a/ Bill left for Rome and Italy.
    /b/ Bill left for Italy and Rome.

Thus, we have to exclude the generation of coordinated structures in which one of the following two relations holds between the conjuncts S_1 and S_2:

/a/ $S_1 > S_2$ or /b/ $S_2 > S_1$. This explains also why one cannot have an implicative verb + complement as one of the conjuncts and the complement (entailed by the implicative verb) as the other conjunct:

/12/ /a/ Sylvia managed to solve the problem and she solved the problem.

    /b/ Sylvia solved the problem and she managed to solve the problem.

/13/ /a/ Sylvia failed to solve the problem and she didn't solve the problem.

    /b/ Sylvia didn't solve the problem and she failed to solve the problem.

Notice that presuppositions behave differently:

/14/ /a/ There was a man whose name was Kepler and he died in misery.

    /b/ Kepler died in misery and there was a man whose name was Kepler.

/15/ /a/ Bill will come and I know that he will come.

    /b/ I know that Bill will come and he will come.

/16/ /a/ John does not have a car and even if he had one he would not drive me home.

    /b/ If John had a car he would not drive me home and he does not have a car.

The /a/ sentences are fully acceptable but not the /b/-sentences. It seems to be quite natural to introduce a presupposition of a second conjunct as the first conjunct of a coordinated structure. In this case the presupposition(s) of the second conjunct will automatically be fulfilled. The second conjunct does not introduce the same presupposition once again.[12] In the /b/-sentences, on the other hand, the first conjunct introduces a presupposition which is identical with the second conjunct. By uttering the first conjunct the speaker would assume that its presuppositions are fulfilled. Why does one then repeat (one of) the presuppositions as the second conjunct? This seems to be at variance with the principle according to which unnecessary redundancy should be avoided whenever possible. Now the second conjuncts in the /b/-sentences seem to be fully superfluous, in contrast to the first conjuncts of the /a/-sentences which are not.

The principle of relevancy just mentioned also explains the unacceptability of /13/. The first conjuncts of the /a/-sentences already *state* the meaning of the second conjuncts. Similarly, the second conjuncts of the /b/-sentences state the same thing as the first conjuncts. The difference between the /a/ and /b/ sentences is purely presuppositional.

The principle of relevancy also prevents us from conjoining sentences whose meanings are not semantically distinct. The repetition of certain constituents is, however, permitted, as we have seen above, since this repetition introduces new information which is connected with the emphatic structure of the repeated constituents.

In some cases entailment seems to be allowed, though only in one direction:

/17/ /a/   I met Lena and the Swedish girls.
     /b/   I met the Swedish girls and Lena.

/18/ /a/   I like Volvos and big cars.
     /b/   I like big cars and Volvos.

/17/ /a/ is quite acceptable even if Lena is one of the Swedish girls. /17/ /b/ cannot have this interpretation. I am not quite so sure about the acceptability of /18/ /a/. One would like to add to the second conjunct something like "in general", i. e. "I like big cars in general." What is, however, really relevant for our discussion is the fact that /18/ /b/ cannot be amended in the above way: it is only acceptable if "Volvo" is not a name for a car. In other words, the entailment $S_2 > S_1$ seems to be allowed in certain cases (the conditions under which this is possible are clearly semantic and quite general) while $S_1 > S_2$ seems always to be excluded.

2.3. Coordinate structures with contradictory conjuncts are in general unacceptable.

/19/ /a/   It is raining and it is not raining.
     /b/   Bill is a bachelor and married.
     /c/   Mary died some years ago and she is reading a newspaper.

Again, whenever the predicates in the conjuncts refer to different evaluative aspects or ambivalent feelings of the same subject the contradiction is only apparent and we get acceptable sentences:

/20/ /a/   Anna is pretty and ugly.
     /b/   John is bright and stupid.
     /c/   This book is interesting and uninteresting.

/21/ /a/   I love and hate Anna.
     /b/   I can and I cannot believe her.
     /c/   I feel and I don't feel like going home now.

It seems to me that apparently contradictory predicates can be coordinated in the case of evaluation (cf. /20/), where the evaluation may refer to different aspects of the person or thing to be evaluated and in the case of *verba sentiendi* or verbs expressing possibility, belief etc. (cf. /21/). Though the details are unclear here one thing seems to be evident: the conditions under which one can depart from the principle of uncontradictoriness are purely semantic, they depend on the overall semantic structure of the conjuncts.

Let us now summarize what has been said so far. Two sentences, S_1 and S_2 cannot be conjoined by "and" if

(U_1) (A) S_1 and S_2 are not semantically distinct,

(B) either $S_1 > S_2$ or $S_2 > S_1$,

(C) S_1 and S_2 must not be contradictory.

. . .

The full stops indicate further conditions. The conditions (U_1) must be supplemented with further conditions which indicate in which cases the conditions (U_1) can be relaxed or cancelled.

(U_2) (A) can be relaxed to the effect that referentially identical terms are allowed to occur in coordinate structures if at least one of the following conditions holds:

(A_1) the terms express different aspects of the subject,

(A_2) the appearance of the terms is linearly ordered in time,

. . .

(B_1) (B) can be restricted to $S_1 > S_2$ if the first term is a name and the second term denotes a group such that the thing or person named belongs to this group (perhaps restricted to animate nouns and/or to certain verbs),

. . .

(C_1) (C) can be cancelled if the predicates denote evaluation,

(C_2) if the predicates are *verba sentiendi*,

(C_3) if the predicate denotes possibility or impossibility,

(C_4) if the predicates denote propositional attitudes,

. . .

The full stops stand for further yet unspecified conditions. It should be made clear that all these conditions are given here in a very preliminary form. Some of them may even turn out to be incorrect. The only thing I am trying to show is the fact that something like (U_1) and (U_2) are needed in order to account for coordination.

It is quite evident now that the conditions (U_1) and (U_2) can easily be accommodated in a theory in which coordinated structures are considered to originate from fully developed sentences by means of certain operations. Each of the conjunctions represents a certain type of operation. On the other hand, (U_1) and (U_2) cannot be made part of a Chomsky-type grammar because there is no way to build into this grammar conditions that would filter out a sentence in dependence of another sentence, or, to put it differently, that would make it possible, given an S, to choose for this S another appropriate S. Selection does not work across sentence boundaries and no such mechanism can be advised in a simple way. It is, of course, possible to have the interpretative component to filter out the unacceptable coordinated structures. In this case, one would expect that all the sentences of a language should be treated in the same way, which means that the syntactic component of the grammar would generate only syntactically well-formed sentences. As a consequence, the main function of the semantic component would be to filter out the unacceptable sentences. Such an approach has long since been considered to be inadequate and we do not have to repeat the arguments against it here.[13] There remains the possibility of having coordinated structures in the semantic base. This is, of course, possible. However, in generative semantics a distinction between sentences and texts can only be drawn on a very superficial level: abstract semantic structures can be realized either as sequences of sentences or as single sentences. Therefore, in the generative semantic approach the placement of coordination is not an issue which decides anything with respect to the relation between sentence and text.[14] For this reason we shall base our considerations on a type of grammar in which sentences and not texts are first generated.

If what has been said so far is correct then coordination is quite different from the regularities usually accounted for in sentence grammar. Coordination consists essentially of semantic operations on sentences. Now, does text constitution require operations of an essentially different kind from those applied in coordination? Text constitution is also a semantic operation. It seems thus to be reasonable to claim that coordination is one aspect of text constitution.

It seems to be the case that sentences of a text may be connected with each other in a way determined by one or another conjunction even if this conjunction does not appear overtly on the surface. In order to disregard the more or less stylistic differences in those cases where a conjunction may be inserted but equally well omitted between two consecutive sentences of a text, let us call a text *closely connected* or say that a text reveals *close connexity* if any consecutive pair S_i, $S_i + 1$ of its sentences are /a/ either conjuncts of a coordinated construction or /b/ they are understood in such a way as if they were. /22/ are examples for close connexity:

/22/ /a/   Peter came into the room. Then he went out again.
        Peter came into the room and then he went out again.

   /b/   Peter thought that Mary would come soon. I don't think that he was right.
        Peter thought that Mary would come soon but I don't think that he was right.

   /c/   Mary got sick. I went to see her.
        Mary got sick, therefore I went to see her.

  or: I went to see Mary because she got sick.

As opposed to close connexity, *loose connexity* cannot be interpreted in the same way as coordinated constructions. /23/ are some examples for loose connexity:

Mood changes.

/23/ /a/ Question-answer
Who knows him? I don't. (I am the speaker of both sentences.)

/b/ Imperative — non-imperative
Be patient! I would like to show you something.

/c/ Dialogues of all types

/d/ 'Common denominator'
Mary is blind, Julia is lazy, Judith is deaf, Lena is stupid. Everybody has got some faults.

It should be made clear that loose connexity should be further differentiated according to the degree of 'looseness'. However, we cannot go into this question here.

Now we can make a more specific statement on sentence combinability.

The conditions (U_1) and (U_2) hold for close connexity but not for loose connexity, or at least, not all of them are valid in the latter case. Thus, (C) of (U_1) holds even for loose connexity since the avoidance of contradiction seems to be a more elementary principle in human language than the avoidance of repetition. Certain communicative situations (for example, if our listener does not seem to get our point) seem even *to require* repetition. Therefore,

/24/ I live in Budapest. I live in the capital of Hungary.

is an acceptable text, the second sentence is meant to convey new information. This was not the case, as we have seen above, in the corresponding coordinate construction which we repeat here as /25/:

/25/ I live in Budapest and in the capital of Hungary.

/25/ is always uttered in one single speech act in contrast to /24/ which is uttered in two different speech acts. The same holds for any other (permitted) repetition.

Close connexity behaves in many other ways differently from loose connexity. Consider the following examples

/26/ Sam likes visiting relatives and so does Bill.[15]

/27/ I am looking for a newspaper and Julia for a book.

/28/ /a/ Peter raucht und Anna trinkt.

/b/ Peter raucht, Anna trinkt und Johann ist pillensüchtig.

/c/ Peter raucht, Anna trinkt und Johann schreibt seine Hausaufgabe für Morgen.

/29/ Julia reminded me of my mother and my work.

/30/ Peter is pulling John's leg and Anna his arm.[16]

These examples show essentially the same phenomenon: the whole sentence has fewer meanings than could be expected on the basis of the meanings of their conjuncts. Thus, /26/ is not four-ways but only two-ways ambiguous, though each of the conjuncts is itself two-ways ambiguous.

But /26/ cannot be interpreted as something like "Sam likes to go to see his relatives and Bill likes if his relatives come to see him." Similarly, /27/ is ambiguous between the specific and nonspecific reading of the indefinite article. So are each of the conjuncts. /27/ thus cannot be interpreted as, for example, "I am looking for a specific newspaper and Julia is looking for any book." /28/ /a/ is ambiguous between the habitual and nonhabitual reading. The sentence cannot be interpreted as, for example, "Peter is smoking now and Anna always drinks." On the other hand, /28/ /b/ and /c/ are unambiguous sentences. One of the conjuncts disambiguates these sentences. This conjunct is in /28/ /b/ "Johann is pillensüchtig," which can only have the habitual reading and in /28/ /c/ "Johann schreibt seine Hausaufgabe für Morgen." which can only have the nonhabitual reading. The verb "remind" is ambiguous, the sentence /29/ is, however, unambiguous because the second conjunct is unambiguous. In /30/ the first conjunct is an idiom but it can also be interpreted literally. The whole sentence /30/ can only have the literal meaning because of the second conjunct's literal meaning. The condition can be formulated in the following way:

(U₃)   Let S' and S" (both S' and S" can be either first or second conjuncts) contain parallel constructions.[17] Then

(D₁) if S' is ambiguous and S" nonambiguous, the conjunction of S' and S" is nonambiguous;

(D2) if both S' and S" are ambiguous then the conjunction of S' and S" is also ambiguous. The number of meanings in the case of the conjunction is equal to the number of meanings of the conjunct that has less meanings.

(D₁) and (D₂) can be formulated as a single principle. Let us denote the number of meanings of S' by n and the number of meanings of S" by m. Furthermore, min (n,m) should mean n, if $n < m$ and m if $n > m$. The number of meanings of the conjunction of S' and S" is then equal to min (m,n).

The principle just formulated reinforces our claim about the semantic nature of coordination. It shows clearly that coordination operates on sentence meanings in specific ways.

3. We can now return to the question formulated at the beginning of this paper. If coordination is part of text constitution then it becomes much easier to delimit texts from sentences. Moreover, a considerable part of text constitution could be accounted for by a theory of coordination. The question as to the differences between sentences and texts could then be reduced to the question as to the differences between close and loose texts. This statement is at the moment not more than an indication of a viable research program, however.[18]

NOTES

[1] A representative sample of recent works on text linguistics can be found in *Petöfi-Rieser*. The text linguistic approach which I have in mind is more or less restricted geographically to Germany where it has been en vogue during the past few years. As far as I can see text linguistics has been equated with either stylistics or with the structural descriptions of literary works by linguists who follow another line of research. I shall not have to say anything about these latter approaches here. I am only concerned with the kind of approach which attempts to generate or to describe texts by the aid of a coherent system of rules which might be called grammar in some sense or another because it is supposed to be an analogon of sentence grammar. This text grammar is often conceived as a kind of generative system that generates texts rather than sentences. Or, alternatively, text grammar is considered to contain a set of rules that determine the coherence of texts, i. e. the grammar is a recognition grammar that recognizes coherent texts and sorts out incoherent texts. My remarks which follow below concern these types of approaches to text linguistics. Of course, many other approaches exist and are conceivable. I would say, however, that they are not quite linguistic or at least not in the same sense as the approaches referred to above. They could very well belong to literary criticism or, to use a more fashionable term, to literary semiotics.

[2] The discussions in *Lang 1973a* and *Dascal-Margalit* cast serious doubts on the validity of the linguistic arguments put forward by 'text linguists' in order to justify text linguistics.

[3] As to the theory of pronominalization see *Ross* and *Langacker*. One of the most serious problems in this connection is that of 'sloppy identity' or 'indirect identity'. For a revealing discussion of this problem see *Schiebe*. I cannot see how any text grammar could solve this problem in such a way that the solution could not be accommodated in sentence grammar.

[4] In other words, the facts that text grammarians describe can also be described by a sentence grammarian. In order to convince sentence grammarians that they are not right one should look for better arguments than those which have been put forward so far.

[5] Of course, many interesting details have been discovered. The emphasis lies here on the systematicity or exactness of the differences between 'sentence' and 'text'.

[6] We know much about how sentences can be 'generated', we also know quite a few things about their structure. Therefore, we can very well speak of sentence grammar. Sentence grammars exist though many details are as yet unknown. In the case of texts the situation seems to be the opposite. Many details are known but nothing seems to be clear as to the overall structure of texts or as to how they could possibly be generated.

[7] Of course, if sentence grammar is part of text grammar, i. e. if sentences are special types of texts, then text grammar contains all the components of sentence grammar. But does a text have morphological, phonological or syntactic properties which go beyond the morphological, phonological or syntactic properties of sentences? I doubt it.

[8] For an interesting and revealing discussion of coordination see Lang 1973b. Lang's monograph contains also a detailed bibliography of works on coordination. Some of the discussion which follows below has been inspired by Lang's work.

[9] This interpretation of 'and' has been taken over from Lang 1973b.

[10] This definition should be made more precise, of course. Only noun phrases have references, consequently condition /b/ pertains to noun phrases but not to adjectives and verbs. Moreover, noun phrases may but need not have references. (They are referentially void in the case of generic sentences, for example.) Thus, for the noun phrases to be conjoined one should require both /a/ and /b/, for adjectives and verbs only /a/.

[11] For the notion of factive verbs see Kiparsky—Kiparsky, for that of implicative verbs Karttunen 1971. For a discussion of performative verbs see Searle, and for the notion of 'propositional attitudes' Hintikka.

[12] One could also say that the presupposition of the second conjunct is not a presupposition of the whole sentence since it is asserted by S₁. This holds *mutatis mutandis* even for the /b/-sentences. The difference lies in the communicative function of the two types of sentences.

[13] In fact, some of the arguments against this approach have given rise to case grammar (Fillmore) and to generative semantics. But even Katz has abandoned this view (see Katz 1973). *Problems in Pragmatic structure. (All?)*

[14] Notice that in generative semantics all semantic information is supposed to be representable in the underlying structures. Apart from the fact that it is not at all clear how this can be done (how are, for example, presuppositions to be represented there? or the differences in meaning which one expresses by different stress placements and intonation? or the different topic-comment structures?) it is, in particular, unclear how the semantic differences between texts and sentences can be accounted for in a semantic deep structure. The transformations, hence the syntactic rules, are all supposed to be meaning-preserving. This means that the meaning differences must already be present somehow in the underlying structure. Would we thus have two different sets of syntactic rules which spell out an underlying semantic representation as a sentence or a text depending on the properties of this representation?

[15] Similar examples have been discussed in a squib by Lakoff. Lakoff wanted to use the phrase 'so does X' as a test for distinguishing real semantic ambiguity from vagueness.

[16] Similar examples can also be found in Lang 1973b.

[17] Here one should specify what 'parallel construction' really means. We take it here simply as referring to the fact that in /26/ we had the same syntactically ambiguous construction in both conjuncts, in /27/ the object phrases were both ambiguous between the readings specific-nonspecific, in /28/ the predicates could express something habitual or actual, in /29/ the verb was lexically ambiguous and in /30/ we had a construction which could be interpreted metaphorically or literally. The sentences below do not contain parallel constructions in this sense:

/i/ I am looking for a newspaper and Anna is preparing coffee.
/ii/ Sam likes visiting relatives and John likes movies.
/iii/ Peter is pulling John's leg and Anna is laughing at him.

[18] A more detailed discussion of some of the problems presented is this paper will appear in the periodical: Általános Nyelvészeti Tanulmányok (Studies in General Linguistics), Budapest, 1975 in Hungarian.

REFERENCES

Dascal, M. and A. Margalit, "A new 'revolution' in linguistics? — 'Textgrammars' vs. 'sentence-grammars'," in: *Theoretical Linguistics*, Vol. I. No. 1/2, pp. 195—213, 1974.

Fillmore, Ch. "The case for case," in: *Universals in Linguistic Theory*, (E. Bach and R. T. Harms, eds.), Holt, Rinehart & Winston, New York, pp. 1—88, 1968.

Hintikka, J. "Semantics for Propositional Attitudes," in: *Studies in Philosophical Logic* (J. W. Davis and D. J. Hockney, eds.), D. Reidel, Dordrecht, 1969.

Karttunen, L. "Implicative Verbs," in: *Language* 47/2, pp. 340—358, 1971.

Katz, J. J. *Semantic Theory*, Harper and Row, New York, 1973.

Kiefer, F. "A szövegelmélet grammatikai indokoltságáról," in *Általános Nyelvészeti Tanulmányok* (Studies in General Linguistics), Budapest, forthcoming.

Kiparsky, P.—C. Kiparsky, "Fact," in: *Progress in Linguistics* (M. Bierwisch and K.-E. Heidolph, eds.), Mouton, The Hague, pp. 143—173, 1971.

Lakoff, G. "A note on Vagueness and Ambiguity," in: *Linguistic Inquiry* I./3., pp. 357—359, 1970.

Lang, E. "Über einige Schwierigkeiten beim Postulieren einer Textgrammatik," in: *Generative Grammar in Europe* (F. Kiefer and N. Ruwet, eds.), D. Reidel, Dordrecht, pp. 284—314, 1973 a.

Lang, E. *Studien zur Semantik der koordinativen Verknüpfung*, Dissertation, Berlin, 1973 b.

Langacker, R. "On Pronominalization and the Chain of Command," in: *Modern Studies in English* (D. A. Reibel and S. A. Schane, eds.), Prentice-Hall, Inc., Englewood Cliffs, N.J. pp. 160—186, 1969.

Petöfi, J. S. and H. Rieser, eds., *Studies in Text Grammar*, D. Reidel, Dordrecht, 1973.

Ross, J. R. "On the Cyclic Nature of English Pronominalization," in: *Modern Studies in English* (D.A. Reibel and S.A. Schane, eds.), Prentice-Hall, Inc. Englewood Cliffs, N. J., pp. 187—200, 1969.

Schiebe, T. "Zum Problem der grammatisch relevanten Identität," in: *Generative Grammar in Europe* (F. Kiefer and N. Ruwet, eds.), D. Reidel, Dordrecht, pp. 482—527, 1973.

Searle, J. *Speech Acts*, Cambridge University Press, Cambridge, 1969.

Ralf Norrman
Åbo Akademi

Reflections on the non-text and
The Bald Soprano

> She has regular features and yet one cannot say that she is
> pretty. She is too big and stout. Her features are not regular
> but still one can say that she is very pretty. She is a little
> too small and too thin.
>
> (Ionesco:*The Bald Soprano*)

It is part of our linguistic competence to distinguish a text from a
non-text.[1] This is such a truism that it seems odd even to pause and
contemplate the fact. Still, from the point of view of a student of literature rather than linguistics, the poetic implications of even the most
basic observation on textuality may be fascinating:

If you take a random-sentence-string — created say by having 50
people each independently write a sentence on index-cards, shuffling the
pack of cards, and writing out the result — and offer it as a text to anybody, it is likely to be rejected immediately — recognized as non-
language. The extent to which textual well-formedness, or textuality,
of a sentence-string is crucial can be seen from a simple experiment:
take a well-written text; write down the sentences unnumbered and unmarked on paper-slips or index-cards; mix the cards and give them to
your linguistic guinea-pig to put together. The ease with which a ver-
bally talented person puts the original text back together, makes clear
the essential importance of textual grammar within our total linguistic
competence.

If you now give a diabolic twist to the experiment and hand your informants a non-text, i.e. random sentences without any order, it is
quite astonishing to watch the amount of frustration they will submit
to in trying to create a text. Such a trivial linguistic experiment gives
a dramatic illustration of that unquenchable desire of man to (as the
critics nowadays never tire to putting it) "impose order on chaos",
or — using the resources of a creative artistic imagination — "make
out a reality in an unreal world". The experiment also gives us a glimpse
of the possible potency of the non-text used as a literary device —
as in absurd drama.

In the same way as everyone is able to create new sentences everyone
is also able to generate new texts or textual patterns in infinite vari-

ation. We all possess a textual grammar in which exists a system of rules that enables us to put our sentences together so as to form texts as well as to discriminate in our intake between language that is textually well-formed and language that is not.

Whatever kind of explanatory model one favours as a means of describing the phenomena of textual grammar it has to include the concept of "textual cohesion". And among the means to achieve cohesion one is bound to recognize one main group of "formal" rules, constituting and governing a system of inter-sentence linkage, and another group which involves the assumption of a rational ordering not only of the linguistic symbols and rules used to describe a material, but of that material itself. These two groups are basic.

II

It is paradoxical that one method of enriching the language of literature should be destroying it. Still it is undeniable that many poets and poetic schools have achieved their greatest triumphs through using highly deviant language (e.g. E.E. Cummings). It is also rewarding to make the intellectual experiment of regarding some age-old established literary phenomena such as the metaphor[2] and irony as the result of a deliberate breaking of certain linguistic rules.

One kind of metaphor would then be the result of breaking a selection rule: E. g. Henry James's "her soft, moist moral surface" *(The Bostonians)* — the semantic matrix of "moral" having + *abstract*, whereas that of "moist" and "surface" having —, which means that they should normally be uncombinable.

Taking this incongruity or breach of a selection rule as essential to the nature of the metaphor we may easily perceive a kinship between the functioning of the metaphor on the word-group level and a certain type of irony on the sentence and text level. Example:

> "Peter was eight. He used to run around, throw sand in the eyes of babies, kick cats and small puppies, set fire to birds' nests while the small birds were still in them and push blind people out into the street against a red light. He was a nice boy."

We are faced here with the sorting out of an extensive cultural/semantic matrix for "nice". If, in the culture we are concerned with, all the things that Peter did have more or less minus-value semantically for "nice", we must conclude that "nice" is irony, and a breach of a selection rule in textual grammar.

Irony here, then, is a secret communication between writer and reader over the head of a "narrator" or "persona". Depending on whether the reader "gets" the irony or not he will see "nice" as + or —.

In this example "nice", the "irony carrier", is only one word but the proportion of the ironically offered material to the key can vary indefinitely. *All* the material may be presented from the narrator's standpoint and the secret communication between author and reader be established only in the shared appreciation of some common views and the too blatant violation of them in the narrator's version. In other words the irony may be embedded wholly in the second layer of cohesion; it need not surface through to "linkage", although usually there will be some "irony signals" in "linkage" too to alert the attention of the reader.

To translate this back into the terms of our model of textual grammar the incongruity is in the representation of one unit from the second layer of cohesion in the first.

Let us, for want of better terms, call the first layer "formal rules" and the second "pragmatic rules". There is nothing wrong with the formal rules in the example above; there are no formal errors. "He was an [adjective] boy" is a perfectly reasonable end to the sequence of sentences.

The pragmatic rules regulate the intercommunication via language of sender and receiver through the shared knowledge of culture, learning, assumptions, prejudices etc. The working of presuppositions is, as we all know, very readily demonstrated in the restraints on the use of "but" and other adversative markers. "She was poor but she was honest" presupposes a shared view that poor people cannot perhaps generally afford to be honest. The sentence "The white rabbit has red eyes but it is not deaf" presupposes a scientific knowledge that white rabbits with red eyes are generally deaf (— are they, by the way?).

Unless the receiver's knowledge of the sender's cultural picture is sufficient he will be reduced to wonder or he will not understand the text (or understand it only partly). Irony depends on the receiver sharing pragmatic rules with the sender. Thus it is often destroyed by time because we cannot be absolutely sure of the pragmatic rules. Are the prioress's eating-manners in Chaucer ironically portrayed, or were these good medieval table-manners? Few readers have missed the irony in Chaucer's portrait of the prioress because Chaucer laid it on thick, but in less obvious cases one reason why we find so little ironic humour in old texts may be our incompetence to read them. We are justly afraid of projecting our own values into the culture of an earlier period.

Pragmatic rules and formal rules are both essential to textuality — they are the blending of life and its representation in language. The breaking of these rules in ironic discourse does *not* destroy textuality. The deviation from normal use is legitimized by tradition, and it is tolerated because it agrees to stay within the limits of carefully regulated possibilities.

What is the potential of non-texts apart from the service of irony? What fictional modes, for instance, could the non-text be made to serve? What are the implications for the author-reader relationship? Does a fictional artist have control of his means of expression when he deliberately sets out to destroy textuality?

What, for example, are we to make of this passage in *The Bald Soprano:*

> Mrs. Smith: Mr. Fire Chief, since you have helped us settle this, please make yourself comfortable, take off your helmet and sit down for a moment.
>
> Fire Chief: Excuse me, but I can't stay long. I should like to remove my helmet, but I haven't time to sit down. [*He sits down, without removing his helmet.*][3]

When words and actions cover each other as they should, but in the wrong order, what are we to make of such a topsyturvy world? What emotions does, and could, this reality or unreality evoke in an audience?

Reflecting on this question seems worthwhile, because the theatre of the absurd forces us to investigate and assess not only the possibilities but also the limitations of the non-text as a literary device.

On the one hand it could be argued that the reasoning of the absurdist writers is sound. Text-linguistically, too, "words should seem an echo to the sense" and if, in what you want to display, there is no sense, then the words should seem an echo to the nonsense. Nevertheless, there is also something definitely self-destructive in the technique as there is in all avant-garde art.

III

What is the effect then of non-texts in *The Bald Soprano?* If irony involves the breaking of textuality rules, is there an element akin to irony in *The Bald Soprano?* Certainly this seems to be so, and remembering that the primary aim of irony is attack, in judging non-textuality in *The Bald Soprano* we have one safe traditional response analogically to fall back on — we can view *The Bald Soprano* as Ionesco's "devastating satire of English suburbia", or a crusade against banality. But is that response sufficient?[4]

Does the use of non-texts enhance the comedy? Certainly non-texts have been utilized for comic purposes before. Non-communication, we all know, may be extremely funny. We only have to recall Corbaccio's and Mosca's dialogues in Ben Jonson's *Volpone.* Having a character who is hard of hearing and thus prone to help create situations of non-communication can be quite funny if you first establish a reason to prefer that the characters misunderstand one another.

But a more complex effect of non-communication can very soon make itself felt. In Henry James's tale *In the Cage* the protagonist, a poor telegraphist, falls in love with one of her customers, a Captain Everard, who does not initially think as much about the telegraphist as she thinks of him. This is how James reports one of their meetings.

> He bade her good-morning always now; he often quite raised his hat to her. He passed a remark when there was time or room, and once she went so far as to say to him that she hadn't seen him for "ages". "Ages" was the word she consciously and carefully, though

a trifle tremulously, used: "ages" was exactly what she meant.
To this he replied in terms doubtless less anxiously selected, but
perhaps on that account not the less remarkable, "Oh yes, hasn't
it been awfully wet?"[5] (204)

To the reader it is obvious that he did not listen to her. He assumed
that she made a remark about the weather. But this is the way the romantic imagination of the girl rationalizes the event:

That was a specimen of their give and take; it fed her fancy that
no form of intercourse so transcendent and distilled had ever
been established on earth. Everything, so far as they chose to consider it so, might mean almost anything.   (204—205)

Undoubtedly the strongest element here is comedy — comedy at the
girl's expense. The tale, too, is one of James's most obvious exercises in
overt comic satire. But at the same time the comedy is rather cruel. The
telegraphist is foolish but she is also in her wistful aspiration far too
much a mirror of ourselves. The comedy of non-communication smacks
of tragi-comedy.

Of course there are works and aesthetic schools where the non-text
is made to serve as clearcut uses in comedy as it does in ironic discourse.
Mark Twain, in "How to Tell a Story":

To string incongruities and absurdities together in a wander-
ing and sometimes purposeless way, and seem innocently un-
aware that they are absurdities, is the basis of the American art,
if my position is correct. Another feature is the slurring of the
point.[6]

Twain gives an example of this:

Artemus Ward . . . would begin to tell with great animation something which he seemed to think was wonderful: then lose confidence, and after an apparently absentminded pause add an incongruous remark in a soliloquizing way; and that was the remark intended to explode the mine — and it did.

For instance, he would say eagerly, excitedly, 'I once knew a man
in New Zealand who hadn't a tooth in his head' — here his animation would die out; a silent, reflective pause would follow,
then he would say dreamily, and as if to himself, 'and yet that
man could beat a drum better than any man I ever saw.' (Twain,
pp. 241—242)

What the Artemus Ward story here exemplifies, is the use of a non-
text, and in this instance it takes the form of presence of formal linkage
("yet") but absence of logical connection.

The potential for pure, healthy comedy is admittedly inherent in the
non-text, and it seems that an audience choking with laughter and slapp-
ing their knees over *The Bald Soprano* cannot be totally wrong. But
again the question is, are they totally right? This is not the "comedy"

of fairy-tale wish-fulfilment (with a happy-end); neither is that hostility of the author against the characters which is characteristic of satire present as the foremost element in the play.

IV

In life non-texts are seldom printed. It is only in manuals of conversation, phrase-books for the tourist, grammar-books and such-like, that sentences without connection are strung together. Predictably enough these books have stirred the poetic imagination of many, and Ionesco's use of the phrase-book atmosphere in *The Bald Soprano* was bound to come. Vladimir Nabokov in *Speak, Memory* recalls his English textbooks:

> I learned to read English before I could read Russian. My first English friends were four simple souls in my grammar — Ben, Dan, Sam and Ned. There used to be a great deal of fuss about their identities and where-abouts — "Who is Ben?" "He is Dan," "Sam is in bed," and so on. Although it all remained rather stiff and patchy (the compiler was handicapped by having to employ — for the initial lessons, at least — words of not more than three letters), my imagination somehow managed to obtain the necessary data. Wan-faced, big-limbed, silent nitwits, proud in the possession of certain tools ("Ben has an axe"), they now drift with a slow-motioned slouch across the remotest backdrop of memory; and, akin to the mad alphabet of an optician's chart, the grammar-book lettering looms again before me.[7]

A textbook in a foreign language progresses from non-text to text. Nabokov:

> On later pages longer words appeared; and at the very end of the brown, inkstained volume, a real, sensible story unfolded its adult sentences ("One day Ted said to Ann: 'let us ...'), the little reader's ultimate triumph and reward. (*ibid.*)

Ionesco's own account of how he discovered the world of textbooks is poetically embellished somewhat in the same manner:

> "... nine or ten years ago, in order to learn English, I bought an English-French Conversation Manual for Beginners. I set to work. I conscientiously copied out phrases from my manual in order to learn them by heart. Then I found, reading them over attentively, that I was learning not English but some very surprising truths: that there are seven days in the week, for example, which I happened to know before; or that the floor is below us, the ceiling above us, another thing that I may well have known before but had never thought seriously about or had forgotten, and suddenly it seemed to me as stupefying as it was indisputably true."[8]

The overriding feeling of Nabokov and Ionesco was one of fascination and curiosity. If Ionesco's aim was to reproduce the same effect in the audience with his play we ought to consider *The Bald Soprano* in the light of the aesthetics of that category or mode of literature which could be called "the Curious".[9]

If one wants to put "the Curious" on the same level as Tragedy, Comedy, the Grotesque, and the Picturesque it is necessary to define the limits and to state the characteristic elements constituting the category. This modal classification, however, is difficult. Clearly the concept of "distance" is crucial. In "comedy" as well as "the curious" the "distance" of the audience from the imitated reality is great. Comedy differs from the curious in that the audience does not take in earnest its imitation of reality whereas in the curious it does take it in earnest but with a feeling of superiority. In tragedy the distance shrinks. The imitation is taken in earnest and the audience identifies and sympathizes with the protagonist. In tragedy fear and pity are evoked, in comedy laughter, and in the curious fascination.

Measured by these distinctions *The Bald Soprano* does not qualify as pure comedy. Distance — the alienation-technique and shock-tactics — is there, but we cannot help sometimes taking the "imitation" in earnest, because it touches spheres of interest too close to us to be ignored.

Comedy and the curious both tolerate incongruity; indeed in many theories incongruity enters the very definition of comedy. But its effect is double-edged and it serves the curious equally well, as indeed, it serves the grotesque.

Although it may not be possible to fix *The Bald Soprano* as belonging to the curious within the categories of fictional representation, still the appeal of the play is ambiguous because of its use of incongruity and non-text, and the lowest common denominator in the multilayered response it evokes, is the curious. That the curious is often overshadowed by other categories, however, is obvious. Before considering whether one of these categories is tragedy let us take a closer look at the text.

V

The play begins its assault upon rationality by frustrating the expectations of the audience in connection with "discourse-markers" from the very first page. In Mrs. Smith's first half dozen monologues (while her husband is reading the paper and clicking his tongue) there are several adversative markers such as "however" and "but still" (*pourtant, mais, cependant*) which are stylistically out of place in small talk between a husband and wife. It introduces immediately the unreal atmosphere of the phrasebook. Contributing further to this effect are the examples of the comparative and the superlative forms of adjectives and adverbs that Mrs. Smith introduces into the mechanical exercise of speaking her mother tongue.[10] Lewis Carroll invented new words but kept the markers (Twas, and, the, -es, did, etc.). Ionesco, by putting apparently "rational" jabberwocky between the markers, but little or no sense in the connection between markers and bulk goes a bit further. The frustration of having nonsense occasionally burst into sense is very great, and it seems that the position of the "argument markers" in the hierarchy of textuality must be quite high.

In brewing his witches' broth of reality and unreality throughout the play Ionesco systematically punctures linguistic presuppositions. There is one type of logical/linguistic rule that Ionesco particularly loves breaking. One instance is the construction: A is X but A is Y, which is impossible if X and Y are antonyms. This is so characteristic that parodists seize upon it; as in " 'Waiting for Pinter': A Play" by Jean Kerr:[11]

> Sybil: You're slow, but you're very quick.

"Another" presupposes a first. Therefore you cannot start a logical chain with the "another" marker. This rule is broken in *The Bald Soprano:*

> "Once upon a time another cow asked another dog: 'Why have you not swallowed your trunk?' 'Pardon me,' replied the dog, 'it is because I thought that I was an elephant.'" (30)

No cow or dog has been mentioned before that.[12] Similarly a comparative form of an adjective, e.g. "more interesting" *(The Bald Soprano*, p. 29) presupposes the positive form of that adjective ("interesting") — a rule which is again broken in *The Bald Soprano*. "Went off in all directions" *(par-ci, par-la)* presupposes a plural subject, but not in Ionesco:

> "He said, 'Goodbye, 'and took them back and went off in all directions." (32)

The presuppositions of *but* as conjunction are violated:

> "It's a useless precaution, but absolutely necessary." (34)

Closely akin to these is

> "Bread is a staff, whereas bread is also a staff." (39)

The construction *A is X whereas A is also X is impossible. So is *A instead of A which Ionesco uses in *The Lesson:*

> Instead of f he said f. Thus, instead of "Birds of a feather flock together," he said: "Birds of a feather flock together." He pronounced filly instead of filly, Firmin instead of Firmin, French bean instead of French bean, go frig yourself instead of go frig yourself ... (Allen 64)[13]

Truths, self-evident to such a degree that pronouncing them is absurd, are gravely paraded in *The Bald Soprano*. In any normal world the ceiling is indeed above and the floor below and little notice taken of either fact; but in phrase-books and *The Bald Soprano* truisms like these are earnestly insisted upon (38) — when they are not denied. A woman is generally more feminine than a man and *The Bald Soprano* parodies tepid and safe non-committal statements in introducing affirmations of such facts:

Mr. Smith: It's true. My wife is intelligence personified. She's even more intelligent than I. In any case, she is much more feminine, everyone says so. (32)

Finally, among the rationality-shattering devices, there is of course flat contradiction:

Mr. Martin: I traveled second class, madam. There is no second class in England, but I always travel second class. (16)

Contradiction is sometimes a denial of the truth of a definition. A widow's husband is, by definition, dead; thus he ought not to be able to sit (apparently alive) and talk about his wife who has been "early left a widow." (33). Ionesco employs contradiction on all levels: On page 12 and 13 the Watsons first have, then do not have, children.

The absurdity created by the assault upon language is reinforced by the absurdity of the whole world of the play. Sometimes the absurdity is just a reversion of normality; vestal virgins extinguish a fire instead of guarding one (29). But the mad clock of the play first strikes seven times, then five times, and so on, until finally it "strikes as much as it likes." (19). The odd irrational beliefs of our daily life reappear as in Mrs. Smith's insistence on the arbitrary rule that "only the first three times count." (25).

All clinging to identify is futile in a world where almost every one is named Bobby Watson,[14] and the careful, scrupulous, intellectual, deductive conclusion reached by the Martins that they are indeed man and wife is sucked into the maelstrom of absurdity by the very fact of its exaggerated nature[15] and the doubt thrown on it later by the maid.[16] The predicament is also shown as universal through the exchange of roles of the Martins and Smiths at the end (— in this version of the play).

Ionesco throughout the play satirizes "proper responses"; clichés of one type or another. By some slight inversion, contradiction or exaggeration he brings out the inherent absurdity of our parrotlike commonplaces. The assumed frame may be a business-discussion where the difficulties of importing fires are gravely pondered ("the tariffs are too high!", p. 28); or the recalling of family history where all the worn-out proper responses are thrown in and destroyed. Finally affirmative exclamations like

Mr. Martin: Yes, that's exactly the word. (35)

are destroyed by the simple trick of letting them be spoken before the "word"! (Similarly in the case of the maid entering, p. 14, whose speech is predictably repeated — except for the piece about the newspaper of course — by Mrs. Smith).

Every attempt at sanity or order is defeated. The accurate placing in time, space and family relationship of the hero of a story is satirized in the 'Headcold', a story which hardly goes beyond the point of trying to pin down the identity of the protagonist. The mad clock defeats any attempt to rely on the regular passing of time as an anchor in reality.

Proverbs, one of the more conspicuous efforts of man to order experience in a concise and maximatic way, are ridiculed, and finally, on page 41, when the strong centrifugal forces, typical of most Ionesco plays, have gathered momentum, the alphabet itself is placed under attack.

Among all the other "breaking-up"-techniques breaking textuality rules is the ultimate imaginable. One's total reaction to the play may vacillate but one senses that the use of the non-text enriches the play thematically.

Tzvetan Todorov in a recent article[17] sums up and discusses two classic attempts at defining literary language. The interest of one approach focuses on "imitation", the relationship of art to "life", and the other on "system", the relationship established between the elements of language. "It is not hard to see," says Todorov, "why, over the ages, these two definitions should have become established in preference to any other . . ." "'Imitation' and 'play' (or system) determine, as we know from Piaget, any symbolic system, hence they determine art too."

In Ionesco's assault on language and on an art form "imitation" is, although somehow accurate, imitation of a very weird world. But he goes beyond this in attacking and destroying "system" from within. He turns one formal rule against another and causes general linguistic havoc and disaster.

VI

Reaction to the play must be ambiguous. You feel that it would be a mistake not to acknowledge comedy, and perhaps the predominance of comedy, in the play; but still you ask yourself whether the core of the play does not after all have the tinge of tragedy. *The Bald Soprano* is one of those increasingly common works of contemporary art in which tragedy can only be achieved through its intermixture with comedy.

Much of the comedy in *The Bald Soprano*, as critics have suggested,[18] is doubtless explicable with Bergson's model "the mechanical imposed upon the living". Human beings behave like puppets in *The Bald Soprano*, but is this realization merely funny for Ionesco and us?

One way of looking at it, is to explain the play's success by its ambiguity. Using the non-text, you may argue, Ionesco consciously or semi-consciously subtly taps several springs of audience response. His play, through the use of the non-text, cannibalistically draws allusive and suggestive strength from all those genres where non-texts have long been legitimate, particularly comedy and satire. But through making an end of a means it also transcends the fun of mockery. Playing with reality through texts and non-texts touches a thematic sphere of supreme contemporary interest, one which insists on the simultaneous existence of both comic and tragic possibilities.[19]

The non-texts are then used for purposes beyond the institutionalized ones. Our response is multilayered. Initially we enjoy the comedy and the satire, we laugh at the characters and their folly. But gradually we are intrigued, made reflective and finally frightened by the nonsense. It sounds too familiar. We are reminded of that often painful aspect of the human condition, the desperate need to maintain a grip on reality, and pathos and terror become elements of the play. By the technique of ultimate negation through the breaking up of language Ionesco implicates the audience deeply. We are first bewildered, then we laugh with selfconfidence, then we are fascinated, and in the end we come more solemnly to realize the full implications of the show and its applicability to everyday life.

We can then regard *The Bald Soprano* as a serious play (disguised as a parody or *jeu d'esprit*); an attempt to restate in contemporary terms, using contemporary techniques, an essential concern of all "romantic" periods, for our period shows many of the characteristics of a "romantic" period. We are fascinated by befogged reality, blurred vision, and impeded communication, all highly characteristic features of romanticism. On the other hand, the characteristics of "classicist" periods which take a no-nonsense-view of reality as that which is in front of you are missing. No longer can a common philosophy be assumed as a means of understanding reality. No longer are we sure that appearances are dangerous delusions; that inability to see through disguises, day-dreaming, drug-taking, and ambiguous language are sins or follies.

As each Classicist period fades into a Romantic age the shift of stress and interest from reality to unreality in subject matter seems to be parallelled with a growing distrust of techniques and forms, a gradual abandoning of them, and a quest for new modes of expression. Classicist periods have never coined new words nor invented new genres. They have sought to make language a precise tool by restricting the number of words and by perfecting existing literary forms.

The aesthetic clash between a romantic and a classicist period often focuses in a conflicting pull towards either extreme of a continuum of artistic possibilities with "concealment" on one hand and "revelation" on the other. It is impossible to have one of these purely; some optimum balance has to be found. Romantics are drawn towards the strategy of concealment and classicists towards that of revelation. Ambiguity means concealment.

Avant-garde art such as absurdism is essentially romantic in this sense. It scorns the over-obviousness of the period preceding. It rebels and destroys. In literature we are still rebelling against nineteenth-century realism and naturalism. Ionesco is rebelling against the petit-bourgeois in all its manifestations, one of these, according to him, being the "social realism" of socialist art.[20]

Tragedy has been defined as "the misfortune of great men". The problem for the nineteenth-century writer was the rapid decline of the hero and the difficulty of depicting "great men" or "misfortunes" convincingly. In England the Victorians put up a brave fight, resorting to pathos and sentimentality (which are now thought of as typical Victorian emotional safety-valves, although sentimentality ought rather to remind one of the end of the eighteenth century). Double standards became odious to the twentieth century; over-obviousness obscene. Sentimentality, pathos and melodrama became taboo. For a while you could have it both ways. You could expose Emma Bovary as a fool and still pity her a little, but soon it was imperative to have anti-heroes, so that, it has been claimed, tragedy became impossible.

Well, did it, or has it been seeking new forms of expression? Is this the context in which we should see *The Bald Soprano*? For a long time now writers have had to mix tragedy with other literary modes in order not to break any of the taboos. Nabokov in *Laughter in the Dark* mixes it with comic cruelty. William Trevor in *The Boarding-House* mixes it with grotesqueness. Only by first reducing expectations to nil, it seems, can you nowadays secure a firm basis upon which to build a tragedy. The tactics of concealment are the key to success throughout. Communication of the tragic elements from the author to the reader has to be clandestine, never open. Our emotional inhibitions, caused by overreaction against our parents and grandparents dictate this. Ionesco criticizes Brecht for over-obviousness. Is not *The Bald Soprano* then, hoax as it may be, a focal point (and perhaps a turning point) in this development in experimentation?

A question arises: Can the art of the theatre, and the theatre-going public, take an assault like Ionesco's on the very basis of rationality, i.e. language? If *The Bald Soprano* were solely and exclusively destructive, the answer would be "yes, but not unconditionally". What the artist gains by the tactics of concealment is an increase in the audience's share in creating the work of art (and thereby the possibility of getting at springs of response in the audience otherwise difficult to reach). "What is the moral," is the question both we and Mrs. Martin ask after the fireman has told his fable. "That is for you to discover," is the fireman's and Ionesco's reply. But there is a limit to the interpretative burden the audience is willing to shoulder. During this century the public has been tolerant to experiments both in drama and the sister arts, but still a writer of absurdist plays must be wary lest he alienate his audience once too often. There must be method in the madness and sense in the nonsense. The breaking up of conventions and the creation of new ones utilizing obscuring techniques (including the non-text) has been highly successful, but even here the bewilderment of the audience may one day give way to frustration and aggression. It is possible that the public will accept one blank canvas at a vernissage, and take upon itself the task of providing a meaning ("The Impossibility of Communication in the Modern World", "The Nothingness of the Universe", "The Terror of Whiteness", "The Painter's Vision of a Void", "A Nadaistic Ultimate" etc.), but the painter who tempts fate with a hundred blank canvasses is quite likely to find his theme of non-communication parallelled in the reaction of the public to himself, critics to his art, and patrons to his agent.

The Bald Soprano resembles a blank canvas in the ambiguity that is inevitable once you decide to employ non-language as a means. The audience may find a titillating luxury at first in loosening its grip on reality, but before long it will retreat in horror from the brink of the abyss of a chaos, where words and texts no longer mean anything (as from the expansive anarchy of the maid's poem), and they will see the horror of linguistic anarchy. The tragedy-starved audiences of today will stay aware of a possible tragedy behind the comedy no matter how much they may laugh.

VII

After one has established one's own ambivalent attitude to the play, it is a relief to turn to the critics and find the confusion fittingly mirrored there.[21] Comedy, satire, tragedy; the interpretations are all there.

Moreover, when you turn to Ionesco's own comments, it is obvious that he cannot make up his mind himself. In *Notes and Counter-Notes* he sometimes says he wrote a tragedy which was understood as a comedy (p. 86). Sometimes he claims what seems to be the opposite (p. 123). However, he states that laughter is not his important object, it is merely a byproduct. "... laughter comes as a reprieve; we laugh so as not to cry..." (p. 122). Asked to give his own definition of the comic he calls it "another aspect of the tragic" (p. 123). It is all a mixture, and the mixing was intentional (pp. 26—27).

Ionesco's comments make it clear that he consciously strove both to convey "fascination" and to preserve "distance" (pp. 127, 27). He sees himself as an innovator, hopes that *La Cantatrice Chauve* will be "a specifically didactic work for the theatre" (p. 183).

But the newspaper debate between Tynan and Ionesco (The "London Controversy"), was bound to come (pp. 90—105). There is both a positive and a negative attitude to be taken to ambiguity. Ambiguity, which means impeded communication, does not lead only to greater suggestiveness but also to greater danger of misinterpretation and a longing for a return to restored communication.

It is of course self-evident that a destruction of language will lead to destruction of communication. To find this out via the labyrinthine way of the absurd theatre may have been a roundabout way but it was a literary path that our generation was destined to wander, and a journey that, after all, may prove to have been worth taking whatever the destination reached.

NOTES

[1] My interest in the problem of the non-text in literature was raised by a series of stimulating lectures given by Professor Enkvist, my teacher. For these impulses, as for much else. I am greatly indebted to him.

² For this approach I am indebted to Mr. Erik Andersson.

³ I shall use the text of Eugène Ionesco: *Four Plays*, trans. Donald M. Allen, Grove Press, Inc., New York, 1958. I use a translation for practical reasons and consider this legitimate since I want to get at generalities and do not attempt a reading that depends upon exclusively French phonetics or syntax. The Allen translation seems the most meticulously direct and literal translation available at the moment. Donald Watson's translation, which is so often used for productions in Great Britain, departs from the original very frequently, often without a discernible reason and not always with happy consequences.

⁴ Ionesco, if one can believe his comments on this, is very anxious to fight the misinterpretation that the play is in any sense anti-British. There is a long critical debate on whether the play is merely an attack on banalities, with Ionesco himself vigourously participating.

⁵ Henry James, *In the Cage & Other Tales*, ed. and introd. Morton Dauwen Zabel. The Norton Library, W. W. Norton & Company, Inc., New York, 1969.

⁶ *Selected Shorter Writings of Mark Twain*, ed. Walter Blair, Houghton Mifflin Company, Boston, 1962, pp. 239—243.

⁷ *Speak, Memory*, An Autobiography Revisited by Vladimir Nabokov. Capricorn Books, New York, 1970, pp. 79—80.

⁸ *Notes and Counter-Notes*, tr. D. Watson, John Calder Ltd., London, 1964, p. 181.

⁹ An example of a recent study of the element of the *curious* in the works of an author is Edmund Nierlich's *Kuriose Wirklichkeit in den Romanen von Henry James* (Bouvier Verlag, Herbert Grundmann, Bonn 1973) which largely follows the definitions of Dietrich Pregel: *Das Kuriose als Kategorie Dichterischer Gestaltung* (Diss. Göttingen, 1957).

¹⁰ This is not the last grammatical drill to appear in the play. The break-neck intricacies of the tangle of pronominal references (multiple "lui":s) in the story about the fiancé and the flowers (31—32) is just one typical case.

A rather interesting absurdity is the story 'The Headcold' (32—34) with all its pronominal references ("who", "whose"). There exist in transformational textual grammar some reiterative or reduplicative transformations, i.e. transformations on the repetition of which the "formal rules" of textual grammar put no limit. The only limit provided is that which lies within the province governed by "pragmatic rules". One of these transformations is the relative-pronominal reference combined with a rheme to theme sentence-transition in linkage. This transformation, curiously sidebranching if repetitive, must have fascinated Ionesco and it was to be expected that he should test out (and exceed) the tolerance limit of the pragmatic rules with a story like "The Headcold'.

It is to be noted that such a reiterative transformation rule does not have the same exasperating effect when excessively applied if the intersentence transition is theme to theme and the typ of link "repetition" rather than "reference". "We went to the park, and then we had some coffee, and then we went to the zoo and then we went..." etc. may incur the wrath of a schoolmaster's red pencil if it occurs in a composition-exercise in secondary school (although in this post-Hemingway stylistic era, who knows!), but it does not produce the same kind of tension. Experience is clearly rationally (which in this case means chronologically) ordered.

In the former example, however, it is to be noted that the use of the reiterative reference theme to theme textual transformation is by common agreement (dictated by the limited resources of the human intellect) restricted to parenthetical passages. After the sidebranching we expect a return to a main line of narrative. The repetitive adding of subsequent sidebranching imposes a strain on one's memory and grammatical retential faculties. It is rationality put to a test. The tension of the cord increases towards (and past) snapping point. What is needed for it to snap is just a comment like Mr. Martin's "I knew that third wife, if I'm not mistaken . . ." The comment is not on anything in the line of the main narrative but on something on one of the plateaus of sidebranching. What is more rational than sticking to the point!

When the fire chief starts his story we expect one of the characters at the beginning of the cat-on-the-mouse-game to become the protagonist because this is usually the case. By the end of the story we have given up, when suddenly it breaks into sense. There emerges a macro-theme and a macro-rheme. There was the grandmother of a priest (macro-theme) and she occasionally caught a cold (macro-rheme). But then we find it absurd that the narrator should get down to business so late and we ask whether the subsidiary text (the establishment, through family relations, of the identity of the grandmother in the secondary themes and the establishment of the identity of these secondary themes by secondary rhemes — bits of information) was necessary, and whether it had to precede the "point" of the story — the relative importance of which, anyway, is out of all proportion to the subsidiary text. In terms of textual "topic" and "comment" the topic is introduced very late — another trick to create absurdity.

[11] *New York Times*, Sunday, December 12, 1971.

[12] Tradition has legitimized specific cases of breaking textuality rules of this kind. In textual linguistics special rules obviously pertain to the first and the last sentences of a text. The first sentence ought to be a topic sentence, a quotation, or it should have a cataphoric link. It cannot contain an anaphoric reference (unless this be to a title or a paralinguistic fact). Thus there should be extensive restrictions on first sentences beginning with the definite article. But writers break this rule, particularly writers of the realistic movement, to achieve the illusion of bringing the reader directly *in medias res* and make him want to find out more.

Similarly with titles; see Harald Weinrich, "The Textual Function of the French Article" in *Literary Style: A* Symposium. Ed. and (in part) trans. Seymour Chatman, Oxford University Press, London and New York, 1971, pp. 221—234.

[13] What the professor teaches his pupil is often curious nonsense, sometimes with a quasi-logic of its own, and always imitating in its general aspect real instruction. The author's purpose with the non-factual nature of the professor's talk is to shift the interest of the audience from the contents of the lesson to the "event" of the lesson — above all to the relationship between the professor and the girl. The language of the professor gives his *function* in the same way as the quasi-medical nonsense-jargon of the doctor in *Commedia dell'arte*.

In *The Lesson,* in contrast to *The Bald Soprano*, it is not often that formal textuality rules are broken. It is mostly pragmatic rules that Ionesco breaks in *The Lesson* and these of such a low hierarchical order that only a professional linguist or a pedant will care. Others will recognize a fictional representation of the contents of a lesson on philology. The absurdity of the contents will soon be overshadowed by the absurdity of the lesson itself.

It is hard to see how this could have been achieved without textual absurdity. As fictional technique it does seem to have a monopoly here.

[14] Cf. *Present Past Past Present*, trans. Helen R. Lane (Calder and Boyars, London 1972), pp. 33—34.

[15] According to H.F. Brookes and C.E. Fraenkel in Eugène Ionesco, *Three Plays*, La Cantatrice Chauve, La Leçon, Les Chaises (Heinemann, London 1965),

Introduction, pp. 14—15, the recognition scene was "inspired by a chance meeting between Ionesco and his wife in the Paris Metro. They happened to enter the carriage by different doors and then enacted a long charade similar to the scene in the play." One obvious way of reacting to the scene is of course to take it as a parody of the Aristotelian concept of anagnorisis.

[16] The recognition-scene and the maid's (or Sherlock Holmes's) quibble about the respective colouring of each child's eye is an absurdification of that rule of scientific inquiry which states that when a hypothesis is put through a series of tests it takes only one result of "falsification" to disprove it, whereas repeated results of "verification" do not amount to proof, only to a higher degree of probability. The characters of *The Bald Soprano* are ridiculous enough when they indulge in their whimsical *non sequiturs;* it is devastating that when once they encounter experience with a truly scrupulous, empirical attitude as in the recognition-scene they should prove not only as ridiculous as usual but arrive at the wrong conclusion!

[17] Tzvetan Todorov, "Artistic Language and Ordinary Language, "*The Times Literary Supplement,* Oct. 5, 1973, No. 3, 735, pp. 1169—1170.

[18] E.g. Jaques Guicharnaud in *Modern French Theatre* (New Haven and London, Yale Univ. Press, 1967). In *Notes and Counter-Notes* (p. 122) Ionesco says that if the characters of *La Cantatrice Chauve* are funny it is perhaps because they are dehumanized.

[19] It is true that *The Bald Soprano* was largely conceived as an attack on contemporary bourgeois theatre. It is subtitled an anti-play and the share of chance in its birth is illustrated by the story of the title. As Ionesco tells us in *Notes and Counter-Notes* it was to have been *L'Anglais sans peine. La Cantatrice Chauve* originated as a slip "une cantatrice chauve" of one of the actors for "une institutrice blonde". Moreover the fact that the enormously suggestive ending of having the play start anew with the Martins and Smiths changing roles was added later. The stage directions in especial illustrate Ionesco's initial mockery of the artform he was to adopt: [He either kisses or does not kiss Mrs. Smith] (32); [the clock doesn't strike] (11); — predictably parodied by Jean Kerr: "*The curtain does not rise because there is no curtain. Lights go up. There is a large bare set which might be a living room. It is a living room . . .*" Evidently *The Bald Soprano* was something of a hoax, but evidently, too, Ionesco stumbled on a success and Saul became a believer.

[20] See *Notes and Counter-Notes,* pp. 95, 125, and especially pp. 108—109.

[21] A bibliography is to be found in Richard N. Coe, *Ionesco, A Study of His Plays,* Methuen & Co. Ltd., London 1971.

János S. Petöfi
Universität Bielefeld

Beyond the sentence,
between linguistics and logic

(Aspects of a partial theory of texts)

0. INTRODUCTORY REMARKS

"A new 'revolution' in linguistics?" — This question is asked by Dascal and Margalit in their study which deals with text linguistics (Dascal and Margalit, 1974). There is no reason to talk about a *revolution*, but it is without doubt an important stage in the *evolution* of linguistics.

Not only linguistic methods can change, the scope of linguistics can change also. And both may happen at the same time. This is true for one part of the present text-grammatical and text-theoretical research. It not only attempts to include all the grammatical phenomena of a text in a description, but it does so by giving full attention to the most recent results of logical-linguistic research. This kind of linguistic research therefore extends beyond the sentence and it tries to combine linguistics and logic.

In the present study I wish to analyse some of the historical and methodological aspects of text-grammatical and text-theoretical research in the hope of contributing to a better understanding of the problems in text grammar and text theory. And a better understanding may help to find better solutions for these problems.

1. A PARTIAL THEORY OF TEXT AS THE SEMIOTICS OF NATURAL LANGUAGES

Semiotics is conventionally divided into three branches: syntax, semantics and pragmatics. Syntax is defined as that branch of semiotics which is concerned with the relation of verbal signs to one another, semantics as that branch of semiotics which is concerned with the relation between verbal signs and those objects to which they refer, and pragmatics as that branch of semiotics which is concerned with relations between verbal signs, those objects to which they refer, and the users or contexts of use of the verbal signs. (Cf. Morris, 1938)

The present development of linguistics represents a development from a *sentence*-centered explicit (formal) *syntactic* theory towards a *text*-centered explicit (formal) *semiotic* theory.

1.1 The foundations of 'modern linguistics' were laid by Chomsky's *Syntactic Structures* in 1957. This work provided the basis for an exact (formal) *syntax*. A semantic component was later added to it (Katz—Fodor 1963); this component, however, cannot be considered to be semantics in a semiotic sense. The generative transformational grammar integrating this semantic component (Chomsky 1965) is, as a matter of fact, a differentiated syntax, which tries to guarantee grammatical well-formedness to a maximal extent by operating with so-called semantic markers. (Katz 1972)

From 1965 onwards different attempts have been made at correcting the Chomskyan theory.

Some of these attempts remained practically within the Chomsky paradigm. Among these one can count generative semantics which has arisen from the criticism of the interpretive character of the semantic component of the Chomsky theory (cf. e. g. Lakoff 1970, Lakoff 1971, McCawley 1972), and the case-grammar of Fillmore (Fillmore 1968), to mention only those two models which had perhaps the greatest effect. (As to the development and change of the generative transformational grammatical paradigm cf. Maclay 1971.)

Much more important, however, are those attempts which aim to develop a 'new paradigm'. Among these attempts one can place the grammatical/semantic research arising from the conceptions of Lewis and Montague, the different kinds of pragmatic investigations, text-linguistics and, finally, text-grammatical/text-theoretical research.

1.2 Lewis and Montague criticize the Chomsky theory from the point of view of *semantics* taken in a semiotic sense, raising the objection that this theory excluded the real semantic questions from research scope (i.e. the relation between the verbal expressions and their denotata). Lewis and Montague claim that all three elements of the triad "form-meaning-referent" (cf e. g. Lyons 1968) (or use other terms: form-intension-extension [cf. e. g. Carnap 1955]) have to be explicitly (formally) described.

In Lewis 1972 a general semantic framework is outlined, in which the investigation of all three above-mentioned elements is guaranteed. It is claimed that in this framework a syntax built up either with or without transformations can function as a syntactic component. The only reservation made is that this syntactic component has to be a categorial-grammatical component.

Montague outlined the construction of a so-called universal grammar, which consists of an intensional logic and an extensional component, and described different fragments of natural language. (Cf. Montague 1968, 1970a, 1970c, 1972.)

A comprehensive survey of the problems of categorial-grammatic/ model theoretical research is given in Cresswell 1973.

Generative semantic studies and the research emerging from the conceptions of Lewis and Montague have had a considerable influence on the investigation of the different non-classical logics, and these investigations again contribute towards the development of different complex (model theoretical) semantics. (As for respective bibliographical information cf.: Petöfi (ed.), in press.)

1.3 The investigation of *pragmatic* questions is twice as complicated as syntactic or semantic considerations. On the one hand, the formalizability of the description of the pragmatic aspects has been much discussed and, on the other hand, even those non-formal researches were not as much concerned with this aspect as with the other two.

Pragmatic questions are partly dealt with by the ordinary language philosophy (Austin 1962, Caton 1963, Searle 1969), and partly by the so-called formal pragmatic investigations (Bar—Hillel 1954, Montague 1968, Stalnaker 1970). The former research is primarily focussed on the performative elements, while the latter is primarily focussed on the so-called deictic indices. Montague calls the theoretical language, by means of which the elements of a natural language and their relations can be described, pragmatic language.

Those socio-linguistic studies which also started with the claim of correcting the Chomsky-conception can also be ranked, in some respects, together with the pragmatic research. However, while among the pragmatic studies there are attempts to treat the syntactic, semantic, and pragmatic aspects in the homogeneous framework of an explicit theory, no such socio-linguistic attempts are known yet.

1.4 The above-mentioned studies are, almost without exception sentence-centered research. The text-centered studies wish to correct the Chomsky-conception from another point of view.

If one wants to evaluate these researches, a basic question must be decided: what is the par excellence basic-unit of verbal communication, the sentence or the text? What should be developed, a sentence-grammar or a text-grammar?

The answer of an ever growing number of linguists to this question is that the basic unit is the text and one must aim at developing a text-grammar (even if only a few of them declare this latter aim explicitly).

Linguistic investigations concerning texts can roughly be divided into two groups: investigations which are focussed on single aspects of texts (these can be called text-linguistic investigations), and investigations aiming at the development of a theoretical framework, within which the single text-specific aspects can be described in a way compatible with each other (these can be called text-grammatical or text-theoretical investigations). Text-specific aspects are, among others, the following: the use of proforms (e. g. pronomina, proadverbs, proverbs), the co-reference, presupposition and consequence, the quantifiers referring to something beyond the frames of the sentence, the connective elements, the topic-comment relation, the modality of texts, etc. (Concerning the text-centered investigations cf. van Dijk 1972, Dressler

1972, Dressler—Schmidt 1973, Petöfi 1971, Petöfi—Rieser (eds.) 1973, Petöfi—Rieser 1974b, Rieser 1974.)

It must be pointed out here that all fields of investigation in which linguistics plays an important role (literary studies, jurisprudence, theology, documentation theory, to mention just a few) support the primacy of investigating texts, too.

1.5 From the above considerations it is easy to conclude that the *semiotic theory of natural languages* must be a *text-centered theory*, the aim of which is to provide an explicit and mutually compatible description of the *syntactic, semantic* and *pragmatic* aspects in a complex theoretical framework. Theoretical research (and its control in practice) seems to substantiate that it is possible to establish such a complex theory. In this complex theory one cannot speak of a syntactic, semantic and pragmatic component as distinct theoretical components, since it does not seem to be justifiable that these aspects should be described separately from one another (cf. Petöfi 1974b).

If we reserve the term 'text theory' for indicating such a comprehensive theory, which aims at describing *all* aspects of texts, the complex text-centered *semiotic* theory can be called a 'partial theory of texts'.

2. BEYOND THE SENTENCE

In this section I wish to analyse briefly two questions which are the basic questions of all theories aiming at a grammatical description and semantic interpretation of texts. These questions are the following: Do we need a grammar with or without transformations? Does text grammar exist at all?

2.1 The question of *transformations* has been much discussed in linguistic research — also in the logic-oriented approaches. If we examine these discussions we find that one equally argues for and against them. As far as the counter-arguments are concerned, none of them is strong enough to preclude the possibility of developing an exact transformational grammar once and for all. Logicians like Lewis and linguists like Partee who aim at constructing a logically-based grammar, not only accept the possibility of applying transformations, they also go into the details of different aspects of transformations (cf. Lewis 1972, Partee 1972).

I, for my part, wish to mention two arguments in favour of the transformations.

First: It is an empirical fact that in the majority of cases the same thought can be expressed in different 'linguistic forms'. This property of natural language must be reflected in grammar too, and this can be done by deriving different linguistic forms of expression from one single (logico-)semantic representation which is indifferent as to the form of expression. (The rules of this derivation are generally called 'transformations'.)

Second: There is no doubt that in those grammars which do not operate with transformations the relationsship between different linguistic forms of expression can also be represented by means of a subsidiary component. However, if a non-transformational grammar claims to represent these relations and contains an appropriate subsidiary component then this complex grammar is a mere notational variant of a transformational grammar and it is certainly much more complicated than a transformational grammar. From this one can conclude that a transformational grammar is much more suitable for the description of natural languages than a grammar without transformations.

The difference between the "different linguistic forms" is, however, not only a difference between elements of the same order. It is not only the case that the same thought can, in many cases, be expressed *either* by different words *or* by different sentences *or* by different texts, but also by different words *and* by different sentences *and* by different texts. The description of this phenomenon requires a special transformational grammar (and a special lexicon).

2.2 I do not wish to deal with the questions of constructing a *lexicon* in detail, I rather want to confine myself to two remarks.

If the lexicon is regarded as a suitable means for revealing and describing semantic relations, (a) it is necessary to assign not mere semantic characteristics but definitions to the theoretical conctructs representing words in the lexicon, and it follows from this that (b) a class of defining elements and a class of elements to be defined must be distinguished within the lexicon, and (c) the definitions must be free of circularity.

The definientes (=explicit intension-representations) in the lexicon permit the construction of explicit sentence-intension and text-intension representations. This means that, on the one hand, it is possible to derive those linguistic forms of expression from a sentence-intension or a text-intension representation, which can be considered as equivalent and, on the other hand, the inferences that can be drawn from the sentence/text, and the presuppositions (or at least one part of the presuppositions) that can be assigned to the sentence/text can be established unambiguously.

Both the linguistic and/or logico-linguistic, and the applied linguistic (documentation-theoretical) research tend more and more to accept this model of a lexicon. (Cf. Petöfi 1974 c.)

2.3 As far as the above-mentioned special grammar is concerned, the opinions of linguists and logicians are divided. The question arising here not only involves the problem whether this special grammar should be a text grammar or a sentence grammar, but also the problem whether a text grammar exists at all or not. Those arguing against the existence or necessity of a text grammar insist on saying that all phenomena which text-grammatical research has claimed to describe so far can also be described by means of a sentence grammar (cf. e. g. Dascal-Margalit 1974).

Though the question what we call a grammar that is capable of supplying a full grammatical description of natural language texts is only subsidiary, I want to show in what follows that it is not justified to call this special grammar a 'sentence-grammar'.

I want to elucidate this question by a short demonstration of a few rules of the formation rule system of the grammatical component of a special partial theory of text. This *partial theory of text* is the so-called 'text-structure-world-structure theory', abbreviated: TeSWeST.

The TeSWeST is an empirically motivated logic-oriented theory aiming at the grammatical description of a text as a complex sign (*intensional semantic description*) and the assignment of the possible extensional interpretations to the intensional-semantically described text structure (*extensional-semantic description*). The intensional-semantic and extensional-semantic descriptions are such that they also contain the description of the pragmatic aspects. (Cf. Petöfi 1973, Petöfi 1974a, 1974b, 1975 and Petöfi—Rieser 1974a.)

The grammatical component of the TeSWeST is a generative transformational text grammar operating with linearly not fixed canonic basic structures.

The formation rule system of this grammar consists of a so-called communicative rule describing a (full or partial) communicative situation and of rules generating an intensional semantic representation (cf. Petöfi 1973.)

The communicative rule (R^C) can be verbalized as follows:

A communicative basis (TB^C) is a communicative predicate-complex; a communicator (C_1) communicates (COMM) to a (potential) communicator/interpreter (C_2) at a given time ($*\varphi^t$) in a given place ($*\varphi^l$) the message TB.

In a formal representation:

$$[R^C] \quad TB^C \ := \ [*\varphi^t \wedge *\varphi^l] \ \{[COMM] \ \{ \ a{:}C_1 \quad e{:}C_2 \quad o{:}TB \}\}$$

In this rule TB is the canonical representation ($=Text\text{-}Basis$) of the message in the form specified by the TeSWeST. The communicative situation is a partial one if the interpretation is produced at another time and/or in another place.

The generative rule system generates intension-representations.

The first generative rule (R_0) is as follows:

The TB is composed of two parts: (1) a normed (implicit or explicit) representation of a text intension (TLeR/TSeR) and (2) an information block (T Ω) which contains all (transformational) informations which determine, how a linearized text (also capable of functioning as an object language unit — cf R^c) has to be derived from this normed representation.

The normed implicit representation of the text intension is called *Text Lexical Representation*/TLeR/; the elements of the TLeR are definienda in the lexicon. The normed explicit representation of the text intension is called *Text Semantic Representation*/TSeR/; the elements of the TSeR are definientes in the lexicon.

In a formal representation:

[R_0]   TB := : TLeR/TSeR + TΩ

The second generative rule (R_1) specifies the structure of the TLeR/ TEsR)

The TLeR/TSeR is composed of the following components:
— the set of the description of those objects which are acting or mentioned in the text ($<d>$);
— the set of the normed representations of the complex or simple propositions manifested in the text ($<P\square>$);
— the connex of the normed representation of simple S-units having the same order as the units which traditional terminology called 'sentences' ($S\square$);
— the set of the thematic nets ($<ThN>$);
  (the number of the thematic nets is equal to the number of the objects; i.e. each object constitutes a net; those propositions are included in one net which contain the object constituting the net in one of their argument places);
— the logical/temporal net ($L\tau N$);
  the logical/temporal net is the net of the logical/temporal relations between the propositions manifested in the text);
— the set of the communicative nets ($<CoN>$);
  (a communicative net contains the propositions which have been communicated in identical communicative situations);
— a reference relation diagram (D_{RefRel})
  (The reference relation diagram indicates, which object has been brought into direct or indirect connection with which other object by the text).

In a formal representation:

[$R1$]   TLeR/TSeR := : $<<d>, <P^\square>, S^\square, <ThN>, L\tau N,$
        $<CoN>, D_{RefRel} >$

(The Roman letter symbols "d", "P", and "S" indicate constants. In later rules they appear in the corresponding Greek letter forms and then stand for variables.)

The third generative rule (R₂) specifies the structure of a Σ -connex: A Σ-connex consists either of one simple Σ-element or more than one Σ -connexes connected by means of connective elements.

In a formal representation:

$$[R2] \quad \Sigma^{\square} :=: \left| \begin{array}{c} \Sigma \\ \varphi^{C(n)} \ \Sigma_1^{\square}, \dots, \Sigma_n^{\square} \end{array} \right| \quad (\ \varphi^{C(n)} \text{ indicates a connective}$$

element (connective functor) which connects "n" elements ("n" arguments) with each other.

In a Σ-connex the "n" elements are, depending on the connective functor, either dependent on or independent of each other. (This is the first recursive rule of the rule system.)

Finally, the last rule that is of interest for us here (R₃) determines/ specifies the structure of a simple Σ-element:

A simple Σ-element is an S-function (an implicit performative predicate-function) containing a complex (or simple) proposition-function $(\Pi\square)$ as its "o"-argument. The task of the implicit performative functor $(\ \varphi^P)$ is to determine the so-called simple modality: assertion (ASS), question (QUE), command (IMP), wish (OPT).

In a formal representation:

$$[R3] \quad \Sigma:=: [\ \varphi^P] \ \{ \text{a:Pers1 e: Pers2 o:} \Pi \ \square \}$$

The other rules of the rule system determine the structure of a complex proposition and that of its constituents. With these rules I do not want to deal here.

Now we can attempt to find an answer to the question "Does text grammar exist at all?" on the basis of the rules R2 and R3.

Let us consider the following text:

Lucky Fisherman

HUSBAND (to his wife): I don't see why you are so cross with me. Haven't I been really lucky in my fishing this time?

WIFE: You have, I am sure. But when you go fishing next time, you will let *me* buy all the fish for you to bring home. If I choose it myself it will at least be fresh.

This text contains the following S-elements (without going into details of the internal structure of the single S-elements):

S_3: [ASS] I don't see why you are so cross with me
S_4: [QUE] I haven't been really lucky in my fishing this time

S_5: [ASS] You have been really lucky, I am sure

S_6: [ASS] You go fishing next time

S_7 [ASS] You will let *me* buy all the fish for you to bring home

S_8: [ASS] I choose all the fish for you to bring home

S_9: [ASS] All the fish for you to bring home will at least be fresh

S_3 and S_4, and S_5—S_9, respectively, are connected to S-connexes ($S_1^{\Box}$ and $S_2^{\Box}$, respectively) in the following way

$S_1^{\Box} \; :=: \; \text{AND2} \; S_3 \; S_4$

$S_2^{\Box} \; :=: \; \text{BUT} \; S_3 \; S_5^{\Box}$

$\qquad S_3^{\Box} \; :=: \; \text{SINCE} \; S_4^{\Box} \; S_5^{\Box}$

$\qquad\qquad S_4^{\Box} \; :=: \; \text{IF -THEN} \; S_9 \; S_8$

$\qquad\qquad\quad S_5^{\Box} \; :=: \; \text{WHEN -THEN} \; S_7 \; S_6$

$S_1^{\Box}$ and $S_2^{\Box}$ are inserted in explicit communicative units in the following way:

$S_1 \; :=: \; [\text{COMMUNICATE}]\{a{:}\text{HUSBAND} \; e{:}\text{WIFE} \; o{:}S_1^{\Box}\}$

$S_2 \; :=: \; [\text{COMMUNICATE}] \{a{:}\text{WIFE} \; e{:}\text{HUSBAND} \; o{:}S_2^{\Box}\}$

Finally, S_1 and S_2 are united to the following S-connex

$S_0^{\Box} \; :=: \; \text{AFTER} \; S_1 \; S_2$

(In these representations "AND2" does not contain any information about the order of the arguments following it, the other connectives do. "BUT X Y" has to be interpreted as "Y BUT X" (and similarly also "SINCE X Y"). "IF —THEN X Y" has to be interpreted as "IF Y THEN X" (and similarly also "WHEN —THEN X Y").

It is not to be questioned that $S^{\Box}$ can also be represented, by means of some 'acrobatics', as a sentence (for instance by transforming the implicit performative elements pertaining to S_3 and S_4 /ASS, QUE/ into explicit performative elements). However, this is not the basic question. The basic question is, in how many and which ways $S^{\Box}$ can be represented as a text. The analysis of those conditions which determine the possible forms of representation, cannot be considered as a sentence grammatical operation. One of the text grammatical operations par excellence is the assignment of all possible interpretations (also the interpretation as a sentence-closing punctuation-mark) to the connective elements of the TSeR.

Even if the question "text grammar vs. sentence grammar" should be nothing else but a terminological question, it is worth considering whether it is not more motivated to call a sentence an "atomic text" rather than calling a text a "complex sentence" (if only because of the operations with punctuation marks!).

2.4 If we examine the discussion and the rule-system fragment demonstrated above, we find four points where this grammar (together with the lexicon of course) operates on structures beyond the sentence.

(a) The first point is the application of the rules R2—R3. These rules can result in an intensional semantic representation which cannot be called a sentence-representation. Even if one can say that the use of pro-forms and the co-reference are phenomena also occurring in sentences, the interpretation of connective elements as *sentence-closing* punctuation marks or intonation *within* a representation can by no means be called a sentence-grammatical operation.

(b) The second point is the derivation of equivalent linguistic expressions, the drawing of inferences and the determining of presuppositions on the basis of an intensional semantic representation. The point is that this grammar does not only permit the derivation of *one* single sentence or text but also of a number of sentences or texts from the same semantic representation.

(c) The third point is the application of the communicative rule (R^c) which enables the explicit representation of certain information referring to the communicative situation of the sentence or text.

In the case of (b) and (c) one could even say that this grammar operates with structures which point not only beyond the sentence but also beyond the text.

(d) The fourth point is the lexicon itself. The structure of the definientes in the lexicon is specified by the formational rule system of the TeSWeST. This means that the representation of the definientes can also be manifested as a text. ((a) and (b) also apply to the definientes.)

3. BETWEEN LINGUISTICS AND LOGIC

The last question I want to discuss in this study is: Is the semiotic theory of texts linguistics or logic — or none of them?

First of all some remarks on 'text theory'. The theory aiming at the description of the semantic (and the pragmatic) aspects of sentences (taking these aspects in the semiotic sense) is given different names by different researchers. Lewis speaks of "general semantics", Montague speaks of a "universal grammar". I call the *semiotic* theory which aims at the same with respect to texts, a *partial theory of text*. This theory contains, as already mentioned, in addition to the grammatical component, an extensional-semantic component as well.

It is rather difficult to establish the theoretical status of this partial theory of text. It cannot clearly be categorised as linguistics, because it applies (modal) logical constructs when representing intensions and it operates with truth values and possible worlds in the extensional semantic component. However, it cannot be categorised as logic either, because it is not (or not in all details) as exact as a logic should be.

The task of the extensional semantic component is to assign possible extensional semantic interpretations (models) to the possible intensional semantic representations of the text. When constructing extensional semantic interpretations, the 'pattern' is the model-theoretical interpretation taken in a logical sense.

This interpretation should be made possible or easier by the rules R_0 and $R1$ of the grammar. The rule R_0 does this by specifying such a TLeR/TSeR which contains all informations that are necessary for the extensional semantic interpretation — and only those. (All other informations are contained in the $T\Omega$ block.)

$R1$ does this by requiring that the structure of the intensional semantic representation of the text be constructed in an immediately extensionalizable form.

The model-theoretical interpretation is, however, only a goal, a possibility, which cannot be realized without further research. The two main tasks of this research are the following:

(a) the elaboration of methods for interpreting *all* S-structures with a simple or complex modality as elements that belong to a TLeR/TSeR;

(b) the assignment of possible worlds to *texts*.

This requires the further development and modification of certain special logics and the integration of all necessary special logics. It is not certain whether this can be solved in a way that will allow the integrated logic to remain a 'logic' that logicians would still be inclined to accept.

To elaborate an empirically motivated and logic-oriented partial theory of text — thus also to elaborate the TeSWeST — the following strategy seems to be expedient:

(a) outline the framework of a general theory on the basis of a thorough analysis of the results of linguistic and logical research,

(b) check the applicability of this general theoretical framework by analysing texts of different languages and/or grammatical/extensional semantic aspects,

(c) a continuous refinement of the theoretical framework on the basis of empirical work and the results of new theoretical research.

Only when the framework seems to be suitable for the descriptions of single aspects in ways compatible with each other within this framework will it be possible to start with a systematic elaboration of partial text theories for different languages.

The research on the TeSWeST is at present in the phase (b)—(c), and it will probably remain in this phase for a long time to come. It is possible that the components of the TeSWeST will not be equally exact even in their final form. This is, however, no crucial point, if we know the achievable grade of exactness with respect to each component.

4. CONCLUDING REMARKS

In this study I tried to present some of the aspects of text-grammatical and text-theoretical research.

From the complexity of the text structures it follows that the full development of a text theory (or a partial text theory, thus the TeSWeST, too) can only be accomplished by *interdisciplinary cooperation*. Only such cooperation can explore the relevance of the results achieved by investigations in single semiotic aspects so far, the integratability of the relevant results into a comprehensive framework, and a satisfactory exploration of those aspects which have not yet been explored at all or have not been resolved satisfactorily.

The TeSWeST is meant to be a first step towards the development of such an interdisciplinary cooperation.

BIBLIOGRAPHY

Austin, J. L., 1962, *How to do things with words*, Oxford: University Press.
Bar-Hillel, Y., 1954, "Indexical expressions". *Mind, 63,* 359—379.
Carnap, R., 1955, "Meaning and synonymy in natural languages", *Philosophical Studies 6,* 33—47.
Caton, Ch. E., 1963, *Philosophy and ordinary language*, Urbana: University of Illinois Press.
Chomsky, N., 1957, *Syntactic structures*, The Hague: Mouton.
    1965, *Aspects of the theory of syntax*, Cambridge, Mass.: M.I.T. Press.
Cresswell, M. J., 1973, *Logics and languages*, London: Methuen & Co Ltd.
Dascal, M.-A. Margalit, 1974, "A New 'Revolution' in Linguistics? — Text-Grammars' vs. 'Sentence-Grammars' ", *Theoretical Linguistics 1*, pp. 195—213.
van Dijk, T. A., 1972 *Some aspects of text grammars. A study in theoretical linguistics and poetics*, The Hague: Mouton.
Dressler, W., 1972, *Einführung in die Textlinguistik*, Tübingen: Niemeyer.
Dressler, W. U.—S. J. Schmidt, 1973, *Textlinguistik: Kommentierte Biblio graphie*, München: Fink.
Fillmore, C. J., 1968, "The case for case". In: Bach, E. and R. T. Harms (eds.), *Universals in Language*, New York: Holt, Rinehart.

Katz, J. J., 1972, *Semantic theory*, New York: Harper & Rom.

Katz, J. J. and J. A. Fodor, 1963, "The structure of a semantic theory", *Language, 39.* 170—210.

Lakoff, G., 1970, "Linguistics and natural logic". Ann Arbor: Phonetics Laboratory, University of Michigan. Revised version in *Synthese, 22* (1971), 151—271.

— 1971, "On generative semantics". In: Steinberg, D. D. and L. A. Jakobovits (eds.), *Semantics, an interdisciplinary reader*, Cambridge: University Press.

Lewis, D., 1972, "General semantics". In: Davidson, D. and G. Harman (eds.), *Semantics of natural language*, Dordrecht: Reidel, 169—218.

Lyons, J., 1968, *Introduction to theoretical linguistics*, Cambridge: University Press.

Maclay, H., 1971, "Overview". In: Steinberg, D. D. and L. A. Jakobovits (eds), *Semantics, an interdisciplinary reader*, Cambridge: University Press.

McCawley, J. D., 1972, "A program for logic". In: Davidson, D. annd G. Harman (eds.), *Semantics of natural language*, Dordrecht: Reidel, 498—544.

Montague, R., 1968, "Pragmatics". In: Klibansky, R. (ed.), *La philosophie contemporaine. I. Logique et fondements des Mathématiques*, Firenze: La Nuova Italia Editrice, 102—123.

— 1970a, "English as a formal language" In: Visentini, B. et al. (eds.), *Linguaggi nella societa e nella tecnica*, Milan: Edizioni di Communita, 189—224.

— 1970b, "Pragmatics and intensional logic". *Synthese, 22,* 68—94.

— 1970c, "Universal grammar". *Theoria, 36.*

— 1972, "The proper treatment of quantification in ordinary English". In: Hintikka, J. et al. (eds.), *Approaches to natural language*, Dordrecht: Reidel, 221—242.

Morris, C. W., 1938, *Foundations of the theory of signs,* Chicago.

Partee, B., 1972, "Some transformational extensions of Montague grammar." In: Rodman, R. (ed.), *Papers in Montague grammar* (=Occasional Papers in Linguistics, No. 2 UCLA) California: University, 1—24.

Petöfi, J. S., 1971, *Transformationsgrammatiken und eine ko-textuelle Texttheorie. Grundfragen und Konzeptionen*, Frankfurt: Athenäum.

— 1973, "Towards an empirically motivated grammatical theory of verbal texts". In: Petöfi, J. S. and H. Rieser (eds.) *Studies in text grammar*, Dordrecht: Reidel, 205—275.

— 1974a, "New trends in typology of texts and text grammars (Aspects of the typology of texts — aspects of a theory of text)", General report delivered at the First Congress of the International Association for Semiotic Studies, Milan, Juni 1974.

— 1974b, "Semantics — pragmatics — text theory" Working Paper, University of Bielefeld. (Also as No. 36 in *Working papers and prepublications*, Centre Internazionale di Semiotica e di Linguistica, Università di Urbino.)

— 1974c "Some aspects of a multi-purpose thesaurus." *International Classification* 1 (1974) No. 2, 69—76.

— 1975 *Vers une théorie partielle du texte* (= Papers in textlinguistics, Volume 9.) Hamburg: Buske.

Petöfi, J. S. (ed.), in press, *Logic and the formal theory of natural language (Selective bibliography)* (= Papers in textlinguistics, Volume 10.), Hamburg: Buske.

Petöfi, J. S. — H. Rieser, 1974a, *Probleme der modelltheoretischen Interpretation von Texten* (=Papers in textlinguistics, Volume 7.), Hamburg: Buske.

— 1974b, "Some arguments against counter-revolution (On Marcelo Dascal's and Avishai Margalit's A new 'Revolution' in Linguistics? — 'Text-Gram-

mars' vs. 'Sentence-Grammars'." Theoretical Linguistics 1. pp. 195—213)".
To appear.

Petöfi, J. S. — H. Rieser (eds.), 1973, *Studies in text grammar*, Dordrecht: Reidel.

Rieser, H., 1974, "Neuere Problemstellungen und Entwicklungstendenzen in der textgrammatischen Forschung (Bemerkungen zur Ausarbeitung einer textgrammatischen/texttheoretischen Konzeption)". In: van Dijk, T. A.—J. Ihwe—J. S. Petöfi—H. Rieser, *Zur Bestimmung narrativer Strukturen auf der Grundlage von Textgrammatiken* (=Papers in textlinguistics, Volume 1.) 2nd edition. Hamburg: Buske.

Searle, J. R., 1969, *Speech acts. An essay in the philosophy of language*, Cambridge: University Press.

Searle, J. R. (ed.), 1971, *The philosophy of language*, Oxford: University Press.

Stalnaker, R. C., 1970, "Pragmatics". *Synthese*, 22, 272—289.

Pauli Saukkonen
University of Oulu

Investigating Finnish textemes and allotexts[1]

The smallest unit of concrete speech that incorporates both a sign component and a meaning component is a morph, and the largest corresponding unit is a text, or the particular concrete speech as a whole. The total grammar of performance is a text grammar, which contains all the rules needed for generation a terminal text. The composition of a text is investigated by text linguistics.

The smallest unit of language, an abstract class composed of infinitely many speeches, that contains both a sign component and a meaning component is a morpheme, and the largest corresponding abstract unit is a texteme, or the particular language, i. e. a class of infinite texts. The total grammar of competence is a texteme grammar. The branch of linguistics dealing with texteme grammar can be called texteme linguistics.

Separate individual languages figure most importantly in the taxonomy of textemes. But they are naturally not the only abstractions: there are both larger subdivisions of human language (e. g. language families) and smaller ones (which I have called microlanguages, see *Linguistics* 108, p. 72). It is not even possible always to say definitely whether we are dealing with a separate language or a subdivision of one language. Textemes thus constitute a hierarchical set, where textemes of all degrees are essentially similar classes of allotexts composed of infinite texts.

Each actual concrete text or imaginary abstract texteme is located in a spatio-temporal frame or context. The context of communication has three obligatory sub-contexts: the sender, the channel and the receiver. The channel is the transferrer element or medium-energy where the signs of the language exist. The signs also reach the sender and the receiver (the speaking, writing, hearing and seeing organs). Bearing in mind that meaning is not transferred, but only exists in the memories of the sender and the receiver, we can draw the following diagram of the total context of communication and the linguistic context as its subset.

---

[1] As background and reference for this article, I recommend Nils Erik Enkvist's excellent books *Linguistic Stylistics* (1973) and *Stilforskning och stilteori* (1974).

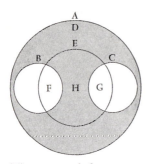

A = context of communication
B = sender
C = receiver
D = (A minus B minus C, the shaded part) channel
E = linguistic context (text or texteme)
F = meaning
G = meaning
H = (E minus F minus G) sign
A minus E = extralinguistic context

The text and the texteme are defined according to one or several characteristics of the context. For example, the hypothetical texteme 'the speech of a Finnish politician of the 1970's to a large undefined group of adults' (which is not restricted to the speeches actually produced) has been defined according to the sender, channel and receiver of the extralinguistic context. An example of a precise, narrow and uniquely concrete linguistic context is this sentence, which can be defined in terms of both signs and meanings. The following are examples of abstract contexts delimited on the basis of extralinguistic content: novel, pop song, subjective information, instructive, reporting and expository information, question, answer, sports commentary, art review, travel book, and research report. Extralinguistic content and its relation to linguistic meaning are not discussed further here.

According to the diagram, the text/texteme is determined by the quality, quantity and location of the sender, channel and receiver, because it is their subset. Generalizing, we can say that each different context requires an appropriate text/texteme and that the differences between texts/textemes are directly proportional to the differences between their extralinguistic contexts.

The ultimate texteme, human language, is divided by considerable extralinguistic differences into individual languages, which are further divided by smaller extralinguistic or linguistic contextual differences into microlanguage textemes. The different types of microlanguage have been given such names as dialect, slang, register, sociolect and style. The use of these terms is not consistent, and the microlanguage delimited according to the temporal context (current language vs. historical forms of language) has no name at all. To eliminate this unnecessary diversity, we might choose, say, the following alternative: that a microlanguage determined by the sender be called a dialect and one determined by the receiver and the channel a style. According to this view, each dialect has different styles and each style different dialects.

Abstract classes of texts can in principle be formed ad infinitum, but not all classes are distinctive from the viewpoint of linguistic rules. Some classes have a greater functional load than the others. For example, the rules for playing badminton (which may consist of innumerable different texts) do not constitute any significant subdivision of language.

They are merely a variant of a larger textemic whole, which is significantly distinctive in regard to normativity. The concept of texteme, including the microlanguage texteme, should be restricted to refer to a set of texts/subtextemes which differs significantly from the other subdivisions of language and which is hence recognized as a functional whole. Textemes can be analyzed by a substitution method similar to that used for phonemes and morphemes. If texts placed in one context all have a function appropriate to this context, they are allotexts of one texteme, but if any text brings about a change in contextual function, it is a variant of another texteme. Since textemes are identifiable wholes formed in the competence of the speakers, they often also have an established name. Among such probable textemes are 'the news', 'the law' and 'the drama'.

No exhaustive account has been given of the textemes of Finnish, or any other language. I therefore initiated a research project towards this objective in the Department of Finnish and Lappish of the University of Oulu in 1967. Our purpose is to find out the different microlanguage textemes in the Finnish of the mass media of the 1960's. The object has been defined contextually according to the principles mentioned above. Though the requirement for exact delimitation of the type of language to be described is quite self-evident, the grammars of Finnish, for example, do not state explicitly what kind of linguistic whole they purport to deal with. The language described in them is primarily current written standard language (even the temporal delimitation is lacking), but, judging from the examples given, it is mainly restricted to the language of fiction, newspapers and periodicals as well as the authors' personal idiolects. It is difficult to say whether this really constitutes a distinct textemic whole.

The abstract basic population for which material has been analyzed is divided according to the type of channel, i. e. the different media. The following categories are included: a) the newspapers and periodicals of 1967, b) the fiction and non-fiction of 1961—1967, and c) the speech programmes originally made for the radio during Sept. 19, 1968 —May 26, 1969. There is also a reference material of informal standard spoken Finnish, for which the basic population consisted of the conversational speech of two populations in 1968. The common basic population defined above was further reduced by excluding the titles, lists, translations and dialectal texts. This original context was classified according to a subjective substitution method into subcontexts corresponding to hypothetical textemes. Altogether 58 subcontexts were obtained, when a minimum of 30 different speakers or writers was required for the material of each subcontext. The final classification is given in the following list, which also shows the size of the material as words.

PERIODICALS
Articles (6 657 words)
News (6 808)

Causeries (6 155)
Religious writings (5 983)
Articles for young people (5 591)
Reviews of non-fiction (7 529)
Art reviews (7 541)
Reportage (6 769)

NEWSPAPERS

Articles (7 005)
News (6 767)
Reportage (6 894)
Columns (7 331)
Art reviews (7 533)
Sports commentaries (6 572)

PERIODICALS AND NEWSPAPERS

Advertisements (6 437)
Picture captions (6 431)

FICTION

Dramas (6 369)
Dramas for young people (6 361)
Poetry (6 771)
Causeries (7 142)
Narrative prose (6 976)
Narrative prose for young people (6 705)
Narrative prose for children (6 643)

NON-FICTION

Religious books (7 139)
Autobiographies (7 433)
Travel books (7 004)
Encyclopedias (7 057)
Laws (7 116)
Books on religion (8 048)
Books on philosophy (8 164)
Books on history (7 908)
Books on society (8 239)
Books on economy (7 832)
Books on administration (8 225)
Books on jurisdiction (12 366)
Reports of commitees (9 477)
Books on mathematics (7 196)
Books on biology (7 335)
Books on medicine (7 410)

Books on agriculture (7 204)
Books on technology (7 360)
Books on housekeeping and hobbies (7 295)
Humanistic research (8 110)
Social research (8 518)
Mathematico-technical research (7 617)
Biologico-medical research (8 422)

RADIO

News reports (7 104)
Current affairs reports (7 238)
Sports commentaries (7 156)
Lectures (7 531)
Radio plays (6 440)
Religious speeches (6 814)
Narrative frames for school programmes (6 687)
Narrative frames for young people's programmes (6 844)
Narrative frames (6 924)
Interviewees' speeches (8 826)
Panel discussions (7 951)

Informal standard spoken language (12 041)

The (con)texts have been delimited mainly on the basis of content. The texts have not been defined according to the sender, though the content is naturally associated with the sender (we know the sender of a news report is a news editor, the sender of a research report a scholar, etc.). All the textemes discovered can be called styles. Among the texts delimited according to the receiver are those intended for young people and children. The channel factor has an effect on all the texts, as implied by the contextual main division.

Each of the 58 (con)texts comprises a random sample of 100 concrete texts, which are extracts of five sentences and a minimum of 60 words. One material text class of this kind, however, represents a whole infinite context. For example, "the articles of periodicals" is an abstract text, and the concrete sample of 6 657 words stands for all the possible, actually produced and imaginary unproduced articles meant for periodicals in 1967. The inferences and generalizations to be made from the material hence apply to this infinite set. In the text — texteme — allotext terminology. such an abstract text refers literally to a text. Whether the text constitutes a texteme (microlanguage) remains to be verified by research. The original classification of texts is only a tentative one, giving classes which may be contextually functional textemes. Our objective has been to establish linguistic wholes which are generally recognized and sufficiently large materially on the one hand, and as delicately classified and homogeneous as possible on the other. The UDK classification of libraries has been used as an auxiliary criterion. Some of the texts will probably turn out as allotexts. One may justly doubt in advance whether, say, the articles of periodicals and newspapers, or the causeries of periodicals and fiction are mutually distinctive.

As is maintained in the present-day stylistics and sociolinguistics, the differences between different texts and different textemes are quantitative. Texts/textemes can be compared by means of relative frequencies. The rules of concrete texts have exact frequencies, while the rules of abstract texts/textemes have probability values. Comparative research is thus always quantitative-statistical. Historical comparative description, which deals with the differences between texts/textemes with different temporal contexts, follows the same principles. The next simple example presents semantically different Finnish one-word "texts" delimited simultaneously according to the temporal context and the social context.

Temporal context		in the year x	in x+200	in x+400
Social context	Meaning of *kynä*	%	%	%
Scholars	1. 'groove e. g. the tip of the shaft of a bird's feather'	50	0	0
	2. 'a shaft of a feather used for writing'	50	100	0
	3. 'a writing instrument, a pen'	0	0	100
		100	100	100
Non-scholars	1. 'groove, e. g. the tip of the shaft of a bird's feather'	100	50	0
	2. 'a shaft of a feather used for writing'	0	50	0
	3. 'a writing instrument, a pen'	0	0	100
		100	100	100

Comparisons can be made between any of the six contexts ($=$ squares). It appears, for example, that the language of scholars in the year x is identical in this respect with the language spoken by non-scholars in the year x+200, but differs by 50 % from the language spoken by non-scholars in that year. Though historical comparison has generally not been based on quantification, the differences are, in fact, quantitative differences of all the common and separate qualities. Thus linguistic changes are also quantitative changes, as shown by the preceding example. The change can be interpreted as follows:

1. 'groove, e. g. the tip of the shaft of a bird's feather	100 %		0 %
2. 'a shaft of a feather used for writing'	0 %	>	0 %
3. 'a writing instrument, a pen'	0 %		100 %

The question of how gradual or sudden the change is remains a matter of descriptive detail, i. e. the answer depends on how gradual or sudden changes of the context are taken into account (the contexts in our example were extreme). The result can be seen as a difference in the quantitative values.

The ultimate goal of the project is to write the grammars of all the enumerated (con)texts according to the quantification principles given above. Such comparative grammars incorporate the field of stylistics, which is based on quantitative description and has existed separately so far, for stylistics is merely a grammar of style. The nature of the qualitative rules to be quantified cannot be discussed here.

The analysis is carried out by a computer. Since the texts are abstract and the material is a sample, the statistical significance of the relative frequencies (%) must be tested. If the relative frequencies of a given phenomenon differ significantly in two texts, the texts are factually different in this respect and the phenomenon acts as an indicator of the text. In the opposite case it is concluded that the texts are homogeneous. Not all statistically significant differences, however, are linguistically significant in the sense that they would be recognized as contextually functional and distinctive. In other words, some of the statistical differences only bring about differences at the allotext level, while some others — when they are sufficiently great and recognizable — give rise to differences at the textemic level. The textemes are eventually identified by substitution tests; the computer analysis only reveals the characteristics and mutual quantitative differences.

A number of analyses made as graduate theses are already available. Though the texts/textemes as a whole cannot be characterized until the entire grammar has been dealt with, I here give some preliminary results as an example. It seems that the different (con)texts combine into the following two fields, when the variables consist of word classes and sentence constituents placed on the coordinate axes in such a way as to correlate negatively with each other.[2]

[2] Similar results are also to be found in the licenciate thesis by Esko Vierikko on the speech of members of the Finnish Parliament ("Parlamenttikielen sanasto- ja lauserakenteesta," Oulu 1947).

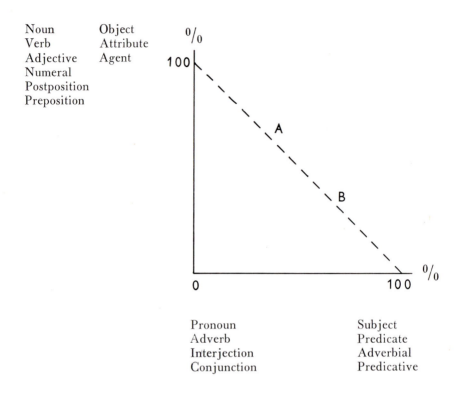

Noun   Object
Verb   Attribute
Adjective   Agent
Numeral
Postposition
Preposition

Pronoun   Subject
Adverb   Predicate
Interjection   Adverbial
Conjunction   Predicative

The total of 58 texts, which in themselves are either allotexts or textemes, hence make up two larger textemes, which can be defined contextually as follows: A = the receivers are numerous or they are undefined and unknown, the temporal distance between the sender and the receiver and that between the thinking process and the communication process are great, the pragmatic function of language affecting the content is merely descriptive; B = the receivers are few or they are known, the temporal distance between the sender and the receiver and that between the thinking process and the communication process are short, the pragmatic function of language affecting the content is descriptive-emotive-controlling. The former set is a typically written, official and formal texteme, whereas the latter is a typically spoken, unofficial and informal texteme.

S. J. Schmidt
Universität Bielefeld

Reception and interpretation of written texts as problems of a rational theory of literary communication

1. INTERPRETATION: AN OPEN QUESTION

1.1 For a long period the "interpretation" of "literary" texts has been widely regarded as the most difficult and at the same time the most important task of the academic "Literaturwissenschaft"[1] (e. g. W. Kayser, E. Staiger, H. O. Burger et al.). Though this position is still held by many scholars its weakness becomes more and more evident through the results of modern research. To illustrate this thesis, I will just mention some of the objections raised against the traditional concept of interpretation:

(a) up to now, the *Literaturwissenschaft* has not been able to develop a method of interpreting written texts which follows the rules of scientific procedure generally accepted in other disciplines;

(b) because of this lack of methodological procedures the results are in nearly all cases idiosyncratic; most of the interpreters do not argue systematically and only some of them try to provide empirically tested or testable data to confirm or refute their hypotheses;[2]

(c) This idiosyncratic character of many interpretations forces the reader to *believe* in the theses of the interpreter because he can all too seldom prove critically the logical value and the empirical content of the interpreter's results.

Consequently, interpretations normally tend to regulate the reception and evaluation of literary texts implicitly; they secretly build up literary canons and establish aesthetic norms which are then taught as "science" in many institutions of the various educational systems;

(d) interpretation concentrates on the literary text as such, at least in all schools of "werkimmanente Interpretation", "close reading", or "explication de texte". Though contextual, biographical, and cultural information is often used for interpretative statements the relation between the text (= the written linguistic materials), its "meaning", and the background knowledge of the interpreter about the production and reception of the text is very rarely treated in an explicit way. Still less is it given systematic treatment anywhere.

1.2   Recently scholars in different countries have tried to change this situation by developing the outlines of a rational *Literaturwissenschaft* which seriously tries to build up empirically testable theories of literary communication.[3] This means that the philosophical orientation and the scope of research have shifted: from hermeneutics to an analytical philosophy of science (as meta-theoretical basis); and from the consideration of (more or less) isolated literary texts to the analysis of complex processes of literary communication.[4] This shift of orientation must seriously affect the traditional concept of interpretation. Strict semioticians of literary communication such as G. Wienold (1972) declare, for instance, that interpretation is an *object* of research rather than a *method* of research, an object which stands on the same level as other textprocessing-operations, such as condensating or paraphrasing. Other scholars try to redefine the concept of interpretation in the framework of a theory of literary communication (cf. W. Kindt and S. J. Schmidt, 1974) or in the framework of analytical philosophy of science (cf. H. Göttner, 1973).

1.3   In the following pages I will concentrate on the question of how it is possible to define the concept of 'interpretation' as opposed to 'reception' in the framework of a rational *Literaturwissenschaft*, and to describe the possible function of interpretation in a theory of literary communication. This investigation presupposes on the one hand that interpretations actually play an important role in various fields of literary communication, and that, on the other hand, a rational interpretation is *possible* and *useful* in an empirical theory of literary communication.

2.   RECEPTION AND INTERPRETATION OF WRITTEN TEXTS[5]

2.1   Many previous scholars of *Literaturwissenschaft* agree with P. Valéry's thesis: "C'est l'execution du poème qui est le poème". Starting from R. Ingarden's theory of "Konkretisation", through the Prague Structuralists' theory of reception as aesthetic realisation, to W. Iser's theory of the "Appellstruktur der Texte" and W. A. Koch's or G. Wienold's theories of textprocessing, many theories try to explain the relation between literary texts, the reader's activities and text-meanings. (For a detailed report see W. Kindt and S. J. Schmidt, 1974, and S. J. Schmidt, 1974a.) I do not know any theory which has explicitly solved this problem; but recent research has made clear — in my opinion — that an empirical theory of reception would amount to a rational reconstruction of the processes of *understanding* verbal texts, and that such a rational reconstruction is an essential prerequisite of any rational theory of verbal communication (and a fortiori of literary communication).[6]

2.2   In our (1974), W. Kindt and I have tried to develop a model for describing the reception of written verbal texts in order to provide a basis for describing the reception of literary texts.

This model (like any other model) necessarily relies upon some general hypotheses concerning the theory of language and the theory of texts involved. The general hypotheses used here are the following ones:

(a) language is not regarded as a set of signs with a fixed meaning but rather as a dynamic system of communicational "instructors" with a variable meaning-potential which is defined by specifying co-texts and contexts;[7]

(b) a verbal text is the result of selective and combinatorial activities of an author (in a specific social and biographical situation at a certain time t) who tries to convey information to others and to realize communicative intentions by specifying the general meaning-possibilities of linguistic materials through the linguistic co-text and verbalized pragmatic context indicators.

Any model of the production and reception of texts must therefore take into account the integrated set of social and biographical conditions of the author and the reader, including their linguistic capacity, their knowledge of other texts and empirical facts, their experiences etc., which all combine to influence the way they are able to produce and receive texts of different kinds.

2.2.1   We now have to deal with the question: What does it mean to say: a reader R_i "receives" a certain written text T_i at a certain time t_x?

A first general answer might look like this: The reception of T_i by R_i can be described a complex process where R_i assigns a structure TW_i to T_i at t_x. This structure may be specified as a "world/worldsystem" in terms of the semantics of a modal logic. TW_i (= the worldsystem R_i assigns to T_i) has the quality of being a model of T_i.[8] In a somewhat loose way of speaking one might say: at t_x a R_i receives a text by "interpreting" the instructors presented in the text in a sequential order to build up a worldsystem in which these instructions are meaningful. This "interpretation" is influenced by a lot of very complicated factors, co-textual, contextual, individual, socio-cultural, and socio-economic.

To reduce this complexity one might *analytically* construct six steps of the process of reception (I here refer to a proposal of W. Kindt in our paper of 1974, 33 ff.).

(1)   First of all a reader must consciously perceive the written linguistic materials (= *physiological act of reading*). Because of mistakes in reading, omitting words or parts of words, changing the sequence etc. he will normally perceive a reduced or modified variant of T_i, a T'_i.

(2) *The syntactic disambiguation*, where R_i assigns a syntactic structure T''_i to T'_i.

(3) *The semantic disambiguation*, where R_i chooses one of the possible meanings of the polysemical text constituents as the one which seems to him most evident. In other words, R_i assigns such an intensional and extensional interpretation (in R. Carnap's sense of the terms) to the text constituents as are possible in his world-model or world of experience (or Etalon-World, in J. S. Petöfi's definition, see his 1974). This means: R_i specifies the meaning-potential of text-constituents in relation to the co-text and to his Etalon-world (EW).

(4) *The organisation and integration* of the data gained in the operations (2) and (3) into a text world TW_i. This operation works under the condition that R_i regards the states of affairs "constituted" by T''_i and his semantic disambiguation as existing in TW_i at t_x.

(5) The *enlargement of* TW_i by the help of assumptions which R_i regards as *probable* in his EW at t_x.

(6) The *enlargement of* TW_i by the help of additional assumptions which R_i regards as *possible* in his EW at t_x, including personal associations, etc.

In order to specify the concept of 'world' used in this paper one might say that 'world' is identical with that structure which contains all the information R_i has at his disposal in the beginning of his reading process. Both the intensions and the extensions of the text constituents he perceives must be implied in his EW at t_x.

2.2.2 In this paper I cannot go into further details of this model of reception. I can only add a few remarks about some general features of the reception. An essential feature is undoubtedly the procedural character of reading. The reader reads a text in "portions" whose length depends on his interests, his presuppositions and predilections, his acquaintance with the style and the content of the text he reads. A second general essential feature seems to be that the reader, in constituting a TW_i as an interpretation (model) of T_i, compares TW_i (and its parts) with his EW and with other textworlds TW_j ,...., TW_x, which he knows from other reading-acts. Thus in a process of reading, there may occur modifications in all the worlds that are (implicitly or explicitly) brought into relation; modifications which may influence the further steps of the process of reading and/or the final construction of a text-meaning.

If a reader meets difficulties in assigning worldsystems to text-structures he can overcome these difficulties

(a) by modifying his EW;

(b) by modifying parts of TW_i as constituted up to the moment where the difficulties arise;

(c) by modifying his dictionary;

(d) by manipulating T_i.[9]

2.2.3   Generally speaking, the process of reading can be described as a process of constituting a worldsystem TW_i which is coherent for a reader R_i at a certain time t_x. That is to say, the meaning must be related to the EW of a R_i (or a group of $R_1, \ldots, R_x$,) at t_x, and to the productive reading activity of R_i. In other words: the meaning of a text is relative to the world of a reader.

2.3   These short remarks were to show how it might be possible to re-construct the process of receiving texts in terms of the semantics of a modal logic.

If one proceeds along this line one has to make use of the *logical* term of interpretation[10] which (fully elaborated) allows covering all varia-tions in assigning intensions and/or extensions to expressions and worlds to propositions and text-structures. Therefore the term 'interpretation' cannot be used in a *Literaturwissenschaft* to denote the operation of assigning a meaning to a text-structure. So we must face the question: what can 'interpretation' mean in a new *Literaturwissenschaft?* The answer cannot be: looking for a coherent reading of a text, because this is now explicitly considered in a theory of *reception.* As I mentioned in the first paragraph the concept of interpretation has never been clearly de-fined in *Literaturwissenschaft* and there exists no explicit method of interpretation.

If one considers the practice of academic interpretation one can see that normal academic interpretations of literary texts are nothing else than demonstrations of the process of reception of a certain person and/ or its results in a verbalised form ($=$ an individual text-concretisation) — or, in some looser way of speaking — reports about an individual act of understanding a text.

A new *Literaturwissenschaft* that intends to develop an empirical theory of literary communication can regard those interpretations only as materials for analysis, i. e. as documentations of individual reading processes at certain times, under special historical and social conditions, etc. But as the aim of a theory of literary communication is not to find out the correct meaning of a literary text but to construe a general theory of literary communication with complement theories for the compo-nents of literary communication (text-production, text-mediation, text-reception), the function of interpretation can no longer be to assign cor-rect meanings to texts but to explain the genesis and the possible func-tions of literary texts in certain constellations of literary communication. In order to explain the possible roles a literary text may play, a theory of literary communication needs of course an explicit text-semantics. This text-semantics must be able to specify under what conditions and in relation to what groups of readers certain texts can be assigned cer-tain interpretations (in the logical sense of the word). But this procedure is only one part of a new concept of interpretation seen as a theory complementary to a theory of literary communication. The full task of this complementary theory is to specify the relations between all components of the process of literary communication (author, text, editor, media, readers, critics, scholars etc.) with regard to an *individual* text or a closed set of texts.

This is a very complicated task, especially if this work is to be done with a clear theoretical foundation and with empirical backing. What sort of methodology can a theory of literary communication develop or what methodology has it to accept from other regions of scientific activities in order to solve these problems?

3. *LITERATURWISSENSCHAFT* AS A PROCESS OF RATIONAL ARGUMENTATION

3.1 In my opinion the development of *Literaturwissenschaft* to a rational science has mostly been retarded by the dogma of the special situation of *Literaturwissenschaft* as a "Geisteswissenschaft".[11] The implications of irrationality of this dogma have prevented most of the scholars of *Literaturwissenschaft* from realising that their work corresponds exactly to that of scholars of other sciences: both have to formulate clear problems and to look for solutions that are accessible to intersubjective criticism. The objectivity of a science consists — as K. R. Popper has put it (1962) — in the objectivity of the critical method; i. e. no part of a theory (either its basic assumptions or special theorems) can be exempted from critical discussion, and deductive logic plays its role as an *organon* of critics. For a *Literaturwissenschaft* this means that its general method must be the method of explicit argumentation, where all the steps or argumentation are exposable to logical criticism and to empirical refutation.

3.2 Such a methodology furthermore implies that *Literaturwissenschaft* must look for *explanations* wherever this is possible. To fulfill this task *Literaturwissenschaft* needs a theory of explanation, e. g. the theory of C. G. Hempel and P. Oppenheim (1948).[12] Many opponents to a rational *Literaturwissenschaft* (as described here) argue that *Literaturwissenschaft* will never be able to obey the rigid rules of an analytical philosophy of science; in particular, *Literaturwissenschaft* will not be able, according to their opinion, to follow the prescriptions of the Hempel-Oppenheim-scheme of explanation. On the other hand many of these opponents are ready to accept the claim that the scholars of *Literaturwissenschaft* too, must argue explicitly and rationally. Is there a way out of this dilemma?

3.2.1 In recent years an increasing interest in theories of argumentation and rhetorics can be noticed. Books like St. Toulmin's *'The Uses of*

Argument' (1958) or Ch. Perleman's and Olbrecht-Tyteca's *'Traité de l'argumentation'* (1958) are frequently cited and discussed as to their possible relevance for *Literaturwissenschaft*.

In this paragraph I will shortly deal with the question of whether Toulmin's scheme of argumentation really — as many scholars write[13] — provides an instrument that fits into the interests of scholars of *Literaturwissenschaft* better than (what Toulmin very generally calls) "formal logics".

The scheme of argumentation as developed by Toulmin is so well known today, I think, that it is sufficient to cite it without further comments:

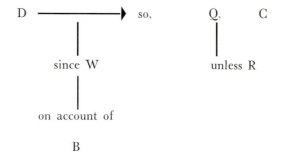

(where: D = data; Q = qualifier; C = claim/conclusion; W = warrant; B = backing; R = rebuttal)

The advantage of Toulmin's scheme is seen in the fact that it allows more complex argumentations than syllogistic patterns of conclusion and that it allows conclusions on the basis of mere plausible arguments — advantages that are very important for a *Literaturwissenschaft*.

3.2.2   At first glance these arguments seem to be correct. But a closer examination of Toulmin's model of argumentation shows some serious shortcomings which — in my opinion — reduce its practical value.

For example Toulmin never sufficiently explains what status the various parts of an argument (backings, qualifiers, claims, datas, warrants) really have. Are they sentences describing observations, or hypotheses, or "Protokollsätze" (in the empiristic sense), or intuitive observations, metatheoretical statements, axioms or something else?[14]

Without a thorough clarification of questions like the following: What is an *observation* (and an observational statement) in *Literaturwissenschaft*? What is a *fact* in a *Literaturwissenschaft*? How can the relation between *object-* and *metalanguage* be defined? Toulmin's model is in no respect better than the eplanation-schemes of "formal logics".

This thesis needs further explanations. First of all I want to point to the fact that all the conclusions we can draw from premises by the help of Toulmin's model are possible, too, in the framework of a logic that works with modal operators and time-indices.

The admittance of mere plausible reasons to theoretical or practical reasoning does not make a decisive difference between Toulmin's model and formal logic models. In any predicate calculus we can work with premises that are marked as only "plausible"; consequently the stringency of the conclusion must be characterised by a modal qualifier according to the certainty of the premises.

Again, as regards complexity, I cannot see any remarkable difference; for even in formal-logical conclusions we can perform complex argumentations where additional assumptions are to be justified. We only need *sequences* of conclusions to reach this goal. E.g. if you want to come from certain data (D) and assumptions (A) to a conclusion (C): D, $A \longrightarrow C$, the assumptions may be backed by a series of new data $(D_1, \ldots, D_n)$. The conclusion of the stringency of A must then be characterised by a modal qualifier (M): $D_1, \ldots, D_n \longrightarrow MA$. A complex argument can then be stated as: D, $MA \longrightarrow M'C$.

3.3   The discussion about adequate and productive models of rational argumentation and empirical testing for a *Literaturwissenschaft* must be intensified in order to transform *Literaturwissenschaft* into an empirically working theory of literary communication. I am convinced that even a serious attempt to accept the standards of rational argumentation as norms of methodology will in itself remarkably change the situation. One of the results of this transformation process must be, I think, that *Literaturwissenschaft* has to develop an *explicit research program* which is able to locate and evaluate the problems and solutions, to correlate and integrate complementary accounts of a theory of literary communication, and to organize interdisciplinary research (cf. S. J. Schmidt, 1973 a).

Only within the framework of such a research program and by being oriented towards the standards of rational argumentation can *Literaturwissenschaft decide* which of its problems can be clearly formulated and solved in relation to explicit theories of literary communication. Without such an apparatus, *Literaturwissenschaft* will remain in its states of a pre-scientific talking about texts.

NOTES

[1] I cannot deal here with the differences between the variant conceptions of academic treatment of literary texts in different countries, and their etiquettes, respectively. What I say here refers to the German, French and Anglosaxon conceptions, at least. For the sake of brevity, I include all of them under the German term "Literaturwissenschaft".

[2] This thesis can be proved by the result of a research group "Theory of literary communication", sponsored by the DFG, at the University of Bielefeld,

which has analysed a series of interpretations as to their argumentative strength. The results will be published in 1975.

[3] The terms 'literary' and 'literature' have not been exactly defined. As it is not my intention to deal with the problems of a definition of literary or poetic qualities or features, I shall use these terms here in a pre-theoretical way (indicated by the use of " "); i. e. 'literary' will denote such texts or communication processes as deal with texts that are at present regarded as literary. — The term 'rationale Literaturwissenschaft' denotes a theoretically based treatment of literary texts (in the broader framework of literary communication), the results of which are empirically testable or refutable.

[4] For details see S. J. Schmidt (1974) and (1975).

[5] I admit that I do not know any exact definition of 'text'. So I have to work with an undefined concept of 'text' as a meaningful coherent integration of linguistic elements into a sequence. (For aspects of a definition of 'text' see my 1973).

[6] A similar view is held by N. Groeben (1972) and the mass-media specialist G. Maletzke (1963).

[7] I use 'co-text' and 'context' in a sense defined by J. S. Petöfi (1973).

[8] This general idea has been elaborated by J. S. Petöfi and H. Rieser (1974), who rely on ideas of D. Lewis (1972) and G. E. Hughes and M. J. Cresswell (1968).

[9] For a detailed textgrammatical description of these operations see J. S. Petöfi, in Petöfi and Rieser (1974).

[10] For a definition see e. g. F. von Kutschera (1972, 255 ff.). — For a closer description of models see H. Schnelle (1972, 22 ff.). — For a detailed text-world-structure-theory in textgrammar see J. S. Petöfi (1974).

[11] For a detailed discussion of this topic see H. Göttner (1973) and S. J. Schmidt (1974) and (1975).

[12] For a serious discussion of this theory see W. Stegmüller (1969).

[13] See e. g. D. Wunderlich (1974).

[14] For this and further critical remarks see R. P. Botha (1970) and Chap. III in my (1975), where I discuss C. L. Hamblin's concept of argument (cf. his 1970), too.

BIBLIOGRAPHY

Botha, R. P., 1970. *The Methodological Status of Grammatical Argumentation*. The Hague-Paris.

Carnap, R., 1955. "Meaning and Synonymy in Natural Languages". In: *Philosophical Studies* 6.

Göttner, H., 1973. *Logik der Interpretation*. München (Münchener Universitätsschriften, Bd. 11).

Groeben, N., 1972. *Literaturpsychologie. Literaturwissenschaft zwischen Hermeneutik und Empirie*. Stuttgart (Sprache und Literatur, Bd. 80).

Hamblin, C. L., 1970. *Fallacies*. London.

Hempel, C. G. + Oppenheim, P., 1948. "Studies in the logic of explanation". in: *Philosophy of Science*, Bd. 15, 135—175.

Hughes, G. E. + Cresswell, M. J., 1968. *An Introduction to Modal Logic*, London.

Kindt, W. + Schmidt, S. J., 1974. *Textrezeption und Textinterpretation* Vorlage zum ZIF-Colloquium "Die Rolle der Grammatik in der nicht-automatisierten und automatiserten Textverarbeitung". 18. — 22.2.1974, Bielefeld.

Lewis, D., 1972. "General Semantics". in: Davidson, D. + Harmann, G., eds. *Semantics of Natural Language*, Dordrecht, 169—218.

Maletzke, G., 1963. *Psychologie der Massenkommunikation*. Hamburg.

Popper, K. R., 1962. "Die Logik der Sozialwissenschaften" in: *Kölner Zeitschrift für Soziologie und Sozialpsychologie*, 14. Jg., 233—248.

Perelman, Ch. + Olbrechts-Tyteca, L., 1958. *La nouvelle réthorique. Traité de l'argumentation*, 2 Bde., Paris.

Petöfi, J. S., 1973. *Towards an Empirically Motivated Grammatical Theory of Verbal Texts*. Bielefeld. (Bielefelder Papiere zur Linguistik und Literaturwissenschaft, H. 1).

Petöfi, J. S. + Rieser, H., 1974. *Probleme der modelltheoretischen Interpretation von Texten*. Hamburg (Papiere zur Textlinguistik, Bd. 7).

Schmidt, S. J., 1973. *Texttheorie. Probleme einer Linguistik der sprachlichen Kommunikation*. München (UTB 202).

— 1973a. "On the Foundations and the Research Strategies of a Science of Literary Communication". in: S. J. Schmidt, ed., "Foundations of Modern Poetics". POETICS 7, 7—35.

— 1974. *Wissenschaftstheoretische Probleme einer theoretisch-empirischen Literaturwissenschaft*. Bielefeld (Bielefelder Papiere zur Linguistik und Literaturwissenschaft, H. 2).

— 1974a. "Literaturwissenschaft zwischen Linguistik und Sozialpsychologie". in: ZGL 2, 49—80.

— 1975. Literaturwissenschaft als argumentierende Wissenschaft. München.

Stegmüller, W., 1969. *Probleme und Resultate der Wissenschaftstheorie und analytischen Philosophie*. Bd. I, Wissenschaftliche Erklärung und Begründung. Berlin—Heidelberg—New York.

Toulmin, St., 1958. *The Uses of Argument*. Cambridge.

Wunderlich, D., 1974. *Grundlagen der Linguistik*. Hamburg. (rororo Studium 17).

Petr Sgall
Charles University, Prague

On the nature of topic and focus

The study of the topic/focus (or topic/comment, theme/rheme) articulation of the sentence, which we consider essential for any account of the relationships between a sentence and a text, has often been rejected or ignored for one of the following two reasons: (i) the vagueness of the methods used and of the formulations of the achievements, (ii) the unclearness of the nature of the given phenomena and of their position in the system of language. We have tried to show elsewhere (see now Sgall, Hajičová and Benešová 1973) that point (i) does not hold any longer, since an operational test (with questions, negation, etc.) can be used to identify the phenomena of the given domain and explicit means of description can serve to render the results of the investigation. Point (ii) also can be refuted, since it has been shown that the topic/focus articulation is conditioned directly by the properties of communication. We want to add here some remarks to point (ii), concerning the communicative basis of the articulation, its necessity for human languages, and the possibility of accounting for it fully, in a pragmatic description.

1. If we start with the Gricean approach to meaning, revised and further elaborated by Searle (1970, pp. 42—50), we may say that a sound basis for an analysis of an illocutionary act does not consist in saying merely that the speaker tries "to tell someone something" or that the speaker, if uttering a sentence (and meaning it), intends to produce in the hearer the knowledge that the state of affairs specified by the rules of the sentence obtain, and that he intends to produce this effect by the hearer's recognition of his intention in virtue of the hearer's knowledge of the rules governing the uttered sentence. A basic characterization of communication must also include an account of the fact that, when uttering a declarative sentence (making a statement), the speaker attempts to make the hearer identify some points of the information stored in the hearer's memory and modify them in some respects,[1] i. e. the speaker not only says something, but says something about this or that.

When formulating an utterance, the speaker specifies those items of knowledge he shares with the hearer that he wants to be modified — we shall call them the established items * and he specifies, further, what properties should be now assigned to them by the hearer, in what relationship with the other items of knowledge they should be introduced, or which other modifications they should undergo.

We must be aware, of course, that human memory is a vast domain, structured in various ways, and if an act of communication is to be

* From the S & BC.

effective, the understanding of the message should not require more than a minimal effort on the part of the hearer. Only some elements of his memory are foregrounded by the situation of the discourse, and the required effort is smaller if some of these elements are chosen as the established items by the speaker and if the lexical units referring to them are marked as such, being (primarily) placed at the beginning of the message. Point after point, the message can be expanded — or, in other terms, the communicative act consists in a structure of messages linking with each other. Thus, in the unmarked case, the established items are referred to prior to the specification of their desired modification.

If the sentence of a natural language is considered the systemic form of an elementary communicative act, its structure may be expected to reflect the basic conditions of communication; this standpoint then makes us understand why the sentence includes, not only the syntactic patterning (consisting in the hierarchy of verbs and their participants, with their inner structure, the finite verb of the main clause representing the central point of this hierarchy), but also the communicative patterning, in which the parts referring to the established items (in the above sense) are distinguished from the parts concerning the modification the speaker has in mind (the added information, in the ideal case). Thus, when formulating a sentence, the speaker has to choose the main predicate and the topic (the established items).

In the elementary case the two hierarchies coincide (in such sentences as *Jack SLEPT.* and *Mary LIVES.* the coincidence is most complete),[2] and they were also put together in the Aristotelian first formulations of linguistic and logical structures. During the development of logic and linguistics they were not only held apart, but the second of them had been neglected almost completely for long centuries; only in the last decades has it been studied in a more systematic way, and attempts have been made to investigate systematically the interplay of the two hierarchies in cases that are not so elementary as the above examples.[3] In these more complicated cases the established items are not always identical with the subject of the sentence (they may include the subject, but also other parts of the sentence, or may even lie outside the subject), the verb need not specify the modification wanted by the speaker completely (it may even refer to some of the established items, if states, activities, etc. are referred to as already known, etc.), the verb may have more participants (with a free choice of those that refer to the established items), some of them may contain other verbs with their participants, and so on.

Thus it is advisable to distinguish the part of the sentence referring to the established items also terminologically (as topic, or theme) from the other part (specifying the desired modification in the above sense, and called comment, rheme, or focus); in other terms, the topic may be called the contextually bound part of the sentence (with embedded sentences, of course, we come to a whole hierarchy, so that it may be advantageous to hold the terms apart for the sake of a more detailed classification). Contextual boundness does not mean co-textual here, since not only items known from the previous portion of the given text, but also those given by the situation of the discourse are included (cf. § 3 below).

2. The question whether the topic/focus articulation, which in any case is useful for communication, also belongs to the structure of natural language as one of its necessary ingredients, can be illustrated in an interesting way by the example of Esperanto — one of the "natural languages" which have not come into being in a quite natural way. As far as we know, during its construction and later history nobody has included the topic/focus articulation into its structure in some way similar to that in which e. g. the distinctions between parts of speech, sentence parts, number, tenses, etc. were included there. It might then be expected that there is no topic and focus in Esperanto (just as there is no Dual Number there, or no Continuative Tense, etc.).

According to some specialists, however, it can be shown that even in Esperanto the topic/focus articulation is one of the main factors determining the word order of written (printed) texts of various kinds:[4] if the goal is contextually bound, it precedes the verb and the agentive — either the passive construction is used (as in English), or only the inverted word order (as in most Slavonic languages); the influence of the native language of the author can be traced here, but it is not decisive; just as in other languages, the definiteness of a noun phrase is correlated, to a certain degree, with its being contextually bound.

The fact that the topic/focus articulation is present also in the structure of Esperanto, though it was not included there deliberately, corroborates the view that the established items, not only "known previously", but introduced by the speaker as points of departure for the message proper, are distinguished systematically, by a natural language, from other items, concerning intended modifications of the established items in the hearer's memory. Not only in languages having morphemic means of expression of contextual boundness (Japanese and some other languages, first of all in Eastern Asia), but even in those where only word order, intonation and certain specific constructions, such as passive or cleft sentences, etc., realise the articulation, it is established to such a degree that it was transferred into Esperanto implicitly. It would be interesting to study also other international languages from this point of view, and, on the other hand, to find out what other subsystems of functions are present in Esperanto or in the other systems due to a similar implicit transfer from European languages.

3. As we have already seen, it is necessary to use, in the description of the structure of sentences, some pragmatic data concerning the stock of knowledge shared by the speaker and by the hearer(s). The elements of the stock of shared knowledge (more exactly, the stock the speaker

himself has and supposes to be shared by the hearer(s), too) should be classified according to the degree to which they are foregrounded (activated) in the situation of the given discourse. This means that besides a (generative or other) description of language itself, a description of the functioning of language in communication (a description of linguistic performance) must also contain another mechanism, describing the stock of knowledge, inside which the elements (or at least some of them) are partially ordered in such a way that the ordering relation may be interpreted as a scale of foregrounding. Some of the elements of the stock of knowledge are, so to say, permanently foregrounded, and thus the speaker can use them as contextually bound, and also as presupposed, at any stage of a discourse; it seems that, first of all, the "indexical elements" *I, you, here, now* belong there, but also other notions closely related to them (*my mother, my wife, my children; my country, my town; this year, this month, today,* etc.), and perhaps even all nouns of unique reference in the universe of discourse (cf. Kuno, 1973, p. 39), including *the sun, the moon.* Other nouns, the reference of which must be specified afresh for every discourse (or even for a certain part of the discourse), can be foregrounded by this very specification (or, if their referents attract the attention of the participants of the discourse, also by deixis).

This mechanism would account for the possible use of *My wife has read, in a German weekly, that* ... as a beginning of a discourse even in a situation where the speaker's wife is not present, and not known to the hearer. As we have said, it would be necessary to work with a hierarchy of the elements of the stock of knowledge, using at least a partial ordering, since, of course, *my aunt, your mother, my third grandson, the Old Town of our capital, last century, Paris,* etc. are noun phrases very suitable for the use inside the topic of a discourse opening (being connected with at most trivial presuppositions), but, under certain circumstances, *my teacher's niece, Aconcagua,* or *the age of Michelangelo* would also do.

The foregrounded elements can be mentioned, in a discourse, in two different ways: (a) as contextually bound, and (b) in the focus, along with elements that are not foregrounded; cf. Czech *Karel viděl JEHO (Charles saw HIM)* with the object foregrounded (and therefore pronominalizable), but included in the focus (and therefore stressed) against *Karel ho VIDĚL (Charles SAW him)*, with the object not only foregrounded (known), but also contextually bound, therefore unstressed (and realized by the enclitical form of the pronoun). Therefore the topic cannot be identified with the known, given (or foregrounded) elements.

If an element of the stock of shared knowledge occupies a relatively low position in the scale of foregrounding, it can be introduced in a discourse as contextually non-bound, i. e. in the focus of a sentence. Such a mentioning gives the element a higher degree of foregrounding; in some respects it is possible to conceive the element mentioned last

412

to be more foregrounded than the elements mentioned before, the fore-grounding of which already shades away step by step (if they do not belong to the permanent part of the foregrounded elements). The order-ing of noun phrases inside the topic in languages with free word order corroborates this view, as well as the opinion according to which an element known from the preceding text is more foregrounded (*ceteris paribus*) than an element known from the situation, but not yet men-tioned in the given discourse. This can be illustrated by the following dialogue in Czech:

A: *Našel už Karel MARII?* (*Has Charles already found MARY?*)
B: *Ne, Marie v tomhle sále asi vůbec NENI.* (*No, Mary probably isn't PRESENT in this room at all.*)

Here, in the utterance formulated by B, the local adverbial could precede the subject only under specific circumstances — either the room was also mentioned before, namely as a stage in the proposed programme (*We'll look for her in this room first*, or similarly), or it would be under contrast.

4. The hierarchical organization of the stock of shared knowledge is relevant also for an investigation of the structure of text. We would like to characterize here quite briefly two kinds of connection between the structuring of the stock of shared knowledge (with its activated and other elements) and the structure of text.

4.1 First, the mentioned change in the degree of foregrounding or activa-tion of individual elements of the stock of shared knowledge is clearly connected with the interplay of themes (chosen among the already acti-vated elements) and rhemes (mostly activated only by the use in the given utterance) of subsequent utterances of the text. What we have in mind here is the aspect of the structure of text which Daneš (1970) calls thematic progression and Enkvist (1973, 117f) analyzes under the heading of patterns of theme movement, also giving types of semantic relationships that make it possible to identify some of the themes of subsequent utterances of a text with each other. Such an identification of themes can be divided, on this basis, into several types, one of them being based on actual identity of reference (repetition, anaphorical re-ference, partly also synonymy), another on contrast (antonymy), with several degrees in between (from hyponymy and synonymy with non-identical reference to co-membership of a class in a list, etc.).

4.2 Second, it may be assumed that any break in the fluent line of discourse or text is connected with a more or less considerable change in the set of the (most) activated elements of the stock of shared know-ledge. The extent of this change depends on whether we are concerned with a simple pause between two paragraphs (after which an issue may be re-evoked that was mentioned not immediatcly before), with a deeper break (e. g. between chapters), or even with a pronounced discontinuity of the text, evoked by an outside interference into the discourse. In the first two cases the change concerned might be characterized as a switch of a common theme or "hypertheme"; these notions, which must be understood as relativized or stretched along some scale, could be analyzed much more explicitly than up to now, if the interplay of themes of utterances, as identified e. g. by the question test, be understood as reflecting the changes in the degree of activation of the corresponding elements in the stock of shared knowledge: typically, an element is activated by its first being mentioned in a rhematic position; by this very fact it becomes available as a possible thematic element, in the following part of the text, and, if the speaker switches to another theme afterwards, the activation of the given element is reduced; after the newly chosen theme has been "exhausted", or saturated, it is possible to return to the former theme again, but this possibility is restricted: if it was the theme of the first utterance of paragraph A, it can well emerge again at the beginning of paragraph B, but if another theme is chosen here, the degree of activation of the original theme is again reduced, and so on.

It seems, from this point of view, as we have already remarked, that often the element mentioned last (i. e. the rheme or focus of the last sentence of the preceding portion of the text) can be conceived as more foregrounded than the elements mentioned before, the foregrounding of which already shades away. This would point to the possibility that the part of human memory corresponding to the foreground of the stock of shared knowledge could be described by a device to some extent similar to a pushdown automaton (but, certainly, restricted to a finite storage). Some examples corroborate the view that an item that has been mentioned later carries a smaller degree of communicative dynamism than another element that was mentioned at some earlier point of the discourse, if — in the present, i. e. repeated occurrence — they both are contextually bound. *i.e. the theme stack!*

In almost every text, of course, the situation is complicated by various factors; in a text having the qualities of a work of art, deviations of different types are possible; in a technical text, the theme is, as a rule, rather complex, consisting of a relatively large number of items activated partly by the belonging of the text to a certain domain of knowledge, and partly by the relationship between technical terms known in this domain.

Concluding our remarks, we would like to stress that a systematic investigation of the structure of text should take into consideration the relationship between the topic/focus articulation of the text (including the patterns of theme movement) and the stock of shared knowledge, as reflecting the changes in the situation of the communication. As Isard (1973) puts it (studying other very important aspects of the communicative situation as changing during a discourse), "a theory which allows a speaker to accomplish something by speaking makes a more promising start toward a larger theory of language use than one which just passes judgements on the propriety of what has been said."

NOTES

[1] Cf. Öim (1973); these points of the stored information may, of course, belong to various sets of psychological phenomena, and we are aware of the simplification we make if we speak, in the sequel, about items of knowledge.

[2] Capitals denote the intonation centre here.

[3] Let us refer only to the writings of Mathesius (1929; 1939), Firbas (1957; 1971) and Halliday (1967); as for the relationships between the topic/focus articulation and the structure of text, investigated by Enkvist (1970; 1973), cf. § 4 below.

[4] These phenomena have been analyzed statistically, to a certain degree, in Verloren van Themaat (1973).

REFERENCES

Daneš, F. (1970), "Zur linguistischen Analyse der Textstruktur," *Folia lingui-stica* IV, 72—78.

Enkvist, N. E. (1970), "Style and Intersentence Linguistics," paper read at the Annual Meeting of the Societas Linguistica Europaea, Prague.

— 1973, *Linguistic Stylistics*, The Hague — Paris.

Firbas, J. (1957), "Some Thoughts on the Function of Word Order in Old English and Modern English," *Sborník prací filos. fakulty brněnské university* A 5, 72—100.

— 1971, "On the Concept of Communicative Dynamism in the Theory of Functional Sentence Perspective," *Sborník prací filos. fakulty brn. university* A 19, 135—144.

Halliday, M. A. K. (1967), "Notes on Transitivity and Theme in English," *Journal of Linguistics* 3, 1967, 37—81, 199—244; 4, 1968, 179—215.

Isard, S. (1973), "Changing the Context," paper read at the Seminar on Formal Semantics, Cambridge; in press in E. L. Keenan (ed.), *Formal Semantics* (Cambridge University Press).

Kuno, S. (1973), *The Structure of the Japanese Language*, Cambridge (Mass.).

Mathesius, V. (1929), "Zur Satzperspektive im modernen Englisch," *Archiv für das Studium der neueren Sprachen und Literaturen* 155, 202—210.

— (1939) "O tak zvaném aktuálním členění věty" (On the So-Called Topic/ Comment Articulation of the Sentence), *Slovo a slovesnost* 5, 171—174.

Öim, H. (1973), "On the Semantic Treatment of Predicative Expressions, in F. Kiefer and N. Ruwet (eds.), *Generative Grammar in Europe*, Dordrecht, 360—386.

Searle, J. R (1970), *Speech Acts*, Cambridge.

Sgall, P., E. Hajičová and E. Benešová (1973), *Topic/Focus and Generative Semantics*, Kronberg/Taunus.

Verloren van Themaat, W. A. (1973), "The Order of the Parts of Speech in Esperanto," manuscript sent to the Internat. Conference on Computational Linguistics, Pisa.

Jan Svartvik and Bengt Törjas
University of Lund

Rhythmic variation
in the use of time references

1. SUPRASENTENCE GRAMMAR

Much has been written on adverbials in English sentences, on their forms, meanings, and positions. But we know comparatively little about adverbials in a wider perspective, for example how they are distributed in larger textual units, such as the paragraph. Yet, according to Enkvist, "style is not merely a quality of sentences but also of texts. If so, we must also devise means of describing style which reckon with textual, intersentential features and not only with terms that refer to phenomena within the confines of single sentences" (Enkvist 1973, 125). Bolinger has pointed to the weakness of our techniques in concentrating, in current grammatical theory on sentences, "which produces a partial blindness both to contextualization within longer sentences ... and to contextualization between sentences. The misjudgments that our contemporaries make simply point, for the most part, to the next great step that must be taken — toward an intersentence grammar. We have not begun to scratch the surface of contextual dynamics" (1968, 38—39).

Assuming that the paragraph is a "sequence of structurally related sentences", that it is a "macro-sentence or meta-sentence" (Christensen 1967, 79 and 54), it should be possible to find some structure in the use of sentence elements such as the adverbial also in paragraphs and perhaps even larger units (the chapter, or the entire discourse). This paper deals with the use of Time References (TRs for short), which, like tense and aspect, are related to the chronological movement of the paragraph.[1]

2. *THE DOUBLE HELIX*

The textual basis for this study is *The Double Helix* by James D. Watson, who was awarded the 1962 Nobel Prize for Chemistry for his contribution to one of the major scientific events of this century, the discovery of the structure of DNA (deoxyribonucleic acid). The book, published in 1968, is a fascinating account of the life of a scientist, describing in a straightforward and arresting manner the path towards the solution of a very difficult scientific problem. In the Foreword, Sir Lawrence Bragg writes: "I do not know of any other instance where one is able to share so intimately in the researcher's struggles and doubts and final triumph" (vii). The text is suitable for this kind of linguistic study for at least two reasons. Firstly, the book contains no dialogue whatsoever, and the paragraphs are thus neatly delimited. Secondly, it gives an almost day-by-day personal account of the research process as experienced by the research worker himself. In addition, the book provides a very human and amusing picture of the scientist, as can be seen in the following example: "One could not be a successful scientist without realizing that, in contrast to the popular conception supported by newspapers and mothers of scientists, a goodly number of scientists are not only narrow-minded and dull, but also just stupid" (18—19).

3. SOME BASIC STATISTICS

The Double Helix contains a Foreword by Sir Lawrence Bragg, a Preface, an Introduction, and an Epilogue, in addition to the main body

Figure 1: Number of chapters containing the different Paragraph No's

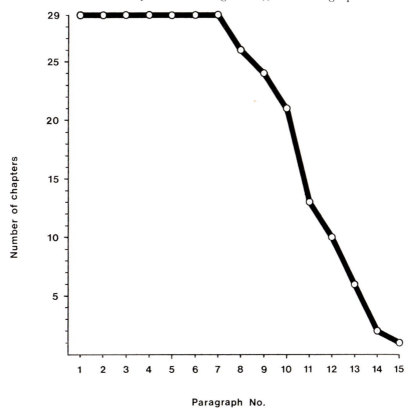

of the book consisting of 29 chapters. It is only these 29 chapters which have been used as our textual corpus.[2]

This body of material contains 306 paragraphs, 1,955 sentences (counting periods and equivalent punctuation marks as boundaries), and 38,949 words (counting hyphenated items and also names consisting of more than one unit as one word). The number of paragraphs per chapter ranges from 7 to 15 (see Figures 1 and 2). The average number of lower units occurring in higher units is as follows:

29 chapters (each consisting of 10.6 paragraphs, 67.4 sentences, and 1,343.1 words);

306 paragraphs (each consisting of 6.4 sentences and 127.3 words);

1,955 sentences (each consisting of 19.9 words).

Figure 2: Length of chapters in terms of paragraphs

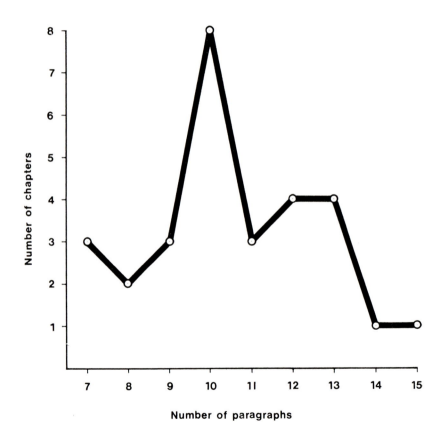

Number of paragraphs

4. TR FORM-CLASSES

The TRs found in *The Double Helix* have been grouped into the following five form-classes:

adv   adverbs
pp   prepositional phrases
np   noun phrases
cl   clauses
x   other types of TRs

The first four form-classes require little exemplification, since they agree with standard classifications (see, for example, Quirk et al. 1972, 420 ff.). Adverbs are e.g. *never, seldom,* prepositional phrases are e.g. *in the evening, at night,* and noun phrases are e.g. *next week, last Sunday.* Clauses include finite clauses, e.g. *until success came,* non-finite clauses, e.g. *when arriving in Italy,* and verbless clauses, e.g. *when young.*

When making an inventory of the TRs in *The Double Helix* it seemed, however, that an analysis of time reference should not be confined to the traditional categories of time adverbials but include also other references to time. A considerable part of the information about time that the reader is given is, in fact, conveyed by other means than adverbials. For example, in the sentence

The only safe course was to ask for funds to spend another year with Herman   (3,7,44)[3]
the object *another year with Herman* denotes time much in the same way as an adverbial in the paraphrase

   ... to ask for funds to work *with Herman for another*
      year.

The subject of the clause may also contain a TR:

The next few days saw Francis becoming increasingly
agitated ...   (25,1,1)

A more usual way to express it would, however, be through an adverbial, as in

The next few days Francis became increasingly agitated.

A complement may be used, as in

Then it was *the spring of 1951* ...   (3,1,3)
which is similar to an adverbial construction:

This happened *in the spring of 1951* ...

Since time adverbials answer the questions *When?, How long?* or *How often?,* it is obvious that the adverbial in

   ... who was just back *from a winter of work at Cal Tech.*   (5,1,6)
is not a time adverbial in the ordinary sense of the term. However, this adverbial serves as a TR. If we try to express the TR by means of an ordinary time adverbial, we might have:

...who was just back *after having worked for a winter at Cal Tech.*

The paraphrases show that the meaning of the utterance is not affected by the choice of form-class in these cases.

Adjectives from which time adverbs can readily be formed frequently serve as TRs. There are numerous examples of this in *The Double Helix:*

...he gave up his *previous* research problem   (3,6,38)

which corresponds to

...he gave up the research problem he had *previously* been engaged on.

Similarly,

But my *subsequent* attempts at crystallization were no more successful ...   (7,3,19)

could be compared with

But the attempts at crystallization that I *subsequently* made were no more successful ...

In many cases, however, there is no adverb corresponding to the adjective:

A *fresh* start would be necessary ...   (14,6,29)

but an adverbial expressing the meaning of the adjective is more or less readily at hand:

It would be necessary to start *again* ...

A noun used as a modifier in a noun phrase, either in the common form or in the genitive, may serve the same purpose as a time adverbial:

...when they had their *morning* coffee.   (2,10,52)

...when they had their coffee *in the morning.*

...as he... surveyed the *afternoon's* effort.   (12,9,55)

...as he... surveyed the effort he hade made *during the afternoon.*

A postmodifier in a noun phrase may be substituted for a time adverbial:

...go out into the foulness *of a heavy, foggy November night* ...   (10,4,25)

...go out into the foul weather *one heavy, foggy November night* ...

Besides the four traditional form-classes (adv, pp, np, cl), a fifth, 'other types of TRs' (x), has therefore been included in the classification to allow for TRs that are conveyed by other means than time adverbials. Type x has the following subgroups:

(A) TR phrases acting as clause elements:

(1) TRs as subjects

Six weeks of listening to Francis had made me realize ...   (10,1,3)

The years of careful... training had left their mark.   (10,3,11)

...*the summer evenings* were more suitable for tennis   (18,2,7)

(2) TRs as objects (including prepositional objects)

Most of my time I spent walking ...   (4,4,21)

...go to the Eagle for lunch, leaving *the afternoon* free ... (13,2,14)

Instead, I used *the dark and chilly days* to learn more
theoretical chemistry ...   (14,7,42)
A number of his colleagues quietly waited for *the day* ... (5,2,19)
(3) TRs as complements
... for it was *a Saturday morning* ...   (24,1,2)
The time of the meeting ... was *the middle of June* ... (15,10,59)
(4) TRs as adverbials (other than in form-class 'pp')
... since, *as an undergraduate* at the University of Chicago, I was principally interested in birds ...   (3,1,7)
Despite the midnight hour, I had no desire to go back ... (18,3,16)
... and *at increasing frequencies* he would look up ...   (24,12,70)
(B) TRs acting as modifiers in a noun phrase
(1) Premodifiers in noun phrases
... would lead to anything of *immediate* interest ...   (3,5,34)
Even if I had to cover my sister's *recent* purchase ...   (6,11,64)
... and he would show equal gusto in telling of his *occasional* mistakes.   (9,7,41)
... his *present* fame.   (1,1,3)
Sir Lawrence flatly denied *prior* knowledge of Francis'
efforts ...   (8,2,12)
His *tenish* entrance, however, did not bring the answer.   (12,4,18)
The high point of each meeting was the *day-long* excur-
sion ...   (4,2,9)
... and even Francis was separated by a *two-hour* rail
journey.   (2,12,67)
(2) Postmodifiers in noun phrases
... certainly a thing *of the past.*   (2,10,51)
... I was asked to propose plans *for the following year.*   (3,7,42)

5. TR MEANINGS

From a semantic point of view the TRs have been grouped according
to a classification mainly based on Crystal (1966). We distinguish the
following six classes of TR meanings:

FREQ	frequency of occurrence
DUR	duration of time
EXPL	explicit time
PREV	previous time
SIM	simultaneous time
FOLL	time following

TRs answering the question *How often?*, e. g. *never, often, usually,
each night,* make up the group called frequency of occurrence (FREQ).
The duration group (DUR) comprises TRs that could be given as answers to *How long?*, e. g. *for some time, briefly, all day.* If a TR is explicit, i. e. if it is not dependent on any other previous TR, it belongs

to the group dealing with explicit time (EXPL), such as *now, in 1952, as an undergraduate, as I set off, when Max telephoned.* References to previous time (PREV) imply that something happened before a specific point of time, e. g. *earlier* (i. e. *earlier than the spring of 1951*), *the previous day* (i. e. *the day before May 12*), *already* in *He had already eaten when we met* (i. e. *he had eaten some time before our meeting*). The time referred to by one TR may be simultaneous (SIM) with that of a previous TR, e. g. *then, at that time, on that occasion.* Reference may also be made to time following (FOLL) a specific point of time, e. g. *soon, immediately, after a while.*

The rank order with percentages of TR form-classes in *The Double Helix* is as follows (see also Tables 1 and 2):

1) adverbs .... 35.6 %
2) prepositional phrases .... 22.0 %
3) clauses .... 18.2 %
4) other types of TR .... 13.6 %
5) noun phrases .... 10.6 %

Table 1: Distribution of TR meaning-classes and form-classes

Form-Classes	Meanings						
	EXPL	FOLL	DUR	FREQ	PREV	SIM	TOTAL
adv	71	173	74	145	68	50	581
pp	115	95	77	8	42	23	360
cl	189	37	25	—	41	5	297
x	91	34	67	17	13	1	223
np	33	50	20	20	25	26	174
Total	499	389	263	190	189	105	1635

Table 2: Rank order of TR meanings in terms of form-classes

Form-Classes	Meanings					
	EXPL	FOLL	DUR	FREQ	PREV	SIM
adv	4	1	3	2	5	6
pp	1	2	3	6	4	5
cl	1	2	4	—	3	5
x	1	3	2	4	5	6
np	2	1	5	5	4	3
Whole book	1	2	3	4	5	6

Most adverbs (29.8 %) are used to refer to time following, and almost as many (25.0 %) to refer to frequency of occurrence. The rest of the adverbs are distributed fairly evenly among the other four meaning-classes.

422

Of the prepositional phrases, almost a third (31.9 %) denote explicit time, 26.4 % denote time following and 21.4 % duration.

An overwhelming majority (63.6 %) of the clauses are used to refer to explicit time, none to frequency of occurrence and between 13.8 % and 1.7 % refer to the other meaning-classes.

40.8 % of other types of TRs (form-class x) denote explicit time and 30.0 % duration. None of the other meaning-classes exceeds 15.2 %.

Noun phrases have the most even distribution among the meaning-classes. The highest percentage (28.7 %) denotes time following, and the percentages for the remaining classes vary between 19.0 and 11.5.

The rank order with percentages of the meaning-classes is as follows:

1) explicit time	30.5 %
2) time following	23.8 %
3) duration	16.1 %
4) frequency of occurrence	11.6 %
5) previous time	11.6 %
6) simultaneous time	6.4 %

Of all TRs denoting explicit time 37.9 % are clauses and 23.0 % prepositional phrases.

Time following is most frequently expressed by adverbs (44.5 %). Prepositional phrases are used in 24.4 % of the cases, whereas the remaining form-classes have a lower, but even, distribution.

Prepositional phrases, adverbs, and other types of TRs are used to denote duration with only small variation in their percentages: 29.3 %, 28.1 % and 25.5 % respectively. The figures for the other two form-classes are far below these.

By far the most common form-class to denote frequency of occurrence is adverbs (76.3 %). In no single case is a clause used to denote frequency of occurrence.

Previous time is most often expressed by adverbs (36.0 %), somewhat less often by prepositional phrases (22.2 %) and clauses (21.7 %).

Simultaneous time is expressed by adverbs in 47.6 % of the cases, followed by noun phrases (24.8 %) and prepositional phrases (21.9 %). The remaining two form-classes are rarely used to express simultaneous time.

6. CHAPTER ANALYSIS

Table 3 gives the number of words and TRs in each chapter of *The Double Helix* and also the ratio of TRs per chapter in relation to the number of words per chapter. The number of TRs per chapter would be informative in itself, provided the chapters were of equal length. However, they differ considerably in this respect, Chapter 8 being the shortest with 864 words and Chapter 18 the longest with 1,844 words. The fact that Chapter 8 contains 44 TRs and Chapter 18 79 TRs is less interesting than their ratios in terms of TRs per chapter in per cent (5,1 % and 4.3 %, respectively). Since many TRs contain more than one word, it would be tempting to count the number of words in each TR and relate the number of words that the TRs are made up of to the number of words in the chapter. This would, however, yield information which must be considered to be of little interest in an analysis of time reference, but which might be relevant to a general stylistic analysis of *The Double Helix*.

It would be misleading to count all the words in a TR in the case of time clauses, which very often contain information about other things than time, such as manner and place. To complicate matters, they may furthermore have an embedded time adverbial, as in ... *before the stopped the car for a while*. No one would deny that this clause contains two TRs, but in counting the words in both TRs one would count the last three words (*for a while*) twice, thus including them in both TRs. It seemed natural therefore simply to count the TRs, paying no attention to the number of words they consisted of and to relate the number of TRs to the number of words in the chapter.

Table 3: Number of words and TRs per chapter

Chapter No.	Words/ Chapter	TRs/ Chapter	TRs/Chapter in per cent
1	874	51	5.8
2	1322	34	2.6
3	1487	63	4.2
4	1190	47	3.9
5	1078	37	3.4
6	1365	62	4.5
7	1514	54	3.6
8	864	44	5.1
9	1133	51	4.5
10	1084	27	2.5
11	1358	49	3.6
12	1749	73	4.2
13	929	41	4.4
14	952	31	3.3
15	1374	66	4.8
16	1387	49	3.5
17	892	23	2.6
18	1844	79	4.3
19	1337	58	4.3
20	1710	83	4.9
21	1507	68	4.5
22	1351	70	5.2
23	1550	67	4.3
24	1769	83	4.7
25	1433	54	3.8
26	1570	65	4.1
27	1584	78	4.9
28	1414	62	4.4
29	1328	66	5.0

Figure 3: Number of TRs per chapter in per cent (see Table 3)

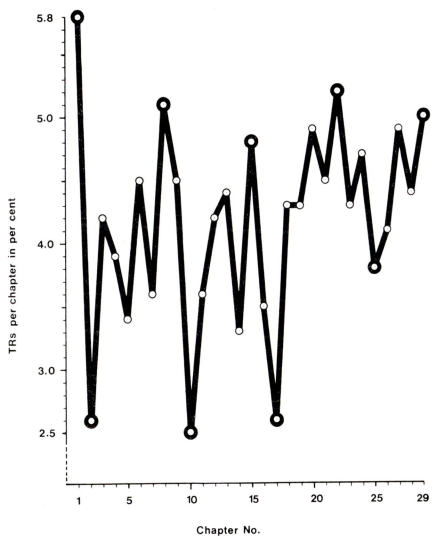

Chapter No.

Fig 3 indicates the percentage of TRs in terms of the number of words in each chapter. A few points should be made in connection with this graph. There are five peaks (Chapters 1, 8, 15, 22 and 29) and four troughs (Chapters 2, 10, 17 and 25). The gap between every two peaks consists of six chapters. The first and the last gap between the troughs cover seven chapters each, whereas the middle gap covers six chapters. The drop from a peak to a trough happens quickly via one, two or no

425

intermediate chapters. The rise from a trough to a peak is slower and is interrupted by intermediate chapters and with at least one 'semi-trough'. These observations highlight the regularity of the variations in the use of TRs throughout the book.

Chapter 1 has the greatest percentage of TRs. This seems natural in an account based on the chronological sequence of events. It is essential that the reader, from the very beginning, should be supplied with the necessary information about the where and when of the story as well as the theme and the characters of the book. After the first chapter with its high percentage of TRs, the author focusses on other matters than time, and the percentage of TRs only gradually rises to another peak. Then again the reader has gained sufficient knowledge of the chronological framework to be able to follow the author's account of the problems discussed, the controversies, the success or failure of experiments, etc.

The regular movement in the graph is, however, somewhat disturbed after the third trough. It is true that the next trough (Chapter 25) occurs with the same regularity as the previous troughs, but it is not as deep as these troughs (3.8 % compared with 2.6 %, 2.5 % and 2.6 %). If, however, the rhythmic regularity in supplying time information can be accounted for in the way we have suggested, the different contours for Chapters 19—29 call for an explanation. Let us look at the text to see whether it can provide a clue. In Chapter 20 Watson remarks that

> ... the vast masses of data now falling into place made me certain that we were on the right track (20, 4, 23).

The prospect of finding the answers to "previously bewildering" facts was attractive:

> Particularly pleasing was the possibility that Joshua might be so stuck on his classical way of thinking that I would accomplish the unbelievable feat of beating him to the correct interpretation of his own experiments (20, 4, 24).

There were other reasons, however, for acting quickly. Like Watson and Francis Crick, Linus Pauling was trying to find the structure of the DNA, and his experiments convinced his competitors in Cambridge that

> ... no further time must be lost on this side of the Atlantic (22, 10, 61).

Although Linus Pauling had committed a blunder as regards the structure of DNA, Watson and Crick knew that they

> ... had anywhere up to six weeks before Linus again was in full-time pursuit of DNA (22, 10, 66).

Time, then, becomes a very important factor in the lives of Watson and Crick after they have realized that they will soon find the secret but that others might find it somewhat earlier. The thought of DNA seldom leaves Watson's mind:

> For over two hours I happily lay awake with pairs of adenine residues whirling in front of my closed eyes. Only for brief

moments did the fear shoot through me that an idea this good could be wrong (25, 9, 64—65).

By the following noon Watson realizes that there was no cause for optimism. In fact he was firmly urged not to waste more time with his "harebrained scheme" (p 122). The last few chapters, then, become a race with time:

> At least two more days were needed before 'they [the models] would be in our hands. This was much too long even for me to remain in limbo, so I spent the rest of the afternoon cutting accurate representations of the bases out of stiff cardboard. But by the time they were ready I realized that the answer must be put off till the next day (26, 7, 45-47).

In no other part of *The Double Helix* is time of such vital importance as in the last ten chapters, and this is probably why these chapters have a higher proportion of TRs than the preceding chapters. Although the variation in TR frequency is here confined to a comparatively narrow range, it is however noticeable that the variation is similar to that of the earlier parts of the book.

7. PARAGRAPH ANALYSIS

The next step, after analyzing the use of TRs in chapter sequence, was to study their use in paragraphs on the assumption that there is some structure of paragraph sequence in the chapters. To this end we numbered the paragraphs 1, 2, 3, etc. in each chapter and added together

Table 4: Number of words per conflated Paragraphs 1, 2, 3, etc.

Paragraph No.	Total sum of words per all Paragraphs No's 1, 2, 3, etc.	Number of chapters containing Paragraph No.	Average number of words per conflated Paragraphs
1	3551	29	122.5
2	3376	29	116.4
3	3677	29	126.8
4	3603	29	124.2
5	3974	29	137.0
6	3800	29	131.0
7	3962	29	136.6
8	3469	26	133.4
9	2916	24	121.5
10	2729	21	129.9
11	1612	13	123.9
12	1079	10	107.8
13	780	6	129.9
14	154	2	77.0
15	155	1	155.0

all Paragraphs 1, all Paragraphs 2, etc. The lengths of the first eleven
paragraphs are fairly even, with a slight rise in the middle (see Table
4 and Figure 4). Since only Paragraphs 1—7 appear in all the chapters,
the right-hand part of the graph from Paragraph 8 and onwards becomes
less representative as we move towards the extreme right.

Now, by adding the number of TRs in all first, second, etc. paragraphs and dividing these totals by the number of chapters containing
these paragraphs, the average TR frequency per Paragraph 1, 2, 3, etc.
is obtained for the whole book (see Table 5). We may call the obtained
value "TR density". As appears in Figure 5, there is a regular variation
of TR density in the paragraphs: high in Paragraphs 1, 6, 10, 13 and 15
and low in paragraphs 3, 8, 12 and 14. We way note, first, that the
"wave-length" decreases as the chapter progresses; second, that the TR
density increases as the chapter progresses. Again, we should point out
that the right-hand part of the graph is less "reliable" than the left-
hand part since it represents fewer chapters. In fact, the extreme right-
hand contour (from Chapters 10 to 15) in Figure 1 closely resembles

*Figure 4: Average number of words per conflated Paragraph No's 1, 2,
3, etc (see Table 4)*

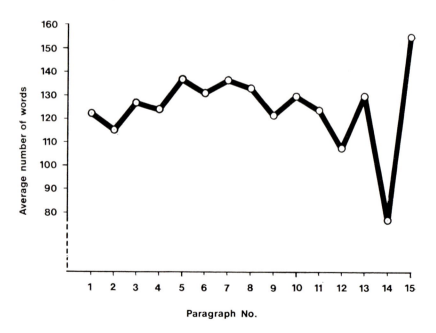

Table 5: Number of TRs per individual paragraphs

Chapter No.	Paragraph No.															No. of TRs/ch.
	1	2	3	4	5	6	7	8	9	10	11	12	13	14	15	
1	11	7	7	9	5	4	8	—	—	—	—	—	—	—	—	51
2	5	1	—	4	4	—	5	1	3	4	5	2	—	—	—	34
3	11	3	10	3	2	8	7	11	4	4	—	—	—	—	—	63
4	1	2	7	5	3	3	6	7	11	2	—	—	—	—	—	47
5	5	7	1	5	4	11	4	—	—	—	—	—	—	—	—	37
6	6	8	6	9	3	4	1	3	4	5	13	—	—	—	—	62
7	7	7	5	7	2	2	3	2	1	3	4	4	7	—	—	54
8	10	3	6	7	7	6	5	—	—	—	—	—	—	—	—	44
9	4	7	5	3	8	7	9	1	5	2	—	—	—	—	—	51
10	4	2	3	4	5	3	2	1	3	—	—	—	—	—	—	27
11	3	5	3	4	9	3	5	3	6	8	—	—	—	—	—	49
12	7	4	6	5	6	14	4	1	5	5	1	4	6	5	—	73
13	9	8	4	1	2	7	3	7	—	—	—	—	—	—	—	41
14	2	7	5	—	2	6	6	3	—	—	—	—	—	—	—	31
15	7	5	4	7	12	10	7	4	5	5	—	—	—	—	—	66
16	3	5	2	5	4	7	3	8	6	6	—	—	—	—	—	49
17	1	2	1	2	3	4	1	—	6	3	—	—	—	—	—	23
18	3	9	7	7	2	4	6	3	4	3	4	6	10	4	7	79
19	9	6	3	2	9	13	6	5	5	—	—	—	—	—	—	58
20	4	10	6	4	5	8	9	6	4	5	10	7	5	—	—	83
21	3	3	1	11	8	8	2	2	7	6	6	6	5	—	—	68
22	2	7	10	4	8	5	3	3	5	14	3	6	—	—	—	70
23	4	7	2	1	6	5	10	10	6	6	6	4	—	—	—	67
24	9	4	6	9	5	2	11	3	9	6	5	6	8	—	—	83
25	7	8	7	5	6	6	3	5	7	—	—	—	—	—	—	54
26	9	5	6	1	4	5	11	6	6	6	6	—	—	—	—	65
27	5	5	2	15	10	5	5	8	1	11	4	7	—	—	—	78
28	8	1	3	3	3	7	3	9	7	11	7	—	—	—	—	62
29	8	4	7	4	9	3	8	6	7	10	—	—	—	—	—	66
Totals	167	152	135	146	156	170	156	118	127	125	74	52	41	9	7	1635
*	29	29	29	29	29	29	29	26	24	21	13	10	6	2	1	
**	5.8	5.2	4.7	5.0	5.4	5.9	5.4	4.5	5.2	6.0	5.7	5.2	6.8	4.5		

* Number of chapters containing the above paragraph No. (see Fig 1)

** Average TR frequency per paragraph (= TR density)

the corresponding section in Figure 4. In this section, then, the TR density is closely related to text length. This, however, is not the case with the major part of Figure 5, where the rhythmic variation in TR density must be attributed to some other factor.

Figure 5: TR density (see Table 5)

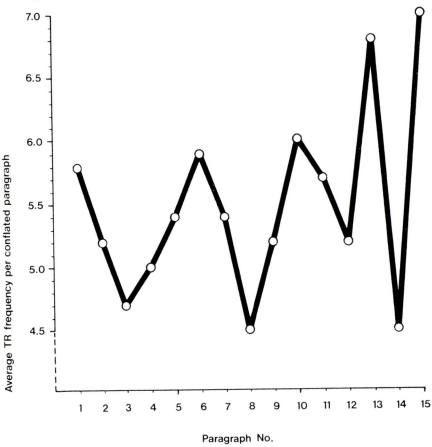

We can now offer an explanation similar to that given in section 6 to account for TR frequency variation in chapter sequence. It seems reasonable to assume that high TR density is essential at the outset of a chapter in order to provide the reader with the necessary chronological information. This need is less pressing in Paragraph 2, and particularly in Paragraph 3, where other types of information are supplied. Hence there is a drop in TR density from Paragraph 1 to 3. In the following paragraphs new chronological data are supplied, resulting in a new TR density peak in Paragraph 6. Then follows a second drop in TR density up to Paragraph 8, when the second upward movement begins, etc.

We may assume that, broadly speaking, this variation reflects the alternation between narrative passages (with high TR density) and descriptive passages (with low TR density). As can be seen in Table 5, this rhythmic regularity is by no means typical of every individual chapter. However, Chapter 19 may serve as an illustration of variation in TR density in an individual chapter whose variation is similar to that of the conflated chapters. The content of the first six paragraphs is, very briefly, as follows:

Paragraph 1 (9 TRs):
A meeting with a colleague at a congress in Paris. The author tries to track down another colleague who had arranged a fellowship for him.
Paragraph 2 (6 TRs):
A conversation with a colleague about Cambridge.
Paragraph 3 (3 TRs):
An account of a lecture by Pauling.
Paragraph 4 (2 TRs):
A conversation with his Cambridge colleague Maurice Wilkins about the lectures they had attended.
Paragraph 5 (9 TRs):
A description of a train journey to Royaumont.
A meeting with friends at dinner and afterwards with Maurice in his room. Maurice leaves for Paris the following morning.
Paragraph 6 (13 TRs):
A colleague mentions that Pauling is coming out to Royaumont. The author tries to arrange a meeting with him. A conversation with Pauling about going to California and about current activities in London.

There is a difference between, on the one hand, Paragraphs 1, 5, and 6 which are largely narrative, i.e. the relate events and have a comparatively high TR density, and, on the other hand, Paragraphs 2, 3, and 4, which are largely descriptive, i.e. they deal with matters of professional interest and have a comparatively low TR density.

8. CONCLUSIONS

Since we have no comparable data available, let alone a norm, to enable us to put features such as TRs at the suprasentence level in perspective, it is obviously difficult to draw conclusions on the basis of this isolated study. We have at present no means of stating to what extent the rise and fall of TRs that we have noted in our counting are relevant to, for example, the distinction made in stylistics between universals and statistical differentials. Consequently, we have made no attempts to determine the statistical significance of our results.

We would, however, like to point to the possibility of studying the feature 'time reference' (TR) in combination with content analysis as a fruitful line of future research. The concepts "narrative" and "descriptive" are widely being used as literary terms without attempting to find objective criteria for the distinction between them. Our results suggest that the variations in TR density in chapters (Figure 3), as well as in conflated paragraphs (Figure 5), are reflections of the alternation between narrative and descriptive passages. It is obvious, however, that much further work, including similar studies of other texts and also more detailed analyses of variations in the use of TR subcategories, remains to be done before any such connection can be established.

NOTES

[1] This linguistic analysis was initially undertaken as part of a larger study of research processes initiated by Dr. Stevan Dedijer, the Research Policy Program, Lund University.

[2] References are to the Signet Book edition, published by the New American Library, Inc., 1968.

[3] The reference numbers denote first chapter, and then paragraph and sentence within the chapter. For example, "3, 7, 44" is to be read as "chapter 3, paragraph 7, sentence 44".

[4] Note that we use the term "Number of paragraphs" to denote "the total quantity of paragraphs" but "Paragraph No." to denote "the place of specific paragraphs in the sequence of a chapter". The parallel terminology "Number of chapters" and "Chapter No." is used in the discussion of chapters.

REFERENCES

Bolinger, Dwight, 1968, "Judgments of Grammaticality", *Lingua* 21, 31—40.

Christensen, Francis, 1967, *Notes Toward a New Rhetoric*, New York.

Crystal, David, 1966, "Specification and English Tenses", *Journal of Linguistics* 2, 1—34.

Enkvist, Nils Erik, 1973, *Linguistic Stylistics*, The Hague.

Quirk, Randolph, Sidney Greenbaum, Geoffrey Leech, Jan Svartvik, 1972, *A Grammar of Contemporary English*, London.

A bibliography
compiled by Torbjörn Söderholm

The published writings of
Nils Erik Enkvist, 1951—1973

1951

1   *Caricatures of Americans on the English Stage Prior to 1870.*
    Diss. Helsinki University. (Societas Scientiarum Fennica. Commen-
    tationes Humanarum Litterarum, XVIII:1.) Helsingfors, 168 pp.
2   "The Folk Elements in Vachel Lindsay's Poetry." *English Studies,*
    XXXII, 241—249.

1952

3   "Charles Dickens in the Witness-Box." *Dickensian,* XLVII, 201.
4   "Gertrude Stein: en amerikansk modernist." *FT,* CLII, 69—75.
5   "Språkvetenskapen av i dag." *FT,* CLII, 161—171.

1953

6   *American Humour in England before Mark Twain.* (Acta Acade-
    miae Aboensis. Humaniora, XXI:3.) Åbo, 107 pp.
7   "The Biglow Papers in Nineteenth-Century England." *The New
    England Quarterly,* XXVI, 219—236.
8   "The Functions of Magic in Milton's *Comus.*" *NphM,* LIV 310—
    318.
9   "The Magnetic Recorder in Foreign Language Teaching." *Via:* Års-
    bok utgiven av Engelska språklärarföreningen i Finland, 1951—52
    (pr. 1953), 45—47.

1954

10 "Hugo Pipping som fonetiker." *FT,* CLVI, 6—17
11 "Två engelska skådespel om Gustav Vasa [Catharine Trotter,
    "The Revolution in Sweden" and Henry Brooke, *Gustavus Vasa, the
    Deliverer of His Country*]." *FT,* CLV, 160—169. (Reprinted in
    Bokvännen, IX (1954), 195—199.)
12 Review of Charles Carpenter Fries, *The Structure of English. An
    Introduction to the Construction of English Sentences*, New York,
    1952, in *NphM,* LV, 149—151.

1955

13 "T. E. Lawrence, en kritiserad hjälte" [review of Richard Al-
    dington, *Lawrence of Arabia,* London, n. d., and T. E. Lawrence,

The Mint, by 352087 A/c Ross, London, n. d.], *FT,* CLVII—CLVIII, 140—144.

14 Review of Erik Erämetsä and Roland Carter, *A Course in Spoken English. Näin puhutaan englantia,* Helsinki, 1953, in *NphM,* LVI, 155—156. (Brief mention of the same work in *Le Maître Phonétique,* No. 104, juillet-décembre, 1955, p. 42.)

15 — James Kirke Paulding, *The Lion of the West,* ed. by James N. Tidwell, Stanford, 1954, in *Western Humanities Review,* IX, 368.

1956

16 "Domen över 'Endymion'. Historien om den unge Keats och hans kritiker." *Bokvännen,* XI, 200—202.

17 "Henry James and Julio Reuter: Two Notes." *NphM,* LVII, 318—324.

18 "The *Octoroon* and English Opinions of Slavery." *The American Quarterly,* VIII, 166—170.

19 "En finsk-engelsk ordbok" [review of V. S. Alanne, *Suomalais-englantilainen sanakirja. Finnish-English Dictionary,* Porvoo & Helsinki, 1956], *FT,* CLIX—CLX, 318—319.

20 "Hundra år Trollopekritik" [review of Rafael Helling, *A Century of Trollope Criticism,* Helsingfors, 1956], *Hufvudstadsbladet,* 15.8.1956.

21 "Marlowe och Shakespeare" [review of Calvin Hoffman, *The Man Who Was Shakespeare,* n. p., n. d.], *FT,* CLIX—CLX, 144—145.

22 Review of Claes Schaar, *The Golden Mirror. Studies in Chaucer's Descriptive Technique and Its Literary Background,* Lund, 1955, in *SNph,* XXVIII, 257—258.

1957

23 *The Seasons of the Year. Chapters on a Motif from Beowulf to the Shepherd's Calendar.* (Societas Scientiarum Fennica. Commentationes Humanarum Litterarum, XXII:4.) Helsingfors, viii, 219 pp.

24 "Samtida engelska omdömen om Runeberg." *FT,* CLXI—CLXII, 7—18.

25 "Harald Jernströms Chaucertolkning" [review of new edition of Jernström's translation of the *Canterbury Tales* into Swedish: Geoffrey Chaucer, *Canterburysägner.* I svensk tolkning av Harald Jernström. I—II, Helsingfors, 1956], *FT,* CLXI—CLXII, 82—84.

26 Review of Rafael Helling, *A Century of Trollope Criticism,* Helsingfors, 1956, in *SNph,* XXIX, 256—257.

1958

27 "Paul Greaves, Author of *Grammatica Anglicana.*" *NphM,* LIX, 277—279.

28 "Porthans 'Försök at uplysa Konung Ælfreds Geographiska Be-

skrifning öfver den Europeiska Norden'." *Årsskrift utgiven av Åbo Akademi*, XXXVIII—XLI (1953—1957) [pr. 1958] 103—122.

29 Summary of discussion, in *Proceedings of the Eighth International Congress of Linguists, Oslo, 5—9 August 1957* (Oslo, 1958), pp. 488—489.

30 Review of Carl L. Anderson, *The Swedish Acceptance of American Literature*, Stockholm, 1957, in *The Modern Language Review*, LIII, 580—581.

31 — Ben Ross Schneider, *Wordsworth's Cambridge Education*, London, 1957, in *MS*, LII, 127—128.

32 — Elizabeth Lutman Gordon, *Puritan, Patriot, and Pioneer. Selections from American Literature to 1900*, Antwerp, n. d., in *MS*, LII, 327.

33 — André Martinet, *Économie des changements phonétiques. Traité de phonologie diachronique*, Berne, 1955, in *Nordisk Tidsskrift for Tale og Stemme*, XVIII, 98—99.

34 — *Tulane Studies in English*, Vol. VII, New Orleans, 1957, in *SNph*, XXX, 275—276.

1959

35 "Edvard [*sic*] Fitz-Geralds Rubaiyat 100 år." *Hufvudstadsbladet*, 8.3.1959.

36 "Ett okänd [*sic*] Ibsenbrev." *Ibsen-årbok*, 1957—59 (Skien, 1959), pp. 185—186.

37 "Två Björnsonbrev." *Nordisk Tidskrift*, XXXV, 400—401.

38 "Borgaren i världslitteraturen" [review of Lorentz Eckhoff, *Borgeren* (De tre kulturformer, II), Oslo, 1958], *FT*, CLXV—CLXVI, 277—279.

39 Review of Simeon Potter, *Modern Linguistics*, London, 1957, in *MS*, LIII, 66—67.

40 — Sir Thomas Browne, *Urne Buriall and the Garden of Cyrus*, ed. by John Carter, Cambridge, 1958, in *MS*, LIII, 164.

41 — J. A. W. Bennett, *The Parlement of Foules. An Interpretation*, Oxford, 1957, in *MS*, LIII, 293—295.

1960

42 *Englannin kielioppi korkeakouluille ja opettajille* [= English Grammar for Universities and Teachers]. Kielihistoriaa ja fonetiikkaa koskevat osat laatinut Nils Erik Enkvist, Helsinki, 270 pp. (With Eino Miettinen.) — 2nd rev. ed., Helsinki, 1970, 274 pp.

43 "Om nykritisk textanalys i språkundervisningen." *Årsbok för Riksföreningen för lärarna i moderna språk* (Stockholm), 1960, pp. 31—55.

44 "Sir Walter Scott, Lord Bloomfield, and Bernadotte." *SNph*, XXXII, 18—29.

45 "Från Brummell till Beerbohm" [review of Ellen Moers, *The Dandy: Brummell to Beerbohm*, London, 1960], *Hufvudstadsbladet*, 17.4.1960.

46 Review of A. C. Cawley (ed.), *The Wakefield Pageants in the Towneley Cycle*, Manchester, 1958, in *MS*, LIV, 98—99.

47 — Alvar Ellegård, *Darwin and the General Reader. The Reception of Darwin's Theory of Evolution in the British Periodical Press, 1859—1872*, Göteborg, 1958, in *MS*, LIV, 136—137.

48 — Axel Wijk, *Regularized English. An Investigation into the English Spelling Reform Problem with a New, Detailed Plan for a Possible Solution*, Stockholm, 1959, in *MS*, LIV, 307—311.

49 — N. E. Osselton, *Branded Words in English Dictionaries before Johnson*, Groningen, 1958, in *SNph*, XXXII, 347—348.

1961

50 Review of Lorentz Eckhoff, *Borgeren* (De tre kulturformer, II), Oslo, 1958, in *Humaniora Norvegica*, V, 291—293.

51 — Teut Riese, *Das englische Erbe in der amerikanischen Literatur*, Bochum—Langendreer, 1958, in *The Modern Language Review*, LVI, 421—423.

52 — G. H. Mair and A. C. Ward, *Modern English Literature, 1450—1959*, London, 1960, in *MS*, LV, 67—68.

53 — Eric Partridge, *A Charm of Words. Essays and Papers on Language*, London, 1960, in *MS*, LV, 104.

54 — E. J. Oliver, *Hypocrisy and Humour*, London & New York, 1960, in *MS*, LV, 158—159.

55 — Robert Gittings, *Shakespeare's Rival*, London, 1960, in *MS*, LV, 269—271.

56 — David Daiches (ed.), *Studies in English Literature*, Vols. 1—4, London, 1961, in *MS*, LV, 319—320.

57 — L. C. Knights and Basil Cottle, *Metaphor and Symbol*, London, 1960, in *MS*, LV, 407—408.

58 — Werner Habicht, *Die Gebärde in englischen Dichtungen des Mittelalters*, München, 1959, in *SNph*, XXXIII, 206—208.

59 — Walter Müller, *Englische Idiomatik nach Sinngruppen. Eine systematische Einführung in die heutige Umgangssprache*, Berlin, 1960, in *SNph*, XXXIII, 217—218.

60 — Eva Sivertsen, *Cockney Phonology*, Oslo, 1960, in *SNph*, XXXIII, 351—353.

1962

61 "The Choice of Transcription in Foreign-Language Teaching." *Proceedings of the Fourth International Congress of Phonetic Sciences ... Helsinki, 4—9 September 1961* (The Hague, 1962), pp. 586—589.

62 "Tillämpad lingvistik." *Hufvudstadsbladet*, 14.1.1962.

63 Review of Norman Mailer, *The Naked and the Dead* (Re-readings, VI), in *MS*, LVI, 60—64.

64 — L. F. Brosnahan, *The Sounds of Language. An Inquiry into the Role of Genetic Factors in the Development of Sound Systems*, Cambridge, 1961, in *MS*, LVI, 71—74.

65 — *The Writer's Dilemma. Essays First Published in The Times Literary Supplement under the Heading 'Limits of Control'*. With an introduction by Stephen Spender. London, 1961, in *MS*, LVI, 102—103.

66 — Raymond Chapman, *The Ruined Tower*, London, 1961, in *MS*, LVI, 103—104.

67 — John Moore, *You English Words*, London, 1961, in *MS*, LVI, 171.

68 — Ian Gregor and Brian Nicholas, *The Moral and the Story*, London, 1962, in *MS*, LVI, 331—333.

69 — James L. Clifford (ed.), *Biography as an Art. Selected Criticism 1560—1960*, London, 1962, in *MS*, LVI, 358.

70 — Kathleen Tillotson, *Novels of the Eighteen-Forties*, London, 1961. — A. O. J. Cockshut, *The Imagination of Charles Dickens*, London, 1961, in *MS*, LVI, 359.

71 — J. M. Cohen, *English Translators and Translations*, London, 1962, in *MS*, LVI, 360.

72 — Jack Dalglish (ed.), *Eight Metaphysical Poets*, London, 1961, in *MS*, LVI, 444.

73 — Bent Nordhjem, *The Phonemes of English: an Experiment in Structural Phonemics*, Copenhagen, 1960, in *NphM*, LXIII, 139—141.

1963

74 "The English and Finnish Vowel Systems: a Comparison with Special Reference to the Teaching of English to Finns." *Via* (Utgivare: Engelska språklärarföreningen i Finland), III, pp. 44—49.

75 "New Words in Roger Barlow's *Brief Summe of Geographie* (1541)." *English Philological Studies*, VIII, 6—23.

76 "Språkmatematik" [review of Alvar Ellegård, *A Statistical Method for Determining Authorship. The Junius Letters, 1769—1772*, Göteborg, 1962, and *idem, Who Was Junius?*, Stockholm, 1962], *Dagens Nyheter*, 6.4.1963.

77 "Toivo Lyys Chaucertolkning" [review of Lyy's translation of the *Canterbury Tales* into Finnish: Geoffrey Chaucer, *Canterburyn tarinoita*. Suomentanut Toivo Lyy. Porvoo & Helsinki, 1962], *FT*, CLXXIII—CLXXIV, 177—180.

78 Review of D. H. Lawrence, *The Symbolic Meaning. The Uncollected Versions of Studies in Classic American Literature*. Ed. by Armin Arnold ... London, 1962, in *MS*, LVII, 105—106.

79 — Geoffrey Bullough, *Mirror of Minds. Changing Psychological Beliefs in English Poetry*, London, 1962, in *MS*, LVII, 186.

80 — Maurice P. Crosland, *Historical Studies in the Language of Chemistry*, London, 1962, in *MS*, LVII,, 342—344.

81 — *Swift's Polite Conversation*. With introduction, notes and extensive commentary by Eric Partridge. London, 1963, in *MS*, LVII, 376.

82 — A. C. Gimson, *Introduction to the Pronunciation of English*, London, 1962, in *SNph*, XXXV, 187—190.

83 — Bertil Malmberg, *Nya vägar inom språkforskningen. En orientering i modern lingvistik*, Stockholm, 1959, in *Via* (Utgivare: Engelska språklärarföreningen i Finland), III, p. 121.

1964

84 *British and American Literary Letters in Scandinavian Public Collections. A Survey.* (Acta Academiae Aboensis. Humaniora, XXVII:3.) Åbo, 110 pp.

85 *Geoffrey Chaucer*. Stockholm: Natur och Kultur, 88 pp. [In Swedish.]

86 "Den amerikanska lingvistiken." *Amerika och Norden*, utgiven av Lars Åhnebrink (Publications of the Nordic Association for American Studies, I, Stockholm . . ., 1964), pp. 195—212.

87 "On Defining Style: an Essay in Applied Linguistics." *Linguistics and Style*, ed. by John Spencer (London, 1964), pp. 1—56. [Translated into Portuguese, 1971, and into German, 1972.]

88 Summaries of discussion, in *Proceedings of the Ninth International Congress of Linguists, Cambridge, Mass., August 27—31, 1962* (The Hague . . ., 1964), pp. 737, 899.

89 Review of John Freeman, *Literature and Locality. The Literary Topography of Britain and Ireland*, London, 1963, in *MS*, LVIII, 78—79.

90 — *T. L. S. 1962. Essays and Reviews from The Times Literary Supplement*, London, 1963, in *MS*, LVIII, 79.

91 — Brita Püschel, *Thomas à Becket in der Literatur*, Bochum—Langerdreer, 1963, in *SNph*, XXXVI, 349—350.

1965

92 "Nya vägar inom engelsk grammatik." *Skola och Hem*, 28:6, 1—5.

93 "Preferences of Phonetic Stimuli" (with R. Lindman), *Language and Speech*, 8, 17—30.

94 Review of *Festschrift für Walter Hübner*, Berlin, 1964, in *SNph*, XXXVII, 221—222.

95 — Emma Vorlat, *Progress in English Grammar 1585—1735. A Study of the Development of English Grammar and of the Interdependence among the Early English Grammarians*, Luxembourg, 1963, in *SNph*, XXXVII, 247—249.

1966

96   *Tre modeller för ljudhistorisk forskning. Föredrag hållet vid Fins-
      ka Vetenskaps-Societetens sammanträde den 20 december 1965.* (So-
      cietas Scientiarum Fennica. Årsbok—Vuosikirja, XLIV B N:o 4.)
      Helsingfors, 20 pp.
97   "Konsten och universitetet." *Vasabladet*, 27.9.1966.
98   "Tal vid inskriptionen den 12 september 1966. Av rektor, profes-
      sor Nils Erik Enkvist." *Årsskrift utgiven av Åbo Akademi*, L
      (1965—1966), 7—28.
99   Review of Jan Svartvik, *On Voice in the English Verb*, The Hague
      and Paris, 1966, in *SNph*, XXXVIII, 387—391.
100   — Gerhard Graband, *Die Entwicklung der frühneuenglischen No-
      minalflexion. Dargestellt vornehmlich auf Grund von Gram-
      matikerzeugnissen des 17. Jahrhunderts*, Tübingen, 1965, in *SNph*,
      XXXVIII, 391—395.
101   — R. C. Alston, *A Bibliography of the English Language from the
      Invention of Printing to the Year 1800*, Vols. 1 and 5, Leeds, 1965
      —66, in *SNph*, XXXVIII, 395—396.

1967

102   "Språkmuren kring vår vetenskap." *Hufvudstadsbladet*, 4.6.1967.
103   Review of Gerhard Nickel, *Die Expanded Form im Altenglischen.
      Vorkommen, Funktion und Herkunft der Umschreibung beon/we-
      san +Partizip Präsens*, Neumünster, 1966, in *SNph*, XXXIX, 194
      —195.
104   — Hans Aarsleff, *The Study of Language in England, 1780—1860*,
      Princeton, N. J., 1967, in *SNph*, XXXIX, 358—360.

1968

105   "Tal vid inskriptionen den 10 september 1967. Av rektor, professor
      Nils Erik Enkvist." *Årsskrift utgiven av Åbo Akademi*, 51 (1966
      —1967) [pr. 1968], 7—27.
106   "Åbo Akademi föddes som en gnista mellan två starka laddning-
      ar." *Åbo Underrättelser*, 26.5.1968.

1969

107   "Tal vid inskriptionen den 10 september 1968. Av rektor, profes-
      sor Nils Erik Enkvist." *Årsskrift utgiven av Åbo Akademi* 52 (1967
      —1968) [pr. 1969], 7—26.
108   "Högskolereform och slagord." *Hufvudstadsbladet*, 24.9.1969.
109   "Stylistics in Sweden and Finland: an Historical Survey." *Style*,
      III, 27—43.
110   Review of Marvin Spevack, *A Complete and Systematic Concor-
      dance to the Works of Shakespeare*, Vol. I, Hildesheim, 1968, in
      SNph, XLI, 184—186.

111 — Wolfgang Kühlwein, *Die Verwendung der Feindseligkeitsbe-zeichnungen in der altenglischen Dichtersprache*, Neumünster, 1967, and *idem, Modell einer operationellen lexikologischen Analyse: Altenglisch 'Blut'*, Heidelberg, 1968, in *SNph*, XLI, 457—459 (with Håkan Ringbom).

1970

112 *Werner Wolf. Minnestal hållet vid Finska Vetenskaps-Societetens sammanträde den 20 januari 1969.* (Societas Scientiarum Fennica. Årsbok—Vuosikirja, XLVII C N:o 2.) Helsingfors, 9 pp.

113 "Kielipalveluopetuksen peruskysymyksiä." (Arbetsstenciler utgiv-na av gruppen för tillämpad lingvistik (AFTIL) vid Åbo Aka-demis Engelska institution, Vol. 3.) Åbo, ii, 67 pp.

114 "Uusien kielten opetus yliopistotasolla." *Vuorovaikutus*, 1970: 5, 21—22.

115 Review of Randolph Quirk, *Essays on the English Language, Medi-eval and Modern*, London and Harlow, 1968, in *SNph*, XLII, 249—250.

1971

116 "Kieliaineiden opetuksesta Ruotsin yliopistoissa syksyllä 1970." *Tutkinnon uudistus. Artikkeleita ja raportteja ... tutkintojen uudistamisen tarpeellisuudesta...,* ed. by Yrjö-Paavo Häyrynen *et al.* (Helsinki, 1971), pp. 103—112.

117 "Korkeakoulujen kieltenopetuksen tavoitteiden määritteleminen." *Virittäjä*, 75, 316—322.

118 "On the Place of Style in Some Linguistic Theories." *Literary Style: a Symposium*, ed. by Seymour Chatman (London and New York, 1971), pp. 47—64.

119 "De vetenskapliga råden behövs. Svåra fall kräver sakkunskap." *Hufvudstadsbladet*, 17.3.1971.

120 "Lingvististä tyylintutkimusta" [review of David Crystal and De-rek Davy, *Investigating English Style*, London and Harlow, 1969], *Virittäjä*, 75, 421—423.

121 Review of A. C. Gimson, *An Introduction to the Pronunciation of English*, 2nd ed., London, 1970, in *SNph*, XLIII, 581.

1972

122 "Applied Linguistics in Finland." *Modern Languages in the Nordic Countries*, ed. by Bertil Malmberg (Council of Europe Report CCC/ESR (72) 22, Strasbourg, 1972), pp. 87—99.

"Något om textuell homoiosemi". Föredrag vid KVAL:s semina-rium den 23—24 oktober 1972. (KVAL PM 733.) Stockholm Re-search Group for Quantitative Linguistics. Reprinted in *Homeosemi* (KVAL Publication 1974:1), ed. by Hans Karlgren, Trelleborg 1974.

124 "Old English Adverbial *þa* — an Action Marker?" *NphM*, LXXIII:1 (= Studies Presented to Tauno F. Mustanoja on the Occasion of His Sixtieth Birthday, I), 90—96.
125 Review of David Crystal and Derek Davy, *Investigating English Style*, London and Harlow, 1969, in *English Studies*, 53, 181—183.
126 — R. W. Zandvoort, *Collected Papers*, II, Groningen, 1970, in *SNph*, XLIV, 206—207.

1973

127 *Linguistic Stylistics*. (Janua Linguarum. Series critica, 5.) The Hague and Paris: Mouton, 179 pp.
128 "Äidinkielen ja vieraan kielen opetuksen ja oppimisen välinen suhde." *Kasvatus*, IV, 3—4.
129 "Should We Count Errors or Measure Success?" *Errata. Papers in Error Analysis*, ed. by Jan Svartvik (Lund, 1973), pp. 16—23.
130 " 'Theme Dynamics' and Style." *Expression, Communication and Experience in Literature and Language. Proceedings of the Twelfth Congress of the International Federation for Modern Languages and Literatures, Cambridge, 20 to 26 August 1972*, ed. by Ronald G. Popperwell (London, 1973), 151—156.
131 Review of Göran Kjellmer, *Context and Meaning. A Study of Distributional and Semantic Relations in a Group of Middle English Words*, Göteborg, 1971, in *SNph*, XLV, 439—443.

NOTE

The items of the bibliography are arranged in chronological order. Under each year books and other separate works are listed first, followed by articles and, in the last place, reviews. Four prominently figuring periodicals have been abbreviated as follows:

FT   *Finsk Tidskrift*
MS   *Moderna Språk*
NphM   *Neuphilologische Mitteilungen*
SNph   *Studia Neophilologica*